Folklore

Folklore

AN ENCYCLOPEDIA OF BELIEFS, CUSTOMS, TALES, MUSIC, AND ART

Second Edition

Volume Three: M–X

Charlie T. McCormick and Kim Kennedy White, Editors

 ABC-CLIO

Santa Barbara, California • Denver, Colorado • Oxford, England

Copyright 2011 by ABC-CLIO, LLC

All rights reserved. No part of this publication may be reproduced, stored in a retrieval system, or transmitted, in any form or by any means, electronic, mechanical, photocopying, recording, or otherwise, except for the inclusion of brief quotations in a review, without prior permission in writing from the publisher.

Library of Congress Cataloging-in-Publication Data

Folklore : an encyclopedia of beliefs, customs, tales, music, and art.
— 2nd ed. / Charlie T. McCormick and Kim Kennedy White, editors.
    p. cm.
  Includes bibliographical references and index.
  ISBN 978-1-59884-241-8 (hard copy : alk. paper) — ISBN 978-1-59884-242-5 (ebook)
  1. Folklore—Encyclopedias. I. McCormick, Charlie T. II. White, Kim Kennedy.
  GR35.F63   2011
   398.03—dc22   2010039858

ISBN: 978-1-59884-241-8
EISBN: 978-1-59884-242-5

15 14 13 12 11   1 2 3 4 5

This book is also available on the World Wide Web as an eBook.
Visit www.abc-clio.com for details.

ABC-CLIO, LLC
130 Cremona Drive, P.O. Box 1911
Santa Barbara, California 93116-1911

This book is printed on acid-free paper ∞

Manufactured in the United States of America

Contents

List of Entries

Standard Folklore Indices
and Classifications

The following works are cited within entries in the short forms shown in brackets.

Aarne, Antti, and Stith Thompson. 1964. *The Types of the Folktale: A Classification and Bibliography.* 2nd rev. ed. Folklore Fellows Communications, no. 184. Helsinki: Academia Scientiarum Fennica. [Cited as AT, Type, or Tale Type, followed by the appropriate number.]

Baughman, Ernest W. 1966. *Type and Motif-Index of the Folktales of England and North America.* Indiana University Folklore Series, no. 20. The Hague: Mouton. [Cited as Baughman Type or Baughman Motif, followed by the appropriate letter or number.]

Child, Francis James. [1882–1898]. 1965. *The English and Scottish Popular Ballads.* 5 vols. New York: Dover. [Cited as Child, followed by the appropriate number from 1 through 305.]

Laws, G. Malcolm, Jr. 1957. *American Balladry from British Broadsides: A Guide for Students and Collectors of Traditional Song.* American Folklore Society, Bibliographical and Special Series. Vol. 8. Philadelphia. [Cited as Laws, followed by the letter J through Q followed by the appropriate number.]

Laws, G. Malcolm, Jr. 1964. *Native American Balladry: A Descriptive Guide and a Bibliographical Syllabus.* Rev. ed. American Folklore Society, Biographical and Special Series. Vol. 1. Philadelphia. [Cited as Laws, followed by the letter A through I, followed by the appropriate number.]

Thompson, Stith. 1955–1958. *The Motif-Index of Folk-Literature.* Rev. ed. 6 vols. Bloomington: Indiana University Press. [Cited as Motif, followed by the appropriate letter and numbers.]

M

Magic

Self-change, communal metamorphosis, and cosmic transformation by ritual and material means, drawing upon the powers of nature and the supernatural. Magic, as it is diversely represented in the cultures of the world, relies upon belief in a universal "sympathy" between all existent things, natural and supernatural, creating a web of meaningful association linking magical knowledge with magical acts. Tapping into the unity of all things, the magical believer gains access to the inherent power or essence of material and spiritual forms and transforms both them and herself or himself. Under James G. Frazer's classic rubric of *sympathetic magic*, there are two main subcategories that express modes of magical efficacy: (1) *homeopathic magic*, that is, magic that operates through the indirect action of similarity, like engendering like, and (2) *contagious magic*, that is, magic that operates through the direct action of contact influencing a desired outcome. Magical action can express both these modes of efficacy simultaneously since they are complementary rather than exclusive in operation. For example, a love charm can employ homeopathic substances (herbs, stones, textiles, etc., which are symbolically or medicinally associated with love and increasing desire) as well as substances that will act by contagion (a lock of hair or a small item worn or touched by the person whom the charm is designed to attract).

An important theoretical question that is part of recent scholarly discussion on magic asks whether the term is itself a proper or useful "translation" in the ethnographic and larger cultural sense of the diversity of historical and contemporary beliefs and practices within discontinuous linguistic, religious, ethnic, and regional communities. In recent theoretical discourse on magic, anthropologist Stanley Tambiah has identified the problems of the "translation" of cultures and the problem of "commensurability" of terms between cultures. In many respects, the anthropologist and the historian are in much the same quandary when it comes to the "translation of magical cultures." However, the historian has no living informant she or he can turn to and query, "Is what you are doing the same as what we mean when we say 'magic'?" and, if so, "What does your word 'magic' mean?" "What does it mean in this context, as opposed to this other?" and "What relationship does your description of what you are doing have to what you are actually performing?" Even with living informants, the anthropologist often has to rely on the social and material context of the magical behavior or speech rather than explicit explanation or description of techniques and verbalizations, just as the historian turns to the texts around the text to provide meaningful context. Instead of turning to an individual and saying, "What does this mean?" the historian can only turn to another text and compare the form and environment of expression trying to establish its semantic field.

The semantic field for magic across the world includes verbal and gestural magic, ritual and ceremonial magic, healing and protective magic, and divination and the mantic arts, as well as magic practiced for ambivalent or openly negative social aims. Verbal magic and gestural magic are the use of mental projection and influence, often called "fascination" or "enchantment," through casting spells, performing incantations, and spellbinding accompanied by gestures such as knot tying to accomplish or prevent an outcome. Ritual magic and ceremonial magic establish sacred time and space in individual and collective terms. Through seasonal and festival ritual cycles, the turning of the solar, lunar, or agricultural year is marked and celebrated. Human ceremonial magic is devoted to ritual cycles that mark the major life passages as well as rites of personal and professional initiation. Rituals of place create and hallow sacred space and effect spatial purification and cleansing. Healing and protective magical tools, materials, and techniques are united in ritual actions that include diagnosis of affliction, spiritual and material prescription, and ritual preparation and administration of prevention or cure. The products of healing magic are religious artifacts such as magical *charms*, *amulets*, and *talismans*, which sometimes have been pejoratively categorized as fetishism. Divination and the mantic arts cover a diversity of intuitive and precognitive techniques and systems of knowledge, including but not limited to oracular and visionary experience; guided dreaming and dream interpretation; the magical use of numbers and numerical calculations, as in numerology and astrology; divination by lots or chance; animal divination, or augury, by sign and omen; elemental divination, by means of water (hydromancy), by means of earth (geomancy), by means of fire (pyromancy), and by means of air (aeromancy); divining by pictographic symbol systems such as tarot and other types of cards; and reading the body (physiognomy and palmistry) and other natural substances (tea leaves, coffee grounds, crystals, and gemstones). Finally, magic is also identified by terms that traditionally carry a negative semantic charge, such as *sorcery*, *demonology*, *necromancy*, and *witchcraft*. These terms often are used for magical and, therefore, potentially dangerous interactions between the human and spirit worlds, as in the theurgic invocation of spirits of nature, gods, or the dead; spirit projection, possession, and mediumship; and the "laying" (to rest) of ghosts and exorcism of evil or troublesome spirits. The range of traditional cursing and malefic magic is often designated as "black" witchcraft, as opposed to healing magic or "white" witchcraft. It is also important to understand that all these activities and categories of magic are not only

Vintage tarot cards. (Carolborreda/
Dreamstime.com)

verbal, physical, and material but also and at the same time mental, emotional, and intentional in method and operation.

Magic has often been associated, in scholarship and in popular awareness, with the supernatural and identified as the *occult*. Magic and the occult share certain qualities and associations. They both rely upon a concept of truth encoded in hidden, secret, inner knowledge and practice that is available only to the initiate, giving the believer extraordinary access to the mysteries of the divinely created and existent universe. The term *occult science* refers to an esoteric, veiled, and transcendent reality, mediated by intuitive inspiration, understanding, and knowledge and interpreted by methods of study, experimental investigation, and disciplinary practice. The "occult sciences," also known as *Hermeticism* or the Hermetic sciences, traditionally have included such diverse systems of magical belief and practice as alchemy, astrology, numerology, magical herbalism, talismanry, and amuletry, as well as systems of divining and dream interpretation, theurgy, and so forth. The occult sciences exist within a mode of knowledge and practice that accepts and even insists upon the parallelism of the natural and supernatural, a chain of causality based on empirical and nonempirical factors, and a system of explanation and instruction that contends that some of the truth (maybe the most important and central part) may not be fully disclosed but must be kept hidden. The mysteries can be interiorly apprehended as "gnosis" and even outwardly experienced in practice, but they cannot be definitively expressed and are thus "occult" or divine secrets. The first term in the expression *occult science* is more about knowledge, the second is more about action. But both share aspects of knowledge and action. There is a need to balance the treatment of the magical, or occult, disciplines as manifestations of "folk" or "primitive" tradition divorced from the theoretical and intellectual strata of communities, cultures, and religious systems by concentrating attention on the links in magic between learned and common belief and practice.

One result of the detailed and mold-breaking ethnographic work in the latter half of the twentieth century is that it has become more difficult, if not impossible, for scholars in anthropology, sociology, the history of religion, and folk religion to speak of magic or the magical arts and occult sciences as *survivals* of earlier unsophisticated, primitive, irrational, or illogical beliefs and practices. To categorize magic and occult phenomena as cultural survivals is to call upon a dichotomous model of cultural development. The concept of survivals belongs to a methodological orientation toward religion and magic that continues to oppose an orthodoxy, embodying the normative values and institutions of official religion, to various heterodoxies, such as folk religious belief and practice. In general, when the beliefs and practices of actual believers diverge from a notion of prescribed institutional norms, they have been judged both heterodox and marginal, whether through the ascription of heterodoxy to sectarian communities or the marginalization of magical practice and occult knowledge.

The history of the scholarly literature on magic may be summarized, in great part, by reviewing the main features of the scholarly debate regarding the definition and relationship of magic, science, and religion; this debate began in the nineteenth century, principally among anthropologists and the pioneers of sociology, and continued through most of the twentieth century. This scholarly debate has revealed a rationalist bias against magic. Magic, like religion, has been predominantly characterized as not real according to the utilitarian approach of functionalist and empiricist scholarship. And the psychologizing of believers' magical worldviews and practices often has been accompanied by an unfortunate stigmatization of magic as individual and/or social illusion, confusion, ignorance, or fraud, justified by a scholarly assumption of an irrational or pathological psychology.

By the same token, the debate regarding the relationship of magic to science has been perhaps most lively in the analysis of the late antique and medieval Hermetic or occult sciences (alchemy, astrology, talismanry, divining, and so forth). In scholarly representation, the relationship of magic to science has often been constrained by the historical "success" of the Western definitions of rationality and empirical method. Science in the Western mode is credited (by early anthropologists such as Edward B. Tylor and James G. Frazer, as well as historians of science) as the empirically based, technically proficient, and experimentally sound realization of its earlier and evolutionary precursor, magic. In this perspective, magic becomes demoted to a pseudo-science. The medieval-based systems of knowledge and experimentation that may be called magical are labeled, therefore, pseudo-science, which is another way of saying "bad science" or "no science." From the perspective of contemporary history of science, the magico-scientific traditions of classical and medieval civilizations for which we have extensive textual records (Hindu, Chinese, Greco-Roman, Islamic, and Christian), for example, become interesting anachronisms, failed cultural and intellectual paradigms, and flawed experimental models based on insufficient empirical evidence and incorrect interpretation of the evidence available.

Magic has also been defined in its most absolute negative—that is, as not religion—in the scholarly debate. It is always something other, usually something less, and it is often assigned the dismissive synonym *superstition*. In turn, magical belief and practice often have been devalued and characterized as primitive, vulgar, crude, material, mechanical, irrational, and nonsensical or, in other words, the opposite of religion, which is characterized as civilized, cultured, pure, spiritual, non-instrumental, rational, and meaningful. A related tendency in the debate has been to see magic as a purely antisocial response by psychologically and socially maladjusted individuals—the repository of the resentment and ill will (if not actual evil) of a society. The classic remedy is countermagic, as in the typical relationship between malicious witchcraft and witch-doctoring of tribal societies, according to germinal anthropological studies and historical studies of witchcraft in early modern peasant societies. The intellectual history of this prejudicial opposition of magic and religion has been described by a number of historians and anthropologists (e.g., Keith Thomas, Frances Yates, Carlo Ginzburg, Jon Butler, and Valerie Flint). They clearly state that the cultural bias against magic in the academic study of religion and magic (in both the humanities and the social sciences) is an inherited one, stemming originally from Christianity's complex and increasingly hostile relationship to magic from the late antique era through the early modern era.

A corrective response to the functionalist and empiricist negation of magic that explains it away as addressing purely human social and psychological needs is the awareness among contemporary scholars that magic (whether defined within a religious system or constituting in itself a religious system) was and is considered real and effective by its community of belief and practice, above and beyond its social and psychological dynamics. The question of effectiveness and its emic criteria has received variable treatment from scholars of magic over time. Earlier anthropological and historical opinion on the efficacy of magical action emphasized the irrationality and illogic of magic, based upon Eurocentric empirical standards of the day. Later and current interdisciplinary opinion has acknowledged that magical belief and practice have a solid empirical basis in physical observation and experience. Magical practice is aimed at ordering and making meaningful human experience and individual and social control or mediation through symbolic representation. Scholarly views that are not grounded in the actuality of magic, as a system of change on the natural and cosmic as well as personal and social levels, are not really engaged with its concerns; they cannot begin to represent what magic practitioners have believed and continue to believe they are doing and what they understand as the results of their practices.

Similarly, in response to the history of science approach to magical systems, there is no reason, based upon the ethnographic evidence available, to continue to dismiss or deny the technological competence, intellectual sophistication, and experimental/observational vigor of the diversity of historical and contemporary magical arts and occult sciences by the standards of the Western sciences. That these magical systems are not conceived to achieve the same results or establish the same paradigms as the modern Western physical sciences does not invalidate or diminish their activities. The history of science approach to them, however, does tend to distort and even block scholarly perception of the meaningful interactions of magical, scientific, and religious systems. To cite a historical example of magical science, medieval Christian and Islamic alchemy utilized the laws of physical causality for both physical and nonphysical goals considered to be outside the purview of modern Western science; thus, it is not surprising that their results should diverge. Viewed from the vantage point of Western results, the actual results achieved become invisible and incomprehensible. The "operation" or "art," as alchemy termed itself, showed not only a philosophical orientation toward nature but simultaneously a material and processual response to nature. Alchemy as a theoretical as well as a practical expression of magic represented the union of nature and artifice.

Historical and contemporary cultures of magical belief and practice have been witnessed by extensive interpenetrating magical traditions of both learned texts (in manuscript and print) and popular/folk texts (in print and manuscript). For example, learned theoretical texts on alchemical talismanry interact with popular chapbooks of talisman and charm recipes, and theoretical texts of philosophical cosmology and astrology are matched by popular manuals of horoscope casting and astrological interpretation, as well as astrological folk almanacs. Although many cultures possess rich traditions of literate magic, all world cultures possess vast treasures of oral and ritual magical devotions expressed by ordinary believers and practitioners, as well as by magico-religious "professionals." In the study of folk religion and folk magic, folklore and folklife scholars have compiled extensive field reports of contemporary magical belief and practice that are, in many cases, the oral observations and testimony of the living remnants of older historical traditions. Oral traditional links of this type (such as that detailed by the scholarship on oral traditional literatures) can potentially assist in the ethnographic reconstruction of magical and other kinds of folklife from earlier historical periods and also enlighten contemporary understanding.

The folkloristic study of magic has focused attention primarily upon collecting ethnographic information on folk healing systems and, in particular, on the interaction of *spell magic* and the material magical techniques and rituals of folk religious healing. Collection and classification of the oral components and contents of these two overlapping categories of folk magic have produced a number of ethnographic studies of the magical practices of individual small communities worldwide and many comparative typologies of magical healing lore by region; the variations of their material and ritual contexts are detailed, but only vestiges of a theoretical approach to magic and a small amount of systematic or rigorous contextualization of magical belief are articulated. Folklore has largely transmitted the inherited theoretical constructs of earlier (and in many cases, now outmoded) anthropological theories on magic, with comparatively little development of its own unique theoretical perspective on the subject. Folklore's strength in the study of magic, however, has been its consistent and detailed attention to the oral and material culture of magic and its delineation of the unique culture of magic expressed by the ordinary believing person and small community.

Folkloristic interest in spell magic is an obvious outgrowth and a parallel development to folkloristics' strong emphasis on traditional oral poetry and the artistry of traditional and received oral forms. Folklore scholarship on the oral epic and other genres of verse and song testifies to the numinous transformative power inherent in the performance of contemporary oral art in the works of Albert Bates Lord and Milman Parry, John Miles Foley, Robin Horton, Ruth Finnegan, and others. These oral traditional arts are reminiscent of and, in many cases, directly descended from rich multicultural historical traditions of the sacred and magical power of cadenced speech; examples include the jinn- inspired gnomic utterance of poetesses and poets of pre-Islamic Arabic, the guided speech of ancient Greek poesy and late Greek oracle possessed and transfigured by an indwelling spirit, and the fiery exhortatory poetry of the ancient Israelite prophets and judges compelled by divine mission. These historical and contemporary conjunctions of the sacred in oral art are strongly akin to the magical use of orality in spell magic, ritual chant, and incantational songs often produced and performed during states of expanded consciousness (trance, conscious dreaming, vision questing, and others) by magico-religious officiants, whether priestesses and priests, medicine workers and shamans, or witches and magicians. The deeply empowered contents, performance, and genres of oral traditional art (particularly epic and other forms of poetic oral art) have substantive and historical affinities with the sacred contents, ritual performance, and verbal genres of folk religion and magic (chant, mantra, spell, and incantation). Word magic is thus embodied for folklore in the universal genres of verbal art: oral poetry, folksong, rhyme, riddle, proverb, folk narrative or story, and memorate.

There is a representative body of folklore material, more often than not labeled *superstition*, relating to the oral lore on magical belief and practice within diverse "folk" or "little" communities, principally in Europe and central Asia, south Asia, Africa, and the Americas. In the United States, folklorist Wayland Hand's systematization of superstitions, for example, has numerous categories and subheadings that are distilled into the cycles of human life, the supernatural, cosmology and the natural world, and "other." Folkloristic conception of and attention to folk magic, exemplified by Hand, most frequently associates magic with the supernatural and beliefs in luck or chance. Oral-literate folk healing systems devoted to oral magic are handled in the contexts of specific small communities, such as the oral healing spells or charms of Serbian women of the Balkans or the dissemination of charm books to use in oral recitation and the performance of cures among the powwowers of the Pennsylvania Germans, based upon earlier European textual precedent.

The material culture of magic is the other major focus of folkoristic interest and study. Within the parameters of a single family or village, individual examples of magical lore have been collected and aggregated to form a network containing the beliefs and practices of an entire region or ethnic group composed of many such small communities. The diverse materials and ritual techniques of magical healing have been cataloged in both sympathetic (symbolic) and contagious (physical) forms of magical efficacy. The concept of transference of disease in American folk medicine, for example, has numerous material and ritual expressions and sites, such as the symbolic or indirect transference involved in the "selling" of warts or the direct transference by contagion involved in rubbing the wart with a piece of potato and throwing it away (when the potato rots, the wart will disappear). Healing also can be effected by transferring disease into material objects or the living bodies of animals or trees by tagging or plugging; in addition, healing can be accomplished by transferring disease into the body of another human by making an image in effigy (symbolic transference) with hair or nail pairings (transference by contagion). Attention to the physicality and instrumentality of magical healing systems has led some medical folklorists into discussions of empirical causality and efficacy, which replicate the larger debate on the relation of magic and science in the modern ethnographic context of the relationship of magical folk healing systems to modern allopathic medicine. More work needs to be done in the interpretation of this material and in the collection and analysis of new living examples of the verbal and material cultures of magic worldwide in order to elicit fully the context of magical practice and to explore issues of magical belief. To expand folkore's attention to contexts of practice and issues of belief, a greater commitment must be made to exploring theoretical concerns such as the redefinition of folklore's understanding of the relationship of magic and religion and magic and science from a truly folkloristic perspective.

For the purposes of a future redefinition of magic within folklore scholarship and within the humanities as a whole, magic may be most profitably viewed as a part of religion or a specific type of religious experience; it may not be understood properly without that relationship being the basis of the definition. This relationship may be stated as follows: Magic is always religious, but religion is not always or only magical. Therefore, magic can be best understood as a subset of religion, and it requires renewed examination as a unique category within the study of religion. As a corollary of this rudimentary definition of the relationship, it may be said that (1) there is a great deal of religious magic (that is, individual beliefs, rituals, and institutions within religions not otherwise dominantly magical in belief or practice, such as systems of belief in and ritual interaction with sacred objects, the magical use of such objects as vehicles of blessing, magical healing systems, and so forth); and (2) there are many magical religions (that is, religious systems that are predominantly magical in belief or practice). Some recent scholars in anthropology, history, and religious studies have addressed the kinship of magic and/or the occult with religion in positive ways, performing a kind of revisionist history on the original revisionist history, which separated magic from religion in the Western perspective in the first place. The need to create scholarly space for magic to be discussed as a legitimate and vital form of religious experience and expression is pressing. The resuscitation of the term *magic* is necessary because it conveys crucial affective qualities (emotional intensity and excitement) embodied by certain types of religious experience and certain religious and cultural systems as a whole, which Valerie Flint, Tom Driver, and others have recently described in the context of magical belief and practice, particularly in ritual forms. When scholarship strips religious culture, particularly religious folk culture, of these affective components by erasing magic or attempting to devalue it by categorizing magical beliefs and practices as not "real religion," our view of that religious culture becomes distorted and diminished. The relatively recent decision among various scholarly disciplines regarding the term *magic*—that it has become too compromised by historical association with Christian and general cultural pejorative to use—has resulted in the substitution of a variety of terms, such as *ritual*, and a recasting of what was called "magic" into new conceptual and descriptive outlines consonant with that very different term. Although there is much subsumed under the term *magic* that is ritual (verbal and material activity, expressive drama, transformation of self and cosmos) and much that magic and ritual share (they are richly affective, powerful, and energetic), the term *ritual* cannot be applied to the mental and emotional features of intentionality, visualization, and interior verbalization that characterize the breadth of magical cultures worldwide.

The redefinition of magic as a part of religion and further ongoing positive attention to the subject of magic will help to clarify the theoretical relationship of magic and science to religion both within particular believing communities and between disparate communities of belief. Further, magic's kinship with science when redefined as a part of religion will highlight the nature of various sciences (whether medieval-based sciences such as alchemy, astrology, and talismanry or modern sciences such as biology, chemistry, and medicine) as systems of belief interacting with parallel, complementary, or competing religious systems of belief. Finally, redefinition of magic as a part of religion by folklorists and other scholars also will highlight the complex and subtle interrelationship between institutional forms of religion and the beliefs and practices of actual believers that often become most visible on the threshold of magic.

Kathleen Malone O'Connor

See Also Assault, Supernatural; Belief, Folk; Charm; Divination; Exorcism; Fairy Tale Heroes; Medicine, Folk; Religion, Folk; Ritual.

References

Butler, Jon. 1979. Magic, Astrology, and the Early American Religious Heritage, 1600–1760. *American Historical Review* 84(2): 317–346.

Douglas, Mary. 1970. *Purity and Danger: An Analysis of Concepts of Pollution and Taboo*. London: Routledge and Kegan Paul.

Driver, Tom F. 1992. *The Magic of Ritual: Our Need for Liberating Rites That Transform Our Lives & Our Communities*. San Francisco: Harper Collins.

Evans-Pritchard, Edward E. 1937. *Witchcraft, Magic, and Oracles among the Azande*. Oxford: Clarendon.

Flint, Valerie I. J. 1990. *The Rise of Magic in Early Medieval Europe*. Princeton, NJ: Princeton University Press.

Frazer, James G. [1890] 1922. *The Golden Bough*. London: Macmillan.

Ginzburg, Carlo. [1966] 1985. *Night Battles: Witchcraft and Agrarian Cults in the Sixteenth and Seventeenth Centuries*. New York: Penguin.

Halpern, Barbara Kerewsky, and John Miles Foley. 1978. The Power of the Word: Healing Charms as an Oral Genre. *Journal of American Folklore* 91: 903–924.

Hand, Wayland D. 1961. Introduction to *Popular Beliefs and Superstitions from North Carolina*. In *The Frank C. Brown Collection of North Carolina Folklore*, ed. Newman Ivey White, Vol. 6. Durham, NC: Duke University Press.

Hand, Wayland D. 1980. *Magical Medicine: The Folkloric Component of Medicine in the Folk Belief, Custom, and Ritual of the Peoples of Europe and America*. Berkeley: University of California Press.

Hufford, David J. 1988. Contemporary Folk Medicine. In *Other Healers: Unorthodox Medicine in America*, ed. Norman Gevitz. Baltimore, MD: Johns Hopkins University Press.

Malinowksi, Bronislaw. [1925] 1954. *Magic, Science and Religion and Other Essays by Bronislaw Malinowski*, ed. R. Redfield. Garden City, NY: Doubleday and Anchor Books.

Mauss, Marcel, and Henri Hubert. [1904] 1972. *A General Theory of Magic*. Trans. R. Brain. New York: W. W. Norton.

Neusner, Jacob, Ernest S. Frerichs, and Paul Virgil McCracken Flesher, eds. 1989. *Religion, Science, and Magic: In Concert and in Conflict.* New York: Oxford University Press.

O'Keefe, Daniel L. 1982. *Stolen Lightning: The Social Theory of Magic.* New York: Vintage.

Tambiah, Stanley J. 1969. The Magical Power of Words. *Man* 3: 175–208.

Tambiah, Stanley J. 1990. *Magic, Science, and the Scope of Rationality.* Cambridge: Cambridge University Press.

Thomas, Keith V. 1971. *Religion and the Decline of Magic: Studies in Popular Beliefs in Sixteenth and Seventeenth Century England.* London: Weidenfield & Nicolson.

Winkelman, Michael. 1982. Magic: A Theoretical Reassessment. *Current Anthropology* 23(1): 37–66.

Yates, Frances A. 1979. *Giordano Bruno and the Hermetic Tradition.* Chicago: University of Chicago Press.

Yoder, Don. 1972. Folk Medicine. In *Folklore and Folklife, An Introduction*, ed. Richard M. Dorson. Chicago: University of Chicago Press.

Magicians

The hero with supernatural powers is a figure found frequently in folk tradition. Often these characters employ their magical abilities in contests with similarly endowed villains, as is the case with the diminutive African hero Fereyel, among many others. Magical powers may also be employed to predict the future, one of Merlin's abilities. They may be employed to immediately transport characters large distances, as in the story of Aladdin. They may enable the magician to cast various spells and charms or to speak with and/or to command animals, as in the Korean story of Marshall Gang Gam-Chan. Heroes with magical powers may also use them to benefit their community, as in the case of the Australian Aboriginal hero Wirreenun. Magicians may also be healers who use their magic to cure illness, as in the case of the Eight Immortals of China.

Magicians are sometimes cast in the role of national or culture hero, as in the case of Saemund Sigfússon the Wise (1056–1133) of Iceland. A priest-prince of Oddi in southern Iceland renowned during his lifetime for his learning and wisdom, Saemund became by the seventeenth century an Icelandic people's hero, symbol of their dislike of and resistance to Danish rule. He was said to have learned his magic at the Black School and was widely credited with cheating the Devil, an attribute often attached to magicians.

Other national figures sometimes attract magical attributes, including Francis Drake, Walter Raleigh, Owen Glendower, and even Oliver Cromwell. Drake, known to the Spaniards as "El Draco," was widely believed to be in league with the Devil, and there are numerous traditions about his use of this connection to protect the nation against the Armada and to provide his local community with a water supply.

Magicians, depending on their positive or negative status, go by various names in folklore, including sorcerers, wizards, wise men or wise women, magi, witches, warlocks, demons, dervishes, and so forth. One of the most commonly encountered magical abilities is the skill of shape-shifting, or transmogrification. Being able to turn oneself, or others, into different forms has many applications, including disguise, invisibility, escape, the attainment of power, and so forth. Believed to have lived in the last half century or so before the Christian era commenced, Vikramaditya was the Raja of Ujjayini. He features in numerous folktales as a magician who can send his soul into any other body and is also able to fly. He is a wanderer and wise man with characteristics similar to those attributed to the biblical Solomon.

Magic is one of the relatively few areas of folk tradition in which heroines approach heroes in number. However, magical villainesses are also extremely common, most usually in the form of the witch, such as the Russian Baba Yaga.

Graham Seal

See Also Fairy Tale Heroes; Helpers, Folk; Hero/Heroine, Folk.

References

Leach, M., ed. 1972. *Funk and Wagnall's Standard Dictionary of Folklore, Mythology, and Legend*. London: New English Library, 1975. Abridged one-volume edition of *Funk and Wagnall's Standard Dictionary of Folklore, Mythology, and Legend,* 2 vols., New York: Funk and Wagnall, pp. 660–663.

Simpson, J., trans. and B. Benedikz, intro. 1975. *Legends of Icelandic Magicians*. London: Brewer/Rowan and Littlefield, The Folklore Society.

Westwood, J. 1985. *Albion: A Guide to Legendary Britain*. London: Granada, pp. 16–18.

Wherry, B. 1904. Wizardry on the Welsh Border. *Folklore* 15: 75–86.

Magic Tale

A lengthy folktale containing elements of fantasy, such as animals endowed with speech, magical objects, monsters and witches, or marvelous helpers and partners. Despite the abundance of fantasy, however, the main character of the tale is a human figure. Magic tales usually have functioned as entertainment. Stories such as "Cinderella," "The Princess on the Glass Mountain," and "Hansel and Gretel" are examples of well-known European magic tales. In Antti Aarne and Stith Thompson's international tale type index, the magic tales fall under the type numbers 300 to 750.

The term *magic tale* (Aarne's *Zaubermärchen*) corresponds to the term *fairy tale*. Certain folklorists and literary critics have suggested the use of the term *magic tale* in order to distinguish oral folktales from literary tales of fantasy. Because oral and literary traditions have intermingled repeatedly in European tales during the past few centuries, favoring the term *magic tale* over the more widely known *fairy tale* is simply a matter of taste.

A number of hypotheses have been raised about the age of the magic tale genre. The suggested time of origin has ranged from the Neolithic Stone Age to the seventeenth century. Contemporary scholars, however, consider the majority of the known European magic tales to have been composed relatively late, in medieval times at the earliest. Nevertheless, magic tales may include elements (images, concepts) much older than the entire plots familiar to us today.

The most famous early anthologies of European fairy tales are Giovanni Francesco Straparola's *I piacevoli notti* (1550–1553), Giambattista Basile's *Il pentamerone* (1634), and Charles Perrault's *Contes de ma mere l'oye* (1697). Jacob and Wilhelm Grimm published their *Kinder- und Hausmärchen* (Children's and household folktales) in several editions from 1812 to 1858.

Magic tales fall into a number of subcategories. The Russian formalist A. I. Nikiforov introduced the distinction between "masculine" and "feminine" magic tales in 1928. The former deal with the feats of male heroes, and the latter concern the vicissitudes of young women's lives. A prototypical example of a masculine tale is the "Dragon Slayer"; feminine tales include "Sleeping Beauty" and "Snow White." Some popular magic tales, however, such as "Strong John" and "Tom Thumb," are founded on hyperbolic, carnivalistic fantasy.

Because of the breadth of the magic tale's plot spectrum, one need not force the tales into the straitjacket of only one plot scheme, as the Russian folklorist Vladimir Propp attempted to do. According to him, all oral fairy tales can be morphologically deduced from the tales about the kidnapping of a princess by a dragon; the hero of these stories travels to the Otherworld, overcomes the monster with his magic object, rescues the girl, and marries her at the happy end. Propp's "mytho-heroic" scheme covers masculine magic tales well; the scheme is, however, less suitable in describing the plots of feminine and carnivalesque tales.

The main protagonists of magic tales are type characters: penniless boys or girls, nameless princes and princesses. The fantasy figures appear as animals, goblins, trolls, witches, spirits, dead people, devils, or human actors endowed with marvelous and incredible abilities. Although Christian or ethnic belief figures may appear in magic tales, the basic attitude or mode found in most oral magic tales is amoral and nonreligious.

Even though the magic tale is a prose narrative, it may include poetic lines or songs. Openings and closings are often formulaic: "Once upon a time" and "Then they lived happily ever after" transport the storyteller and audience in and out of the fictitious world. A familiar feature of this type of folktale's style and structure is repetition: the presentation of the same element in two or three versions.

Although we usually regard the magic tale solely as a source of amusement, some are didactic and moralistic. Because magic tales were entertainment for all age groups in preindustrial communities, narrators would alter tales to accommodate their audiences. A survey of European folklore collections and archives reveals powerfully erotic, humorous, and satirical magic tales that could hardly pass as entertainment intended for children.

Satu Apo

See Also Folktale; Motif; Tale Type.

References

Aarne, Antti. 1910. *Verzeichnis der Märchentypen* (The types of folktale). Folklore Fellows Communications, no. 3. Helsinki: Academia Scientiarum Fennica.

Aarne, Antti, and Stith Thompson. 1961. *The Types of the Folktale: A Classification and Bibliography.* Second revision. Folklore Fellows Communications, no. 184. Helsinki: Academia Scientiarum Fennica.

Apo, Satu. 1994. *Narrative World of the Finnish Fairy Tale: Structure, Agency, and Evaluation in Southwest Finnish Folktales.* Folklore Fellows Communications, no. 255. Helsinki: Academia Scientiarum Fennica.

Dégh, Linda. 1969. *Folktales and Society: Story-Telling in a Hungarian Peasant Community.* Bloomington: Indiana University Press. (Originally published as *Märchen, Erzähler und Erzählgemeinschaft: Dargestellt an der ungarischen Volksüberlieferung,* Berlin, 1962.)

Jason, Heda. 1977. *Ethnopoetry: Form, Content, Function.* Bonn: Linguistica Biblica.

Lüthi, Max. 1985. *The European Folktale: Form and Nature.* Trans. John D. Niles. Bloomington: Indiana University Press. (Originally published as *Das europäische Volksmärchen: Form und Wesen,* Bern and Munich, 1947.)

Moser, Dietz-Rüdiger. 1975. Alterbestimmungen des Märchens. In *Enzyklopädie des Märchens,* ed. Kurt Ranke et al., Vol. 1. New York: Walter de Gruyter.

Nikiforov, A. I. 1975. Towards a Morphological Study of the Folktale. In *The Study of Russian Folklore,* ed. and trans. Felix J. Oinas and Stephen Soudakoff. Paris: Mouton. (Originally published as *K voprosu o morgologiceskom izucenii narodnoj skazki,* Leningrad, 1928.)

Propp, V. 1970. *Morphology of the Folktale,* 2nd ed. Trans. Laurence Scott. Austin: University of Texas Press. (Originally published as *Morfologija skazki,* Leningrad, 1928.)

Thompson, Stith. 1946. *The Folktale.* New York: Holt, Rinehart and Winston.

Martial Arts and Folklore

Back when fighting arts operated at the village or family level, all knowledge was folk knowledge—stories were told over drinks, around the campfire, and so on, much as family stories are told and retold today, at every holiday. At the village or family level, changes to the existing narrative only occurred with the tacit agreement of the listeners. Change the story without the agreement of listeners, and the listeners would soon start telling new stories about the silly person who tried to change the narrative.

Today, few martial arts operate solely at the village or family level. Instead, most of them are regulated by bureaucracies. Bureaucracies produce formalized curricula, sanctioned histories, and so on, and change is approved from above. The advantage of this system is that it standardizes practices and curriculum, thereby allowing an art to survive, reasonably intact, even during times of rapid expansion.

A bureaucracy keeps money and power flowing to the center. Thus, the people nearest the center (the elite) tend to rewrite their practices and curricula to protect their own political and economic interests. For example, elite members are usually given disproportionate coverage in official histories, whereas people who have displeased the elite are written out of the official histories altogether. Nonetheless, even in the most bureaucratic systems, folklore continues to circulate informally. Some people still have the old text, or the old curriculum, or simply dislike the central leaders, and have no problem telling anyone who will listen.

Martial arts provide a rich medium for folklore studies. For traditional systems, folklore provides insight into a worldview, whereas for bureaucratic systems, folklore provides clues into what may have actually happened (as opposed to what the elite wishes had happened).

Put another way, folklore consists of a store of traditional knowledge embodied in the customs (e.g., rituals and costumes) and art forms (e.g., proverbs and tales) that are transmitted among members of a group. The folklore in turn helps build and maintain group identity. In this context, the label "folk" is not a prejudicial comment on the validity of the material so labeled. Neither should anything labeled "folk" be discounted as nonsense. Even if folk stories cannot be proven using historical documents, the stories often lead researchers to more concrete data. Even when documentation and archaeological evidence actually disproves individual stories, such elements of expressive culture reflect qualities of self-image and worldview current at the time the story was told. Thus, folk perspectives warrant our respect and attention.

Narrative

Martial folk narratives should be viewed as efforts to "flesh out" the practical aspects of the system of which they are a part. Although many of the tales eventually find their way into print, the tales frequently exist apart from written media. Committing a narrative to print, however, does not change the folk status, but print versions do give the impression of the story being genuine.

At one level, orally transmitted narratives are suspect. As any trial lawyer, police officer, or parent can attest, stories change once you get somebody on the stand. In addition, if we tell the story enough, we start to believe it ourselves. Moreover, the

A nineteenth-century depiction of Minamoto Yoshitsune, a famous and chivalrous warrior, being taught martial arts by the tengu (mountain goblins) on Mount Kurama, outside Kyoto. (Asian Art & Archaeology, Inc./Corbis)

"same" story often exists in different versions: folktales change to respond to changing social situations and audience feedback during performance.

At another level, however, orally transmitted narratives give us insight into motivations that may never have been put on paper. This happens because the fundamental goals of the storytelling are to reinforce group identity, legitimize the worldview arising from that identity, and support a common bond among members of the folk group. Thus, orally transmitted narratives are best considered as gauges of attitude rather than as funds of historical fact.

In the martial arts, lineage is a traditional means of establishing credibility for a system. As in the Bible, who begat whom? Therefore, origin narratives are among the most common types encountered in martial arts systems.

Many origin legends maintain that the point of the art's origin lies outside the human realm. For example, Japanese tradition preserves legends of warriors who attained martial skill by contact with supernatural figures called *tengu*, meaning goblins that combined the physical attributes of men and raptors. *Tengu* had a particular talent for swordsmanship, a gift they passed along to humans who won their favor. One such fencer was Minamoto Yoshitsune (1159–1189). While Prince Yoshitsune was training to become a monk at Tokobo Monastery, an apparition of his mother visited him in a dream, and implored him to avenge his father who had died at the hands of the rival Taira clan. Although little more than a child, he resolved to answer his mother's call by roaming the mountainous area around the monastery after dark, striking stones and trees with his wooden practice sword. In this manner, he intended to teach himself the art of swordsmanship. The King of the Tengu, observing his dedicated practice, appeared to the youth, defeated him using only a feathered fan, and then took on the task of teaching him to master the sword.

Another common motif credits the animal world with laying the foundation of a new martial art or technique. For example, although the particulars of the surrounding events vary, tradition indicates that Praying Mantis *quanfa* was developed after a Chinese martial artist known as Wang Lang heard a ferocious hissing from the bushes. He went to look, and witnessed a struggle between a praying mantis and another insect (a cicada, grasshopper, or fly, depending on the version).

Many other martial creation legends hinge on the founder witnessing a life and death struggle between different animal species. Indeed, some plots recur so frequently and are dispersed so widely that they should be considered international tale types. For instance, a clash between a snake and a bird has been claimed as the origin legend of the Chinese arts of taijiquan and *yongchun* (wing chun) and the Sumatran art of *pencak silat*; the clash also appears on the Mexican flag.

The animal-modeling motif incorporated into the taijiquan, *yongchun*, and Silat legends is not limited to Asia. In the Gidigbo wrestling of the Yoruba of West Africa, there is a technique of snatching an opponent's arm in an attempt to dislocate the shoulder or elbow. The technique is called *ja-di ilafa* ("he who fights like a gorilla"), and is said to have been derived from watching the gorilla's attempt to intimidate rival gorillas by snatching and breaking young trees.

The reasons for basing martial arts on animal models are open to speculation. More important at this point is the fact that these origin narratives provide a point of common reference and a source of core attributes (e.g., strength, ferocity, or endurance) that encourages bonding among practitioners of a martial art.

Another common genre consists of stories about the system's heroes. For example, a traditional history of *yongchun* maintains that this system was created by the Buddhist nun named Wu Mei (Ng Mui) who had escaped from a destroyed Shaolin Temple (various locations are identified) following an attack by the forces of the Qing dynasty (1644–1911). The widely spread legend continues that Wu Mei created a simple, quickly learned fighting system that she transmitted to Yan Yongchun, after whom the martial art was named.

In the United States, a unique variant of the Wu Mei legend is perpetuated within the contemporary Won Hop Loong Chuan (WHLC) system. According to this group's traditional history, Ng Mui (their preferred pronunciation) was allowed to leave the temple at the conclusion of the battle because she was "only a woman." (This feature was emphasized by one of the WHLC's female senior instructors.) Ng Mui was accompanied by her children: one who held her hand, one she bore in her arms, and a third whom she carried in her womb. The oldest child was named Soy, and the fact that the family was later attacked by Qing troops is commemorated in a WHLC form called Inky Toy San Soy, a name said to mean "The Three Steps of Little Soy." To continue the WHLC story, Ng Mui was said to have raised a family of ten sons and several daughters (the number varies). She developed Wing Chun (their preferred pronunciation) as a relatively low level art (in contrast to the secret family styles taught to the sons) so that the daughters could barter these arts to their husbands (famous martial artists all) in exchange for learning the spouse's superior arts. Thus, thanks to Ng Mui, students of WHLC are ultimately heirs to the "best of the best" martial arts (Green 1997).

In Brazil, King Zumbi (1655–1695) is both a historical figure and a legendary hero, especially for capoeiristas of African descent. According to oral tradition, Zumbi was the last leader of the *quilombo* (runaway slave colony) of Palmares, in what is now the state of Alagoas, Brazil, and for years, Zumbi led resistance against conquest of his *quilombo* and recapture of his people using his skills as a capoeirista. Like the WHLC version of the Ng Mui saga, the legends of Zumbi argue for a truly superior martial art, one that enabled unarmed resistance against swords and guns. Solid early evidence connecting Zumbi to capoeira is lacking. Nevertheless, Zumbi's central role in the African Brazilian martial arts community is attested to both by the persistence of his legends and by the commemoration of November 20, the anniversary of his execution, as a day for African Brazilian awareness.

In some cases, legendary heroes cross beyond specific martial arts groups and become the property of most of the martial arts community. Following the U.S. releases of the films *Fists of Fury* (Golden Harvest, 1971) and *The Chinese Connection* (Golden Harvest, 1972), Bruce Lee (Li Xiaolong, 1940–1973) "mania" generated a spate of contemporary legends focused on Lee's martial prowess. Among these was a narrative that was transmitted from Hong Kong by students studying at the University of Texas at El Paso in 1972. This tale described a challenge to Lee by a cast member in one of Lee's films who was an accomplished martial artist. In response to the invitation to combat, Lee was said to have walked over to an oil drum and pierced its metal side with a single thrust of his index finger. This act squelched the fight before it began. Both the narrator and his audience were active practitioners of *yongchun*, the system Lee had studied in Hong Kong, and, most important, the performer was an instructor and the audience members were his students. The tale used Lee as an example of what diligent practice could produce.

Counter claims regarding Lee's superhuman abilities also have surfaced within the martial arts community. For example, Gene LeBell (1932–), a former Amateur Athletic Union judo champion, professional wrestler, and stunt man, allegedly gave Lee a beating while working on the set of Lee's *Green Hornet* television series (ABC, 1966–1967). According to some versions, LeBell choked the actor into unconsciousness. The actual event, according to LeBell's Web site, was a prank during which the stunt man lifted Lee onto his shoulders and refused to put him down until the actor promised not to kill him. The two then became close friends (LeBell). The tale entered oral circulation around 2000 (probably as a result of its being posted on LeBell's Web site in that year), long after Bruce Lee's death and virtual canonization by his admirers. Reasons for the story's popularity include debunking the Lee mythology and exemplifying the maxim that no one is invulnerable.

Folk Belief

Unsurprisingly, folktales embody folk beliefs. Folk beliefs in the martial arts can range from the mundane to the fantastic, and tend to articulate relationships between the fighting system itself and larger belief systems, such as religion, politics, or medicine. Folk belief may be cast in narrative form, exist as a succinct statement of belief, or simply as allusions to common knowledge within the group.

A mundane folk belief is the one common among martial arts that the cloth belt or sash used as a mark of rank should not be washed. The usual folk explanation for this custom is that the white belt of the beginner eventually turns black through years of wear, and then, after countless more hours, turns back to a threadbare white. Thus, the natural (dis)coloration represents the effort expended in developing one's expertise, and washing unnaturally changes the color, thereby leading to a misrepresentation of the wearer's place in the martial order.

Beliefs in esoteric powers are also common. Examples are the concept known as *qi* (in Chinese) or *ki* (in Japanese). Other martial arts have comparable beliefs. For example, Southeast Asian Silat preserves a concept of supernormal power. The sources vary but are internally consistent with the prevailing religious systems (in this case, Islam). Gurus in the Sumatran style of Silat, called *Silek Bayang* (shadow Silat), reportedly have the power to kill opponents by directing their power at the victim's head, neck, stomach, or navel; some even claim to have the ability to kill with a glance. Equally esoteric Silat is said to render a practitioner invulnerable. The signature weapon of Silat, the *keris* or kris, is believed to have an animating presence akin to a soul that can trap a slain victim's soul at the moment of death, thus increasing its own power (Farrer 2006, 32–33). Some krisses are said to have the ability to rattle inside their sheaths, thereby warning their owners of danger, and some are said to leap from the sheath unbidden (Draeger 1972, 86). In the drive for Indonesian independence following World War II, some nationalists who were Silat practitioners credited the supernatural powers of their art (rather than international political pressure) for the success of their efforts to force the Netherlands in 1949 to abandon colonialism in Southeast Asia.

Similarly, belief in the *anting-anting* (a physical charm or amulet) persists among some practitioners of the Filipino martial arts. The *anting-anting* is said to confer invulnerability on the bearer, as long as it remains in his possession. The belief in the animate nature of weapons that was noted in the Indonesian

Silat community is also found among some members of the Filipino martial arts community. For example, a particular bladed weapon can have the power to cut the person who removes it from its sheath. Protection against being cut is provided by ownership of an *anting-anting* or by personal charisma that confers protection against such a "malicious" weapon.

In capoeira, the power of *corpo fechado* ("closed body"), a practice by which the body becomes invulnerable not only to the blows encountered in the *roda* (the circle in which capoeira is played) but against blades and bullets, is sometimes claimed. The closed body was achieved by the use of amulets. Oral tradition also attributes the power of shape-shifting to some capoeiristas of the past, claiming that they had the power to transform into an animal or tree, or to vanish into thin air.

Folklore, as a consequence of arising from members of a group needing to crystallize and express identity, reflects the preoccupations of the group, embodies collective self-image, projects images of others, and crystallizes worldview. Wherever it exists, folklore serves the ends of defining the group and the group's relationships to a given social, cultural, or historical environment.

Thomas A. Green and Stanley E. Henning

See Also Art, Folk; Asian American Humor and Folklore; Chinese Folklore; Japanese Folklore.

References

Chozanshi, Issai. 2006. *The Demon's Sermon on the Martial Arts*. Trans. William Scott Wilson. Tokyo: Kodansha International.

Draeger, Donn. 1972. *The Weapons and Fighting Arts of Indonesia*. Rutland, VT: Charles F. Tuttle.

Farrer, Douglas. 2006. Deathscapes of the Malay Martial Artist. *Social Analysis* 50(1, Spring): 25–50, DOI: 10.3167/015597706780886076.

Green, Thomas A. 1997. Historical Narrative in the Martial Arts: A Case Study. In *Usable Pasts: Traditions and Group Expressions in North America*, ed. Tad Tuleja. Logan: Utah State University Press, pp. 156–174.

Green, Thomas A. 2003. Sense in Nonsense: The Role of Folk History in the Martial Arts. In *Martial Arts in the Modern World*, ed. Thomas A. Green and Joseph R. Svinth. Westport, CT: Praeger, pp. 1–11.

Henning, Stanley. 1994. Ignorance, Legend and Taijiquan. *Journal of the Chen Style Taijiquan Research Association of Hawaii* 2(3, Autumn/Winter): 1–7. http://seinenkai .com/articles/henning/il&t.pdf (accessed October 26, 2008).

LeBell, Gene. Stories. http://www.genelebell.com/stories.html (accessed October 29, 2008).

Lewis, J. Lowell. 1992. *Ring of Liberation: Deceptive Discourse in Brazilian Capoeira*. Chicago: University of Chicago Press.

Ozaki, Yei Theodora. 1909. *Warriors of Old Japan and Other Stories*. New York: Houghton Mifflin.

Spiessbach, Michael F. 1992. Bodhidharma: Meditating Monk, Martial Arts Master or Make-Believe? *Journal of Asian Martial Arts* 1(4): 10–27.

Talmon-Cvaicher, Maya. 2007. *The Hidden History of Capoeira: The Collision of Cultures in the Brazilian Battle Dance.* Austin: University of Texas Press.

Un, H. B. 1974. *Praying Mantis Kung Fu.* London: Paul H. Crompton.

Wiley, Mark. 1997. *Filipino Martial Culture.* Rutland, VT: Charles F. Tuttle.

Wilson, James. 1993. Chasing the Magic: Mysticism and Martial Arts on the Island of Java. *Journal of Asian Martial Arts* 2(2): 10–43.

Marxist Approach

Various methodological approaches to the study of folklore that are based on the writings of Karl Marx (1818–1883) and Friedrich Engels (1820–1895). There is no unified Marxist approach in the study of folklore, nor is there any Marxist school allied with the study of folklore. Instead, scholars have incorporated various aspects of Marxist philosophies either in their interpretive methodology or in the selection of the folklore that they study. A great number of the Marxist theories and Marxist-informed studies in folklore are closely related to the interpretation of Marxism in the study of anthropology.

Marxism, which is generally considered to be a critique of capitalism, views capitalism as historically bounded and not a natural, universal system. Marxist theories engage several key concepts important to the study of culture and cultural expressions. Perhaps the most important among these concepts is that of dialectal historical materialism. Marxism is based on a dialectical model—one that accepts the often contradictory nature of phenomena. Materialism, usually contrasted with idealism, posits the primacy of matter. Thus, in Marxist dialectical historical materialism, the consciousness of humanity stems from the relationships with material existence. By incorporating the concept of dialectics—a theory of contradiction—with materialism, Marx and Engels provided a basis for the evaluation of history based in materialism. Nature, in this view, is not considered static; furthermore, the often contradictory phenomena of rapid change compared to slow development can be accounted for in this theory. Dialectical historical materialism thus forms the foundation for the critique of the development of capitalism and the concomitant effects of this development on cultural expressions.

Capital, in Marxism, is not a "thing" but rather both a process and a social relationship. Capital is based on the commodity. All commodities have use value and exchange value. The use value of a commodity stems from its ability to satisfy human needs, and the exchange value stems from its fixed-sum distribution. The concept of surplus value, the difference between the worker's wages and the exchange value added to the commodity, allows for the accumulation of capital.

Mode of production and social and economic formation also are essential terms in the Marxist social critique and are used to describe stages in the development of capitalism, a system that suggests both the existence of alienable labor and global exchange networks. The term *mode of production* incorporates both the technical, physical processes of commodity production and the social relationships that underlie production in a society. This level of relationships is referred to as the infrastructure. The term *social and economic formation* refers to the interrelatedness of several coexisting modes of production in a given society. This level of relationships is referred to as the *superstructure*. Given this intense focus on processes and relationships, Marxism can be viewed as primarily concerned with the analysis of social relationships and how they are articulated. Thus, in Marxism, there is an intense scrutiny of class, ethnicity, family organization, and the division of labor along gender lines.

Neither Marx nor Engels wrote specifically on folklore or its study, although they were aware of problems associated with the study of folklore. Perhaps the two works that come closest to folklore studies in these original Marxist writings are Marx's *Ethnological Notebooks of Karl Marx* and Engels's *Origin of the Family, Private Property and the State*. The former work engaged the concept of primitive society and precapitalist modes of production, and in the latter, Engels provided a critique of the development of the division of labor between men and women in the preindustrial household. The household, for Engels, was the original economic unit of organization, one in which all of the work was done for the benefit of the entire household. Although Marxist anthropologists have been actively engaged in the study of the development of modes of production and social and economic formation throughout history, Marxist folklorists have generally been interested in how these developments are expressed in or articulated as folklore.

One can make several major divisions to describe the practice of Marxist theories in folklore. The first major division is that between Western Marxism and Soviet-bloc Marxism. Although there has been a generally consistent development in Western Marxism and its application to the study of folklore, the development of Soviet folkloristics has been somewhat fragmented. Therefore, it may be useful to view the study of folklore in the Soviet Union and the Eastern-bloc countries in several periods: immediately following the Russian Revolution, the years under Stalin, and the years after Stalin. Given the breakup of the Soviet Union in the early 1990s, there will undoubtedly be a significant change in the study of folklore in the years ahead, particularly in regard to the Marxist analysis of folklore. In recent years, two major trends in the study of folklore have emerged that are closely linked to Marxist-informed approaches. The first of these trends is the documentation and analysis of "workers' folklore." The second of these trends is the increased interest in Third World folklore, particularly expressions associated with colonialism, imperialism and state-sponsored oppression.

Western Marxism is reflected in the works of a number of scholars, most notably those influenced by Antonio Gramsci, Ernst Bloch, Georg Lúkacs, and the Frankfurt school. Primary among those who reflect this influence are Theodor Adorno, Herbert Marcuse, and Walter Benjamin—none of whom lived or worked in Soviet-controlled countries. Thus, these scholars were able to develop Marxist theories that did not necessarily need to reflect the beliefs or views of the Soviet Communist Party. Although they did not engage the study of folklore except in passing, they were generally aware of the potentially subversive orientation of folklore as a collective expression inherently opposed to state capitalism. Although Western Marxism is, at times, evaluated as a reaction to Stalinism—an attempt to rescue Marxian thought from unfortunate associations with Stalinist brutality—it also engages the historical dialectic of post–World War I Europe and the United States, namely, the inability of the workers there to develop a revolution as occurred in Russia. Since the early years of the Institute of Social Research, Western Marxism has become a well-developed approach to cultural criticism, which includes the analysis of folklore at least to some degree. In the United States, José Limón and Jack Zipes are the scholars most engaged in the application of Western Marxist thought to the analysis of folklore. In his analysis of German fairy tales, a study influenced by the writings of Bloch, Zipes relied on Marxist theories to reveal social contradictions in Western culture that, in turn, find expression in the fairy tales. He suggested that "the commodification of Western culture creates a magic spell over society . . . so that, enchanted and blinded by commodity fetishism, we act against our own humane interests" (Zipes 1979). Limón also suggested that the Western Marxist interpretation of folklore is particularly allied with a performance-centered approach to folklore, noting that "in the very aesthetic act of performance may be found an inherent oppositional quality of all folklore. . . . All such performances may be displays of the possibility of hanging on to the use and value of things . . . in face of those who would turn all of life into acts of consumption" (Limón 1984).

The study of folklore in Soviet Russia and other Soviet-bloc countries does not reflect a consistent development. Prior to the Russian Revolution in 1917, the subject and methodologies of folklore were similar to those in the West, with a significant focus on the study of the byliny (epic). Immediately following the revolution, there was little focus on the study of folklore. It was not until the 1920s that it was once more engaged, and at that time, there was a flowering of formalist studies, Vladimir Propp's *Morphology of the Folktale* being among the most notable works in folklore from that period. Nevertheless, ideology did not comprise a major aspect of these works. Formalism quickly fell out of favor, however, and, along with Western methodologies such as those of the Finnish School, it was abandoned on ideological grounds. In the late 1920s, Maxim Gorki's formulation of the classical Marxist view that folklore reflected the collective spirit of the working classes and therefore was a valuable achievement gained acceptance and influenced the direction of Soviet folkloristics.

In the 1930s, folklore studies moved toward an examination of both ideology and social problems as expressed by the workers in their songs and stories. The study of individual narrators and the interplay between ideology and individual creativity became a major area of study, as evidenced by B. M. Sokolov's study of byliny singers. The prior view of the aristocratic origins of the byliny was rejected and replaced by the new interpretation of the genre as a creation of the people. Another area in which Soviet folklorists began to work was the collection and analysis of previously ignored folk genres, such as satires on religious figures and aristocrats, skazy (or personal experience narratives), the folklore associated with the revolution, and the folklore of workers. Folklore also was used as a source for and an object of propaganda. Not only was there an interest in the folklore of the workers and the revolutionary spirit expressed in traditional genres, there were also new ideological songs and stories composed in folkloristic style.

With the advent of Stalinism, the study of folklore in the Soviet Union became somewhat constricted, and folklorists were forced to abandon all forms of comparative studies and focus instead on the uniquely Soviet aspects of revolutionary cultural expression. After de-Stalinization in 1956, Soviet folklorists were once again allowed to make reference to Western works in their scholarship. Also, folklorists attacked the manifestly nonfolkloric forms of byliny that detailed the exploits of heroes of the revolution and Soviet leaders. Soviet folklorists also began to study the folklore of ethnic minorities living in the Soviet Union. The ideological slant of these studies was closely linked to the dialectical historical materialism of classical Marxism. By studying the folklore of the minority populations, their cultural expressions could be included by folklorists in the analysis of the historical development of societies. With the collapse of the Soviet Union, it is unclear what the future holds for Marxist approaches to both the analysis and collection of folklore in these previously Marxist-informed societies.

The study of workers' folklore also has become a significant object of study outside of Soviet-influenced countries. In Scandinavia, numerous scholars have been involved in both the collection and analysis of workers' lore, and throughout the 1980s, several conferences were held specifically concerned with workers' culture inside and outside of Scandinavia. In the United States, the study of workers' folklore is often considered under the rubric of "occupational folklore." Studying the folklore of workers contrasts with the romantic project of studying the folklore of peasants, dominant in nineteenth- and early twentieth-century folklore studies.

The fastest-growing field of study in Marxist folkloristics involves the Third World countries and their development. The transition from precapitalist to capitalist modes of production is a significant historical change. Michael Taussig, in his study of Latin American plantation and mining communities, examined how precapitalist symbols, particularly the devil, are used to negotiate the fearful transition to capitalism. In his study, he linked the devil as manifest in the folklore of the workers to commodity fetishism. According to Marxist theory, abstractions and social relations tend to become regarded as things—they are objectified. In the extreme case, the objectified becomes reified and appears to take on its own agency—it becomes fetishized. In the Marxist critique of capitalism, commodities are seen as becoming fetishized, and this fetishism, in turn, finds expression in folklore, according to Taussig. Precapitalist symbols, such as the devil, are then used to express phenomena of the emergent capitalism. Studies based on Taussig's evaluation of the use of precapitalist symbols to explain emergent capitalist phenomena could include the examination of economic exchange in peasant societies as expressed in their oral narratives.

Timothy R. Tangherlini

See Also Cultural Studies; Historical Analysis.

References

Bausinger, Hermann, Felix J. Oinas, and Carl Stief. 1972. Folklore. In *Marxism, Communism and Western Society: A Comparative Encyclopedia*, ed. C. D. Kerning. New York: Herder and Herder.

Choi, Chungmoo. 1993. The Discourse of Decolonization and Popular Memory: South Korea. *Perspectives* 1: 77–102.

Hemmersam, Flemming. 1991. Worker's Folklore and Worker's Ethnology in Scandinavia in the 1980s. *ARV* 47: 59–118.

Jay, Martin. 1973. *The Dialectical Imagination: A History of the Frankfurt School and the Institute of Social Research 1923–1950*. Boston: Little, Brown.

Limón, José. 1983. Western Marxism and Folklore: A Critical Introduction. *Journal of American Folklore* 96: 34–52.

Lombardi-Satriani, Luigi. 1974. Folklore as Culture of Contestation. *Journal of the Folklore Institute* 2: 99–121.

Marx, Karl. 1974. *The Ethnological Notebooks of Karl Marx*. Ed. and trans. Lawrence Krader. Assen, Netherlands: Van Gorcum.

Oinas, Felix J. 1973. Folklore and Politics in the Soviet Union. *Slavic Review* 32: 45–58.

Oinas, Felix J., and Steven Soudakoff, eds. 1975. *The Study of Russian Folklore*. The Hague and Paris: Mouton.

Taussig, Michael. 1980. *The Devil and Commodity Fetishism*. Chapel Hill: University of North Carolina Press.

Zipes, Jack. 1979. *Breaking the Magic Spell: Radical Theories of Folk and Fairy Tales*. Austin: University of Texas Press.

Zipes, Jack. 1984. Folklore Research and Western Marxism: A Critical Reply. *Journal of American Folklore* 97: 329–337.

Mask

Any sort of facial transformation or adornment and the costume and behavior that necessarily accompany it. In this sense, masks can range from the application of makeup to the use of elaborate head coverings. As the basic sites of communicative expression and identity, the head and face are subject to extremely diverse forms of masking in cultures throughout the world. Masks and masking techniques can be viewed as arts and crafts, but their cultural function of altering the faces of individuals in everyday life, drama, ritual, and celebration also must be considered. The concept of "face" implies more than anatomical features. It includes all of the social and symbolic meanings members of a society associate with specific physical appearances. The considerable social significance of the face accounts for stereotyping based on facial features, such as eye shape, nose size, and skin color, and for the human propensity to distort these features through masking. By simultaneously releasing individuals from their accustomed face and burdening them with expectations associated with another, masking reveals individual and cultural explorations of personality.

The production of masks consists of several stages: collection of raw materials, preparation of the materials, crafting the mask from them, and application of the mask. Materials for mask making include wood, shells, grasses, feathers, and

Actor wears a 200-year-old wooden mask in a carnival parade in Bad Hindelang, Germany, 2010. (Filmfoto/Dreamstime.com)

other natural products, papier-mâché, ceramic, treated animal skins, plastic, rubber, and metal. The raw materials may be carved, shaped, combined, painted, or otherwise manipulated. In some contexts, any member of the given society may perform each of these preparatory tasks; in others, the tasks may be restricted to professionals and those in other specialized roles. For example, although many participants in European carnivals purchase their masks from professional craftspeople who use materials procured commercially, their New World counterparts more readily construct their own, original masks from materials at hand. Application and use of certain masks may likewise be restricted to specific individuals, groups, or occasions, such as shamans in some rituals. Some masks may be reserved for use by one gender.

The functions, meanings, and significations of masks must be determined in relation to the specific cultures and events of which they are a part. A surgical mask means something very different in an operating room than on the street at Halloween. Many Native American masks have religious significance restricted to specific rituals and dances, including healing and puberty ceremonies. Some masks have the power to transform the person wearing them into the figures they represent.

Traditional occasions for masking generally cluster at points of transition in the annual cycle and the life cycle, such as changes in seasons, birth, and death. Most European scholars formerly took this as an indication that all masking events originated in a primitive, pre-Christian mentality geared toward spirits of nature that govern fertility and renewal or spirits of the dead that can affect the living. From a different perspective, transitional points can be seen as pauses in the productive cycles. The increased leisure time during these phases allows for eased structures of social engagement. In this context, masking occasions, like other forms of play and fantasy, provide a possibility for the exploration of alternative identities. This exploratory operation often focuses on inversions, opposites, and exaggerations. Some of the most common masking strategies involve the conflation of incompatible binaries: male/female in cross-dressing and androgynous masks; human/beast in the many animal masks found globally, in wild man figures, and in the Kwakiutl man within a raven within a bull; plant/animal in vegetation demons made of agricultural waste or excessive local natural products, such as bog moss creatures; insider/outsider in the frequent, stereotyped depiction of ethnic groups, such as Jews, Gypsies, and Moors in Europe, Indians and Africans in North America, and white anthropologists in Africa; and human/supernatural in masked depiction of deities.

Exaggeration takes the form of extended and exploded features. Bulbous noses, puffy cheeks, and monstrous mouths appear on masks in many societies. Giant figures walking on stilts or carried in processions also utilize this trope, as do "big-heads" with their oversized heads dwarfing the bodies on which they sit. Jewelry, implants, and means of extending features offer other techniques for facial distortion. Rarely does a mask attempt an accurate representation of a human face. Seemingly human masks often involve subtle caricature or reduction of distinctive features. Some masks, such as stockings or plastic Halloween faces, take the reduction of facial features to an extreme, creating eerie effects.

Although the disguise afforded by masks frees wearers from their conventional personalities, it does not allow unrestricted exploration of alternative roles. Cultural expectations, explicit or perceived, also impose restrictions on the sounds, gestures, and movements made when wearing certain masks. In the carnival of Elzach, Germany, masked Schuttig figures must speak in a falsetto or emit gruff growls. In ritual and drama, maskers often have precisely choreographed roles. A child dressed for Halloween is likely to behave in a manner associated with the figure represented by the mask, just as the performer of a Navajo bear has specific duties and roles. However, the behavior of these maskers may tend toward caricature and exaggeration, much like the facial features presented in their masks.

Outside of their culture contexts, masks often retain elements of their power and fascination. The booming market for masks as art pieces, the popularity of plastic surgery, even the effect of dismembered heads displayed in various ways all reaffirm the significance of the face in human communication and thought.

Peter Tokofsky

See Also Carnival; Costume, Folk; Drama, Folk; Festival; Mumming.

References

Alford, Violet. 1978. *The Hobby Horse and Other Animal Masks*. London: Merlin.

DeMott, Barbara. 1982. *Dogon Masks: A Structural Study of Form and Meaning*. Ann Arbor, MI: UMI Research.

Goonatilleka, M. H. 1978. *Masks and Mask Systems of Sri Lanka*. Colombo, Sri Lanka: Tamarind.

Hammoudi, Abdellah. 1993. *The Victim and Its Masks*. Trans. Paula Wissing. Chicago: University of Chicago Press.

Leach, Edmund. 1961. Time and False Noses. In *Rethinking Anthropology*, ed. Edmund Leach. London: Athlone.

Lévi-Strauss, Claude. 1982. *The Way of the Masks*. Trans. Sylvia Modelski. Seattle: University of Washington Press.

Napier, David. 1986. *Masks, Transformation and Paradox*. Berkeley: University of California Press.

Material Culture

A mode of cultural expression in which technological means are used either to produce artifacts or to modify segments of the natural landscape. Frequently described as including food, shelter, and clothing and therefore as essential for the maintenance of human life, material culture also includes objects that may be classed as amenities, such as varieties of household implements, and luxuries, such as paintings or items of jewelry. Since human beings are constantly making or using things, a person's entire biography from birth to death can effectively be monitored by following the flow of objects throughout his or her life. Larger social themes can be investigated as well by making similar observations across the experience of an entire community. Thus, students of material culture, though they are expected to pay close attention to the description and evaluation of artifacts, are even more concerned with how people use objects and assign meanings to them. The thought and behavior associated with material items is, in the end, considered more important than their physical attributes.

Within the phrase material culture, culture is ultimately the more significant term, for no matter how intriguing or emotionally satisfying an object's form, color, or texture, its deepest significance will not differ in any fundamental way from the prime messages of music, oral literature, dance, or any other expressive form. Material culture specialists should be seen, then, as students of a segment of human conduct. They even may play the lead role in the study of particular locales where things and property are deemed crucially important or where artisans are highly esteemed. In materialistic places where the production, accumulation, and display of goods are central to social definition, it would seem most prudent to concentrate the greater share of scholarly inquiry on aspects of material culture. And where there is little in the way of firsthand data about a group, particularly for those vanished historical communities that have left little or no legacy in written or documentary form, material culture provides the most secure means for retrieving salient features of everyday life. This is because an object, unlike a story or a song, does not require the presence of a living performer; an artifact can be said to "perform" its biography by the simple fact of its presence. Although the mission of material culture study may complement a wide array of disciplines, including art history, the decorative arts, architectural history, geography, and social history, the greatest similarities are found with the objectives of anthropology, particularly with its subfield archeology. Indeed, material culture research is, because of its utility as a means of historical recovery, often referred to as "aboveground archaeology."

The study of any object proceeds via the analysis of its components or attributes. Although these may be prioritized in different ways, all objects, it is agreed, have a physical form, a method of manufacture or construction, and a pattern of use. Of these features, form is usually the first to be considered since it provides the most trustworthy basis for developing a typology and then for making assessments about definitive characteristics and relevant comparisons. Through formal analysis, one develops a three-dimensional description of an object, and once a particular object—a chair, for example—is compared with other objects of a

Artifact

Any object made or modified by humans. The term derives from the Latin *arte factum*, meaning something made with skill. The object expresses the mental template of its maker and the culture at large, through the shaping of raw materials that result in the artifact's tangible form. The attributes seen in an artifact are based on traditional, functional, and/or technological requirements of the user and culture. For these reasons, few artifacts have only one attribute or meaning.

The varied approaches used during the last century to study artifacts began with the description and classification of objects, usually by museum curators. The artifacts were grouped according to type, based on their morphological features. Nineteenth-century evolutionary theory, combined with the diffusionist theories of early twentieth-century anthropologists, contributed to the development of stylistic analyses of artifacts, as well as interest in the techniques and technology used in making them. The early fieldwork of cultural anthropologists such as Bronislaw Malinowski, Franz Boas, and Ruth Benedict and archaeologists such as A. V. Kidder focused on the interrelationship of objects to sociocultural patterns and structures.

Since the 1960s, the study of artifacts has drawn on a number of disciplines in the physical and social sciences to extract information not readily apparent to the observer. The most recent efforts now inform an integrated approach that includes aspects of the previous approaches. Artifacts now "speak" to the observer as repositories of human communication and interaction. Reading the text of an artifact, rather than just focusing on its physical attributes, is another way of accessing the culture being studied.

Although artifacts occupy a central place in anthropology and folklore studies, each discipline differs in its approach and analyses. It is understood that through artifacts, researchers in both disciplines can attempt to comprehend the beliefs, values, attitudes, ideas, and assumptions of a society or group of people at a given point in time. So the main distinction that separates the two disciplines is the factor of time.

For the archaeologist, the *processes* (both mental and physical) by which an artifact is produced are less tangible than for the folklorist since archaeologists often study cultures that are extinct. At best, the archaeologist can only hope to accurately guess at these processes through the reconstruction of events and scientific study.

For the folklorist, however, the artifact or folk object is part of an informal learning process whereby, through tradition, the mental and physical aspects of the object's manufacture are seen in the creative process of the producer and are recorded by the folklorist. In turn, when the artifact's form is read like a text, then certain motifs can be recognized and compared to known traditions. In this context, the artifact is complete and historical, so there is no mystery as to its relative context or creator.

Regardless of disciplinary orientation, the artifact continues to play a central role in bringing the culture to the researcher. In this sense, the artifact, as reference point, mirrors for posterity the ideas and systems of the culture that produces it purposefully or accidentally.

Georgia Fox

similar class—the chairs produced in a given region—one can determine, with reasonable confidence, if the particular object is representative of local practice, an extraordinary masterwork, or only a quirky aberration. All of an object's features bear cultural meaning, but features of form connect most directly to the process of design and thus to the idea of form rather than to physical appearance or social usage. This is so because traditional forms derive from deeply coded notions of order and propriety. These ideals are less likely to be revealed by secondary attributes, such as color, finish, or materials. In looking at form, one engages the cultural rules that govern the way an artifact is conceived in the mind of its creator.

How an object is constructed involves not only the tools and techniques employed but also the selection and procurement of materials. In studying a potter, for example, one would first determine what type of clay is used, how it was obtained, and how it was prepared for use. Usually, it would be mined, transported to the workshop, mixed with water, weighed out into units known by experience to produce vessels of a conventional size, and kneaded into solid lumps. The investigator would then follow the sequence of steps required to transform the raw clay into a vessel, noting how the lump of clay is pinched and pulled while being turned on the potter's wheel. Next follows the drying and glazing process (sometimes repeated twice), and finally, the brittle pot would be loaded into the kiln and fired to rocklike hardness. If one had an expert knowledge of ceramics, many of these steps could actually be inferred from the examination of a finished pot. However, it is best to observe the processes of construction or manufacture firsthand, for there are always procedures that leave no telltale marks, and more important, an individual artisan's personality is likely to be manifested more clearly in the production rather than the design stage. Although a traditional potter might make a particular type of churn according to the dictates of local custom, the curvature of its sides, its height, the position of handle attachments, its color, and many other attributes are mainly the result of personal taste and habit. In studying production techniques, one encounters numerous opportunities for innovation, however modest. Some of these opportunities will show up as features in the finished artifact, and others only in the skilled use of tools, as the so-called tricks of the trade.

How an object is used is most likely to reveal more about its destination and consumer than its circumstances of creation. An artisan may have intended that an object be used in a particular way and thus may have designed it with special attributes. Some potters, for example, place an extra handle near the bottom of their storage crocks so that their contents can be more easily poured out. However, if this same crock is purchased by a contemporary urbanite, it might end up as an umbrella stand or serve as a base for a lamp, so that the extra handle is rendered functionless. Once an object leaves its creator's hand, it can serve purposes or acquire associations that he or she never imagined. Thus, compiling the

Traditional quilt from the 1930s. (Marilyn Stevens Photography)

"social life" of an artifact is a distinct task of material culture research that may take one well beyond an object's apparent function.

A quilted bedcover, for example, is generally understood as an item of sleeping equipment meant to protect and comfort a sleeping person through a cold night. Yet a quilt does so much more than that. The design of its top side, often colorful and geometrically complex, warms the spirit as much as the body. Intriguing to look at, it may even affect the overall look of the space in which it is used, simply by being the largest item in the room. Further, since quilts are usually produced by women, their decorative impact brings a woman's signature to a building that was likely constructed by men. A quilt may then constitute a crucial feminizing component in the effort to transform a house into a nurturing home. Since the materials used in quilts frequently were scavenged from other sewing projects, various bits of cloth will serve as mnemonic devices that awaken recollection of poignant moments in the family's history. A quilt may then enhance solidarity by encouraging the telling of important narratives. Because any artifact will simultaneously serve several purposes, there is an obligation in material culture research to portray something of the daily life of objects. Consequently, one is inevitably led beyond discussions of expected pragmatic functions to considerations of such aspects as aesthetics, ethical responsibilities, gendered social roles, or the preservation of memory. This is because in studying how artifacts are used, one is soon drawn into the social contexts that surround objects. In considerations of form and construction, the artifact is the center of attention, but in discussions of use, the artifact may only serve as a means of entry into other social concerns. In this sort of inquiry, the artifact even may seem to fade into the background as other matters are highlighted.

The study of the social contexts surrounding artifacts provides the most common meeting ground for the various disciplines with proclaimed interests in material culture. But if the commentary about material culture is not grounded in things—in the concrete experience of the artifact—objects are reduced to mere illustrations, to pictures that serve only to adorn the pages of a scholar's text. It is a fundamental assumption in material culture research that artifacts are texts, albeit in tangible form. Thus, they have to be treated as vital, firsthand evidence and not as ornaments that will enhance accounts generated primarily from written records. That the reputation of the artifact still lags well behind the document as the datum of choice is due to a long-standing bias in scholarly tradition that favors words over things. There is, consequently, a general lack of what might be termed "artifactual literacy" among scholars who, though they can read documents, do not know how to look beneficially at material evidence. Until the ability to "read" objects is more widespread, the study of material culture will continue to be snubbed as "pots and pans history."

Since material culture is so pervasive in human history, it makes little sense to ignore the ever-present, ever-constant messages that it provides. Folklorist Henry Glassie argues that via the artifact, scholars might recover truly scientific procedures for their enterprise, avoid the biases of elitism, and develop more convincing explanations—all of which should lead to what he calls a "more human history." Such a laudatory project, however, is not easily achieved. Artifacts are complex texts layered with subtleties and the seeming contradictions of simultaneous functions. Although all objects convey cultural meaning, some convey that meaning more effectively and with greater impact. Therefore, in selecting an object or class of objects to study, it is important to choose well. One should select things that are complex and thus invested by their makers with considerable effort in design and manufacture: The investment of time, resources, and energy provides assurance of significance. The most preferable object also should be tied to a place, that is, rooted to a locale in the case of a building or intimately connected to a family in the case of a cherished keepsake. In either instance, the object is less likely to be removed from its original context and will more readily allow access to the circumstances of its creation and use and therefore to its social meanings. Finally (and this is perhaps obvious for historically motivated projects), one should select artifacts that are durable and enduring. Things that have survived the assaults of time have the capacity to take us back directly to the periods when these items were first made. They thus are quite useful in developing an accurate historical baseline. Things that continue to be made according to the dictates of traditional authority and in large numbers illuminate well the satisfactions of custom and the dynamics of social identity. Used together with very old items, they facilitate confident analysis both of origins and subsequent developments, involving a complex balance of continuity and change over time.

Material culture research is, among American folklorists, a relatively young enterprise. Even though a number of the founding members of the American

Folklore Society in the late nineteenth century were associated with museums and were thus students of artifacts, it was not until the 1960s that material culture began to be more fully accepted. However, studies of folk architecture, art, craft, foodways, costume, and agriculture published since then have effectively demonstrated the value of this specialization. Indeed, material culture courses have become regular offerings in university curricula, and papers on tangible aspects of traditional culture are now a staple of academic conferences. One suspects that in the future, it will be normal practice for folkloric ethnographies to incorporate and blend together evidence of oral, musical, and material traditions.

John Michael Vlach

See Also Architecture, Folk; Art, Folk; Costume, Folk; Craft, Folk.

References

Appadurai, Arjun. 1986. *The Social Life of Things: Commodities in Cultural Perspective*. New York: Cambridge University Press.

Armstrong, Robert Plant. 1971. *The Affecting Presence: An Essay in Humanistic Anthropology*. Urbana: University of Illinois Press.

Babcock, Barbara A. 1992. Artifact. In *Folklore, Cultural Performances, and Popular Entertainments*, ed. Richard Bauman, pp. 204–215. New York: Oxford University Press.

Bronner, Simon J., ed. 1992. *American Material Culture and Folklife: A Prologue and Dialogue*. Logan: Utah State University.

Bronner, Simon J. 1992. The Idea of the Folk Artifact. In *American Material Culture and Folklife: A Prologue and Dialogue*, ed. Simon J. Bronner. Logan: Utah State University Press.

Csikszentmihaly, Mihaly, and Eugene Rochberg-Halton. 1981. *The Meaning of Things: Domestic Symbols and the Self*. New York: Cambridge University Press.

Deetz, James. 1967. *Invitation to Archaeology*. New York: Natural History Press.

Glassie, Henry. 1968. *Pattern in the Material Folk Culture of the Eastern United States*. Philadelphia: University of Pennsylvania Press.

Glassie, Henry. 1975. *Folk Housing in Middle Virginia: A Structural Analysis of Historic Artifacts*. Knoxville: University of Tennessee Press.

Jones, Michael Owen. 1989. *Craftsman of the Cumberlands: Tradition & Continuity*. Lexington: University Press of Kentucky.

Schlereth, Thomas J., ed. 1982. *Material Culture Studies in America*. Nashville, TN: American Association for State and Local History.

Upton, Dell, and John Michael Vlach, eds. 1986. *Common Places: Readings in American Vernacular Architecture*. Athens: University of Georgia Press.

Vlach, John Michael, and Simon J. Bronner, eds. 1992. *Folk Art and Art Worlds*. Logan: Utah State University.

Walls, Robert E. 1990. Folklife and Material Culture. In *The Emergence of Folklore in Everyday Life*, ed. George H. Schoemaker. Bloomington, IN: Trickster.

Medicine, Folk

"Unofficial" health practices and beliefs found in all societies. These are both religious (e.g., the use of prayers for healing or the belief that sin is a cause of disease) and material (e.g., the belief that eating a hot breakfast will prevent winter colds or the use of jewel weed to treat poison ivy). These beliefs and practices exist as complex systems related to the other beliefs, values, and attitudes of those who hold them. Folk medicine is not considered "false belief," and conventional medicine has, in fact, adopted many items from folk tradition. The oldest modern conception of folk medicine placed it within a system of layers, lying between official, scientific medicine (the top layer) and primitive medicine (the bottom layer). This scheme reflected the nineteenth-century view of cultural evolution in which medicine, like the rest of culture, was seen as having developed from its crudest, most primitive form into its modern, Western, highly sophisticated state. All that was most effective in medicine was retained during this evolutionary ascent, while discarded and obsolete ideas drifted downward and were preserved in the lower layers. This notion is summed up in the German term *gesunkenes Kulturgut* (sunken cultural materials). Although this model remains influential in popular thought, the evolutionary view of culture on which it was based has now been discarded or extensively revised by most scholars.

Current definitions of folk medicine show two main influences. Folklorists interested in health beliefs and practices in modern, technologically advanced societies have focused primarily on those found in specific cultural and subcultural groups and transmitted, in large part, by oral tradition. Examples would be the brauche, or "powwow," tradition among Pennsylvania Germans, curanderismo among Mexicans and Mexican Americans, and the herbalism traditions found in Appalachia. Anthropologists usually have studied folk medicine in developing countries. This setting has led them to emphasize the culture-exchange relationship of folk medical systems both with local, indigenous traditions and with the official medical system of the politically dominant national culture. The latter is often modern, Western medicine. From the fieldwork of these two disciplines, a general definition of folk medicine has evolved, encompassing health traditions that exist alongside but at variance with whatever other medical system is recognized as "official" in the local context. As a result, the concept of folk medicine has broadened.

If folk medicine is unofficial health beliefs and practices, it must be recognized that *officialness* is a relative term, rooted in context. Something is official if it is authorized in a formal way. Scientific medicine is the official medicine of the United States through authorization by a host of government sources (e.g., the office of the surgeon general), the bodies that accredit medical schools, and so forth. Folk health traditions are not given official standing by such agencies, and many lack formal authority structures of their own. There is no office or agency among folk herbalists in a region that can specify standard procedure or regulate practice. Oral tradition has processes that support standards and constrain practice, but they do not speak with one voice. They also do not command the resources and power that more formal institutions do. Therefore, folk medicine tends to rely heavily on oral tradition, and this is one reason why it tends to develop locally distinct forms, whereas official medicine shows much greater consistency across large distances.

Folk Medicine Traditions as Health Systems: Consensual and Individual

Systematic organization is one feature of folk medicine traditions that tends to produce stability, and this is a characteristic that is shared with other kinds of belief traditions. In the old concept of folk medicine as obsolete notions from "high culture," there was a tendency to view beliefs and practices as individual pieces. However, recent students of folk medicine have recognized that these diverse elements actually operate within an orderly set of relationships, forming a "health system." Health systems may be viewed in either of two ways: as the consensus among a number of people or as an individual's collection of health-related information and attitudes. For example, scientific medicine, Pennsylvania German powwow, and classical Chinese acupuncture are consensual health systems; the beliefs and practices of a particular doctor, powwow, or acupuncturist are individual health systems.

It is the relationships among the elements of a system that tend to give it stability and coherence. Many herbalists, for instance, believe that the special virtue of plant medicines lies in their "naturalness," which is considered desirable because nature is inherently reasonable; that is, things are as they are in nature for functional reasons. Some attribute this inherent reasonableness to the goodness of the divine plan, and others cite the operation of evolution. Many see the two as indistinguishable. However this natural order is understood, it is coupled with the belief that when humans attempt to increase productivity or comfort or to speed up and amplify natural effects without an appreciation of the real reasons for that order, the order becomes deranged, with unhealthy consequences. Heart disease is believed to result, in part, from the increase of refined foods in the diet—a change that is convenient (longer shelf life, easier preparation) but unhealthy. Similarly, although the treatment of heart disease by synthetic digitoxin is faster and more profitable than treatment using the leaf of *Digitalis purpurea*, the herbalist believes that the leaf is safer and has a broader effect. So an herbalist health system may embody an entire set of attitudes, values, and beliefs that constitute a philosophy of life, not merely a batch of remedies. This systematic view even extends explicitly to the moral questions of disease and healing, with laziness and greed being considered important contributors to sickness.

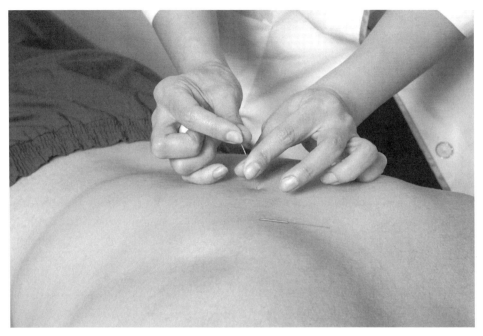

Acupuncture is a traditional Chinese medical procedure in which practitioners insert hair-thin needles through the skin to stimulate points of the body. (iStockPhoto.com)

The more complex and the more integrated such a health system is—that is, the greater the number of orderly relationships among its parts—the more stable it will be. One very important element that adds complexity is the tendency of folk medicine traditions to combine both natural elements, such as herbs, massage, and dietary rules, with supernatural elements, such as divine sanction for the natural approach, the efficacy of prayer, the idea of supernaturally caused disease, witchcraft, or the evil eye. The division of folk medicine into "natural" and "magico-religious" domains, common through much of twentieth-century scholarship, misses the powerfully integrative tendency of most traditions. This integration of material and spiritual elements is one of the great attractions of folk medicine to many of its users.

No matter how complete and exclusive a consensual health system may appear, the individual systems of those who comprise it will be somewhat eclectic. The individual systems of most folk healers and their patients will include ideas not only from their folk tradition but also from modern medicine, from religion, and so forth. By the same token, most medical doctors hold some folk beliefs along with their scientific beliefs and values. This individual diversity encourages the constant flow of influences among the health systems within a society because each person actually constitutes a bridge connecting two or more traditions.

The Dynamic Interaction of Folk Medicine Traditions

Folk medical systems are vigorous in the modern world, and they are in a constant state of dynamic interaction with each other and with official cultural institutions. As a result, they contribute elements directly to official medicine, and some develop their own official structures.

Given the definitions of folk medicine discussed earlier, all religious healing is folk medicine within the context of most modern societies because religious beliefs and practices are very different from the beliefs and practices of official medicine. However, certain religious healing beliefs do achieve varying levels of official religious, as opposed to medical, status. Thus, for example, a belief in miraculous, divine healing is simultaneously a folk medical belief and an official religious belief within several major Christian denominations. This simply reflects the complex and context-bound nature of the folk-official distinction. Further, specific kinds of beliefs in religious healing vary along the folk-official continuum within particular religious traditions and over time. For instance, since the 1960s, the charismatic movement has risen to widespread popularity among Christians around the world, and a central feature of the movement is a strong belief in miraculous healing through prayer. Although it began as a grassroots movement, its broad appeal eventually produced accommodation and change within the established denominations, including a reemphasis of the healing mission of religion. In this process, prayer healing, which has always been a major feature of folk medicine, was returned to at least semiofficial status within many Christian denominations.

Herbal healing traditions have existed in most regions of the world. The most widespread healing system currently serving as a vehicle for herbal healing in North America is the health food movement. Until the counterculture revolution of the 1960s, health food stores remained predominantly Seventh Day Adventist enterprises, a carryover from the health reform movements of the turn of the century, and their clientele was primarily an older and rather conservative group. With the development of the ecology and back-to-the-land movements, this picture changed radically, and by the 1970s, the character of the natural food stores, with their young clientele, had a major impact on the health food industry. Today, one can find herbs coming from traditions all over the world in U.S. health food stores. These stores are not only commercial concerns, they also serve as important links in folk medical oral networks. Like the religious healing revival before it, the natural healing complex burst its original cultural bounds and became an influential force in American health belief. And now, the American Botanical Council has been established to serve a variety of political, commercial, and scientific purposes, representing herbalists from a great variety of traditions. The council also publishes a peer-reviewed journal called *HerbalGram*. Many herbalists do not even know the council exists, and the official power of the council is relatively small compared to such structures in conventional medicine. Nonetheless, herbalism is clearly becoming more formally organized, and this change further enhances its influence.

In 1992, the National Institutes of Health established, under congressional mandate, the Office of Alternative Medicine (OAM) to fund studies of the efficacy of all sorts of popular treatments. Many of the practices that the OAM is seriously investigating are among those that have been traditionally considered folk medicine, ranging from herbal treatments to laying on of hands and distant prayer for healing. Internationally, the World Health Organization has recognized the importance of folk medicine and has developed programs intended to help folk healers and medical doctors to work together in delivering health care in underserved areas of the world. Clearly, official approbation and the development of internal official structures does not mark a sharp boundary that separates folk medicine from all other health beliefs and practices in the modern world. The category of folk medicine constitutes a range within which traditions differ from one another and change over time with regard to their "officialness," and folk, commercial, and official institutions influence each other constantly.

Although oral tradition is relatively important, especially in less formally organized traditions, it cannot be used as a definitional requirement of folk medicine. Most of the traditions studied as folk medicine use print to some extent. For example, in the Pennsylvania German powwow tradition, *Der lang verborgene Freund*, a book of charms and recipes compiled and published in 1820 by a German immigrant named John George Hohman, has remained in print and in use to the present day in both German and two English translations. This book and others, including manuscript charm collections by individual practitioners, have not only helped preserve the tradition but also implemented its spread, especially since Hohman's book was sold through the Sears Roebuck catalog around the end of the nineteenth century. Although oral tradition remains an important aspect of folk medicine, the use of magazines, books, television, and the Internet by traditional health systems today is a mark of their vigor and adaptability.

The Persistence and Prevalence of Folk Medicine

The modern picture of who uses folk medicine also has undergone radical changes. It was long assumed that folk medicine persisted in places where modern, scientific medicine was not available or as a survival among early generations of immigrants from traditional societies. It was assumed that higher education and familiarity with scientific medicine would result in sole reliance on medical doctors and hospitals. It is no doubt the case that isolation and lack of acculturation tend to reduce the rate at which any cultural institution changes, but change and adaptation are the natural state of tradition. It is now evident that the changes in folk medicine brought about by modern communication, geographic mobility, and other forces that reduce cultural isolation have not led to the demise of folk medicine—quite the contrary. A study published in the *New England Journal of Medicine* in 1993 found that 34 percent of Americans had used what the investigators called "unconventional interventions" within the preceding 12 months. Among those practices mentioned in the survey were several forms of folk medicine, including herbs and spiritual healing. This high rate of use came in spite of the exclusion from the survey of basic prayer for healing, probably the most widely used variety of folk healing. The survey also found, as have other studies in the United States and Europe, that use of these traditions was positively associated with higher education.

This finding comes as no surprise to scholars who do fieldwork in contemporary folk medicine. Although the children and grandchildren of some immigrant groups have rejected traditions including folk medicine as impediments to "Americanization" and their social aspirations, others in the community have shown great interest in folk medicines with which they did not grow up. The Caribbean traditions of spiritism, *espiritismo* (Puerto Rican) and *santeria* (Cuban), both with strong healing elements, now attract supplicants and members from the Anglo community in the northeastern United States. In Puerto Rico and the northeastern United States, there have even been projects to bring spiritists and mental health professionals into a collaborative, collegial relationship to work together in community mental health. Like acupuncture (which it accompanied to the United States), classical Chinese herbalism is sought out by patients from all kinds of ethnic groups and social classes. Psychotherapists and psychoneuroimmunology researchers are turning to the techniques of shamans to treat both psychological illnesses and physical diseases such as cancer. There is, in fact, a "neoshamanic movement" whose members seek to use drumming and other shamanic techniques to attain trance states both for self-fulfillment and for the treatment of others.

In the 1960s, cross-traditional influence and the adoption of beliefs and practices by people not raised with them would have been seen as "contaminating" tradition. The result, especially when it began to be transmitted in books and magazines, might have been called "fakelore." But it is clear that this view is outmoded today, particularly concerning folk medicine. Folk medicine always has exchanged materials and ideas with official medicine, and it always has been an important competitor with official medicine. In the nineteenth century, it was, in fact, almost impossible to tell which tradition was the official and dominant one. At present, a variety of factors, including the increasing costs of high-tech medicine, a widely expressed desire for a philosophy of healing that is more "holistic," and ready access to many cultural traditions due to modern communication and migration patterns, have led to an efflorescence of folk medicine traditions.

The Efficacy of Folk Medicine

Folk medicine persists because people believe that it helps them. Conventional physicians often reject or even seek to eradicate folk medicine because they believe that it is useless at best and dangerous at worst. The issue of efficacy is an inevitable aspect of inquiry into folk medicine. Understandably, this question is often asked in the terms of scientific medicine: How does a particular treatment compare with no treatment (a placebo control) in a controlled trial? Although such trials have been rare in the study of folk medicine per se, some have, in fact, been conducted, and there have been other sources of scientific evidence that bear on this question. In 1785, the British physician William Withering published *An Account of Foxglove with Its Medical Uses*. This marked the entry of digitalis into the pharmacopoeia of medicine, and Withering had made his discovery through the observation of an herbalist's successful treatment of a patient with "dropsy," using an herbal tea. Furthermore, numerous scientific studies have shown that various herbal traditions contain plant medicines that have real effects against some forms of cancer.

Dietary advice with a long history in folk medicine recently has attained medical acceptance. An excellent example of this is the new medical consensus concerning the importance of fiber in the diet. This development is credited largely to Denis P. Burkitt, the surgeon whose work in Africa included definitive research on the disease that bears his name: Burkitt's lymphoma. His observations of the high-fiber diet of certain West African tribes, the decreased transit time of food in their intestines, and the low rates of certain diseases among them led him to urge an increase of fiber in the modern Western diet. This proposition now has received substantial medical endorsement, particularly for the reduction of risk for gastrointestinal cancers. However, rarely, if ever, has any medical reference acknowledged that this has been a major folk medical belief in the United States at least since the nineteenth century. As recently as the 1970s, this belief was derided in medical circles, and it is cited in many descriptions of folk medicine along with such other unconventional notions as "bad blood." More recently, in 1994, Jerry Avorn, MD, published a study in the *Journal of the American Medical Association* documenting the usefulness of cranberry juice to prevent bladder infections, a long-standing folk practice. Such observations are numerous and add greatly to the credibility of natural healing beliefs and the popular idea that they are "forgotten knowledge" rather than obsolete medical beliefs or ignorant superstition.

Perhaps most surprising from the medical view, several medical journals have published randomized, double-blind studies of the efficacy of intercessory prayer, carried out at a distance. In 1988, cardiologist Randolph Byrd, MD, published a study in the *Southern Medical Journal* reporting a consistent and statistically significant advantage among seriously ill cardiac patients in a "prayed for" group as compared to a control group. The fact that such studies are being carried out and published by medical doctors is perhaps as significant as their results.

But a consideration of folk medical efficacy cannot be restricted to medical definitions. Several researchers have reported that even when the clients of folk healers show no objective improvement in their symptoms, they often say they feel better and may say that they have been healed. Such observations indicate that folk medicine does more than address physical malfunctions. That broader effect is indicated by healing, a central concept in many folk medicine systems. Healing is one in a series of English words that have developed from the single, ancient, Indo-European root word *kailo*, meaning "whole, uninjured, or of good omen." The linguistic descendants of *kailo* include the following: *hale* (as in "hale and hearty"), *health*, *whole*, and *holy*. The ancient connections of health with wholeness and holiness give some indication of why the connotations of healing have always been larger than those of curing or treating, to choose words more readily associated with medicine. One may or may not be made whole by being cured of a particular condition, but no cure or remedy is likely to be said to have rendered the patient more holy. Many forms of folk medicine deal directly with the metaphysical issues raised by illness and the social disruption that it often brings. So even when physical disease remains, the peace and satisfaction of having one's spiritual welfare and one's continuing place in the community affirmed may constitute the most personally important form of healing.

David J. Hufford

See Also Midwifery; Religion, Folk.

References

Block, Eric. 2010. *Garlic and Other Alliums: The Lore and the Science*. Cambridge: RSC Publishers.

Cavender, Anthony. 2003. *Folk Medicine in Southern Appalachia*. Chapel Hill: University of North Carolina Press.

De la Portilla, Elizabeth. 2009. *They All Want Magic: Curanderas and Folk Healing*. College Station, TX: Texas A&M.

DeStefano, Anthony M. 2001. *Latino Folk Medicine: Healing Herbal Remedies from Ancient Traditions*. New York: Ballantine Books.

FC&A Medical Publishing. 2004. *The Folk Remedy Encyclopedia: Olive Oil, Vinegar, Honey and Other Health Remedies*. Peachtree City, GA: FC&A Medical Publishers.

Hand, Wayland D., ed. 1976. *American Folk Medicine: A Symposium*. Berkeley: University of California Press.

Hand, Wayland D., ed. 1980. *Magical Medicine: The Folkloric Component of Medicine in the Folk Belief, Custom, and Ritual of the Peoples of Europe and America—Selected Essays of Wayland D. Hand*. Berkeley: University of California Press.

Hatfield, Gabrielle. 2004. *Encyclopedia of Folk Medicine: Old World and New World Traditions.* Santa Barbara, CA: ABC-Clio.

Hufford, David J. 1983. Folk Healers. In *Handbook of American Folklore*, ed. Richard M. Dorson. Bloomington: Indiana University Press.

Kirkland, James W., Holly F. Mathews, C. W. Sullivan III, and Karen Baldwin, eds. 1991. *Traditional Medicine Today: A Multidisciplinary Perspective.* Durham, NC: Duke University Press.

Kleinman, Arthur. 1980. *Patients and Healers in the Context of Culture: An Exploration of the Borderland between Anthropology, Medicine, and Psychiatry.* Berkeley: University of California Press.

McClenon, James. 1994. *Wondrous Events: Foundations of Folk Belief.* Philadelphia: University of Pennsylvania Press.

McGuire, Meredith. 1988. *Ritual Healing in Suburban America.* New Brunswick, NJ: Rutgers University Press.

Mitchem, Stephanie. 2007. *African American Folk Healing.* New York: New York University.

O'Connor, Bonnie Blair. 1994. *Healing Traditions: "Alternative" Medicines and the Health Professions.* Philadelphia: University of Pennsylvania Press.

Rubel, Arthur J., Carl W. O'Nell, and Rolando Collado-Ardón. 1984. *Susto: A Folk Illness.* Berkeley: University of California Press.

Sieling, Peter. 2003. *Folk Medicine.* Broomall, PA: Mason Crest.

Trotter, Robert C., and Juan Antonio Chavira. 1981. *Curanderismo: Mexican American Folk Healing.* Athens: University of Georgia Press.

Yoder, Don. 1972. Folk Medicine. In *Folklore and Folklife*, ed. Richard Dorson. Chicago: University of Chicago Press.

Memorate

An experiential narrative, a description of a supranormal experience undergone by the narrator or a person close to him or her. The term *memorate* was introduced by C. W. von Sydow in 1934 but was later redefined for analytical purposes. As firsthand accounts, memorates provide reliable data for the scholar studying the affective experiential aspects of religion as they reveal the situations in which the religious tradition was actualized and began effecting behavioral patterns. They also give information on the social contexts of beliefs, on religious experiences, on interpretation and transmission processes, and on the society that preserves the religious traditions in question.

Memorates are regarded as having no fixed formal characteristics. One way of recognizing a memorate is through its perception of psychological authenticity: By taking into account perception and social-psychological factors, one can judge how authentically the memorate under study describes the supranormal experience.

Another useful aid to comprehending the genre is offered by content analysis. Memorates containing many unique features that are "unnecessary" and secondary from the point of view of the narration and plot are primarily "fresh" and authentic and likely to give a most reliable picture of local folk belief.

The third means concerns a detailed study of the transmission process. On the basis of in-depth research concerning memorate materials, it seems to be expedient to show the links in the chain from the experiencer to the narrator. Most memorates are either firsthand (personal) or secondhand narratives, which implies that the actual religious tradition described must be continually renewed. It also is clear that in memorates, the details describing the supranormal experience (but unnecessary from the point of view of the plot) are more sparse when there are more links in the chain and when one gets further from the place and moment of experience. Memorates can be grouped into three categories: individual (based on the narrator's personal experience), group (family or age-group), and collective (stereotyped narratives that have been subjected to the social control of a society). The memorate describing an encounter with an unidentified supernatural being (numen) is called a numen memorate.

The part played by the tradition learned from previous generations (vertical tradition) and that learned from other members of the group (horizontal tradition) is of great importance at every stage of the transmission of a traditional message. One cannot experience or interpret an event as religious if one is not already acquainted with the religious experience and explanatory models of a tradition. A religious experience is always a question of the actualization of a belief within some supernatural frame of reference. The patterns of content, style, structure, and language, already familiar from the learned tradition, regulate oral communications in a chain of transmissions. It is through these patterns that the tradition is preserved and gradually assumes its stereotyped form. In studying religious events, there is an important problem of the processes of interpretation; these may be individual or social events controlled or regulated by individuals who exercise some kind of authoritative power in their social groups. In this way, a uniquely experienced event is partly absorbed into the traditions of the society. Studies of the preliterate stage of religious traditions presuppose that the chain through which the experience or event has been communicated is examined in detail. Each informant in the chain plays an important part, but of particular significance are the eyewitness to the event and the last informant, that is, the person who actually relates the oral message or converts it into a written form. It is at this point that the oral stage begins. The analysis of the written stage, however, is just as interesting a task as that of studying the oral process of transmission.

It is worth noting that different genres seem to transmit information about various aspects of a religion in different ways. Thus, myths, folk beliefs, and legends deal chiefly with the cognitive aspects of religion. At the same time, the cognitive level manifests itself, above all, in rites and the ritualistic descriptions of such rituals as sacrifices, prayers, or charms.

Juha Pentikäinen

See Also Anecdote; Belief Tale; Legend.

References

Dégh, Linda, and Andrew Vázsonyi. 1974. The Memorate and Protomemorate. *Journal of American Folklore* 87: 225–239.

Pentikäinen, Juha Y. 1978. *Oral Repertoire and World View: An Anthropological Study of Marina Takalo's Life History*. Helsinki: Academia Scientiarum Fennica.

Stahl, Sandra Dolby. 1989. *Literary Folkloristics and Personal Narrative*. Bloomington: Indiana University Press.

von Sydow, Carl Wilhelm. 1948. *Selected Papers on Folklore: Published on the Occasion of His 70th Birthday*. Copenhagen: Rosenkilde and Bagger.

Memorial Shrine

Informal assemblage constructed in commemoration of sudden death in a public space. In the context of folkloristics, the concept of the memorial shrine, in contrast to structures formally erected through a religious, educational, or governmental institution, is indicated by several terms including: *improvised memorial*, *memorial assemblage*, *makeshift memorial*, *spontaneous memorial*, *spontaneous shrine*, *temporary memorial*, *vernacular shrine*, and so on. Many have pointed out the implications of each term, with care being taken to recognize the emotional investment indicated by such assemblages. Therefore, some scholars discourage the use of terms such as *makeshift*. Moreover, others question the degree to which such memorials may currently be considered spontaneous, as their appearance at sites of unexpected death and attendant characteristics are now, in the early twenty-first century, tending toward the predictable. One of the earliest folkloristic treatments of the subject was Jack Santino's 1992 examination of memorials placed at sites of politically motivated murders in Northern Ireland, which he designated *spontaneous shrines*. The usage of *assemblage* in relation to memorial shrines may also be connected to Santino's use of the term with regard to Halloween decoration in a 1986 article published in the *Journal of American Folklore*.

Just as the terms signifying these assemblages are used interchangeably in both popular and academic writing, they may be applied to a number of subtypes of constructions. These range from small groups of items around a generally two-foot high Latin cross marking the site of a fatal automobile accident, to the vast numbers of bouquets and other artifacts left at various sites in memory of a public figure, such as a politician (Dutch politician Pim Fortuyn), a member of a royal family (Princess Diana of Wales), an actor (River Phoenix), or a professional athlete (Los Angeles Angels pitcher Nick Adenhart). The memorials often develop at the site of death within hours, but may also appear at other sites related to the life of the deceased. Memorials to Pim Fortuyn were assembled at the base of a statue of William the Silent, recognized as the father of the Netherlands, as well as in front of Fortuyn's home in Rotterdam. Memorial shrines for Princess Diana proliferated throughout the city of London, while mourners also left flowers and other mementos at the site of the fatal automobile accident in Paris. In April 2009, Los Angeles Angels fans left tributes for Nick Adenhart at the scene of the accident that killed him and three friends, and at the entrance to Angel Stadium of Anaheim. If the accident site is not accessible to mourners, a memorial may be constructed somewhere nearby, such as the memorial that developed on the fence outside a helicopter base in St. John's, Newfoundland, after a helicopter transporting workers to offshore oil platforms crashed in the Atlantic Ocean. Virtual memorial shrines are also found in various forms on the Internet, including social networking sites such as MySpace and Facebook.

In addition to flowers, visitors leave a wide range of items, both sacred and secular, universal and highly individual in meaning and apparent communicative intent: handwritten letters addressed to the deceased, photographs in protective plastic sleeves, rosaries, angel figurines, candles, canned beverages (e.g., the deceased's favorite soft drink or beer), food, signed baseballs and T-shirts, stuffed animals, coins, holy cards, saints' medallions, cigarettes, guitar picks, and so on. Whether handmade or mass-produced, the items often reflect particular interests or occupations of the deceased. The memorial shrines constructed for the victims of a school shooting may include ephemera such as spirit ribbons, graduation tassels, and group portraits of orchestras, choirs, and athletic teams. As well, people may leave items that directly address the circumstances of the accident or tragedy. American flags, notes and posters bearing nationalistic statements, toy fighter planes, and other items expressing patriotism dominated September 11th shrines in both New York City and near the Pentagon, in Virginia. Similarly, memorial shrines that developed after the terrorist train bombings in Madrid featured banners used in anti-terrorism demonstrations and posters that called upon the Spanish government to be truthful in its communication with the public about the attacks. Mourners also left posters and letters that expressed solidarity with the victims and between nations in a desire for peace.

Although memorial shrines are generally initiated by someone well known to the deceased (e.g., a relative or close friend), acquaintances and strangers, such as passersby who witness an automobile accident, may also contribute items and spend time at a memorial. Immediately after an accident or murder, people may gather at a memorial shrine to express their grief and commiserate with other mourners. Individuals may also visit the memorial to see what others have left.

Kathleen Olivo of Stroudsburg, Pennsylvania, who lost her sister on September 11, 2001, looks at a memorial wall in front of St. Paul's Chapel in New York City, blocks from the World Trade Center site. (AP/Wide World Photos)

This interaction between visitors and items left at the shrine—as each item contributed changes the memorial, if only slightly—has led scholars to theorize about memorial shrines' communicative and performative qualities.

Memorial shrines are temporary constructions, generally remaining at a site for a few months to a few years if the assemblage is not considered a hazard to public safety or commerce. The highest levels of re/creation and visitation generally occur right after the death(s) commemorated, and to a lesser extent on holidays, birthdays of the deceased, and anniversaries of the incident. Activity at the memorial may decrease due to the transference of material culture–centered mourning to the cemetery or home. In other cases, memorial shrine creators may fix a specific date for its termination, such as the date the deceased would have graduated from high school. However, activity at the site may be prolonged if: decorating at the cemetery is prohibited or restricted; the shrine commemorates a public figure whose burial site is not accessible to the general population; a large number of people are memorialized at the same site; the incident causing the death(s) is controversial in some way; or the shrine itself becomes a political statement. Memorial shrines constructed following terrorist attacks are examples of the latter three conditions, although roadside memorial shrines are also a frequent focus of local or regional controversy and lead to official policy creation or change.

Some of these same conditions may also discourage or prevent a memorial shrine from developing. As a matter of policy, vernacular memorial shrines are sometimes banned by municipal or regional authorities. Death sites related to recent or ongoing political or military conflict may be considered too dangerous to visit, both physically and politically. Concerns for the maintenance of commerce near a death site may also dissuade the construction of a memorial shrine. If family and friends live far away from the site of death, the construction and maintenance of a shrine is less likely. Finally, surviving family and friends may wish to avoid the death site altogether and therefore have little or no interest in constructing and maintaining a memorial.

Considering the factors that contribute to or discourage the construction of a memorial shrine leads to contemplation of the social meanings of such assemblages. The roadside memorial tradition, perhaps one of the earliest forms of memorial shrines, developed as a material focus for prayers for the souls of the deceased, to assist those who may have been spiritually unprepared for death. Individuals interviewed regarding contemporary memorials speak of the assemblages' role in reclaiming a site that has been tainted by accidental or intentional violence. In this way, memorial shrines may function as both physical and psychological healing mechanisms. Scholarship on contemporary vernacular memorial shrines has also identified them as a way of expressing grief in a public and participatory manner, a break from the conventional Western denial of death. The interaction between people and artifacts at memorial shrines also supports the interpretation of these shrines as a new kind of mourning. Other scholars have focused on the political or more broadly social declarations communicated both by the artifacts and those who visit the shrines—statements about the dangers of drunk driving; the importance of religion, patriotism, or public safety; affection for a particular school or team; condemnation of politically motivated violence.

However, memorial shrines are not always judged positively. Some journalists and academics view these assemblages as manifestations of excessive or even pathological grief, narcissism, and consumer culture at its worst, telling the viewer more about the people that visit the memorial than those they commemorate or the circumstances that led to their death. By visiting and contributing items to memorial shrines, some argue, individuals prolong and make public emotion that has historically been expressed in more private contexts. Moreover, the accumulation of artifacts at a shrine may be interpreted as: a demonstration of consumer culture excess, a fetishistic display of consumer goods meant to rehabilitate a scarred site and assuage feelings of loss and vulnerability, as well as an element identified in the impulse to transform accident victims into heroes or heroines, regardless of the circumstances of their death. Such interpretations, however, are often at odds with ethnographic readings of memorial shrines, as they negate the highly individual motivations that shrine visitors express verbally, kinetically, and materially. Fieldwork with memorial participants reveals the crucial role of these shrines in facilitating communication with the dead. Thus, both individuated and broad sociocultural expressions are significant in the construction, maintenance, and analysis of memorial shrines.

Holly Everett

See Also Art, Folk; Belief, Folk; Custom; Material Culture; Performance; Pilgrimage; Popular Culture.

References

Doss, Erika. 2008. *The Emotional Life of Contemporary Public Memorials.* Amsterdam: Amsterdam University Press, 2008.

Everett, Holly. 2002. *Roadside Crosses in Contemporary Memorial Culture.* Denton: University of North Texas Press.

Grider, Sylvia. 2001. Spontaneous Shrines: A Modern Response to Tragedy and Disaster. *New Directions in Folklore* 5(October). http://www.temple.edu/isllc/newFolk/shrines.html.

Margry, Peter Jan. 2007. Performative Memorials: Arenas of Political Resentment in Dutch Society. In *Reframing Dutch Culture: Between Otherness and Authenticity,* eds. P. J. Margry & H. Roodenburg. Aldershot, UK: Ashgate, pp. 109–133.

Santino, Jack, ed. 2006. *Spontaneous Shrines and the Public Memorialization of Death.* New York: Palgrave Macmillan.

Metacommunication

Communication that refers to or comments on relationships among aspects of the communication process. These aspects include: speaker, addressee (i.e., the person spoken to), topic and message, contact, and code. For instance, some metacommunication refers to the *speaker's* attitude toward what he or she is talking about (e.g., "I'm serious!") or comments on the speaker's act of speaking itself (e.g., "I've just come from the dentist and am having trouble talking"). In folklore study, Richard Bauman has pointed to tall-tale-teller Ed Bell's use of a metacommunicative aside to bridge the gap between Bell's "real world" identity—the "I" as a narrator of events (in the quote that follows, events centering on a tree filled with honey)—and Bell's fictional identity—the "I" as a character within the story being told: "That's what I always think of, get some honey, you know, or get whatever's there to be gotten." Other metacommunication may refer, for instance, to the nature or timing of the *addressee's* response relative to the speaker's utterances—for example: "Repeat after me . . ." or "Don't interrupt!" Storyteller Bell used metacommunication specifically addressed to his audience (as in the phrases "you've heard" and "you know") to suggest an explanatory link between the huge tree of his story and his audience's knowledge of large trees in the "real world": "*You've heard* o' those big ol', uh, trees in California, *you know*, bein' so big" (italics added). Metacommunication focusing on *topic* or *message* can deal, for example, with the contextual appropriateness of topic (e.g., "Johnny, we don't talk about such things in public") or with the repetition of message for the purpose of clarification or emphasis (e.g., "I said, 'Pass the butter'"). For his part, storyteller Bell used a metacommunicative aside to comment humorously on his own ability to provide a convincing story, on the problem of whether his audience was convinced, and on the believability of the story (i.e., the message) itself: "And I don't blame y'all if you don't believe me about this tree, because I wouldn't believe it either if I hadn'ta seen it with my own eyes. I don't know whether I can tell ya how you could believe it or not, but that was a big tree."

Metacommunication dealing with communicational *contact* between the participants can announce the opening of a communication channel (e.g., saying "Hello" after picking up a telephone receiver), or it can check whether the channel is indeed open (e.g., "Can you hear me?"). In folklore performance, a blues singer's line, "Hear me singing to you," refers to the singer, the audience, and the communication channel (oral channel, or singing), as well as offering a request for communicational contact ("Hear me"). Metacommunication treating *code* (i.e., a system of information) might refer to whether the participants share a particular cultural code. For example, the mother's utterance in the following exchange comments metacommunicatively on an ambiguous message and thus on a lack of cultural sharing: Adolescent son: "That's bitchin' [a term of approbation], Mom!" Disconcerted mother: "What do you mean?"

Metalinguistic utterances focus on aspects of the linguistic code (e.g., grammar, lexicon, orthography). For instance, they may refer to words *as words* (e.g., "I can't find *macabre* in the dictionary") or to the spelling of words (as in the spelling riddle "How do you spell *enemy* in three letters?—N M E"). *Metageneric* utterances refer to conventions associated with a particular generic code. In the following catch riddle, for example, the riddler "catches" the addressee in the conventional assumption that riddlers already know the answer to the questions they pose: A: "What's red, purple, green, yellow, gray, sky-blue, and green?" B: "I don't know." A: "I don't know either, that's why I'm asking you."

Metanarration is metacommunication that refers to or comments on aspects of a narrative or on aspects of a storytelling event. Excerpts given earlier from storyteller Ed Bell illustrate some metanarrational functions. In addition, Barbara Babcock has distinguished two types of metanarration. *Explicit metanarration* calls attention deliberately to the narrative and/or to the storytelling event. For instance, narrative beginning and ending formulas (e.g., "Once upon a time" and "they lived happily ever after") establish and conclude, respectively, a metanarrational frame in terms of which the contained utterances are to be understood (i.e., as a fairy tale). Explicit metanarrative-framing utterances also include stories that contain within themselves reports of the telling of other stories, as illustrated in the narrative set of *1001 Nights*. *Implicit metanarration* operates both as part of the story (e.g., it may advance the story's plot) and as metacommunication that calls attention to the story as a story (i.e., as constructed artifice). Examples include the use of syntactic and thematic parallelism.

Alan Dundes has called for folklorists to record and study *oral literary criticism*—that is, folk performers' and audience members' own interpretations of and commentaries on the meanings and uses of folklore. Such criticism would include, among other things, a storyteller's metanarrational asides offered during storytelling as well as participants' comments solicited apart from the storytelling act itself. For example, narrator Ed Bell has commented on his rhetorical purpose in drawing out his storytelling at folk festivals. He has said that such drawing out keeps the audience in suspense a bit longer and thus makes the listening experience better.

By commenting on aspects of the communication process, metacommunication facilitates participants' understanding of communicational structure, focus, and content and gives participants the means to talk about their communicative relationships to each other and to the ongoing discourse.

Danielle M. Roemer

See Also Frame.

References

Babcock, Barbara. 1977. The Story in the Story: Metanarration in Folk Narrative. In *Verbal Art as Performance*, ed. Richard Bauman. Rowley, MA: Newbury House.

Bauman, Richard. 1986. *Story, Performance, and Event*. Cambridge: Cambridge University Press.

Dundes, Alan. 1966. Metafolklore and Oral Literary Criticism. *The Monist* 50: 505–516.

Midwifery

The knowledge and practices associated with the experience of pregnancy and childbirth. Ritual birth practitioners exist in all cultures. Since birth is a complex cultural and biological process, midwifery encompasses belief systems about healing as well as medical treatment. In some societies, midwives function as an occupational group, often in conjunction with other medical personnel in the public sphere. Traditional midwives, in contrast, aid the birth process in the private realm as unpaid work or for a nominal or in-kind fee. In all cases, midwifery involves prenatal and antenatal care as well as aid with the birth process. Prenatal practices include massage, the use of steam baths, and nutritional advice regarding proper foods and/or medicinal herbs. Assistance with birth often requires emotional as well as physical support, "catching" the baby, cutting the cord, and treatment of the afterbirth, which has sacred significance in many cultures. In caring for the mother and infant, midwives may stay with a woman for a week or more. Traditional midwives perform a wide variety of other social functions, which may include circumcision, preparation of the dead for burial, and quasi-legal services such as establishing claims of virginity or alleged rape. Despite tremendous cultural variation, midwifery practices underscore birth as a universal and often highly structured ritual in modern industrial cultures as well as in traditional societies.

Early folk medicine scholarship in the United States and Europe incorporated midwifery under studies of superstition and folk belief. At the turn of the twentieth century, a number of articles appeared in the *Journal of American Folklore* on myths, rituals, and beliefs surrounding childbirth. Early collections offer a compendium of beliefs about the evil eye, breech births, being born with a "caul," foods to eat to avoid miscarriage, and similar topics.

Recent analysis of midwifery reflects the shift in folkloristics from collection of static phenomena and classificatory schemes to the study of dynamic processes and context. Often structural and comparative in nature, many studies contrast ethnomedical and biomedical worlds or compare midwifery as folk healing with popular and academic medicine.

Early research concentrated on folk practitioners in rural settings and among specific ethnic groups, such as African American midwives, Native American practitioners, and Hispanic women who practice midwifery as part of *curanderismo* (folk healing). Comparative studies have expanded to include the practice of nurse-midwives, who exist between the folk and biomedical worlds. A number of scholars have moved beyond particular ethnic groups to examine birth as a widespread rite of passage in technological societies.

Complementing and sometimes replacing comparative views, hermeneutic/interpretive approaches focus on the meaning of midwifery practice. In the convergence of studies of folk healing and systems of meaning, gender is pivotal. Although early studies assumed gender, it was not an analytic focus. More recent work problematizes gender, seeing midwives as *women* healers whose practice exists in a web of gender/power relations. Focus shifts to the midwife as social actor, recruitment to her role, and her place in the larger social order. Gender-focused studies also look at informal healing roles in order to include a broader range of women's experiences and pose new questions about gender and healing. In some studies, midwives are marginal figures, mediating between public and domestic worlds and nature and culture; in others, midwives' knowledge is central but "coded" by their subordinate position in male-dominated social worlds and medical structures.

Other works examine myths, other narratives, and broader cosmologies related to creation and procreation. These offer a movement beyond nature/culture divisions that contrast the female realm of procreation as "merely physical" with the creative realms of art and ritual that constitute culture.

Joanne Mulcahy

See Also Childbirth and Childrearing; Family Folklore; Feminist Perspectives on Folklore Scholarship; Gender; Medicine, Folk.

References

Davis-Floyd, Robbie E. 1992. *Birth as an American Rite of Passage*. Berkeley: University of California Press.

Hand, Wayland, ed. 1975. *The Frank C. Brown Collection of North Carolina Folklore*. Vols. 6 and 7. Durham, NC: Duke University Press.

Jordan, Brigette. 1983. *Birth in Four Cultures: A Cross-Cultural Investigation of Childbirth in Yucatan, Holland, Sweden and the United States*. Montreal: Eden.

Kay, Margarita, ed. 1982. *Anthropology of Human Birth*. Philadelphia: Davis. Martin, Emily. 1987. *The Woman in the Body*. Boston: Beacon.

McClain, Carol S., ed. 1989. *Women as Healers: Cross-Cultural Perspectives*. New Brunswick, NJ: Rutgers University Press.

Michaelson, Karen, ed. 1988. *Childbirth in America: Anthropological Perspectives*. South Hadley, MA: Bergin and Garvey.

Susie, Debra Ann. 1988. *In the Way of Our Grandmothers: A Cultural View of Twentieth Century Midwifery in Florida*. Athens: University of Georgia Press.

Weigle, Marta. 1989. *Creation and Procreation: Feminist Reflections on Mythologies of Cosmology and Parturition*. Philadelphia: University of Pennsylvania Press.

Migration

The movement of people, animals, or things from one location to another. Human migration refers to the movements of people, often in large groups or along specific routes. In folkloristics, migration usually refers to human migration. Migration can refer to the movement of people from one country to another, or movements of people within a country, for example, migration from rural areas to urban areas. Motivations for migration are often economic though they can also be political or religious. Nations, towns, or communities from which migrants originate are referred to as "sending" nations, towns, or communities. The destinations or migrants are referred to as "receiving" nations, towns, or communities. "Immigration" refers to settling in another nation or area; "emigration" refers to the act of leaving one's region of residence to settle elsewhere.

Not all migration is intended to result in permanent settlement. Workers may migrate seasonally; this is common among agricultural laborers. In early twentieth-century Argentina, large numbers of Italian agricultural workers referred to as *golondrinas* (swallows) traveled back and forth between Italy and Argentina in order to work the harvest season in both countries. In larger, geographically diverse nations such as the United States, migrant workers travel within the country to work on the harvesting and planting of different crops. Workers may also migrate temporarily seeking other forms of employment, usually because of higher wages or availability of jobs in the receiving location. Since credit is more difficult to obtain in Mexico, for example, workers often migrate from Mexico to the United States in the hopes that higher wages will allow them to accumulate savings for large expenses such as buying a house or starting a business. A recent trend in migration is university students seeking higher paying jobs abroad; such jobs are usually only short term, lasting only during the students' break between terms at school. Even when migration is intended to be temporary, however, migrants may settle permanently into a community or nation.

Migration is not always voluntary. One of the largest forced migrations in recent history was that of Africans who were sold as slaves to Europe and the Americas during the seventeenth, eighteenth, and nineteenth centuries. The Highland Clearances refers to the forced migration of highland Scots by British authorities in the eighteenth and nineteenth centuries. In the nineteenth century, indigenous populations in the United States were forced to migrate from their traditional lands to reservations designated by the United States government. The Soviet Union under the leadership of Joseph Stalin engaged in a number of forced resettlements and population transfers, usually targeting specific ethnic or religious groups.

Another common form of migration is that of refugee populations seeking escape from natural disasters such as drought or famine or political turmoil or persecution. The civil wars in Central America during the 1970s and 1980s led to a large numbers of refugees immigrating to the United States. Terrorism in the highland regions of Peru in the 1980s caused refugees from affected rural areas to migrate to urban centers.

Industrialization increased the trend of rural to urban migration within nation-states. Industrialization of agriculture meant that less labor was needed to achieve desired agricultural yields while the growth of factories in urban areas provided an increase in the number of unskilled jobs (Leeds 1971, 165–166). Rural to urban migration is also often stimulated by economic depressions or crises such as natural disasters that hinder agriculture.

The United States has defined itself as a nation of immigrants, as have Canada and Australia. In the United States, the traditional metaphor for this history of immigration has been that of the "Melting Pot"—the idea behind this being that upon arrival in the United States all cultures melded into one another to create a homogenous new identity. More recent scholarship has challenged this metaphor, arguing that ethnic groups retain at least part of their inherited identity. The first

German immigrants arrive in Topley, Canada, ca. 1910. (Corel)

major wave of European migration to the United States was one of settlement, taking place in the seventeenth and early eighteenth centuries. These migrants were almost exclusively from Western Europe, primarily the British Isles. Studies of migration, however, have tended to focus on later waves of migration occurring in the nineteenth and twentieth centuries. The next major wave of migration began in the mid-nineteenth century, and though these migrants were still primarily European peasants, they became an increasingly diverse group than before, including Southern, Northern, and Eastern Europeans. The Irish Potato Famine (1845–1852) led to mass emigration from Ireland, primarily to the United States. Growing population pressures in the East and the lure of economic opportunity in the West created an internal western migration in nineteenth-century America as well. In the twentieth and into the twenty-first century, the largest number of immigrants entering the United States has come from Mexico. The United States Immigration Reform and Control Act (IRCA) in 1986 had a significant impact on this migrant population by granting amnesty to certain undocumented migrants on the condition of continuous residency in the United States. It impacted the immigration process for both documented and undocumented immigrants (Hondagneu-Sotelo 1994, xiv).

In Europe, the two World Wars caused massive shifts in political boundaries, which in turn prompted an increase in human migration. The years after World War II marked the highest point of migration within Europe since the eighteenth century (Dégh 1975, 122). The creation of the European Union has changed the face of migration, making it simpler for citizens of member nations to migrate to other member nations. This has made it easier for migrants to return to their nation of origin rather than settle permanently in the new country. The creation of the nation-state of Israel in 1948 sparked the migration of Palestinian refugees out of Israel, and the migration of Jews from Europe, the United States, and other parts of the world to Israel. War, "ethnic cleansing," and famine have caused large refugee migrations in Africa in the late twentieth and early twenty-first centuries.

Folkloristics has approached and incorporated migration in numerous ways. Immigrant folklore has been the subject of American folklore studies almost from the inception of the discipline. "Immigrant folklore" usually refers to the traditions and lore of more recent immigrant groups, rather than the initial migration wave of settlers. Following the migrations caused by the World Wars in Europe, European folklorists and ethnologists increasingly examined the impact of migration as well (Dégh 1975,122).

In some cases, folklore is studied with the goal of determining past migrations. Studies of folk narrative have been used in comparative mythology and the historic-geographic method, in part, to trace the movements of people through the spread of narrative. Similar elements in myth, narrative, music, or art are held up as evidence of past contacts between separate groups.

Folklorists have examined the impact of migration on aspects of traditional culture including foodways, dress, belief, speech, and music. Availability of ingredients can make continuation of migrant foodways difficult, but this sometimes leads to the creation of specific grocery stores or restaurants to service migrant populations. Such business can become important centers for migrant communities. Similarly, churches can become hubs for migrant communities, particularly when the religion of the migrant culture differs from the religion of the dominant culture. As cultures interact they absorb aspects of each others' folklore so that immigrant groups develop a folklore that is their own, belonging neither to the sending nor receiving cultures. Ethnicity becomes a major theme, particularly in studies of international migration. Ethnic practices may be maintained symbolically as a way of maintaining differential identity and creating cohesion among an immigrant community (Dégh 1975, 115).

The concept and rates of acculturation have been a major theme in many folklore studies of migration. Linda Dégh has shown that the histories of the United States and Europe have created different patterns of acculturation. The high rate and diversity of immigration in the United States has caused less dominance of any one group, which speeds acculturation of all groups. Although immigrant enclaves are created, they usually become acculturated within two generations (1975,115). In Europe, however, migrant enclaves have greater endurance and the cultural persistence of some immigrant groups enables them to achieve the official status of national minorities (1975, 117).

In the United States, studies of immigrant folklore previously focused mostly on traditional "gateway" locations: urban centers such as New York City or the southern border states in the case of Mexican migration. Recent studies have increasingly examined populations outside of the traditional points of entry in suburban locations and throughout the country. Scholars have also looked at the impact of migration on sending communities.

Much recent folklore scholarship has also addressed the issue of gender, showing that men and women have fundamentally different experiences of migration owing to differences in cultural gender norms and the types of employment most accessible to different genders. This is further complicated by the fact that many married couples may migrate separately, with one spouse arriving sometimes decades before the other. This separation causes an impact on traditional family structure when families are reunited; gender norms, spousal relationships, and parent-child relationships may have to be renegotiated, often incorporating norms of the receiving culture (Hondagneu-Sotelo 1994).

Beginning in the latter half of the twentieth century, folklore studies of migration began to shift focus away from specific items or orientation and onto the process of migration itself (Dégh 1975,115). The study of immigration networks has been essential to understanding patterns of migration. When migrants move along networks they use personal connections to find employment, housing, and community in the destination location. This provides the migrant with resources that facilitate the migration and often results in the creation of an ethnic enclave. This means that many immigrants in a particular location will not only be from the same nation of origin, they will be from the same community of origin.

Immigration narratives have been studied as oral histories. These narratives can be examined to show how knowledge is passed along regarding the immigration process with regard to tactics for obtaining visas, cultural beliefs regarding the receiving culture, and tips for adjusting to life in the new environment. Folklorists studying immigration often focus on the points of contact between immigrant groups and the host culture. Folklore related to immigration also encompasses the beliefs and attitudes of the receiving culture toward the immigrant group.

Kristina Downs

See Also Ethnic Folklore; Immigration.

References

Dégh, Linda. 1975. The Study of Ethnicity in Modern European Ethnology. *Journal of the Folklore Institute* 12(2-3): 113–130.

Georges, Robert A., and Stephen Stern. 1982. *American and Canadian Immigrant and Ethnic Folklore: An Annotated Bibliography*. New York: Garland.

Hondagneu-Sotelo, Pierrette. 1994. *Gendered Transitions: Mexican Experiences of Immigration*. Berkeley: University of California Press.

L'Estoile, Federico Neiburg, and Lygia Sigaud, eds. 2005. *Empires, Nations, and Natives*. Durham: Duke University Press.

Leeds, Morton. 1971. The Process of Cultural Stripping and Reintegration: The Rural Migrant in the City. In *The Urban Experience and Folk Tradition*, ed. Américo Paredes and Ellen J. Stekert. Austin: University of Texas Press.

Peregrine, Peter N., Ilia Peiros, and Marcus Feldman. 2009. *Ancient Human Migrations: A Multidisciplinary Approach*. Salt Lake City: University of Utah Press.

Pozzetta, George E., ed. 1991. *Folklore, Culture, and the Immigrant Mind* in the series American Immigration & Ethnicity. New York: Garland Publishing, Inc.

Stern, Stephen, and John Allan Cicala, eds. 1991. *Creative Ethnicity: Symbols and Strategies of Contemporary Ethnic Life*. Logan: Utah State University Press.

Mnemonic

Aid for memory. Many professions and academic specialties use mnemonics for teaching and remembering, and educators endorse them for classroom and other formal educational contexts. Some mnemonics, especially those in oral circulation, have currency as folklore. They may assume several forms that encourage the memorization of facts or procedures that are otherwise difficult to retain.

Mnemonics often assume the form of rhyming verse. The rhyme that begins "Thirty days hath September," for example, helps to recall the number of days in each month. A rhyme that assists in spelling certain English words reminds us that it is "i before e except after c." Those faced with emergency situations can remember the proper treatment for accident victims by recalling, "If the face is red, raise the head. If the face is pale, raise the other end" (alternatively, "raise the tail").

Memorization of some facts may receive assistance from songs. Children often learn the alphabet by singing "The Alphabet Song," for example. Setting the multiplication table to the tune of "Yankee Doodle" once facilitated arithmetic instruction in New England classrooms. Matching geographical facts to familiar tunes was once a favorite mnemonic device, and some traditional songs—such as "The Brazos River," which lists the principal rivers of Texas—aided the memory of such information.

Less complex mnemonic devices include acronyms. The name "ROY G. BIV," for example, enables one to remember the colors of the light spectrum. "HOMES" is a mnemonic acronym for the names of the Great Lakes. The initial letters of the words comprising certain traditional sentences may form an acrostic that recalls difficult facts: "George eat old gray rat at pa's house yesterday" reminds one how to spell *geography*. The names of the lines on the musical scale in the treble clef correspond to the beginning letters in "every good boy does fine." The initial letters of "my very educated mother just served us nine pickles" represent the names of the planets in order, moving away from the sun.

In addition to identifying traditional mnemonic devices of the types just described, folklore studies concerns itself with memory aids that assist the performance of verbal art. Among nonliterate groups—for example, certain Native American peoples—items such as wampum belts, carved sticks, and pictographs have assisted storytellers in recalling incidents for their narration. Singers, especially those with extensive repertoires, often maintain manuscript collections of songs to stimulate their memories. Perhaps the most thorough studies associated with mnemonics and folklore performance involve the oral-formulaic theory, which suggests that performers of long, rhythmic folklore forms such as epics or chanted sermons rely upon verbal formulas. Other approaches to the mnemonics of oral performance focus on the ways in which memory differs in oral and literate societies.

Folklore research into mnemonic devices has seldom gone beyond simply reporting them and possibly noting how their form and style help in the process of memorization. Studies of a "folk art of memory," analogous to the techniques for memorization developed by the Greeks (which flourished as a rhetorical study through the Renaissance), provide a rich, largely unexplored research topic.

William M. Clements

See Also Oral-Formulaic Theory; Performance.

References

Dundes, Alan. 1961. Mnemonic Devices. *Midwest Folklore* 11: 139–147.

Finnegan, Ruth. 1977. *Oral Poetry: Its Nature, Significance, and Social Context.* Cambridge: Cambridge University Press.

Foley, John Miles. 1988. *The Theory of Oral Composition: History and Methodology.* Bloomington: Indiana University Press.

Lord, Albert B. 1960. *The Singer of Tales.* Cambridge, MA: Harvard University Press.

Ong, Walter. 1982. *Orality and Literacy: The Technologizing of the Word.* London: Methuen.

Yates, Frances A. 1966. *The Art of Memory.* Chicago: University of Chicago Press.

Zumthor, Paul. 1990. *Oral Poetry: An Introduction.* Trans. Kathryn Murphy-Judy. Minneapolis: University of Minnesota Press.

Mobility

The principle that people, objects, and ideas are in motion, and a corresponding set of ethnographic practices and sensibilities employed by researchers to represent this complex reality.

The last two decades have witnessed an unprecedented rise in the mobility of peoples, objects, and ideas as a consequence of increasingly sophisticated communication technologies, tourism networks, wars, and dispossession. The networks constituting our information society challenge traditional anthropological practice: Research on migrants "at home," Internet communication, and the proliferation of special-interest communities may not require the researcher to set foot outside of her city, but necessitate more sophisticated concepts and ethnographic strategies than we have employed in the past. Urry proposes a post-disciplinary paradigm of social science research to study both human subjects and the "underlying physical or material infrastructures" (Urry 2007,19) that belie their movement in this century when mobility is central. He employs the term *mobilities* "to refer to the broader project of establishing a movement-driven social science" (2007,18) and argues for the incorporation of "everyday" activities like car driving, holiday-making, telephoning, and flying that social research has largely disregarded. The journal *Mobilities* was established in 2006 to address such issues through multidisciplinary approaches, including those of human geography, tourism, sociology, and communication. Additionally, the premise that the body's mobility impacts subjectivity implies that identity becomes malleable, displaced, and on-the-go. The body's movement—in both face-to-face communicative actions like gestures and mimicry, as well as in its travel to and from places—entails "shifting the gears" among aspects of one's identity. Researchers can harness this notion of mobility by drawing on different facets of their affiliations and experiences to establish rapport and proximity with their informants.

Traditional anthropological practice has posited the scholar's travel to distant, unfamiliar places as a "rite of passage and marker of professionalism" in contrast to locality of the informant, whose native village became an accepted unit of analysis (Clifford 1997, 21). For much of the twentieth century, evolutionary and structural-functionalist theories viewed oral and/or non-Western societies as frozen in time, immobile. Localizing culture in a delimited space and time was convenient and taken to represent a microcosm of the whole society (idem). At the same time, the mobility of the researcher, in terms of his or her travel from home and the university to the research site, from city to the village, has been masked. Since the 1980s, social scientists and historians have questioned the notion that culture is a local phenomenon and have devised methods to capture the complex historical and contemporary social and spatial interactions of people, images and objects, and the relationships between local and larger-than-local contexts. Folklorists have made strides toward studying this facet of mobility, albeit from the opposite direction. The discipline has long been marked by the scholarly trajectory known as the historic-geographic method, which involves mapping versions of oral narratives, technologies, and customary behaviors onto points on a map where they were found to exist and as they move across spaces, to answer basic questions about the human mind's propensity to manifest in similar cultural expressions across broad geographical swathes. While the movement of lore, materials, and ideas through space (and to a lesser extent, time) is at the heart of the method, it was schematic and did not account for the situated performances of narratives or customs.

The intersection of the post-spatial turn in the social sciences and as of the 1990s the "bodily turn" manifested in more reflexive research trajectories and methodologies aimed at understanding the interaction between subjectivity and the world "out there," as well as the networks and flows of ideas, goods, armies, and migrants that animate history. De Certeau (1984) reinvigorated the study of mobility with his premise that spaces are animated by people's activities or "spatial practices," which must be captured in representations of a locale. Questionnaires, interviews, observation, and mapping quotidian routes are used to examine the embodied practices and navigation habits of residents in different cities. This approach hearkens to earlier social theorists like Georg Simmel and Mikhail Bakhtin, whose concepts of proximity and distance in social relations in the city and in the novel, respectively, were recently taken up by social scientists. Feminist scholarship on the body has contributed to the conceptual and methodological shift from participant-observation to observant-participation: Researchers move along with people being studied to explore the role of physical motion in subjective experience, disclosing their own mobility to ethnographic sites and mimicking the motions of locals in an attempt to gain insights into their experiences of place and community. Their shared premise is that corporeality, emotion, and abstraction are intertwined in movement that embodies socially constructed cultural knowledge.

Sklar (1994) espouses mimetic bodily movement as a fundamental way of knowing and a complementary method to reading, watching and listening. She notes how bodily movement in religious rituals expresses symbols, one's relationships to the divine and to members in the faith community, and ultimately one's identity. Sklar employs "kinesthetic empathy," writing of her own corporeal mimesis of worshippers in two distinct settings of religious worship: a Christian chapel and an orthodox synagogue. Similarly, Del Negro's (2004) ethnography of an Italian town focuses on nonlinguistic behavior in the performance event of the *passeggiata*, or ritual promenade. The event includes a spectacle of gesture and comportment, dress, grooming and accessories, and their interpretation by local observers. Del Negro ties ideas about modernity and cosmopolitanism in the town to the body's performance, which is judged according to displays of moral character, suggesting the traditional association with Mediterranean values of honor and shame. This study of expressive acts is articulated as a legacy of the folklife movement and its incorporation of performance theories. Lastly, Noy (2009) attunes to the interface between the mobility of people and objects, as well as the constant shift between roles of driver-passenger and parent-child, in experiencing of automobile travel as a family. Noy's auto-ethnographic approach considers how we incorporate transportation modes into our subjectivity when we operate (in) them, dovetailing into a new terrain of *automobilities*. As mobility, connectivity, displacement, and diaspora increasingly define our world, social science will continue to refine its concepts and methodologies to keep up with its complexities.

Dana Hercbergs

See Also Ethnography; Ethnology; Historic-Geographic Method.

References

Clifford, James. 1997. *Routes: Travel and Translation in the Late Twentieth Century.* Cambridge, MA: Harvard University Press.

De Certeau, Michel. 1984. *The Practice of Everyday Life.* Trans: Steven F. Rendall. Berkeley: University of California Press.

Del Negro, Giovanna P. 2004. *The* Passeggiata *and Popular Culture in an Italian Town: Folklore and the Performance of Modernity.* Montréal: McGill-Queen's University Press.

Noy, Chaim. 2009. On Driving a Car and Being a Family: A Reflexive Ethnography. In *Material Culture and Technology in Everyday Life: Ethnographic Approaches,* ed. Phillip Vannini. New York: Peter Lang Publishing, pp. 101–113.

Sklar, Deidre. 1994. Can Bodylore Be Brought to Its Senses? *Journal of American Folklore* 107: 9–22.

Urry, John. 2007. *Mobilities.* Cambridge: Polity Press.

Modernization

Modernization is a form of social and cultural change, usually involving the rapid transition of premodern or traditional societies or the adaptation of specific cultural forms to modernity.

Modernization is closely connected to rationality, science, universalism, mass literacy, technology, industrialization, and urbanization. According to the romanticized ideas of the nineteenth century, folklore was thought to embody the premodern past and cultural specificity and to constitute a counterworld to modernity. Therefore, the fact that folklore changes, is subjected to processes of modernization, and can thus reflect modernity received attention only late, especially with Hermann Bausinger's seminal book *Volkskultur in der technischen Welt* (1961; English translation: 1990). Modernization is relevant for folklore and folkloristics in several ways.

The growing interest in folklore and mythology in the nineteenth century can be understood as a reaction to rapid modernization, rationalization, and social breakdown. At the time William J. Thoms coined the English term *folk-lore* in 1846, the material encompassed by his neologism was perceived and studied as a treasury of survivals and relics of antiquity; "genuine folklore" could be gleaned only in remote rural areas uncontaminated by modernity. This emphasis on archaic elements placed folklore in direct opposition to modernization and even celebrated it as an antidote to its perils. In industrial societies, folklore offered a counterworld to modernization—a nostalgic realm of "wholesome" tradition, stability, continuity, orality, and authenticity, which—while serving as escape, refusal, or protest—was more often utilized for very modern purposes, such as folklorism (displaying folklore for the purposes of celebrating and preserving national identity and often to promote tourism) and fakelore (identifying and promoting as "folklore" materials that have little relationship to the processes of traditional creation and dissemination). Collecting, archiving, and preserving that which folklorists feared was soon to fall prey to modernization became the major preoccupation of folklore studies, in which anti-modernist attitudes, national orientation, and the assumption of folklore's imminent demise prevailed for a long time.

Because of the impact of modernization, it was inevitable that the process itself became a topic of folklore. Technical innovations (such as the railroad, telephone, and automobile) and the processes of industrialization and urbanization became part of oral or printed folklore as early as the nineteenth century, so that through folklore, the modern technical world was transformed into a "natural" life world. By taking up elements of modernity; by placing legends, tales, and songs in modern (urban) settings; by addressing the problematic aspects of modernization (e.g., anonymity, moral decay, crime in the big cities, and alienating work in factories and offices); and by expressing people's anxieties and fears (e.g. of trains, electricity, car accidents, airplanes, and computers), folklore serves the vital social function of familiarizing people with modernization and its hazards.

In a process of adaptation (which was long regarded as destructive), modernization soon extended to the contents and themes of folklore. Songs and tales, even fairy tales, incorporated elements of modern life, replacing magic carpets and horses with airplanes, messengers on horseback with telegrams, and swords with pistols. The adaptation concerned not only the material objects, the props of narrative action, but also the actions and actors, plots, subject matter, and contexts—not to mention the underlying values and worldviews. Apart from everyday narrating, the joke and the modern legend are those genres that incorporate and reflect modernity most strongly and answer the needs of modern society. Modern elements in folklore can represent a straightforward adaptation to the present, but they can also be ironic—in parodies or in literary adaptations, for example. On the other hand, folklorism—though a modern phenomenon—tends to stress archaic elements and plots.

Modernization also concerns the forms and genres of folklore. It has replaced the traditional tale of magic with the more realistic novella; the longer humorous tale (jest, tall tale) with the short, pointed joke and slur; the traditional legend with the modern or urban legend; and the "ballad of tradition" with topical street ballads and ditties. The print and electronic media in particular have changed the forms and genres of folklore and produced new forms and subgenres, such as broadside ballads, newspaper legends, movie *Märchen*, political jokes, black humor, and Internet witchcraft tales.

Modernization has deeply affected the means and media, the performances and contexts, of folklore. Contrary to romantic ideas, literacy and print have been highly important for folklore ever since the Renaissance, through broadsides, chapbooks, dime novels, newspapers, and other reading material. In the twentieth century, electronic devices and media (the telephone, the phonograph, radio, movies, television, audio and video recorders, and the Internet) became important means of transmission, diffusion, and performance as well as of collection and preservation of folklore. Alongside festivals, exhibitions, concerts, and shows, the modern media have created new stages and contexts that allow folklore to reach larger audiences at a faster pace than ever before in history. Folklore as part of mass culture has become a public commodity that can be technically reproduced and used almost infinitely in advertising, sports, tourism, politics, and other contexts, while contents of the mass media enter everyday narrating and oral tradition. There is a permanent exchange between oral, literal, and visual representations of folklore; between tradition and modernity; and between folk culture and modern mass culture.

Klaus Roth

See Also Urban Folklore; Worldview.

References

Abrahams, Roger. 1964. *Deep Down in the Jungle: Negro Narrative Folklore from the Streets of Philadelphia*. Hatboro: Folklore Associates.

Bausinger, Hermann. 1971. *Volkskunde*. Darmstadt: Habel.

Bausinger, Hermann. 1990. *Folk Culture in a World of Technology*. Trans. Elke Dethmer. Bloomington: Indiana University Press.

Bausinger, Hermann. 1991. Tradition und Modernisierung. *Schweizerisches Archiv für Volkskunde* 87: 5–14.

Bausinger, Hermann. 1999. Modernismen. In *Enzyklopädie des Märchens*, eds. Rolf Brednich et al. Berlin: Walter de Gruyters, vol. 9, pp. 747–750.

Brednich, Rolf W. 1990. *Die Spinne in der Yucca-Palme: Sagenhafte Geschichten von heute*. Munich: C. B. Beck.

Brunvand, Jan H. 1981. *The Vanishing Hitchhiker: American Urban Legends and Their Meaning*. New York: Norton.

Dégh, Linda. 1971. The "Belief Legend" in Modern Society: Form, Function, and Relationship to Other Genres. In *American Folk Legend: A Symposium*, ed. Wayland D. Hand. Berkeley: University of California Press, pp. 55–68.

Dégh, Linda. 1994. *American Folklore and the Mass Media*. Bloomington: Indiana University Press.

Dégh, Linda. 2001. *Legend and Belief. Dialectics of a Folklore Genre*. Bloomington: Indiana University Press.

Dégh, Linda, Henry Glassie, and Felix Oinas, eds. 1976. *Folklore Today: A Festschrift for Richard M. Dorson*. Bloomington: Indiana University Center for Research in Language and Semiotic Studies.

Dundes, Alan. 1969. The Devolutionary Premise in Folklore Theory. *Journal of the Folklore Institute* 6: 5–19.

Dundes, Alan. 1971. A Study of Ethnic Slurs: The Jew and the Polack in the United States. *Journal of American Folklore* 84: 186–203.

Dundes, Alan, and Carl R. Pagter. 1975. *Urban Folklore from the Paperwork Empire*. Austin: University of Texas Press.

Dundes, Alan, and Carl R. Pagter. 1987. *When You're Up to Your Ass in Alligators: More Urban Folklore from the Paperwork Empire*. Detroit: Wayne State University Press.

Fine, Gary A. 1992. *Manufacturing Tales: Sex and Money in Contemporary Legends*. Knoxville: University of Tennessee Press.

Fischer, Helmut. 1991. Kontinuität oder Transformation: Die mündliche Volksüberlieferung im Zeitalter der Massenkultur. *Schweizerisches Archiv für Volkskunde* 87: 93–106.

Giddens, Anthony 1990. *The Consequences of Modernity*. Stanford: Stanford University Press.

Jason, Heda. 1966. Jewish Narrating Art in Yemen and Israel. *Fabula* 8: 93–106.

Köstlin, Konrad. 1991. Folklore, Folklorismus und Modernisierung. *Schweizerisches Archiv für Volkskunde* 87: 46–66.

Paredes, Américo, and Ellen J. Stekert, eds. 1971. *The Urban Experience and Folk Tradition*. Austin: University of Texas Press.

Röhrich, Lutz. 1964. *Märchen und Wirklichkeit*. Wiesbaden: F. Steiner.

Röhrich, Lutz. 1977. *Der Witz: Figuren, Formen, Funktionen*. Stuttgart: Metzler.

Roth, Klaus. 1983. Märchen als Lesestoff für alle. Populare Märchenbüchlein in Bulgarien. In *Dona ethnologica monacensia*, eds. H. Gerndt et al. Munich: Institut für Deutsche und Vergleichende Volkskunde, Universität München, pp. 267–288.

Roth, Klaus. 1992. Narrating in Socialist Everyday Life: Observations on Strategies of Life Management in Southeast Europe. In *Creativity and Tradition in Folklore*, ed. Simon Bronner. Logan: Utah State University Press, pp. 127–139.

Roth, Klaus, and J. Roth. 1996. Modernisierungsprozesse in der bulgarischen Gesellschaft im Spiegel der Popularliteratur (1880–1914). *Narodna umjetnost* 33(2): 325–355.

Schenda, Rudolph. 1991. Folklore und Massenkultur. *Schweizerisches Archiv für Volkskunde* 87: 15–27.

Monogenesis/Polygenesis

Origin from a single source (mono) or from multiple sources (poly), or the theory that an item has a point of beginning or origin (its genesis) and that the beginning may have been from one single source (monogenesis) or from two or more sources (polygenesis). Drawn from the sciences and social sciences, the theories of monogenesis and polygenesis are used to explain the origin of such diverse phenomena as species, government, ethnicities, and aesthetics. In folkloristics, the theories are used to explain the origins of specific items of folklore and their variants.

Monogenesis, or monogenetic transformation, holds that for any given artifact, there is one and only one point of origin. For example, most religions hold that mankind came about as the creation of a supernatural power. From that original creation came all of the members of the group and all of the others who inhabit the earth. In the sciences, monogenesis has been used to support theories of species evolution from one common ancestor to the forms now known. In folklore, the Finnish, or historic-geographic, method of narrative research relies on the theory of monogenesis. In this method, the Ur-form, the archetype for a narrative, is the result of a conscious act of creation at a specific time and location. From this Ur-form came all known variants. For example, some scholars hold that the similarities in the creation stories of various religions point to a common point of ancestry from which all people and their religions spring. In like manner, languages are thought to have one point of origin. The group of languages classified as Indo-European is sometimes used as evidence for monogenesis of language. A few scholars hold that, given enough time and data, they can find a proto-Indo-European language from which all known languages of this stock emerged.

In 1524, Paracelsus argued for the theory of polygenesis. Using the available scholarly evidence, he posited that all the known varieties of mankind could not have evolved solely from the union of Adam and Eve. Proponents of the theory of polygenesis, or polygenetic transformation, and the allied parallel evolution hold that similar needs and development can create similar cultural artifacts in different, independent groups. Under the theory of polygenesis, the similarities in language groups or creation stories are just that—similarities. Antidiffusionist folklore scholars argue that linguistic barriers are too hard for an item of oral folklore to overcome. Instead, they believe that similar items arose in divergent language areas independently. The Swedish folklorist C. W. von Sydow held that the unique qualities of history and culture in various regions pushed the creation of similar types of tales, or regional oikotypes, each with its own unique history. Similar creation stories, under the theory of polygenesis, arose out of similar needs to explain the universe rather than out of a single point of origin.

The use of monogenesis and polygenesis as analytical tools has its merits and limitations. Certain items of folklore may be traced to an original source and support the theory of monogenesis. Other items, though similar among diverse groups and locations, are the result of similar needs and multiple creations and thus support the theory of polygenesis.

Randal S. Allison

See Also Historic-Geographic Method; Oikotype/Oicotype.

References

Dégh, Linda. 1972. Folk Narrative. In *Folklore and Folklife: An Introduction*, ed. Richard M. Dorson. Chicago: University of Chicago Press.

Dorson, Richard M. 1972. Introduction: Concepts of Folklore and Folklife Studies. In *Folklore and Folklife: An Introduction*. Chicago: University of Chicago Press.

von Sydow, C. W. 1965. Folktale Studies and Philology: Some Points of View. In *The Study of Folklore*, ed. Alan Dundes. Englewood Cliffs, NJ: Prentice-Hall.

Motif

A unit of content found in prose narratives or in poems. According to the American folklorist Stith Thompson, motifs were "those details out of which full-fledged narratives are composed." The term *motif* came into use in comparative textual studies at the turn of the twentieth century. For the practitioners of the historic-geographic method, narrative plots (tale types) were made up of episodes and motifs.

Thompson expanded the motif's range of meaning. He argued that some motifs, such as "Creation of the sun," can be a narrative's highly abstract subject or the main theme. The term *motif* also can refer to the narrative plot; the myth "Sun and moon from belly of a fish," for example, is unit A 713.1 in Thompson's motif-index.

Motif also can refer to a smaller narrative unit such as an episode, a sequence of several events, or a single event or action. Some of these "action motifs" can be linked to a variety of plots. An example of this kind of motif is "The obstacle flight," whereby the fleeing protagonist throws back a brush, a stone, and a bottle of water; the objects miraculously turn into a dense wood, a mountain, and a lake in order to ensure an escape from the pursuer.

The term *motif* also has been used in reference to the descriptions of the narrative world and its inhabitants. For example, Thompson's motif "Abode of the dead" and its realization "Land of dead across river" describe the supernatural setting of the narrative. The motif "Mermaid has white skin" refers to the physical attributes of a supernatural actor.

Thompson's motif-index is a six-volume reference work of themes and other elements of content that appear mainly in the folklore and early literature of Eurasia. The index also includes some information on Oceanic, indigenous North and South American, and African myths and other narratives.

Thompson's index is hierarchical: Abstract themes and broad categories ("Cosmogony and Cosmology," "Animals") are divided into subcategories ("The Heavens," "The Earth," "Mythical Animals," "Magic Animals"). The last volume of the index contains more than 10,000 main terms.

Thompson's motif-index prevails as an effective reference book, especially for scholars of European folklore and folk belief. His way of defining the term *motif*, however, has been strongly and justifiably criticized. Thompson's *motif* is both vague and ambiguous; it variously refers to theme, plot (tale type), actor, item (object), or descriptive element. A precise application of the term requires that it refer to only one kind of unit.

As folkloristic textual analysis developed alongside narratology (i.e., the structural study of narratives and narrative techniques) in the 1960s, scholars saw that the hierarchical set of terms *theme, tale type, episode,* and *motif* was inadequate for describing a story's essential structures. New solutions and concepts were first created in the morphological and structural analyses of folktales and later in the linguistic study of narrative discourse in the 1970s and 1980s.

Satu Apo

See Also Folktale; Historic-Geographic Method; Motif; Structuralism; Tale Type.

References

Dundes, Alan. 1962. From Etic to Emic Units in the Structural Study of Folktales. *Journal of American Folklore* 75: 95–105.

Finnegan, Ruth. 1992. *Oral Traditions and the Verbal Arts: A Guide to Research Practices.* London: Routledge.

Goldberg, Christine. 1986. The Construction of Folktales. *Journal of Folklore Research* 23: 163–176.

Krohn, Kaarle. 1971. *Folklore Methodology.* Trans. Roger L. Welsh. Austin: University of Texas Press. (Originally published as *Die folkloristische Arbeitsmethode*, Oslo, 1926.)

Siikala, Anna-Leena. 1990. *Interpreting Oral Narrative.* Folklore Fellows Communications, no. 245. Helsinki: Academia Scientiarum Fennica.

Thompson, Stith. 1946. *The Folktale.* New York: Holt, Rinehart and Winston.

Thompson, Stith. 1966. *Motif-Index of Folk-Literature: A Classification of Narrative Elements in Folktales, Ballads, Myths, Fables, Mediaeval Romances, Exempla, Fabliaux, Jest-Books, and Local Legends.* Second printing. Bloomington: Indiana University Press.

Mumming

Seasonal custom in which one or more disguised figures intrude into private households with the purpose of engaging in traditional, convivial interaction with the residents. Observance is invariably associated with the season of winter revels, encompassing (in Christian communities) Christmas, New Year's, and Twelfth Night. Interaction takes the form of various pastimes, many of which might figure in the revelry of a festive gathering independently of the intrusion by the visitors—for example, singing and dancing. In late medieval and Renaissance Europe, interaction usually took the form of gambling with dice; in recent Newfoundland tradition, the pastime comprises the attempts of the hosts to guess the identity of the visitors.

Since it involves the intrusion of disguised visitors into the private space of a domestic household, the custom has particularly powerful social perspectives, with the transgressing of significant social and psychological (as well as physical) thresholds. The nature of this transgression will vary according to the ambient social conventions, as the mummers challenge whatever is normal during the rest of the year. In the comparatively homogeneous communities of Newfoundland, where neighbors normally enter a house without ceremony, the Christmas mummers (those same neighbors in disguise) draw attention to their otherness by knocking at the door as if they were strangers. In the hierarchical and comparatively anonymous society of Tudor London, in contrast, it was the prospect of strangers (by implication, individuals of lower rank) penetrating the private homes of gentlefolk that provoked legislation against mumming in disguise.

Whatever the etymology (currently disputed) of the English term *mumming* and its cognates in other languages, the terms' connotations imply, in one direction, the refusal to communicate in normal speech. Medieval mummers were silent; the Newfoundland mummers speak by breathing inward; and elsewhere, mummers are recorded as making humming noises (i.e., murmuring). In another direction, the word *mumming* implies disguise or at least a masking of the face, and in scholarship, *mumming* is sometimes used to describe customs involving disguise but within other frameworks than the house visit—a procession, for example, as in the Philadelphia mummers' parade.

On a different axis, the term can, with varying legitimacy, be extended to house-visit customs during other seasons or in which the interaction between disguised visitors and hosts involves something other than or more than a convivial pastime. Some visits seem to be designed as a courtesy to the householder, involving the expression of greetings and goodwill or even the proffering of gifts (the most extravagant and literary manifestation of this trend being the Elizabethan and Stuart court masque). In others, the visitors' motivation may focus on receiving refreshment and/or financial largesse, making their visits effectively begging visits or (in the conventional euphemism) *quêtes*. In either of these cases, the visitors are likely to entertain their hosts with a show, comprising a display of disguised figures (a fool, a grotesque female, animals), dance, song, speeches, or even a short but essentially dramatic interlude, qualifying the custom concerned as a *mummers' play*.

Thomas Pettit

See Also Drama, Folk; Festival; Mask.

References

Alford, Violet. 1978. *The Hobby Horse and Other Animal Masks*. London: Merlin.

Halpert, Herbert, and G. M. Storey, eds. 1969. *Christmas Mumming in Newfoundland: Essays in Anthropology, Folklore and History*. Toronto: University of Toronto Press.

Lovelace, Martin J. 1980. Christmas Mumming in England: The House-Visit. In *Folklore Studies in Honour of Herbert Halpert*, eds. Kenneth S. Goldstein and Neil V. Rosenberg. St John's, Newfoundland: Memorial University of Newfoundland.

Welsford, Enid. 1927. *The Court Masque: A Study in the Relationship between Poetry and the Revels*. Cambridge: Cambridge University Press.

Museum, Folk

A museum devoted to the study, collection, and interpretation of materials pertaining to local or regional culture. Generally, folk museums consist of two parts: an outdoor gathering of reconstructed buildings placed in an authentic natural contextual setting and a building that houses static exhibits of folk material culture. In some countries, the term *folk museum* refers to those museums also known as "open-air" or "living-history" museums.

The rise of folk museums coincided with several trends in the middle to late nineteenth century in both northern Europe and the United States. Perhaps the most important was the growing interest in ethnography, folklore, and the study of objects within those fields of inquiry. Victorian scholars dedicated to the study of the customs of traditional groups began to examine the "objective culture" or the material world, along with their studies of more intangible features of these groups. Among the scholars who turned their attention to the study of the material aspects of local culture and played prominent roles in the development of significant museum collections were Stewart Culin, Henry Mercer, and Fletcher Bassett in the United States and Artur Hazelius and Bernard Olson in Scandinavia.

During the latter part of the nineteenth century, exhibitions of arts and industries were extremely popular on both continents. From the World's Columbian

Museum of Liptov Village in Pribylina, Slovakia, 2009. (Elesuc/Dreamstime.com)

Exposition in Chicago to trade fairs in small towns, many of these exhibitions were devoted to the display of new industrial and agricultural goods. However, spurred on by widespread national romanticism, organizers also presented static displays of materials that reflected keen interests in "bygone days" or the contributions of local culture. In northern Europe, these displays often featured artifacts of the peasants or farmers. In the United States, they frequently highlighted the contributions of the immigrants to the new nation through "homeland exhibits."

Artur Hazelius, the man credited with developing the concept of the folk museum, initially mounted an exhibition of Swedish folk arts at the 1878 World's Fair in Paris. He sought to present a more authentic representation of Swedish culture by basing his displays on artifacts collected through extensive fieldwork and by incorporating figures "arranged in a highly emotional tableaux similar to the way it is done at a waxworks." Upon seeing the way in which Hazelius had constructed the room settings, Bernard Olson, founder of the Danish Folk Museum, exclaimed that the exhibit "clearly sets itself apart from the rest of the exhibition with its amassed industrial wonders and trifles, manufactured for the occasion and worthless afterwards. Here was something new—the emergence of a fresh museum concept associated with a class, the life and activities of which had heretofore been disregarded by the traditional and official view of what was significant to scholarship and culture."

Hazelius founded two museums in Stockholm—*Nordiska* and *Skansen* (literally, open-air)—that became the models for national, regional, and local folk museums around the world. At *Nordiska*, Hazelius used his vast collections of folk materials in room settings or in displays arranged systematically according to type of material, historical period, function, and geographical region. Today, *Nordiska* is home to a folklife research institute operated in conjunction with the University of Stockholm, and it hosts temporary exhibitions that interpret materials from a variety of perspectives. At *Skansen*, Hazelius brought together entire farmsteads removed from their original locations and reinstalled in one outdoor location in central Stockholm. The variety of structures represented each of Sweden's regions, classes, and major historical periods and were placed in settings that included native plants and animals of the regions and periods. By adding traditional musicians, craftspeople, and farmers to perform and demonstrate their skills, Hazelius created the first "living museum." There, he was able to portray regional variations in Sweden's built environment through a variety of historical periods.

So popular was this new form of museum that major national open-air museums were quickly established in Norway (*Norsk Folkemuseum*, 1894), Denmark (*Frilandmuseet*, 1887), and the Netherlands (*Nederlands Openluchtmuseum*, 1912), and regional museums sprang up all over northern Europe. In 1974, Adelhart Zippelius was commissioned by the Association of European Open-Air

Museums to compile a guide to 314 open-air museums in twenty-one European countries, and the model has now been adopted by nations around the world.

By the latter part of the nineteenth century, interest in the collection and display of folk material culture was also rising in the United States. In 1876, Hazelius sent six of his folklife tableaux to the United States Centennial Exposition. Subsequently, the Newark Museum in New Jersey organized a series of "homeland exhibits," and by 1893, Stewart Culin had developed a series of exhibits on folk objects for the World's Columbian Exposition held that year in Chicago (the Chicago World's Fair).

By the early twentieth century, Hazelius's model for folk museums was used to guide the development of such museums as Old Sturbridge Village and Plimoth Plantation in Massachusetts; the Farmer's Museum in Cooperstown, New York; Mystic Seaport in Connecticut; Colonial Williamsburg in Virginia; the vast Henry Ford Museum and Greenfield Village in Michigan; and numerous smaller complexes across the country. All of these institutions shared the primary features of *Skansen*: the development of collections reflecting a preindustrial society, the assemblage of buildings in a re-created natural setting, and the use of costumed interpreters and craft demonstrations to selectively simulate the lives of ordinary people. In all, the pedagogical intent is clear—to give visitors an idea of life as it was lived in the past.

It is this conception of the past, however, that has proved to be one of the most difficult flaws in the formation and operation of folk museums. Folk museums have a tendency to depict generalized rather than specific experiences, to represent agricultural rather than urban life, and to deal with a historical past and not an ethnographic present. In reality, the collecting and interpretation activities of folk museums represent only very small slices of any national or regional cultural history. Folk museums generally rely on the reconstruction of a building to reconstruct and communicate information about life in a particular place in a moment in time. Yet, even undergirded with the most comprehensive of historical and folklife research, this reconstruction process will ultimately result in an interpreted re-creation or simulation of that life. The degree of authenticity achieved by a folk museum relies on both solid research and an interpretation or education staff that seeks to clearly communicate information. The best of the folk museums are those that focus on narrowly defined periods and regions, have research programs that support continued investigation on those defined periods and regions, and have well-developed educational programs.

Marsha MacDowell

See Also Folklife; Material Culture.

References
Anderson, Jay. 1984. *Time Machines: The World of Living History*. Nashville, TN: American Association for State and Local History.

Bronner, Simon J., ed. 1982. *American Material Culture and Folklife: A Prologue and Dialogue*. Logan: Utah State University Press.

Bronner, Simon J., ed. 1987. *Folklife Studies from the Gilded Age: Object Rite, and Custom in Victorian America*. Ann Arbor, MI: UMI Research Press.

Hall, Patricia, and Charlie Seemann, eds. 1987. *Folklife and Museums: Selected Readings*. Nashville, TN: American Association for State and Local History.

Higgs, J. W. Y. 1963. *Folklife Collection and Classification*. London: Museums Association.

Ice, Joyce, ed. 2009. *On Collecting: From Private to Public, Featuring Folk and Tribal Art from the Diane and Sandy Besser Collection*. Santa Fe, NM: Museum of International Folk Art.

Jenkins, J. Geraint. 1972. The Use of Artifacts and Folk Art in the Folk Museum. In *Folklore and Folklife: An Introduction*, ed. Richard Dorson. Chicago: University of Chicago Press.

Loomis, Ormond. 1977. *Sources on Folk Museums and Living History Farms*. Folklore Forum Bibliographic and Special Series. Bloomington: Indiana University Folklore Institute.

McLerran, Jennifer. 2009. *A New Deal for Native Art: Indian Arts and Federal Policy, 1933–1943*. Tucson: University of Arizona Press.

Owen, Trefor. 1972. *Welsh Folk Museum Handbook*. St. Fagans: National Museum of Wales.

Steenberg, Axel. 1966. *Dansk Folkmuseum and Frilandsmuseet*. Andelsbogtrykkerirt and Odense, Denmark: Nationalmuseet.

Zippelius, Adelhart. 1974. *Handbuch der Europäischen Freilichtmuseen* (Handbook of European open-air museums). Cologne: Rheinland-Verlag GMbH.

Music, Folk

Tunes sung, with or without verbal texts, or played on instruments in folkloric performance settings. Contemporary perspectives stress the idea that such music, whatever its origins and previous usages, can be considered folk music when its use is primarily for the enjoyment of performers and listeners in noncommercial settings. This definition, like many recent definitions of folklore in general, stresses *behaviors* in *contexts*—in particular those that are more informal than formal—that exist outside performance settings typically associated with popular and elite or art music in Western cultures.

Earlier definitions of folk music stressed *textual* aspects. Thus, the often quoted definition promulgated by the International Folk Music Council (IFMC) in 1954 described folk music as "the product of a musical tradition that has been evolved through the process of oral transmission," a process entailing continuity, variation, and communal selection. This definition views folk music as a special kind of text, shaped unconsciously in a Darwinian manner by a community to fit its own needs and values. Here, melodies are considered as texts, too, and those that are transmitted aurally are privileged over sight-readable music "texts." The formative scholarship on folk music stressed its value as a representation of a special kind of community, one imagined to exist among a homogeneous group of non-elite people within a peasant, working-class, ethnic, or regional community. These types of communities were held to be particularly important by early folklore scholars who were strongly influenced by populist cultural nationalist agendas. Thus, through processes of borrowing, co-optation, and canon formation, the music associated with non-elite communities became an important symbol of identity for intellectual elites involved in nationalist enterprises.

Consequently, folk music was analyzed in terms of musical elements thought to be characteristic of such national/communal settings. Because one type of verbal folksong text, the ballad, was recognized in the eighteenth century as having important connections with elite literature, its musical aspects received considerable scholarly attention. The ballad, as performed in Western Europe and in other parts of the world colonized from this region, was typically performed solo and a cappella. Consequently, musicologists who focused upon folksong generally concerned themselves with monophonic sound. This concern reflected, as well, the limitations of data collection in the era prior to the widespread use of sound recordings, for at that time, it was rarely possible to accurately notate more than a single line of melody. In this context, certain aspects of melody—particularly scale and, to a lesser extent, melodic contour—were thought by influential scholars such as Cecil Sharp to be diagnostic of cultural *geists* (spirits). So, for example, considerable weight was given to tunes with scales that, because they had less than a full octave or were modal rather than harmonic, might be considered to be survivals of very old music practices. Considerable attention was also paid to developing the idea of the "tune family," utilizing selected aspects of melody for comparative analysis that paralleled the research into the history of verbal folksong texts that led to schemes of classification and typology, such as those of Francis James Child and Malcolm Laws.

The growth of the discipline of ethnomusicology in the twentieth century, coupled with the advent of convenient sound-recording technology, led to a broadening of perspective. Alan Lomax, studying the relationships between folksong style and culture, developed cantometrics, a system of analysis designed to describe recorded musical performances using standardized terminology. Cantometrics' thirty-seven different parameters encompass a variety of factors, including: the social organization of vocal groups and orchestras, levels of cohesiveness and explicitness, rhythmic organization, melodic complexity, embellishment, and vocal stance. Lomax sought to describe aspects of *texture* as well as text.

As a descriptive system, cantometrics is much more inclusive than previous musical analysis systems, most of which have suffered from the fact that they

Lightnin' Washington, an African American prisoner, singing with his group in the woodyard at Darrington State Farm, Texas, April 1934. From the Lomax collection of photographs depicting folk musicians, primarily in the southern United States and the Bahamas. (Library of Congress)

utilize the prescriptive notation developed by Western art music, which biases the description. Lomax's analytic uses of his descriptive system, however, also have proven contentious. Utilizing Freudian ideas about human behavior, he suggested certain relationships between aspects of sound and musical organization, on the one hand, and broadly conceived cultural patterns, on the other. This reflected Lomax's own preference for theory-driven survey research rather than in-depth, data-driven field studies.

Nevertheless, Lomax's work served to broaden the scope of musical description, something that was necessary given the contemporary approach described at the beginning of this entry. Indeed, the problem folk music scholars now face is one of the boundaries of their field. Is, for example, the music made by of a group of friends who gather occasionally to play Bach or Beethoven for their own enjoyment to be considered folk music? One argument against calling such performances folk music is that in these performances the musicians intend to follow closely the composer's original score; the emphasis in folk music, by contrast, is upon a variety of intentions related to the perceived history, meaning, and uses of the music. Clearly, though, the differences between these intentions are a matter of degree rather than of opposition, for folklorists have shown that noncommercial musical traditions such as fiddling and Sacred Harp religious singing often place considerable emphasis upon the score as a document of the intention of the composer. However, such musics tend to fall outside the realm of elite art music, which is perpetuated through formal training based not just upon scores but also upon an extensive interpretive literature.

A second parallel dilemma is raised by the fact that there are many examples of musical performance that are called folk music but that take place in commercial or formal settings. These examples may reflect an understanding of folk music in cultural nationalist terms. Or they may be using folk music as a metaphor for the values associated with informality and noncommercialism. Whatever the case, when one analyzes the musical aspects of such performances, one usually finds considerable differences, particularly in terms of textures, in comparison with the same musics in noncommercial and informal settings. So, for example, when folk-lorist MacEdward Leach collected "The Blue Velvet Band" from folksinger William Riley of Lance au Loup, Labrador, in 1960, Riley closely followed the lyrics and melody of the song as first recorded by its author—professional country music singer Hank Snow—in 1937. But in terms of texture, there is a world of difference: Riley sings a cappella in a rubato parlando style; Snow accompanies himself with a guitar to a faster fixed tempo. Further, Riley's performance omits both Snow's opening spoken introduction, which contextualizes the song as a fictional cowboy bunkhouse performance, and Snow's closing yodel, an ornamental feature characteristic of his commercial musical domain.

This example reminds us that folk music researchers continue to focus upon issues of variation—whether in text, texture, or context—reflecting an underlying assumption that individual folk music pieces are, to a greater extent than other forms of music, constantly changing. The idea of viewing folk music as a mode of expression that frees singers and instrumentalists to re-create and improvise within the arena of a collective or shared *music-culture* (a term coined by Mark Slobin and Jeff Titon) recalls the IFMC's communalist definition mentioned earlier and suggests the importance of a perspective that moves beyond individual items and performances to consider entire repertoires.

Many studies of individual folk tunes exist, but folk music is nonetheless conventionally thought of in a plural sense as an aggregation of tunes. Although contemporary scholars tend to follow the strategy of viewing folk music in terms of individual behaviors in specific contexts (as suggested in the definition offered at the outset), a considerable number of those who speak of folk music think of it in these aggregational terms. It is useful to think of such aggregations as *canons*. Philip Bohlman suggests that canon formation is an essential aspect of folk music in the modern world. He offers several models of canon formation, ranging from local to national, in his discussion of the ways in which groups of people participating in folk music performances perceive their repertoire. Such canon formation is assessed critically and analytically by contemporary scholars as a source for data about the realities of folk music from a contextual point of view. Beyond this, however, it must be recognized that the entire body of writing about folk

Fiddling

Playing traditional folk music on the violin, generally without the aid of written music (although many a fiddler is musically literate to some degree). Wherever the remarkably versatile violin has traveled to play art music, from Italy to Scotland to South India, fiddling has gone too. Fiddling is differentiated from formal violin performance by customary functions, venues, and repertoires. Also, in several locations in the North Atlantic sphere, including the southern United States, playing techniques are distinctive, as are uses of the scordaturas that American fiddlers call "cross-tunings" (ones other than the usual low-to-high G-D-A-E, for example, A-E-A-E, which allows easy double-stops and maximum overall resonance in the key of A Major). In comparison to the violin, the fiddle is more loosely defined in construction materials and techniques, and, especially, in range of desirable timbres. In fact, in many times and places, the relatively nasal and penetrating timbres of fiddles have been favored because this helps the music be heard above the clatter of dancers' feet.

Today, in North America, Britain, Ireland, and Scandinavia, fiddling constitutes the most vigorous surviving folk music. Fiddlers in the American British colonies drew especially on Scottish traditions for tunes and for ways of writing their own new tunes (playing and composing new tunes within established dance genres, then retaining each new generation's dance types as those faded in urban popular use). In 18th-century America there was not always a clear line between violin performance and fiddling, since plenty of what were already traditional dance tunes—plus

Naomi Martin, age six, of Willmar, Minnesota, competes in the fiddle contest, August 8, 2003, at the Iowa State Fair in Des Moines. (AP/Wide World Photos)

tunes that would become traditional—were fashionable and in print, both in Britain and the United States. But during the first half of the nineteenth century, American fiddling took on an identity of its own partly due to rural fiddlers insisting on drawing idiosyncratically on repertoires that had fallen out of fashion, and partly due to the widespread popularization of blackface minstrelsy, which incorporated white performers' interpretations and caricatures of slave fiddling.

Fiddlers usually play in styles specific to the regions where they live, though those regions are more broadly defined today than formerly. 'Old-Timey' fiddlers in the Southeast still perform rustic 'breakdowns' in heterophony (approximate unison) with banjos that are played with techniques invoking nineteenth-century blackface minstrelsy (tunes such as 'Sail Away Ladies' and 'Cluck Old Hen'), while Texas fiddlers in 'contest style' vary breakdowns, waltzes, polkas, and rags systematically and virtuosically (a pair of common tunes: 'Sally Johnson' and 'Dusty Miller'). Most of English-speaking North America replicates the Texas contest model or imitates it to some degree; regional forms of the Texas-based contest style are emerging, particularly in the Pacific Northwest and in the Tennessee Valley.

Today, most fiddlers' repertoires still focus on genres of bipartite dance tunes and songs stemming from the eighteenth through early twentieth centuries, even though during the last half-century bluegrass venues and especially fiddle contests have supplanted actual dances as the focus for most public fiddle performance. These contests represent different flavors of a pan-North-Atlantic matrix of nativistic folk revivals, in which a rainbow of blends of rural and urban brands of nostalgia, the modern luxury of plentiful practice time, and adjustments made for more attentive listeners in this concert-like venue have again obscured the line between art and folk performance and between the cultivated violin and the rough-and-ready fiddle.

Chris Goertzen

---

music, scholarly and otherwise, constitutes the most important and influential canon that shapes perceptions about what is and what is not folk music.

Neil V. Rosenberg

See Also Ballad; Broadside Ballad; Cantometrics; Ethnomusicology; Folksong, Lyric; Folksong, Narrative.

References

Alves, William. 2010. *Music of the Peoples of the World*. Boston, MA: Schirmer Cengage Learning.

Bohlman, Philip V. 1988. *Folk Music in the Modern World*. Bloomington: Indiana University Press.

Child, Francis James. 1965. *The English and Scottish Popular Ballads*. New York: Dover. International Folk Music Council. 1955. Resolutions: Definition of Folk Music. *International Folk Music Journal* 7: 23.

Dunaway, David King, and Molly Beer. 2010. *Singing Out: An Oral History of America's Folk Music Revivals*. New York: Oxford University Press.

Epstein, Lawrence J. 2010. *Political Folk Music in America from Its Origins to Bob Dylan*. Jefferson, NC: McFarland.

Goertzen, Chris. 1996. Balancing Local and National Fiddle Styles at American Fiddle Contests. *American Music* 14(3): 352–381.

Laws, G. Malcolm. 1957. *American Balladry from British Broadsides*. Philadelphia: American Folklore Society.

Laws, G. Malcolm. 1964. *Native American Balladry*. Philadelphia: American Folklore Society.

Leach, MacEdward. 1965. *Folk Ballads and Songs of the Lower Labrador Coast*. Ottawa: National Museum.

Ledgin, Stephanie P. 2010. *Discovering Folk Music*. Santa Barbara: Praeger.

Lomax, Alan. 1968. *Folk Song Style and Culture*. Washington, DC: American Association for the Advancement of Science.

Moore, Robin. 2010. *Music in the Hispanic Caribbean: Experiencing Music, Expressing Culture*. New York: Oxford University Press.

Slobin, Mark, and Jeff Todd Titon. 1992. The Music-Culture as a World of Music. In *Worlds of Music*, ed. Jeff Todd Titon et al. New York: Schirmer.

Titon, Jeff Todd. 2001. *Old-Time Kentucky Fiddle Tunes*. Lexington: University of Kentucky Press.

Musical Instrument, Folk

In their most basic denotation, traditional objects used to produce and control musical sound. Folk musical instruments are tools or technological extensions to the sound-producing capabilities and kinetic expressions of the human body. Although instruments often are viewed as distinct from the human body and voice (manifest in culture-based distinctions between instrumental and vocal musics), they effectively intensify and complement communicative facets of speech and song and the rhythmical features of movement and dance.

Comparable to distinctions between music and nonmusic, the precise factors that differentiate any sound-producing object from a musical instrument result from the beliefs and practices of individual cultures. Whatever their design—from common objects to those of elaborate construction—musical instruments generally exhibit characteristic timbres appropriate to music performance, as well as some degree of pitch and loudness variation, and they allow for the control of sound over an interval of time. Widely distributed conch-shell trumpets, the hourglass-shaped *kotsuzumi* drum of the Japanese *noh* orchestra, the African plucked lamella instrument *sanza* or *mbira*, the lute of East Asia and North Africa known as the '*ud*, and the mechanically bowed hurdy-gurdy from medieval Europe all illustrate distinctive sound colors and allow control of pitch, loudness, and rhythm. Such acoustical properties neither limit a musical instrument to one use nor require that music performance be the instrument's primary purpose. Music performance may employ ritual articles, cooking utensils, agricultural tools, or any number of other objects, temporarily or otherwise. Moreover, depending upon its cultural context, distinctions between a musical use and any other use of an object need not be demarcated clearly. Although long a debated issue, African musical bows resemble hunting bows in form and suggest another purpose, as does the *ghatam* (literally, waterpot), a clay-pot percussion instrument of the Indian subcontinent.

With historical depth extending from prehistory to the present and a geographic scope encompassing six continents and nearly all societies, musical instruments challenge holistic considerations. Several cultures have developed instrument classifications to account for their instruments and performance ensembles, most notably China, which uses eight divisions based on the material that produces the sound or contains the vibrating air, and India, which has four instrument divisions organized by the sounding element. However, like the European classification with its divisions of winds, strings, and percussion (still applied to the Western orchestra), they all fail to adequately explain basics of design or to clarify relationships for the large number of instruments known today. Museum curators, instrument collectors, and scholars have sought more systematic and comprehensive means to describe and categorize the vast array of musical instruments; the standard that has emerged comes from a system developed by Erich M. von Hornbostel and Curt Sachs.

To distinguish and organize musical instruments, most systems of classification take as a fundamental principle the importance of the vibrating, or sounding, material. Drawing examples from historically and geographically disparate cultures, the Hornbostel and Sachs classification system, published in 1914 as the "*Systematik der Musikinstrumente: Ein Versuch*," follows this principle to divide instruments into four groups, based on their physical characteristics of sound production; further subdivisions are based on the form of the instrument. With some modifications and extensions, the Hornbostel and Sachs classification remains the most influential today. Its four large categories are *aerophones,* wind instruments or instruments with a vibrating column of air such as trumpets and flutes; *chordophones*, or string instruments; *idiophones*, instruments of self-sounding materials such as scrapers or bells; and *membranophones*, drums with stretched skin or other membranes.

Aerophones are subdivided into types according to the manner of producing vibration. The first group, free aerophones, consists of whirling instruments such as the bullroarer in which the vibrating air is not confined. An instrument found in ancient Greece, among aboriginal Australians, and among Native Americans, the bullroarer's thin blade of wood rotates at the end of a swung chord that excites the air to produce its characteristic roaring sound. The second group of aerophones contains those in which the air is constrained by a tube or vessel,

Two Chinese men blow their suonas (Chinese reeded horn) to accompany a group of folk dancers on a Beijing sidewalk, during the city's first snow of the winter, November 30, 1997. (AP/Wide World Photos)

with the vibration created by the breath or wind. This is a much larger group of instruments, with three further subdivisions. First, flutes consist of instruments in which the air is blown against an edge of the tube, such as with the Andean notched flute of cane, the *kena*. The next are reeds, such as the Western clarinet or oboe, in which the airstream is excited by a beating reed or reeds. The *khaen*, from Southeast Asia, is an example of a reed aerophone. Similar to the Chinese *sheng* and Japanese *sho*, the *khaen* is a mouth organ made of up to sixteen bamboo pipes arranged into two rows, each with a brass reed. Finally, there are trumpets, such as the aforementioned conch-shell trumpet or the large, wooden Swiss alphorns, in which the airstream is blown through a player's vibrating lips.

The term *chordophone* refers to instruments with one or more strings stretched between supporting structures or across a resonating body or sound box. Common examples include the guitar and Appalachian dulcimer. Although chordophones are sometimes grouped by how the strings are set in motion (struck, plucked, or bowed), they first subdivide by the shape of the sound box and neck, if the instrument has one. The simplest chordophone is the musical bow, a string stretched between two ends of a flexible stick. Some musical bows have attached resonators, such as the Brazilian *berimbau* and its small gourd that amplifies the sound of the single, struck string. Harps are plucked instruments with strings stretching between a sound box and a straight or curved neck. The small Celtic harp, for instance, has a triangular frame, one side of which is a sound box, the other a pillar, and the third a curved neck. Strings of graduated lengths connect the sound box to the neck. Zithers, such as the Appalachian dulcimer, have strings attached parallel to the sound box. The Hindustani *bîn*, also a zither, has seven strings (three of which sound sympathetically as drones) stretched above a fretted, bamboo tube, with two large gourd resonators attached below and near the tube's ends. Lutes and fiddles have one or more strings across a sound box and a straight neck, as with the ancient Chinese *pipa*, a strummed, pear-shaped lute. The *pipa* has four strings that run from a bridge on the flat-topped sound box to tuning pegs at the head of the neck. One fiddle from Iran, more precisely a spike fiddle, is the *kamanche*. Across this instrument's neck stretch three strings played with a bow; the neck pierces a round wooden resonator, forming a spike at the end of the instrument.

Drums with stretched skins or membranes are membranophones. Various criteria distinguish the subdivisions of membranophones: whether the instrument is a percussion drum or a friction drum, the number of vibrating heads, the shape of the drum frame, the material of its construction, the manner in which the membrane is attached to the frame, and so forth. Examples of percussion drums—those struck with the hand, sticks, or something else—include *kalangu* and *kendang* drums. The *kalangu* of the Hausa of Nigeria is a kind of talking drum, a double-headed, hourglass-shaped drum laced so that, when squeezed, its pitch changes. Another example, this one from Indonesia, is the *kendang*. This is the laced, double-headed, barrel-shaped drum of the Gamelan orchestra. The *kendang* derives from the South Indian *mrdanga*. The *cuíca* is a friction drum from Brazil played with a stick attached to the membrane and rubbed with wetted hands or a damp cloth to create its sound.

Idiophones are instruments that produce sound by the material of their construction, without the addition of strings or membranes. Structural features of idiophones do not distinguish subcategories, as with the other divisions. Instrument shape has little significance for the subdivisions of idiophones; rather, playing techniques subdivide the group: by concussion, striking, stamping, shaking, scraping, friction, or plucking. The number of instruments that fall within these various subdivisions is immense. A few illustrative examples include: the solid-body concussion sticks, or *claves,* of Latin America; the struck, fixed-keyed xylophones, such as the *balo* of West Africa and the *marimba* of Guatemala; the *ganbo* stamping tubes of Haiti; the *angklung* rattle of Java and Bali (played by shaking its sliding bamboo tubes); the scraped African American washboard; the tortoise-shell *áyotl*, a friction idiophone of the Maya-Quiche of Central America; and the plucked lamellaphones or *mbiras* of South Africa and *sanzas* of Cameroon, which consist of sets of graduated metal tongues on boards or sound boxes.

The large-scale classification of musical instruments attests to the wide range of instrument designs while giving insight into commonalities of acoustical/ physical features. Musical instruments, however, exhibit more properties than classification alone suggests. Isolated, classification does little to show the historical and cultural import of an instrument, its musical function within performance, or its social functions.

At an intersection of artifact, behavior, and belief, a musical instrument carries significance and meaning beyond its physical characteristics. Garnered from a society's material and ideological resources, musical instruments are often viewed as technical achievements, celebrated for their beauty of workmanship and renowned for their quality of sound. More significantly, musical instruments exist as complex cultural phenomena that resonate with a society's history and beliefs and its perceptions of music and music making. The ways instruments connect and merge with a society are myriad. John Baily, for example, relates how changes in a musical instrument of Afghanistan, the Herati *dutâr*, reflect pressures to include music from outside its traditional repertoire. These changes—most fundamentally seen in the addition of more strings to this long-necked lute—correlate to changing political alliances within and outside Afghanistan and a shift, for musicians and audiences alike, from lives focused on rural activities to more urban ones. From the Solomon Islands, Hugho Zemp explains that the basis of 'Are'are music theory—the notion of melodic interval—derives from the different lengths of tubes within bamboo panpipes and panpipe ensembles. In another example, Thomas Turino demonstrates how the performance of the *charango*, a small lute with a sound box often made from an armadillo shell, carries an essential role within courtship in the Peruvian province of Canas. Drawing upon the power, beauty, and music of the mythological *la sirena* (the mermaid), young males use the *charango* in courtship to signal intent, make contact, and ultimately woo young women. And as a final example, the performance of a Javanese *gamelan*, an ensemble of mostly sets of tuned gongs, corresponds to the interlocking cycles that delineate the lives of the Javanese. Briefly, *gamelan* music is organized around a recurring melodic/rhythmic cycle built in successive layers of sound from low to high, from larger gongs to smaller ones, with the melodic/rhythmic complexity literally doubled at each layer of sound. According to Judith Becker, these gong cycles from the *gamelan* orchestra show an isomorphic relationship to the way in which time is represented in Java, as overlapping simultaneous cycles in which smaller cycles move within larger ones. Such examples affirm that, more than just integral to music and musical behavior, musical instruments exist as a fundamental part of the human condition.

Leslie C. Gay Jr.

See Also Ethnomusicology; Folksong, Lyric; Folksong, Narrative; Music, Folk.

References

Baily, John. 1976. Recent Changes in the *Dutâr* of Herat. *Asian Music* 8(1): 29–63.

Becker, Judith. 1979. Time and Tune in Java. In *The Imagination of Reality*, eds. A. L. Becker and A. A. Yengoyan. Norwood, NJ: Ablex.

Buchner, Alexander. 1972. *Folk Music Instruments*. New York: Crown.

Buchner, Alexander. 1973. *Musical Instruments: An Illustrated History*. New York: Crown.

Dournon, Geneviève. 1992. Organology. In *Ethnomusicology: An Introduction*, ed. H. Myers. New York: W. W. Norton.

Kartomi, Margaret J. 1990. *Concepts and Classifications of Musical Instruments*. Chicago: University of Chicago Press.

Lysloff, René T. A., and Jim Matson. 1985. A New Approach to the Classification of Sound-Producing Instruments. *Ethnomusicology* 29(2): 213–236.

Marcuse, Sibyl. 1964. *Musical Instruments: A Comprehensive Dictionary*. Garden City, NY: Doubleday.

Sachs, Curt. 1940. *The History of Musical Instruments*. New York: Norton.

Schaeffner, André. [1936] 1968. *Origine des instruments de musique: Introduction ethnologique à l'histoire de la musique instrumentale*. New York: Johnson Reprint Corporation.

Schaeffner, André. 1946. Les Instruments de musique. In *La Musique des origines à nos jours*, ed. N. Dufourcq. Paris: Libraire Larousse.

Turino, Thomas. 1983. The Charango and the *Sirena*: Music, Magic, and the Power of Love. *Latin American Music Review* 4(1): 81–119.

von Hornbostel, Erich M. 1933. The Ethnology of African Sound Instruments. *Africa* 6(2): 129–157, 277–311.

von Hornbostel, Erich M., and Curt Sachs. 1914. Systematik der Musikinstrumente: Ein Versuch. *Zeitschrift für Ethnologie* 46: 553–598. Translated in 1961 by Anthony Baines and Klaus P. Wachsmann as Classification of Music Instruments. *Galpin Society Journal* 14: 3–29.

Wachsmann, Klaus P. 1961. The Primitive Musical Instruments. In *Musical Instruments through the Ages*, ed. A. Baines. New York: Walker.

Zemp, Hugo. 1979. Aspects of 'Are'are Musical Theory. *Ethnomusicology* 23(1): 5–48.

Myth

Narrative of cultural or religious beginnings. Myths refer to beginnings, in a sacred sense, and their definitions and analyses have plagued and fascinated folklorists and other scholars for centuries.

The brothers Wilhelm and Jacob Grimm, best known for their collections of *Märchen,* or fairy tales, were scholars who wanted to demonstrate that (German) national character was embodied in the folklore of a people. They distinguished

Mixtec creation myth showing the fire god at the center of the universe being fed the blood of sacrifice, which emanates from the head, hand, leg, and ribs of the god Texcatlipoca. (Werner Forman/Art Resource, NY)

among myth, folktale, and legend, as have many other scholars in several parts of the world.

The eminent Austrian psychoanalyst Carl Gustav Jung, who worked in the late nineteenth and early twentieth centuries, proposed that myth arises from the collective unconscious—that portion of the unconscious mind common to all human beings. In his formulations, myth shares common archetypes (or deeply and mentally embedded recognizable patterns) with dreams and other workings of the unconscious. Archetypes are to psychological processes as instincts (such as sucking) are to physiological ones. It is the archetypes, Jung advocated, that account for commonalities in mythic stories and events that are seen across cultures and time periods.

Others, such as Max Müller (who worked in Great Britain in the middle and latter parts of the nineteenth century), have believed myths to be metaphors for processes of nature. For example, Müller, a Sanskrit scholar and comparative philologist, believed that the folklore and especially the mythology of his day in England were the survivals of a presumed Aryan past, which he thought retrievable through careful comparisons of languages, beginning with Sanskrit. He noted similarities among the metaphorical names of the ancient gods of ancient civilizations from India to Greece to Rome. Through what he termed the "disease of language," processes of forgetfulness, and improper translations, myths were coded metaphoric mnemonics not only for the gods and their actions but also for the natural processes of the world, especially the movements of the sun. He believed that myths arose when people were capable of reasoning but not capable of very abstract thinking. Both a number of words and a particular god, he suggested, could symbolize one natural process: the movement of the sun through the day and year. Thus, for Müller and others who reasoned in a similar vein, myths were metaphors that, through time, lost their original meanings and became entities that seemed to stand for themselves. Only scholarly, comparative linguistic work could unravel the mysteries of which gods stood for which natural phenomena.

Franz Boas, credited with establishing the study of anthropology and mythology in the United States, saw all folklore as mirroring culture, both in what is allowed and what is prohibited. He specifically stated, in 1916, that the thought processes leading so-called primitive man to concoct myths were the same processes that modern man used. (It was the fashion of that day to speak in terms of "man" and "men" to mean "people.") He prefigured arguments Claude Lévi-Strauss would make thirty years later.

In 1965, William Bascom published a proposed solution to the definitional problem. His definition has both formed the basis for acceptance of a narrative as myth and served as the beginning point to argue against classifications of myth. It was his intention to provide analytic constructs—for myth, legend, and folktale—that had cross-cultural validity.

Bascom considered myth to be a form of prose narrative, believed to be true by the members of the society whose culture holds the myth. Bascom further noted that myths deal with events of the remote past from a world that is different from or earlier than the one in which the myth is related; myths have a sacred component (if they are not considered to be totally sacred), and they have mostly nonhumans as principal characters. He also maintained that, though there are many fewer myths present in any given culture than there are folktales or legends, the myths are held to have importance exceeding their numbers in that they are sacred and provide the rationale for existence and ways of doing things within the culture. Finally, he said that myths have explanatory and etiological functions.

In Bascom's cataloging of societies and cultures from around the world, he noted that it was often difficult to use an ethnographer's or folklorist's work on myth or narrative in general because the researcher had not included sufficient information on belief in the generating group. Therefore, it seems that the issue of belief was key for Bascom. He did note that the categories of myth, legend, and folktale were often collapsed in some cultures but added that, since his definition was part of an analytic scheme imposed from outside the culture, the people's own categories were not important for purposes of analysis and comparisons by outsiders to the culture.

Recently, Claire Farrer proposed a term—the *mythic present*—in an effort to characterize to Euro-American students and scholars the attitudes most Native Americans have toward the time element in myth. Although some of Bascom's criteria for myth hold true for Native Americans and their mythology, there is a collapse of time in Native American society that does not conform to Euro-American understandings of the various phenomena of time. Specifically, that which is known to have occurred in the long-ago past (often expressed as "when the world was in the process of being made") is conflated with that which is occurring now, at this moment, in our own time-space: This is the mythic present.

Some other researchers, particularly those who work with Native Americans, have found difficulties with Bascom's categories because myths are not always prose narratives and because the issue of time is not so clear-cut as Bascom proposed. Oftentimes, myths are in poetic language and follow the canons of poetics for the culture in which the myths are present. Both Dell Hymes and Dennis Tedlock are credited with forcing folklorists to recognize the poetic structure not only of myths but also of other forms of narrative through their insistence that rendering the narratives of other cultures in prose, rather than seeking to present them in the manner in which they are spoken, robs those narratives of their poetic structure and power. Their work demands careful typesetting and reading in order to assist a reader in appreciating the quality of the spoken, in contrast to the written, word.

A cross-culturally sound and minimal definition of the term *myth*, as distinct from other forms of narrative, is that it is sacred narrative that is most often believed to be true. Because myth is of such a sacred nature, many people object to the very word *myth* when it is attached to their own sacred narratives. For those in whose culture the myth is embedded, the truth of the myth may be literal or figurative. Literalists believe fully in the absolute truth of myth, whereas figurativists believe in myth as metaphor.

For example, believing Jews, Christians, and Muslims who consider themselves to be fundamentalists assert that the biblical Genesis is literal truth: Yahweh/God/Allah created the world and universe in which we live in six of our experienced days (twenty-four hours, more or less) and rested on the next, the seventh day.

By contrast, believing Jews, Christians, and Muslims who consider themselves to be less doctrinaire assert that the biblical Genesis is to be understood as a metaphor: Yehweh/God/Allah created the world and universe in which we live in six episodes called "days" that do not correspond to our experience of days; further, the creator (whatever name is given in the particular culture) inaugurated a pattern of alternating work (creation and creative effort) and rest.

This latter view of Genesis as metaphor allows for accommodation between religion and science in that the biblical Genesis of separation of light and dark, water and firmament, with the further differentiation of species culminating in human beings, follows evolutionary theory precepts as well.

For some people, the very words of myth are in themselves sacred. Even to utter such words is to call into presence, if not being, the referent. For example, recitations of the "beginningtime" by Mescalero Apache religious specialists are done in vernacular Apache or in English on most occasions; only during important ceremonials is the ritual language used, for that language had its own genesis in the "beginningtime" and, therefore, is intrinsically powerful. When speaking in the ritual language, religious specialists are extremely cautious, obeying many injunctions, speaking only in allusion and metaphor, and explaining to the powers that be that they are welcome among their people once again, for the speaking of them in the ritual language—the language of myth—calls them and demands their presence. It is also this power of word in sacred context that gives rise to the mythic present, the re-creation of mythic past in contemporary time and experience. By such a process of speaking/calling into being, myth is accorded an importance not only in the long-ago past but also in the here and now.

The power of the word was used very effectively by a mesmerizing speaker, the late Joseph Campbell. During the 1980s, no one was more closely associated with myth in the popular mind than Campbell. Not only a captivating speaker, he was also a fine storyteller, whether in lectures or on television. In general, Campbell's approach to myths and mythology (the study of myths) was a universalist one. He maintained, much as had the psychologist Jung before him, that myths embody the same stories for disparate cultures and that they were retellings of each other; his data were garnered from pieces of myths taken out of context from many narrative traditions. Because of his selective comparisons, he is usually not granted much scholarly credence. His lack of analysis of complete myths in their appropriate contexts has lessened his credibility, especially among folklorists and anthropologists.

Yet there is a certain appeal to a universalist explanation of myths. The French scholar Claude Lévi-Strauss is perhaps the best-known scholarly student of the world's mythology; although, if the truth be told, most of his data are from Native American sources in all the Americas. Lévi-Strauss has reached his audience primarily through the written word rather than through visual media. But, like Campbell, he has been roundly criticized for taking material out of context and comparing what may roughly be termed apples and bricks. However, in Lévi-Strauss's rationale, the lack of contextualization is permissible since he avers that all myths, wherever they are found, share a common structure that he has reduced to an algebraic formula. He also maintains that myths are binary structures, setting up and resolving contrasts and contradictions within the culture and society. For Lévi-Strauss, the universalist position is an acceptable one since all people in the world share common brain structure—structure that he sees replicated in myths. Therefore, myths become both good to think and a reflection of the thought process itself. His is a complex argument, and it often seems that no one can utilize the Lévi-Strauss analytic technique quite as well as can Lévi-Strauss.

Alan Dundes, a contemporary folklorist, also has devoted considerable effort to the analysis and explanation of myth. Rather than a universalist approach, however, he utilizes a neo-Freudian schema for analysis, finding that myths (products of adult minds, he avers) are one of the adult projective systems. As such, they are universal, in that all adults around the world use projective techniques that often are expressed in myths. Whereas followers of Jung maintain that archetypes are the same throughout the world, followers of the Freudian analysis of myth maintain that the symbols found in myth will be culturally relative but nonetheless a projection of infantile and child socialization systems. Many non-Freudian-oriented scholars marvel at the number of times neo-Freudians, such as Dundes, find that the myth under analysis has a sexual component somehow related to toilet training and Oedipus or Electra complexes.

The links among symbols and myths, myths and rituals, and heroes and myths also have been explored. Similarly, the syntagmatic (ordering) and paradigmatic (substituting) aspects of myth have been of interest to scholars. In the latter part of his career, the late Edmund R. Leach, a British social anthropologist, turned to a consideration of Christian and Jewish myths. Utilizing biblical myths, he demonstrated the redundancy in myth, maintaining that the episodes within myths make the same essential point or points over and over again as a means of reinforcing the importance of the message. His work has been said by some to be both a distillation and an extension of that of Lévi-Strauss, although Leach did not make claims to the universality of myth messages in general. But it was his earlier work that had a greater impact on those who study myth, for he demonstrated how myth is fluid, rather than being fixed for all time, in his discussion of the manipulation of myth and genealogy to reinforce land claims or settle other political issues.

Indeed, the permeability of myth is one of its essential characteristics. If myth, once constructed, were immutable, it would soon lose its value for people since it would not be able to accommodate changes in culture or the society's knowledge base. Myth lends itself to reinterpretation, but myth also adjusts to incorporate the new as well as celebrate the old—at least in the societies where myth is alive in verbal tellings and not subject to the orthodoxy that accompanies the fixing of myth in writing. In the 1960s, LaVerne Harrell Clark provided examples of myth's permeability through a study of how horses, a late postcontact phenomenon, were thoroughly incorporated into Navajo and Apache narrative.

Most folklorists and anthropologists continue to consider myth in its cultural context rather than simply as literature or philosophy. Sometimes, it has been the fashion for myth to be termed a mirror of culture, and at other times, it has been fashionable to subject myth to computer analyses. At still other times, myth has been pointed to as the philosophy of the unlettered, completely ignoring that the lettered also have and believe in their own myths. What is enduring is myth itself. It does not vanish with increased complexity of social life. Worldwide trade and politics do not cause it to wither and die from lack of use. It can stand—indeed, it has stood—scrutiny as metaphor, as literal truth as well as a synonym for untruth, as lessons for life, as components in an algebraic system, as manifestations of psychological processes, as exemplar of properness and simultaneously as warning of the consequences of impropriety, as philosophy of the Other, as engaging literature, as being universal as well as being particular to a group of people at a specific time. Whatever else it may be, myth authorizes the present in terms of the past. Myth, quite simply, is.

Claire R. Farrer

See Also Anthropology, Symbolic; Comparative Mythology; Cosmology; Culture Hero; Hero/Heroine, Folk; Myth-Ritual Theory; Religion, Folk; Ritual; Romantic Nationalism; Structuralism; Trickster.

References

Bascom, William. 1965. The Forms of Folklore: Prose Narratives. *Journal of American Folklore* 78: 3–20.

Boas, Franz. 1916. The Development of Folk-Tales and Myths. *Scientific Monthly* 3: 335–343.

Campbell, Joseph. 1949. *The Hero with a Thousand Faces*. New York: Pantheon Books.

Campbell, Joseph. 1969. *The Masks of God, Vol. 1: Primitive Mythology*. New York: Viking.

Clark, LaVerne Harrell. 1966. *They Sang for Horses*. Tucson: University of Arizona Press.

Dundes, Alan. 1962. Earth-Diver: Creation of the Mythopoeic Male. *American Anthropologist* 64: 1032–1050.

Farrer, Claire R. 1994. *Thunder Rides a Black Horse*. Prospect Heights, IL: Waveland.

Frazer, Sir James G. 1958. *The Golden Bough* (abridged edition). New York: Macmillan.

Hymes, Dell. 1981. *"In Vain I Tried To Tell You"*: Essays in Native American Ethnopoetics. Philadelphia: University of Pennsylvania Press.

Jung, Carl Gustav. 1958. *Psyche and Symbol*. New York: Doubleday Anchor.

Jung, Carl Gustav, and Carl Kerényi. 1963. *Essays on a Science of Mythology*. Trans. R. F. C. Hull. Princeton, NJ: Princeton University Press.

Kearns, Emily. 2010. *Ancient Greek Religion: A Sourcebook*. Chichester: Wiley-Blackwell.

Leach, Edmund. 1965. *Political Systems of Highland Burma*. Boston: Beacon.

Leach, Edmund. 1976. *Culture and Communication: The Logic by Which Symbols Are Connected*. Cambridge: Cambridge University Press.

Lévi-Strauss, Claude. 1969. *The Raw and the Cooked: Introduction to a Science of Mythology*. Trans. John Weightman and Doreen Weightman. New York: Harper & Row.

Lévi-Strauss, Claude. 1967. The Story of Asdiwal. In *The Structural Study of Myth and Totemism*, ed. Edmund Leach. London: Tavistock Publications.

Middleton, John, ed. 1967. *Myth and Cosmos: Readings in Mythology and Symbolism*. New York: Natural History Press.

Müller, Max. 1889. *Natural Religion: The Gifford Lectures Delivered before the University of Glasgow in 1888*. Oxford: Oxford University Press.

Peregrine, Peter N., Ilia Peiros, and Marcus Feldman. 2009. *Ancient Human Migrations: A Multidisciplinary Approach*. Salt Lake City: University of Utah Press.

Rank, Otto. 1964. *The Myth of the Birth of the Hero and Other Writings*. New York: Alfred A. Knopf and Random House.

Sebeok, Thomas A., ed. 1972. *Myth: A Symposium*. Bloomington: Indiana University Press.

Tedlock, Dennis. 1983. *The Spoken Word and the Work of Interpretation*. Philadelphia: University of Pennsylvania Press.

Myth-Ritual Theory

Primarily, a critical approach to literature that was influential in the English-speaking world during the first half of the twentieth century and that sought to uncover prehistoric ritual forms or patterns underlying literary works. Its germ is to be found in the work of the Scottish historian of religion William Robertson Smith (1846–1894), who, in *Religion of the Semites* (1890), asserted that what mattered most to the ancient worshipping community was action rather than belief, the correct performance of ritual rather than intellectual acceptance of creedal myth. This insight was developed at length by a group of British classical scholars at the turn of the century who were seeking the formal origins of Greek tragedy. This group, usually called the "Cambridge Ritualists" because all but one (Murray) were Cambridge dons, was comprised of Jane Ellen Harrison (1850–1928), Gilbert Murray (1866–1957), Francis Macdonald Cornford (1874–1943), and Arthur Bernard Cook (1868–1952). The well-known historian of religion James George Frazer (1854–1941), influenced by his mentor Robertson Smith, was sympathetic to myth-ritualism early in his career and definitely influenced the Cambridge Ritualists' work, but he soon disavowed the theory and its partisans and returned to a rationalism that he found more congenial. By 1921, his antipathy had grown so great that in the preface to his translation of the ancient mythographer Apollodorus's collection of myths called *The Library*, the normally unpolemical Frazer went out of his way to attack myth-ritualism.

Myth-ritualism is a collectivist and irrationalist explanation of the origin, development, and meaning of myth and ritual, and as such, it represents a deviation from the main line of British theorizing, which has always emphasized the individualist and intellectualist aspects of religion. From the moment of its enunciation, myth-ritualism has been controversial, and even in its heyday, it never appealed to more than a small number of scholars and literary critics. The main reason for this antipathy among classicists, historians, and folklorists always has been the quality of the evidence that its advocates have been able to marshal. Because (the theory goes) the forms that have come down to us in ancient literary texts derive from prehistoric rituals, which by definition are inaccessible, most of the data illustrating the argument have been (and have had to be) inferential and comparative, drawn from the behavior and beliefs of so-called primitive peoples who became known to Europeans during the imperialist expansion of the nineteenth century and who, it was claimed, stood at the same stage of mental evolution as did the peoples of classical antiquity. Generally speaking, scholars in disciplines with historical methodologies have regarded such evidence as excessively speculative and have refused to make the intellectual leaps that are often called for by myth-ritualists.

From the point of view of the history of ideas, myth-ritualism was part of the wave of irrationalist thought that crested throughout Europe just before World War I. The movement passed through two phases. The founding generation, the aforementioned Cambridge Ritualists (1890–1914), analyzed Greek drama (both tragedy and comedy) and found its "deep structure" to consist of a ritual pattern of death and rebirth based ultimately on the reconstructed stages of the Dionysian mysteries. In a series of publications leading up to Harrison's *Themis* (1912)—a volume that included chapters by Murray and Cornford—the group, led by Harrison and basing itself on the anthropology of J. G. Frazer, the vitalism of Henri Bergson, and the sociology of Émile Durkheim, turned away from the traditional image of the bright, shining Greeks and instead presented them and their religious belief and behavior as essentially "primitive." By the late 1920s, most classicists had, in turn, dismissed the Cambridge Ritualists' general theory of Greek religion and their specific analysis of the historical and formal origins of drama. By then, however, the theory had already been picked up elsewhere in the intellectual world, most notably by biblical critics (among whom it was in vogue in Scandinavia from the late 1920s through the 1940s) and especially by English-speaking literary critics.

Although a few scholars (such as the Marxist classicist George Thomson) continued to embrace myth-ritualism, the second phase of myth-ritualism (1930–1965) was essentially literary-critical. During those years, a number of critics rejected the classicists' rejection, simply assumed the correctness of the Cambridge Ritualists' method, and proceeded to apply it to postclassical texts, mostly dramatic but also including medieval poems, folk ballads, and novels. As time passed, myth-ritualism, when used at all, was increasingly encountered as only one element in a complex critical approach. The most notable critics associated with the second phase were the Americans Kenneth Burke, Francis Fergusson, and Stanley Edgar Hyman and the Canadian Northrop Frye. When the members of this second generation died or became inactive, no successors emerged. Perhaps because it was essentially a formalist method, myth-ritualism seems to have died unnoticed and unmourned in the mid-1970s, as the energy and attention of literary criticism in North America turned toward politics, in the forms of poststructuralism and especially deconstruction.

Robert Ackerman

See Also Evolutionary Theory; Myth.

References

Ackerman, Robert. 1991. *The Myth and Ritual School: J. G. Frazer and the Cambridge Ritualists*. New York: Garland.

Cornford, F. M. 1914. *The Origin of Attic Comedy*. London: Edward Arnold.

Else, Gerald F. 1965. *The Origin and Early Form of Greek Tragedy*. Cambridge, MA: Harvard University Press.

Harrison, Jane Ellen. [1912] 1927. *Themis*. 2nd ed. Cambridge: Cambridge University Press.

Hyman, Stanley Edgar. 1968. The Ritual View of Myth and the Mythic. In *Myth: A Symposium*, ed. T. A. Sebeok. Bloomington: Indiana University Press.

N

National Folk Heroes

Often synonymous with culture heroes and heroines, national heroes are those figures who are widely considered by the members and government of a nation-state to be especially outstanding. They tend to have a strong presence in the formal apparatus and activities of government, especially in education, civic observances, and public holidays, and in statues, place-names, and other public memorials. They may also feature in official national projections and expressions, on postage stamps, for instance. While the status of these figures as folk heroes is sometimes uncertain, depending on political and social circumstances, they may have a purchase in the popular consciousness and feature in folk expressions.

In some cases these heroes are historical figures, like the English Alfred the Great (849–899) or the American Betsy Ross (1752–1836), designer and maker of the American flag, the "Stars and Stripes." In other cases, they are legendary figures or icons, such as the American Uncle Sam.

National heroes, historical or not, may be stereotypes of national characteristics, real or imagined. The figure of "the jolly swagman" in Australia, for instance, is representative of the pioneering, antiauthoritarian values many Australians consider to be part of their national identity. Australia is perhaps unique in boasting as a national hero the figure of Ned Kelly, a bushranger or outlaw hero who murdered three policemen and robbed banks. More often, national heroes are associated with resistance to foreign domination. Typically such heroes are warriors who fight valiantly and cleverly, heroes of struggle who represent their people in their hour of need. Some examples of this type include Rákóczi of Hungary, Holger Dankse of Denmark, and El Cid of Spain.

Wars are often the source of national folk hero stereotypes, which include the American "doughboy," the British "tommy," the French "poilu," and the "digger" of Australia and New Zealand. Such generic figures, all male, have a good deal in common with the warrior hero as well as with the culture hero. National heroine types exist in the figure of the nurse, the mother who weeps and waits, and the brave young woman who prefers death to sexual capitulation, as in the story of the Serbian heroine Dojrana.

National heroes are frequently the "discoverers," claimers, and explorers of New World nations. Thus Christopher Columbus has this role in the United

Yankee Doodle

The earliest reference to the well-known ditty and its eponymous hero seems to be in a Boston periodical, *Journal of the Times*, in September 1768, though the tune, at least, was apparently well known for some time before this date. Various claims for the origins of the catchy tune (which was used by both the British and American sides during the War of Independence) and words have been made, and there are many different versions of the lyrics. Yankee Doodle's reported exploits, the best known of which is to "stick a feather in his hat and call it macaroni," are whimsical rather than heroic.

The term itself originally referred to a person from the New England states and was used by the Confederate forces in the Civil War as a slur against the Union side. As often happens in such cases, the Yankees took up the insult and wore it as a badge of pride, further developing the character into something of a roguish trick-ster figure. As is usual with such widely known and culturally significant names, its origins are the subject of considerable folk etymologizing. There are claims for a Native American origin and, perhaps more likely, for an origin in the nicknames Dutch settlers gave their English neighbors in the New England region. Over time, the name 'Yankee Doodle' became synonymous with the national spirit and identity of the United States and came to personify the American way, both at home and abroad.

Graham Seal

Cover of *Yankee Doodle Children's Book*, published by McLoughlin Bros., New York, NY, 1880. (Transcendental Graphics/Getty Images)

States of America, while Captain Cook has it in Australia. Such figures, as well as other types of national hero, are frequently held in high esteem as representatives of national identity, actual or imagined.

Heroes who have been chosen or developed as national figures are often said to be sleeping until their nation needs them once more. The king of Spain who died in 711, Roderick or Roderigo, was the last of the Visigoth monarchs. He was killed by the North African Muslims under Tariq ibn Ziyad and became the center of numerous legends. In some stories, he ends his days as a hermit, devoured by snakes, and in others he is a sleeping monarch, waiting to come again in the time of his country's need.

The processes by which real and mythic folk heroes become national heroes are generally complex and of considerable historical duration. These processes involve an ongoing and often intense interaction between the folk traditions that celebrate such figures and their representation in nonfolkloric form, including formal art, literature, and popular culture.

Graham Seal

See Also Children's Folk Heroes; Hero/Heroine, Folk; Local Heroes; Occupational Folk Heroes.

References

Alver, B. 1989. Folklore and National Identity. In R. Kvideland and H. Sehmsdorf, eds., *Nordic Folklore: Recent Studies*. Bloomington and Indianapolis: Indiana University Press.

Botkin, B., ed. 1944. *A Treasury of American Folklore: Stories, Ballads, and Traditions of the People*. New York: Crown Publishers.

Clough, B., ed. 1947. *The American Imagination at Work: Tall Tales and Folk Tales*. New York: Knopf.

Dorson, R. 1959. *American Folklore*. Chicago: University of Chicago Press, pp. 41, 47.

Hosking, G., and J. Schöpflin, eds. 1997. *Myths and Nationhood*. London: Hurst and Co.

Neck Riddle

A genre integrating traditional enigma and narrative. The neck riddle is usually thought of as a riddle told by the hero of a tale, either to win the hand of a princess (AT 851, "The Princess Who Cannot Solve the Riddle") or to save his neck from a sentence of death (AT 927, "Out-Riddling the Judge"). The riddle also contains a narrative. Its solution lies in the recent experience of the hero. Since the experience is private and always of a bizarre character, the princess or the executioner is unable to solve the riddle, and the hero triumphs. For example, the hero (like the biblical Samson) has seen a bird's nest or beehive in the carcass of an animal:

> Ten tongues in one head,
> Nine living and one dead;
> One flew forth to fetch some bread
> To feed the living in the dead.

Other neck riddles have to do with inversion—a man walking under gravel and on top of leaves, a daughter suckling her father—or more explicitly with incest, as in the Greek romance of Apollonius of Tyre, the source for Shakespeare's *Pericles*. Still other grotesque solutions relate to posthumous birth, dismembered bodies, or poisoned meat.

Many commentators have remarked upon the relationships of neck riddle themes to the imagery of carnival as described by Mikhail Bakhtin. Unlike the true riddle, which describes ordinary things in unexpected language, the neck riddle uses simple language to speak of the most shocking fusions of incompatibles: parent and child, life and death. Its challenging of culturally decreed separations reinforces the action of the frame narrative, in which a structurally weak challenger gains power over the powerful by the use of wit.

Recent scholarship has addressed the generic status of the neck riddle. John Dorst proposes that the neck riddle is not a stable genre but "an arena of intergeneric conflict" in which narrative and riddle struggle to impose their respective orientations on reality. Thus, the atemporal compression of the riddle reduces the narrative solution to a static tableau, but the narrative's unfolding in time opens up the riddle to the instabilities of experience. As Dorst notes, the same material emerges as narrative and as riddle in the West Indies. Seizing the West Indian examples, Roger D. Abrahams points out that there, as in other creole cultures, the neck riddle's generic flexibility is more the norm than the exception. Perhaps the neck riddle, and not tightly framed European genres such as the "true riddle," should be our model and point of departure in examining the history of folklore forms.

Dorothy Noyes

See Also Enigma, Folk.

References

Abrahams, Roger D. 1980. *Between the Living and the Dead.* Folklore Fellows Communications, no. 225. Helsinki: Academia Scientiarum Fennica.

Abrahams, Roger D. 1985. A Note on West Indian Neck-Riddles as They Comment on Emergent Genre Theory. *Journal of American Folklore* 98: 85–94.

Dorst, John D. 1983. Neck-Riddle as a Dialogue of Genres: Applying Bakhtin's Genre Theory. *Journal of American Folklore* 96: 413–433.

Night Hag

A phenomenon during which an individual senses the presence of a malevolent agent, is unable to move, is consciously aware of their surroundings, experiences a sense of fear or dread, and often feels a pressing or strangling sensation. In addition to these core elements, auditory and visual hallucinations and respiratory difficulty are common. The attack terminates when the victim is finally able to move. Traditionally, the word *nightmare* is used to describe this phenomenon. *Nightmare* comes from the Anglo-Saxon *neaht* or *nicht* (night) and *mara* (incubus or succubus). *Mara* is the agent form of the verb *merran* and literally means "a crusher." Because *nightmare* is commonly used to refer to a "bad dream," folklorists employ more restrictive terms, such as *night hag* or the terms used by the group under study, to refer to the syndrome.

The night hag has been documented throughout history and in a variety of cultures, suggesting a universal distribution. Victims of classic hag attacks wake to find themselves paralyzed, with a malevolent form astride their chests attempting to strangle them. Many cultures have an established interpretation that categorizes the classic form in particular. Representative examples are *augumangia* and *ukomiarik* (Eskimo), spirit possession that occurs while the soul wanders during sleep; *dab tsog* (Hmong), nocturnal pressing spirit; *cauchemar* (African American French-Catholics in Louisiana), a spirit that "rides" the victim; witch riding (Europe, Colonial America), oppression by a witch "riding" the victim to the witches' sabbath; and *kokma* (St. Lucia), the spirit of a dead, unbaptized infant who attempts to strangle the victims while sitting on their chest. Many traditions maintain that a night-hag attack can result in the victim's death if the attack is not terminated soon enough. In communities where attacks are attributed to witchcraft, a protective cutting instrument (e.g., razor, knife, shears, scythe) placed under the pillow or bed of the victim is believed to injure or kill the attacker, thus revealing the perpetrator's identity.

Individuals in groups that lack a folk taxonomy for the attack must rely on worldview, personal beliefs, and personal experience for interpretation. This results in idiosyncratic explanations. For example, many Americans familiar with the stories and images of unidentified flying objects (UFOs) and extraterrestrial beings prevalent in popular culture have interpreted hag attacks as abduction by creatures from outer space.

The Greek physician Galen (CE 130?–200?) diagnosed the night hag as a symptom of gastric disturbance, providing one of the earliest recorded medical references to the syndrome. This explanation persists today in the popular belief that attributes bad dreams and nightmares to "something I ate." Physiologically, the night hag occurs when symptoms of the rapid eye movement (REM) stage of sleep, specifically the suppression of muscular activity and characteristic brain activity, intrude upon either the hypnagogic (falling asleep) or the hypnopompic (waking) phase of sleep. Recent research indicates that the night hag may play a role in the sudden unexpected nocturnal death syndrome (SUNDS) afflicting Hmong refugees in the United States.

Leah Carson Powell

See Also Assault, Supernatural.

References

Adler, Shelley R. 1991. Sudden Unexpected Nocturnal Death Syndrome among Hmong Immigrants: Examining the Role of the "Nightmare." *Journal of American Folklore* 104: 54–71.

Hufford, David. 1982. *The Terror That Comes in the Night*. Philadelphia: University of Pennsylvania Press.

Jones, Ernest. 1931. *On the Nightmare*. London: Hogarth.

Obscenity

An act or expression that transgresses a culture's ordinary norms of social decorum. Obscenity may take the form of a word (e.g., *fuck*), a gesture (e.g., "flipping the bird"), an artifact (e.g., a tattoo, graffiti), a concept not normally mentioned in polite conversation (e.g., impotence), or a behavior (e.g., oral sex). Although by definition transgressive, obscenity is often shaped by tradition; in fact, most cultures include recognized means and occasions for the performance of obscene behaviors. Since identification of obscenity is based on prevailing social sentiment and judgment at any given time, precise definitions vary from group to group within a culture and may show marked alteration over time as well.

Within the folklore of Europe and America, obscene humor plays an important, if sometimes obscured, part, especially in certain genres, such as the folksong (particularly the ballad), folktale, and riddle. In these cases, obscenity often consists of scatological humor, sexual innuendo, and references to castration, impotence, sexual appetite, bestiality, and stamina or capacity. Many genres, such as riddles, possess both obscure and innocent answers, allowing the performer to suggest obscene topics while claiming innocence. For instance, a Finnish riddle asks what swells when held in the hand. The innocent answer—a ball of yarn—elicits laughter and embarrassment when compared to the implied but unspoken answer—a penis. Other genres, such as folksongs, sometimes substitute sound-alike alternatives for expected obscene words, creating a similar tongue-in-cheek humor that suggests but does not fully employ obscene material. In other cases, however, such as some folksongs, folktales, graffiti, jokes, and toasts, the item of folklore may prove openly bawdy, describing normally taboo subjects in great detail and with great gusto. Good examples are ballads such as "Our Goodman" (Child 274), which details the singer's discovery of his wife's infidelity, and folktales such as AT 850—variants of which contain a suitor test involving the identification of the color of the princess's pubic hair. Obscene toasts and verbal dueling have also been studied, particularly within African American folklore.

Traditional performers generally made a strong distinction between single-sex and mixed-company contexts, avoiding at least some sorts of obscene folklore when in the presence of children, clergy, disapproving collectors, or the opposite sex. By contrast, some folklore items that might be considered obscene by contemporary standards in the United States today were openly performed in mixed company in the past. Examples are *Märchen* and legends containing descriptions of the dismembering or torture of women. Customs such as *bundling*—a courtship pastime in which a couple slept together in the same bed, although clothed—were considered innocent in many agrarian communities in the past but are regarded as illicit in similar communities today.

In many cultures the world over, obscenity—particularly lewd behavior—correlates with sacredness. Deities are represented as lascivious, and calendar customs marking the agricultural or ritual year may include days of obscene license (e.g., *carnival*). Such moments may include lewd dancing, cross-gender behaviors, nudity, and sexually explicit masks or costumes. Initiations to college fraternities often contain similar occasions. Obscene folklore was an important part of Irish wakes as well. In all of these cases, obscenity plays a part in the ritual inversion of everyday life; after the completion of the ritual or outside of the celestial pantheon, such behaviors may again be strongly censured by the community at large.

Folklorists often have faced difficult decisions when collecting and presenting obscene lore. In the past, many collectors rejected such items at the time of performance or conveyed to the performers beforehand an unwillingness to record such materials. Other collectors recorded obscene items but decided against publishing them, presumably out of deference to the sensibilities of the reading audience or the reputation of the editor or performers. Still others devised methods of obscuring or diluting the force of the items, bowdlerizing explicit passages, translating key words into Latin, or replacing letters of obscene words with dashes (e.g., *c—t* for *cunt)*. Early collectors, such as the Englishman Sabine Baring-Gould, even occasionally supplied entirely new texts for folksongs they collected. Folklorists involved in the systematization of folklore often avoided classification of obscene materials altogether; Stith Thompson includes a section for obscene erotic materials in his *Motif-Index of Folk-Literature* (X700–799, "Humor Concerning Sex") but refrains from further detailing of elements that might belong under the rubric.

During the nineteenth century, folklorists occasionally circulated obscene materials in "gentlemen's editions," with limited subscriptions, plain covers, and little or no advertisement. Robert Burns's *Merry Wives of Caledonia*—a collection of bawdy folksongs from Scotland—is a particularly noteworthy private edition that appeared posthumously. The great Russian folktale collector Alexander Afanas'ev grouped his informants' bawdy tales together into a single final volume of his extensive anthology, labeling the material "secret tales" and marketing the volume to a limited circle of scholars. Limited-circulation scholarly series, such as the French and Italian *Kryptadia*, sought to present examples of the entire world's erotic folklore for the benefit of interested scholars. The American journal *Maledicta* seeks to accomplish a similar goal in a more open manner and for a broader audience today and includes treatments of erotica, verbal obscenities, insult, and off-color humor.

Although folklorists today may smile at the seeming prudishness or reserve of previous collectors, many of the same questions remain difficult for field-workers in contemporary contexts. Considerable public debate and legal dispute, for instance, has centered on the appropriateness of publishing or marketing obscene lines in contemporary rap music. Various forms of pornography remain illegal to publish or sell, limiting the editorial decisions of even the most liberal-minded collector. Questions of interracial or interdenominational slurs often pose problems to editors concerned with presenting lore that conveys a positive image of the informants and their community. Is it right or fair to the informant to publish remarks that may have seemed appropriate in the locker room or around the campfire but that may brand the informant as racist, sexist, or coarse when appearing in print? Are there genres of behavior that have become traditional— for example, sadism or the making of obscene phone calls—that do not merit inclusion in general anthologies of folklore? Should one anthologize a case of "mooning" (showing the buttocks) by fax or a case of "flaming" (writing a litany of coarse insults) by e-mail? Some newer technologically mediated obscenities pose problems for editors today equivalent to those facing nineteenth-century collectors of folktales and ballads. The transgressive nature of obscenity itself makes such questioning inevitable; when an item ceases to arouse a reader's surprise (if not consternation), its significance as true obscenity has probably come to an end. Folklorists, as members of cultures, participate in the same processes of definition and decision as their informants and readers, even if they would sometimes prefer to stand outside or above such debates. Thus, the decision to publish obscene materials may change their reception within the source community, altering, for better or worse, the culture under examination.

Thomas A. DuBois

See Also Carnival; Scatology; Verbal Duel.

References

Abrahams, Roger. 1964. *Deep Down in the Jungle: Negro Narrative Folklore from the Streets of Philadelphia*. Hatboro, PA: Folklore Associates.

Afanas'ev, Alexander N. 1970. *The Bawdy Peasant*. Ed. Gordon Grimley. London: Odyssey.

Brand, Oscar. 1958. *Bawdy Songs and Backroom Ballads*. Sound recording. New York: Audio Fidelity.

Burns, Robert. 1959. *The Merry Muses of Caledonia*. Ed. P. Ferguson. Edinburgh: Macdonald.

Goldstein, Kenneth S. 1967. Bowdlerization and Expurgation: Academic and Folk. *Journal of American Folklore* 80: 374–386.

Jackson, Bruce. 1974. *Get Your Ass in the Water and Swim Like Me: Narrative Poetry from Black Oral Tradition*. Cambridge, MA: Harvard University Press.

Legman, G. 1964. *The Horn Book: Studies in Erotic Folklore and Bibliography*. New Hyde Park, NY: University Books.

Legman, G. 1990. Erotic Folksongs and Ballads: An International Bibliography. *Journal of American Folklore* 103: 417–501.

Randolph, Vance. 1976. *Pissing in the Snow and Other Ozark Folktales*. Urbana: University of Illinois Press.

Randolph, Vance. 1992. *Blow the Candle Out: Unprintable Ozark Folksongs and Folklore,* vol. 2. Ed. G. Legman. Fayetteville: University of Arkansas Press.

Randolph, Vance. 1992. *Roll Me in Your Arms: Unprintable Ozark Folksongs and Folklore,* vol. 1. Ed. G. Legman. Fayetteville: University of Arkansas Press.

Occupational Folk Heroes

One of the most prolific fields for the creation of folklore is work. Since the industrial revolution defined work as we know it, trades, professions, and occupations of all kinds have developed. Many of these have long histories and proud traditions of struggle and development. An important aspect of these traditions may be a heroic, larger-than-life figure, usually a male, who represents the skills, values, and beliefs of an industry, trade, or occupation. Typically these figures are superhuman axmen, shearers, train drivers, sailors, or cowboys about whom numerous tall tales are woven.

In English-language tradition at least, there is sometimes a close connection between occupational folk heroes who are the product of working groups and heroes who are inventions of fiction writers. The controversy about whether Paul Bunyan was an "authentic" folk hero of timber workers or a literary creation has been echoed in studies of a number of lesser-known American figures. One of these figures is the African American Annie Christmas, who is said to be almost seven feet tall, to have twelve even taller sons, and to run a floating brothel. Neither her prodigious drinking nor her wild ways ended her days, though. Instead, she is said to have killed herself for the love of one who did not want her. According to folklorist Richard Dorson, Annie was solely the creation of Louisiana writer Lyle Saxon. The legendary Febold Feboldson, occupational hero of Scandinavian American farmers, is probably based on the stories told about Olof Bergstrom, a Swedish immigrant to America who appears in newspapers and comics of the early twentieth century and about whom many local tales were told around Stromsburg and Gothenburg, Nebraska. Paul Beath put many of these tales in literary form, furthering the Paul Bunyan–like legendry of Febold, which included such widely told tall tales as hitching a bee to a plow to plow a "beeline," along with a host of traditional lies involving giant mosquitoes, hoop snakes, and the business of cutting and selling frozen postholes. The steel mill worker Joe Magarac, created by writer Owen Francis in the 1930s, is a similar instance of an invented hero. Joe, whose surname means "jackass" in Slovak, is seven feet tall, works all day and night, eats enormous meals, molds molten steel through his fingers, and finally melts himself down into steel to prove that he can, literally, make a higher quality product than iron ore.

A number of other occupational heroes have similarly murky folkloric provenances. Old John was said to be the hero of American printers. All printers knew someone who had seen him, or even spoken with him. Old John was so supernaturally skilled that he could wave his hand across the composing desk and all the type would fall magically into its proper place. He always quit at the most critical moment of a job, when the type was being placed. According to the traditions of the printing trade, when John died, he, along with all other printers, would go to compositor's heaven, a print room with all new presses and type. Another example is the occupational hero of American signwriters, Slappy Hooper. Slappy was a larger-than-life character who painted the biggest, best, and fastest signs. He painted on the sky using "skyhooks" to hold his scaffold, and he once painted a red stove that was so realistic it radiated enough heat to make flowers and weeds bloom in winter. Doubts have been raised from time to time about the authenticity of some occupational heroes of other cultures, such as the Australian figure Crooked Mick, who first came to light in literary rather than folkloric contexts.

Despite the largely, perhaps solely, literary origins of many of these characters, some of them so convincingly echoed the interests and concerns of the occupational groups they purported to represent that they were adopted by those very groups. This was certainly the case with Paul Bunyan and Febold Feboldson and is very much in accord with the processes of folklore, where ideas, characters, and other information originating in nonfolkloric sources may be taken over and adapted by members of folk groups for their own ends and purposes. Broadly distributed themes and story elements of the kind found in most of these occupational hero traditions may be adapted to local places, events, and characters. To describe tales about characters who do not have "authentic" origins within a particular folk group as "fakelore" is to ignore this important aspect of cultural process and implicitly to denigrate those groups who have adopted such characters as occupational heroes.

Occupational heroes should not be confused with the patron saints of many industries and occupations. Such saints are often selected on the basis of the relationship between their skills or attributes and the tasks they perform. So, for example, St. Nikolai is the patron saint of Russian seafarers because he rescues the musician and merchant Sadko of Novgorod from the clutches of the sea czar.

Graham Seal

See Also Children's Folk Heroes; Hero/Heroine, Folk; Local Heroes; National Folk Heroes.

References

Beath P. 1948. *Febold Feboldson: Tall Tales from the Great Plains*. Lincoln: University of Nebraska Press.

Botkin, B., ed. 1944. *A Treasury of American Folklore: Stories, Ballads, and Traditions of the People*. New York: Crown Publishers.

Dorson, R. 1959. *American Folklore*. Chicago: University of Chicago Press.

"Febold Feboldson." In Leach, M., ed. 1975. *Funk and Wagnall's Standard Dictionary of Folklore, Mythology, and Legend*. London: New English Library.

Francis, O. 1931. Joe Magarac, *Scribner's Magazine* 90(5. November): 505–511.

Pound, L. [1913] 1987. *Nebraska Folklore*. Lincoln: University of Nebraska Press.

Occupational Folklife/Folklore

Expressive aspects of the workplace with special emphasis upon informally learned narrative, skill, and ritual passed from one generation of workers to the next. In Europe, the study of occupational folklife is concerned with both work culture and labor ideology, but parallel work in the United States has concentrated more on cultural expressions (stories, songs, skills, and customs) in the workplace with less emphasis upon the social and political contexts within which these expressions are formed and used.

The Industrial Revolution drew into sharp contrast industrial urbanism and the agrarian divisions of labor and social order that had characterized Europe and the English-speaking world since the early medieval period. In the nineteenth century throughout Western Europe and the British Isles, this contrast suggested to many intellectuals the importance of documenting and preserving these earlier ways of life or modes of economic production and their unique social and spiritual responses before the "dark Satanic mills" wiped them from the face of the earth. It was out of this impulse that Victorian intellectuals and aristocrats on the continent and in England began to conceive of "folklore" as a body of traditional materials that could be collected, documented, and preserved. Ironically, the very industrial trades and occupations that were emerging from this historical epoch (and that, to a great extent, defined the market and industrial era) were themselves unexamined since, in effect, they were seen as antithetical to the very customs, beliefs, songs, and narratives that interested these early scholars. Looking primarily at the theoretical development of American folklore but with an occasional glimpse at research efforts in Europe and Britain, a more comprehensive view of the development of occupational folklife—verbal and material aspects of work—can be drawn.

In both Europe and the United States, early students of occupational and industrial folklore were drawn toward resource-based trades that established regional and national identities linked to the need for raw materials. Mining, fishing, building construction, farming, ranching, and timber harvesting became the foci of the first occupational researchers. In Europe, particularly Scandinavia and Germany, this early research focused on preindustrial technologies and occupational structures linked to traditional village economies. The emphasis in much of this research was on craft and traditional forms of technology that were viewed in an evolutionary context, from the earliest periods of settlement to more contemporary, nineteenth-century occupational complexes. This focus on craft as a part of community and family life created a holism in European folklife studies that continues today. Occupational folklife—the entire range of verbal and nonverbal traditional expression—continues to shape this approach. Early occupational folklorists in Denmark, Sweden, England, and the Soviet Union drew direct connections between craft and guild solidarity and the "aristocracy of labor." More elaborate forms of political resistance and class formation during the industrialization period created a linkage of worker and labor consciousness that continues to shape much research in this field throughout the world.

In the United States, this historical response to emergent forces of work in a new physical environment resulted in a more nationalistic and romantic view of work culture. John Lomax and N. Jack Thorp, collected and reinterpreted the songs, stories, and verbal arts of the American buckaroo (cowboy) as an embodiment of a frontier, democratic ideal. These early American folklorists paid little attention to the economic or structural responses of buckaroo employment, with its nomadic uncertainty and state capitalist support of the railroads. Ironically, the occupational folklore of this group continues to contain much material expressing workers' opposition to these various forms of exploitation. Lomax and Thorp focused instead on popular concepts of the trade, paying particular attention to the way in which the western landscape and the expansive hardships of frontier life in America created new and unique forms of traditional expression or provided opportunities for the adaptation of Anglo or European traditional forms to the American context. The ballad, tall tale, and etiological legend forms of Europe were transformed to depict the heroic exploits of cowboy lore. Lomax, Thorp, and later Frank Dobie relegated the craft, techniques, and structural concerns of this trade to virtual invisibility in order to foreground a popular mythology of primitive romanticism that more closely reflected their externally derived concepts of class and culture. In contrast to European folklore collections of this period, however, there was some diversity and internal ethnic confrontation within these early collections. Whereas the European scholars focused more on work craft and traditional technology in homogeneous communities as an embodiment of national or regional character, the Americans devoted some of their energies to collecting verbal forms that depicted women, African Americans, Mexican Americans, and Native Americans in a more diverse, but often ethnocentric manner. In general, occupational folklorists in Europe evinced a more sophisticated view of the ideological aspects of work culture; the development of occupational folklore in the United States was less politically sophisticated and more closely linked to a more culturally diverse yet stereotypical concept of workers.

During the post–World War I period, regional folklorists in continental Europe, the United Kingdom, and the United States greatly expanded their respective collections of occupational folklife. In Europe, these documentary efforts often were conducted as part of nationally supported programs designed to preserve disappearing material and architectural heritage. In England and throughout the British Isles, researchers set about developing more systematic strategies of collecting and archiving a wide array of cultural materials, and the technical concerns of work were simply viewed as a segment of these wider collecting efforts. In the United States, regional folklore societies collected primarily verbal material, with linguistic and etymological interests leading some researchers into urban and industrial trades. The jargon, or *argot*, of the prostitute, grifter, and pickpocket that appeared in linguistic and sociological journals soon led regional collections into the listing of other work languages, from that of firemen and policemen to that of painters and actors.

In the 1930s, the depression and the ensuing economic collapse throughout the West resulted in a refocusing of occupational folklife. The industrial worker had, up to this point, been considered either a contemporary embodiment of a craftsmanship continuum as in Europe or the urban carrier of surviving verbal traditions in the United States, but massive urban migration and the collapse of previous conceptualizations of work culture forced a reformulation of these perspectives. In Europe, this transition resulted in an immersion of occupational folklife studies within ideological and political frames of reference, affecting larger concepts of class formation and labor history. In the United States, this transition laid the groundwork for more comprehensive documentation of occupational culture through which work culture was represented multivocally by individual workers, songwriters, fiction and nonfiction writers, and filmmakers. American folklorists paralleled European and British folklorists in their interest in agency and class formation, but they lacked acceptance within the labor movement itself as allies in trade union ideology. This distrust on the part of organized labor in the United States has continued to fractionalize occupational folklife studies within and outside the academy. In Europe and Britain, the inclusion of occupational folklife as a part of wider structural and ideological frames of reference within the labor movement and the academy has resulted in the establishment of archives, museums, and labor studies centers that subsume occupational folklife studies under various local, regional, and national jurisdictions. In his international review of occupational folklore studies, Flemming Hemmersam noted that early occupational folklorists in the Soviet Union used early collections of workers' folklore as means of "folklorism," the use of folk material for political purposes. In Germany, according to Hemmersam, Robert Michels and Will-Erick Peuckert paralleled the politically motivated work in the Soviet Union, but the historical and comparative methods of German linguistic and etymological research drew these earlier studies into more academic and less politically oriented collections. The contemporary research of Lutz Rohrich and Herman Bausinger reflects these influences. British and Italian interests in workers' songs, stories, and popular media led occupational folklorists into more careful examinations of the relationship between mass media and local work cultures, and Scandinavian scholars, drawing on regional and nationalist frameworks for the identification and collection of agricultural and resource occupations, developed a systematic method for documenting both the material and the verbal aspects of work culture that continues to inform occupational folklore researches in those countries.

Turning to developments in the United States, one of the earliest American folklorists interested in industrial folklore, George Korson, was drawn to collecting miner's lore and personal experiences through his journalistic focus on regional lore in Pennsylvania. As Archie Green stated in his two overviews of occupational folklore, unlike many of his colleagues before and since, Korson was able to work with the United Mine Workers, publishing collected songs and stories in its journal and relying on contacts and union support to make contact with individual miners. In his many books and articles, Korson walked a fine line between describing actual work experiences (dangers of the work, songs, and customs of above- and underground experience, customs, and work traditions) and making various political characterizations of the mine workers' resistance to capitalist exploitation. Korson recorded protest songs, strike ballads, and laments for workers killed in disasters and labor struggles, yet he never overtly aligned himself or his work ideologically with the causes expressed in these materials. In bringing miners and their occupational folklore to the attention of a national audience, Korson led the way toward state-supported programs designed to document occupational folklore as a means of articulating emergent and resilient forms of national character. At the same time, his populist and progressive political motivations remained largely implicit in his writings and public presentations.

In the 1930s, the Works Progress Administration provided an opportunity for writers and intellectuals in the United States to develop an array of public projects aimed at restoring a sense of national pride in the everyday experiences of American citizens. As a part of this movement, folklorist Ben Botkin and writers Nelson Algren and Jack Conroy began to collect and present aspects of worker stories and perspectives that they termed "occupational folklore." These collections paralleled the approach of Korson in their attention to the words and stories

Poster by Isadore Posoff for the Works Progress Administration, featuring a Pennsylvania miner, 1937.(Library of Congress)

of industrialized, urban workers, but they did not have the sophistication and holistic sweep of Korson's work. Wayland D. Hand, a folklorist from Utah, extended his interest in the folklore of hard rock miners into an international, comparativist study of occupational folklore—primarily verbal arts and legends—that linked American research to European antecedents and parallels. Unfortunately, this comparativist approach remains one of the few international studies of occupational folklore written by an American scholar, and Hand's call for more cross-cultural research in this area largely has gone unanswered.

In the 1960s, a former shipwright in the United States and a historian in England reformulated the field of occupational folklore. With a background in both an industrial trade and organized labor, Archie Green's research into labor and occupational folklore reflected a division between the political and ideological culture of the labor movement itself. What is most important in Green's work, particularly his early descriptions of labor and occupational folklore and his investigation of the relationship between popular and local working-class culture in the production of popular/folk music, is his ability to bring together academic interests in occupational traditional culture with an appreciation within the labor movement for cultural expression and ideology through folklore. Green's innovations in occupational research led to the first collaboration between the American Federation of Labor and Congress of Industrial Organization (AFL-CIO) and occupational folklorists at the Smithsonian Institution's 1976 Festival of American Folklife; in addition, he also drafted and lobbied for the passage of the American Folklife Act that established a permanent American

Folklife Center at the Library of Congress. This foray into public support of occupational folklife parallels museum and archival networks already well established in Europe and Great Britain.

In England, E. P. Thompson's view of class formation within British society shifted historical and cultural studies away from the somewhat mechanical forms of Marxist interpretation, which had characterized earlier exploitations of work culture for socialist ends, and toward a more processural, humanist social history of work culture. Raphael Samuel, Thompson, and a whole generation of working-class intellectuals sought to identify and describe the contexts within which cultural resistance to capitalism on a local, regional, and international scale took place. Folklorists within this emergent social and critical reshaping of the intellectual relationship between academics and the world of work emerged from the workplace itself, with miners, industrial laborers, and building trades workers becoming the collectors and interpreters of working-class culture within these various trades.

In the United States, Archie Green's ability to bridge the academic-labor public contexts, within which occupational folklore and the more inclusive folklife have developed, has brought us to the current generation of occupational folklorists in Europe and the United States. Hemmersam, in his summary of European and American research in workers' folklore, stated that there are basically four divergent approaches to the field. Interestingly, he divided these approaches into their respective ideological strategies, that is, with regard to the "system of attitudes, concepts and ideas behind the researcher's concern with workers' culture." The four ideological approaches are: (1) the classic folkloristic and ethnological approach, (2) bourgeois research of workers' culture, (3) a socialist/communist-oriented school, and (4) empirical research on workers' culture.

Viewed from this perspective, the classic folkloristic approach maintains the antiquarian's ideological commitment to a peasant model of work. Here, the researcher adopts a historical, regional, and often nationalistic theoretical position, through which surviving work traditions of the past are maintained and/or represented through material culture into the present. Flemming Hemmersam cited the work of Europeans Vesa Kurkela and Matz Rehnberg. In the United States, the work of Bruce Nickerson and Michael Owen Jones fell into this category.

This is contrasted with a more contextualized, ethnographic approach to work culture that maintains some of the elements of folkloristic research in its emphasis upon specific expressive forms within broader social and political contexts. In Europe, this approach is exemplified in the work of Birgitta S. Frykman in England and Hemmersam in Sweden. In the United States, it is evident in the work of Robert McCarl, Jack Santino, and Paula Johnson.

Bourgeois research of workers' culture maintains the position that mass media, public schooling, and the uniform experiences of urban life have penetrated

working-class culture to the point that there are virtually no unique or opposi-
tional forms remaining. Hemmersam cited the work of German scholar Herman
Bausinger as a proponent of this approach, and in the United States, the works of
Richard Dorson, Hennig Cohen, and Tristram Coffin fall into this category.

Socialist/communist approaches to workers' culture see a culture that has been
created exclusively in opposition to capitalism and capitalist modes of production. In Europe, this approach has a rich and deep history, and Hemmersam cited
Anders Björklun and Gösta Arvastson as the two main proponents of this
approach. In the United States, the approach has not been as actively expressed,
although certainly more Marxist views of work culture, from the work of Harry
Braverman and Archie Green to the folkloristic writings of José Limón and
Manuel Peña, have been informed by a more oppositional view of cultural formation in working-class communities.

Finally, the empirical approach has produced large collections of the cultural
materials of work with little attention to social or ideological context. Hemmersam noted the work of Simo Laaksovirta and Ulla-Maija Peltonen as providing a
useful description of how this approach is employed in Europe. In the United
States, this type of research has been conducted primarily by Wayland Hand and
Horace Beck.

It is difficult to summarize all of the approaches to occupational folklore to
date, but beyond discussing Hemmersam's useful divisions, it might be helpful
to suggest how these various forms of research are related. In this era, Marxism
has virtually disappeared as a viable political structure, yet the theoretical tools
of Marxist analysis provide a useful perspective from which to critically evaluate
the development of occupational folklore in the West, and Renato Rosaldo has
provided a theoretical framework that might pull these disparate elements together. In brief, Marx stated that the mode of production—the technology and
practices of producing food and energy—to a great extent determine or influence
all other forms of social life. Human reproduction, social organization, economic
life, and belief or "superstructural" aspects of a culture are based on these structural constraints. The following characterization simplifies this culturally materi-
alist approach to an examination of structure—the received circumstances of a
particular historical response to economic and physical conditions that result in
forms of social, political, and demographic response within a particular work organization. Beyond simply a labor market, the inherited structure of a particular
type of work generates a mode of production that elicits a specific, concrete historical response. This response is made up of two elements, the relational and the
practical. A worker responds to and becomes a part of the forces of production
(the tools, techniques, hierarchies, and economic constraints of a particular type
of work); at the same time, he or she creatively and informally participates in an
informal world of human relations that, to a great extent, responds to and resists

the very forces of production in which the work is conducted. A welder in the Portland shipyards in World War II, for example, acquiesced to the speedup and shortcuts of a wartime economy and its concomitant demands on production, while at the same time, the subculture of welders within the shipyard work culture determined the limits and boundaries of their complicity in this process. Work culture and its resulting occupational folklore is shaped by the forces of production, but it is born and given life by the informal relations of production that put a human face to work experiences and provide the technical means of opposition.

In addition to structure, it also is important to investigate *agency*—the informally held value system that is born at the point where the primary work group defines its independence from and opposition to all other hierarchies and groups within the workplace. Agency is the collective expression of specific individual choices that are made by workers as they form a class response to the constraints imposed by supervisors, union representatives, other workers, and even family and community members. Agency is defined by the primary work group, that face-to-face ensemble of individuals who respond to the occupational constraints of structure, and it defines the informal boundaries of cultural experience within that structure. A firefighter, for example, must respond to the physical realities of a high-rise building fire using the technical (structural) techniques of his or her trade. At the same time, however, he or she does so using knowledge and ideologies (agency) engendered by fellow workers, who inform and evaluate the performance.

Finally, there are border zones and boundaries that are constantly shifting in the world of work and are irreducible to a particular category or characterization as aspects of work structure or agency. Underemployed workers, the arrival of various ethnic, generational, or sexual preference groups, radical shifts in labor markets that export entire industries and relegate an entire generation of skilled tradespeople to obsolescence, as well as the depictions of workers in the media and in the representations created by folklorists—these are transition points or boundaries within the global economy that create the dynamic fluidity of work in the contemporary world. Increasingly, the worker today has no security but exists in a liminal context of tension between his or her historical preparation for a particular work structure, a set of personal values and ethos born of informally generated responses (agency) that reflect the primary work group's ability to accept or reject, assimilate, or alter the internal and external assaults on its collective will. New workers, loss of a labor market, or de-skilling force all workers into a daily reappraisal of how the unavoidable evolution of structure will affect our ability to survive. For their part, women, people of color, and a new generation of workers with new values experience internal boundaries caused by a denial of communication across the ever-increasing number of challenges to the status quo. Hemmersam noted the general shift in studies of occupational folklore worldwide from studies of lore to studies of the workers themselves, from externally conceived attempts to document occupational folklore for any of the various theoretical or ideological reasons mentioned earlier to a more internally generated concern for and articulation of the workers' own point of view. Stating this within the framework previously outlined, the concentration upon structural concerns in the study of work culture (survival of skills and materials from previous modes of production or a concentration on the historical evolution of a particular work process, for example) has given way to greater attention to various forms of agency (resistance to particular labor markets, the formation of oppositional forms directed at a further de-skilling or rationalization of work). This movement has created, in turn, an international context within which newer, oppositional forms from cultures outside of the workplace are creating new boundaries. Taken together, the structure, agency, and boundaries within any occupation create a cultural framework that is central to our understanding of contemporary life but irreducible to an individual representation of that life.

Robert McCarl

See Also Occupational Folk Heroes; Organizational Folklore.

References

Botkin, Benjamin. 1949. Industrial Lore. In *Standard Dictionary of Folklore, Mythology and Legend,* ed. Maria Leach. New York: Funk and Wagnalls.

Beck, Horace. 1973. *Folklore and the Sea.* Middletown, CT: Wesleyan University Press.

Coffin, Tristram, and Hennig Cohen. 1973. *Folklore from the Working Folk of America.* Garden City, NY: Doubleday.

Dorson, Richard. 1981. *Land of the Millrats.* Cambridge, MA: Harvard University Press.

Green, Archie. 1971. *Only a Miner: Studies in Recorded Coal Mining Songs.* Urbana: University of Illinois Press.

Green, Archie. 1978. Industrial Lore: A Bibliographic-Semantic Query. In *Working Americans: Contemporary Approaches to Occupational Folklife,* ed. Robert H. Byington. Smithsonian Folklife Studies No. 3. Washington, DC: Smithsonian Institution Press.

Green, Archie. 1993. *Wobblies, Pile Butts and Other Heroes: Laborlore Explorations.* Urbana: University of Illinois Press.

Hand, Wayland D. 1969. American Occupational and Industrial Folklore: The Miner. In *Kontakte und Grenzen: Probleme der Volks-, Kultur-, und Sozialforschung: Festschrift fur Gerhard Heilfurth,* ed. Hans Foltin. Göttingen, Germany: Verlag Otto Schwartz.

Heilfurth, Gerhard. 1976. Work in Industrial Culture—Aspects and Trends. In *Folklore Today: A Festschrift for Richard Dorson,* eds. Linda Dégh, Henry Glassie, and Felix Oinas. Bloomington, IN: Research Center for Language and Semiotic Studies.

Hemmersam, Flemming. 1985. Worker Lore and Labor Lore. *ARV: Scandinavian Yearbook of Folklore* 41: 17–29.

Hemmersam, Flemming. 1988. Workers' Folklore and Worker Culture. *ARV: Scandinavian Yearbook and Folklore* 44: 49–102.

Hemmersam, Flemming. 1991. Worker's Folklore and Worker's Ethnology in Scandinavia in the 1980s. *ARV: Scandinavian Yearbook of Folklore* 47: 59–117.

Holtzberg-Call, Maggie. 1992. *The Lost World of the Craft Printer*. Urbana: University of Illinois Press.

Johnson, Paula. 1988. *Working the Water*. Charlottesville: University Press of Virginia.

Jones, Michael Owen. 1984. Introduction—Works of Art, Art as Work, and the Arts of Working. *Western Folklore* 43: 172–178.

Korson, George. 1938. *Minstrels of the Mine Patch*. Philadelphia: University of Pennsylvania Press.

Limón, José. 1983. Western Marxism and Folklore: A Critical Introduction. *Journal of American Folklore* 96: 34–52.

Lomax, John, and Allen Lomax. [1910] 1948. *Cowboy Songs and Other Frontier Ballads*. New York: Macmillan.

McCarl, Robert S. 1978. Occupational Folklife: A Theoretical Hypothesis. In *Working Americans: Contemporary Approaches to Occupational Folklife*, ed. Robert Byington. Smithsonian Folklife Studies No. 3. Washington, DC: Smithsonian Institution Press.

McCarl, Robert S. 1985. *The District of Columbia Fire Fighters' Project: A Case Study in Occupational Folklife*. Smithsonian Folklife Studies No. 4. Washington, DC: Smithsonian Institution Press.

Nickerson, Bruce. 1974. Is There a Folk in the Factory? *Journal of American Folklore* 87: 133–139.

Peña, Manuel. 1985. *The Texas-American Conjunto*. Austin: University of Texas Press.

Rosaldo, Renato. 1989. *Culture and Truth: The Remaking of Social Analysis*. Boston: Beacon Press.

Santino, Jack. 1989. *Miles of Smiles, Years of Struggle: Stories of Black Pullman Porters*. Urbana: University of Illinois Press.

Thompson, E. P. 1963. *The Making of the English Working Class*. London: Victor Gollancz.

Thorpe, N. Jack. 1968. *Songs of the Cowboys*. Variants, Commentary, Notes and Lexicon by Austin and Alta Fife. New York: Clarkson Potter.

Oikotype/Oicotype

The local form of a text type (known as either oikotype or oicotype). C. W. von Sydow, who introduced the concept into folklore studies, borrowed it from biology, where *ecotype* means a variety of a species that possesses inherited characteristics that enable them to thrive in a particular habitat. Usually applied to longer folklore forms such as folktales and ballads, oikotypification occurs when regular changes occur in a text type's content, style, or structure as it adapts to the preferred patterns of a particular locality or culture group. Von Sydow's concern was the manner in which folktale performers who moved across regional and national boundaries told their stories in ways that conformed with the story-telling norms of their new cultural milieus. If a story caught the imagination of storytellers native to the new environment, it gradually would change from its original form while assuming characteristics suitable for its adopted locale.

An oikotype may be thought of as a special kind of subtype, one that is tied explicitly to a particular cultural setting. The process of oikotypification resembles localization, but the latter phenomenon usually refers to relatively superficial adaptations of a text type to a locality, such as changes in place- or personal names. Oikotypification suggests changes that affect the text type's narrative core. For example, the repetition by threes that characterizes most traditional narratives from Indo-European traditions may become repetition by fours when a tale is taken up by narrators from Native American cultures such as the Navajo, whose pattern number is four. Von Sydow's borrowing from biology was refined in the work of Roger Abrahams. Working with the narrative folklore of urban African Americans, Abrahams sought an approach to identifying what was culturally characteristic of the material these people performed. Many of their jokes, for example, were versions of international tale types, but Abrahams believed that an examination of their folklore would reveal particular ways of narrating that the African American performers found especially attractive. These tropisms might involve the content that had been von Sydow's principal interest but could also include structural properties, diction, framing devices, imagery, and symbols. Once the oikotypal pattern for a particular locality or group had been isolated, Abrahams noted, examination of a single piece of lore might reveal whether it came from that group.

Versions of the British ballads anthologized by Francis James Child that have been encountered among American traditional singers often reflect the process of oikotypification. For example, the texts may be shorter than their British counterparts, often pared down to what has been called the "emotional core." Moreover, supernatural elements may become rationalized, and topics of high seriousness may be treated with earthy matter-of-factness. Moral preachments may be added to those ballad narratives that lend themselves to such homiletics.

Although von Sydow's approach to folklore studies was exclusively textual, the concept of oikotype may have applications for performance-oriented folklorists. The geographically distinct styles of singing identified by Alan Lomax's cantometrics project, for instance, may amount to an identification of oikotypes of approaches to song performance.

William M. Clements

References

Abrahams, Roger D. 1970. *Deep Down in the Jungle: Negro Narrative Folklore from the Streets of Philadelphia*. First revised edition. Chicago: Aldine.

Coffin, Tristram P. 1977. *The British Traditional Ballad in North America*. Revised edition with supplement by Roger deV. Renwick. Austin: University of Texas Press.

Lomax, Alan. 1976. *Cantometrics: A Method in Musical Anthropology*. Berkeley: University of California Extension Media Center.

von Sydow, C. W. 1948. *Selected Papers on Folklore*. Copenhagen: Rosenkilde and Bagger.

Onomastics

From the Greek word *onoma*, meaning "a name," the term *onomastics* (or *onomatology*, as it is sometimes called) means the study of names. Onomastics has two chief subdivisions, *toponymy* (the study of place-names) and *anthroponymy* (the study of personal names). Each of these categories can be further subdivided, and the relationship of these divisions to folklore may vary considerably.

Historically, the scholarly study of names was begun by European linguists toward the end of the nineteenth century, and it acquired a solid scientific basis in the early years of the twentieth century. The first meeting of the International Congress of Onomastic Sciences was held in Paris in 1938, but it was not until 1987 that the eminent folklorist and onomastician W. F. H. Nicolaisen proposed, at the sixteenth congress, held at Laval University in Quebec, that onomastics be treated as a distinct discipline with its own philosophy and its own theories, rather than as a subspecialty of linguists, philosophers, folklorists, sociologists, psychologists, geographers, historians, and students of literature and aesthetics. Nicolaisen outlined a framework in which like-minded scholars could pursue this goal.

The study of place-names certainly became an important adjunct to nineteenth-century language studies. At the end of the eighteenth century, it was discovered that Sanskrit, the sacred language of ancient India, was, in fact, related to Greek and Latin. This discovery initiated a period of intense research into European languages, resulting in the development of a comparative approach to language—it was soon realized that modern European languages such as French, Italian, Spanish, Portuguese, and Romanian, for example, could all be traced back to earlier forms of Latin. By the end of the nineteenth century, a very refined methodology existed that enabled scholars to pinpoint sound changes as they occurred in time and the concomitant changes to the shape and meaning of words. Theories could be tested because there was a substantial body of data attesting to the nature of Latin during the centuries of Roman domination of Europe and the Mediterranean world. Modern French and Spanish words, for example, could be traced back by applying the laws that seemed to have governed their evolution, with known Latin forms acting as a control.

As comparative methodology was refined, a second important discovery was made—that not only were many modern European languages sister languages descended from Latin but also that other, seemingly unrelated language families were also related to Latin, Greek, and Sanskrit. Thus, the many Germanic languages, including modern English, Dutch, German, and Scandinavian languages, were seen to be connected, with the Romance tongues, to Celtic languages such as Welsh, Irish, Cornish, and Breton and the great family of Slavic languages, including Russian, Polish, Serbo-Croat, and Bulgarian. All these languages and others not mentioned here were, in turn, related to Iranian and languages of India—hence the term *Indo-European* used to indicate the geographical spread of these distant but related languages. Awareness of this Indo-European family of languages was to influence the study of the folktale in the latter half of the nineteenth century and much of the twentieth.

The reason linguists turned more and more to the study of toponymy is not hard to find. It soon became apparent that contemporary place-names often incorporated elements whose meaning was now opaque, the careful study of which, however, suggested the influence of languages now dead or no longer spoken in a given geographical region.

Building a hypothetical picture of primitive or proto-Indo-European languages by careful comparison of root words common to all, scholars began hypothesizing about the spread of these languages, finding in place-names the earliest evidence of language movement. Indeed, the existence of non-Indo-European roots in certain place-names was the first clue about even earlier human settlement in some countries. As a result, the use of comparative linguistic methodology was seen as central to the study of place-names, the more so because careful analysis revealed considerable layering of languages. Thus, in France, for example, it was possible to isolate place-name roots predating the arrival of Celtic-speaking peoples, who, in turn, adapted earlier forms to their language, only to have their own forms adapted and modified by subsequent external influences—of Latin with the colonizing Romans and later by Germanic speakers. Much of Europe shows this kind of depth and richness with its toponyms, be they towns and cities, rivers, lakes, mountains, or hills. This explains why so much onomastic research in Europe has been focused on unraveling the etymologies or history and meaning of place-names and so dominated by linguists. That historians have been so intimately connected with European place-name study is also logical since they were the scholars whose study of ancient documents produced the earliest known or attested forms of place-names.

This same preoccupation with the history of place-names led to a growing interest in personal names. All personal names seem to have meant something when they were first applied, but few contemporary names drawn from European languages have transparent meanings. Nowadays, people give names to their children that may come from any European language, regardless of the language spoken by the namer. Yet people often want to know what their names mean. Using the same principles applied to tracing the history of place-names, scholars are usually able to suggest the original meaning of personal names; the diversity of popular books available to facilitate the choice of names for new babies suggests that many people attach great importance to the names they choose, believing perhaps that names have power and that the name's original meaning somehow imprints itself on its bearer.

Underlying this desire to know the origin and meaning of names, be they place-names or personal names, is the fundamental need felt by humans to identify the physical world around them and to identify other humans. The naming and identifying of individuals creates a sense of social order and establishes sets of relationships; the naming of places helps make the unknown and potentially threatening known and familiar. Naming thus allows humans to domesticate the world about them, to acquire a sense of control, however illusory in reality that control might be. The fact remains that all human societies name themselves and name features of the world around them, as they perceive the world to be. As such, naming is therefore a very ancient and a very traditional preoccupation. And since tradition remains a central concern of the folklorist, the folklorist is interested in names and the process of naming. However, since tradition is not immutable but instead subject to the forces of change, the folklorist is also interested in the patterns that develop and emerge in space and time, though focusing more on the informal process than, for example, on the institutionalized processes established by governmental bureaus and boards of names and naming that are in charge of official naming (though even formally constituted naming institutions are subject to the vagaries of fashion).

It is not easy to establish how very ancient place-names were first given or, indeed, how very ancient personal names were first attributed, though one may find ample clues in the naming processes still functioning among many non-European peoples (the 1990 movie *Dances with Wolves* owes its title to just such a process). European place-names and personal names were very much in their present form, however, when, at the end of the fifteenth century, Europeans first came to the New World, as they quickly named the Americas.

European exploration and subsequent settlement drew on contemporary European patterns of naming in the wake of post-Renaissance voyages around the world. Wherever Europeans passed and wherever they settled, the place-names they created tended to follow recognizable trends. Prominent features, at first observed from the sea, were named to reflect their appearance, the date on which they were encountered (and were often named after that day's saint in the

Catholic calendar), after royal patrons, or after some fortuitous circumstance. Settlements were named in a similar fashion or, with increasing frequency, to recall the home town or city of prominent early settlers. As settlements grew in number, whole regions were named in memory of the home country, and subdivisions likewise often reflected European administrative units such as counties.

Relationships with native peoples were both good and bad, though in many parts, more bad than good—as is attested by native names existing only in corrupt forms, the originals of which can only be established by comparison with native languages that were not wiped out by war or disease.

Indeed, the number of Native American toponyms is sparse throughout most areas of North America, remaining only in the names of some states, rivers, and occasional settlements. They are most numerous in areas that remained unsettled until comparatively recent times, although recent official policy in Canada, for example, has seen a trend toward the reestablishment of native names or the substitution with native names of European forms; this is especially true in the Arctic regions.

The most striking feature of North American place-names is the linguistic diversity of toponyms of European origin. Early European explorers included the French, the British, the Spanish, the Portuguese, and the Basques, all of whom have left a greater or lesser imprint on contemporary maps. Changing patterns of domination, however, have muddied the toponymic waters. Newfoundland, one of the earliest regions of the continent to be influenced by Europeans, has place-names of French, British, Spanish, Portuguese, and Basque origins, though not infrequently, the oldest forms have undergone considerable transformation. Place-names of apparent French origin are, in fact, Basque names that were given French forms; seemingly English names are anglicized versions of earlier French or Portuguese names. Names of native origin are often the most recent, given by nincteenth-century explorers of the Newfoundland interior accompanied by Micmac guides.

This pattern is reflected across the continent. French explorers were often the first Europeans to set foot in many parts of North America, and there are few states and no Canadian provinces where the French did not leave their mark. The Spanish influence in Florida and the Southwest has been well documented. To these earlier settlements' names were later added names given by eighteenth- and especially nineteenth-century immigrants. In the same period, new patterns in the naming of settlements began to appear, one notable example being the application of names drawn from classical antiquity, reflecting the then new interest in the classical age. Similarly, religiously inspired settlement names stud the maps with biblical terms, and other names reflect the revolutionary period in Europe and North America. Some mapping of settlement patterns based on linguistic toponyms is very instructive not only about ethnic movement but also about regional and dialectal European influences and philosophical views popular at a given period.

Because of the relatively recent settlement in the New World that has given rise to place-names whose earliest forms are readily identifiable if one has sufficient knowledge of post-Columbian history, place-name studies have, with the exception perhaps of names of Native American origin, been a good deal less etymologically oriented in North America than in Europe. Interest has tended to focus more on social and historical factors in the patterns of naming, rather than on the original meaning of names. To this end, though it is still necessary to make the best use of all available documents in order to identify the earliest and subsequent forms of names, contemporary onomastic studies recognize that names are far more than the meaning of the words that become names and that central to the study of names today should be the namer, the name, the naming process, and name usage. Such an approach requires familiarity with a wide variety of humanistic disciplines, not simply with the history of languages or of colonization.

It was noted earlier that folkloristic interest in naming is fundamental but that not all subdivisions of onomastics are necessarily of equal interest to the folklorist. What follows is an outline of most of the main and some of the minor areas of naming that may concern the folklorist, beginning with the broad subfield of toponymy.

Among the oldest features named by humans must stand elevations, be they mountains, hills, ridges, or crests, since elevations have always been convenient reference points. The technical term for the study of elevations is *oronymy*; it includes not only the names of heights but also the terms used to name kinds of geographical elevations. These reflect settlement patterns, insofar as early settlers would have used their native, dialectal terms. It is possible to use a knowledge of, for example, regional English terminology as a clue to the peopling of the regions of North America. The folklorist will be particularly interested in the etymologies offered by locals to explain or justify the use of such-and-such a name, as when the name seems to refer to a historical event or when its meaning is not immediately evident and a story is created to provide an apparently satisfactory meaning.

Alongside the naming of elevations stands the naming of bodies or courses of water, or *hydronymy*. Folklorists are particularly interested in microhydronymy, the names given to small bodies of water or water courses not usually large enough to figure on maps but to which some significance is attached by the local population. These may range in size from duck ponds and swimming holes to alleged bottomless lakes or holes, about which there frequently is a body of anecdotes of legendary nature.

An area of naming that seems to have attracted little scholarly attention until recently is what one might term *hydroronymy*, or naming used to designate the contiguity of land and water features. This is of particular significance to people whose work places them on water, be it sea, lake, or river, for whom a water-borne perspective is important. Thus, sandbanks in rivers, reefs, or shallows in a lake or sea, inlets, bays, landings, and landmarks will all be given names. But the most important aspect of land-sea features is perhaps those features that are not visible to either a land- or sea-based observer: undersea features that are significant to fishers, for example, the careful location of which enables them to know when a vessel is poised over a fruitful fishing ground. Today, of course, with modern technology, it is possible to pinpoint such locations with incredible accuracy, for satellites and miniature computers allow the most precise location finding in the thickest of fogs. But before the advent of such technology, fishers had to rely on traditional forms of location finding, often using a system of triangulation based on landmarks seen from the sea or lake.

So far, the focus has been on natural features of land and water; geopolitical names and naming bring toponymic concerns into the lap of the everyday. But though the folklorist may have only limited interest in the naming of countries or continents, states, provinces, and other official subdivisions established by governments, interest grows when one considers the local, regional subdivisions. Thus, patterns useful to understanding local context emerge in an examination of school districts and the naming of schools, for example, all of which will give some insight into prevailing local perspectives. It is, however, when one comes to the level of community, be it city, town, village, hamlet, or whatever term is used locally to designate types of community, that tradition is most clearly at play.

Thus, any reasonably large agglomeration will be divided into informal but no less real (to their inhabitants) neighborhoods; the boundaries of such neighborhoods are marked by streets (whether they are called avenues or boulevards, lanes or alleys, or any of the myriad such terms available); the study of *odonymy* casts much insight into historical development, fashions of naming, and, indeed, contemporary thinking in urban planning. Of no less importance are the patterns in the naming of all public buildings, from schools to hospitals, churches to malls, cinemas to sports fields.

Here, the formal overlaps with the informal. In some communities, people favor naming their homes instead of or in addition to using a sanctioned street number, and patterns reflecting prevailing fashions are nowhere more visible than in the names given to shops and stores. The importance to the individual's cognitive map of local but unofficial features is often only accessible to the careful folklorist who seeks information on the names of fields, street corners, and other unofficial sites.

Such place-name features not only draw the formal into the informal, they also draw the inanimate of the toponym to the animate of the anthroponym or personal name. Personal names are given to inanimate objects such as boats, cars,

Phyllis Wheatley Elementary School in the northwest area of Miami. (AP/Wide World Photos)

trucks, spaceships, and ocean-going vessels; the process is clearly both personal and important since people also name stuffed toys, plants, and even "pet stones." Insofar as insight can be gained both on an ancient and traditional practice and on very personal processes, such study is clearly of interest to the folklorist.

The second major element of onomastics, anthroponymy, also deals with a wide range of naming practices. Although contemporary surnames are generally inherited and of interest chiefly for historical reasons, first names are of interest for very immediate reasons. Depending on a community's history and its openness to innovation, different patterns of naming can be observed. In some families, for example, there is a very strict adherence to tradition, with the eldest son taking his father's or grandfather's name; male and female children may be named according to a strictly observed hierarchy. The folklorist will attempt to uncover such patterning, in addition to noting changes in the pattern. In the last few generations, there has been, in some segments of society, considerable innovation based on the influence of the cinema, television, and popular music (although there is nothing new about naming children after famous, powerful, or otherwise influential people).

More interesting perhaps to the folklorist is the field of nicknaming. Nick-names, often attributed at an early age by one's peers, are not infrequently pejo-rative, brutally reflecting a perceived flaw of character, appearance, or behavior. All manner of anecdotes are told explaining the origin of such names. However, various systems exist in small communities to identify individuals who may share their name with one or more people in the same area; three women with the same first name and the same surname may be identified with reference to men in their families or to the places where they live; the same process is, of course, found with males sharing the same names. Identification may make use of this system in conjunction with personal nicknames. As an extension, rela-tional designations are sometimes used, calling male elders "Uncle" or female elders "Aunt" as terms of respect; at times, hypocoristic terms, or terms of endearment, may acquire the value of a first name or nickname.

An extension of nicknaming is encompassed in the French phrase *blason populaire*, used to refer to nicknames applied not to individuals but to whole communities. Nicknames and the related anecdotes usually poke fun at the bearers of the *blason*, often going from the purely local rivalry between neigh-boring communities to the regional and, indeed, the national level.

Given the traditional importance of animals in people's lives, it is hardly sur-prising to find patterns in the naming of domestic animals. A distinction can be drawn between farm or working animals, on the one hand, and pets, on the other. The former may still maintain traditional patterns; in recent years, however, pet names have been as subject to the influences of education and the media as have the names of their owners. As a corollary to pet names, patterns of naming in pedigree animals also should be examined.

To conclude with humans, however, a final area of interest concerns names given to groups. These may include the ephemeral, such as pop music groups, to the more durable, such as sports teams, and the less well known, such as military units. In all cases, names are given in order to promote a specific image. Of inter-est to the student of contemporary society are the names found in literature and the media. Pen names, comic book characters, and names of characters in car-toons, movies, and videogames can all, in their own way, inform the scholar about change in society and about the enduring significance of names as a reflec-tion of evolving cultural preoccupations.

Gerald Thomas

See Also Ethnic Folklore.

References

Baker, Ronald L., ed. 1991. *The Study of Place Names.* Terre Haute: Indiana Council of Teachers of English and Hoosier Folklore Society.

Boulanger, Jean-Claude, ed. 1989. *Proceedings of the XVIth International Congress of Onomastic Sciences.* Quebec: Presses de l'Université Laval.

Nicolaisen, W. F. H. 1976. *Scottish Place-Names.* London: B. T. Batsford.

Reaney, P. H. 1967. *The Origin of English Surnames.* London: Routledge and Kegan Paul.

Rennick, Robert M. 1984. *Kentucky Place Names.* Lexington: University Press of Kentucky.

Seary, E. R. 1971. *Place Names of the Avalon Peninsula of the Island of Newfoundland.* Toronto: University of Toronto Press.

Oral-Formulaic Theory

The approach to the study of oral tradition and works with roots in oral tradition that prescribes a specialized language or idiom as the basis of composition in performance. Also known as the Parry-Lord theory, after its founders, this approach puts a premium on the utility of patterned phraseology (*formulas*), typical narrative scenes (*themes*), and large-scale organization (*story-patterns*) in providing ready solutions to the performer's ongoing challenge of maintaining fluent, intelligible composition. In addition to applying the theory to living traditions, chiefly poetry, scholars have retrospectively analyzed ancient and medieval works to determine the extent of their dependence on such paradigms and, in some cases, their "oral" or "literary" character. With typical structures demonstrated in more than 130 separate language areas, the most pressing question has become how to interpret works composed in this specialized idiom.

The oral-formulaic theory began with Milman Parry's pioneering studies of the Homeric epics, the *Iliad* and *Odyssey*, which reveal systematic patterning behind the recurrence of particular phrases, especially noun-epithet expressions such as "swift-footed Achilleus" and "goddess bright-eyed Athena." Instead of explaining the great epics as either conglomerate editions of smaller poems (according to the analyst school) or the personal and individual achievements of a single genius (the unitarian school), Parry argued that a poetic diction as systematized as the language of the Homeric poems must be the legacy of generations of bards, who perfected the idiom over centuries. His fundamental insight was thus that the language of Homer was traditional.

The core of Parry's theoretical proposal was the formula, which was defined as "an expression regularly used, under the same metrical conditions, to express an essential idea." Parry eventually enlarged this definition beyond the noun-epithet phrase to include any metrically determined unit of Homeric diction. Thus, for example, recurrent expressions for speech introduction (e.g., "As so he/she spoke") were shown to combine with recurrent names for mortals or gods to produce predictable—and in terms of oral-formulaic theory, useful—hexameter lines.

Theme

Narrative "words"—recurrent actions or scenes—in oral-formulaic theory; defined by Albert Lord as "groups of ideas regularly used in telling a tale in the formulaic style of traditional song." First suggested by Milman Parry in his review of Walter Arend's 1933 monograph on typical scenes in Homer, the theme has a heritage in earlier studies of repeated actions in various narrative works, just as the Parry-Lord formula can be traced to the earlier analysis of *Parallelstellen* (parallel passages) in ancient and medieval poetry. What distinguishes both formula and theme from this background is the insistence that they constitute a performance idiom, a special compositional language that was both traditional, in the sense of inherited and collective, and oral, in the sense of unwritten or pretextual. Examples of themes in various traditions include: assembly, arming for combat, boasting before battle, sea voyage, feasting, exile, and the "beasts of battle" (carrion animals).

Lord, to whom the concept of theme should largely be attributed, conceived of the unit as an idea pattern together with a relatively stable core of verbal expression. As he demonstrated in Homer and in the south Slavic epic tradition, occurrences of themes in those traditions correspond in terms of the actual formulas employed, with predictable flexibility due to different singers or regional dialects. South Slavic bards also were shown to adapt their thematic patterns to individual songs or performances. Likewise, narrative inconsistencies—cases of Homer or his counterparts ignoring content and thereby allowing apparent contradictions within a given work—were explained in terms of themes that have lives of their own. A contradiction within a single performance fades in importance when weighed against the expressive impetus of a theme in the tradition as a whole. That is, the individual instance always draws its most fundamental meaning from the larger traditional context, which dwarfs any single performance.

As with other aspects of the oral-formulaic theory, studies of theme spread outward from ancient Greek and south Slavic traditions, especially to Old and Middle English, Old French, Biblical studies, Hispanic, central Asian epic, Irish, Welsh, and other traditions. With that growth, the original definition and concept shifted somewhat, coming to emphasize idea pattern over verbal correspondence among instances; eventually, efforts were mounted to understand the theme within its many different, tradition-dependent contexts. Questions of what mechanisms control aesthetics and whether thematic mechanisms persist when epics become transmitted by writing rather than orally can, as with the formula, be put to rest by viewing themes as metonymic of the tradition at large, with the concrete part standing for a much larger implied whole. One particular feast or battle, for example, is always echoic of other feasts or battles in the audience's experience of the tradition at large.

John Miles Foley

For Parry, utility in formulaic diction derived from the participation of individual phrases in larger, generative *formulaic systems*, groups of items fitting the same metrical slot that also are related by common semantic and syntactic features. Although this aspect of the poetic idiom furnished the composing poet a flexibility in line-to-line construction, the simplicity of the diction was attributed to an overall *thrift*—"the degree to which [a formulaic system] is free of phrases which, having the same metrical value and expressing the same idea, could replace one another" (Parry 1971). Formulaic language, therefore, was understood as serving the poet's needs not only in providing ready solutions but also in productively limiting compositional options.

This approach began as an analytical procedure to prove the traditional nature of ancient Greek texts. But Parry, under the influence of his mentor Antoine Meillet and of Matija Murko, a Slovenian academic familiar with south Slavic epic poetry from his own fieldwork, soon added the criterion of *orality* as a necessary implication of the traditional character of verse making. In order to confirm his hypothesis of an oral tradition from which the Homeric poems stemmed, Parry and his assistant, Albert Lord, conducted a large-scale fieldwork expedition to the former Yugoslavia from 1933 to 1935 (continued by Lord from 1950 to 1951 and later) to study firsthand the living phenomenon of south Slavic oral traditional epic. They recorded acoustically or by dictation more than half a million lines of epic from preliterate *guslari* ("bards; those who play the *gusle* [a single-stringed lute]"), now deposited in the Milman Parry Collection of Oral Literature at Harvard University; Lord and David Bynum have published selective contents in the series *Serbocroatian Heroic Songs* (*SCHS*, 1953–).

Aside from writing a few shorter papers, Parry did not carry out the comparative analyses of Homer and south Slavic epic that he had envisioned. After Parry's death in 1935, Lord assumed responsibility for that planned enterprise and, in fact, moved well beyond the original analogy to make the oral-formulaic theory a truly multidisciplinary undertaking.

The most influential of Lord's writings, in many respects the touchstone for the entire field, is *The Singer of Tales*, completed as his dissertation in 1949 and published in 1960. This book uses the *guslar* in performance as a model for Homer and also for Anglo-Saxon, Old French, and Byzantine Greek narrative poets. In addition to illustrating formulaic composition in the south Slavic songs, *Iliad* and *Odyssey*, *Song of Roland*, *Beowulf*, and *Digenis Akritas*, he also described narrative units called *themes*, or "groups of ideas regularly used in telling a tale in the formulaic style of traditional song." These included, for example, such typical actions as arming a hero, readying a horse, summoning guests to a wedding or battle, and so on. He also identified *story-patterns* that were coextensive with the work as a whole, the most familiar example being the Return song, essentially the story of the *Odyssey*, that also appears in Turkish, Bulgarian, Albanian, Russian, medieval English, and other traditions. At every level, the key concept is multiformity, the mutability of phraseological or narrative patterns within limits, as an aid to composition in performance.

Of Lord's later contributions, Volumes 3 and 4 (1974) of *SCHS* and *Epic Singers and Oral Tradition* stand out as exemplary. The first of these consisted of his translation and Bynum's edition of *The Wedding of Smailagi'c Meho*, a

12,311-line oral epic performed for Parry and Lord in 1935 by the preliterate singer Avdo Medjeovi'c of Bijelo Polje in Herzegovina. The latter volume is a collection of some of his most wide-ranging and important essays, treating Homer, south Slavic, Finnish, Old English, Bulgarian, and central Asiatic epic.

In the wake of the publication of *The Singer of Tales*, the Parry-Lord theory underwent vigorous translation and application to Old English, Middle English, Old French, Hispanic, American folk preaching, biblical studies, and scores of other areas; it also continued to expand in ancient Greek studies. A history of the comparative methodology is available in John Miles Foley's *Theory of Oral Composition*; an annotated bibliography appears in his *Oral-Formulaic Theory and Research*, with updates in *Oral Tradition*.

With formulas, themes, and story-patterns identified in traditions worldwide, new questions began to arise about the implications of oral-formulaic theory for interpretation, especially in relation to texts with extensive prior critical histories, such as the Homeric poems. One of the central tenets of the approach as originally stated held that a certain percentage of formulas and formulaic systems constituted proof of the ultimately oral provenance of a given text, independent of any supporting testimony for that claim. The reasoning proceeded from the criterion of utility: If a poet had regular recourse to ready-made diction and narrative patterns, then he or she was composing traditionally and thus orally. Quantitative measurement of this sort did not take into account the inevitable differences among languages, traditions, or genres, nor did it consider the persistence of the formulaic idiom after the introduction of writing.

Indeed, as the oral-formulaic theory has expanded to more and more traditions, many of them still living, it has become increasingly apparent that an absolute dichotomy of oral versus written does not fit the evidence. Manuscript works that presumably represent freestanding compositions by individual authors still show extensive use of the formulaic language, and different rules govern the structure and texture of formulas and themes from one language to another or even from one genre to another. Additionally, the issue of performance and all that it entails has come to the fore: Oral tradition presents many channels for communication (linguistic, paralinguistic, and nonlinguistic), only a limited number of which are reflected in what we conventionally reduce to a transcribed text.

Another area in which the theory has been modified is in response to the charge of mechanism, that is, the perception that formulas and themes imprison a verbal artist, restricting originality and diluting expressivity. Although based primarily on literary criteria, not all of them applicable to oral tradition, this objection has stimulated a reexamination of what is meant by the "essential ideas" of formulas and the "typical" content of themes. One proposed answer to the quandary consists of understanding the oral-formulaic idiom as a highly focused species of communication, one that encodes complex information in simple forms within the enabling event of performance and by institutionalized reference to the immanent tradition. By employing this special register of language, in other words, performer and audience (and later, writer and reader, if properly prepared) communicate with greatly enhanced economy. Of course, the traditional language cannot accomplish all of the quotidian tasks normally assigned to a much more generalized register, but as long as audience and reader are fluent in the traditional tongue, its dedicated function promotes a unique economy of expression and reception.

John Miles Foley

See Also Bard.

References

Amodio, Mark C. 2005. *New Directions in Oral Theory.* Tempe, AZ: Arizona Center for Medieval and Renaissance Studies.

Culley, Robert C. 1986. Oral Tradition and Biblical Studies. *Oral Tradition* 1: 30–65.

Edwards, Mark W. 1986–1992. Homer and the Oral Tradition. *Oral Tradition* 1: 171–230, 3: 11–60, 7: 284–330.

Foley, John Miles. 1985. *Oral-Formulaic Theory and Research: An Introduction and Annotated Bibliography.* New York: Garland.

Foley, John Miles. 1988. *The Theory of Oral Composition: History and Methodology.* Bloomington: Indiana University Press.

Foley, John Miles. 1990. *Traditional Oral Epic: The Odyssey, Beowulf, and the Serbo-Croatian Return Song.* Berkeley: University of California Press.

Foley, John Miles. 1991. *Immanent Art: From Structure to Meaning in Traditional Oral Epic.* Bloomington: Indiana University Press.

Foley, John Miles. 1995. *The Singer of Tales in Performance.* Bloomington: Indiana University Press.

Lord, Albert B. 1960. *The Singer of Tales.* Cambridge, MA: Harvard University Press.

Lord, Albert B. 1991. *Epic Singers and Oral Tradition.* Ithaca, NY: Cornell University Press.

Parry, Milman. 1971. *The Making of Homeric Verse: The Collected Papers of Milman Perry.* Ed. Adam Parry. Oxford: Clarendon Press.

Parry, Milman, Albert B. Lord, and David E. Bynum, colls., eds., and trans. 1953. *Serbocroatian Heroic Songs (Srpskohrvatske junacke pjesme).* Cambridge, MA, and Belgrade: Harvard University Press and the Serbian Academy of Sciences.

Oral Tradition

A Brief Definition

Whether we define the utterances of an oral tradition broadly, as any customary oral expression, or more specifically, as verbal arts using a "poetic" form of spoken language unlike everyday speech, it is generally recognized that oral traditions may encompass a wealth of verbal genres of enduring value to their communities. The scope of oral-traditional expressions extends from oral histories and folktales to epic poetry; from stylized, lengthy greeting ceremonies to religious invocations, mourning songs, medical recipes, and many other genres. To understand as accurately as possible each oral-traditional expression, we—ideally—learn the language in which it is spoken and the special idioms of that culture's oral tradition, and we listen to what the tradition bearers have to say about it.

The term *oral tradition* underscores two important aspects of these specialized expressions: their orality and their connection to a tradition. The *oral* half of the label "oral tradition" points to the use of vocal cords (versus pen and paper, keyboard and monitor, etc.) and also the demands upon the narrator or "tradition bearer" that accompany the act of composing "in real time," without the option to erase, shuffle paragraphs, or cut and paste. An oral performance places demands upon an audience, which participates by listening and, often, by responding. Orality shapes the composition and dissemination of the many forms of performed verbal expressions and art—both narrative and non-narrative.

The *tradition* half of the term "*oral tradition*" balances out the emphasis, implied by the word *oral*, upon the present moment of the utterance, which is shaped by the oral-aural dynamic between the tradition bearer and the other participants, by the sound of a voice, by attentive listening, and by people being present to each other. "Tradition" calls to mind, as far as memory reaches, all of the previous performances of a particular story or song. It also calls to mind the interrelationships between many different genres of oral expression, which, within a particular community, may share a set of related themes, ideals, characters, proverbs, and story patterns, including those appearing in folktales and fairy tales. "Tradition" may also be carried in the register of language that tradition bearers draw upon to recollect and reinvent verbal expressions in performance. Often this register can easily be differentiated from everyday speech. Like "once upon a time," it sets the stage for a specialized form of communication. The mere intonation of "once upon a time" may invoke the generic expectations intrinsic to fairy tales and the narrative content of those stories known to a community where these tales form a vital part of its culture.

Those who study oral traditions may work with ancient and medieval manuscripts, with the records of anthropologists, folklorists, and linguists, or with living performers and their communities.

Oral Traditions and Folklore

Studies in the twin fields of folklore and oral tradition inevitably converge. The oral performance of a poet, shaman, matriarch, healer, or any other sort of tradition bearer helps to create and re-create the knowledge of a community (its "folklore"). A sophisticated verbal technology, oral traditions encode historical legends, place-names, detailed medical, botanical, and agricultural information, moral and ethical teachings, games, mourning songs, proverbs, myths, epics, praise songs, and wisdom sayings. The foregoing—and far from comprehensive—list reveals that oral traditions encode highly diverse types of information. It should also be stressed, however, that oral traditions often privilege the performative power of language—sometimes saying is doing. A medical charm incanted by a South Slavic *bajalica* ("conjurer") may heal the suffering patient, just as the recitation of a genealogy placates ancestors, or Baul devotional songs of mystic minstrels enact the sacred. Thus, the *process* of an oral-traditional performance may bear as heavily upon its significance as the *product*—and we would be mistaken to equate an oral tradition with knowledge that may be distilled into discrete, paraphrasable (written) concepts. Oral-traditional lore is both particle and wave, never solely one or the other.

Although oral-traditional lore may be frozen in writing or recorded by other media, it is usually executed in real-time enactments. Just as *saying* cannot always be parted from *doing*, the lexical content (what is said) during such performances may not be separated from its physicality (how it is said). Such physicality includes the emergent and ephemeral medium of the tradition bearer's voice (for instance, vocal tone, rhythm, and silence punctuating sound) and, depending on the tradition, his or her gestures, stance, facial expressions, and use of props. Furthermore, oral traditions depend largely upon the face-to-face relationships shared by performer and audience. An audience's attentive comprehension and feedback vitally contribute to the oral-traditional performance; in turn, a skilled verbal artist adapts his or her performance to the context and the responses of those present. The people's lore—neither solely process nor product—thus emerges within the community and potentially transforms or maintains it.

Texture

A general term for the poetic devices of the surface level of texts, such as *alliteration*, *assonance*, *consonance*, *anaphora*, and *rhyme*. Sometimes, the term *texture* has been used to cover even broader concepts of diction and meter. According to some authors, *texture* is distinguished from *structure*. The former comprises the organization of prosodic and stylistic features and syntax, and the latter encompasses the large-scale elements such as organization of narration, plot, and story. Heda Jason, in her narrative structural model, separates texture from such categories as *wording*, *narration*, and *dramatization*.

According to some tenets of text linguistics, texture is imbued with cohesive relations. As M. A. K. Halliday and R. Hasan maintain, the text is distinguished from something that is not a text because the parts of a text form a coherent whole: A text has a texture.

Lauri Harvilahti

Diversity and Fluidity in Oral Traditions

The term *oral tradition* does not indicate a homogenous entity—a static and monolithic collection of stories and sayings to which speakers subserviently give voice. Rather, from one culture's traditional practices to the next, we find that oral traditions are, in fact, highly diverse in terms of function, genre, style, and transmission. A single oral tradition may include a wide variety of important genres, whose tradition-specific parameters will shift from culture to culture and from language to language.

Even the recounting of a single narrative or epic song within one language group's tradition reveals that there is enormous room for creative expression as well as continual re-tailoring to fit the demands of the performance context. For example, the Tibetan epic *Gesar* (also known as *Geser*, *Gesar of Ling*, and *King Gesar*) may be sung by a traveling bard for a household for the twofold purpose of entertainment and moral instruction or, at the other end of the spectrum, by a solitary Buddhist as he traverses a mountainside chanting *Gesar* "hymns" that are believed to manifest purificatory and protective powers. In the former case, an audience in the typical sense is present, while in the latter, a virtual audience composed of "all sentient beings" witnesses and receives the benefits of *Gesar* prayers. The *Gesar* epic has shown remarkable adaptability in response to both oral and written media, traveling fluidly between the two. Over the past two centuries, literary poems and written rituals (*pujas*) have emerged that reframe *Gesar* for aristocratic and monastic audiences, resulting in more diverse renderings of this oral epic.

Oral Traditions and the Literary Arts

The study of oral traditions has shed light on important features that differentiate them from literary works. Expectations associated with the literary arts do not adequately take into consideration how oral traditions work and may even obscure their aesthetic vitality. The following list, while neither complete nor universally applicable to all oral traditions, provides an overview of key contrasts between oral and literary compositions.

1. Oral traditions do not supply the crude, "primitive" prototype of a written literature; they are a sophisticated form of communication in their own right.

2. In place of the literary tradition's "original" poem produced by a single author, we find many versions of a well-known narrative, song, or other instances of oral expression that has no ur-form. Each evanescent version may differ according to the talent of a performer and the context of the performance. Even a single storyteller may re-create many versions of "the same" fairy tale or folktale.

3. From a literary perspective, the reuse of a common phrase runs the risk of sounding flat and clichéd. Conversely, recurring traditional "formulas"

Tibetan actor in costume prepares to perform King Gesar in Naqu, Tibet, China, July 7, 2007. (AP/Wide World Photos)

(phrases and verses that sometimes vary little from telling to telling) resonate idiomatically with far greater meaning than would, say, the same number of words utilized in everyday, nontraditional conversation. The same holds true for images, motifs, type-scenes, and story patterns. Consider, for example, such tale types as the Cinderella story or the narrative etiologies that recur in folktales. Rather than being trite, the ongoing reframing of a tale draws its power from a simultaneous responsiveness to the newness of the immediate situation and the traditional weight of a narrative that resonates with prior instances of its telling and reception.

4. While we think of words as units delimited by white space upon the page, a traditional poet or storyteller often conceives of whole units of acoustically encoded information as "words," whether this means a line of verse, a scene, or an entire story. Each "word," long or short, forms a part of the performer's repertoire. Thus, to understand oral expressions properly, we need to learn the working vocabulary, the "words," of the tradition.

5. A "great divide" was once imagined to exist between oral-folkloric and written-literary works, but the actual practices of tradition bearers have debunked this myth. Artists (among others) negotiate ongoing alliances between the literary and the oral in their creation of verbal expressions. Hybrid compositions in written form—the Middle English *Pearl* and *Sir Gawain and the Green Knight*, for instance—employ an oral poetics. Literate tradition bearers and their audiences could (and can) use resources

provided by both the oral-traditional and literary paradigms, much the same way that communities of bi- and trilingual speakers may switch languages multiple times within a single conversation.

6. The following "media morphology" (Foley, 39–53) addresses the adaptability of oral traditions with respect to writing: "voices from the past" (e.g., Homeric epics, the medieval Japanese *Tale of the Heike*, and the Old French *chansons de geste*), "voiced texts" (slam poetry), "written oral poems" (*Pjevannija*, Finnish *Kalevala*, and the works of Lydia Cabrera), and "oral performance" (Tenore Song, Mongolian Long Song [*Urtiin Duu*], Palestinian Hikaye, and Tibetan *Gesar*). "Oral performance" contains by far the most diverse species of oral traditions, and the features of oral traditions in the foregoing section derive mainly from the study of oral performances. Due to their various relationships with the technology of writing, performances and works in the other categories—"voices from the past" and "written oral poems"—may be mistakenly treated as literary. Recognition that these pieces rely upon oral-traditional modes of composition helps audiences reframe their expectations, avoid depending too heavily on the wrong set of interpretive tools (that is, the literary), and learn a new set (the oral).

The Study of Oral Traditions

From the eighteenth century, when oral tales first became the object of enduring scholarly interest, to the present, scholars have attempted to describe the products (and, to some extent, the process) of oral-traditional expression (primarily storytelling, folktales, and oral histories) in light of a growing appreciation for their aesthetic and cultural value. Along the way, as certain ethnocentric prejudices and literary expectations have been recognized, scholarship in this field has gradually paid more attention to what communities and tradition bearers have to say about what they say. There has been a general transition from the appropriation of folktales, epics, and songs for literary collections or ideological agendas toward the study (and perpetuation) of living traditions within their own contexts and according to their own rules. The following survey of approaches to the study of oral traditions is informed by Rosemary Lévy Zumwalt's in-depth article on the subject, "A Historical Glossary of Critical Approaches."

During the eighteenth and nineteenth centuries, solar mythology (Friedrich Max Müller), cultural evolutionary studies (Edward B. Tylor, Andrew Lang), and, the most far-reaching of these, Romantic nationalism (Jacob and Wilhelm Grimm, Johann Gottfried Herder) treated oral tales as newfound objects of serious study. The nineteenth century witnessed a burgeoning interest in oral traditions for the purpose of defining national identity—an interest that resulted in fieldwork within national boundaries and the transplanting of oral expressions from indigenous habitats to the more prestigious realm of literature. At their worst, solar mythology, cultural evolutionary studies, and Romantic nationalism problematically stripped agency from the folk, failed to assess the dynamic relationship between performer and audience, and assumed an urtext—an original text—that could be rediscovered through redaction and editing.

Two fruits of the Romantic-nationalist movement in Europe are the Grimm brothers' German *Kinder- und Hausmärchen* (*Children's and Household Tales*, 1812–1815) and Elias Lönnrot's Finnish epic, *Kalevala* (1835, 1849). The Grimms' early editions of their folktales and fairy tales treated oral storytelling as *Naturpoesie* ("natural poetry") that ought to be collected and published in a relatively unmodified form. However, due to the poor reception of these early editions and their emerging expectations for the *Märchen*, the Grimms gradually replaced many of the tales with either those that were told by more talented storytellers or their own rewritten versions that blended texts or added content and structure of a more literary style. The result is that the final 1857 edition shines with the polish of literary stories recounted for an audience with literary expectations. The Grimms' careful notes on their collections and their attempts at classification inspired later motif and tale type indices. Like the Grimm brothers, Elias Lönnrot performed fieldwork to gather oral Finnish tales (these recounted in verse), which he then prepared according to the rubric of literary standards. However, Lönnrot was fluent in the traditional oral register of Karelia, and, using the poems he had collected, he both compiled *and* composed the *Kalevala*, which is now considered the Finnish national epic. Lönnrot became the first secretary of the Finnish Literature Society, which to this day promotes the study of Finnish and international folktales and publishes such indices as those set in motion by the Grimm brothers' annotations.

The excesses of Romantic nationalism were countered by twentieth-century "mechanical" approaches: the Finnish historic-geographic method (Antti Aarne and Stith Thompson), where extensive catalogs of geographically dispersed folklore themes served to deflate Eurocentrism, and the age-area hypothesis approach (Franz Boas), which sought to map the migrations of cultures and their traditions, paying little heed to national boundaries. Cultural approaches—culture reflector (Boas), culture and personality (Ruth Benedict, Edward Sapir), and functionalism (William Bascom)—analyzed the relationship between the content of oral-traditional performances and the needs of communities, thereby attempting to bridge the gap that the previous approaches introduced between folk and folkways. The mechanical and cultural approaches could, however, be criticized for not heeding the artistry of oral traditions.

The issue of aesthetics was initially addressed by approaches that explored the patterning of text: epic laws (Axel Olrik), myth-ritual approach (Lord Raglan), morphological approach (Vladimir Propp), and oral-formulaic theory (Albert Lord and Milman Parry). For the aesthetic interpretation of oral expressions, the first three of these approaches have proven to be rather blunt instruments: "epic laws," mythic features, and morphological functions describe commonalities among epics and folktales irrespective of their tradition-specific differences. Their generalizations, largely imposed from the outside, often risk being reductive. However, the work of Milman Parry and his assistant Albert Lord transformed the study of oral traditions by generating the first oral theory—*oral-formulaic theory*—that truly took into account the role of oral performance in the process of composition.

Parry, whose dissertation demonstrated that a large percentage of the *Iliad* and the *Odyssey* (nearly 27,000 lines of ancient Greek hexameter combined) relied upon oral-formulaic phrases, decided to record and interview living epic poets in the former Yugoslavia who maintained a tradition similar to that of the ancient Greeks. With Lord as his assistant, Parry sought to understand the role of memory in the recitation of epic-length poems. Without Parry and Lord's discoveries, we would still have very little insight into the complexities of surviving records of ancient epic poetry and the practices of oral poets and other tradition bearers to this day. They found that, rather than a feat of superhuman memory, a narrative oral poem is composed *in situ* using a repertoire of templates: stories, passages, and lines (also called story patterns, themes, and formulas). To meet the demands of improvisation, a bard re-creates entire stories by expanding or compressing these templates of various duration—as long as they remain recognizable to their audience (Foley's concept of "variation within limits" in *The Traditional Oral Epic*). Furthermore, an oral poet draws upon a virtual cultural repository ("the tradition") of shared stories, characters, and idioms familiar to his or her audience. These findings switched attention from the generic patterns common to stories in many languages (patterns perceived by a scholar in isolation from the actual communities that use such tales) to specific traditions, a community's commentary on the tradition (if possible), and the poet's process of composition.

Alongside oral-formulaic theory, other approaches have been brought to bear upon the study of oral traditions: structuralism (Claude Lévi-Strauss), the symbolic-interpretive (Richard Geertz), psychoanalysis (Alan Dundes), feminism (Susan Tower Hollis, Susan Slymovics), authenticity (Regina Bendix), ethnopoetics (Dennis Tedlock, Dell Hymes), performance theory (Richard Bauman), and immanent art (John Miles Foley) (for more information, see Zumwalt). Ethnopoetics, performance theory, and immanent art examine the nexus of performance, tradition, and the specialized, idiomatic registers of language that form oral traditions. Proponents of ethnopoetics ask how oral performances may be recorded in writing and read (or re-performed) on their own terms. Dell Hymes has searched for those structural units within a poem that are constitutive of its

Repertoire

In general, the stock of skills a person or persons are prepared to execute; with specific relevance to folklore, the complex sets of interrelated skills, knowledge, and achievements that highlight a person or group's unique abilities in a particular genre (or genres) of traditional performance.

A performer's repertoire is generally used to denote an individual's particular skill, achievement, or knowledge. The term *repertoire* also applies to the same areas on a group level. An example of the former would be the narrative repertoire of a particular raconteur who is recognized for a knowledge of trickster tales or, in the latter case, the craft repertoire of a group known for particular skill at producing specific types of pottery in a style in which the designs and techniques are common to the entire group.

Though generally seen as a discrete set of forms, a person or group's repertoire is built upon a complex of interrelated items that both shape and are shaped by the particular skill being focused upon. For example, the narrative repertoire of the storyteller known for trickster tales not only reflects a learned set of traditional tales but also calls forth a variety of questions about the performer's social and artistic backgrounds. From whom were the narratives learned and how? Were they passed orally from a particular relative, or were they acquired from a number of sources? What were the circumstances surrounding the performance of each particular tale? Was there an associated task or event that precipitated the performance, such as weaving a rug, quieting a child, or entertaining and educating the group? What other skills and activities reinforce or detract from the performer's narrative skills? What is the performer's individual and family status in the community? These are among the variables that affect individual repertoires.

The study of a person's or a group's repertoire requires a multifaceted approach that accounts for as many of the variables involved as possible. The study also requires a recognition of the multiple genres involved in a repertoire. Folklorist Barre Toelken describes repertoire in terms of multiple repertoires. That is, a person's or group's repertoire is a collection of interrelated genres of folklore that reflect and are shaped by the aesthetics of the performers' folk group. On occasion, a specific genre may be the main focus of the performance, but the rendering of each individual item is shaped by the full range of identifiable folklore genres that a particular individual or group possesses, and these are shaped by the aesthetics of the group with which the performers identify. This ideational context thus informs us what the genres of a particular performance are, as well as the realities of the aesthetics and traditions of the group in which the performers live. In addition, it is necessary to be aware of the roles of not only active bearers of tradition (i.e., performers) but also inactive bearers (i.e., those who know but do not actively perform folklore). Both sorts of tradition bearers are vital to the development and perpetuation of repertoires. Thus, the term *repertoire* refers to the full range of knowledge and abilities of the performers as shaped by the relationship among the folk genres in their repertoire and to the traditional aesthetics of the group to which the performers belong.

Randal S. Allison

meaning, working to rediscover the effaced poetic structures of Native American tales recorded in writing by anthropologists and linguists who paid little attention to their artistic value. In contrast, Dennis Tedlock seeks to graphically represent paralinguistic performative traits—such as volume, rising and falling tones, pauses, and so on—by modifying typefaces and spacing. In performance theory, Richard Bauman and others have argued that performance plays an integral role in the meaning of an oral "text." Bauman's "keys to performance" (special codes, figurative language, parallelism, appeals to tradition, special formulae, disclaimers of performance, and others) all call attention to performance per se. Immanent art, developed by John Miles Foley, builds upon Parry and Lord's oral-formulaic theory by exploring examples of the agency and creativity of oral-traditional bards. Foley demonstrates how a verbal artist may modulate and even recombine traditional "words"—individual words, phrases, lines, half-lines, themes, type-scenes, and story patterns—for special effect. His research on ancient Greek, South Slavic, and Anglo-Saxon oral traditions also incorporates the findings of performance theory and ethnopoetics to investigate performance, traditional idioms, and translation practices.

At present, scholars and policy makers are concerned about safeguarding traditional cultures threatened by globalization, cataloging "intangible heritages" worldwide, and giving communities the opportunity to define their own traditions and choose the best means to safeguard them. For example, in 2001, a transnational association was founded for the preservation of oral epics: Mezhdunarodnaya Assotsiatsia "Eposy Narodov Mira" (MAEN)/International Association "Epics of the World's Peoples" (IAEWP). The majority of participants hail from central Asia (Turkey, Iran, Mongolia, Kyrgyzstan, and Kazakhstan, but also Germany and Armenia), where tradition bearers continue to recompose epics in performance. This association addresses those factors that threaten to undermine the ongoing existence of epic traditions. On a global scale, UNESCO's 2003 Convention for the Safeguarding of the Intangible Cultural Heritage (ICH) seeks to support and bring recognition to such cultural heritages as oral tradition, ritual and social practices, traditional knowledge, performing arts, and traditional craftsmanship—domains that inevitably overlap. The UNESCO 2003 Convention asks member nations to amass inventories of their communities' ICHs, while promoting community-based (versus scholarly) definitions of ICH.

Future directions for the study of oral traditions include preserving the conditions that allow for the continued existence of oral traditions; defining and translating the idiomatic vocabulary ("words" such as phrases, poetic lines and line segments, type-scenes, story patterns, and so on) of a tradition for a reader or listener outside that tradition; the relationship between performance context and genre, and the issue of "gentrification" in folklore studies; hybrid oral and literary works of verbal art; contributions from cognitive science concerning memory and performance; cultural studies approaches that question the relationship between tradition and political authority; and many more. Volume 18 of the journal *Oral Tradition* offers a collection of short articles written by more than eighty scholars addressing the state of the field with respect to individual traditions worldwide.

Heather Maring

See Also Ethnopoetics; Historic-Geographic Method; Legend; Literary Approach; Myth; Performance; Proverb; Romantic Nationalism; Storytelling; Structuralism.

References

Amodio, Mark C. 2004. *Writing the Oral Tradition: Oral Poetics and Literate Culture in Medieval England*. Notre Dame, IN: University of Notre Dame Press.

Del Giudice, Luisa, ed. 2009. *Oral History, Oral Culture, and Italian Americans.* New York: Palgrave Macmillan.

Falola, Toyin, and Fallou Ngom, eds. 2009. *Oral and Written Expressions of African Cultures*. Durham, NC: Carolina Academic Press.

Fine, Elizabeth C. 1994. *The Folklore Text: From Performance to Print*. 1984. Bloomington: Indiana University Press.

Foley, John Miles. 1990. *Traditional Oral Epic: The* Odyssey, Beowulf, *and the Serbo-Croatian Return Song*. Berkeley: University of California Press.

Foley, John Miles. 2002. *How to Read an Oral Poem*. Urbana: University of Illinois Press. eCompanion at http://www.oraltradition.org/hrop.

Folklore Fellows, Finnish Academy of Science and Letters, University of Helsinki. http://www.folklorefellows.fi.

Honko, Lauri. 1998. *Textualising the Siri Epic*. Helsinki: Suomalainen Tiedeakatemia.

Lord, Albert Bates. 2000. *The Singer of Tales*. Revised edition. Cambridge, MA: Harvard University Press.

Oral Tradition: An Interdisciplinary Academic Journal. http://www.oraltradition.org.

UNESCO Culture Sector. Intangible Heritage. http://www.unesco.org/culture.

Zumwalt, Rosemary Lévy. 1998. A Historical Glossary of Critical Approaches. In *Teaching Oral Traditions*, ed. John Miles Foley. New York: Modern Language Association, pp. 75–94.

Organizational Folklore

Forms and examples of folklore as instances of organizing, folklore about organizations, and folklore originating in the organizational workplace. An organization comes into being when two or more people communicate and contribute action to accomplish a common purpose. Many instances of games and play, festive events and celebrations, and picketing with slogans and singing exemplify spontaneous organization. Increasingly, folklorists document and analyze the organizational processes in religious activities, ethnic display events, and customs or rituals involving food, especially in "temporary communities." One study of the Passover seder considers how foodways and ritual can determine *communitas* and define who in a family exercises control, who the guests really are, and ultimately, who is and is not "family." Another describes behavior of people on soup night, a contemporary small-group festive gathering, suggesting implications for better understanding the tension and balance between individual and shared power as well as the process by which a sense of community and group identity is generated. A third focuses on an annual family clambake, exploring how celebrations often serve as instruments for community, fellowship, and intimacy achieved, in part, through leadership, teamwork, joking behavior, and the sharing of knowledge about the tradition.

The overwhelming presence and impact of formal institutions in people's lives—schools, utility companies, law enforcement, government at all levels, the entertainment industry, the workplace, and purveyors of consumer goods—have produced a spate of stories, rumors, jokes, sayings, and even terms ("Ma Bell," "Mickey Mouse" products). Many narratives revolve around the quality of service, including the difficulties posed by the absence of sales personnel in large discount stores, the slowness of the postal system, and the problems of communicating with computers (such as the bill for $0.00 for which the customer is dunned until he or she finally sends a check in that amount). Stories describing the flood of gobbledygook, foul-ups in paper shuffling, obscure offices (and people) with no present function, and glutted warehouses indict government or other institutions with inefficiency, wastefulness, or ineptitude.

Numerous legends and rumors concern big business or particular corporations. Historically, attitudes toward the businessperson in American folklore have ranged from resentment or hostility toward merchants and bankers to viewing the traveling peddler with an admixture of condescension and sympathy and according respect toward the petty capitalist master-worker employer (the individual entrepreneur working alongside his or her employees). The portrait of business organizations today is ambiguous, and peoples' feelings about these institutions are ambivalent. Some accounts depict a careless organization, as in stories describing bottles of Coca-Cola or other brands of soft drink contaminated with decomposed mice, cigarette butts, or putrid peanuts. Others portray a dangerous or deceptive organization, for example, alleging that Kool-Aid is carcinogenic, that Pop Rocks explode, that Corona Beer has been urinated in by Mexican workers, that the garments made in the Third World and sold in discount stores are infested with snakes, and so on. Another image is the evil organization as presented in accounts about religious cults kidnapping prospective members and allegations that certain corporations are linked with extremist groups (Arm & Hammer, Proctor & Gamble, and Exxon with satanists; Adolph

Coors Company with the American Nazi Party; and Uncle Ben's Rice and Church's Fried Chicken with the Ku Klux Klan). A fourth image sketches the beneficent organization, particularly in redemption rumors claiming that a certain company will purchase expensive medical equipment (a dialysis machine, an iron lung) for a needy child if customers send discarded items such as cigarette packages, the pull tabs from aluminum cans, or the tags from tea bags.

Folklorists have documented and analyzed such stories, hypothesizing that some reflect major structural changes in society as communities move from self-sufficiency to dependency on large, impersonal organizations, which generate anxieties or fears expressed symbolically (e.g., legends about "Kentucky Fried Rat" in which a patron of a fast food franchise discovers a crispy coated rodent in the bucket of chicken because of unsanitary conditions or a prank by a disgruntled employee). Other accounts may convey concern over an invasion of foreign goods and threats to a country's economy by competitors abroad (allegations of contaminated, defective, or dangerous products from Third World countries). Some likely involve transference (the redemption rumors can assuage feelings of guilt over unhealthful habits). Whether or not accounts are based on actual experience, they are significant in their pervasiveness.

Folklore also pervades the organizational workplace. Much of photocopier lore focuses on points of strain inherent in formal organizations, occasioned by institutional controls, supervision, and structure at the expense of individual freedom and personal power. The familiar drawing of a person with an enormous screw through the midriff and the caption "Work hard and you shall be rewarded" communicates the feelings that organizational life can produce much too easily. Fake memos, usually ascribed to the personnel office, set forth changes in policies. For example, one describes a new restroom trip policy limiting use of facilities to twice a day and warning of a thirty-second buzzer that will sound before the roll of paper automatically retracts, the toilet flushes, and the stall door opens. Another informs employees of a forced early retirement plan called RAPE (Retire Aged Personnel Early). A third presents a new sick leave policy stating that a physician's statement will no longer be accepted as proof ("if you are able to go to the doctor, you are able to come to work") and that death will not be accepted as an excuse for absence unless it is the employee's own (in which case, "we would like a two-week notice as we feel it is your duty to train someone else for your job"). Sometimes, photocopier lore evincing criticism circulates sub rosa; on other occasions, members of an organization openly display it (feeling, perhaps, that it refers to the larger organization but not their department or to other institutions but, thankfully, not their own).

Many people decorate their work area with mementos, posters, postcards, cartoons, photocopier lore, or other items. Placement may be as important as content in regard to function (whether something expressing criticism is hidden or in public view, where items that one looks at for diversion or reverie are located, and so on). The nature and extent of personalization reveals a great deal about the individual, management attitudes, and organizational climate.

In addition, much talk (illustrated with numerous stories) about beating the system, engaging in prohibited behavior, and so forth suggests worker dissatisfaction. The presence of celebratory events, festive occasions (such as birthday parties), joking, and food sharing signal cordial relations, cooperativeness, and ready communication. Recounting oft-told tales about a worker insulting an impudent customer, getting back at a supervisor, or violating rules and regulations express frustrations and serves as a means of coping with stress. Stories about critical incidents in the organization's history can reveal beliefs about the institution and its environment as well as the organization's preparedness for and responsiveness to change. Traditional expressions and metaphors often encapsulate values and influence perceptions, decisions, and actions; consider, for example, cowboy management metaphors ("earning his spurs," "gunning for the opposition," "a Smith & Wesson beats four aces") that justify extreme behavior, in contrast to what is conveyed by frequent reference to "family," "teams," or "nurturing." In sum, stories, ceremonies, rituals, rites of passage, festive events, play, metaphorical language, and other examples of folklore in organizational settings may instruct, persuade, entertain, express the ambiance of the workplace, help an individual cope, protect personal integrity, stimulate a sense of community, guide decision making and action, reinforce factionalism, and help or hinder organizational effectiveness. Folklore can serve the researcher as a source of information, a diagnostic tool to uncover problems and their causes, and a means of improving organizational functioning and the conditions under which people labor.

Michael Owen Jones

See Also Occupational Folklife/Folklore.

References

Collins, Camilla. 1978. Twenty-Four to the Dozen: Occupational Folklore in a Hosiery Mill. PhD dissertation, Indiana University, Bloomington.

Dundes, Alan, and Carl Pagter. 1978. *Work Hard and You Shall Be Rewarded: Urban Folklore from the Paperwork Empire*. Bloomington: Indiana University Press.

Fine, Gary Alan. 1992. *Manufacturing Tales: Sex and Money in Contemporary Legends*. Knoxville: University of Tennessee Press.

Humphrey, Theodore C., and Lin T. Humphrey, eds. 1988. *"We Gather Together": Food and Festival in American Life*. Ann Arbor, MI: UMI Research Press; reprinted by Utah State University Press, 1991.

Jones, Michael Owen. 1987. *Exploring Folk Art: Twenty Years of Thought on Craft, Work, and Aesthetics*. Ann Arbor, MI: UMI Research Press; reprinted by Utah State University Press, 1993.

Jones, Michael Owen, ed. 1990. Emotions in Work. Special issue of *American Behavioral Scientist* 30(January-February): 3.

Jones, Michael Owen, Michael Dane Moore, and Richard Christopher Snyder, eds. 1988. *Inside Organizations: Understanding the Human Dimension.* Newbury Park, CA: Sage Publications.

Nickerson, Bruce. 1976. Industrial Lore: A Study of an Urban Factory. PhD dissertation, Indiana University, Bloomington.

Porter, Kenneth. 1944. The Business Man in American Folklore. *Bulletin of the Business Historical Society* 18: 113–130.

Santino, John Francis. 1978. The Outlaw Emotions: Workers' Narratives from Three Contemporary Occupations. PhD dissertation, University of Pennsylvania, Philadelphia.

P

Paradigmatic/Syntagmatic

Distinctive dimensions of linguistic structure applicable to phonology, grammar, and other aspects of language, including folklore forms. As defined by linguist Ferdinand de Saussure, the syntagmatic relationship between elements in language refers to their occurrence in a linear sequence. An element's meaning depends upon its place in the sequence. The syntagmatic relationship (sometimes referred to as *diachronic*) may be represented by a series of words strung out along a horizontal axis. The paradigmatic relationship (sometimes called *synchronic*) refers to the association between all elements that could fill a particular place in a sequence—for example, words with the same grammatical function or the same or similar denotation. Words stacked up and down a vertical axis may represent paradigmatic relationships.

Syntagmatic and paradigmatic distinctions help to differentiate two approaches to the structuralist study of folklore, especially narratives. The perspective associated principally with Russian formalism—manifested in Vladimir Propp's morphological analysis of the folktale—treats structure from a syntagmatic perspective. Propp identified a sequence of thirty-one actions that constitute the Russian wonder tale. These actions always occur in the same order, even if some are omitted. Each action, no matter what character in the narrative performs it, takes its meaning from its sequential position. Propp's syntagmatic approach to Russian folktale structure contributed to Alan Dundes's identification of recurrent syntagmatic patterns in Native American folktales. Dundes and others have also analyzed non-narrative genres, including proverbs and riddles, from a structuralist approach influenced by Propp.

The paradigmatic approach to folk narrative structure has found its fullest expression in the work of Claude Lévi-Strauss, who identified a paradigmatic pattern of mediated binary oppositions underlying the linear structures of myths from North and South America. This paradigm may accommodate a variety of elements. The Zuni creation myth, which attempts to mediate between the oppositions life and death, for example, may do so by substituting other oppositions (such as horticulture and war), which may then be mediated by a single concept, the hunt. Lévi-Strauss's work had less immediate impact on folklore studies than the syntagmatic approach, but examples of other structural analyses of folklore from a paradigmatic perspective include Edmund Leach's treatments of Old Testament narratives and a theory of genres developed by Elli Köngäs-Maranda and

Pierre Maranda. The concept of paradigmatic structure also has influenced work in ethnopoetics by Dell Hymes and others, who have applied it to texts of Native American verbal art. Using an approach he called "verse analysis," Hymes, for example, discovered repeated patterns in narratives from Native American people along the northwest coast that provide the molds by which storytellers shape their specific performances.

The oral-formulaic theory of Milman Parry and Albert Lord exemplifies the combination of paradigmatic and syntagmatic approaches. On one hand, Parry and Lord argued, epic singers work from syntagmatic outlines of the epics they spontaneously compose. On the other hand, they plug into the outlines various formulas, many of them interchangeable paradigms, that fit the poems' metrical and narrative needs.

William M. Clements

See Also Diachronic/Synchronic; Ethnopoetics; Folktale; Linguistic Approach; Oral-Formulaic Theory; Structuralism.

References

de Saussure, Ferdinand. 1966. *Course in General Linguistics*. Trans. Wade Baskin. New York: McGraw-Hill.

Dundes, Alan. 1975. On the Structure of the Proverb. *Proverbium* 25: 961–973.

Dundes, Alan. 1980. *The Morphology of North American Indian Folktales*. Helsinki: Academia Scientiarum Fennica.

Georges, Robert A., and Alan Dundes. 1963. Toward a Structural Definition of the Riddle. *Journal of American Folklore* 76: 111–118.

Hymes, Dell H. 1981. *"In Vain I Tried To Tell You": Essays in Native American Ethnopoetics*. Philadelphia: University of Pennsylvania Press.

Köngäs-Maranda, Elli, and Pierre Maranda. 1971. *Structural Models in Folklore and Transformational Essays*. The Hague: Mouton.

Leach, Edmund R. 1961. Lévi-Strauss in the Garden of Eden. *Transactions of the New York Academy of Sciences* 23(4): 386–396.

Lévi-Strauss, Claude. 1955. The Structural Study of Myth. *Journal of American Folklore* 67: 428–444.

Lord, Albert B. 1960. *The Singer of Tales*. Cambridge, MA: Harvard University Press.

Propp, Vladimir. 1968. *Morphology of the Folktale*. 2nd ed. Trans. Laurence Scott. Austin: University of Texas Press.

Parody

Parodia, the Greek term from which the English word *parody* derives, is composed of two morphemes, *par-*, which can be translated as "beside, against or counter," and -*odia*, meaning song. Hence in its original usage it appears to be a type of song that imitates another song for humorous effect. The important point is that the listener or audience is able to recognize the pale reflection of the more serious original in the imitation. As Humberto Eco notes in *Carnival!* "the law [meaning in this case the song, narrative, etc.] must be so pervasively and profoundly introjected as to be overwhelmingly present at the moment of its violation" (1984, 6). Or as any standup comedian knows, it's always helpful to have a straight man.

This process can be seen clearly in the Mexican *coloquios* or traditional nativity plays described by Bauman (1996, 318). Here the parody is effected by enabling the audience to hear both the narrator or prompter's rendition of a written, religious text (the straight verse) and the actor's parodic counterstatement, a type of word play in which syntactic and phonological parallelism foreground humorous semantic differences. For example, while the prompter states, "It appears that I am getting out without losing a step" (*Parece que voy saliendo sin perder una pisada*), the Hermitano, the parodic figure of the drama, remarks, "Now I am getting used to it without missing even a single fuck." (*Ya me estoy poniendo sin perder ni una pisada.*)

Parody is, of course, no longer limited to song if it ever was. It can be found in all of the arts and the humanities—literature, painting, poetry, theatre, dance, and more recently in film. One that readily comes to mind is Charlie Chaplin's *The Great Dictator*, which ridiculed Adolf Hitler through exaggerated imitation of the Fuhrer's violent gestures and shrill tone. An oft-cited theatrical example is Tom Stoppard's *Rosencrantz and Guildenstern Are Dead*, an absurdist drama first staged in 1966, which borrows two minor characters from Shakespeare's *Hamlet* and turns tragedy into comedy.

Ironically, some literary parodies, such as *Don Quixote*, live on long after the work on which it was based; *Amadis de Gaula*, has been forgotten. Moreover, thanks to new technologies that allow us to juxtapose photographic images, visual parodies that require few if any words can be found all over the Internet. One famous or infamous example, depending on your political perspective, is the side-by-side photos of George Bush and a variety of chimpanzees that appeared sometime after the 2000 election. Although the person who designed the Web site claimed he was not politically motivated—he supposedly just thought Bush looked like an ape—the author's intentions are probably less important than the reader's response.

Among the "folk," parodies not only abound during carnival, but also during the "profane" activities that precede or follow processionals held in honor of the patron saint of a town or village. On September 29, following the mass said in honor of St. Michael the Archangel, the patron saint of Maxcanú, Mexico, the congregants pour into the street behind the church and reassemble in their respective *cofradias* (religious brotherhoods). Once in place, the image of St. Michael is lowered from his pedestal and set on an altar at the front of the procession. Then, with the utmost solemnity, an altar boy leads the procession, swinging a ball of incense. Close behind are the priest and four litter bearers who agonize in silence under the tremendous weight of the altar and image, for this is an act of penitence. From the church the procession enters the main square, silently circles the plaza in a slow, deliberate manner and returns to the starting point marking the end of the "pilgrimage." After a rosary is recited, the patron saint is returned to his pedestal.

However, in nearby San Bernardo, the hallowed *santa procesión* (procession of the saints) becomes the object of humor in the *k'ub pol*, or dance of the pig, which occurs on St. Bernard's special day in liturgical cycle. The similarity between the *santa procesión* and the San Bernardo *k'ub pol* is revealed through a series of indexical relationships: the raiment of the pig with jewelry (e.g., earrings) and ornaments in emulation of Catholic images that must be properly dressed before they go out in public; the placement of the finely manicured beast on a portable altar similar to those used to carry religious images; her association with the images of St. Anthony of Padua, the Virgin of the Conception and St. Bernard in the corner of the hacienda's outdoor shelter, and, finally, her incorporation into the procession that enters the church. Indeed, the procession that Luis Pérez Sabido witnessed in San Bernardo in 1974 included the three Catholic saints named herein as well as a two hundred kilo pig (1983, 140).

At the same time, the satirical nature of the *k'ub pol* is revealed through a series of paradigmatic shifts: the insertion of a raucous shoving contest in place of the dignified pilgrimage described previously, the cascades of laughter and shouting in lieu of silence, and, of course, the substitution of a raw, corpulent beast for a handsomely carved wooden saint.

The most seditious act, however, is the recitation of vulgar Maya/Spanish quatrains or *bombas* during the procession of the saints. The latter, in fact, is doubly subversive since they not only evoke the festive image of the *jarana* (a sensuous, colorful folk dance) in what would normally be an extremely solemn affair, but debase the refined character of the Spanish *cuarteta* (quatrain) itself. The *bomba's* predictable rhyme scheme, consistent meter, and long association with genteel courtship rituals have, in recent years, become so attractive to the Yucatecan middle class that its poetic form is now frequently used in advertising jingles on television. Urban consumers are entreated to purchase anise liquor and other goods through clever *bombas*. However, in the *k'ub pol*, the quatrain is irreparably damaged. Its gentle sexual allusions are rendered overt, and its poetic form

A scene from *Don Quixote*, Miguel de Cervantes's great tale of adventure published in 1605. (Library of Congress)

is distorted almost beyond recognition as the drunken leader stumbles through each verse.

Oxp'e dia ma' haantken tinwatan	For three days my wife doesn't eat me
Mix inwatan tsenken xan	Nor does my wife feed me either
Yaan tun kubo'otik bin up'ax	She must, then, pay the debt she owes
[inaudible] *ko'olibi bo'otik xan*	[inaudible] the virgin pays it too

(Translated from Yukatek Maya by author).

Another type of parody that should be of interest to folklorists is the newly revised folktales that have flooded the market in recent years. For functionalist ethnographers like Bronislaw Malinowski and Margaret Park Redfield the purpose of folk literature was simply to reinforce community norms. In the *Folk Literature of a Yucatecan Town*, for example, Park Redfield notes that the *ejemplo* or example, a more or less true story, was a tool for teaching children to avoid saying inappropriate things. "People said that I had twins because the children had two fathers. But God punished them for talking this way. It is not good to talk about other people, and so these same women had twins too" (1937, 26).

In contrast, revised folktales, like Bob Hartman's *The Wolf Who Cried Boy* (2004), Susan Meddaugh's *Cinderella's Rat* (1997), Simon Puttock's *Big Bad Wolf Is Good* (2002), Jon Sciezka's *The True Story of the Big Bad Wolf* (1999), and my favorite, Eugene Trivizas's *The Three Little Wolves and the Big Bad Pig* (1993), show little concern about upholding community standards or maintaining wholesome "family values." The goal may be to question the nature of stereotypes, poke fun, raise contemporary political issues, or simply use an old story to create a new one.

In Trivizas's revision of the Three Little Pigs, for example, the roles are entirely reversed. Three tender, fluffy wolves seek refuge from a maniacal pig by building successively stronger houses. Beginning with brick, they move on to reinforced concrete, and, finally, a house made out of iron bars, armor plates, and heavy metal padlocks. Pig, however, is able to destroy all of them with the help of a sledge hammer, a pneumatic drill, and dynamite. The wolves are saved only by the beautiful scent of flowers they get from Flamingo. The scent is so enticing that Pig sniffs and sniffs until he decides to become a good pig, and he and the wolves become friends. Trivizas's tale may very well be a belated celebration of flower power as Amie Doughty argues in *Folk Tales Retold* (2006). However, as a child of Dr. Seuss and the *Butter Bean War*, I can't help but see a comment on the massive growth of prisons or the Star Wars Defensive Initiative—both of which were costly and controversial issues in the 1990s—and an admonition that we will either learn to live together or we will surely die together.

The relationship between the original tale and the revised tale, of course, varies from tale to tale. In some cases, the original is retold with a few new twists or a different ending; in other cases, as in *Cinderella's Rat*, minor characters are elevated to major characters to create a "new" tale. In either case, however, it is the intertextual play between the old and the new that lends rhetorical force to the tale and helps it succeed.

Although parody is often used to address social or political issues of the day, not all parodies are satires, and not all satires involve parody. Satire often involves a variety of different rhetorical devices such as sarcasm, irony, burlesque, and innuendo, and may or may not be parodic. The question that is more difficult to answer is whether parody must be humorous. In the last year or so, side-by-side images comparing the mistreatment of the Jews by the Nazis and the mistreatment of Palestinians by Israelis have been circulating on the Internet. Although the juxtaposition of these images can be viewed as poignant, provocative, or even inflammatory, neither side views them as humorous.

Ronald Loewe

See Also Asian American Humor and Folklore; Carnival; Folktale; Joke.

References

Bauman, Richard. 1996. Transformations of the Word in the Production of Mexican Festival Drama. In *Natural Histories of Discourse*, eds. Michael Silverstein and Greg Urban. Chicago: University of Chicago Press, pp. 301–328.

Doughty, Amie. 2006. *Folktales Retold: A Critical Overview of Children's Stories.* Jefferson, NC: McFarland and Company.

Eco, Umberto, V. V. Ivanov, and Monica Reed. 1984. *Carnival!* (Approaches to Semiotics). New York: de Gruyter.

Hartman, Bob, and Tim Raglin. 2004. *The Wolf Who Cried Boy.* New York: Puffin Press.

Loewe, Ronald. 2003. Yucatan's Dancing Pig's Head: Icon, Carnival and Commodity. *Journal of American Folklore* 462: 420–443.

Meddaugh, Susan. 1997. *Cinderella's Rat.* Boston: Houghton Mifflin.

Pérez Sabido, Luis. 1983. *Bailes y Danzas Tradicionales de Yucatán.* Mérida, México: DIF.

Redfield, Margaret Park. 1937. The Folk-Literature of a Yucatecan Town. *Contributions to American Archaeology.* Vol. 3. Washington, DC: The Carnegie Institute of Washington.

Puttock, Simon, and Lynne Chapman. 2002. *Big Bad Wolf Is Good.* New York: Sterling Publication Company.

Scieszka, Jon, and Lane Smith. 1999. *The True Story of the Three Little Pigs.* New York: Viking Juvenile Press.

Trivizas, Eugene. 1993. *The Three Little Wolves and the Big Bad Pig.* New York: Mammoth Press.

Participant-Observation Method

The method typically employed in conducting field research. This method, as it has been applied by folklorists, traces its origins to anthropology, which developed the technique in an effort to conduct thorough and reliable ethnographic research in the field by requiring field-workers to be both participants in a target community and objective observers who translated their participant experience into a formalized summary. The method's goal is to account for the subject's point of view within a general theoretical framework.

The participant-observation method necessitates a long-term approach, for it usually takes field-workers an extended period of time in order to become functioning members of the target community. Until the researcher achieves this status, the data obtained by using the method will reflect an abnormal routine since the target community is likely to change its routines when outsiders impose on or cross its boundaries. These anomalies will appear for a number of reasons, including the suspicion of the field researcher and strangers in general, the attempt to hide secrets from the outsider, the fear of being mocked because of so-called primitive ways, and the desire to remain insulated from the forces of change. However, once the field-worker becomes accepted by the target community and is allowed to participate in its daily affairs, he or she is able to accumulate data from which an accurate ethnography can be written or a particular problem can be studied.

Although the researcher must become accepted by the target community for this method to be productive, complete acceptance is rare. Furthermore, it is useful for the researcher to maintain some distance from the target group so that the second dimension of the method, the observation, can be undertaken with as much integrity and objectivity as possible. Nonobjective observations result in data that cannot be verified; therefore, they are useless except as commentary on the field researcher's experience itself.

Proponents of the participant-observation method have recognized the need to reconsider some of the basic premises surrounding the approach. Primary among the assumptions that must be questioned is the idea that field researchers can be objective, for field-workers themselves are born into situations that imbue them with particular ways of perceiving, with particular agendas, and with particular biases. Many field-workers, in response to this situation, make their reflexivity, the revelation of themselves, a strength of the research by providing their audience with data that aids in interpreting their work. Additionally, these field-workers are acknowledging the voice of the Other as a significant factor in the participant-observation method. This voice—which is not only the voice of the subjects being studied but the field-worker's voice as well—is made manifest in the presentation of the field research, and it acknowledges that the field-worker's objective observation is always incomplete. This incompletion implies that understanding and interpretation emerge from participation in the experience itself, and accurate representation will result only from the field-worker's acknowledgment that participation is nonrepresentational in any objective sense.

Charlie T. McCormick

See Also Fieldwork.

References

Jackson, Bruce. 1987. *Fieldwork*. Urbana: University of Illinois Press.

Kerr, David. 1991. On Not Becoming a Folklorist: Field Methodology and the Reproduction of Underdevelopment. *Folklore* 102: 48–61.

Kodish, Debora. 1987. Absent Gender, Silent Encounter. *Journal of American Folklore* 100: 573–578.

May, Tim, ed. 2002. *Qualitative Research in Action*. London: Sage.

Murchison, Julian. 2010. *Ethnography Essentials: Designing, Conducting, and Presenting Your Research*. Hoboken: John Wiley & Sons.

Okely, Judith, and Helen Callaway, eds. 1992. *Anthropology and Autobiography*. New York: Routledge.

Turner, Edith. 1992. *Experiencing Ritual: A New Interpretation of African Healing*. Philadelphia: University of Pennsylvania Press.

Pennsylvania Dutch Folklore

A widespread North American ethnic group, also known as Pennsylvania Germans, with roots in the colonial British colonies. Beginning in 1683, with the foundation of Germantown, German-speaking emigrants from Central Europe flooded into Philadelphia, settling in Southeastern Pennsylvania, from whence they occupied additional areas of Pennsylvania. Their culture area, usually called the Pennsylvania Dutch Country, covered approximately one-third of Pennsylvania's total area, the exact equivalent of the geographical area of Switzerland. From Pennsylvania, diaspora settlements were planted in the Upland South as far as the Carolinas, northward into Ontario and New Brunswick, and directly west, into many areas of the Midwestern and Plains states. The emigration from Europe of Pennsylvania Dutch ancestral families continued until about the close of the Napoleonic Wars in Europe, or the Treaty of Paris that settled the American War of 1812, in 1815.

The European areas that produced the emigrants to colonial Pennsylvania centered in the Rhineland, and involved German, Swiss, and French Huguenot emigrants, as well as significant groups from a wider periphery—the Moravian Brethren from Sexy, the Schwenkfelders from Silesia, and many Austrian Protestant refugee families. The culture that the Pennsylvania Dutch created on American soil was a sturdy American hybrid culture, blending Continental European with British Isles and American cultural traits. So creative was this culture that Southeastern Pennsylvania is considered in cultural geographical terminology an American "culture hearth," influencing other regions of early America with material culture elements such as the Pennsylvania bank bar, the Pennsylvania rifle, and the Conestoga wagon. In addition, Pennsylvania Dutch religious

A rural red barn with Pennsylvania Dutch hex signs. (Cynthia Farmer/Dreamstime.com)

patterns, both churchly and sectarian, were planted in all the diaspora settlements. The German language was spread via sermon, everyday speech, and print (newspapers, books, and broadsides). In all the diaspora areas, Pennsylvania Dutch foods and foodways, customs of the year, and other folkloric elements spread widely with the transplanted Dutchmen of the nineteenth century: Pennsylvania's manuscript art called "fraktur," its legacy of fantastic quilt patterns on the distaff side, traditional pottery, and, for those who can appreciate it, that vast store of native wit and humor, folksongs, folktales, and other folkloric elements, preserved in the dialect, now properly a language, called Pennsylvania Dutch.

Research Survey

America's rediscovery of itself through the trauma of the Civil War and the centennial of the American Revolution in 1876 with the unparalleled Centennial Exposition in Philadelphia, exercised a catalytic effect in all American ethnic groups, including the Pennsylvania Dutch. With the upswing in ethnic pride that produced such late nineteenth-century institutions as the Scotch-Irish Society

(1888) for the Ulster heritage, the Welcome Society (1889) for Pennsylvania Quakers, the Pennsylvania Dutch followed in 1891 with their own Pennsylvania German Society. The intellectuals among the founders of this society—ministers, lawyers, and others—were influenced also by the national foundation of the American Folklore Society in 1898, which brought the concept of "folklore" in the British Thomsian sense, with its division into "genres," to the attention of several native Pennsylvania Dutch scholars, who began to apply the concepts to their own culture. Among these was Dr. Walter J. Hoffman of the Smithsonian Institution, whose folkloric surveys of Pennsylvania Dutch culture appeared in the *Journal of American Folklore* in its very first volume (1888–1889). This influence of the American Folklore Society on selected scholars continued in the work of John Baer Stoudt, whose seminal work, *The Folklore of the Pennsylvania Germans*, appeared in 1916. The pioneer work of such scholars as Marion Dexter Learned and his pupil and successor Edwin M. Fogel at the University of Pennsylvania in Philadelphia furthered the cause, with Dr. Learned's ethnographic questionnaires (the first in the nation) focused on folksongs and other genres of Pennsylvania Dutch folklore, in 1899–1900, followed by Dr. Fogel's equally seminal volumes on Pennsylvania Dutch folk beliefs, proverbs, and "superstitions."

The discovery of "Elizabethan" balladry existing in Appalachia spurred on much work on the Pennsylvania Dutch folksong traditions, with a Dutch Country–wide recording of dialect folksongs by Thomas R. Brendle, reformed clergyman, and William S. Troxell, Allentown journalist and prolific producer of dialect literature under the pen name of "Pumpernickle Bill." A selection of their recordings appeared in George Korson's *Pennsylvania Songs and Legends* (1949), although the first complete book on the subject, *Songs along the Mahantongo*, appeared in 1951.

In the 1930s, centering in Allentown and Lehigh County, a strong dialect-speaking area, a renaissance of Pennsylvania Dutch studies began that extended into the people's sector with dialect radio programs, dialect church services, and the invention of the "Grundsow Lodch" (Groundhog Lodge)—an all-dialect evening banquet and performance where amid the festivity and feasting, one was fined for speaking English! At the same time, the team of Preston A. Barba and Harry S. Reichard, both dialect-speaking professors of German at Muhlenberg College in Allentown, Pennsylvania, produced Dr. Barba's long-lasting (1936–1969) weekly newspaper column, '*S Pennsylfawnisch Diesch Eck* (The Pennsylvania Dutch Corner), which is a treasure trove of folklore as well as historical material. Dr. Reichard also joined the Lehigh County folk artist and dialect playwright Paul R. Wieand in a weekly radio dialect skit called "Assebe and Sabeina," reporting very amusingly on the ups and downs in the life of a typical Dutch farmer and his wife and their circle of archetypical Dutch friends.

At the same time in the 1930s, the folk festival movement was brought to Pennsylvania by George Korson, America's first industrial folklorist. In 1935, he began the Pennsylvania Folk Festival at Allentown, which later moved to Bucknell University at Lewisburg in central Pennsylvania. These festivals featured Pennsylvania Dutch singing groups, Conestoga waggoners, miners' songs, and other products of Pennsylvania's rich ethnic heritage. This led eventually to the Pennsylvania Dutch Folk Festival at Kutztown, founded in 1950 and still going strong sixty years later.

The ethnographic work begun at Franklin and Marshall College at Lancaster, Pennsylvania, in 1949 by the research triumvirate of Alfred L. Shoemaker, J. Willim Frey, and Don Yoder, led to the establishment of the journal *The Pennsylvania Dutchmen* (1949; it became *Pennsylvania Folklife* in 1968), the Pennsylvania Dutch Folklore Center (1949; which was incorporated in 1958 as the Pennsylvania Folklife Society), and the Pennsylvania Dutch Folk Festival at Kutztown (1950). This concerted approach united all phases of Pennsylvania Dutch folklore, but broadened it into the European "folklife" approach, using both current ethnography (interviews and questionnaires) and historical ethnography (using historical documentation to reconstruct past levels of the culture). The "folklife studies movement," which began in America with the work of these three scholars, has had a wide influence on the American folklore research scene, with the establishment of such national institutions as the American Folklife Center at the Library of Congress and the Folklife Program of the Smithsonian Institution.

Folksong Research

The first genre of Pennsylvania Dutch folklore to be investigated thoroughly was the folksong. The culture's song repertoire represented three historical strands. First are the songs, jingles, and rhymes that are so widespread they were obviously brought to Pennsylvania in the memories of the eighteenth-century emigrants. The second layer, drinking songs and other amusing genres, were evidently brought here by the nineteenth-century emigrants and spread through the countryside by itinerants like the colorful *Fritter mit der Zitter*—a zither-playing emigrant-German tramp who sang often raunchy songs in the country taverns—veritable men's clubs of the culture—until his lamented death, reported in the Lebanon County newspapers in 1880. This tradition of the lone singer-entertainer continued into the twentieth century, represented by such memorable figures as Willy Brown of Klingerstown in Schuylkill County, whose songs—such as those sung in the Klingerstown tavern to audiences of Dutch farmers and workmen—I recorded half a century ago, along with some of his traditional folktales. The third category of Pennsylvania Dutch folksongs includes those composed in America, often sung to American pop culture tunes. These chronicle local characters like "Bully Lyons," a nineteenth-century Reading constable. Other songs sided with Democrats or Republicans in the nineteenth-century gubernatorial political campaigns.

The ballad repertoire of the culture also was spread by individual singers like the slightly aberrant Polly Schrob of Pine Grove in Schuylkill County, who in the early decades of the nineteenth century had her songs printed as broadsides, for sale in the towns where she performed. Schoolmasters of the German parochial church schools were the usual authors of the German-language ballads, songs of murder and suicide, and unrequited love, all with a heavily accented moral warning in the last verses. These tragedy songs usually were printed as broadsides, and sold by the schoolmasters to eke out their meager wages as teachers.

Ballads were also sung in the family circle, often by the grandmothers, to warn the children against following the path trod by Susanna Cox or Wicked Polly. And there is evidence that some of the grandmothers accompanied their singing on the Pennsylvania Dutch zither.

The "Susanna Cox" ballad was written in 1809 to chronicle the hanging in Reading of a twenty-four-year-old hired servant on an Oley Valley farm. This unfortunate soul had a bastard child, did away with it, and was discovered and sentenced to death. Her death was witnessed by the largest crowd that had ever gathered in Berks County's capital of Reading, and the song went through over a hundred different broadside printings in German and English. One memorable day in 1961, at the Pennsylvania Dutch Folk Festival at Kutztown, I was able to hear, and record, the singing of the original German ballad—all thirty-two verses and to the original tune—as remembered by a ninety-year-old farm wife from Lehigh County.

For the folktale repertoire of the Pennsylvania Dutch culture, see the pioneering treatment by Thomas R. Brendle and William S. Troxell, *Pennsylvania German Folk Tales, Legends, Once-upon-a-Time Stories, Maxims and Sayings Spoken in the Dialect Popularly Known as Pennsylvania Dutch* (1946). Unfortunately, the tales are given only in English translation, not in their original recorded dialect form.

Additional folktale materials center around the many "characters" the Dutch culture has produced—the hermits who rejected human society, the powwow doctors, the alleged witches, and yes, even the "saints" like "Mountain Mary"

(*Die Berg-Maria*, Maria Jung) of the Oley Hills, whose benevolence to her neighbors, her freely given healing procedures, and other virtues were noted and written about throughout the nineteenth century long after her death in 1819.

Finally, the folktale repertoire of the Pennsylvania Dutch was often mirrored in the local color fiction by such early twentieth-century writers as Elsie Singmaster, especially in the volume *Bred in the Bone* (1925), Fred Lewis Pattee's *The House of the Black Ring*, and even some of Henry W. Shoemaker's books, although many have found his attempts to write about folklore too fictionalized for the taste of an academic folklorist.

The numerous collections of folktale recordings by individual scholars, most of them unpublished, deserve to be surveyed, and more recording needs to be pursued while significant numbers of Pennsylvania Dutchmen still speak full and perfect Dutch. Also, more of the printed literature of the culture, especially from the nineteenth- and twentieth-century newspapers, needs to be culled for folktale materials.

Proverbial Lore

Proverb research among the Pennsylvania Dutch was largely initiated by Edwin Miller Fogel of the University of Pennsylvania, with his *Beliefs and Superstitions of the Pennsylvania Germans* (1915). Fogel's materials were gathered by interviews in the Dutch Country, and then collated with the European proverb collections. Typical of the times is the fact that Fogel omitted from his book a substantial corpus of "erotic" materials, which he allowed to appear in a "Supplement" (1915) "for private distribution, not for public perusal." The translations of the Pennsylvania Dutch originals appeared in decorous Latin. Inevitably, the "Supplement" found its way into print, the Latin rendered into very readable English.

In 1925, Dr. Fogel's major proverb collection, *Proverbs of the Pennsylvania Germans*, appeared. This was reprinted later in the century in two different annotated editions, by Wolfgang Mieder, proverb scholar of the University of Vermont, and C. Richard Beam of Millersville University.

Proverbs and proverbial sayings exist by the thousands in the literature of the Pennsylvania Dutch people, whether in dialect, High German, or English, and a concerted effort to cull them from the printed sources and record them from living speakers of Pennsylvania Dutch is overdue.

Folk Medicine

Pennsylvania's most distinctive form of folk medicine is the ancient procedure called in English "powwowing" or "powwow medicine." The term *powwow* itself is from an Algonquin word that, according to the Oxford English Dictionary, came over into English in New England in the 1640s. It was used first for Indian healers and healing procedures, then applied to the colonial healers. While the practice was once universal in the states, under various names, the Pennsylvania Dutch culture would seem to be its center and fountainhead today.

While certain Indian herbal remedies were appropriated and used by the colonial white settlers, the name alone is the only element of powwowing that has any connection with the American Indians. Powwow medicine involves the use of magical formulas (*Zauberformeln* in German) brought from Central Europe by the emigrants. The charms were put into print, and therefore canonized, by the 1802 emigrant John George Hohman (Homan), whose book *Der Lang Verborgene Freund* (usually translated "The Long Lost Friend") appeared at Reading, Pennsylvania, in 1819/1820, and spread widely.

The Pennsylvania Dutch word for powwowing is *Brauche* or *Braucherei*, and for powwow practitioners, *Braucher*. Synonyms in English include "to use" and "to try for," although my most important powwow contact, Sophia Bailer of Tremont in Schuylkill County, preferred "calling a blessing on" the patient.

In the past few decades, there have been several new and novel developments in the field of powwow medicine. The proliferation of "Indian Readers" and "Healers by Prayer" in the Eastern cities following World War II also has been registered in the Dutch country. Several of these practitioners have subtly added the word *powwow* to their printed advertisements, usually broadsides, distributed in parking lots and other city venues to attract susceptible Dutchmen to their services.

There also seems to be an upswing in the number of practicing powwow doctors, several of whom have written books describing and defending their healing techniques. It appears also that some of the newer, younger practitioners have been reading anthropological literature, since they are attributing their therapeutic powers to a "soul journey" similar to those claimed by the Asian shamans. Such claims, of course, were never part of the classic powwower's understanding of his craft.

Folk Religion

The Pennsylvania Dutch essentially was a Protestant culture. In its own terminology, it was divided down the middle into "churchmen" and "sectarians." The churchmen included the major denominations of the Protestant Reformation, the Lutherans and the Reformed. The sectarians, led by the Mennonites and their stricter offshoot the Amish, included the Church of Brethren (Dunkards), the River Brothers, and the Schwenkfelders. There were, in addition, revivalist sects modeled on Methodism—the United Brethren, the Evangelical Association, and the Church of God, and their late nineteenth-century offspring the Holiness groups. In between the *Kirchenleute* and the *Sektenleute* were the Moravians, or *Herrnhuter*, who operated with episcopacy and liturgical services, but originally were communitarian. Finally, there were two strictly defined communitarian groups, the Ephrata Cloister and the Harmony Society.

Apart from these organized, official forms of Pennsylvania Dutch religion, there existed vast areas of folk religion or folk spirituality—beliefs and customs held by the people but not necessarily condoned or applauded by the clergy. A prime example is the document, usually printed as a broadside, called the *Himmelsbrief* or Heaven-Letter. Said to have been written by Jesus himself and sent down to earth mysteriously, the text gives a kind of Protestantized version of the Ten Commandments, urging the hallowing of Sunday as the Sabbath, avoidance of fancy dress, pride, and so forth. But the document had a magical side and attraction that has kept it in print into this century. It specifically states that anyone who copies it and spreads it will be blessed, and whoever keeps it in his blouse or on his person will be safe from flood, pestilence, and violent death. The letters were carried by Pennsylvania Dutch soldiers in all of America's wars from the Revolution on, and printed in innumerable editions, in German or English, by upstate country printers.

But folk religion involves more than personal and household protection. Practical matters involved seating in the churches and burial patterns in the churchyards. Since the Pennsylvania Dutch individual, as in European peasant society, was in earlier days subsumed under the community concept, men and women sat apart in the churches, not in family groups as today, and the dead were buried not in family plots, as today, but in the time slot beside the last community member buried. In the older cemeteries, the dead were buried facing eastward, symbolically toward the rising sun of the Resurrection morning.

On the negative side, the Pennsylvania Dutch folk worldview included, as did every ethnic community of early America, a strong belief in witchcraft, the transfer of evil from person to person by occult means. Every Dutch community has nineteenth-century stories of persons accused of witchcraft and their devious, devil-inspired doings—plus stories of how one countered witchcraft by going to the local "witch doctor" (*Hexe-Doktor*) for a written country charm. See Richard M. Dorson's *Buying the Wind* for several examples of witch tales recorded from a believer in the 1950s, including the classic Central Pennsylvania folktale "The Bewitched Automobile."

Customs of the Year

The folklore patterns of the Pennsylvania Dutch people included numerous colorful customs of the year, some of which have influenced the larger American scene. The principal examples are Christmas and Easter customs. The first American evidence for both the Christmas tree and the Easter rabbit come from Pennsylvania sources. However, the Pennsylvania Dutch Christmas involved many more folkloric elements in the past. The modern Santa Claus was absent from the earlier Pennsylvania Dutch Christmas celebration. In his place were the gift-giver, the Christ-Child (Pennsylvania Dutch *Grischtkindel*), who left gifts for the children, unseen, during the night, and the frightening Belsnickel, of which there were two varieties.

On Christmas Eve, the father of the house, often masked and dressed in tattered clothing, went outside, tapped on the window, was let in, scattered nuts and candy on the floor, and when his children scurried to pick them up, gave them a token switching, all in fun. But the Belsnickel concept had other dimensions—in some cases groups of masked and sometimes cross-dressed teenagers and unmarried young people went around from farm to farm on Christmas Eve, put on various acts, and collected goodies that were divided at the end of the circuit. Most frequently, these bands of masked and curiously dressed people paraded or rode into the neighboring towns on "Second Christmas," the day after Christmas, or on New Year's Day. This satisfied the human yen for dressing up and masking, which other Americans confined to Halloween, and in Europe, to Fastnacht (Shrove Tuesday). Striking photographs of troops of Belsnickels from the period 1900–1915 have recently turned up and have been used to illustrate the third and fiftieth-anniversary edition of Alfred L. Shoemaker's *Christmas in Pennsylvania*. Alas, the colorful Belsnickel custom has faded from history, and most Pennsylvania Dutch families now honor Santa Claus. The custom, however, occasionally has been revived by local museums, in celebrations called "Belsnickel Days."

Another custom, now unfortunately gone, is the New Year's shoot—shooting in the New Year, with the accompanying chanted German blessing. A group of eight to ten men, one with a rifle, circulated to neighboring farms on New Year's Eve. At each home, after asking permission to shoot, the shot was fired into the winter sky, and then there was the *Neujahrswunch*, blessing the family, the household, the animals in the barn, and extending the blessing to "all of Christendom." This was a folk-religious ritual that was looked forward to from year to year, and any family that was missed on the rounds was insulted! Recordings exist form traditional "wishers" like Willy Brown, mentioned in the folksong section. A few contemporary Dutchmen, like Peter V. Fritsch of Longswamp Township in Berks County, are carrying on the tradition at the present time.

A third Pennsylvania Dutch holiday celebration, of more recent origin, is "Groundhog Day," February 2, and has spread widely in the United States and Canada. Known as Candlemas in the medieval European church calendar, the day united two Christian festivals, the Purification of Mary (forty days after the birth of Christ) and the Presentation of Christ in the Jerusalem Temple. In continental Europe, the day developed into a weather predictor. An animal, the badger (*Dachs*) and originally the sacred bear of the alpine cultures, both hibernators, were believed to issue from their winter quarters on February 2. If the day was sunny and the animal saw its shadow, the winter weather was predicted to continue for six more weeks. If the day was cloudy, rainy, or snowy, and the animal did not see its shadow, this was taken as a sign of an early spring.

The Pennsylvania Dutch brought the custom to America, and lacking badgers, chose the native groundhog or woodchuck in its place, likewise a hibernating animal. There are two Pennsylvania centers of the cult at present—Punxsutawney in Jefferson County in northwestern Pennsylvania, and Quarryville in Lancaster County in southeastern Pennsylvania. In both cases, talented, innovative journalists created the outline of the current holiday through their columns. In Punxsutawney, the movement began in the 1880s, and in Quarryville after 1900. Both centers developed elaborate scenarios—Punxsutawney's ritual begins at 3 A.M. on Gobbler's Know outside the city. And, of course, the clever film Groundhog Day helped the cause and the custom has now spread to at least twenty-five states and several Canadian provinces. It is a fun and tongue-in-cheek holiday, providing some ritualistic humor in the calendric doldrums between New Year's Day and Easter.

Recent Developments

There have been three major research developments in the study of Pennsylvania Dutch folklore. Professor C. Richard Beam, founder and director of the Pennsylvania German Center at Millersville University, has recently completed and published his lifetime work, the eleven-volume Pennsylvania German Dictionary. This is now the ultimate authority on vocabulary and its usage in Pennsylvania Dutch, besides being full of traditional sayings, proverbial lore, and folklore in general.

Across the Atlantic, the Palatine linguist Dr. Michael Werner of the University of Mainz, Germany, has established an international journal devoted to the Pennsylvania Dutch language. Called *Hiwwe wie Driwwe*, the title—"over here like over there"—reflects the frequent feeling experienced by a Pennsylvania Dutchman in the Central Rhineland, where his language is understood, and the same for the visiting Rhinelander over here. The journal is entirely in Pennsylvania Dutch, except for occasional letters in High German or English. And the letters are sent from every area in the United States and Canada where Pennsylvania Dutch is still spoken and appreciated.

The third noteworthy item is Kutztown University's Pennsylvania German Cultural Heritage Center, founded by Dr. David Valuska and now headed by Dr. Robert Reynolds. The center offers academic work, a major in Pennsylvania German Studies with a minor in the language, and a twenty-two-acre open air museum of Pennsylvania Dutch folklife on the northern edge of the university campus. Plans for a major research library are in the works, and numerous research projects in Pennsylvania Dutch folklife have been outlined and commissioned.

Pennsylvania Dutch folklore will continue to be an important regional component of American folklore even after the culture has shifted linguistically from Pennsylvania Dutch to English. But fortunately, at the present time, there are sufficient active speakers of Pennsylvania Dutch in Pennsylvania and the diaspora to keep many folk-cultural specialists at work recording and analyzing the multilayered marvel that has in the last three centuries developed into the Pennsylvania Dutch culture.

Don Yoder

See Also Custom; Ethnic Folklore; Folktale; Medicine, Folk; Religion, Folk.

References

Kirchner, Audrey Burie, and Margaret R. Tassia. 1996. *In Days Gone By: Folklore and Traditions of the Pennsylvania Dutch.* Englewood, CO: Libraries Unlimited.

Kriebel, David W. 2007. *Powwowing among the Pennsylvania Dutch: A Traditional Medical Practice in the Modern World.* University Park: Pennsylvania State University Press.

Varr, Richard. 2007. *Philadelphia and the Pennsylvania Dutch Country.* New York: DK.

Yoder, Don. 1989. *Hex Signs: Pennsylvania Dutch Barn Symbols and Their Meaning.* New York: E. P. Dutton.

Yoder, Don. 1990. *Discovering American Folklife: Studies in Ethnic, Religious, and Regional Culture.* Ann Arbor, MI: UMI Research Press.

Yoder, Don. 2003. *Groundhog Day.* Mechanicsburg, PA: Stackpole.

Yoder, Emma Jean S. 2006. *Cooking as Cultural Communication: How Pennsylvania Dutch Women Construct Cultural Identities and Group Membership through Cooking.* Dissertation.

Performance

In folklore, a mode of presentation in which a party or parties utilize conventional artistic techniques to stage actions for others. In theory and in method, the concept of performance builds upon the range of meanings the term has in common use. These emphasize actualization versus potentiality, demonstration versus knowledge, ritual versus belief, observable behavior in prescribed circumstances, and, in particular, artistic display in words, music, dance, and drama. In its initial use in folklore scholarship, the term *performance* evoked the gap that exists between presentation and its documentation. William J. Entwhistle, for example, associates mime, music, and dance with performed ballads. For him, they project authenticity and antiquity that are inevitably lost in the printed text or the affectation of drawing room singing. Performance connotes the vigor of delivery that is knowable through experience only. Methodologically, Kenneth S. Goldstein defines *performance* as the occurrence of folklore in its "normal social context" prior to being collected.

The technology of recording and the emerging theories in the humanities and social sciences have contributed to a renewed inquiry into the dynamics of folklore performance. This quest builds upon the concept of orality that has dominated folklore research from its inception and recognizes the primacy of any performed act over any form of its abstracted documentation. It also has recovered the meanings of performed speech associated with such terms as *epic* and *myth* that connote discourse as distinguished from action, colored by its context.

The study of performance has shifted the claims folklore has had on national traditions and histories, on cultural cosmologies, and on social ethos. The notion has been rethought in terms of searching for a dynamic, interactive force in society that is an agent of communication subject to the wills of its performers and to the contingent interpretations of its audiences. From this perspective, folklore no longer studies tradition as a superstructure or as an expression or mirror of national culture but as a set of artistic acts that are an integral part of the fabric of social life and religious and political rituals. The application of the concept of performance to folklore, hence, has transformed its subject from being a cultural metanarrative to becoming acts of narrating, singing, and speaking.

There are two basic assumptions that guide the different approaches to performance analysis. First, is the idea that a society has a set of systemic conventions and rules that regulate and generate folklore acts. Second, is the notion that while speakers are in performance mode, their verbal behavior has an acceptable range of deviance from the common use of language in society. Native speakers, whether performers or listeners, adhere to the rules of performance and to its socially accepted margin of variance. Methodologically, in the presence of an outsider, speakers may heighten the principles of performance or seek to present certain aspects of their culture through the selection of themes, genres, and modes of folkloric display they deem as markers of their ethnic identity.

Ethnography of Performance

The fundamentals of any performance analysis require an adequate ethnographic description of speech acts in a given society, accounting for the reasons and purposes of speaking, the participants and performers in the occasion, and the speech genres they employ. All these aspects of performance are interdependent, and there is a degree of correlation between them that a description must make explicit. Therefore, the description of performance focuses on the relations within the occasion as much as on the nature and meaning of each of its

Catch Question

A type of traditional enigma designed to "catch" the respondent by frustrating expectations. The catch question may exploit syntactic ambiguities: "I saw Esau sitting on a see-saw, how many s's in that?—None" (the word *that* has no s's). Or the catch question may use homonyms: "I know three monkeys. One's called Doh, one's called Ray. What's the third one called?—Me.—Oh, I didn't know you were a monkey." Or the question may give a personal application to an apparently general question: "What do virgins eat for breakfast?—I don't know" (thus, the respondent must not be a virgin).

Just as it shifts the frame of reference, the catch question also shifts the performance frame. Its efficacy results from a surprising emergence in another kind of discourse. In the middle of a riddling session, someone asks, "What has four legs, a tail, and barks?" The respondent, expecting a metaphorical or punning solution, ponders, gives up, and at last volunteers, "A dog?" The poser gives a condescending smile and replies, "Oh, you've heard that one." The catch question may break into ordinary conversation: "You know your great-grandfather?—Yes.—No you don't, he's dead!" Sometimes, it comes disguised as a clever question with a recondite answer: "Where did King John sign the Magna Carta?—At the bottom."

The catch question is used to embarrass, obliging the respondent to utter an obscenity, make an unintended admission, or simply appear foolish. It may serve to upset the accepted hierarchy of wit, pulling the rug from under a clever person. Or it may simply introduce variety into a riddling session.

A subtype of the catch question is the mock-obscene or double-entendre riddle, found widely around the world and often in cultures with strict norms of sexual propriety. The mock-obscene riddle presents a question with an apparently sexual solution. The respondent betrays awareness by offering this answer or by blushing; the poser then provides an innocent solution. An example is this Italian riddle: "You stick it in hard, it comes out soft. What is it?—Spaghetti." Such catches are generally exchanged among children, as a way of introducing a forbidden but endlessly interesting topic, and in cross-gender gatherings of adolescents, among whom, as Anniki Kaivola-Bregenhøj has said, the mock-obscene riddle acts as "kindler of an erotic atmosphere."

Dorothy Noyes

components. Performances vary in society in terms of the social, religious, and political reasons that generate them and the purposes toward which their performers and participants strive. The qualifications of performers also depend on the needs of each occasion. For example, though a highly structured ritual or a lengthy poetic text requires rigorously trained performers, casual verbal exchanges are accessible to any native speakers with no more than a mild inclination for verbal play. The exploration of the relations within a performance event involves an exposition of the observable characteristics of the performers and the participants, such as gender and age, as well as those features that require specific inquiry or knowledge. These involve the training of the performer, his or her position in the society (and in any sect or cult organization), and the existence or absence of any patronage system. Also correlated with any performance are the locations and times that a society designates for performance, as well as the genres, themes, and speech modes that are appropriate for each occasion.

Performance as Quality

To a degree, the ethnography of performance adheres to the theoretical and methodological principles of the "ethnography of speaking," which considers speech as an activity in its own right. Yet the former has a narrower focus in concentrating upon a particular mode of communication. The elucidation of the qualitative nature of performance is central to the understanding of folklore in society. William Hugh Jansen proposes that "performance does not exist until the "doer," the speaker, or the reciter of the bit of folklore steps outside himself as an individual and assumes a pose toward his audience, however small, that differs from his everyday, every-hour-in-the-day relationship to the same audience." Theatricality, however minute and fleeting, has become a key quality in the folklore performance. The quality can manifest itself when an individual adopts the role of performer by engaging in conventional behaviors dictated by tradition (e.g., introducing a proverb by "you know what they always say . . . "). Most instances of folklore performance fall between these two minimal and maximal acts, when speakers take upon themselves, for a limited time and on a specific occasion, the role of singers, narrators, and riddlers. In those roles, they assume responsibility for presentation to an audience, as Dell Hymes has said, or they display communicative competence, as Richard Bauman asserts. These two conceptions of performance share the principle of display and involve a transformation of the performing self and a transition from an everyday mode of communication to an exhibitory one.

Performance and Knowledge

The formal and social qualities of performance have been the primary features for its description, so much so that they have obscured the question of its substance. Partially because of the broad thematic range of folklore, as well as its diversity and multifariousness, there is a purposeful vagueness in the discussion of the contents of performances.

To compound matters, the influential terminological use in linguistics that contrasts *performance* with *competence,* setting the terms as two paradigms representing the vagaries of language in speech against its ideal rule-generating symbolic cognitive system, diverted the discussion into a rebuttal of generative linguistics. Hymes and Charles L. Briggs argue that competence involves mastery of communication that extends beyond the utterance of sentences into the social and cultural rules that generate performance.

Coping with similar issues, albeit not within the discourse of linguistics, Roger D. Abrahams proposes considering performance and enactment as the heightened performance of cultural experiences in rituals and festivals, and John Miles Foley suggests regarding performance as immanent art, displaying the images of the mind. These and other solutions point to a synthesis that encompasses cultural knowledge and experience—as they are available to members of the community in verbal, visual, musical, and mimetic symbolic forms—as the substance of performance. The knowledge accumulated in the collective memory becomes the subject of performance in society. Both the substance and the rules for its communication are essential knowledge for socially responsible performances.

In practice, it is possible to paraphrase or report such cultural knowledge, squeezing out its performative quality, but such an account becomes a secondary representation of the knowledge that is culturally available for performance.

The Languages of Performance

Speakers, narrators, and singers heighten the poetic function of language. On the phonetic level, alliteration, rhyme, and measured speech attain a more prominent position in performance than they would have in common conversation. In fact, one or all of these features could function to highlight a proverb when it occurs in daily conversation.

Parallelism, paired words, and formulas are also used in the language of performance. They could function mnemonically, as Milman Parry and Albert B.

Barney McKenna from the Irish folk group The Dubliners performs at the "Donauinselfest" open-air festival in Vienna, Austria, on June 27, 2010. (AP/Wide World Photos)

Lord have suggested regarding the formula in epic, but their occurrence in a broad range of genres is indicative that they are intrinsic to performance, distinguishing them from everyday discourse. The marking of performance language from everyday discourse has a scale of deviation in which prose narration is most similar to speech and the language of magical formulas is most removed from it, often jumbling sounds into utterances whose meaning is known only to the speaker. On the semantic level, there is an increased use of metaphors, allusions, and quotations that construct the themes in performance into interwoven domains and images that are connected to other principles of "interperformance," to use Lee Haring's term. They constitute the narrated, the sung, and the recited cultural experiences and imagined worlds.

The Presentation of Performance

More than any other approach to folklore, the focus on performance has highlighted the gap between experience and its representation. No matter how comprehensive the documentation of performance might be, it cannot replace performance as experience. Any representation of folklore performance implies a selective abstraction of the event as a process. Even the use of audiovisual documentation of performance does not replace the experience itself. Furthermore, observation alone is often insufficient for the comprehension of performance, and inquiry into the meaning of its symbols must follow. Therefore, although all available means to present the experience of performance are welcome, an interpretive analytical narrative that relates its component parts is essential for adequate presentation.

Universals of Performance

The study of folklore performances is grounded in the ethnographic descriptive tradition, yet because such performances occur in societies all over the world, the search for universals is inevitable. Although the definition of a human characteristic as universal logically implies that it has a biological basis, it is possible to describe a behavior as universal without defining its biological foundation in the case of cultural performance.

Victor Turner proposes that performances are universally playful, framed, symbolic, and in the "subjunctive mood"—that is, they assume an "as if" position toward their substance. The applicability of these four features is most appropriate to ritual and drama, yet the features are relevant to verbal genres as well. Narratives require verbal frames that open and conclude them as specific social discourse, and so do songs. In fact, the frames have the capacity of being cultural identity markers for specific genres, indicating to speakers and listeners the attitudes they could assume toward a narration or a song. The performance of other speech genres, such as proverbs, requires at least an introductory formula that serves as a framing device, distinguishing it from the preceding discourse. The illusionary quality of performance, universal as it is, does not detract, however, from its affective psychological and political power, which can potentially have real rather than fictional consequences. Further studies may identify other universals of performance, but on the basis of currently available knowledge, it is possible to conclude that performance itself is universal. It is a fundamental mode of communication that may have a variety of cultural manifestations, but in each society, performance defines and generates folklore.

Dan Ben-Amos

See Also Ethnopoetics; Frame; Linguistic Approach; Metacommunication; Oral-Formulaic Theory; Verbal Art.

References

Abrahams, Roger D. 1977. Toward an Enactment-Centered Theory of Folklore. In *Frontiers of Folklore*, ed. William Bascom. Boulder, CO: Westview Press.

Bauman, Richard, ed. 1977. *Verbal Art as Performance*. Rowley, MA: Newbury House.

Bauman, Richard, and Charles L. Briggs. 1990. Poetics and Performance as Critical Perspectives on Language and Social Life. *Annual Review of Anthropology* 19: 59–88.

Blackburn, Stuart H. 1988. *Singing of Birth and Death: Texts in Performance*. Philadelphia: University of Pennsylvania Press.

Briggs, Charles L. 1988. *Competence in Performance: The Creativity of Tradition in Mexicano Verbal Art*. Philadelphia: University of Pennsylvania Press.

Dégh, Linda. 1995. *Narratives in Society: A Performer-Centered Study of Narration*. Folklore Fellows Communications. Helsinki: Academia Scientiarum Fennica.

Dougherty, Carol, and Leslie Kurke, eds. 1993. *Cultural Poetics in Archaic Greece: Cult, Performance, Politics*. Cambridge: Cambridge University Press.

Drewal, Margaret Thompson. 1991. The State of Research on Performance in Africa. *African Studies Review* 34: 1–64.

Entwhistle, William J. 1939. *European Balladry*. Oxford: Clarendon Press.

Fabian, Johannes. 1990. *Power and Performance: Ethnographic Explorations through Proverbial Wisdom and Theater in Shaba, Zaire*. Madison: University of Wisconsin Press.

Fine, Elizabeth C. 1984. *The Folklore Text: From Performance to Print*. Bloomington: Indiana University Press.

Foley, John Miles. 1991. *Immanent Art: From Structure to Meaning in Traditional Oral Epic*. Bloomington: Indiana University Press.

Foley, John Miles. 1992. Word-Power, Performance, and Tradition. *Journal of American Folklore* 105: 275–301.

Foley, John Miles. 1995. *The Singer of Tales in Performance*. Bloomington: Indiana University Press.

Fox, James J., ed. 1988. *To Speak in Pairs: Essays of the Ritual Languages of Eastern Indonesia*. Cambridge: Cambridge University Press.

Goldstein, Kenneth S. 1963. Riddling Traditions in Northeastern Scotland. *Journal of American Folklore* 76: 330–336.

Haring, Lee. 1988. Interperformance. *Fabula* 29: 365–372.

Hymes, Dell. 1974. *Foundations in Sociolinguistics: An Ethnographic Approach.* Philadelphia: University of Pennsylvania Press.

Hymes, Dell. 1981. *"In Vain I Tried To Tell You": Essays in Native American Ethnopoetics.* Philadelphia: University of Pennsylvania Press.

Jansen, William Hugh. 1957. Classifying Performance in the Study of Verbal Folklore. In *Studies in Folklore in Honor of Distinguished Service Professor Stith Thompson,* ed. W. Edson Richmond. Bloomington: Indiana University Press.

Kapchan, Deborah A. 1995. Performance. *Journal of American Folklore* 108: 479–508.

Kratz, Corinne. 1994. *Affecting Performance: Meaning, Movement, and Experience in Okiek Women's Initiation.* Washington, DC: Smithsonian Institution Press.

Kuipers, Joel C. 1990. *Power in Performance: The Creation of Textual Authority in Weyewa Ritual Speech.* Philadelphia: University of Pennsylvania Press.

Lord, Albert B. 1960. *The Singer of Tales.* Cambridge, MA: Harvard University Press.

Lord, Albert B. 1995. *The Singer Resumes the Tale,* ed. Mary Louise Lord. Ithaca, NY: Cornell University Press.

Martin, Richard P. 1989. *The Language of Heroes: Speech and Performance in the Iliad.* Ithaca, NY: Cornell University Press.

Okpewho, Isidore, ed. 1990. *The Oral Performance in Africa.* Ibadan, Nigeria: Spectrum Books.

Opie, Iona, and Peter Opie. 1959. *The Lore and Language of Schoolchildren.* Oxford: Oxford University Press.

Ortutay, Gyula. 1959. Principles of Oral Transmission in Folk Culture. *Acta Ethnographica* 8: 175–221.

Reynolds, Dwight F. 1995. *Heroic Poets, Poetic Heroes: The Ethnography of Performance in an Arabic Oral Epic Tradition.* Ithaca, NY: Cornell University Press.

Sherzer, Joel. 1990. *Verbal Art in San Blas: Kuna Culture through Its Discourse.* Cambridge: Cambridge University Press.

Sherzer, Joel, and Anthony Woodbury, eds. 1987. *Native American Discourse: Poetics and Rhetorics.* Cambridge: Cambridge University Press.

Turner, Victor. 1987. Are There Universals of Performance? *Comparative Criticism: An Annual Journal* 9: 47–59.

Turner, Victor. 1987. *The Anthropology of Performance.* New York: PAI Publications.

Personal Experience Narrative

Prose narrative account of the performer's personal experience. This consciously constructed narrative not only recounts the experiences of the narrator but also follows accepted norms for traditional performance, such as form, function, or style. The personal experience narrative also has been labeled *personal experience story* or *personal legend*.

The interest in and study of this narrative type has gained in popularity since the 1970s. Few other forms of narrative expression can provide the same depth of revelation of the social life of a community as can the personal experience narratives of its members. As a narrative form, the stories arise out of the experiences of their individual performers—and out of a felt need to relate those experiences. Performers develop their own repertoire of narratives, and individual personal experience narratives are readily identifiable by group members as to their "owners." Like other narrative genres, their form and structure—though it is always relatively loose, especially when compared to genres such as the *Märchen*—may become more polished over time with retelling. Conversely, they arise within conversational contexts, may be communally constructed within such settings, and may be so closely tied to a given interaction that their texts almost disintegrate outside the original setting.

As a separate genre, personal experience narratives do not necessarily fit neatly within the traditional canons of folklore. By their nature as personal accounts, they may not be correlated to a stock of identifiable narratives, and these accounts are necessarily idiosyncratic. Folklorist Sandra K. D. Stahl counters, though, that these narratives do fit within the context of folklore. Personal experience narratives have long been a part of the oral tradition but as a genre have been ignored in favor of more established areas of narrative research. Stahl asserts that this general type of folklore (the new label for the type notwithstanding) has long been of interest, as evidenced by research into first-person anecdotes, tall tales, and jokes, for example.

Moreover, personal experience narratives do manifest characteristics of many of the recognized oral narrative genres. Like legends, they recount an experience of a particular person or group; they follow accepted structural and performance patterns; and they rely on a set of understandings common to the group in their transmission of meaning. Personal experience narratives, like other smaller narrative categories such as family stories or anecdotes, have a limited circulation and, in certain instances, a limited lifespan. The standardization in form of the personal experience narratives has prompted some researchers, such as Juha Pentikäinen and Linda Dégh, to suggest that it is nearly impossible to distinguish between early forms of legends and those having roots as personal experience narratives or as narrative accounts told in the first person.

As a genre for scholarly research, personal experience narratives provide an opportunity to learn about the functional norms of a group on a micro level. As performances, these narratives reflect what is important to the group in terms of performance style, narrative content, and social concerns and norms of the group. These narratives also reflect how individual performers interpret these performative and social standards in order to present the narratives for group approval. Yet, unlike other types of narrative performance, personal experience narratives place fewer demands on the performer. Whereas many narrative types require performers who have a polished repertoire to draw upon for performance and are thus recognized for their skills, personal experience narratives can be performed by any group member. Personal experience narratives also may reveal more of the day-to-day realities of group standards than other traditional narrative forms in that they are drawn from (or at least are alleged to be drawn from) the real experiences of their performers in the present, rather than from the near or distant past life of the group or its legendary figures.

Randal S. Allison

See Also Anecdote; Family Folklore; Legend; Memorate.

References

Dégh, Linda, and Andrew Vázsonyi. 1974. The Memorate and the Proto-Memorate. *Journal of American Folklore* 87(2): 225–239.

Mulrooney, Kristin J. 2009. *Extraordinary from the Ordinary: Personal Experience Narratives in American Sign Language.* Washington, DC: Gallaudet University Press.

Pentikäinen, Juha. 1973. Belief, Memorate, and Legend. *Folklore Forum* 6: 217–241.

Pentikäinen, Juha. 1983. Personal Experience Stories. In *Handbook of American Folklore*, ed. Richard M. Dorson. Bloomington: Indiana University Press.

Pentikäinen, Juha. 1989. *Literary Folkloristics and Personal Narrative.* Bloomington: Indiana University Press.

Stahl, Sandra K. D. 1977. The Personal Narrative as Folklore. *Journal of the Folklore Institute* 14: 9–30.

Phenomenology

One of several traditions of philosophical discourse coming out of nineteenth-century Hegelian thought. Without discountenancing the claims of idealism—witness Hegel's own work *The Phenomenology of Mind*—phenomenology begins its investigations in phenomena, the material substances of the world, rather than in mental processes, the ethereal forms of thought. It thus shifts the footing of European metaphysical philosophy from idealism to materialism. Philosophies apart from phenomenology that are heir to this shift include existentialism, structuralism, structural linguistics, semiology, Marxism, feminism, ethnomethodology, and sociolinguistics.

The world adumbrates itself around the embodied person as its centrality. "My body," writes the American phenomenologist Maurice Natanson, "is the unique instrument through which I experience my insertion in the world" (Natanson 1962).

This characteristic use of the phenomenological "I" acknowledges the locus of perception in the body of the perceiver. The usage does not refer to any particular individual but to an incarnated self. From that perspective, the world is not only differentiated in substance but differential in significance: Where I look from is tied up with how I see. It is the centrality of embodied experience in phenomenology that has given the term *phenomenological* its narrow interpretation in folklore and the social sciences as "subjective."

But to distribute the distinction between subjectivity and objectivity over a contrast between the body and things, phenomenologists contend, would be a misunderstanding. Things are entangled with the body. I enter as a material object a world rendered intelligible by virtue of my presence in it. The French phenomenologist Maurice Merleau-Ponty writes, "We grasp external space through our bodily situation. A 'corporeal or postural schema' gives us at every moment a global, practical, implicit notion of the relation between our body and things, of our hold in them. A system of possible movements, or 'motor projects,' radiates from us to our environment. Our body is not in space like things; it inhabits or haunts space" (Merleau-Ponty 1971).

The body is a central term in the old philosophical dispute between materialism and idealism. It partakes of the nature of both things and thoughts. To keep the mind/body problem unsolved by coming down neither on the side of materialism, which grants objects priority, nor on the side of idealism, which privileges consciousness, is one of the tricks of phenomenology. The haunting body and the incarnated mind are modes of being in a world in which subjects materialize in the flesh. Bodylore is one of the areas of inquiry in contemporary folklore that investigates the symbolic properties of the body and the corporeal properties of thought.

The world holds me bodily as consciously I hold it, "consciousness, understood as a directional force sustaining the entire range of perceptual experience," as Natanson puts it. Consciousness is not a mental event secreted in the cranium but a constitutive act, the invention of a world. I am, Natanson continues, a "self constructing for itself the world it then finds and acts in" (Natanson 1970). The constructedness of my world becomes explicit in narrative and ritual genres that describe or fabricate a reality. This constitutive gesture is what phenomenologists call *intentionality* or the *intentionality of consciousness*. Over the course of its recent history, folklore, like other humanistic disciplines, has become more inclined to take meaning out of the artifact and reinsert it in the intentionality of its perceiver or producer.

The world I intend becomes fixed or typified so that the phenomena I retrieve from it take on the quality of objects. In this undertaking, the American phenomenologist Alfred Schutz notes, "the constituting process itself is entirely ignored, while the objectivity constituted by it is taken for granted" (Schutz 1973).

Typifications of persons become culturally visible as stereotypes; typifications of objects become visible as material culture; typifications of acts become visible as customs; typifications of talk become visible as genres; and arguably, typifications of groups become visible as ethnicities or national traits. Such typifications form what the ethnomethodologist Harold Garfinkel calls the "background expectancies" of everyday life. Part of the enterprise of folklore is to excavate such typifications from the matrix of the ordinary. As a consequence, new genres continue to appear in the field.

Typifications are among the "metaphysical constants" Schutz takes to constitute the world. Natanson writes, "The world I inhabit is from the outset an intersubjective one. The language I possess was taught to me by others; the manners I have I did not invent; whatever abilities, techniques, or talents I can claim were nourished by a social inheritance; even my dreams are rooted in a world I never created and can never completely possess" (Natanson 1971). Metaphysical constants can be said to take the folkloristic form of traditions, customs, practices, and ways of thinking, moving, and speaking that are culturally informed. Schultz calls the taken-for-granted world thus constituted the primary "realm of experience" or "paramount reality."

A shift of attention transfers the perceiver to another realm, a different universe of discourse, an alternate reality that Schutz, following the American philosopher William James, calls a "subuniverse" or "finite province of meaning." Thus, he writes, "all these worlds—the world of dreams, of imageries and phantasms, especially the world of art, the world of religious experience, the world of scientific contemplation, the play world of the child, and the world of the insane—are finite provinces of meaning" (Schutz 1967). Peter Berger and Thomas Luckmann, who have translated phenomenology for the social sciences, write:

> Different objects present themselves to consciousness as constituents of different spheres of reality. I recognize the fellowmen I must deal with in the course of everyday life as pertaining to a reality quite different from the disembodied figures that appear in my dreams. . . . Put differently, I am conscious of the world as consisting of multiple realities. As I move from one reality to another, I experience the transition as a kind of shock. This shock is to be understood as caused by the shift in attentiveness that the transition entails. Waking up from a dream illustrates this shift most simply. (Berger & Luckmann 1967)

Some genres elaborate and so inscribe the realm of the ordinary as gestures; for instance, elaborate body movement and costumes expand the expressive capacity of skin, architecture reconstitutes the world as a bony carapace around the body, or foodways inflect ingestion. All of these genres carry the imprint of the body on the world, most articulately in the form of tools or weapons, one end of which fits the body and the other the world. Speech forms, as it were, use the voice to lift thought out of the body and convey it to our social others. Thus, greetings and farewells acknowledge the boundaries of social encounters. Some genres close themselves off from the realm of the ordinary as separate realities, as when gesture is formalized as dance, sound transpires as music, or tools produce crafts. Folklorist Susan Stewart, perhaps following the title of Merleau-Ponty's book *Sense and Non-sense*, calls genres that catch ordinary phenomena and uproot them from their ordinary ground *nonsense*.

Representational genres invoke and fabricate other realms. Not only narrative genres such as myths, epics, legends, folktales, anecdotes, and jokes, but also folk painting, folk costume, folk theater, and such cross-genres as folk poetry and folksong conjure up alternate realities. Some representational genres invoke two realities at once: Fables, proverbs, puns, riddles, and folk metaphors offer their own fictive worlds and also direct attention to the realm of the ordinary. Other genres reframe reality. Genres from cosmologies to confidence tricks represent reality under a different description, a particular set of assumptions about the nature of the given, the apparent, the real. Some of these reframings of the realm of the ordinary themselves become inhabitable worlds. Rituals and religious ceremonies, feasts, festivals and carnivals, and games and play are experienced as realities, at least temporarily. Mary Hufford, for instance, reconstitutes the domain of hunting over the topography of the ordinary. Sometimes, fragments of alternate realities appear to be embedded in the realm of the ordinary as what Schutz calls "enclaves" of a different ontological status. Thus, superstitions, charms and amulets, curses, blessings, and oaths, along with such entities as gods, ghosts, angels, devils, or witches, trail through the fabric of the real, ephemera of a different domain. So Erving Goffman, heir to the phenomenological tradition in the social sciences, writes, "Realms of being are the proper objects here for study; and here the everyday is not a special domain to be placed in contrast to the others, but merely another realm" (Goffman 1974).

Katharine Young

See Also Frame.

References

Bazerman, Charles, ed. 2010. *Traditions of Writing Research*. New York: Routledge.

Berger, Peter, and Thomas Luckmann. 1967. *The Social Construction of Reality*. Garden City, NY: Anchor.

Garfinkel, Harold. 1977. Background Expectancies. In *Rules and Meanings*, ed. Mary Douglas. Middlesex, England: Penguin.

Goffman, Erving. 1974. *Frame Analysis*. New York: Harper Colophon.

Hezekiah, Gabrielle A. 2010. *Phenomenology's Material Presence: Video, Vision and Experience*. Chicago: Intellect.

Hufford, Mary. 1991. *Chaseworld: Foxhunting and Storytelling in New Jersey's Pine Barrens*. Philadelphia: University of Pennsylvania Press.

Merleau-Ponty, Maurice. 1964. *Sense and Non-sense*. Trans. Hubert Dreyfus and Patricia Dreyfus. Evanston, IL: Northwestern University Press.

Merleau-Ponty, Maurice. 1971. *The Primacy of Perception*. Ed. James M. Edie. Evanston, IL: Northwestern University Press.

Natanson, Maurice. 1962. *Literature, Philosophy and the Social Sciences*. The Hague: Mouton.

Natanson, Maurice. 1970. *The Journeying Self: A Study in Philosophy and Social Role*. Reading, MA: Addison, Wesley.

Schutz, Alfred. 1967. *The Phenomenology of the Social World*. Trans. George Walsh and Frederick Lehnert. Evanston, IL: Northwestern University Press.

Schutz, Alfred. 1973. *On Phenomenology and Social Relations*. Ed. Helmut Wagner. Chicago: University of Chicago Press.

Stewart, Susan. 1979. *Nonsense*. Baltimore, MD: Johns Hopkins University Press.

Young, Katharine. 1987. *Taleworlds and Storyrealms: The Phenomenology of Narrative*. Dordrecht, Netherlands: Martinus Nijhoff.

Young, Katharine, ed. 1993. *Bodylore*. Knoxville: University of Tennessee Press.

Philological Approach

Conceptual models and research practices applied to the analysis of folksongs, ballads, proverbs, folktales, epics, and other oral narratives from historical linguistics, literary history, and classical scholarship.

Part of so-called literary folkloristics or the European orientation, the philological approaches in folklore studies focus on the folklore text, contextualizing its semantic and linguistic texture to other, similar texts. The main focus of philological approaches lies in the comparison of folklore texts for their various textual-linguistic elements in order to: (1) classify the texts according to genres, types, variants, and motifs, (2) determine their origin, genealogy, historical development, and geographical distribution, or, more recently, (3) study on the textual level the nature of their oral composition.

Drawing analogy from the study of classical and medieval literature as well as language history, the philological research tradition provided, in the early modern Europe of the eighteenth, nineteenth, and early twentieth century, the first scientific systematization of oral traditions and a model for their conceptualization as artifacts of unwritten literature.

Most philological research in folklore has been conducted within the framework of the historic-geographic method. This approach is also known as the

Finnish method, named after the country in which the method was codified. As implied by its name, the method is concerned with the historical development and geographic dissemination of folklore. It is diachronic in nature, using the comparison of folklore texts as a means to elucidate and reconstruct textual histories.

The methodological basis of the historic-geographic method lies in philological text criticism, a branch of literary research that goes back some 2,000 years to the comparisons between different Homeric texts. Since the Renaissance, this method has been much employed in the study of biblical and medieval manuscripts.

The application of text criticism to materials recorded from oral tradition, especially folktales, myths, and ballads, was popular among nineteenth-century philologists. Even earlier, the method had been employed on, for example, Finnish folk poetry, by Henrik Gabriel Porthan. Some of the best-known nineteenth-century scholars in this field were Elias Lönnrot in Finland, the brothers Jacob and Wilhelm Grimm in Germany, Svend Grundtvig in Denmark, and Francis James Child in the United States.

In text criticism, the scholar aims at establishing a relationship between two or more manuscript versions of the same text, studying whether manuscript A is the source of manuscript B or vice versa, or whether they are both derived from a common source. Analogically, the text-critical folklorist makes comparisons between a number of versions of a given folklore item in order to determine their relationship of descent. The underlying postulate here is that the paradigmatic variation of similar traits in different versions indicates a linear process of change.

Since the manuscript is the cognitive and conceptual model for the explanation of variants in oral tradition, a folklore item in text-critical logics is a text that is a copy of another text. As is often the case with manuscripts, copies contain errors made by the copyist, and analogically, difference in folklore variants is regarded as due to errors, flaws, and other alterations made in their replication. In error analysis, the text-critical scholar uses errors as clues pointing to the relationship between different copies and establishes their chronological order. The perceived gaps and errors in one version are then eliminated with material taken from another version, by replacing, say, a flawed line with one that is considered more correct. The scientific aim is to reconstruct a text that could be considered complete and original and that would then give information about the customs and beliefs of earlier generations. To meet the other scientific requirements, a publication of such a study must contain a critical apparatus that lists the alternative folklore sources and their variant readings.

Text criticism was developed and codified into the historic-geographic folklore method by Julius and Kaarle Krohn, father and son, in the 1870s and 1880s in Finland. Although originally designed for the study of Finnish *Kalevala* metric oral poetry, the new method became internationally known as a tool mainly to be used in folktale scholarship, primarily because Kaarle Krohn applied it first to animal tales in his influential dissertation of 1889, and his pupil Antti Aarne wrote the method's guidelines (1913) with a focus on the comparative study of folktales. With these and other publications, especially those published in the Helsinki-based series entitled Folklore Fellows Communications, they set a new course for the already well-established line of comparative-philological research into folktales, whose best-known nineteenth-century representatives had been Jacob and Wilhelm Grimm and the Indologist-linguist Theodor Benfey.

Influenced by Herderian romanticism, the Grimm brothers believed that folktales—or fairy tales, as they have also been called—are not mere products of imagination but aesthetically structured historical documents about the ways in which people in ancient (especially medieval) times thought. As anonymous products of a collective national spirit and as survivals of forgotten myths, folktales, as well as other oral poetry, are subjected to both historical-mythological research and artistic-philological reconstructions. The brothers' famous collections of tales, especially *Kinder- und Hausmärchen* (Children's and household tales; 1812, 1815), became evergreens as children's literature and, as such, models for many later publications in the literary fairy tale genre. In addition to following their own artistic intuition in order to make the tales, as it were, speak the "voice of the folk," the brothers employed text-critical principles to combine different versions of the same tale and reconstruct them in their alleged "essential" and authentic form.

The comparative emphasis in European folktale study had received a dramatic impetus from the discovery of the relationship of Sanskrit to Greek, Latin, and many other major European languages. By analogy, the Indo-European linguistic connection was soon extended, as suggested by the Grimm brothers, to fables, folktales, and other oral narratives whose origins, it was thought, were to be looked for in India. While Max Müller, a student of Vedic texts and Aryan mythology, theorized on the relationship between language and myth and on the origin of religion, Theodor Benfey compared Greek fables, traditionally credited to Aesop, with Indic texts and came up a with a diffusionistic theory according to which India was the source of most folktales in the world. Much of this diffusion took place, according to Benfey, as early as the Middle Ages, through the many oral and literary readaptations and translations of the *Panchatantra* collection of tales, which he himself translated into German in 1859.

As far as the migration of folklore is concerned, one of the main issues for the Krohns and other historic-geographers in the Finnish context was the politically charged question of whether the *Kalevala*-metric runes originated in western or eastern Finland—in other words, whether they had been composed under medieval Scandinavian or Russian influence. Although migration of folklore on a general level concerns intercultural and international relations and contacts, it is, at the same time, directly related to the issue of land control and its symbolism. Indeed, the Finnish concern had many precedents in the royal collections of antiquities in the seventeenth and eighteenth centuries, as well as in the textual collections of *naturpoesie* by Johann Gottfried von Herder and the Grimms in the early nineteenth century, which all purported to create a natural link between the land, the past, and a particular nation or social group. Thus, the significance of the new method for the international study of folktale lay, on the one hand, in the Finnish scholars' explicit interest in the continuation and consolidation of the basic folkloristic ideology and, on the other hand, in its methodological reformism as the historic-geographers questioned India as the common source of folktales and insisted that origins and migratory routes had to be established for each tale type separately, with the help of a detailed scientific analysis.

In accordance with the then popular theories of monogenesis and diffusionism, all folklore texts were regarded in historic-geographic assumptions as having an original form, an *Ur-form*, composed at a specific historical moment in a specific historical place. This then migrated from one locality to another, transforming in such a way that one version developed from another in a geographic order. As in the so-called age-area theory in anthropology, the versions recorded in the opposite ends of such a chain of development were, in terms of both their content and their locality, furthest apart from another—and as a result of this logic, they were also judged to be the oldest variants of a particular tale type. For this reason, according to Kaarle Krohn, it is possible to follow the historical and geographical chain in a reversed order and, in the same manner as in the study of sound changes in historical linguistics, to deduce the birthplace of a folklore item and reconstruct its original form.

In addition to the historic-geographic method's role in creating and consolidating disciplinary identity for the study of folklore, one of the main factors in the significance of the method was its systematic approach—or rather, what seemed to be systematic according to the contemporary standards of scholarship—to philological comparisons and folklore migrations. In contrast to earlier text-critical research, historic-geographic methodology emphasized the source-critical argument that scholars had to assemble a full collection of versions before an adequate comparative analysis could be done. In addition to extensive recordings of oral materials, this would include the sources available in print and in manuscripts. The materials would then be arranged both chronologically and by region, and the texts would be broken down into a series of episodes and other narrative components and then tabulated and compared within the whole body of versions.

Such methodology created a need not only for extensive collections of texts—and big folklore archives—but also for a uniform system of reference for the making of comparisons between materials from different geographic and cultural areas. Already in text-critical folklore scholarship, materials were organized into types and subtypes and published with type numbers. Now it became the trademark of the historic-geographic comparative approach to compile and publish national and international indexes and registers. In addition to the canon of English and Scottish popular ballads, compiled by Francis James Child in the late nineteenth century, some of the most famous of these are *The Types of the Folktale*, first compiled by Antti Aarne in 1911 and later revised by the American folklorist Stith Thompson, and Thompson's *Motif-Index of Folk-Literature.*

The interest that the historic-geographic folklorists showed in origins and historical developments was a reaction to the romantic notion of a collective national ethos as the creator of folklore. The method's premises also followed the Darwinist arguments concerning cultural evolution. Although cultures were seen to be progressing, most of folklore was regarded as survivals from earlier cultural stages, subjected to a process of degeneration as more variants emerged and cultures modernized.

In accordance with the then dominant positivistic premises, the method also drew on natural sciences for models of explanation and scientific language. The interest in folklore classification and taxonomies followed a model taken from botany, and the conceptualization of the relationship between different versions as "genetic" came from biology. The tendency to view social processes in biological terms was also evident in the scholars' habit of speaking of transformations in folklore as either following rules comparable to "natural laws" or as being "mutations."

Some of the method's major theoretical ingredients were criticized and refuted early on, by both the so-called typological school of post-Krohn Finnish folklorists and scholars in many other countries. One of the early objects of criticism was the automigration theory, according to which folklore travels like rings on the surface of water or like a stream. This was regarded by the Estonian German Walter Anderson, among others, as both mechanistic and invalid, and instead, more emphasis was put on human factors in the diffusion process, including ethnic, political, national, linguistic, and religious boundaries. The distinction between active and passive tradition bearers, stressed by the Swede Carl Wilhelm von Sydow, became an important modification, as did his emphasis on *oicotypes*, or regionally adapted forms. The reconstruction of the *Ur-form* was rejected either as a methodological impossibility or on the grounds that the archetype never existed. Instead, folklorists were to strive for what could be considered the original thematic contents and construct normal forms that would, for technical purposes, serve as standardized abstractions.

None of this criticism, however, questioned the textualist tradition itself or the objectivist or natural scientific premises of philological folklore research. The historic-geographic approach continued to be the dominant paradigm in folkloristics worldwide until new influences from anthropology, sociology, and comparative religion in the 1960s moved folklore studies away from philology and toward psychological and social scientific research problems. In the United States, as folklore became an independent university subject, philology-based, item-centered, and comparative literary folkloristics at least partially blended with anthropological folkloristics.

Despite this development, philological and postphilological approaches continue their influence to this day. In Finland, the role of text criticism in folklore methodology was promoted and further developed by Matti Kuusi as recently as in the 1970s and 1980s. In many parts of the world, even though the question of when and where a folklore item was first invented and how it migrated no longer interested folklorists, monographs on textual histories were still being written and published in the 1990s; in addition, large amounts of material are still collected for archival and comparative purposes, and typologies and indexes are compiled. For many, literature still forms the conceptual framework for oral traditions, and literary folklorists still tend to regard themselves as the only "real" folklorists.

Yet literary folkloristics is bound to change as both philology and literary research change. For example, after being the center of philological folklore study in the United States in the early decades of the twentieth century, Harvard University became the birthplace of a new type of philology as Milman Parry and later his pupil Albert Lord developed a synchronic and ethnographic approach to textual comparativism. Convinced that the Homeric epics were products of oral tradition—a theory that, in the nineteenth century, had caused Lönnrot and his followers in Finland to take up text-critical reconstructions and epic compilations—Parry and Lord set out to study textual elements that would indicate how the Homeric epics had been orally composed. Their major finding was the formulaic structure of oral epic language.

With the help of fieldwork among contemporary epic singers in Yugoslavia, Parry and Lord formulated the oral-formulaic theory, according to which epics are produced in performance by means of compositional textual elements, such as memorized traditional formulas, around which thematic units are woven. Instead of regarding a folklore text as a copy of another text, the oral-formulaic theory treats it as a product of active oral composition created in interaction between the performer and the audience.

In some oral-formulaic studies, the performance aspect has been surpassed by the theory's philological foundation, as scholars have focused on elucidating formulas and other compositional elements through textual comparisons instead of actual performances and performer-audience interactions. For the most part, however, the theory is emphatically directed toward the study of composition in performance, as occurs in textual-linguistically oriented performance studies, such as ethnopoetics. In fact, the oral-formulaic theory functions as both a historical and a methodological link between performance-oriented folkloristics, present-day research into oral literature in anthropology and classical studies, and the philological folkloristics proper—that is, text-critical and historic-geographic studies.

Pertti Anttonen

See Also Diachronic/Synchronic; Folktale; Historic-Geographic Method; Linguistic Approach; Literary Approach; Monogenesis/Polygenesis; Oikotype/Oicotype; Romantic Nationalism; Text; Tradition Bearer.

References

Aarne, Antti. 1913. *Leitfaden der vergleichende Märchenforschung*. Helsinki: Academia Scientiarum Fennica.

Abrahams, Roger D. 1993. Phantoms of Romantic Nationalism in Folkloristics. *Journal of American Folklore* 106: 3–37.

Briggs, Charles L. 1993. Metadiscursive Practices and Scholarly Authority in Folkloristics. *Journal of American Folklore* 106: 387–434.

Cocchiara, Giuseppe. 1981. *The History of Folklore in Europe*. Trans. John N. McDaniel. Philadelphia: Institute for the Study of Human Issues.

Dundes, Alan. 1986. The Anthropologist and the Comparative Method in Folklore. *Journal of Folklore Research* 23: 125–146.

Foley, John Miles. 1988. *The Theory of Oral Composition: History and Methodology*. Bloomington: Indiana University Press.

Goldberg, Christine. 1984. The Historic-Geographic Method: Past and Future. *Journal of Folklore Research* 21: 1–18.

Hautala, Jouko. 1969. *Finnish Folklore Research, 1828–1918*. Helsinki: Academia Scientiarum Fennica.

Holbek, Bengt. 1983. Nordic Research in Popular Prose Narrative. In *Trends in Nordic Tradition Research*, eds. Lauri Honko and Pekka Laaksonen. Studia Fennica, no. 27. Helsinki: Finnish Literature Society.

Honko, Lauri. 1979. A Hundred Years of Finnish Folklore Research: A Reappraisal. *Folklore* 90: 141–152.

Krohn, Kaarle. 1971. *Folklore Methodology, Formulated by Julius Krohn and Expanded by Nordic Researchers*. Trans. Roger L. Welsch. Publications of the American Folklore Society, Bibliographical and Special Series, Vol. 21. Austin: University of Texas Press.

Kuusi, Matti. 1974. "The Bridge and the Church": An Anti-Church Legend. In *Finnish Folkloristics* 2nd ed. Pentti Leino, with the assistance of Annikki Kaivola-Bregenhøj and Urpo Vento. Studia Fennica, no. 18. Helsinki: Finnish Literature Society.

Taylor, Archer. 1928. Precursors of the Finnish Method of Folk-Lore Study. *Modern Philology* 25: 481–491.

von Sydow, C. W. 1948. Folk-Tale Studies and Philology: Some Points of View. In *Selected Papers on Folklore* by C. W. von Sydow. Copenhagen: Rosenkilde and Bagger.

Zumwalt, Rosemary Lévy. 1988. *American Folklore Scholarship: A Dialogue of Dissent*. Bloomington: Indiana University Press.

Photography, Folk

Folk photography is concerned with photography—an artistic and documentary element of both material and popular culture—as it is used by ordinary people to document everyday life. The commercialization and technological democratization of photography for non-elite consumption has made photography a shared life experience and presence for most North Americans, as well as an expressive medium strongly associated with women, families, and the domestic sphere. If not from photography's arrival in 1839, certainly since the latter part of the nineteenth century with the introduction of the Kodak camera and the rise of amateur photography, photographs have chronicled the lives of common persons. As an artifact that resides in a context—a literal and figurative frame—the photograph should be considered for both its surface qualities and the more subtle information it holds about the human condition.

By treating photography customarily as a flat art, photographic scholarship has privileged surface analysis, accomplished exclusively by scrutinizing its composition and other formal characteristics of the picture plane. While this is one appropriate level of appreciation and understanding of photos, in considering folk photography it is equally necessary to adopt methods for the contextual study of photographic images, in which women would represent not merely the subject matter for, or the creators of, images, but the chief (though not exclusive) guardians of generational stories catalogued in photograph files, albums, scrapbooks, slideshows, and, most recently, household items featuring digitized images, ranging from personalized calendars to customized mouse pads.

Photographs act as visual cues for the behavior of persons connected with them; that is, they frequently encourage an intimate viewer to engage in a dialogue specifically corresponding to the imagery. Pictures may serve as a catalyst to the viewer-listener's sharing of narrative memories, or even tangentially related stories, as is common in the ritual act of presenting the contents of a family album to a guest as after-dinner entertainment. However, if not fastidiously tended, family photographs risk becoming pedestrian, devoid of emotional meaning, and become artifacts, collections of images whose specific importance resides in their function within social and historical memory.

Because photography is a relatively new phenomenon, the context of its making sometimes remains accessible, at least in part. Often, the photographer or others linked directly to the photographic event are still available to researchers.

A woman touches the wall of a highway underpass where some believe an apparition of the Virgin Mary has appeared, April 19, 2005, in Chicago, Illinois. Police were posted in the area to keep traffic flowing as hundreds of people have been drawn to the site. (Getty Images)

Interviews, oral histories, and other records of personal contact may then accompany visual scholarship. With good fieldwork, the student of photography and its lore can capture and preserve interactions between people and their contexts through material images. Daniel Wojcik's study of photographs purportedly representing apparitions of the Virgin Mary is a good example.

While photography receives explanation and embellishment from verbal expression, it is a language in itself. Every photographic image has a surface and a deep structure. The communication of a photographic message is coded, containing a subtle set of rules for the transmission and reception of visual information. People assign their own meanings to images, and yet, when viewed in large numbers, snapshots begin to resemble each other, falling into recognizable categories. Photographic images are, therefore, generalizable, signaling social and aesthetic meanings using consensually agreed upon patterns (e.g., obligatory smiles, the group shot with an identifying placard placed in front) and visual tropes (newlyweds with all the reception guests, the new baby peering from beneath a crib blanket), at once showing the unique faces of family members and the familiar poses and occasions American viewers have come to regard as emblems of a family's history.

In this sense, the study of photographs concerns itself with the history of everyday life. Once the hand-held camera had freed photographers from costly and cumbersome tripods and flash units, shooting in more remote locations and with quicker exposure times became achievable. The revolution in technology inevitably influenced both choices of photographic subjects and their manner of representation. Prints became affordable and plentiful, and thus less formally posed. Marianne Hirsch and Jerald Maddox, among others, approach homemade photography as a folk medium, concerned more with documenting vernacular culture than with technological savvy or pretensions to art. To the extent that women have traditionally been charged with the role of culture bearer, they are similarly the keepers of most homemade photographic images. Whether generating, arranging, displaying, or exchanging photographs, women preserve the images, and with them the memories, that have become mainstays of family folklore. However, since few well-developed studies on women and folk photography are available, the field remains open to further study.

Linda S. Watts

See Also Folk Culture; Material Culture.

References

Adams, Timothy Dow. 1999. *Light Writing and Life Writing: Photography in Autobiography*. Chapel Hill: University of North Carolina Press.

Coke, Van Deren, ed. 1975. *One Hundred Years of Photographic History*. Albuquerque: University of New Mexico Press.

Hirsch, Marianne, ed. 1997. *Family Frames: Photography, Narrative, and Postmemory*. Cambridge, MA: Harvard University Press.

Hirsch, Marianne, ed. 1999. *The Familial Gaze*. Hanover, NH: University Press of New England.

Ohrn, Karen Becker. 1980. *Dorothea Lange and the Documentary Tradition*. Baton Rouge: Louisiana State University Press.

Rosenheim, Jeff. 2009. *Walker Evans and the Picture Postcard*. New York: Metropolitan Museum of Art.

Sayre, Maggie Lee. 1995. *"Deaf Maggie Lee Sayre": Photographs of a River Life*. Ed. Tom Rankin. Oxford: University Press of Mississippi.

Wojcik, Daniel. 1966. "Polaroids from Heaven": Photography, Folk Religion, and the Miraculous Image Tradition at a Marian Apparition Site. *Journal of American Folklore* 109: 129–148.

Pilgrimage

The journey of individuals in homage to highly esteemed places, individuals, or artifacts with the aim of deriving some benefit therefrom. Pilgrimage operates at the juncture of the spiritual and material worlds as both a mapping of a sacred landscape onto physical space and as the amelioration of bodily illness and injury through arduous physical exertion with a spiritual focus.

Although the term *pilgrimage* may be used in a secular sense to denote a sojourn or personal odyssey and is often invoked in discussions of tourist experiences, the word most often describes an act of piety, penitence, or thanksgiving—an ascetic journey of religious obligation to obtain healing and purification. *Pilgrimage* is also used to describe the interiorized journey of the religious mystic.

Pilgrimage, at the nexus of official and local religious systems, often generates vehement ecclesiastical responses. Though strongly rooted in popular tradition, pilgrimage is a displacement of individuals from their local communities and may be in tension with the usual hierarchies of religious organization and administration.

Pilgrimage has been described by Victor Turner and Edith Turner as a tripartite rite-of-passage experience: *the journeying to* (separation), *the experience of the destination* (liminality), and *the returning home* (reaggregation).

The pilgrim's departure may be marked by special preparations, consecrations, and celebrations. Arduous means of travel (e.g., procession) and/or bodily posture (e.g., walking on the knees) may often be prescribed (although technological advances in transportation have transformed the pilgrimage route). Pilgrims may be sick and travel with the assistance of others, or a proxy may make the pilgrimage on behalf of an ill person. The temporary exile of the pilgrim and the difficulties and dangers of the pilgrimage route are endured in exchange for the ultimate rewards of the journey.

The travel route is highly marked, often dotted with signs, sacred precincts, and facilities to provide for the traveler's corporeal and spiritual needs. The journey out is often characterized as an ascent, a time for exploration and greater freedom than subsequent phases of pilgrimage. As the destination is neared, rituals of preparation may be intensified: Special interdictions, ablutions, and prayers may commence, and special vestments may be donned. The destination of pilgrimage may be surrounded by a sacred precinct, often a set of lesser shrines that direct visitors toward their ultimate goal.

The pilgrim's destination may be a site where something extraordinary occurred, such as a miracle or an apparition, or a place where a revered individual was born, lived (or lives), or died. The material representation of such an individual might take the form of relics. A shrine may be seen as a specially energized place. The spiritual efficacy of a shrine as an auspicious place for communication between humans and deities is seen to be enhanced by the visits of successive waves of pilgrims. The visitor will typically leave some form of offering as witness to the pilgrimage: a consecrated object brought from home or a representation of self such as a snippet of hair or clothing, money, or food.

Returning home, the pilgrim brings something of the experience back, possibly in the form of a tangible souvenir, token, or relic. The returning pilgrim may experience an enhanced status in his or her community of origin.

The Kaaba is a shrine that houses the Black Stone of Mecca, the focal point for Muslim prayer and final destination for pilgrims to Mecca. (Ayazad/Shutterstock)

The force of pilgrimage is often described as centripetal: The individual travels from a peripheral location to a highly significant religious center. This convergence on a shared cosmic center is the reverse of diaspora, reuniting coreligionists from diverse ethnic, linguistic, political, and social backgrounds. The communitarian elements of pilgrimage may include simplicity in dress and diet, common endurance of a physical ordeal, and general meditation on the common faith. Yet there has been much recent debate over describing pilgrimage as *communitas*, a leveling process characterized by a spirit of fellowship, bonding, and temporary release from mundane social differences.

Some current writers suggest that, rather than dissolving social boundaries, pilgrimage actually maintains and reinforces them. Pilgrimages exist on a variety of scales and cover a range of distances. Although the collective nature of pilgrimage assures the existence of a range of interpretations and practices, the authoritarian discourse of shrine controllers and patrons may, in some instances, mediate the behavior of devotees visiting the shrine.

Pilgrimage routes map a sacred topography upon secular space and have profound historical consequences affecting artistic, commercial, and religious interchanges on both the global and local scales. Often occurring during certain seasons and accompanied by festivals, fairs, or specialized markets, pilgrimage may be a religious tourist attraction. The relation of the sacred and secular market systems have profound effects on the local community at the pilgrimage destination.

Central pilgrimage destinations in world religion include Jerusalem (Jewish, Christian, Muslim) and Meron (Jewish). Popular Catholic destinations include Rome, Lourdes, Santiago de Compostela (Spain), and the Basilica of Guadalupe (Mexico City). *Hajj*, the pilgrimage to Mecca in Saudi Arabia (including shrines at Medina and Arafat), is a religious duty to be completed, if possible, by all adult Muslims. Hindu pilgrims visit the purifying waters of the Ganges in Varanasi (Benares), India, and Mount Kailas, Tibet (China). Bodh Gaya and Sarnath in India and Saikoku, Japan, are destinations for Buddhists, and Ise, Japan, is visited by Shintos. Countless other pilgrimage traditions exist in every corner of the globe. Pilgrimage is also an important theme in literary allegories, such as *Pilgrims' Progress* (Bunyan), *Divine Comedy* (Dante), and *The Canterbury Tales* (Chaucer).

Emily Socolov

See Also Medicine, Folk; Religion, Folk.

References

Eade, John, and Michael J. Sallnow, eds. 1991. *Contesting the Sacred: The Anthropology of Christian Pilgrimage*. London: Routledge.

Jha, Makhan, ed. 1991. *Social Anthropology of Pilgrimage*. New Delhi: Inter-India Publications.

Kamal, Ahmad. 1961. *The Sacred Journey: Being a Pilgrimage to Makkah*. New York: Duell.

Morinis, E. Alan. 1984. *Pilgrimage in the Hindu Tradition: A Case Study of Rural Bengal*. Delhi: Oxford University Press.

Munro, Eleanor. 1987. *On Glory Roads: A Pilgrim's Book about Pilgrimage*. New York: Thames and Hudson.

Nolan, Mary Lee, and Sidney Nolan. 1989. *Christian Pilgrimage in Modern Western Europe*. Chapel Hill: University of North Carolina Press.

Ousterhout, Robert, ed. 1990. *The Blessings of Pilgrimage*. Urbana: University of Illinois Press.

Sallnow, Michael J. 1987. *Pilgrims of the Andes: Regional Cults in Cusco*. Washington, DC: Smithsonian Institution Press.

Sumption, Jonathan. 1975. *Pilgrimage: An Image of Medieval Religion*. Totowa, NJ: Rowman and Littlefield.

Turner, Victor, and Edith Turner. 1978. *Image and Pilgrimage in Christian Culture: Anthropological Perspectives*. New York: Columbia University Press.

Place

Denotes the ways locations are made meaningful through the experiences of inhabitants; closely associated in folkloristics with notions of "regionalism" and the "sense of place," sometimes contrasted with concepts of "space" or "landscape," which indicate more abstract or outsider perspectives.

In the early years of American folkloristics, little attention was given to the idea that a place or region could have a relationship to the expressive culture being collected. However, by the mid-1900s, the concept of regionalism began to develop, and the work of folklorists such as Herbert Halpert, Benjamin Botkin, and Américo Paredes moved the field closer toward a coherent regionalist approach, which solidified in the 1960s with the revolution in folklife studies, the reconceptualization of folklore as process, and expanded notions of the folk (Allen 1990,7–10). Folklorists began to look at region as a geographical boundary that constructed a shared identity for folk groups and thus a shared body of lore and to see, for example, the regionalization of folklore as a rhetorical strategy (see Jones 1976).

More recently, influenced by the work of Yi-Fu Tuan and Edward Casey, among others, the contributions of folklore as a discipline have been especially central to the study of how collaboratively produced and continually reproduced forms of (artistic) expression and communication generate a "sense of place," the subjective and emotional attachment people have to a place (as examples of a few different types of approaches, see Glassie 1982, Pocius 1991, Hufford 1992, Feld and Basso 1996, and Dorst 1999; see Ryden 1993 for the relationship between folklore's emergent studies of place and humanistic geography).

At the same time, folklorists have also called attention to the rather "unmarked" construction of locality (Shuman 1993) sometimes characterized by these studies and have turned to the concept of "critical regionalism" (see the work of Hufford 2002, Reid and Taylor 2002, Miller 2007, Thorne 2004) to address the relationship between local and global constructions of place and the connections between people characterized by the "global sense of place" (Massey 1994).

Another productive strand of place studies, indebted to the work of Michel de Certeau, Edward Soja, and Henri Lefebrve, envisions places as events or performances that make available the human practices and processes involved in their construction, as a way to understand that places are never "finished" or complete but are always becoming. As Cresswell articulates, "Place in this sense becomes an event rather than a secure ontological thing rooted in notions of the authentic. Place as an event is marked by openness and change rather than boundedness and permanence" (Cresswell 2004, 39). See also the special issue of *Western Folklore* (2007), "Space, Place, Emergence," for more detailed discussions of perspectives on place.

In the realm of public folklore, exciting projects that map personal experiences and places in very local and interactive ways are being carried out online through nonprofit organizations. For example, "Place Matters," a project of City Lore and New York's Municipal Art Society, "seeks to promote and protect places that connect us with the past, sustain community life, and make our surroundings distinctive" (http://www.placematters.net). PhilaPlace, a multimedia project of the Pennsylvania Historical Society, connects stories by people of all backgrounds and historical records with places across time in different Philadelphia neighborhoods to present an interpretive picture of the rich history, culture, and architecture of neighborhoods, past and present (http://www.philaplace.org).

Rosina S. Miller

See Also Folk Culture; Material Culture.

References

Allen, Barbara. 1990. Regional Studies in American Folklore Scholarship. In *Sense of Place: American Regional Cultures*, eds. B. Allen and T. J. Schlereth. Lexington: University Press of Kentucky.

Cresswell, Tim. 2004. *Place: A Short Introduction.* Malden, MA: Blackwell Publishing.

Dorst, John. 1999. *Looking West.* Philadelphia: University of Pennsylvania Press.

Feld, Steven, and Keith Basso, eds. 1996. *Senses of Place.* Santa Fe, NM: School of American Research.

Gabbert, Lisa, and Paul Jordan-Smith. 2007. Introduction: Space, Place, Emergence. *Western Folklore* 66(3-4): 217–232.

Glassie, Henry. 1982. *Passing the Time in Ballymenone: Culture and History of an Ulster Community.* Philadelphia: University of Pennsylvania Press.

Hufford, Mary. 1992. *Chaseworld: Foxhunting and Storytelling in New Jersey's Pine Barrens.* Philadelphia: University of Pennsylvania Press.

Hufford, Mary. 2002. Interrupting the Monologue: Folklore, Ethnography, and Critical Regionalism. *Journal of Appalachian Studies* 8(1): 62–78.

Jones, Suzi. 1976. Regionalization: A Rhetorical Strategy. *Journal of the Folklore Institute* 8(1): 105–120.

Massey, Doreen. 1994. *Space, Place, and Gender.* Minneapolis: University of Minnesota Press.

Miller, Rosina. 2007. Sharing Prosperity: Critical Regionalism and Place-Based Social Change. *Western Folklore* 66 (3-4): 351–381.

Pocius, Gerald. 1991. *A Place to Belong: Community Order and Everyday Space in Calvert, Newfoundland.* Athens: University of Georgia Press; Montreal: McGill-Queen's University Press.

Reid, Herbert, and Betsy Taylor. 2002. Appalachia as a Global Region: Toward Critical Regionalism and Civic Professionalism. *Journal of Appalachian Studies* 8(1): 9–32.

Ryden, Kent C. 1993. *Mapping the Invisible Landscape: Folklore, Writing, and the Sense of Place*. Iowa City: University of Iowa Press.

Shuman, Amy. 1993. Dismantling Local Culture. *Western Folklore* 52(2-4): 345–364.

Thorne, Cory. 2004. Come from Away: Community, Region, and Tradition in Newfoundland and Expatriate Identity. Dissertation, Folklore and Folklife, University of Pennsylvania, Philadelphia.

Poetry, Folk

Rhythmic and/or rhyming texts, intended for reading, chanting, recitation and/or singing, including local compositions as well as traditional verse, often highly symbolic and relevant to a community's knowledge, beliefs, and views, are considered folk poetry.

Folk poetry is an extremely diverse genre. It can include verse for or by children—nursery and skipping rhymes; materials related to particular occupations from peddlers' cries and military cadences to cowboy poetry; written short verses communicated in graffiti and autograph books; lyric, narrative, and epic song texts; traditional as well as event-specific recitations, including African American toasts; and written verses for family and community circulation. Arguably, many kinds of folk poetry—ballads, lyric folksongs, epics, and newer forms like rap—are distinctive because of the integral importance of tunes and musical accompaniment. However, folklorists have often considered together verses intended for singing, recitation, and reading, and the line between them is a particularly difficult one to draw in current societies, as it was in literate cultures of the past. The texts or the rhymical/verse structures of songs may be the bases for both serious and parodic folk poetry for singing, reciting, or reading, suggesting that the distinctions between them may be detected primarily in terms of performance. And the same tunes can be used for entirely different song texts, suggesting a less-than-unbreakable link between music and verse content.

Folk poems of various types—original and traditional, irrespective of performance mode—say a great deal about the perspectives of women and men on their society, and about sociocultural organizations of gender in general. Many religious poetic texts like the *Ramayanas* of India are recited, and probably also authored, by men. In Iran, historical battle poetry is associated with men, dirges and laments with women, and wedding verse is recited by both sexes. Seven of the fifteen "amateur poets" whose gender could be identified in Cynthia Lamson's collection of Newfoundland counterprotest verse about seal hunting are women; one used a feminine pseudonym "Minnie Ha-Ha." However, in the additional categories of published, performer, and public-figure poets, only one

---

Lament

An improvised folksong or poem following a traditional pattern in metaphorical language to express sorrow and other strong feelings and states of mind. Functionally, laments can be classified into wedding laments, death laments, going-to-war laments, autobiographical laments, and recompensive laments.

Laments are nearly always chanted by women and often by professional mourners at funerals, for example. In Europe, the tradition of lamentation has been preserved at its best within the Russian Orthodox Church. Lament chants are encountered, for the most part, east of a line drawn from Greece to Finland, but in earlier periods, they were not uncommon in Western Europe as well. Laments are associated with funerals, weddings, and the departure of soldiers to military service or battlefields. Above all, they are the ritual poetry of parting and separation. Laments belong to the sacred language of a rite. They make it possible to ensure that social relations and values of a delicate nature are handled correctly and with due respect. Although laments are primarily performed in rites of passage, they can also be improvised to be used on particular occasions—for example, when friends meet or part, as thanks for hospitality, as a means to break the monotony of a long and boring job, or just to provide an outlet for a mood of depression. At its best, the performance of a lament is a channel to ecstatic anarchy, helping to penetrate deeply into the spirit of the occasion and normally accompanied by tears, with the chanting interrupted at intervals by sobbing.

Laments originated as a form of ritual poetic keening that comments on social relations. When lamenting, the chanter regularly brings into focus either the subject or the object of the lament. Laments reveal clearly the social position and interaction of participants. Lamenting is regularly practiced during wedding ceremonies and rites for the dead, thus referring to the most important transition periods in social relations. Wedding laments and death laments represent ritual poetry and are a form of sacred communication within these critical moments of transition. By means of these performances, the lamenters and the community seek to pass safely through these delicate periods of transition.

Juha Pentikäinen

---

woman is found, leaving a maximum of nine out of twenty-six writers who could be women.

Though some Eastern European folk poetic traditions have historically been restricted to male bards, many others are strongly associated with women. Women often perform ritual songs associated with weddings, funerals, and calendar customs—Christmas, Easter, Saints' Days, and so forth. In Brazil, the broadside *literatura de cordel* is almost exclusively masculine, since it is a professional activity requiring literacy and conflicting with women's traditional roles. But many forms traditionally associated with men, and misogynist lyrics like those found in many forms of male rap, also offer sites wherein women can express themselves.

The gendering of folk poetry can be deceptive. It might seem that cowboy poetry, relating to a quintessentially masculine occupation, would not be written or performed by women; however, they are performers as well as audience members at cowboy poetry gatherings in Canada and the United States. In the Canadian province of Alberta, women and men write and perform poetry about pioneer life—farming and homesteading—more than about ranching. Much of what is called "cowboy" poetry in the United States may similarly refer to any and all aspects of life on the western plains.

The groups or communities to which folk poetry is directed are extremely diverse. They may be ethnic groups, rural communities, age groups, religious congregations, or special populations like prisoners, friends, families, and so on. Folk poetry is read, recited, or sung because of its expression of ideas and sentiments that the poet or presenter feels will be useful to the community or group to which it is directed. Since gender relations are pervasively significant in all cultures, folk poetry often says a great deal about women and men and their interactions with one another. Take, for example, this song text from nineteenth-century Iran:

Daughters? One is enough.
If there are two, well, Mother is not without help.
If there are three, the ceiling beams will break down.
If there are four, calamity is complete.
If there are five, it is a deep darkness.
If there are six, send out a crier.
If there are seven, think of husbands.
Still, may God bless the girls;
Still, may God's name protect the girls. (Soroudi 1990, 552)

Folk poetry may at times reflect social relations, but it may sometimes also address them adversarially, as in this Brazilian *folheto*, based on the Jorge Amado novel, *Tereza Batista*, in which the male author counters conventional views of sex workers:

The prostitute is a human being
like any other,
Therefore, if treated with respect
she can tomorrow lead
a more honorable life as wife
and mother, no longer dimming
the radiance of the Immaculate
Virgin-Mother of Christ. (Slater 1982, 157)

While not the most progressive view imaginable, this perspective counters the notion that all sex workers are irredeemably damned.

Not all folk poetry by men shows women in a negative light, but such presentation is not uncommon, as in Texas prisoner Johnny Barone's poem about his life experiences:

Once in jail he came to know,
Of his wife and best friend Joe,
She told his sons that he was dead,
Married Joe and shared his bed. (Burns 1993, 45)

The poet makes his wife directly responsible for most of the evil in his life. However, as Roger Renwick noted, folk poets may extol the conventional virtues of women, too, as in verses composed to nurses as thank-yous after a hospital visit, praising their nurturance, kindness, and so on.

A Macedonian wedding text speaks eloquently about the bride's situation:

Give me your blessing, Oh darling father,
for I must leave you for a strange household,
for a strange household, and for strange people.
Though not my father, I'll call him father,
I'll call him father, he'll not say daughter.
Though not my mother, I'll call her mother,
I'll call her mother, she'll not say daughter. (Sazdov 1991, 193)

Many ritual occasions call for focus upon particular female participants. In Luri (Macedonian) wedding verse, the mother-in-law is an ambivalent figure:

O girl, get up, get up, it is better there than here.
The mother-in-law you'll have is sweeter than sugar.
O girl, get up, get up, it is better here than there.
The mother in law in store for you is worse than a viper. (Amanolahi and Thackston 1986, 108)

The previous text also reflects the structuring of much folk poetry in terms of parallels and opposites, as will be discussed following. Luri dirges also reflect gender relations between women:

A mother dies, and a daughter next to her
Spreads her black tresses over the body.

Or:

A daughter and her mother are at the riverbank
When they do not see each other they pine for each other.
And between the sexes:
My grave is narrow, for no brother dug it.
The mourning for me is cold, for no sister wailed.

Or:

Girls with fathers sit in honor;
Girls without fathers welter in blood.

There are often touching commentaries on the importance of women:

Mother, mother, I shall never call you mother again.
You have left me behind like a mountain ewe's lamb.

Cross-culturally, women are frequently placed in the role of mourners, often as semi-professionals extemporizing chanted dirges and/or mourning songs. Irish Gaelic lament poetry—keening—allows a mourning woman to express praise for the deceased. But a woman can also direct anger against a priest who tells her to accept her lot as a widow, against her husband for dying and leaving her, or against the abuser she is burying:

You used to give me
The thick end of the stick,
The hard side of the bed,
The small bit of food,
—That was all I expected. (Bourke 1993, 174)

Much folk poetry paints a bleak picture of women's lives. Ingrian (Finnish/Russian) wedding songs advise the groom to beat his wife, but not to injure her excessively, and indoors rather than publicly. Women ethnographers often un/dis/cover resistance in verse-making traditions. Lila Abu-Lughod shows that Bedouin women's poetry does not indulge in the stereotypical representations of compliant, invisible Islamic women. She cites a Bedouin wedding verse that offers a negative view of polygyny:

Better death, blindness, poverty, and destitution
than a match with a married man. (Abu-Lughod 1986, 217)

Folk poetry about heterosexual relationships is abundant cross-culturally. The Serbian "Death of Omer and Merima" is a tale of family opposition to lovers that ends, as so many of this story type do, with their deaths. In one version, the parallels so often evident in folk poetry take another form familiar cross-culturally—plants growing from the lovers' graves that link the two:

When just a little time had passed,
From Omer springs a young green pine,
Another springs from Merima:
About young Omer's Mera's wreathes,
Like silky thread a nosegay binds;
About both trees, the wormwood climbs. (Zimmerman 1986, 141)

Indeed, much love poetry expresses misery:

Tears won't bring your sweetheart
endure your malady patiently
Tears won't bring your sweetheart
pay no mind and be quiet. (Abu-Lughod 1986, 263)

Or:

The wounds, oh beloved, of your love
heal some days then open again. . . .
My wounds were just about healed
and today oh my torment, they tore open. (Ibid., 264)

But heterosexual relationships are not always unhappy. "Maiden of Kosovo" is about lovers reunited on the battlefield because he recognizes the gold ring he gave her, and she recognizes the gold shawl she gave him.

Misogyny is rampant in folk poetry, especially that which is composed and/or presented by men. But alternative visions are also possible. Dianne Dugaw found cross-dressing ballads throughout Anglo-European and North American traditions, in which bold women become sailors, highway robbers, and soldiers. Though these songs appear to be particularly popular with women singers, men also perform them. Indeed, the almost exclusively male-performed Brazilian *literatura de cordel* includes many texts with a woman-warrior theme. But the attitudes expressed toward such women in these songs cannot be generalized; one singer and audience member might see them as personal role models, where another finds them abhorrent and unfeminine.

In a genre as diverse as folk poetry, it is difficult to locate specific common qualities. Indeed, folk poetry's symbolic and communicative aspects make it richly interpretable. For example, a series of verses that appear in as diverse a group of genres as ballad, lyric folksong, and African American blues, are these:

Who's gonna shoe your pretty little foot,
Who's gonna glove your hand,
Who's gonna kiss your ruby red lips,
Who's gonna be your man?
Papa's gonna shoe my pretty little foot,
Mama's gonna glove my hand,
Sister's gonna kiss my ruby red lips,
And I don't need no man. (Greenhill 1997)

This traditional Euro–North American song text exemplifies the repetitive and paralleling structures that make folk poetry so easy to remember, but it also says much about gender assumptions and relations in Euro-North American society. Most readers/listeners would assume that the first speaking persona is male. He is probably addressing a woman who is his lover or some other relative, questioning her about her economic situation, but also about her sexual availability. The woman's response in the second verse implies familial dependence but sexual autonomy—or even lesbianism.

Folk poetry is highly adaptable to circumstances. Note the extreme semantic shift when the identities your/my are reversed (as is frequently the case in traditional versions of this text):

Who's gonna shoe my pretty little foot,
Who's gonna glove my hand,
Who's gonna kiss my ruby red lips,
Who's gonna be my man?
Papa's gonna shoe your pretty little foot,
Mama's gonna glove your hand,
Sister's gonna kiss your ruby red lips,
And you don't need no man.

Now the first speaker is female, and her questions have become somewhat plaintive, while the second speaker could be male or female, the tone either dismissive or reassuring. The structures of folk poetry make it not only memorable, but also multiply interpretable.

Pauline Greenhill

See Also Ballad; Ethnopoetics; Folksong, Lyric; Performance.

References

Abu-Lughod, Lila. 1986. *Veiled Sentiments: Honor and Poetry in a Bedouin Society.* Berkeley: University of California Press.

Amanolahi, Sekandur, and W. M. Thackson. 1986. *Tales from Luristan: Tales, Fables and Folk Poetry from the Lur of Bâlâ-Garîva.* Cambridge, MA: Harvard University Press.

Bourke, Angela. 1993. More in Anger than in Sorrow: Irish Women's Lament Poetry. In *Feminist Messages: Coding in Women's Folk Culture*, ed. Joan Newlon Radner. Urbana: University of Illinois Press, pp. 160–182.

Dugaw, Dianne. 1989. *Warrior Women and Popular Balladry.* Cambridge: Cambridge University Press.

Green, Chris. 2009. *The Social Life of Poetry: Appalachia, Race, and Radical Modernism.* New York: Palgrave Macmillan.

Greenhill, Pauline. 1989. *True Poetry: Traditional and Popular Verse in Ontario.* Montreal: McGill-Queen's University Press.

Greenhill, Pauline, ed. 1993. Special Issue: Folk Poetry. *Canadian Folklore canadien* 15(1). Also see *intra* Richard A. Burns, "Prison Folk Poetry: The Barone Trilogy," pp. 41–53.

Greenhill, Pauline. 1997. "Who's Gonna Kiss Your Ruby Red Lips?": Sexual Scripts in Floating Verses. In *Ballads into Books: The Legacies of Francis James Child*, eds. Tom Cheesman and Sigrid Rieuwerts. Berne: Peter Lang, pp. 225–236.

Lamson, Cynthia. 1979. *"Bloody Decks and a Bumper Crop": The Rhetoric of Sealing Counter-Protest.* St. John's, NF: ISER.

Renwick, Roger. 1980. *English Folk Poetry: Structure and Meaning.* Philadelphia: University of Pennsylvania.

Sazdov, Tome. 1991. Macedonian Folk Poetry, Principally Lyric. *Oral Tradition* 6(2-3): 186–199.

Slater, Candace. 1982. *Stories on a String: The Brazilian Literatura de Cordel.* Berkeley: University of California Press.

Soroudi, Sorour S. 1990. Folk Poetry and Society in Nineteenth-Century Iran. In *Proceedings of the First European Conference of Iranian Studies*, eds. Gherardo Gnoli and Antonio Panaino. Rome: Instituto Italiano Per Il Medio Ed Estremo Oriente, pp. 541–552.

Zimmerman, Devrnja. 1986. *Serbian Folk Poetry.* Columbus, OH: Kosovo Publishing.

Popular Culture

Materials and activities widely disseminated in a society. Like *folklore*, the term *popular culture* is also used as the name of a scholarly discipline. Popular culture studies involves the scholarly investigation of expressive forms widely disseminated in society. These materials include but are not restricted to products of the mass media—television, film, print, and recording. Thus, popular culture studies may focus on media genres such as situation comedies, film noir, bestselling novels, or rap music. Other, nonmediated aspects of popular culture would include such things as clothing styles, fads, holidays and celebrations, amusement parks, and both amateur and professional sports. Ideally, the study of these or any other popular materials should be done holistically, viewing them both aesthetically and also within the social and cultural contexts in which the materials are created, disseminated, interpreted, and used. In this way, the study of popular culture, like the study of folklore, involves the use of methodologies from both the humanities and the social sciences in the effort to interpret expressive cultural forms, specifically those that are widely disseminated (that is, popular) in a group as part of dynamic social intercourse.

Many definitions of folklore have tended to be enumerative, naming genres such as beliefs, customs, ballads, and proverbs as examples of folklore, thus assuming a self-evident, inherent similarity among them. Some scholars have suggested that folklore is that portion of a culture or society that is passed on orally or by imitation. In 1972, Dan Ben-Amos defined the term *folklore* as artistic communication in small groups. In this formulation, the concept of the small group replaces the "folk" determination, and the "lore" becomes identified as artistic communication. This communication need not necessarily be verbal, but it will be stylized and expressive, thus calling attention to itself. The "small groups" referred to requires that the genre be performed in company small enough in number and in close enough proximity to be able to affect the performance and to contribute to it.

Popular culture, by contrast, has often been equated with the mass media: products of film, television, recordings, and print that are widely disseminated in society or at least created with widespread dissemination in mind. Thus, when a friend tells us a joke, this is, by the preceding definition, a folk event. When we watch a comedian on television tell the same joke, we have entered the realm of popular culture. We can have only indirect influence on the products of mass media, but we can have direct effects on small-scale, interpersonal communications. American scholars often distinguish folklore, or folk culture, from popular culture along many lines, including the communicative nature of the materials themselves: Are they mediated or unmediated? That is, do we hear the story, or listen to the music, or see the dance directly? Can we join in, or are we watching a film, listening to a recording, or looking at a videotape?

Many of those who consider folklore as unmediated, small-group, face-to-face expressive culture and popular culture as large-scale, mass-mediated forms view the two as antithetical. That is, simply put, folklore thrives where the mass media have not taken hold. Conversely, by this formulation, popular culture kills folklore: Where once people entertained each other with storytelling, instead they now watch television. Many see a moral dimension here: Storytelling (or whatever genre of folklore we are talking about) is seen as active and creative, whereas consuming mass-mediated forms is described as passive and numbing. Thus, the former is said to be superior to the latter. Other scholars might view the folk genres pejoratively, describing them as unsophisticated, primitive, or naive.

However, some scholars use the terms *folklore* and *popular culture* more or less interchangeably. Social historians, for instance, who have researched everyday life in medieval, late medieval, and early modern societies (frequently reconstructing popular rituals, festivals, and celebrations), generally prefer the term *popular culture* to *folk culture*, possibly owing to romantic or pejorative associations of the concept of folk. In these cases, culture and society are more likely to be viewed in dichotomous terms, with allowances for overlap between the courtly culture of the socially elite and the popular culture of the masses. Some popular culturalists accept this view, maintaining that only after the Industrial Revolution and its attendant urbanization and the development of a middle class does it make sense to speak of a tripartite model of culture that includes folk, popular, and elite. In this formulation, the folk represent peasant society—a semiautonomous group that depends on a nation-state for at least part of its subsistence.

The point here is not to argue for a specific definition but to indicate some of the ranges of thought that accompany the terminologies employed herein. To a large extent, definitions indicate methodologies: The definitions one works with influence both what is studied and how it is studied. In recent years, many scholars, folklorists included, have begun to look at popular culture not simply as the mass media but also as the popular use of the mass media. Janice Radway's study of a group of women who read romance novels is an example of the application of social science and ethnographic techniques to an area that had been dominated by humanities approaches. In the past, popular genre fiction such as romances would be studied as texts only and found lacking in aesthetic merit as defined by Western European high art critics. Radway (and other cultural studies scholars) expanded the area of study to transcend the written text and to include ethnographic considerations, such as who exactly was reading the novels, when, for what purposes, and what meanings and values they derived from them. In order to determine such things, the readers were interviewed to ascertain their own perspectives on and understandings of the materials. Instead of condemning a genre in which millions of people find something of value, Radway attempted to understand what aesthetic principles were at work and how readers of popular romances themselves understand the texts.

Radway's work and that of others has shown that people are not as passive as was once thought in their interactions with mass or popular forms. In addition, there are a great many areas of overlap between folk and popular culture. As

Youths wearing Halloween masks receive candies and sweets during the "Trick or Treat" tradition in Manila's Makati city in the Philippines, on October 31, 2008. (AP/Wide World Photos)

concepts that refer to social dynamics rather than things, the two feed off each other. The examples in this regard are too numerous to attempt to quantify, but two brief illustrations will suffice. Children's jump-rope rhymes, a folk genre, commonly use well-known celebrities, popular songs, and commercial jingles for their subject matter, and the converse is also true: Many popular songs and commercial jingles are derived from the poetry and song of the streets. Another example would be the relationship of the so-called slasher or stalker films, such as *Nightmare on Elm Street*, to the modern legends in oral circulation that tell of similar horrific killings.

Celebrations of contemporary holidays, life passages, and other special occasions are an area in which many of the various aspects of culture are coterminous. The use of yellow ribbons publicly displayed during wartime is one such example. Holidays such as Halloween are good examples of contemporary phenomena that combine customary behaviors and traditions carried out on the personal level (e.g., trick-or-treating, learning to carve a jack-o'-lantern) with the tremendous commercialization having to do with the marketing of cards, candies, and costumes; media products such as episodes of television programs with Halloween themes or specials such as *It's the Great Pumpkin, Charlie Brown*; mass behavior; and even church-sponsored events and, in certain cases, condemnations.

Both folklorists and popular culture scholars study created, expressive, and artistic materials as their primary data, much as literary scholars take the novel or the sonnet as their primary data. In this way, they are both within the tradition of the humanities. However, the disciplines of folklore studies and popular culture studies differ from traditional humanities studies in that they recognize the existence of alternative systems of aesthetics that guide the creation of popular materials and the evaluation of those materials by an audience. Albert Lord, in his important work *The Singer of Tales* (1960), identified the ways singers of epics in Eastern Europe learn their art orally and how they compose as they perform. He suggested that these performances and the poems themselves be judged according to the specific goals of the artists and the audiences and according to an understanding of the problems unique to an oral poet. In other words, oral poetry is a different genre than written poetry. Each has its own aesthetic standards, and it is misguided to judge one by the standards of the other. Popular culture scholars recognize this principle and extend it to the popular arts, such as television programs, popular films, popular music, best-selling novels, genre fiction (e.g., mysteries or romances), and so on.

Each medium or genre has an audience that can and does make evaluations according to aesthetic criteria. These criteria are usually unarticulated, but they are no less real because of it. People regularly make choices as to which book to read or movie to see and just as regularly evaluate the experience: This was a good thriller, this is a great party song. Because these aesthetic criteria are generally unarticulated, it is the task of the researcher to identify them through ethnographic methods such as interviews and participant observation, as well as humanities techniques such as textual analysis. The term *ethnography* refers to the cultural description of any event or artifact, usually as expressed and perceived by those people who are participants in the event, by producers, consumers, or users of the artifact, or by members of the cultural group in question. After these insider (or native) perceptions and categories are documented, the researcher may undertake the scholarly analysis of the materials as components of a dynamic social and cultural field of behavior. These methods enable the scholar to situate the discussion of any aspect of folklore or popular culture within the larger context of the meanings and values of the society within which it exists—to determine, as Clifford Geertz has suggested, what we need to know in order to make sense of something. Social science methodologies enable the popular culture scholar to root an expressive form in its social context and to uncover the aesthetic system upon which it is judged. Humanities approaches provide models for the appreciation of aesthetic forms and enable the scholar to apply theories of genre and make comparative analytical statements. As social science and humanities methodologies are combined in the study of artistic forms of expression that are broadly based in society, scholars can begin both to provide an understanding of the social and cultural significance of these artistic forms and to determine the aesthetic, social, commercial, and technological considerations that underlie their creation, distribution, and reception. Rather than attempting to determine ultimate worth or meaning according to an imposed value system, scholars have begun investigating the ways in which meaning is created and creativity evaluated. This requires ethnographic research, and it is in the ethnographic study of the everyday uses of mass cultural forms that folklore and popular culture merge.

Jack Santino

See Also Folk Culture; Legend, Contemporary; Legend, Urban.

References

Burke, Peter. 1978. *Popular Culture in Early Modern Europe*. New York: Harper and Row.

Gans, Herbert. 1974. *Popular Culture and High Culture*. New York: Basic Books.

Geertz, Clifford. 1984. *The Interpretation of Cultures*. New York: Basic Books.

Le Roy Ladurie, Emmanuel. 1979. *Carnival in Romans*. New York: George Braziller.

Lord, Albert B. 1964. *The Singer of Tales*. Cambridge, MA: Harvard University Press.

Nye, Russel. 1970. *The Unembarrassed Muse: The Popular Arts in America*. New York: Dial.

Paredes, Américo, and Richard Bauman. 1972. *Towards New Perspectives in Folklore*. Austin: University of Texas Press.

Perez, Domino Renee. 2008. *There Was a Woman: La Llorona from Folklore to Popular Culture*. Austin, TX: University of Texas Press.

Toelken, Barre. 1979. *The Dynamics of Folklore*. Boston: Houghton Mifflin.

Possession

The taking over of a person by an outside spirit. The possessed person may undergo hysterical fits, show drastic changes in physiognomy, go into a catatonic state, show no reaction to pain, or speak in an altered voice that is taken for the voice of the possessing spirit. Often, the subject professes total ignorance of what has taken place during the fit, although the possessing spirit is usually aware of the existence of the subject. The transition into and out of possession is often abrupt.

Possession can occur because, in the traditional view, the human spirit has only a tenuous connection to the body, so that it may be dislodged and replaced by another spirit. This spirit may be seen as a demon, as a spirit of disease, or as a spirit of the dead, sometimes an ancestor of the possessed, that may be either inimical or helpful. Such a spirit is not necessarily exorcised—it may be tamed and domesticated. Also, spirits of disease do not necessarily displace the spirit of the patient; they may simply dwell in part of his or her body and cause pain. I. M. Lewis argues that, where religions have become established and ritualistic, possession is generally most common among people with low status and little power, who may use possession to protest their situation safely since they are presumed to be under the control of another entity. In such religions, an amoral spirit, rather than a representative of the deity, generally takes over the victim. The latter form of possession is discouraged by the episcopal authorities, perhaps because it could alter the revelation on which the religion is based. Joan of Arc was burned at the stake largely for claiming that she was responsible only to God, who communicated with her through the voices of saints and not to the church.

In Western tradition, marks of possession have typically included the ability to speak and understand languages foreign to the patient; a knowledge of things unknowable by natural means; bodily strength exceeding the normal capacity of the possessed; and a revulsion for sacred things, such as relics, the host, and holy water. Such objects may not only prove the possession but also cure it. Typically, however, involuntary possession is ended via the exorcism of the spirit by a shaman or priest. In some cultures, the exorcism may itself be a form of possession: The shaman enters a trance and is taken over by a spirit that causes the offending spirit in the patient to depart.

In Christian history, there have been occasional cases of fraudulent possession. A sixteenth-century woman, for example, went into convulsions on hearing a bishop intoning the first line of the *Aeneid* while pretending to read from a book of exorcisms. It also was recognized, as early as the sixteenth century, that illness might account for the symptoms of possession. Epilepsy was considered a common cause, and many historical cases of possession look very much like what psychologists now call "multiple personality syndrome."

Attempts to view possession strictly as a nervous disorder founder on the fact that possession is sometimes not peripheral, as in Christianity, but actually central to a religious movement, being viewed as a religious experience open to all participants. In Haiti, the *loa*, or god, may take up residence in any participant in a ceremony. Thus, one would have to view entire populations as quite mad in order to uphold the thesis that possession is merely mental illness. Indeed, its principle element, worldwide, seems to be an altered state of consciousness either deliberately or incidentally induced in the subject. Many of the phenomena associated with deliberate possessions (e.g., rhythmical dance and drumming, sleep deprivation, the use of psychedelic drugs) are known to bring about a state of consciousness characterized by dissociation, subjective feelings of timelessness, an alteration of body image, an increased sense of meaningfulness, and greater suggestibility. These experiences, however, are given their particular form and meaning by the individual's culture.

Paul Barber

See Also Divination; Exorcism; Medicine, Folk; Religion, Folk; Shamanism.

References

Lewis, I. M. 1989. *Ecstatic Religion: A Study of Shamanism and Spirit Possession.* London: Routledge.

Ludwig, Arnold. 1968. Altered States of Consciousness: Trance and Possession States. In *Proceedings of the Second Annual Conference, R. M. Bucke Memorial Society,* ed. Raymond Prince. Montreal: R. M. Bucke Memorial Society.

Métraux, Alfred. 1972. *Voodoo in Haiti.* Trans. Hugo Charteris. New York: Schocken.

Oesterreich, T. K. 1974. *Possession, Demoniacal & Other, among Primitive Races, in Antiquity, the Middle Ages, and Modern Times.* Secaucus, NJ: Citadel.

Siikala, Anna-Leena. 1978. *The Rite Technique of the Siberian Shaman.* Folklore Fellows Communications, no. 220. Helsinki: Academia Scientiarum Fennica.

Walker, D. P. 1981. *Unclean Spirits: Possession and Exorcism in France and England in the Late Sixteenth and Early Seventeenth Centuries.* Philadelphia: University of Pennsylvania Press.

Postfolklore

Urban cultural traditions that developed over the twentieth century independently of, or parallel to, archaic and agricultural traditional folklore. The term was introduced by Russian folklorist Sergey Neklyudov in his 1995 article "After Folklore" to denote "city traditions that create their own texts and that function in oral and written forms equally actively." Neklyudov and his adherents consider twentieth-century urban oral traditions to differ from earlier archaic and village oral traditions, and to not fit the traditional canons of folklore, while still manifesting some characteristics of traditional folklore genres.

Other folklorists have suggested terms such as *urbanized folklore, anti-folklore,* and *folklore of the third culture* to denote the state of folk culture in recent decades. Common to all these terms is the idea that the (e.g.) folklore of the New Times differs substantially from what we know as traditional folklore genres. Postfolklore's main characteristics are its urban and marginal nature, its close connection to mass culture, and the frequent "birth" of new genres and texts. Anatoly Kargin and Sergey Neklyudov wrote that postfolklore is "ideologically marginal, polycentric and fragmented, in accordance with social, professional and even age divisions of city residents. . . . In contrast to the local phenomenon of agricultural folklore, postfolklore is becoming national and in some forms even global" (Kargin & Neklyudov 2005).

A postfolklore text is less accessible to those outside a particular urban folk group, for example, prisoners, graffiti writers, or street gangs. For instance, symbolic language and cultural codes of graffiti can be readily understood only by members of particular urban youth groups. Because these traditions function primarily among younger, technologically adept bearers, they are more readily transmitted internationally than is traditional agricultural folklore. Such folk communities are no longer limited geographically, but rather can be global and virtual, as long as members are aware of the symbols and signs of the transmitted texts. As a result, postfolklore becomes more international (universal) then national (ethnic).

Postfolklore is regarded as arising in cities and later spreading to agricultural communities. As a cultural product, postfolklore represents a "combination of urban mass culture, created by 'professionals for sale' and oral traditions, created by urban performers for their own use" (Kargin & Neklyudov 2005). As a result, the main characteristics of postfolklore texts depend on their functions within urban communities. Contemporary urban communities are very different from traditional village communities and this greatly impacts the performers and transmission of contemporary folk culture. In the city, traditional plots do not function as part of an artistic communicative event as actively as they do in the village, due to differences between those communities: in the village, the territorial closeness, the similarity of lifestyle and spiritual interests, make the community much stronger as a traditionally oriented, tradition-preserving unity. In the city, members of a particular folk community are much more flexible, mobile, and influenced by many different factors. Urban folk communities are more mobile and open than are traditional, agricultural folk communities, which are formed by those who are deeply interested in traditional plots and eager to share them with neighbors, friends, or colleagues. In cities, for instance, demonological prose functions as a set of beliefs and superstitions corresponding to the traditional plots and pagan beliefs of previous generations. Communities influence the style, repertoire, and texts of performers.

The fact that the postfolklore concept arose in Russian scholarship is not coincidental. Kargin, Neklyudov, Panchenko, and other Russian folklorists characterized Russian urbanized folk culture as a substitute for traditional agricultural genres and texts, the "death" of which was hastened by urbanization in the 1970s. They wrote that the disappearance of villages and small towns caused the disappearance of an agricultural oral tradition. Alexander Panchenko, for example, argued that as urbanites became a majority of the Russian population (with villagers being "only" 26.7 percent), traditional village culture was marginalized and bound to die out. Large cities absorbed small towns and in the process developed their own oral traditions. As traditional folk communities began to disappear, traditional archaic folklore genres were replaced with a new type of folk culture: "The twentieth century appears to be the period of the final receding of classical agricultural folklore, which is being pushed out by the folklore of other social groups, including social[ly] marginal [individuals] . . . the texts and facts of the traditional agricultural culture are becoming a part of the life of ethnographical museums. This concerns, first, epic genres (historical songs) and fairy tales. Those genres are labeled 'nonproductive,' or 'incapable of creating new forms'" (Kargin & Neklyudov 2005).

The concept of postfolklore prompted active discussion among Slavic folklore theorists. Some supported it with great enthusiasm, some opposed it completely, and some argued merely against the term. V. Pozdneev, in his article "Third Culture. Folklore. Postfolklore," wrote that "the contemporary state of folklore can be characterized as a system of circles which go from the center out: in the center we have archaic genres; farther out, new genres. The old archaic genres are narrowing because new ones are circling around." He characterized the beginning of the twenty-first century not as "postfolklore" but rather as "postfolklore culture," in which all traditional genres are secondary and borrowed from literature. Anikin, an adherent of the literary model of folklore, opposed both the term and concept of postfolklore completely. Panchenko agreed with the concept of the death of traditional folklore but argued that "village culture of the New Times is not much more 'folkloric' or 'traditional' than is the mass culture of the modern city. This is why the terms 'anti-folklore' and 'postfolklore,' suggested by N. Tolstoy and S. Neklyudov . . . do not make much sense."

It is uncertain how well-received the postfolklore idea would be among folklorists of societies in which villages did not play such a persistently overwhelming role historically, or by contrast in which agricultural lifestyles still dominate. Despite twentieth-century urbanization, the mentality of the people is still fundamentally traditional, and it will take a very long time before postfolklore displaces folklore. More likely, they will continue to develop independently and in parallel.

Inna Golovakha-Hicks

See Also Postmodernism.

References

Anikin, Vladimir. 1997. Ne "Postfolklore" a Folklore: K Postanovke Voprosa o ego Sovremennykh Traditsiyakh (Not "Postfolklore" but Folklore: On the Problem of Contemporary Traditions). In *Slavyanskaya Traditsionnaya Kultura: Sbornik Materialov Nauchno Practicheskoy Konferentsii, Vypusk 2*. Moscow: State Republican Center for Folklore.

Kargin, Anatoly, and Sergei Neklyudov. 2005. Folklore i Folkloristika Tretyego Tysyacheletiya (Folklore and Folkloristics in the Third Millennium). In *Pervy*

Vserossiyskiy Kongress Folkloristov: Sbornik Dokladov, Vypusk 1. Moscow: State Republican Center for Folklore: 14–28.

Neklyudov, Sergey. 1995. Posle Folklora (After Folklore). *Zhivaya Starina* 1: 1–5.

Panchenko, Aleksander. 2005. Folkloristika kak Nauka (Folkloristics as Science). In *Pervy Vserossiyskiy Kongress Folkloristov*: Sbornik Dokladov, Vypusk 1. Moscow: State Republican Center for Folklore: 72–95.

Pozdneev, V. 2005. Tretya Kultura. Folklore. Postfolklore (Third Culture. Folklore. Postfolklore). In *Pervy Vserossiyskiy Kongress Folkloristov*: Sbornik Dokladov, Vypusk 1. Moscow: State Republican Center for Folklore: 300–308.

Postfolklore (online folkloristics society). http://community.livejournal.com/postfolklore.

Postmodernism

Various aesthetic and cultural trends that arise in the context of advanced consumer culture and that stand in contrast to modernism. The rapid spread of the term *postmodernism* in academic and increasingly in popular discourse suggests that it has all the attractions and defects of a superficial fashion but also perhaps that it is a response in language to a legitimate perception that our current historical moment has distinctive qualities for which we need a new name. This latter possibility makes a consideration of postmodernism worthwhile in general and of some relevance to folklore studies in particular.

Amid the welter of its applications, one can distinguish three broad uses of the term *postmodernism* that folklorists might want to keep in mind. The most recent and most problematic is its use as an umbrella term for all of the new theoretical and methodological strands that now crisscross the academic terrain of the human sciences. These strands, first woven firmly together in the 1970s (though many of them were spun earlier), are associated particularly with the triumvirate of French theorists Jacques Derrida, Jacques Lacan, and Michel Foucault. Their work forms the foundation of *poststructuralism*, so called not because these scholars reject and abandon the structuralist project but rather because they carry it to some of the logical conclusions that high structuralism did not pursue. In doing so, the poststructuralists have called into questions many of the stabilities upon which previous cultural analysis depended—stabilities of language, of empirical inquiry, and even of the human subject itself. These largely philosophical insights have had a profound effect on the intellectual practice of many disciplines, not to mention on the very nature of disciplinarity itself. Most prominently in literary studies—but for folklorists perhaps more importantly in historical and ethnographic studies—this wholesale reorientation stands at the heart of much current intellectual debate. It is worth noting that whereas structuralism significantly influenced folklore studies, poststructuralist trends have had only marginal impact on the field, though there are indications this may be changing. Of course, the readiness of folklorists to entertain structuralist ideas reflects the fact that structuralism concerned itself early on with folkloric genres such as myth and folktale. Poststructualism has operated largely in the rarified atmosphere of philosophical discourse.

One thing the term *postmodernism* has come to designate, then, is the whole shake-up in academic theory and practice, at the core of which are such concepts as the ultimate undecidability of meaning, the insistence on the "textual" nature of all reality, and the characterization of the human subject not as a vessel to be filled but as an unstable effect of the play of signifiers. In the least appropriate application of the term, *postmodernism* is sometimes used as an equivalent to *poststructuralism*, which refers to a much narrower theoretical phenomenon.

If *postmodernism* has most recently come to refer to the general post-1960s "turn toward theory," its oldest application was in the arena of aesthetics. Dating back as far as the mid-1930s, the term has designated, sometimes positively, sometimes negatively, certain trends in elite culture running counter to the reigning modernism. By the mid-1960s, there began to coalesce an aesthetic stance, if not a single coherent movement, that rejected some of the more austere aspects of modernism in the arts. This new aesthetic privileged fragments rather than wholes, glossy surfaces rather than depth, vulgar ornamentation and bizarre juxtapositions rather than minimalist purity. It also actively blurred the line between elite and mass cultural forms. So-called pop art, best exemplified by the early work of Andy Warhol, was perhaps the clearest expression of what has come to be called Postmodernism in the arts, with the upper case appropriate to its usage as an art historical designation. Although all the standard artistic media— literature, film, theater, music—have generated Postmodern movements analogous to those in the plastic arts, architecture is the medium in which this aesthetic has been most fully developed, to the point that one can legitimately speak of various "traditions" within Postmodern architecture.

In this second application of the term, then, *postmodernism* designates a set of aesthetic inclinations, if not formal principles, manifest in stylistic features that stand in marked contrast to what came before and constitute, at least implicitly, a critique of modernism. Although certainly legitimate in its limited sphere, this usage names only one among many phenomena, including the developments in theory discussed earlier, that are all related as enactments of a whole sociohistorical order. It is as a name for the culture of this embracing historical moment that "the postmodern" seems most interesting for folklorists.

In this regard, a useful distinction can be made between the terms *postmodernism* and *postmodernity*, the former appropriate to specific trends in current culture such as the movements in academic theory and fashions in aesthetic style mentioned earlier, the latter a designation for the whole cultural regime of the late twentieth century. The multiple and various postmodern*isms* are to be understood, then, as local expressions or stagings of a single and pervasive Postmoder*nity*.

The classic statement about postmodernity as a distinct moment in sociocultural history is Frederic Jameson's 1984 essay, "The Cultural Logic of Late Capitalism." Working out of a Marxist tradition, he uses *postmodern* to designate the cultural formations that are inextricably bound up with the most recent phase of the capitalist mode of production. The central institutions and mechanisms of this phase include advanced consumer social relations (the penetration of the commodity form into virtually all spheres of life), a global economic order dominated by massive corporate entities whose power transcends national polities, and a rapidly evolving technology, best characterized by the tele-electronic media, which have made instantaneous information exchange a reality.

The definitive characteristic of postmodernity, an equivalent term for which might be *advanced consumer culture*, is a new and subtly pervasive "depthlessness." Jameson traces this quality in the most fundamental categories of cultural experience: space, time, and human subjectivity. He finds spatial dislocation and intense, "schizophrenic" focus on surface images, an equally intense focus on the present moment and a proliferation of flattened, "historicist" images of past periods, and a new, blankly ironic and unlocalized emotional register to be hallmarks of postmodernity. These and related qualities coalesced as an identifiable cultural formation in the 1960s, though one might argue that the conditions necessary for such a formation were already in place in the 1950s.

Until quite recently, folklore studies had not been significantly affected by the debates over postmodernity, in part, no doubt, because postmodern theorists have focused their attention on elite and mass cultural forms and ignored vernacular expression. This separation may be coming to an end, as folklorists confront the impact of advanced consumer culture on their traditional objects of study. Theorists of postmodernity, by contrast, have been slow to recognize that folklore studies have something to offer their project.

There seem to be two general responses that are the most obvious for folklorists wishing to take *postmodernity* seriously as a name for the cultural environment of advanced consumer capitalism. One is the liberal extension of folklore studies to accommodate the postmodern; the other is a recognition that postmodernity implies a radical shift in thinking about the very status of folklore as a cultural and analytical category. If one accepts that *postmodernity* names an actual cultural phenomenon emergent by the 1950s and now firmly in place in advanced consumer society, then by the liberal principle that folklore adapts to and emerges in all cultural formations, one should be able to speak of a *postmodern folklore*. One might expect, for example, to find new folkloric genres that are made possible by these new postmodern cultural conditions. Mass-communications technologies are the most obvious arena of such emergent forms. Computer networks that allow interactive personal exchanges have shown themselves to be particularly fertile as a new kind of folkloric space.

Another version of this liberal view is a recognition that postmodernity implies new social roles, new classes, and a new political economy that collectively allow for the reframing of traditional folklore forms in the new space of advanced consumer culture. The "folklorized festival" and the various therapeutic movements that draw on the imagery of traditional ritual and other folk practices might be considered examples of this postmodern(ized) folklore, at the heart of which is the commodification of folk images.

Standing somewhat apart from these liberal conceptions of a postmodern folklore that awaits inventory and analysis is the more radical recognition that postmodernity also might imply a condition of culture that discomfits the whole idea of an identifiably separate domain of folklore. The point here is not, as in the old mass culture argument, that folklore is disappearing under the onslaught of homogenized, highly mediated cultural productions but rather that it is increasingly difficult to distinguish the distinctly vernacular sphere one normally associates with folk culture from everything else. Jean-François Lyotard's classic statement about the "postmodern condition" associates postmodernity most basically with the discrediting of the "grand narratives," both cultural and scientific, that heretofore served to represent modern society's collective experience. In their wake, we are left with the fragmentary and circumscribed expressions that are responses to more immediate and localized circumstances. In this view, culture looks increasingly like a collection of pieces—a *pastiche*, to use a favorite term of postmodernists—rather than a comprehensible whole.

Following this line of thinking, one might consider a central feature of postmodernity to be, depending on one's political inclinations, either the thorough colonization of everyday and vernacular experience by the commodity relations of a fragmented but pervasive advanced consumer order or a thorough "vernacularization" of consumer experience in which cultural life becomes increasingly local, personalized, and immediate. In either case, the lines between cultural domains—folk, popular, mass, elite—become blurred more thoroughly than ever before. And whether one accepts these scenarios of postmodernity—indeed, whether one accepts postmodernity as a distinct cultural formation at all—it does seem that local cultures and vernacular experience are coming to occupy a new and more prominent place both in contemporary cultural life as lived and in the academic arena of cultural analysis. Folklorists have some stake in these developments since their training equips them particularly well to deal with such cultural phenomena.

John Dorst

See Also Computer-Mediated Folklore; Deconstruction; Tradition.

References

Connor, Steven. 1989. *Postmodern Culture: An Introduction to Theories of the Contemporary*. New York: Basil Blackwell.

Dorst, John D. 1989. *The Written Suburb: An American Site, An Ethnographic Dilemma*. Philadelphia: University of Pennsylvania Press.

Jameson, Frederic. 1984. The Cultural Logic of Late Capitalism. *New Left Review* 144: 53–92.

Jencks, Charles. 1986. *What Is Post-Modernism?* London: St. Martin's Press.

Lyotard, Jean-François. 1984. *The Postmodern Condition: A Report on Knowledge*. Minneapolis: University of Minnesota Press.

Warshaver, Gerald E. 1991. On Postmodern Folklore. *Western Folklore* 50: 219–229.

Protest

Expression of objection or nonacceptance of a policy, institute, event, or situation. Protest enables an individual or group to make their feelings and opinions of an issue known publicly. Protest is often outside of the realm of political action that is accepted as legitimate.

Protest can be either an individual or a collective effort. It can be either violent or nonviolent in nature. The targets of protest are varied but often constitute a condition or entity that people are unable to escape from or too weak to negotiate with directly. Issues of social justice and ethics are often the motivation behind

Antiwar protesters gather outside the British Parliament in London in 2003 to voice their concern about the Iraq War. (iStockphoto.com)

demonstrations. Protest movements offer commentary on human existence within society and provide opportunities to voice dissent and convey reaction. Movements are diverse and many involve creative means in expressing sentiments and beliefs. Protest carries a connotation of suspicion of authority. Participants in demonstrations are often viewed as subversive and antagonistic. Interests and beliefs held in common unite individuals who rally around these shared values to organize in opposition. An act of protest can simply broadcast an opinion, or it can go as far as individuals taking direct action in an effort to fix or eliminate the problem themselves.

Protest is a common occurrence during periods of war and economic recession. The restriction of self-expression or other rights can also create an atmosphere conducive to protest movements. Such conditions cause feelings of civil unrest among the population of a society and passion or desperation may motivate them to band together and take action. Protest can develop into a major social or political upheaval if it is not addressed properly. An example of this progression is the American Revolution, which evolved from colonial protests over British taxation.

Folklore is an important form of the expressive culture of human beings that folklorists are eager to study. Organized protest movements serve as opportunities for politics and folklore to mix. Banners, buttons, flags, bumper stickers, and posters are several examples of the protest ephemera that is produced. Folklorists also focus on power relationships in societies. Clashes between those with great authority and those who are powerless are common causes and effects of protest.

Types of Protest

Protest comes in various forms including public demonstrations, written demonstrations, and other creative modes. Marches and rallies are public demonstrations that are visible and energizing. Protests at places of employment include picketing, lockdowns, strikes, and walkouts. Occupational protest has an important place in labor lore. Written demonstrations include petitions and letter-writing campaigns. Sometimes protestors circulate censored materials, known as samizdat, as a way of spreading a message. Numerous protests involve the use of civil disobedience as a strategy to communicate opinions and effect change. People may erect tents on government property, refuse to pay taxes, or boycott certain goods. More extreme means of protest include flag desecration, suicide, and hunger strikes. Protest also uses artistic vehicles to convey messages in a powerful way, whether through the performance of a protest song or the creation of literature, paintings, and films that focus on themes of dissent. There are protests within religious traditions, certain occupations, and social groups.

A single person may conduct a quiet protest, passively refusing to accept something he or she believes is unjust. An individual can also carry out a vocal protest by himself or herself. In most cases, however, individuals come together over common feelings of objection and unite to express their emotions.

Major Protest Movements

There have been various protest movements in the history of the United States. The labor movement that followed the industrial revolution in the early nineteenth century was significant. Through the formation of unions and demonstrations such as strikes, the people of the working class were able to protect their rights and negotiate better working conditions and higher salaries. It is important to note that this labor movement set a precedent for the widespread use of civil disobedience as a protest tactic used by large groups of people. America also witnessed the abolition movement that ended slavery and the women's suffrage movement that won women the right to vote. The animal rights movement, the right to life movement, and the fair trade movement are examples of protest movements with a narrow focus.

The largest and most influential protest movement in U.S. history was the civil rights movement of the 1960s. Americans expressed their objection to and abhorrence of the Jim Crow laws that segregated blacks from whites. Important in the American civil rights movement was the use of music as protest ephemera. The "freedom songs" used in this movement were often spiritual hymns that the people modified to use as tools of political protest.

Music and Protest

Protest movements have used music as propaganda and a means of uniting those who hold strong objections to aspects of society. Folk music serves to reaffirm people's beliefs and strengthens existing attitudes in its audience. This genre of music can be used by the disenfranchised and downtrodden to achieve political ends. Folk music was popular in the 1930s and 1940s but lost its momentum as a result of McCarthyism. A revival of the genre occurred in the 1960s.

The protest songs of the 1930s and 1940s were different from those in the 1960s. The earlier songs engendered feelings of connectedness with one another in the face of adversity and support for ideologies. The songs of the revival focused more on cultivating feelings of individualism, independent thinking, and discontent with society overall. The former were composed during a severe economic depression while the latter emerged during a period of relative affluence and growth of the middle class. The adolescents of the 1960s were filled with the spirit of nonconformity and idealism.

Protest songs include those of the civil rights movement. They are an example of both expressive culture and folk art. Protest songs are centered on the concerns and struggles of the ordinary people. Through their lyrics the artists purport to express social and political ideas.

The folk protest movement encompassed a group of individuals who believed that folksingers should act as spokesmen for the common people by expressing their feelings and opinions to the general public. Among its prominent leaders was Alan Lomax, a folklorist. Another important figure was Moses Asch, who owned Folkway Records and had committed himself to recording and preserving the expressions of minorities. Pete Seeger, a well-known folksinger, cofounded the periodical *Broadside* alongside Agnes Cunningham and Gordon Friesen, who were spouses and former members of the Almanac Singers. *Sing Out!* magazine was the key medium for the movement. Its editor, Irwin Silber, was passionate about advocating for the common people and using folk music to give them a voice. The leaders of the movement criticized the vagueness they felt permeated the folk music of the 1960s. Famous folk musicians who wrote and performed protest songs included Woody Guthrie, Bob Dylan, Phil Ochs, and Joan Baez.

Jaclyn Ozzimo

See Also Folk Culture; Folksong, Narrative.

References

Brown, Stuart M. 1961. Civil Disobedience. *Journal of Philosophy* 58: 669–681.

Denisoff, R. Serge. 1970. Protest Songs: Those on the Top Forty and Those of the Streets. *American Quarterly* 22: 807–823.

Denselow, Robin. 1990. *When the Music's Over: The Story of Political Pop*. London and Boston: Faber & Faber.

Dunlap, James. 2006. Through the Eyes of Tom Joad: Patterns of American Idealism, Bob Dylan, and the Folk Protest Movement. *Popular Music and Society* 29: 549–572.

Greenway, John. 1970. *American Folksongs of Protest*. New York: Octagon Books.

Rodnitzky, Jerome L. 1976. *Minstrels of the Dawn: The Folk-Protest Singer as a Cultural Hero*. Chicago: Nelson-Hall.

Proverb

A concise traditional statement expressing an apparent truth with currency among the folk. Defined more inclusively, *proverbs* are short, generally known sentences of the folk that contain wisdom, truths, morals, and traditional views in a metaphorical, fixed, and memorizable form and that are handed down orally from generation to generation. Numerous scholars have tried to formulate *the*

Ukiyo-e print illustration showing Rokurokubi and Mikoshi-nyudo, demons from Japanese folklore, frightening noodle shop customers to illustrate the proverb that "resistance is futile," ca. 1863. (Library of Congress)

proverb definition, ranging from abstract mathematical formulas based on symbolic logic to Archer Taylor's almost proverbial claim that "an incommunicable quality tells us this sentence is proverbial and that one is not." Two major aspects of what amounts to proverbiality should be part of any proverb definition, but they cannot be ascertained from the proverb texts themselves. The elements of traditionality and currency always must be established before a particular short sentence can indeed be called a proverb. This situation is especially vexing when the question arises whether such modern formulaic statements as "Different strokes for different folks" or "Garbage in, garbage out" have reached a proverbial status.

There are, of course, some clear "markers" that help to establish that certain short utterances of wisdom or common sense are, in fact, proverbs. Such markers also assure the memorability and recognizability of the texts as traditional wisdom. In addition to their fixed (and usually oppositional) structure, their relative shortness, and their common use of metaphors, proverbs usually contain some if not all of the following poetic or stylistic features: alliteration—"Many a little makes a mickle"; parallelism—"First come, first served"; rhyme—"No pains,

Wellerism

Traditional expression that includes both a quotation and a putative speaker of that quotation. Most commonly, some contrast, incongruity, or other relationship between speaker and spoken creates humor or irony in the Wellerism, as in such well-known examples as "'I see,' said the blind man, as he picked up his hammer and saw" and "'Neat but not gaudy,' as the monkey said when he painted his tail blue." Wellerisms may also involve punning or other word play. Although the term *Wellerism* is derived from the name of a character who used such phrases in Charles Dickens's *Pickwick Papers* (1836–1837), the genre itself is much older, examples being found in classical writings.

Wellerisms have been considered a type of proverb and have much in common with other types. However, little attention has been given to how Wellerisms may actually function in oral contexts, and their usage may differ in some respects from that of other proverbs. They may be used solely as witticisms, as their appearance in nineteenth-century newspapers along with other humorous filler material suggests (this also suggests that some Wellerisms may have subliterary rather than oral currency). However, like other proverbs, they can be used rhetorically or to comment on life situations. If proverbs in general distance a speaker from a situation commented on (by providing a traditional observation that gives a generalized rather than a personal statement), so may Wellerisms create even greater distancing by providing a fictional speaker. Such may certainly be the case when the quotation element is itself a traditional proverb, as in "'All's well that ends well,' said the monkey when the lawnmower ran over his tail."

Frank de Caro

no gains"; ellipsis—"Once bitten, twice shy"; personification—"Love laughs at locksmiths"; hyperbole—"It is easier for a camel to go through a needle's eye than for a rich man to enter the kingdom of God"; and paradox—"Absence makes the heart grow fonder."

In addition to proverbs that, as complete thoughts, can stand by themselves, there are such subgenres as proverbial expressions ("To hit the nail on the head"), proverbial comparisons ("As drunk as a skunk"), proverbial exaggerations ("He is so tight, his eyelids squeak when he winks"), and twin (binary) formulas ("Safe and sound"). Such proverbial phrases (or phraseological units, as linguists call them) are but fragmentary metaphorical utterances that do not contain any complete thought or wisdom. Although they add color and expressiveness to oral and written communication, they cannot stand alone, as proverbs and Wellerisms do. The latter is yet another proverb subgenre, which is based on the triadic structure of (1) a statement (often a proverb), (2) an identification of the speaker, and (3) a phrase that puts the utterance into an unexpected situation, resulting in a humorous, ironic, or satirical comment. Wellerisms delight in wordplay and puns, and an example such as "'Everyone to their own taste,' as the cow said when she rolled in the pig pen" illustrates how folk humor overcomes the seemingly sacrosanct wisdom of traditional proverbs.

Proverbs in actual use are verbal strategies for dealing with social situations. As speech acts, they must be viewed as part of the entire communicative performance. This is true not only for proverbs employed in oral speech but also for proverbs that frequently appear in literary works, the mass media, advertising, popular songs, cartoons, and comic strips. Only the analysis of the use and function of proverbs within particular contexts will determine their specific meanings. In fact, proverbs in collections without contexts and annotations are almost meaningless or "dead," but they become quite significant and alive once they are used as a strategic statement that carries the weight and authority of traditional wisdom. Proverbs clearly include various semantic possibilities due to their different functions in varying situations. It is precisely this intangible nature of proverbs that results in their continued and effective use in all modes of human communication.

Proverbs have often been grouped according to their content, some major groups being legal proverbs, medical proverbs, and weather proverbs (of which many are mere superstitions couched in proverbial language). Other groups would be proverbs dealing with such topics as the body, health, marriage, and work. Groupings are often rather arbitrary and ignore the multisemanticity of proverbs. Based on structural and semiotic considerations, scholars have begun to group proverbs more systematically, according to linguistic and logical types. This methodology permits scholars to group together proverbs of the same structure (i.e., "Like X, like Y") or of the same logical thought pattern (i.e., texts based on such oppositions as one:two or short:long). Although they might have completely different metaphors and realia, such proverbial signs express fundamental human thought patterns. Grigorii L'vovich Permiakov in Russia, Matti Kuusi in Finland, Peter Grzybek in Austria, and Alan Dundes in the United States have been particularly interested in fitting thousands of proverbs into a limited number of universal proverb types. This structural and semiotic research will facilitate the work of scholars interested in comparative and international paremiology (study of proverbs) and paremiography (collection of proverbs).

It is difficult to know which came first—the study or the collection of proverbs—but clearly, these two major branches of proverb scholarship are closely linked. The earliest proverb collections are found on Sumerian cuneiform tablets from the third millennium BCE. Since then, literally thousands of proverb collections of various sizes and different values have been published. Otto Moll's international *Sprichwörterbibliographie* lists over 9,000 collections and is certainly not comprehensive. The annual bibliography of "New and Reprinted Proverb

Proverbial Phrases and Proverbial Comparisons

Stock conversational phrases that, like proverbs per se, have conventionalized forms but that, unlike proverbs, are not complete statements in themselves. Common English examples are "to kick the bucket" (meaning to die) and "to cross that bridge when we come to it" (meaning to be concerned about some problem or issue when it is actually encountered and not before). Whereas proverbs show little variation, proverbial phrases necessarily change to fit larger grammatical structures used in conjunction with the phrase ("He/She/It kicked/might kick/will kick the bucket"). Closely related proverbial comparisons are phrases that consist of conventionalized comparisons, such as "mad as a hatter" (meaning very mad, i.e., insane) and "dead as a doornail" (meaning definitively dead).

Proverbial phrases and comparisons facilitate spoken communication by providing a kind of "shorthand," that is, by providing speakers with ready-made phrases that identify or "name" recurring situations. Proverbial comparisons always involve metaphor, and proverbial phrases almost always do so also. Thus, a speaker uses a readily understood metaphor to make a point, comparing, for example, not being concerned with crossing a bridge not yet arrived at to some real-life situation in which a problem has not yet been actually encountered. Proverbial phrases may sometimes be used like proverbs to teach a lesson or win an argument or press a course of future action, but they are more likely to be used simply to observe or comment or characterize succinctly. Proverbial comparisons in particular are used primarily to intensify meaning, by introducing into a discourse an expanded frame of reference involving some similitude.

Frank de Caro

Collections" in *Proverbium: Yearbook of International Proverb Scholarship* adds about sixty collections each year that have been published throughout the world. Among those are small popular collections that are produced with the mass and tourist markets in mind. But there are also excellent regional collections that assemble dialect proverbs and provide detailed etymological and cultural notes. Major collections also have been assembled for virtually all languages, from tribal languages in Africa to world languages such as English.

The significant collections differ widely in their lexicographical setups and their materials. Anthropologists, in particular, have collected proverbs from oral tradition, and they usually provide invaluable ethnological annotations without paying much attention to the origin or history of their texts. These collections often are thought of as indicators of cultural values and worldview, and the best among them even present the relatively small number of proverbs in their actual speech acts. This is, however, hardly possible when folklorists, lexicographers, and phraseologists try to amass the entire national corpus of proverbs from different countries. How was Karl Friedrich Wilhelm Wander, for example, to include contextual materials with his 250,000 German proverbs in his massive, five-volume *Deutsches Sprichwörter-Lexikon*? But like other historically interested paremiographers, Wander does include references to all major German proverb collections from the Middle Ages to the nineteenth century, and he also presents dialect variants and parallels from numerous foreign languages.

The U.S. paremiographer Bartlett Jere Whiting has developed a lexicographical methodology for diachronic proverb collections that is now considered as *the* model for any national language collection. In his classic collection *Proverbs, Sentences, and Proverbial Phrases from English Writings Mainly before 1500*, he has arranged the proverbs alphabetically according to their key words (usually the subject noun or a verb). Each entry starts with a lemma that lists the proverbial text in its standard form and is preceded by the first letter of the key word and a consecutive number (e.g., F194 "No fire without some smoke"). The many references that Whiting has located in various early English publications follow in chronological order, and at the end, the author adds cross- references to other scholarly proverb collections. Whiting also uses this system in his invaluable *Early American Proverbs and Proverbial Phrases*, which records the proverbial language used in American writings from the first decades of the seventeenth century to about 1820. Other scholars have followed Whiting's lead, and a number of excellent national proverb collections based on historical principles now exist for French, Polish, and other languages.

There is yet another type of proverb collection that deserves to be considered. People in general and scholars in particular often have wondered about the similarities and differences among proverbs of different languages. Those proverbs that go back to Greek or Roman antiquity or to biblical traditions for the most part have been loan translated into many languages, and they usually exist as identical texts from one language to another (loan translation is the direct translation of a foreign proverb into the "borrower" language). The same is true for many medieval European proverbs that became current as loan translations due to social and commercial intercourse. The tradition of serious comparative and polyglot proverb collections goes back to the late Middle Ages. Today, scholars have assembled impressive collections for the Germanic, Romance, and Slavic languages, for example. A particularly valuable collection of this type is Matti Kuusi's *Proverbia Septentrionalia: 900 Balto-Finnic Proverb Types with Russian, Baltic and German Scandinavian Parallels*. This collection represents a major step toward identifying those universal proverb types that have an international and perhaps global distribution. Proverbs such as "One hand washes the other" and "Big fish eat little fish" are examples of widely disseminated proverbs. But much work remains to be done by comparative paremiographers. A similar collection for the proverbs of the African continent is sorely needed, and there are also no polyglot collections of this value for the Oriental languages.

Although all of this paremiographical work is of great importance, it does, for the most part, ignore the social, cultural, and psycholinguistic significance of contextualized proverbs. Paremiologists and, with them, scholars from such varied disciplines as anthropology, art history, ethnology, folklore, history, linguistics, literature, philology, psychology, religion, and sociology have all looked at proverbs from their particular vantage points. Clearly, paremiologists make it their particular business to study proverbs from as broad a perspective as possible, but the interdisciplinary, international, and global involvement by other scholars is gaining momentum and has resulted in valuable advances in this field of study. Proverbs are basically used by everyone; everyone is confronted by them, and they are verbal nuggets deserving everyone's attention.

As a paremiologically interested folklorist, literary historian, and philologist, Archer Taylor clearly brought his bias to the writing of his undisputed classic work, *The Proverb*. The four major parts of this book deal with questions of origin (classical literature, the Bible, folk narratives, fables, literary works), content (customs and superstitions, history, law, weather, medicine, national stereotype), style (form, poetics, proverb types), and subgenres (proverbial phrases, proverbial comparisons, Wellerisms). The value of this compact volume lies in the fact that Taylor approaches the proverb with an international and cross-cultural perspective and that the work reviews the most important proverb scholarship prior to its publication. It is thus a broad survey of proverbs that, to this day, serves as the best introduction to the fascinating and complex world of these traditional verbal expressions. Similar volumes have been published in Finnish, French, German, Russian, Spanish, and other languages, but those usually concentrate on the paremiological and paremiographical state of research for that particular national language.

The breadth and depth of proverb scholarship is immediately evident from the 4,599 annotated bibliographical entries in Wolfgang Mieder's comprehensive, three-volume *International Proverb Scholarship: An Annotated Bibliography*. His annual supplementary bibliographies of "International Proverb Scholarship" in *Proverbium* list, on average, 200 new entries, an overwhelming indication of the interest in proverbs by scholars from multiple disciplines and countries. Although proverbs can and must be studied regionally and nationally, there is no doubt that comparative international research will lead to additional and more comprehensive insights, as it does in the study of folklore in general. Some proverbs are indigenous to a particular region or country, but there are also hundreds of generally known proverbs that cross national boundaries in their geographical distribution. Classical and biblical proverbs gained such wide currency throughout most of the world, and the process of internationalizing certain proverbs can still be observed today. In fact, twentieth-century American proverbs such as "A picture is worth a thousand words," "It takes two to tango," and "Garbage in, garbage out" have been accepted in English or as loan translations in numerous foreign cultures through the powerful influence of the mass media.

Although anthropologists continue to study the use and function of proverbs among so-called primitive peoples (i.e., those in remote areas of the world where literacy has not yet replaced the reliance on oral communication), scholars have also become interested in the manipulative power of proverbial language in political discourse (debates, speeches, interviews, etc.). Much work remains to be done by anthropologists, especially as regards the apparent dearth of proverbs among the Native Americans, but it is of equal interest to understand how world leaders of the democratic or dictatorial persuasion, such as Winston Churchill, Adolf Hitler, Vladimir Ilich Lenin, and Franklin D. Roosevelt, have used proverbial speech as an effective political tool. The authority of tradition and the inherent claim of expressing truth and wisdom give proverbs in political argumentation a rhetorical power that can make them into manipulative and aggressive weapons. This is particularly the case when proverbs expressing national stereotypes are employed as slurs against certain ethnic or religious minorities, as was done with despicable results against the Jewish people in Nazi Germany.

Scholars studying popular culture and mass media also have begun to include the analysis of proverbs. Quite a number of investigations exist concerning the use and function of proverbs in popular songs (folk, country-and-western, rock-and-roll), in advertising (as traditional or innovative slogans), in journalism (especially as newspaper and magazine headlines), and in various illustrations (caricatures, cartoons, and comic strips). Varied proverbs also appear as so-called anti-proverbs on lavatory walls as graffiti expressing new wisdom, and they certainly have become very popular as humorous messages on greeting cards and T-shirts. The applicability and adaptability of proverbs seem to be without limit. The moment that a traditional proverb does not appear to be appropriate, its wording is consciously changed, though the underlying proverbial structure is maintained. Quite often, popular proverbs are simply reduced to their basic structures, as, for example, "Where there is X, there is Y," and this formula can then serve for an advertising slogan by replacing the variables with the product name. There is thus a steady interplay of tradition and innovation at work here, as Wolfgang Mieder has shown in various chapters of his book *Proverbs Are Never out of Season: Popular Wisdom in the Modern Age.*

Exciting work also is being done by literary scholars, linguists, and psychologists. Formerly, literary proverb investigators were satisfied with publishing mere lists of proverbs found in the works of a particular author, but now they ask far more detailed questions regarding the function, meaning, and communicative relevance of proverbial language in poems, dramas, and novels. Impressive studies exist on such world-renowned authors as Miguel de Cervantes Saavedra,

Geoffrey Chaucer, Agatha Christie, Charles Dickens, Johann Wolfgang von Goethe, François Rabelais, William Shakespeare, and Lev Nikolaevich Tolstoy, but work also is being done on non-European authors such as African playwright Chinua Achebe. Linguists and psychologists join forces in psycholinguistic studies using "proverbs tests" as tools for detecting schizophrenia, measuring intelligence, and establishing employment aptitudes. The whole question of metaphor comprehension and cognition is being addressed through proverbs, as can be seen from Neal R. Norrick's valuable study *How Proverbs Mean: Semantic Studies in English Proverbs*. Paremiology finds itself at the intersection of poetics, linguistics, and psychology, and the resulting studies are significant steps toward a better understanding of human thought processes.

Finally, mention must be made of what Grigorii L'vovich Permiakov has called the "paremiological minimum." This concept describes those proverbs that have the highest frequency in a particular language group. Such minima have already been established through questionnaires for the Russian and German languages, and they consist of about 300 proverbs and proverbial expressions that every native speaker knows well. These findings have, of course, important ramifications for the question of cultural literacy. Clearly, these proverbs belong to the store of knowledge of a culturally literate person, and it behooves language instructors (both native and foreign) to teach them so that citizens as well as immigrants and foreign visitors can communicate effectively. Lexicographers and phraseologists also need to find better ways of including this proverbial language in various types of language dictionaries. With English being *the* world language, its paremiological minimum is indeed of major importance to anybody making use of it. With this issue, the pragmatics of paremiology attempt to find universal proverb types, and perhaps some day scholars even will speak of a global paremiological minimum, that is, a small set of proverbs that everybody knows.

Wolfgang Mieder

See Also Belief, Folk; Speech, Folk.

References

Bryant, Margaret M. 1945. *Proverbs and How to Collect Them*. Greensboro, NC: American Dialect Society.

Carnes, Pack, ed. 1988. *Proverbia in Fabula: Essays on the Relationship of the Fable and the Proverb*. Bern: Peter Lang.

Dundes, Alan, and Claudia A. Stibbe. 1981. *The Art of Mixing Metaphors: A Folkloristic Interpretation of the "Netherlandish Proverbs" by Pieter Bruegel the Elder*. Helsinki: Suomalainen Tiedeakatemia.

Krikmann, Arvo. 2009. *Proverb Semantics: Studies in Structure, Logic, and Metaphor*. Burlington, VT: University of Vermont.

Kuusi, Matti. 1972. *Towards an International Type-System of Proverbs*. Helsinki: Suoamalainen Tiedeakatemia.

Mieder, Wolfgang. 1982, 1990, 1993. *International Proverb Scholarship: An Annotated Bibliography*. 3 vols. New York: Garland.

Mieder, Wolfgang. 1993. *Proverbs Are Never out of Season: Popular Wisdom in the Modern Age*. New York: Oxford University Press.

Mieder, Wolfgang, ed. 1993. *Wise Words: Essays on the Proverb*. New York: Garland.

Mieder, Wolfgang, and Alan Dundes, eds. 1981. *The Wisdom of Many: Essays on the Proverb*. New York: Garland.

Norrick, Neal R. 1985. *How Proverbs Mean: Semantic Studies in English Proverbs*. Amsterdam: Mouton.

Oxford Dictionary of Proverbs. 2008. Oxford: Oxford University Press.

Permiakov, Grigorii L'vovich. 1979. *From Proverb to Folk-Tale: Notes on the General Theory of Cliché*. Moscow: Nauka Publishing House.

Proverbium: Bulletin d'information sur les recherches parémiologiques (Proverbium: Newsletter of paremiological research). 1965–1975. Eds. Matti Kuusi et al., Nos. 1–25: 1–1008. Helsinki. Reprinted in two vols. 1987. Ed. Wolfgang Mieder. Bern: Peter Lang.

Proverbium: Yearbook of International Proverb Scholarship. 1984–. Eds. Wolfgang Mieder et al. Burlington: University of Vermont.

Taylor, Archer. [1931] 1985. *The Proverb*. Introduction and bibliography by Wolfgang Mieder. Bern: Peter Lang.

Taylor, Archer. 1975. *Selected Writings on Proverbs*. Ed. Wolfgang Mieder. Helsinki: Suoamalainen Tiedeakatemia.

Whiting, Bartlett Jere. 1994. *The Origin, Nature and Study of Proverbs*. Eds. Wolfgang Mieder and Joseph Harris. Cambridge, MA: Harvard University Press.

Psychoanalytic Interpretations of Folklore

Technique based upon psychoanalysis, a scientific discipline begun by Sigmund Freud in the last decade of the nineteenth century. Psychoanalytic analysis proposes that (1) events in mental lives are not random, being determined by preceding events; and (2) unconscious mental processes are of great frequency and significance in normal and abnormal mental functioning. According to Freud, consciousness is only a part of mental life, developed out of the unconscious during the early life of the individual and in the evolution of the human species. The approach posits that dreams, neurotic symptoms, myth, legend, fairy tales, jokes, and daily behavior are symbolic substitutes for what we unconsciously desire. To Freudian psychoanalysts, the roots of folklore are to be found in repressed conflicts pertaining to an individual's life experiences. According to the psychoanalytic model, the existence of a universal human psychic unity allows dreams and fantasies of an individual to become incorporated into the folklore of the group.

Freud's work is steeped in anthropological interests as an attempt to show how psychoanalysis could help to explain the origins and functioning of cultural institutions. In the Freudian view, culture is to society as neurosis is to the individual. Freud's followers Ernest Jones and Erich Fromm were practicing psychoanalysts who took an interest in cultural matters. Géza Róheim, George Devereux, and Erik Erikson, trained as psychoanalysts, carried out ethnographic fieldwork. Various studies of folklore have shown that oral, artistic, religious, and gestural expressions of tradition hold clues for the understanding of social structure, socialization processes, and aspects of the mental functioning of groups.

Freud's analysis of the Oedipus myth is perhaps the best-known example of psychoanalytic involvement in folklore. This analysis, presented in *Totem and Taboo*, has influenced attitudes toward applied psychoanalysis. Its principal thesis linked totemism with exogamy and incest with taboo.

Early criticism of the psychoanalytic approach was strong, and it was subsequently dismissed as unrealistic. One of the difficulties in applying classical psychoanalytic theory to folklore is the assumption that the theory is universally applicable. More recent modifications include consideration of cultural context, including expressive culture (e.g., folklore). Folklorist Alan Dundes is among those who believe that important psychological studies of American folklore are made by psychologists and psychiatrists conducting studies among peoples within the context of their own cultures. Thus, Dundes has employed psychoanalytic theory to study folklore as well as popular culture.

According to folklorist Elliott Oring, Freud explained the suffering of one's past, how suffering was engendered, and how the past was divested. The psychoanalytic approach has contributed to the study of folklore in a number of areas. Psychoanalytic models of narrative have yielded understanding not only of performers but also of aspects of socialization and social structure. Fairy tales are recognized in the content of dreams. Myth is deemed a special form of shared fantasy that, constituting a type of adaptation to reality, serves to bring the individual into relationship with members of the culture group on the basis of common psychological needs. Myths and related phenomena are recognized as culturally shared images that serve as screening devices in the defensive and adaptive functions of the ego, reinforcing the suppression and repression of individual fantasies and personal myths. Shared daydreams, when they emerge as expressive culture, are instruments of socialization that lead to a sense of mutual identification on the basis of common needs. From psychoanalytic perspectives, folklore, art, and religion are institutionalized instruments that bolster the social adaptation ordinarily made possible by the dream.

Margaret Bruchez

See Also Freudian Psychology; Jungian Psychology; Psychological Approach.

References

Devereux, George. 1980. *Basic Problems of Ethnopsychiatry*. Chicago: University of Chicago Press.

Dundes, Alan. 1962. Earth-Diver: Creation of the Mythopoeic Male. *American Anthropologist* 64: 1032–1051.

Erikson, Erik. 1963. *Childhood and Society*. New York: W. W. Norton.

Freud, Sigmund. 1965. *The Interpretation of Dreams*. New York: Basic Books.

Jacobs, Melville. 1959. *The Content and Style of an Oral Literature*. Chicago: University of Chicago Press.

Jones, Ernest. 1959. *On the Nightmare*. New York: Grove.

Oring, Elliott. 1984. *The Jokes of Sigmund Freud: A Study in Humor and Jewish Identity*. Philadelphia: University of Pennsylvania Press.

Róheim, Géza. 1950. *Psychoanalysis and Anthropology*. New York: International Universities Press.

Psychological Approach

The systematic application of concepts derived from psychology—such as human cognition, learning, motivation, affect, behavior, unconsciousness, defense mechanisms, and image making—to the study of folklore. Although there are numerous approaches in the discipline of psychology, we may speak of three different types of psychological theories, each adopting an essentially different model of man. These three models are the *Homo volens*, which views man as a creature of striving motivated by unconscious inner urges, the *Homo mechanicus*, which views man as a machine that can be programmed to produce certain responses to specific stimuli, and the *Homo sapiens,* which views man as a rational cognitive creature capable of guiding his own behavior. These models represent psychoanalytic, behavioristic (in the connectionist mode), and cognitive (including "cognitive behaviorism") psychologies, respectively.

Interest in psychological explanations for folklore (particularly in its striking stability) began early in the twentieth century. Psychological speculations by folklorists Antti Aarne, Walter Anderson, and Albert Wesselski and subsequent experimentation on the nature of learning folkloric materials undertaken by psychologist F. C. Bartlett and folklorists such as Anderson and Wesselski did not have much impact on folklore scholarship as a whole. Of the various types of psychological approaches, the psychoanalytic and its derivatives have dominated scholarship in folklore and related fields. This dominance continues to the present, in spite of the often stinging criticisms directed against these approaches. The first systematic challenge to the dominance of the psychoanalytic school in folklore came in 1967 with suggestions for viewing folklore as "behavior" and offering alternate explanations and research processes and methods.

The work of Sigmund Freud, C. G. Jung, Franz Boas, Otto Rank, and other psychologists and anthropologists during the late nineteenth and early twentieth centuries set the stage for more recent approaches to the psychological study of folklore. These pioneering figures viewed folklore and folklife as products of inner psychodynamic processes, such as unconscious imagery and repressed feelings, that function as catalysts for folkloric expressions as well as for personal and culturewide psychological dynamics. During this period, for instance, Freud and his disciples used folklore for much of their analytic work with dreams, fairy tales, jokes, and slips of the tongue. Freud observed the ambivalent reactions of modern people to "something familiar and old-established in the mind which has been estranged only by the process of repression." For him, the distant past, hidden in the unconscious and reflected in folkloric symbols, was particularly evident in folklife and childhood and was regarded as the key to understanding present repressed feelings and urges. This general view of the ties between childhood, the past, and folklore was reflected in the thinking of early American folklorists such as Alexander Chamberlain (1865–1914), editor of the *Journal of American Folklore*, who emphasized this perspective in *The Child and Childhood in Folk-Thought*.

The psychoanalytic approach to folklore around the turn of the twentieth century borrowed the concept of "survivals" from evolutionary theory and psychoanalysis. Although existing in altered form and generally beyond conscious awareness, the traditions of the hidden past were seen to survive for the individual as dreamlike images reflecting a developmental sequence and amenable to mythic interpretation by an analyst. Likewise, folklorists saw a unified cultural past reflecting a series of human developmental stages, or "the varieties of man." Even after this notion had waned in folklore studies, the related idea of a personal past lived on.

In the work of the Swiss psychologist C. G. Jung, for example, notions of a personal and cultural past took on a central position. Delving into folklore and the past represented a significant human activity by which individuals could derive inner symbols and imagery for use in the process of psychospiritual integration, or *individuation*. Jung's influence on folklore studies is still being felt.

The impact of Charles Darwin can be seen in the psychological approaches of folklorists during this period as well, in frequent references to folklore's links with the "history and psychology of man," and the "psychic unity of man" maintaining the natural evolution of culture. At the time, psychological views of folklore conceived of psychology as developmental, addressing the discontent, alienation, and anxieties of modern industrial society.

During subsequent decades, these approaches were countervailed in anthropology and, by extension, folklore studies by behavioristic analyses involving the learned or acquired aspects of cultural and folklore expressions as responses to a given environment. For example, in 1944, Bronislaw Malinowski, in *A Scientific Theory of Culture*, established the "functional analysis" of culture within the framework of a broadly based behavioristic approach. Concerning the scientific perspective of the fieldworker operating under a behavioral model, he wrote, "We understand the behavior of another person when we can account for his motives, his drives, his customs, that is, his total reaction to the conditions in which he finds himself." And two decades later, Melville Herskovits stated that, in psychological terms, culture could be defined as "the learned portion of human behavior."

Concern for the behavioral or acquired aspects of folkloric expressions involved questioning of the individual's role in the postwar Western world. In the impersonal mass culture that arose during the 1950s and 1960s, individuals came to be known less for their backgrounds than for their social behaviors, which could involve multiple identities and roles, and the ability to "put on a front" became a valuable skill in social and cultural relations.

In this context, a greater degree of authenticity seemed to exist in subcultures and traditional folk behavior, which were seen to possess a level of intimacy and value that was missing in mass society. Thus, behavior became an increasingly important object of study for folklorists during the 1960s, a period that witnessed rapid social action and change. Many researchers made forays into the area of day-to-day behavior that was not bound by class considerations. In folklore studies, research methods moved toward the objectivity of behaviorism and away from theory. In such work, researchers drew conclusions from behavioral observation and analysis, which they hoped would lead to a greater understanding of the psychology of folkloric expressions.

Seeking to shift the emphasis in folklore theory from the product to the process, Hasan El-Shamy called on folklorists to "initially concern themselves with folkloric responses (narrating, believing, singing, applying a proverb, or dancing) and relevant social and cultural factors before proceeding to the study of the folklore items themselves (narratives, beliefs, songs, proverbs, or dances)." To achieve the goal, he introduced the concept of "folkloric behavior," noting direct links between behavioristic learning principles such as motivation, context (cues), rewards, and punishments on the performance of established folk traditions (e.g., customs, lifestyle, and verbal lore such as lyric songs, ballads, and proverbs) of an ethnic community in the United States (Egyptian immigrants in Brooklyn, New York). By applying these learning principles, the study established observable and quantifiable relationships between the stability and subsequent continuity of certain folklore items or their disintegration and ensuing disappearance. The learning and retention of folkloric expressions also are affected by factors such as repetition, recency, structure, and ego involvement (or self-reference); this latter factor calls into play individuals' attitudes toward themselves and their possessions, social groups, values, and institutions.

El-Shamy's analysis of Egyptian storytellers revealed that certain folkloric items are ego-involving for particular individuals who view them as their own property and thus are more likely to be learned and remembered. Similarly, entire social, religious, vocational, and ethnic groups or even entire communities or nations may be ego-involved with particular folk items, which they see as reflecting their own identity. The genres or subclasses of responses that are subject to such communal ego involvement include beliefs, myths, legends, memorates, and proverbs. Moreover, El-Shamy showed that the learning and memorization of folktales is a function of the behavioral "law of effect," in which rewards have a "stamping in" effect on an individual's memory and punishments have an opposite, "stamping-out" effect. Similarly, the "law of exercise" operates in folkloric behavior in that learning and retention of folklore items are functions of repetition and recency as well as of the meaning inherent in the structural qualities of the learned material. These latter principles are, in turn, functions of ego involvement, in which folkloric materials offer greater behavioral rewards and thus are more meaningful to the individual.

In another cognitive behavioristic study, El-Shamy applied concepts such as stimulus and response (S-R) theory in discussing the analysis of folk texts. He argued that in using the S-R approach in folklore studies, two aspects of a folkloric response need to be differentiated: (1) the initial response per se such as narrating, singing, dancing, or performing (i.e., the initial action), and (2) the style, "texture," form, and content of that response, which involves examination of the folklore item itself as a whole, or what may be called its *measurement*. In terms of the folktale, this notion may be stated as follows: what makes (stimulus and cues) a person (organism) tell (response) a tale (the measurement of the response), under which conditions (cues), and with what results (effect). This approach holds true for other forms of lore as well, such as folk art and dance.

Around the same time, El-Shamy combined cognitive behaviorism with the psychology of perception and cognitive systems in a study of "the brother-sister syndrome" as embodied in the folktales of traditional Middle Eastern groups. In this work, narratives related to brother-sister interactions and their related cognitive and affective states were shown to reveal a pattern of brother-sister love and affection, husband-wife hostility, sister-brother's wife rivalry, and niece/nephew-maternal uncle affection. El-Shamy used concepts from behavioral and cognitive psychology to show how the narrative components of tale telling in Arab folk groups—that is, the gender and age of the narrator and audience, the direction and routes for communicating a story, the narrative's structure and content, the semantics involved in expressing its various aspects, and the symbols contained in it—all relate to the tale's affective content, as well as to the expression of sentiments within the traditional Arab family.

Taken separately, each of these factors by itself may not have sufficient power to determine the motivating force for telling a tale, but together, they reflect the general nature of that force. In other words, the folk narrative is viewed as a response to specific stimuli or an integrated behavioral event in which motivation (stimuli, wants, or goals) and intermediary stimuli (cues, or the context in which narration occurs), as perceived by the narrator, invoke the tale. Thus, the folktale as a whole may be seen as the measurement of that response and an instrument for accomplishing the narrator's goals. Moreover, both the affective and cognitive elements of the narrative are seen to parallel other cognitive systems, schemata, or worldviews typical of the narrator and his or her cultural group.

The motivating force that determines the sequencing of events in traditional Arab tales reflecting the brother-sister syndrome is that the brother and sister desire to be together. The narrator perceives this force and behaves within its framework. With the fulfillment of the brother's and sister's wishes at the end of the tale, the underlying motivation diminishes in power, and the story reaches a conclusion that is emotionally satisfying to both narrator and listeners.

El-Shamy supported his views on the brother-sister syndrome in Arab folktales through numerous examples from the Middle East and North Africa, all of which reflect the international folktale type AT 872: "Brother and Sister." His study aimed to establish the extent to which this tale type is "an integrated cognitive system," in which the various parts of the tale are interconnected and congruent with each other and the tale operates as functional social behavior that helps to realize the narrator's goals. Thus, El-Shamy combined concepts from cognitive psychology (e.g., "integrated cognitive system") and behaviorism (e.g., the narrator's goals) to show that AT 872 represents an interpersonal behavioral event and is "an integrated instrumental (goal-oriented) social act."

In recent decades, directly cognitive approaches to folk expressions and symbols have emerged in folklore studies as well. Henry Glassie, for example, examined the trend toward symmetry and enclosure in folk housing in colonial Virginia as a cognitive-affective need for order in the midst of perceived chaos during the American Revolution. Similarly, Michael Owen Jones has analyzed the transformations in the cognitive schemata of a folk artisan, a maker of handmade furniture. Jones noted that when this craftsperson worked near crowded urban areas, his cognitive schemata and work reflected a sense of enclosure. But when "drawn back into the countryside, his chairs opened up," which Jones interpreted as a change in cognitive-affective states.

Another area of inquiry derived from cognitive psychology that has been addressed recently in folklore scholarship is memory storage and retrieval, specifically, memory for stories. Robert A. Georges examined the complementarity and conflict between folklorists' and psychologists' views on memory, challenging the long-standing notion that individual folklore items are simply stored in "inventorylike fashion" for subsequent retrieval on command. In contrast to this view, Georges stated that many folklorists and psychologists are adopting a more dynamic, generative, context-specific model of memory, supported by data from neuroscience. And yet others favor neither the static storage-and-retrieval model nor the dynamic and generative view. Instead, these researchers posit that memory may be both stable and variable, depending on the situation. Implicit in such a view are the assumptions that what is most readily remembered in a given item of folklore is its "basic plot or central theme, while what is likely to be forgotten and perhaps replaced are specifics and details." This approach is widespread in folklore studies, with those parts of stories or songs that are best remembered being identified variously as "normalforms," "kernel stories," "emotional cores," or "ideational cores." Georges pointed out that, whatever the model or approach a folklorist adopts, memory is a central concept in folklore studies and deserves to be examined and discussed more vigorously in future research and theory in the field. He stated that folklorists have the experience and skills needed to test hypotheses and assess generalizations made by nonfolklorists, as well as the responsibility to reveal to nonfolklorists theories about memory that have guided and emerged from their own inquiries.

Other psychological concepts that have influenced folklore studies in recent years have come from the area of social psychology. For instance, the concept of "conduit" proposed by Linda Dégh and Andrew Vázsonyi, in their influential "The Hypothesis of Multi-Conduit Transmission in Folklore," is essentially the social psychological technique of "sociogram." Robert A. Georges discussed "communicative role and social identity in storytelling," noting that since the 1970s, folk narratives have begun to be studied as social behaviors, such as "communication," "interaction," "performance," and "art." And folktales have been seen as "situated in" and "emergent from" cultural or social contexts, with narrators being described as "performers," "artists," and "followers or trans-formers of rules." Georges saw such trends as a move toward a new model of folklore studies emphasizing the social behavior of participants in storytelling, as opposed to the older text-transmitting-and-receiving model. He felt that the conceptualizing and identifying of tale narration or storytelling as a panhuman, role-based communication mode, with participants' behaviors being determined by manifestations of their communicative roles and identities, "provide part of the intellectual foundation for an alternative model for folk narrative research." Such a psychologically based approach counters the culture-based construct that has dominated folklore studies for many decades, which assumes that folk narrators and other performers identify themselves exclusively in cultural terms.

The emotional aspects of folk narrative also have been discussed in the psychological approaches of numerous folklorists, who have used ideas and principles derived mainly from psychoanalysis and neopsychoanalytic schools. Such efforts generally have focused on the panhuman, hereditary, or archetypal bases for the origin and continuity of "emotional" patterns in folktales. Other work has employed vaguely defined concepts, such as feelings, attitudes, love, hate, and affect.

However, two general aspects of the emotional experience are of special importance in folklore research and may be defined and used precisely: *emotions* and *sentiments*. These terms have been used in the folklore literature interchangeably, but recent psychological research differentiates them from each other. Emotions may be defined as complex arousals that stem from an organism's attempts to cope with a given environment. They emerge through disturbance or sudden success in activities basic to biological survival and well-being, being acute, intense, and often disruptive in nature. By contrast, sentiments are affective experiences with a cognitive basis, such as patriotic, religious, ethical, aesthetic, or intellectual ideas, and they are based on past life experiences and education. They are usually enduring and should be distinguished from transient cognitive experiences, such as the memorization of facts for academic purposes. Given these definitions, behavior in folk narratives that depicts sudden, intense, disruptive affective experiences largely connected with basic biological needs may be seen as describing emotions. Examples of this group include AT 1119 ("The Ogre Kills His Own Children") and AT 931 ("Oedipus"). Another application of the psychological approach to folklore is the recent adoption of key principles from cognitive psychological literature as classificatory devices, especially as motifs recurrent in "folk literature" and other facets of traditional community life. The assumption here is that if a psychological theory is "correct," with reproducible results, it must be applicable to instances of actual living experiences as portrayed in the cultural sphere that emphasizes the stable reproducibility of traditions (i.e., folklore). Although Stith Thompson had expressed some doubts in this regard (probably with reference to the psychoanalytic approach), there are indications that such psychological (and sociological) concepts do recur in folk expressions as a matter of empirical observation by folk groups and that they can be of significant classificatory (indexing) usefulness. Examples of these newly devised motifs are the following:

- A1241.5.1§, "Physical and personality attributes (temperament) are determined by characteristics of the earth from which the first man was created"
- J10.1§, "Persistence of first (primary) impressions"
- J10.1.1§, "Unforgettable first experience"
- J19§, "Knowledge acquired from experiencing the suffering of others"
- J20§, "Conditioning: effects associated with past experience cause man (animal) to respond accordingly (conditioned response)"
- J20.1§, "Memory of painful experience causes animal to flee (feel pain)"
- J148§, "Teaching (learning) through repetition"

- P798§, "Characteristics of social interaction within triads"
- P798.1 §, "Unbalanced (unstable) triads"
- P798.1.0.1 §, "Triads revolving around father and mother as unbalanced (Oedipus)"
- P798.1.0.5§, "Triads revolving around brother and sister as unbalanced (Sethian syndrome)"
- P798.1.1 §, "Conflict within a triad: one party is removed so as to restore stability (balance)"
- P750.0.1 §, "Basis for social differentiation and stratification"

The application of these psychologically oriented motifs (and related tale types) to bodies of cross-cultural primary data should help bridge the gap between the data used in theory building in folklore scholarship, on the one hand, and the contents of lore itself, on the other.

Besides the realm of research and theory in psychology, the applied areas of the field also have had an impact on folklore studies over the decades. For instance, Freudian psychoanalysis and Jungian analytic practice, as noted earlier, have had a noticeable influence on folklorists.

Also, the general topic of mental health and illness in traditional cultures has been examined by numerous researchers and theorists. Preventive and therapeutic folk practices, including the beliefs, values, and techniques of shamans and faith healers as well as the contrast between ideas and methods used in scientific psychiatry and folk treatments in traditional settings and the successes and failures of folk healing all have been addressed.

Another area of applied psychological theory is the use of folklore in curriculum development in elementary and high school education. It is hoped that the ego-involving aspects of lore will induce students to learn more and faster.

Clearly, folklorists need not seek explanation in a single type of psychological theory adopting only one of the three models of humans cited earlier and excluding the other two. As psychology has matured as an intellectual discipline, there is recognition that humans are a synthesis of all three models: *Homo volens*, *Homo mechanicus*, and *Homo sapiens*.

Hasan El-Shamy

See Also Freudian Psychology; Jungian Psychology; Psychoanalytic Interpretations of Folklore; Worldview.

References

Bronner, Simon J. 1986. *American Folklore Studies: An Intellectual History*. Lawrence: University of Kansas Press.

Dégh, Linda. 1995. *Narratives in Society: A Performer-Centered Study of Narration.* Folklore Fellows Communications, no. 255. Helsinki: Academia Scientiarum Fennica.

Dundes, Alan. 1979. *Analytic Essays in Folklore.* The Hague: Mouton.

El-Shamy, Hasan M. 1967. Folkloric Behavior: A Theory for the Study of the Dynamics of Traditional Culture. PhD dissertation., Indiana University, Bloomington.

El-Shamy, Hasan M. 1979. *Brother and Sister Type 872*: A Cognitive Behavioristic Analysis of a Middle Eastern Oikotype.* Folklore Monograph Series, no. 8. Bloomington, IN.

El-Shamy, Hasan M. 1995. *Folk Traditions of the Arab World: A Guide to Motif Classification,* 2 vols. Bloomington: Indiana University Press.

Georges, Robert A. 1990. Communicative Role and Social Identity in Storytelling. *Fabula* 31: 49–57.

Glassie, Henry. 1975. *Folk Housing in Middle Virginia: A Structural Analysis of Historic Artifacts.* Knoxville: University of Tennessee Press.

Herskovits, Melville J. 1964. *Man and His Works: The Science of Cultural Anthropology.* New York: A. A. Knopf.

Jones, Michael Owen. 1975. *The Hand Made Object and Its Maker.* Berkeley: University of California Press.

Jung, C. G. 1958. *Psyche and Symbol: A Selection from the Writings of C. G. Jung.* Ed. Violet S. de Laszlo. New York: Doubleday.

Luchins, Abraham S. 1964. *Group Therapy: A Guide.* New York: Random House.

Public Sector Folklore

The presentation and interpretation of folklore outside its original context. The term *public sector folklore*, in use since approximately 1980, can be taken in either a narrow or a broad sense, according to Archie Green. The narrow sense emphasizes certain types of activities carried out by folklorists to present folklore to "the public," together with the host institutions that house and support such activities. In this sense, public sector folklore includes distinctive research and presentation activities (including the production of festivals or live performances, media programming, exhibitions, publications, and other educational programs) that have flourished in large part since the early 1970s but that have important earlier roots; these activities are carried on by folklorists working primarily outside academic life, in arts councils, museums, historical societies, and other public or quasi-public institutions.

Robert Baron and Nicholas Spitzer's *Public Folklore* gives a concise statement of a broader view of the term: "Public folklore is the representation and application of folk traditions in new contours and contexts within and beyond the communities in which they originated, often through the collaborative efforts of tradition bearers and folklorists or other cultural specialists."

In this instance (though these authors use a slightly different term), public sector folklore includes *all* activities, since the beginning of the discipline over a century ago, that have represented or applied folk traditions in some new way or to some new audience. In this light, any or all of the following contemporary phenomena can be understood as public sector folklore:

- an audio-illustrated class lecture on polka music
- a demonstration of a Cajun-style *boucherie* (traditional hog butchering) by south Louisianans to a busload of northern tourists
- a book-length study published by a university press about folk traditions in women's domestic work
- a collaboration among traditional sweet grass basket makers, folklorists, and natural resource specialists to ensure that those artists' access to necessary materials, threatened by urban development, is ensured
- a community-sponsored project to find and document the work of local quilters and other needle artists for exhibition at the local library or historical society

Though the following comments concentrate on public sector folklore work in the United States, it is important to remember that there is a long history of such work abroad, often stressing what European scholars call *folklife*: the material and customary culture of (increasingly marginal) rural groups. Since the early years of this century, European governments in particular have supported intensive, systematic folklore research and the maintenance of national archives of documentary materials drawn from that research. What is more, they also have developed living folk museums representing historical periods in material and cultural life through reconstruction and reenactment. And, especially during the Iron Curtain era in the former Eastern bloc nations, they have trained and toured performing ensembles, presenting nationalized amalgams of regional music and dance styles as governmentally sanctioned evidence of a proud peasant past undergirding the socialist present and future.

In the United States perhaps even more than abroad, the history of public sector folklore is coextensive with the history of the entire field of folklore. For its first fifty years, the field was broadly public in its orientation, though the term *public sector folklore* was not used to describe any folklore work until around 1980. During its earliest years of development (circa 1880 to 1900), the discipline of folklore in the United States was shaped as much by folklorists working in public institutions (e.g., the Smithsonian Institution, the Bureau of American Ethnology, and the American Museum of Natural History) and by talented, thorough, and articulate amateurs as it was by university faculty or by private scholars. During the depression years, several branches of the Works Progress Administration's arts projects—most notably, the Federal Writers' Project, the folklore activities of which were coordinated by Benjamin Botkin in the late 1930s—devoted attention to collecting and disseminating American folk expression.

However, between the late 1940s and the late 1960s, public sector folklore generally fell out of favor within the larger field. During these years, many university scholars involved in focused, dedicated efforts to establish folklore as a significant university discipline argued that public sector folklore's "popularization" of folk expression weakened not only the material of folklore but also the discipline's own chances for academic respectability—and the departmental territory, research grants, and other professional benefits that respectability could bring. In effect, the increasing power of the field of folklore as an academic discipline was purchased at the cost of the wholeness of that part of the discipline and of its connection with a broader public. At the same time, however, the products of the "popularizers" of folklore—including Botkin's various *Treasuries* volumes, Sarah Gertrude Knott's annual National Folk Festivals (which began in 1934 and continue in changed form today), and local folk dance participation activities throughout the country—were indeed popular, then and now. To this day, Americans' ideas about folklore have been shaped and reinforced far more by such popular work than by the academic activities of folklorists.

A movement toward *applied folklore*, the use of folklorists' skills and knowledge for projects of social reform in the communities they study, took place within the American Folklore Society in the late 1960s and early 1970s. Based in leftist movements of the 1960s joining intellectual and political life, such work went beyond the presentational activities of public sector folklore. But once again, voices idealizing "detached, objective" scholarship held sway, and the applied folklore movement effectively ceased to be, not to be resurrected until the "cultural conservation" movements of the middle 1980s.

Even viewed in the context of this long history, the 1970s saw an unprecedented explosion of work in the public sector, most of it funded by federal and state governments. In 1967, the Smithsonian Institution began presenting an annual Festival of American Folklife, directed by Ralph Rinzler, on the National Mall—the nation's ceremonial axis—in Washington, DC. Initially a weekend's performance of traditional music, it soon grew into a two-week exploration of various forms of folk performing, material, narrative, and customary traditions from throughout the United States and the world. In the nation's bicentennial year of 1976, in fact, the festival ran for twelve weeks and featured the folk traditions of scores of cultural groups from all the states and territories and dozens of other countries. Moreover and equally important for the history of public sector

Colombian women's singing group at a Las Americas venue at the Smithsonian Folklife Festival on the Mall in Washington D.C., July 2, 2009. (Richard Gunion/Dreamstime.com)

folklore, the festival (particularly the enormous 1976 undertaking) has served as the annual training ground for young public sector folklorists.

Their mid-1970s Smithsonian experience enabled these young folklorists to occupy the dozens of "state folklorist" posts and other more local public sector folklore positions that were created between 1975 and 1990. Most of these positions are located in state arts councils (and a minority in state humanities councils, historical societies, departments of culture, or other similar agencies), and, like state arts councils themselves, they were a direct result of the initiative of the Folk Arts Program (now renamed the Folk and Traditional Arts Program) of the National Endowment for the Arts (NEA).

The Folk and Traditional Arts Program began in 1974 and, over the next several years, grew from within the NEA's special projects office to take on independent status. It was headed until 1976 by Alan Jabbour, folk music scholar and former head of the Library of Congress's folk music archive, and from 1977 to 1992 by Bess Lomax Hawes, who joined the NEA following an extensive career in folklore as a collector, performer, teacher, and writer. Longtime deputy Dan Sheehy took over direction of the program after Hawes's departure.

Early in the program's history, the staff set several objectives, including that of firmly establishing folklore in the landscape of public support for culture and the arts. In part, they went about achieving that objective by offering grants to state arts councils to establish folk arts programs, staffed by professional folklorists, to serve artists and art forms not served by state councils' more typical music and visual arts programs. In this way, the Folk and Traditional Arts Program has attempted to do in the world of government what academic folklorists had attempted to do in the world of universities: establish institutional territory but, in this case, without needing to disparage other aspects of folklore work.

For reasons ranging from a belief in the necessity of support for folk expression to a desire for federal funds, many state arts councils and other agencies took advantage of this NEA support. Among the first states to begin folk arts programs were Alabama, Florida, Maryland, North Carolina, Ohio, Oregon, Tennessee, and Utah. These programs' early activities—more often than not, statewide folk festivals or folk arts exhibitions, both based on field research and documentation—were intentionally chosen to establish visibility and territory for folk arts, folk artists, and folklorists. Since both were considered comparable in impact, the choice between them, in fact, was often determined by the interests of the new state folklorist or by the preferences of state arts council directors or boards.

Each of these presentational modes has its advantages and disadvantages. Folk festivals tend to be large and therefore highly visible, and as celebratory media, they are associated in the public mind with fairs, outdoor concerts, and other visually and programmatically similar events. To be sure, exposure and celebration are powerful cultural tools, especially when festival artists and audiences come from different cultural backgrounds. Nevertheless, festival producers' educational aims are often frustrated by audience perceptions of these events as primarily for entertainment—again, as are state fairs and other celebratory events. Festivals' presentational settings and techniques have concentrated on (and the wandering behavior of festival audiences favors) performing artists as opposed to craftspeople and large-scale events as opposed to intimate ones. Finally, festivals tend to be quite expensive and can be short-lived and ephemeral unless plans are made to build more lasting community programs on the foundation of festival celebrations or to extend the life spans of festivals by tours, residencies, and other movable or smaller-scale presentational activities.

Exhibitions, by contrast, favor the presentation of material culture. They can be broader and more flexible in approach, devoting attention to dimensions of medium, theme, cultural and social context and the development of a tradition over time that are often difficult to convey effectively in live events. Exhibitions can travel to several sites and thus reach more diverse and larger audiences, and exhibition catalogs, when carefully prepared, become valuable, permanent educational products. Without creative conception and design, however, exhibitions can become only static inventories of objects that do not convey the vitality and depth of their home traditions and communities.

Since the mid-1970s, state folk arts programs have built on this heritage to design and produce their own locally appropriate repertoire of activities. These include conducting and documenting field research; providing advice and assistance to folk artists; producing festivals, exhibitions, media programs, publications, educational residencies, and other public presentations; and giving grants to artists and community-based organizations. Committees of public sector folklorists conducted surveys of these state programs' funding and activities in 1983, 1984, 1989, and 1994 for the Folk and Traditional Arts Program and the Public Programs Section of the American Folklore Society (the society's interest group for public sector folklorists).

At present, forty-eight of the fifty-six states and territories have such programs. Their increasing establishment and maturity—and funding—also has supported the growth, especially since the mid-1980s, of a significant number of public folk cultural programs in cities and counties that concentrate on local artists and traditions. Finally, several of the regional consortia of state arts councils, which foster cooperative activities among the states (the Mid-Atlantic Arts Federation, the New England Foundation for the Arts, the Southern Arts Federation, and the Western States Arts Foundation), now include folk arts among their presentations and folklorists on their staffs.

Since the mid-1970s, the NEA Folk and Traditional Arts Program has shaped the public sector folklore landscape in other ways. The program gives grants throughout the country to community-based nonprofit organizations for the presentation and media documentation of traditional arts and artists, as well as for various services to the field. In the late 1970s and early 1980s, the program supported regular meetings of state folklorists in Washington, DC, and more recently has convened meetings and designed projects on support for crafts and craftspeople, on folk arts in education, and other special topics. The program pioneered the awarding of small grants to support apprenticeships in the folk arts, and it has passed on to many states the responsibility and the funding to continue such programs. In 1982, the program began honoring the nation's finest and most respected practitioners of tradition through an annual set of a dozen or more National Heritage Fellowships, thereby also giving larger visibility to folk tradition and the field of folklore.

During this same period, other federal programs were created or expanded. An intensive lobbying effort, spearheaded by Archie Green, for a federal institution specifically devoted to folklore led to the passage of the American Folklife Preservation Act in 1976, which established an American Folklife Center to be housed in the Library of Congress to "preserve and present American folklife," in the language of the act. In 1978, the center incorporated the Library's Archive of Folk Culture, created in 1928 as the Archive of Folksong and directed, over the years, by several of the most significant "popularizers" of American folk culture: John Lomax, Alan Lomax, Benjamin Botkin, and Duncan Emrich. The center, directed by Alan Jabbour since its establishment, carries out its own program of team field research projects, archival organization and preservation, reference services, conferences, educational programs and publications, and services to the field.

Since the publication in 1983 of its study *Cultural Conservation: The Protection of Cultural Heritage in the United States*, the center also has devoted effort to working out the implications of the concept of "cultural conservation." This concept is both an end—the expression of an ideal, in thinking and planning, of concern for the processes and products of everyday culture—and a means—a way of saying "folklore" to professionals and policy makers in other fields in a manner they are more likely to understand.

The National Endowment for the Humanities, since it is not internally organized according to humanities disciplines, has no folklore program or staff positions per se. However, NEH has had folklorists on its staff for some years who serve as important advisers to and conduits from the field.

The Festival of American Folklife, originally produced by the Smithsonian's Division of Performing Arts, became a production of the newly created Office of Folklife Programs in 1976. In 1987, the office acquired the enormous recorded holdings of Moses Asch's Folkways Records after Asch's death. It now both distributes existing Folkways recordings and vigorously issues new recordings under its Smithsonian Folkways label.

In line with the recent development of interdisciplinary university programs and scholarly journals in "cultural studies," the office was renamed the Center for Folklife Programs and Cultural Studies in 1992. In addition to the annual festival and ongoing recording activities, the center produces documentary publications and films and works closely with the cultural groups featured in the festival to plan continuing folk cultural programs in their home communities. Among its other activities is an annual workshop, coinciding with the festival, to bring folklorists together with "community scholars" (those many skilled and devoted nonprofessionals with a long history of commitment to documenting, presenting, and supporting local folk traditions) to exchange the useful philosophies and practices developed by both groups.

This same twenty-year period has seen the development of energetic private, nonprofit organizations engaged in local, state, or national folklore research and programming. The oldest of these—actually founded well before this period—is the National Council for the Traditional Arts (NCTA) in Silver Spring, Maryland. Founded by Sarah Gertrude Knott in 1934 as the National Folk Festival Association to produce the event of the same name, the organization was essentially devoted only to that project until recently. Since beginning in the early 1970s, NCTA (under the direction of Joe Wilson) has designed and tested many new models for the presentation of (mostly performing) folk arts. Most notable among these is the "inreach" tour, which presents respected local performers to other communities around the country or world that share the performers' culture (as opposed to "outreach" tours, much more common in the mainstream arts world, that present performances to culturally unfamiliar audiences).

Several private, nonprofit organizations, headed by former state folklorists, carry on work once done by public sector programs in their state's government, as well as newer, unique programs. These include the Alabama Center for Traditional Culture, Texas Folklife Resources, the Vermont Folklife Center, and the Western Folklife Center in Elko, Nevada. Similar organizations focused at the community level include City Lore and the Ethnic Folk Arts Center in New York City, Cityfolk in Dayton, and the Philadelphia Folklore Project. In addition, many other arts, cultural, and educational institutions support their own public sector folklore and folk arts programs, from the California Academy of Sciences in San Francisco to the Institute of Texan Cultures in San Antonio and the McKissick Museum at the University of South Carolina in Columbia. Finally, several folk museums and historical archaeology sites—among them the Conner Prairie Pioneer Settlement outside Indianapolis, the Jensen Living Historical Farm in Logan, Utah, the Museum of American Frontier Culture in Staunton, Virginia, and Plimoth Plantation in Plymouth, Massachusetts—carry on in the European tradition by presenting reconstructions and reenactments of rural folklife.

This network of public sector folklorists and institutions keeps written track of itself through the twice-yearly issues of the *Public Programs Newsletter*, the periodical of the American Folklore Society's Public Programs Section. A typical example of the *Newsletter*, the first issue of 1993, ran to eighty-seven double-column pages and contained discussions of cultural conservation matters and other professional issues, news of public sector activities throughout the country, and a directory of 177 entries for public sector folklore programs and independent folklorists. By contrast, the American Folklore Society's *Journal of American Folklore (JAF)*, as well as other significant American folklore serials (*Western Folklore, Southern Folklore*) have devoted relatively little attention to public sector folklore, at least until recently. *JAF*, for instance, now prints reviews of some public sector presentations—exhibitions, festivals, and the like—and has included several articles on issues of authenticity and representation that draw on public sector experience.

The society's annual meeting in late October, however, is the largest gathering of public sector folklorists in the country. Since the late 1980s, about one in every eight sessions at the meeting has been explicitly "about" public sector folklore. (At the 1993 meeting, for example, 14 sessions of 115 total, at least one during every time slot in the program fit this description.) Many others are informed by current work in this area but have been given some other title. Other regional meetings offer more focused gatherings: Public sector folklorists from the Western states have met in parallel with Utah State University's annual Fife Folklore Conference since around 1980, and the Southern Arts Federation sponsors biannual retreats for folklorists from the Southeast.

Thus, there are many indications that the entire field of folklore and related fields of cultural study are again positively incorporating public sector work and are again incorporating as central those issues that have been at the heart of the public sector enterprise from the start. These include issues of *representation* (How are folk traditions, artists, and communities depicted through the work of folklorists and others?), *authority* (By whom are folk traditions, artists, and communities depicted and in whose terms?), *responsibility* (for informed, sensitive, and accurate representation), and *collaboration* (among tradition bearers, other community members, and folklorists or other outside workers to achieve the most appropriate representation).

Responding to these sorts of issues requires integrative education: extensive fieldwork experience; a solid grounding in the materials, history, theories, and techniques of the entire discipline of folklore (including the discipline's always-present public aspects); and direct experience in public sector folklore work, from teaching to presentation planning and community service, along with reflection on that work. For the most part, graduate programs in folklore and folklife do not provide public sector experience or reflection as a formal part of their curricula, though this is changing, especially at younger programs. The effective collaboration of community members and folklorists that is a goal of contemporary public sector folklore work also requires shared and integrative learning, based in carefully planned projects that serve communities well.

Timothy C. Lloyd

See Also Archives and Archiving; Folklife; Folklore; Museum, Folk.

References

Baron, Robert, and Nicholas R. Spitzer, eds. 1992. *Public Folklore*. Washington, DC: Smithsonian Institution Press.

Bronner, Simon J. 1986. The Usable Hidden Past of Folklore. In *American Folklore Studies: An Intellectual History*, Simon Bronner. Lawrence: University Press of Kansas.

Byington, Robert H. 1989. What Happened to Applied Folklore? In *Time and Temperature*, ed. Charles Camp. Washington, DC: American Folklore Society.

Camp, Charles, and Timothy Lloyd. 1980. Six Reasons Not to Produce Folk Festivals. *Kentucky Folklore Record* 26: 1–2, 67–74.

Dwyer-Shick, Susan. 1975. The Development of Folklore and Folklife Research in the Federal Writers' Project, 1935–1943. *Keystone Folklore* 20(4): 5–31.

Feintuch, Burt, ed. 1988. *The Conservation of Culture: Folklorists and the Public Sector*. Lexington: University Press of Kentucky.

Green, Archie. 1992. Public Folklore's Name: A Partisan's Notes. In *Public Folklore*, eds. Robert Baron and Nicholas R. Spitzer. Washington, DC: Smithsonian Institution Press.

Hufford, Mary, ed. 1994. *Conserving Culture: A New Discourse on Heritage*. Urbana: University of Illinois Press.

Loomis, Ormond, coord. 1983. *Cultural Conservation: The Protection of Cultural Heritage in the United States*. Washington, DC: Library of Congress.

Siporin, Steve. 1992. *American Folk Masters: The National Heritage Fellows*. New York: Harry N. Abrams.

Teske, Robert T. 1988. State Folk Art Exhibitions: Review and Preview. In *The Conservation of Culture: Folklorists and the Public Sector*, ed. Burt Feintuch. Lexington: University Press of Kentucky.

Williams, John Alexander. 1975. Radicalism and Professionalism in American Folklore Studies: A Comparative Perspective. *Journal of the Folklore Institute* 11(3): 211–239.

Puppetry

The manipulation of material images by human hands in dramatic or narrative performances. The world's peoples have devised a broad range of puppetry traditions over the centuries, some quite familiar and others virtually unknown outside of their originating communities. A number of well-known examples fit the definition precisely, ranging from the European glove puppets of the Punch-and-Judy type to the multi-stringed marionettes of Burma or Thailand, from the snake puppets of Hopi ritual dramas to the shadow puppets of the Malayo-Indonesian world, from the rod puppets of western Africa to the Japanese *bunraku*. But there are other performing traditions that challenge the boundaries of the definition, such as elaborate, larger-than-life-sized masquerades common throughout Africa or the processional giants of Western Europe, icons and other images used in sacred rituals that may not be conceived by their practitioners as "performances," the use by storytellers of scroll paintings or pictures to illustrate their narratives, or traditions of "flesh-and-blood" puppetry in which performers—often small children—imitate the stiff and conventionalized movements of puppets. Despite its global ubiquity, puppetry remains a relatively unstudied performance tradition (with some few exceptions), perhaps because it is often considered as a trivial genre of greatest interest to children. Increasingly in recent years, folklorists and other scholars have moved from simple historical accounts tracing the evolution of genres and characters to studies of actual performances and their dynamics.

Colorful puppets on a market stall in Kathmandu, Nepal. (Jeremy Richards/Dreams time.com)

Although puppetry traditions can be classified functionally (e.g., sacred versus secular forms, serious versus humorous ones) or according to features of their performance (e.g., mute versus speaking puppets, those with music or those without, improvised versus scripted content), they are most often considered comparatively in terms of their formal-structural elements and means of animation. Marionettes are operated by means of strings or rods hanging from above (for instance, the *kathputli* puppets of Rajasthan or the *pupi* of Sicily, both of which enact historical legends). In glove puppets (or hand puppets), the puppeteer's hand fits inside the puppet's head, as for instance the French Polichinelle or Russian Petrushka (two cousins of the Punch-and-Judy family that also includes the German Hanswurst, Italian Pulcinella, and Egyptian Aragouz). Shadow puppets include opaque or translucent images, usually two-dimensional, that are displayed behind or in front of a screen, casting a shadow or being illuminated in relief; this form has been highly elaborated in China, India, the Middle East, and Southeast Asia. Rod puppets are distinguished from marionettes because the rods that are used to animate the puppets are operated from below rather than above; among the more familiar forms are the Japanese *bunraku*, the Indonesian *wayang golek*, and the Thai *khun lakhon lek*.

Cutting across these formal-structural categories are certain characteristics of puppetry performance traditions. Within each tradition, puppeteers have evolved various ways of giving voice to the puppet characters. Typically, the puppeteer provides distinct voices for each of the puppet characters, who engage in dramatic dialogue with one another. The voices may be distinguished by speaking style, vocabulary, voice quality, or the use of distinct dialects or languages. The Indonesian *dalang* (puppeteer) makes use of different levels or styles of language (from colloquial to royal, informal to elegant) as well as different vocal qualities (smooth and gentle for refined characters and rough and abrupt for ruffians or clowns). Similarly, the chivalric marionettes of Liège or Palermo are endowed by their operators with identifiable voices and appropriate vocabularies and speaking styles. In other cases, the puppeteer is assisted by actors who provide the voices for each of the characters, as one or more manipulator operates the puppets. In many traditions (especially those of the Punch-and-Judy family), the puppeteer makes use of an instrument in his or her mouth that distorts the natural voice and produces a semi-nonsensical squeaking or buzzing voice. The puppeteer will then carry on a dialogue between the distorted voice and a natural one, often assisted by an interlocutor or musician who takes one of the parts in the dialogue. In other traditions, the spoken element of the performance takes the form of a narrative rather than a dialogue, and there is no effort to make it appear that the puppets are carrying on conversations among themselves.

The subject matter of puppetry performances may range from slapstick, topical humor, and ribaldry to highly serious sacred rituals. Often, puppets are used to enact semi-historical legends, such as the chivalric epics of Roland or Orlando or the Indic *Ramayana* epic. Such extended works may be presented serially, with each performance featuring a single episode, or in performances that last all night or several days. The dramatis personae may be numerous or relatively few. The Punch-Pulcinella-Petrushka tradition of glove puppets typically includes a handful of characters who engage the hero in dyadic encounters. These forms also typically feature a substantial degree of involvement by one or more members of the audience, and they often make humorous reference to the events of the day or the attributes of the spectators or their context. In repressive sociopolitical settings, puppets are a favorite voice for the downtrodden or rebellious since they may be granted a degree of license to make critical remarks that would be punished if uttered by human actors. And because they are not human, puppets can easily be beheaded or otherwise victimized. Folk puppetry traditions often have been taken up by elite artists and writers, who find them a flexible medium through which to engage in theatrical experimentation or innovation.

Frank Proschan

See Also Mask.

References

Darkowska-Nidzgorska, Olenka. 1980. *Théâtre populaire de marionettes en Afrique sudsaharienne* (Folk puppet theater in sub-Saharan Africa). Bandundu, Zaire: Centre d'Études Ethnologiques.

Keeler, Ward. 1987. *Javanese Shadow Plays, Javanese Selves*. Princeton, NJ: Princeton University Press.

Malkin, Michael R. 1977. *Traditional and Folk Puppets of the World*. New York: A. S. Barnes.

Pasqualino, Antonio. 1977. *L'Opera dei pupi*. Palermo: Sellerio Editore.

Proschan, Frank. 1981. Puppet Voices and Interlocutors: Language in Folk Puppetry. *Journal of American Folklore* 94: 527–555.

Sherzer, Dina, and Joel Sherzer, eds. 1987. *Humor and Comedy in Puppetry*. Bowling Green, OH: Popular.

Speaight, George. 1990. *The History of the English Puppet Theatre*. 2nd ed. Carbondale: Southern Illinois University Press.

R

Rapunzel

Long-haired heroine of a well-known folktale. Versions of this story are told throughout Europe, the Americas, and the West Indies, though the best-known version is probably the much-embellished fairy tale popularized by the Grimm brothers in 1812. In their telling, a man and wife wish for a child but have long been unable to have one. They live in a house overlooking a beautiful garden that belongs to a fearsome witch. One day, the woman looks into the fine garden and wishes for some radishes. Her obliging husband overcomes his fear of the witch, climbs over the high wall of the witch's garden, and helps himself to some radishes. He takes these home to his wife, who enjoys them so much that she desires more and cannot rest until she has them. Once again screwing up all his courage, her husband climbs into the witch's garden. But this time the witch is waiting for him. She is angry and threatens to cast an evil spell on the man. Hastily he explains his wife's desire for the radishes. The witch has an apparent change of heart and says that she can have all the radishes she wants on condition that the man and his wife allow the witch to have their child. In return, the witch promises she will care for the child. The man, in fear and confusion, agrees, probably thinking that as they have no child there is no need for concern.

However, a child is born to the man and his wife. They named her Rapunzel and "she grew to be the most beautiful child under the sun." On her twelfth birthday, the witch claims her according to the agreement with her father and locks her in a tower deep in the forest. The tower has no door and no stairs, only a small window at the top. When the witch wants to enter the tower, she stands down below and calls out, "Rapunzel, Rapunzel, let down your hair." Rapunzel then throws her long, golden tresses through the small window. Reaching down to the ground, Rapunzel's hair forms a silken ladder that the witch can use to climb in and out of the tower.

After a few years, a king's son happens to go near the tower and hears Rapunzel's lovely voice in song. He finds the tower but cannot enter and so rides home again. But every day he comes back and hides in the forest, listening to the entrancing melodies of Rapunzel's singing. One day he sees the witch approach the tower and call out to Rapunzel to throw her hair down; in this way he learns the secret of entry to the tower. The next day, he goes to the foot of the tower and calls out, "Rapunzel, Rapunzel, let down your hair." She does, and he climbs

Illustration from the Brothers Grimm's *Rapunzel* by Anne Anderson (1874–1930). (The Bridgeman Art Library International)

up. At first Rapunzel is frightened because apart from her father she has never seen a man before. The prince then seduces Rapunzel—though the Grimm tale says simply that he "talked in a loving way to her"—and the lovers plot Rapunzel's escape. She tells the prince that each evening when he comes to her, he should bring a skein of silk, which she will then weave into a ladder that will allow her to escape with the prince. This plan proceeds happily until Rapunzel lets slip to the witch that the prince makes a visit on the day the witch is elsewhere. In a fury, the witch hits Rapunzel, cuts off her hair, and takes the girl to a desert, leaving her "to die in great misery and grief."

Back at the tower, the witch ties the tresses to the window, and when the prince returns in search of his love, the witch throws the hair down as if all is well. When the prince reaches the top, he finds the witch waiting for him, and she tells him that his beloved is lost. In grief and fear he throws himself out the window, falling into thorns that break his fall but blind him. He then wanders the wild wood in mourning, living off berries and roots for many years, until one day he arrives at the desert where the witch had left Rapunzel to die. Hearing a familiar voice, he makes his way toward it. By some miracle, Rapunzel has survived and given birth to twins, a boy and a girl. Rapunzel recognizes her prince and embraces him, weeping for joy. Her tears fall upon his eyes, freeing him of blindness. The prince then takes Rapunzel (and, presumably, the twins) back to his kingdom "where he was received with great demonstrations of joy."

In the usual manner of the fairy tale, events in this story occur with little or no motivation, preparation, or even logic. Rapunzel is inexplicably born to a previously barren couple for no good reason other than to fulfill the witch's condition that she should have the couple's child. The witch then locks Rapunzel away for no apparent purpose, in an isolated tower to which entry and exit is unnecessarily difficult. Rapunzel and the prince's escape plan is annoyingly long-winded. Why can't he simply bring back a rope on his next visit? Rapunzel, who shows no other signs of idiocy, blurts out the secret of her lover to the witch and then somehow survives in the desert, giving birth to twins and keeping them alive until the prince miraculously stumbles across his new family some years later. Her tears magically cure the prince's blindness, and he is free to take her back to his kingdom in the traditional fairy tale manner, though in the Grimms' version we are not told whether he also takes his two children or leaves them to perish in the desert.

Of course, in collusion with the genre of the fairy tale we suspend our disbelief for the reward of having the tension resolved in the happy ending, which, after all, is what these narratives are all about. The means by which the hero and heroine reach the end of the story are less important than the fact that they reach it and that things conclude with smiles all around. Even the defeat of the villain has not anywhere near the same importance as reaching the happy ending. In the fairy tale of Rapunzel, the pointlessly malevolent witch suffers no punishment for her actions.

We are, it seems, meant to interpret these stories and the often odd events that constitute them as metaphors. In the story of Rapunzel, the common motifs of the promised (usually female) child, the imprisonment to preserve the heroine's virginity, the rescue by the handsome prince (well, almost), the mutilation of the hero, his wandering in the wilderness, the abandonment in the desert, the healing power of the heroine's tears, and the inevitable happy closure are all classic elements of fairy tale fantasy—even though there is not a fairy in, or out, of sight.

Our need for such narratives has ensured their perpetual popularity. In the form we call the "fairy" tale, such stories date from the seventeenth century, and the earthier folktales on which many of the fairy tale encounters of princes, beautiful singing maidens, and the like are based date from some considerable number of centuries earlier. Scholars will continue to offer new interpretations of the significance of such fairy tales ("Rapunzel" being an obvious favorite for psychoanalytic approaches), while we continue to read them, turn them into films, and, sometimes, tell them to our children.

Graham Seal

See Also Cinderella; Fairy Tale Heroes; Jack and the Beanstalk; Sleeping Beauty; Snow White.

References

Bettelheim, B. 1976. The *Uses of Enchantment: The Meaning and Importance of Fairy Tales*. New York: Knopf.

Bottigheimer, R., ed. 1986. *Fairy Tales and Society: Illusion, Allusion, and Paradigm*. Philadelphia: University of Pennsylvania Press.

Hallett, M. and B. Karasek, eds. 1996. *Folk and Fairy Tales*. Ontario: Broadview Press.

Hunt, M., trans. and ed. 1884. *Grimm's Household Tales* (with the author's notes and an introduction by Andrew Lang), 2 vols. London: George Bell and Sons.

Lüthi, M. 1976. *Once upon a Time: On the Nature of Fairy Tales*. Trans. L. Chadeayne and P. Gottwald. Bloomington: Indiana University Press.

Minard, R. 1975. *Womenfolk and Fairy Tales*. Boston: Houghton Mifflin.

Opie, I. and P. Opie. 1974. *The Classic Fairy Tales*. London: Oxford University Press.

Rebus

A term used to signify the representation of language "by means of things." It is important to distinguish between the rebus principle, what I. J. Gelb calls the "principle of phonetization," by which words or syllables are represented by drawings of homonyms, and the enigmatic representation of a name or phrase—or even whole texts—which employ the same, or similar, principles. The former was a stage in the development of writing systems, and the ancient Sumerians, out of practical necessity, represented their word *ti* (life) by a drawing of an arrow, which was also *ti* in Sumerian. The enigmatic representation of written language, a test of a reader's ability at mental gymnastics, clearly differs from a practical system of writing, which requires speed and accuracy.

Because Western societies have become increasingly linear in their conception of language since the invention of print—a phenomenon intensified not only by the Reformation, with its insistence upon the "word," but also by the relatively recent emergence of computer technology, with its assumption of strings of alphanumerics—mention must be made of what is called *pattern poetry*, the combination of the visual and the linguistic or literary. Like the term *shaped poetry*, *pattern poetry* was coined in the nineteenth century in an attempt to signify the variety of similar attempts at cojoining the visual and the verbal in different cultures and in different eras. *Hieroglyphic poetry* is yet another term for the same phenomenon. The overall shape of these texts either suggests or reinforces their meanings, as, most literally, in George Herbert's well-known poem, "Easter Wings."

Rebuses may be seen to be hieroglyphic poems in style but with a larger proportion of enigma involved. Rather than reinforcing meaning, rebuses seem more often to distract from it because they are literal puns. A drawing of an eye followed by a drawing of a saw does not necessarily suggest "I saw." That example, of course, conforms to Gelb's notion of the principle of phonetization, with one word or syllable represented by a drawing of a more concrete homonym. In more modern societies, however, words are sufficiently stable that they have become things, and as a result, a nonpictorial rebus (i.e., a literal rebus) is the following: HAbirdND = BUtwoSH ("A bird in the hand is worth two in the bush"), with the only clue to its resolution being the change in type. A different kind of rebus, WORL signifies "world without end." It is of no little significance that the word processor used to write this entry makes it impractical to represent less linear rebuses, such as those that signify "back-up lights" and "John Underwood, Andover, Mass." Such rebuses, playing as they do upon our left-to-right linear concept of language representation, violate assumptions about language that underlie our word-processing software. Thus, the workaday-world practicality of computer technology reinforces the "enigmatic" quality of rebuses. Rebuses today are generally considered humor for children or, at best, "language arts" exercises in elementary schools; illustrative examples are David A. Adler's *Happy Thanksgiving Rebus* and Lisa Rojany's *Story of Hanukkah: A Lift-the-Flap Rebus Book*. In the late eighteenth century, however, a number of "hieroglyphic epistles" were printed on broadsides for adult readers. One of these was printed by W. Allen, Dame Street, Dublin, in 1779. It begins as follows (an interpretation is enclosed in brackets following each word that involves rebuses of the various kinds):

> Ewer [Your] H-eye-ness's [Highness's] E-pistol [Epistle] Came Safe toe [to] hand [hand], eye [I] Have S-hoe-n [Shown] it toe [to] awl [all] m-eye [my] friends on ear-th [earth], w-hoe [who] r [are] glad toe [to] hare [hear] t-hat [that] T-hare [there] Is so good an Under-stand-ing [understanding] bee-tween [between] us, and t-hat [that] eye [I] am lick-ly [likely] toe [to] bee [be] ass [as] grate [great] a favor-ite [favorite] bee-low [below] ass [as] eye [I] am hare [here].

Printed in Ireland and on a topic that concerns England, this hieroglyphic epistle lends itself to a pro-revolution reading through its many uses of "pistol" and even "hoe," weapons of the Irish peasantry that were not included in the printing of a variant of this broadside in Scotland. Thus, such rebus writing may contain a higher level of meaning than the literal, but on the literal level, this item illustrates a range of practices that contradict Gelb's idea of one syllable or word for one image. Here, there is a mixture of ways of representing spoken syllables and words (Under-stand-ing) and their spelling (t-hat). Indeed, this text plays off of the various ways we read and speak. If we consider its possibly revolutionary intent, we should not consider its arbitrary mix of rebus applications out of line. In its complexity, it contrasts strikingly with the various "hieroglyphic" Bibles and love letters of the period.

Rebus writing has a long history, and the play with those principles has a shorter history. That certain words, word fragments, and syllables were represented in conventional ways within a given culture should surprise no one because the fit between the available visual images and the current state of language is ever-shifting. That a subversive representation should have developed in a country as repressed as Ireland also should surprise no one.

Michael J. Preston

See Also Enigma, Folk.

References

Augarde, Tony. 1984. *The Oxford Guide to Word Games*. Oxford: Oxford University Press.

Céard, Jean, and Jean-Claude Margolin. 1986. *Rébus de la Renaissance: Des images qui parlent* (Renaissance rebus: Images who speak), 2 vols. Paris: Maisonneuve and Larose.

Dupriez, Bernard Marie. 1991. *Gradus: Les Procedes litteraires* (Gradus: The literary proceedings). Trans. and adapted by Albert W. Halsall. Toronto: University of Toronto Press.

Gelb, I. J. 1952. *A Study of Writing*. Chicago: University of Chicago Press, reprinted in 1963.

Higgins, Dick. 1987. *Pattern Poetry: Guide to an Unknown Literature*. Albany: State University of New York Press.

Preston, Michael J. 1982. The English Literal Rebus and the Graphic Riddle Tradition. *Western Folklore* 41: 104–138.

Recitation

Orally performed and rhetorically mannered spoken delivery of verse or prose text, usually prepared and often memorized. Cross-culturally, recitation is ancient in practice, transglobal, and considerably varied in secular and sacred performance evidence. Presumably, the historically distant roots of recitation reside in face-to-face encounters dependent largely, if not exclusively, upon spoken rather than inscribed dissemination of public oratory, collective oral history, oral-formulaic verse, entertaining and edifying passages, and the like. Oral recitation is not restricted by gender or age, and it pertains to many genres of verbalized folk and popular culture literature. As performed rhetoric, recitation lends itself to a range of oratorical style options based on a combination of text content, conventional norms, and individual predispositions. The term *recitation* is widely employed in reference to rhythmic chanting, metered declamation, and "theatrically" stylized oral performance of texts, though straightforward and understated renditions occur as well. Often, recitation offers opportunities for showcasing self as performer, while accompanying vocal inflections and body gestures inform and encourage within audience members the reciter's interpretation of and emotive response to the text.

Pluralized, the term *recitations* refers to folk verse, rhymed popular poetry, and prose either specifically intended in composition for recitation delivery or subsequently lending itself to it. A closely related term, *monologues*, refers more narrowly to narrative prose or narrative poetic selections rendered as recitation. In usage, the latter term appears primarily identified with late-Victorian and early twentieth-century British Isles popular culture, notably in England, where allusion to "monologues" appears in the titles of numerous printed elocutionary manuals, anthologies, and folios. Intended for mass-audience appeal and dissemination, these sources feature recitation texts often identified with renowned and professionalized public entertainers (e.g., Billy Bennett and Stanley Holloway) affiliated with music halls, burlesque, vaudeville, and early commercial sound recordings. To some extent, as in Newfoundland, Canada, and elsewhere in anglophonic tradition, the inclusive terminology *recitations and monologues* exists in popular culture and scholarly currency as an accepted alternative to recitations per se (hence, analogous to the usage "folksongs and ballads"). However, many performers and most folklorists opt for the latter term, *monologue*, when referring to both the materials and the performance of recitations.

Considered internationally, recitation among adults includes oral epics and sagas; accolades and memorial tributes; formulaic incantations and sayings; mock-serious and parodic speeches; rhymed verse such as toasts and limericks; and innumerable dramatic, descriptive, sentimental, and homiletic poems and prose passages in whole or part attributable to anonymous or known authorship. Humorous, erotic, bawdy, and obscene recitation texts exist as well, sometimes coincident with the aforementioned examples. Adult recitation is also found as an alternative to the singing of lyrical, descriptive, or narrative song texts; for Western Europe, Scandinavia, Great Britain, and North America, evidence includes recited folk ballads. Elsewhere and documented during the twentieth century, adult recitation traditions in North America include folk verse circulated among occupational workers and within rural communities; urban street vendors' "spiels"; prison inmate verse; and chanted oral sermons found in various white and African American Protestant religious service observances. In the British Isles, recitations are presented (as in, "I'll give you a humorous poem") at social drinking pubs, folk clubs, and staged heritage festivals. In the British West Indies, Afro-Caribbean declaimed speeches occur at "tea meeting" social gatherings; in Australia, there are "bush recitations" ("bush verse," "bush ballads") at social drinking pubs; and in Canada, dialect poems and monologues are recited at house parties and community entertainment events ("times"). The preceding examples single out reports from the English language; a more comprehensive and indicative survey would include a vast compilation of evidence from additional world culture areas, countries, linguistic traditions, and folk groups. This observation holds as well for documented recitation evidence among children.

Numerous collections and accompanying commentary have dealt with childlore recitation. In its Western European, British Isles, and North American manifestations, examples include childhood recitations of traditional verse accompanying folk games; recited parodies of well-known, adult literary passages and revered songs; "tangle-talk" mock speeches and nonsense verse; chanted boasts and taunts; and, primarily among urban adolescents and young adults affiliated with street gangs, reciting of mini-epic rhymed folk verse that boasts of real or fantasized contest and conquest.

Since the 1970s, a number of folklorists in Great Britain, Australia, and the United States—together with recitation performers—have singled out, for greater attention, late-Victorian, Edwardian, and twentieth-century English-language popular poetry as a primary source for reciters dually influenced by anglophonic folk tradition and popular culture antecedents. Whether labeled *popular poetry*, *vernacular popular poetry*, or *poetry of the people*, such rhymed verse compositions are distinguishable from *elite poetry* by their commonplace diction and tendency to present subject matter dealing with real or fictional adventure, faraway dramatic encounter, community happenstance, or rural domestic experience. Narrative and humorous popular poetry recitation texts, often authored and performed by men, appear to outnumber others; women's authored and performed texts, at least in anglophonic tradition, are frequently lyrical, sentimental, and homiletic. Many widely circulated popular poetry compositions are attributable to regionally, nationally, and internationally known authors: in England, notably Rudyard Kipling and George R. Sims; in Canada, Robert W. Service and William Henry Drummond; in Australia, A. B. Paterson and Henry Lawson; in the United States, Eugene Field and Will Carleton. In the western United States, rhymed popular poetry suited to oral recitation has flourished among cowboys and ranchers since the late 1800s, and there are numerous renowned and lesser-known self-identified "bunkhouse folk poets" within their ranks. In the late twentieth century, American "cowboy poetry" in four-line or longer stanzas vies with Australian "bush verse" as ongoing, freshly creative, and commercially evolving oral recitation within conventions and precedents found worldwide. Representative and widely heralded twentieth-century American cowboy and rancher poet-reciters include Curley Fletcher, Baxter Black, and Waddie Mitchell; Australian counterparts include C. J. Dennis and others who have foregrounded their continent's history, popular culture, and western Queensland bush.

In all, oral recitation endures from ancient times into the present in diversified textual evidence and situated occasioning. Increasingly, inquiries into the phenomenon among adults need to contend with expanding global public access to printed publications, audio recordings, radio and television, videotape, emerging electronic and computer media, and commercial popular culture generally. Tourism-related displays and events that serve nostalgia sometimes introduce new and wider audiences to reciters and the recitation format. Emergent commercial outlets also may bring established recitation tradition to mass-public familiarity, as happened with the rhymed "rap" recitations found in American popular music since the late 1970s, which derived from African American "street poetry" current a generation earlier. Scholars might also consider the indebtedness, interconnections, or departure of childlore recitation texts and performances from those of culture-sharing adults. Whatever and wherever the evidence, recitation continues as one of the major oral performance varieties in global consideration.

Robert D. Bethke

See Also Oral-Formulaic Theory; Performance; Popular Culture.

References

Cannon, Hal, ed. 1985. *Cowboy Poetry: A Gathering*. Layton, UT: Gibbs M. Smith.

Cunningham, Keith, ed. 1990. *The Oral Tradition of the American West: Adventure, Courtship, Family, and Place in Traditional Recitation*. Little Rock, AR: August House.

Goldstein, Kenneth S. 1993. Recitations and Monologues. In *Folk Literature: Voices through Time*, eds. Bill Butt and Larry Small. St. John's, Newfoundland: Breakwater Books.

Goldstein, Kenneth S., and Robert D. Bethke. 1976. *Monologues and Folk Recitation*. Special issue, *Southern Folklore Quarterly* 40(1-2).

Greenhill, Pauline. 1989. *True Poetry: Traditional and Popular Verse in Ontario*. Montreal: McGill-Queen's University Press.

Jones, Sanford W., ed. 1976. *Great Recitations*. New York: Hart.

Kochman, Thomas, ed. 1972. *Rappin' and Stylin' Out: Communication in Urban Black America*. Urbana: University of Illinois Press.

McHenry, Keith. 1993. Folk Poetry and Recitation. In *The Oxford Companion to Australian Folklore*, eds. Gwenda Beed Davey and Graham Seal. Melbourne: Oxford University Press.

Opie, Iona, and Peter Opie. 1959. *The Lore and Language of Schoolchildren*. Oxford, UK: Clarendon.

Rosenberg, Bruce A. 1988. *Can These Bones Live?: The Art of the American Folk Preacher*. Urbana: University of Illinois Press.

Regional Approach

An approach that considers distinctive constellations of traditional expressive forms performed in a specific area, with a particular emphasis on those that exist in a mutually responsive relationship with the area. Although *all* of the folklore of a particular place is important and can reveal much about its inhabitants, contemporary folklorists distinguish between *the folklore of regions* and *regional folklore*. Regional folklore, unlike traditions that appear and function widely, exists in what Archie Green calls a "reflexive" relationship with a spatially defined group, rather than one conceptualized on the basis of such other factors as age, gender, occupation, ethnicity, avocation, or lifestyle. Truly regional folklore expresses and articulates a place's worldview, while at the same time shaping and informing it. In other words, as Green puts it, "Lore delineates region and region delimits lore. In either direction each turns back, or is bent, to the other" (Green 1978). This reflexivity is not operative insofar as the folklore of regions is concerned. For example, catastrophe jokes, the proverb "Haste makes waste," the ballad "Barbara Allen," and the belief that a copper bracelet cures arthritis are part of the traditional inventories of many regions, but *corridos* (Mexican American folk ballads), stories about the Brown Mountain lights, sneakboxes (small boats made and used by duck hunters in southern New Jersey), sang hoes (three-pronged hoes for extracting ginseng), and the ballad "Talt Hall" are most certainly not. Moreover, these latter forms are inextricably connected to the specific geographic contexts in which they appear, both expressing regionality and informing it. As Barre Toelken puts it: "We learn our culture by hearing its expressions, and we in turn express our culture whenever we engage in performing any of its vernacular genres" (Allen & Schlereth 1990). Indeed, regional analysis provides excellent insights into the relationships between people, their place, and their lore. Understanding spatially defined groups enhances our understanding of their folklore, and the regionally bound folklore facilitates our understanding of the group: To know Appalachian folklore, we must know Appalachia; to know Appalachia, we must know its folklore. Whether concerned with the folklore of regions or regional folklore, however, most folklorists would agree with Howard Odum and Harry Moore, who write in *American Regionalism* that the "geographic factor" is the "mudsill" of the concept of regionalism and that "social phenomena may best be understood when considered in relation to the area in which they occur as a cultural frame of reference" (Odum & Moore 1938).

During the first few decades of American folklore scholarship, many folklorists were interested in the "geographic factor," framing the traditions they collected in spatial terms. These studies focused on the folklore of regions, paying little attention to regional theory or analysis, but they nevertheless afforded valuable texts and indicated that scholars were at least thinking about the connections between land and lore. Perhaps the first regional folklore collection in the United States was the 1867 book *Slave Songs of the United States*, in which the authors, William Francis Allen, Charles P. Ware, and Lucy M. Garrison, arranged 136 songs according to a geographical scheme, presenting them as belonging to either the "South-Eastern Slave States," the "Northern Seaboard Slave States," or the "Inland Slave States." A few years later, the folklore of such regions as New England, the Southwest, and Appalachia began appearing in the *Journal of American Folklore*. Many of these articles provided excellent texts but very little else, sorely frustrating modern folklorists. For example, in 1925, Isabel Gordon Carter published several Jack tales (*Märchen* that had been "regionalized") in the *Journal of American Folklore*. After an introductory paragraph, she included only four more short paragraphs of contextual data, pointing out only that her informant, Jane Gentry, learned the stories from her grandfather, who had learned them from his mother. Was Gentry referring to "Old Counce" Harmon, her mother's father, or to her *paternal* grandfather, who was a Hicks? And what relationship was there between the stories and the title of Carter's article "Mountain White Folk-Lore: Tales from the Southern Blue Ridge"? The texts in the article are unquestionably important; they are perhaps the purest Jack tales we have from the rich Hicks-Harmon family repertoire. But fuller contextual information and some discussion of the connections between the stories and the Appalachian experience would have made Carter's study even more valuable.

Among other early collections of the folklore of regions were those of Alcée Fortier in Louisiana (1895), E. C. Perrow in the South (1912), E. M. Fogel in the Pennsylvania Dutch country (1915), and Aurelio M. Espinosa in the Southwest (1915). Important regional work in the 1920s includes studies by Fanny Hardy Eckstorm and Mary Winslow Smyth in Maine, Josiah H. Combs in Appalachia, and Newbell N. Puckett and John H. Cox in the South.

No doubt motivated by widespread dissatisfaction with collective American society, scholars produced an explosion of regional studies during the 1930s, with the "Twelve Southerners" setting the charge in their 1930 document "A Statement of Principles," which proclaimed that the South was indeed a distinctive section, defined primarily by its agrarianness, and that it deserved the right to determine itself and to resist "joining up behind" the American industrial way of life. Writers, historians, geographers, economists, and the federal government all embraced the concept of regionalism. Leading the way for folklorists was Benjamin A. Botkin, editor from 1929 to 1932 of *Folk-Say: A Regional Miscellany*, who became folklore editor for the Federal Writers' Project, a New Deal effort to celebrate the culture of ordinary Americans. Botkin coordinated intense collecting activities, later publishing the materials in several regional "treasuries": New England (1947), the South (1949), the West (1951), and the Mississippi River (1955). A golden age of folklore collecting within regions, the 1930s produced numerous works grounded in spatial dimensions. Collectors and their respective regions include Harry M. Hyatt in Adams County, Illinois; Phillips Barry in Maine; Frank C. Brown and Ralph Steele Boggs in North Carolina;

Thomas Brendle in southeastern Pennsylvania; J. Frank Dobie and Mody Boatright in Texas; Hans Kurath in New England; Louise Pound in Nebraska; George Pullen Jackson in the upland South; and Richard Chase, John Jacob Niles, and Cecil Sharp in Appalachia. The best of these collections was Emelyn E. Gardner's *Folklore from the Schoharie Hills, New York*, published in 1937. In addition to providing some excellent texts, Gardner included brief impressions of the region's people, gave a geographical description of the area, discussed local history, and distinguished between folklore "collected elsewhere in the United States" (e.g., "Pretty Polly") and "Schoharie localizations," such as place-name legends, tall tales relating to a local hero, legends concerning area resistance to rent collectors, and four "crude" ballads about local characters. Gardner's work was a firm step in the direction toward the maturation of regional folkloristics.

Collecting organized according to state boundaries continued into the 1940s—John Lomax in Texas, Henry M. Belden in Missouri—but, like Gardner, some folklorists concentrated on cultural and physiographic regions: George Korson in the mining districts of Pennsylvania, Austin E. and Alta S. Fife and Levette J. Davidson in Mormon Utah, Vance Randolph in the Ozarks, and Lelah Allison

Localization

The process by which folklore develops to conform to the preferred patterns of folk cultural regions; alternatively, the products of such a process. Folk cultural regions are self-conscious, multileveled assemblies of folk as specific as "Arizona White River Apache" and as broad as 'the Southwest,' but members of all regions share a traditional aesthetic sense that regulates folklore. Localization reshapes lore to fit these varied senses of form.

Literary folklorists analyzed texts as products of localization and found that characters' names and the settings of oral folklore were frequently localized. One of the most notable Anglo-American ballad localizations, for example, is the substitution of familiar names for unfamiliar ones, so that names acceptable to audience and performers replace characters of long ago or far away in localized versions.

The settings of folk narrative are also frequently localized in response to the traditions of folk cultural regions. Most Anglo-American urban legends, for example, are introduced as having happened recently and nearby, but they lack exact settings.

Field-based folklorists and anthropologists concentrated upon the localization of folklore performance and upon the process by which localization took place. Field researchers investigating localization focused on the unconscious process of selection and adaptation by which folk cultural regions create their lore. Localization, in both the literary and field research senses of the term, is an important concept in cultural studies, explaining one of the major ways in which folklore develops and examining the results of this process.

Keith Cunningham

Uncle Billy McCrea (right) with John A. Lomax (center), and friends, at Billy's home in Jasper, Texas, September 1940. (Library of Congress)

and Grace Partridge Smith in the twenty-five-county area in southern Illinois known as "Egypt."

But in these studies, there was no consistency in the use of the term *region*, collecting was generally haphazard rather than systematic, scant attention was given to contextual data, and there was very little reflexive (or any other kind of) analysis. Surveying these collections in 1947, Herbert Halpert, who had himself advanced the status of the field in his dissertation on the New Jersey Pine Barrens a few years earlier, reported that most of them were little more than lists of texts with inbred notes and that the collectors failed to provide adequate descriptions of the cultures with which they were concerned. Halpert went on to call for more sophisticated regional studies.

Halpert's call was answered in 1952 with Richard M. Dorson's *Bloodstoppers and Bearwalkers*, a study of Michigan's Upper Peninsula region. Basing her comments largely on Dorson's "analysis of the place and the people who live there," reviewer Thelma James referred to the book as "the pattern for regional collections and studies in American folklore." Dorson indeed discussed the regional context in the book, and he devoted over a third of it to "The Native Tradition," exploring at length local beliefs, customs, legends, and anecdotes. Barbara Allen, in commenting on the importance of the book in *Sense of Place*, pointed out that its implicit message "is that the folklore of the Upper Peninsula is truly a regional product, a response to residents' experiences there." Though perhaps not as paradigmatic as *Bloodstoppers and Bearwalkers*, regional collections continued to appear in the 1950s, including those of Harold E. Briggs (Egypt), Horace P. Beck (Maine), Don Yoder (Pennsylvania), J. Mason Brewer (Texas), Ray B. Browne (Alabama), Harry Oster (Louisiana), and Leonard Roberts (eastern Kentucky). The jewel in the crown of regional folklore scholarship in the 1950s, however, was Américo Paredes's *"With His Pistol in His Hand": A Border Ballad and Its Hero.* "It was a peculiar set of conditions," wrote Paredes (1958), "that produced the Lower Border *corrido,*" a ballad form typical of the Lower Rio Grande Valley region, half in Mexico, half in the United States. Devoting the entire book to the ballad about the outlaw Gregorio Cortez, Paredes provided detailed discussions of the history, geography, and culture of the region, explaining how the song dramatized cultural conflict along "the Border." As Allen observed, the book was "pivotal"; it moved regional folkloristics even further from the folklore of regions to a study of truly regional folklore.

Paredes's book had not appeared, however, when, in 1957, Richard Dorson delivered to an impressive symposium of scholars his "theory of American folklore," in which he complained that most of the regional collections still remained "on the level of text-hunting motivated chiefly by convenience and emotional identification with a locality." Dorson, like Halpert ten years earlier, urged that American regional collecting "be tied to theoretical questions," insisting that "a series of planned and coordinated field trips is necessary in place of the casual and haphazard collecting that is now the practice." Two years later, in the "Regional Folk Cultures" chapter of *American Folklore*, Dorson offered as a model the results of his own fieldwork in two communities in Maine, along with what others had collected in German Pennsylvania, the Ozarks, Spanish New Mexico, and the Utah Mormon region. By the end of the 1950s, regional folklore studies had established a secure position in American folklore scholarship.

This position was strengthened in 1964 with Dorson's *Buying the Wind: Regional Folklore in the United States*, a book-length expansion of his regional folklore chapter in *American Folklore*. One reviewer called this work "the first scholarly anthology of regional American folklore." Omitting the Ozarks, perhaps because Vance Randolph had published five books on the subject, Dorson added units on Egypt, Appalachia, and the Louisiana Bayou. The subtitle notwithstanding, the book focused as much on ethnicity as it did on geography, but at the time, it was nevertheless the most responsible collection of American folklore considered on the basis of "place," and it provided an excellent bibliography of regional folklore studies. Dorson mulled over the idea of regional folklore for the next several years, eventually persuading two of his graduate students to pursue the topic.

Regional collections continued to appear throughout the 1960s—S. J. Sackett and William E. Koch's *Kansas Folklore* and Ruth Ann Musick's book on West

Virginia ghost tales, for example—but the decade is best characterized by the integration of folkloric and geographic approaches. Geographers had been interested in the concept of regionalism since the publication in 1789 of Jedidiah Morse's *American Geography*, in which the author attempted to make explicit implied assumptions about major American "sections," but oddly, substantial geographically oriented folklore studies did not appear until 1968. That year saw the publication of the cultural geographer E. Joan Wilson Miller's "Ozark Culture Region as Revealed by Traditional Materials," in which Miller argued that "regionalized" folklore (specifically, narratives collected by Vance Randolph) could contribute to "an understanding of forms and processes of settlement" within a cultural region. Miller (1968) later suggested that superstitions, too, could facilitate the discovery of a region's "resource base," which supplies the physical and spiritual needs of a folk group. Also in 1968, Alan Lomax published *Folk Song Style and Culture*, a collection of essays supporting his thesis that singing styles defined large, worldwide musical regions. And 1968 was the year that Henry Glassie, following Fred Kniffen's groundbreaking work on the diffusion of folk house types, published his influential *Pattern in the Material Culture of the Eastern United States*. Like Lomax, Glassie identified regions on the basis of folk cultural expressions, in this case, architecture and artifacts. The book represents the high watermark of geographical folklore scholarship.

This geographically oriented folklore approach carried over into the 1970s, especially in the work of W. F. H. Nicolaisen, who became involved with the Society for the North American Cultural Survey, a consortium of geographers, folklorists, anthropologists, and historians that has as its mission the production of an atlas of North American cultures. Nicolaisen's interest in "the reciprocal ways in which folklore creates region while at the same time being shaped by it" mirrored exactly Archie Green's thinking outlined in "Reflexive Regionalism," which appeared in 1978. Regional theory also was advanced by Suzi Jones in her 1976 article "Regionalization: A Rhetorical Strategy," in which she, like Miller, emphasized the importance of transformations of folk materials based on a response to a specific place. Other important regional studies in the 1970s were those of Henry Glassie on folk housing in Middle Virginia, Roger Welsch's work on tall tales in the northern plains, and George Carey's study on the folklore of both Maryland and the Eastern Shore. Moreover, Richard Dorson, perhaps thinking about his upcoming handbook on American folklore, encouraged two of his graduate students, Howard Marshall and William E. Lightfoot, to undertake regional projects for their dissertations at Indiana University. Marshall, in "The Concept of Folk Region in Missouri: The Case of Little Dixie" (1976), analyzed both verbal and nonverbal traditions, especially those that tended to reveal "regional personality," concluding that architecture most clearly expressed Little Dixie's identification "as an island of Southern folk culture in the lower

Midwest." (Marshall's study was published in 1981 as *Folk Architecture in Little Dixie: A Regional Culture in Missouri.*) Lightfoot concentrated on "Folklore of the Big Sandy Valley of Eastern Kentucky" (1976), also focusing on traditions that displayed regional integrity. Two studies emerging from this work were "The Ballad 'Talt Hall' in Regional Context" (1978) and "Regional Folkloristics" (which appeared in Dorson's 1983 *Handbook of American Folklore*); in this piece, Lightfoot proposed a methodology for regional folklore scholarship that he applied to an analysis of the Big Sandy local ballad "Sam Adams." Dorson was keen on having regional folklore represented in the *Handbook*, and he included several more essays on the subject.

The essays in the *Handbook* were grounded deeply in the notion of *reflexivity* and were indeed analyses of regional folklore rather than the folklore of regions. Marta Weigle, for example, pointed out that traditional materials of the Southwest both *affect* and *effect* Southwesterners' expressions of themselves and their region's distinctiveness. Jan Harold Brunvand discussed the esoteric-exoteric dimensions of folk speech in Utah and the Mountain West, and Edward D. Ives explored the nature of locally composed songs that share "a special provenience," Maine and the Maritime Provinces of Canada. José E. Limón analyzed "the special regional experience" that generated an extensive body of folklore concerning social conflict along the U.S.-Mexico border, and Robert B. Klymasz examined the generally friendly folklore of the Canadian-American border. In his introduction to the unit, Dorson referred to such concepts as *identity* and *consciousness*, terms that were then becoming characteristic of regional folklore scholarship. Mention should also be made of Dorson's *Land of the Millrats* (1981), a coordinated team effort to record and analyze the folklore of an urban region—northern Indiana's Calumet complex. Another major source of work in regional folklore in the 1980s was the Library of Congress–based American Folklife Center, part of whose mission is the preservation of regional cultures. The center has sponsored intensive folklife projects in such regions as "Wiregrass" Georgia, northern Nevada, the Blue Ridge Mountains, and the New Jersey Pinelands.

Regional folkloristics was advanced further in 1990 with the publication of *Sense of Place: American Regional Cultures*. Framed with essays by its editors, Barbara Allen and Thomas J. Schlereth, the book's ten studies all focused on the reciprocal interaction between place and folk, showing how folklore is both a product of and stimulant to regional group consciousness and how it simultaneously reflects and reinforces regional identity. Roughly half of the essays were concerned with verbal traditions. Barre Toelken, for example, explained how vernacular expressions—jokes, tall tales, legends, and anecdotes—"grow out of, and give voice to" the collective value system of the American West. Larry Danielson discussed the ways in which beliefs, sayings, and stories "crystallize" profound concerns about weather in the Great Plains "breadbasket" area, expressing "a distinctive identification with one's regional home." Local historical legends were found by Polly Stewart to be vehicles for the expression of strong "us-versus-them" attitudes among residents of Maryland's Eastern Shore, and Barbara Allen showed how folk speech in a Kentucky community reflects Southerners' intense sense of place, perhaps the "hallmark" of their regional identity. Illustrating his thesis with both verbal and nonverbal examples, John Michael Coggeshall explained how speech, legends, religious rituals, foodways, and material culture establish bases for regional identity in southern Illinois' "Egypt." Three of the essays focused on material culture exclusively. Mary Hufford, for example, described the Barnegat Bay sneakbox, a small skiff used for duck hunting in coastal New Jersey, as a boat comprising "a distinctive response to distinctively regional conditions, a tool whereby local men distinguish themselves as inhabitants of a singular region." Richard E. Meyer explored the ways in which both visual and verbal images on grave markers form a significant part of collective regional self-image not only of people in Oregon's Willamette Valley but also of Pacific Northwesterners in general. Charles E. Martin analyzed the power of a collective Appalachian regional aesthetic that prohibits individual self-expression, forcing artists to conceal personal expressivity within utilitarian productions. Another study of how regions define form was that of William E. Lightfoot, who described the concatenation of historical, demographic, and physiographic forces in a two-county area in western Kentucky that produced the distinctive regional guitar-playing style known as "Travis-picking," which became a prominent instrumental element of commercial country music. Finally, Erika Brady suggested that the traditional skill of fur trapping represents the nexus of many aspects of regional identity among residents of the southern Missouri Ozarks. In characterizing these studies, editor Barbara Allen once again evoked the idea of "reflexivity," writing that the subjects of the essays were "regional cultures and the regional consciousness that both shapes and is shaped by them." The reflexive process is indeed the very heart of regional folkloristics.

The essays in *Sense of Place* had a profound impact on the thinking of the American studies scholar Kent C. Ryden, whose 1993 book *Mapping the Invisible Landscape: Folklore, Writing, and the Sense of Place* explored the ways in which narratives—both oral and written—create and communicate what he called a regional insider's "invisible landscape," a term that he suggested is identical to "regional consciousness." Believing that folklore "vivifies" geography, Ryden analyzed field-collected narratives in order to better understand the culture of northern Idaho's Coeur d'Alene mining district.

Another important regional study by a nonfolklorist that nevertheless relied heavily on traditional materials was the 1989 book *Albion's Seed: Four British*

Folkways in America, by the historian David Hackett Fischer. Indeed, it was Fischer's thesis that four sets of British folkways—from East Anglia, southern England, the northern Midlands, and the Borderlands—became the basis of the four original regional cultures in America: the Massachusetts Puritans, the Virginia Cavaliers, the Delaware Valley Quakers, and the Backcountry borderers, respectively. Fischer illustrated this thesis by extensive analyses of the folklore of the four regions.

Although regional folklore studies have matured considerably and have proven useful to scholars in several other disciplines, there is still very little consistency in regional folklore theory. The concept of "region" is so ambiguous and imprecise as to virtually undo itself. For example, the "regions" mentioned here range from the 5,500-mile Canadian-American border to large groups of states (the South) to smaller groups of states (the Southwest) to areas that include parts of states (Appalachia) to single states to clusters of several counties (Egypt) to small groups of counties (Big Sandy) to single counties (Adams County, Illinois). Regions are defined willy-nilly on the bases of physical characteristics, states of mind, political maneuverings, uniformity of cultural traits, distinctiveness, collective personality, consciousness, and single-trait variables. In forty-one definitions of region listed by Odum and Moore, twenty-five were based on notions of "uniformity," with eight emphasizing "distinctiveness"; four combined the two ideas. "Consciousness" and "identity" would appear frequently. But "uniformity" or "homogeneity" would certainly not characterize Egypt or Appalachia, both of which contain several ethnic groups and social classes within their boundaries. It is doubtful that Glassie's upland South region, which extends from southern Pennsylvania to Birmingham, Alabama, and includes portions of fourteen states, has a distinct personality or consciousness. The practice of snake handling helps to define Appalachia, but it is not exclusive to that region, and even if the ritual were performed there, it would not define Salina, Kansas. Most people in Central City, Kentucky, are probably unaware that they belong to the "Shultz-Travis" region. Although theoretical concepts may be fuzzy, the notion of "place" and folk responses to place remain central to regional folklore scholarship.

William E. Lightfoot

See Also Localization; Oikotype/Oicotype.

References

Allen, Barbara, and Thomas J. Schlereth, eds. 1990. *Sense of Place: American Regional Cultures.* Lexington: University Press of Kentucky.

Dewhurst, C. Kurt, and Marsha MacDowell. 1984. Region and Locality. In *American Folk Art: A Guide to Sources*, ed. Simon J. Bronner. New York: Garland.

Dorson, Richard M. 1959. A Theory for American Folklore. *Journal of American Folklore* 72: 197–242.

Dorson, Richard M., ed. 1964. *Buying the Wind: Regional Folklore in the United States.* Chicago: University of Chicago Press.

Dorson, Richard M., ed. 1983. *Handbook of American Folklore.* Bloomington: Indiana University Press.

Gardner, Emelyn E. 1937. *Folklore from the Schoharie Hills, New York.* Ann Arbor: University of Michigan Press.

Green, Archie. 1978. Reflexive Regionalism. *Adena* 3: 3–15.

Jones, Suzi. 1976. Regionalization: A Rhetorical Strategy. *Journal of the Folklore Institute* 13: 105–120.

Miller, E. Joan Wilson. 1968. The Ozark Culture Region as Revealed by Traditional Materials. *Annals of the Association of American Geographers* 58: 51–77.

Odum, Howard W., and Harry E. Moore. 1938. *American Regionalism.* New York: Henry Holt.

Paredes, Américo. 1958. *"With His Pistol in His Hand": A Border Ballad and Its Hero.* Austin: University of Texas Press.

Religion, Comparative

An academic discipline devoted to the general study of religions on a comparative basis. The approach is characterized by nondenominational and interdisciplinary research into the phenomena classified as religions, worldviews, and similar systems of thought. Other labels for the discipline are *comparative study of religions*, *the academic study of religions*, *history of religions*, *religious studies*, or *Allgemeine* or *Vergleichende Religionswissenschaft* in German. As an independent academic discipline and an approach to the study of humanity in relation to mind, society, and culture, the approach dates back to the second and third quarters of the nineteenth century. Although such materials for the study of human religiosity as, for instance, rock paintings, archaeological findings, and historical reports of travelers, explorers, and missionaries were available prior to the nineteenth century, the intellectual atmosphere did not support the independent general study of religions as an expression of human concerns over the uncertainty and mysteries of life and limitations of human existence.

The comparative study of religion emerged in Western Europe, and for that reason, it has a very close link with ideological and social developments in the Western world. In fact, the concept of religion in its present use stems from the Age of Enlightenment, when it was first used in the present Western sense as a discrete sphere of activity. The intellectual atmosphere, however, was not congenial to the fostering of comparative and non-dogmatic study of other religions until the nineteenth century.

An ambitious effort to study religious phenomena from a comparative perspective was impossible before the realization of the existence of non-Judeo-Christian religions. The acceptance of non-Western sources of interpretation of the social and physical universe coincided with the discovery of the vast new territories and enabled the realization of the great variety of human religious experiences and beliefs in, particularly, Asia and Africa. The idea of regarding Christianity as merely one of the religions, with no need to label other beliefs as heretical or pagan, preceded and enabled the development of the comparative study of religions. The whole appearance of the concept of religion as a plural phenomenon required a shift from the monopoly of the Roman Catholic Church into a plural interpretation of Christianity itself in Europe. It is also important to realize that comparative religion is not an atheistic discipline but includes atheism as an object of study as well. It should be added that comparative religion, maintaining the goal of a greater understanding of both religions and secularization processes, does not advocate any single faith or ideology.

Comparative religion originated in two different fields of inquiry: philology and anthropology. German scholar F. Max Müller is credited with establishing the philological strand of comparative religion in the 1860s. He was a specialist in Indian classical languages and the "science of religion." The philological study of that period relied mainly on the textual sources of such great Asian religions as Hinduism and Buddhism. The anthropological approach to the study of religion was developed by British scholars E. B. Tylor (1832–1917) and James G. Frazer (1854–1941). This orientation was based on the theory of nonlinear cultural evolution, and the research material consisted of reports produced by people other than the scholars themselves and centered on the problems of the origin of religion and so-called primitive religion.

The term *study of religion* is usually qualified as *general* or *comparative*. In German-speaking countries, for example, the field is referred to either as *Allgemeine* or *Vergleichende Religionswissenschaft*; in the anglophonic world the terms *comparative religion* or *(academic) study of religions* are predominant. In the Scandinavian languages, *religionshistoria* has gained an established position, denoting the study of religion in general even though *history of religion* is usually defined as only one of the five main branches of the study of religion, along with the phenomenology of religion, the sociology of religion, the psychology of religion, and the anthropology of religion. The term *comparative religion* is thus a kind of an umbrella for many different approaches to and methods of dealing with religion as a historical, cultural, and individual phenomenon considered in space and time. This list of subjects reveals how varied the viewpoints and problems encountered in the study of religion are. The methods used in different branches of religious study often are not profoundly different from those applied in the corresponding general disciplines.

The *history of religion* focuses on the central problems of the origins of religions and their historical development. Thorough source criticism of the obtained material in order to prove its historical and religious value is a fundamental part of such study, and the methods used depend on the nature and quality of the material. It is common practice to divide religions into two categories, depending on whether their sources are principally in written documents or oral traditions. In the former case—in the so-called historical, or literate, religions—the study is based primarily on the historical analysis of texts and documents. In the case of cultures not based on written materials, known as primitive or illiterate (nonliterate) religions, conclusions concerning their history have to be arrived at on the basis of oral tradition.

The *phenomenology of religion* is principally a comparative discipline. Its task is to seek out regularly occurring patterns, repeatedly encountered phenomena, and recurring structures and functions in the religious field. The phenomena studied need not necessarily be interdependent from the point of view of their genetic history. The phenomenology of religion is more interested in the phenomena than in the historical relationships among them. The material is usually arranged not chronologically but systematically. The task of religious phenomenology is to classify various forms, structures, and functions of religions. The approach corresponds, to a large extent, to the study of structures and substructures in cultural anthropology. Methods of typological comparison have been very important for this kind of study. As in cultural anthropology, cross-cultural research occupies a prominent position, offering more-exact methods for measuring differences between cultural mechanisms and finding common denominators. In contemporary practice, the phenomenology of religion aims to ensure that neither the social nor the cultural context of those phenomena is neglected. To draw up a workable religio-phenomenological model, in general, presupposes historical, ecological, and sociological analysis within a relatively homogenous cultural area. Regional phenomenology of religion as practiced by Scandinavian and Finnish scholars has incorporated the methods of folkloristics into religious studies.

Sociology of religion is a branch of the study of religion that occupies a rather independent position; its methods and problems are much the same as those in general sociology. From the sociological viewpoint, religion is principally a group phenomenon that has been adopted by a limited, cohesive group. Sociologists examine religion as a social system that maintains certain ideas about what is sacred and what is not, as well as the norms and roles associated with sacred and secular phenomena and beings, together with regular patterns of behavior that recur at fixed intervals.

Psychology of religion, on the one hand, forms a sector of the wide field covered by modern psychology; on the other hand, it is a branch of the study of religion. Most of the methods employed today in the psychology of religion have been developed in other branches of psychology. Examples of these methods are questionnaires together with accompanying interviews, laboratory experiments, psychoanalysis, and tests. A new trend is exemplified by questionnaires about people's attitudes and the use of autobiographical interviews. With a greater emphasis on empirical research methods, scholars within the psychological and sociological trends in the study of religion have labeled their discipline as the *scientific study of religion*.

Anthropology of religion is focused broadly on humankind in its problematic scope: Religion is viewed within the terms of the concepts and behavior of individuals and societies. This method is anthropological in the sense that it attempts to portray religion holistically, either as a part the cultural totality to which it belongs or as a part of the learned social tradition of man. The central problem concerns religious communication, that is, the transmission of religious tradition, the crucial object of the study being interactions between the individuals and societies. The religio-anthropological approach is also ecological, as it concerns itself with the interdependence between religions and the environments in which they exist. Such studies strive to eliminate changes resulting from contacts with other factors (acculturation) in order to arrive at an explanation of whether, for example, membership in a group engaged in a particular trade or occupation influences the way in which religion, religious tradition, and religious behavior are molded into a certain shape and, in the final analysis, the way in which a religious person's character is formed in a particular culture. Religio-anthropological study is based primarily on the materials collected in intensive fieldwork. The problems of the holistic study of culture, religious interaction systems, religious communication, and ecological questions make such great demands as regards the material under study that collecting in-depth in any field is central to religio-anthropological research.

Juha Pentikäinen

See Also Evolutionary Theory; Religion, Folk.

References

Evans-Pritchard, E. E. 1965. *Theories of Primitive Religion*. Oxford: Oxford University Press.

Kitagawa, Joseph M. 1987. *The History of Religions: Understanding Human Experience*. Atlanta, GA: Scholars.

Pentikäinen, Juha Y. 1978. *Oral Repertoire and World View: An Anthropological Study of Marina Takalo's Life History*. Folklore Fellows Communications, no. 219. Helsinki: Academia Scientiarum Fennica.

Segal, Robert A. 1989. *Religion and Social Sciences: Essays on the Confrontation*. Atlanta, GA: Scholars.

Sharpe, Eric J. 1975. *Comparative Religion: A History*. London: Duckworth.

Sharpe, Eric J. 1983. *Understanding Religion*. London: Duckworth.

Smart, Ninian. 1989. *The World's Religions: Old Traditions and Modern Transformations.* London: Cambridge University Press.

Tambiah, Stanley Jeyaraja. 1990. *Magic, Science, Religion, and the Scope of Rationality.* Cambridge: Cambridge University Press.

Religion, Folk

Religion as it is believed, practiced, and experienced in everyday life. Many humanistic and social scientific disciplines have examined the kinds of religious belief and practice found among the common people and categorized them as *folk religion*. The discipline of folklore has employed this term to describe a variety of rural, urban, historical, and contemporary religious phenomena that are directly influenced by, develop alongside, and exist within "official," institutional religious contexts and forms.

Folklorists continue to prefer *folk religion* as a term of choice to describe the religion of small, homogeneous communities of believers in place of *popular religion*, the religious expressions of the masses or religion transmitted by means of mass communication. Many other designations share a conceptual kinship with folk religion. Some of these expressions in English are: *popular religion, people's religion, practical religion, local religion, common religion, the religious life of the laity, domestic religion, extra-ecclesiastical religion, pragmatic religion, subterranean theologies and superstitions, nonofficial religion, lived religion,* and *actual religion*. Terms specifically used by folklore/folklife scholars are *superstition, unofficial religion, religious folklife, religious folklore, religious folk tradition, the folk church,* and *oral, traditional religion*.

Whatever confusion there is navigating the plethora of terms folklorists have used in their study of religion, they share one essential idea: that a concern for religion as it is manifested in everyday life is essential for a complete apprehension of human religiosity. This point is crucial because of the overemphasis of scholarly interest in the institutional dimensions of religious history, structure, laws, polity, community, education, texts, and architecture. Folk religion scholarship has examined, instead, religion expressed in individual and community systems of belief; speech, story, and song; private devotions and practices; public ritual activities; and the material culture of clothing, food, domestic space, religious objects, and the life of the body.

When folklorists study religion, they tend to see it as involving explicit references for people to conceptions of deities or the supernatural. Their eclectic study of religion has centered on complex societies and mainly emphasized Christian contexts. Conceptualizations of folklore and religion have been divided between the study of lore, that is, the oral (and sometimes behavioral and material) expressions concerning or emanating from a particular religious tradition,

Animism

Term derived from the Greek *anima*, meaning spirit or soul, and used to signify either: (1) the belief in indwelling spirits (souls, ghosts, and other invisible beings) inherent in people, animals, plants, or even lifeless things and often presented in personalized or anthropomorphized images, or (2) the theory that accounts for the origin of religion on the basis of this kind of anima. The anima is believed to be like a soul, a self, or an ego, able to leave the body either temporarily (e.g., in sleep, ecstasy, or fright) or permanently (e.g., on the occasion of death).

The theory of animism as the basis of the earliest form of religion was set forth by the pioneer English anthropologist E. B. Tylor (1832–1917) in his book *Primitive Culture*. Tylor bridged the evolutionary and diffusionist theories of culture of his times in his own psychologically inspired reasoning. The general evolutionary perception of that age proposed a gradual development of the natural, social, and spiritual worlds toward more complex and higher modes of existence. In the evolution of man's religious ideas, monotheistic Christianity was placed at the pinnacle of the developmental scale as the highest form of spirituality.

Tylor stated that primitive religion was rational in its own way, supporting his premises with an image of the 'ancient savage philosophers.' The theory of animism was thought to reveal the psychological mechanisms of primitive man and the original form of religion in human history. However, Tylor's hypotheses were not based on reliable scientific data, and the premise of unilinear cultural evolution ultimately could not prevail in the face of accumulating evidence regarding early man. Scientific accumulation of knowledge on the so-called primitive religions and on continuous contacts between these tribes and peoples of different modes of production and belief systems forced scholars to abandon the theory that claimed that the nineteenth-century aboriginal tribes represented the pristine state of human cultural evolution.

Despite the fact that the theoretical value of animism has been disproved, it played an influential role in the study of man for decades before the rise of functionalism in the field of anthropology. It also made an important contribution to the search for the origins of human civilization.

Juha Pentikäinen

and the study of the folk (a group of religious people). This can be called "religious folklore." Folk religion also has represented for folklorists a specific group of religious people, such as "the folk church," which stands independent of a culture's normative religious communities or organizations. Finally, "folk religion" has been conceived as the entire body of interpreted and negotiated religious beliefs and practices of individuals and communities fluidly interacting with organized religious traditions. The diverse subjects examined have included the collection and analysis of Christian saints' legends; supernatural narratives from

Mormon Utah; American regional spirituals; witch tales from eastern Pennsylvania counties; popular beliefs concerning the cycles of human life, luck, magic, and the supernatural given the pejorative designation "superstitions"; and the cultural continuities categorized as survivals of distinct ethnic and linguistic regions and peoples, such as the ancient Celts, Germans, Mediterranean peoples, Eastern Europeans, Middle Eastern and Far Eastern communities, Africans, and Native Americans. The breadth of folkloristic interests in religion is shown in the range of other historical and contemporary work, such as the study of Bavarian pilgrimage devotionalism and its associated material culture of medals and badges; French, French Canadian, and German holy cards and other religious prints; Holy Week processions of southern Italians; Swedish Lutheran peasants' use of the Bible; devotion in Newfoundland to particular Roman Catholic saints; healing narratives associated with a European or American saint's shrine; the use of talismans in Greek American culture; New England tombstone designs; oral expression of Pentecostal women in Indiana, Illinois, and Missouri; speech, chant, and song in an Appalachian Independent Baptist congregation; voudon and other African Caribbean syncretized forms of belief; urban and rural Italian and Italian American home altars and street and lawn shrines; apparitions of holy persons in Europe and the Americas; contemporary Wicca and goddess religion in England and the United States; and the negotiated beliefs of gay and lesbian urban Roman Catholics.

Folklorists have studied religion and religious material in a number of ways. The earliest research into folk religion was accomplished by German folklife scholars, and it was the Lutheran minister Paul Drews who coined the term *religiöse Volkskunde* in 1901 to prepare young seminary graduates for the radically different religious ideas of their rural congregants. Throughout the twentieth century, German, Austrian, Swiss, and Swedish folklife scholars (Georg Schreiber, Wolfgang Brückner, Richard Weiss, and Hilding Pleijel among them) studied the religious customs of Roman Catholic and Protestant peasant and rural (and gradually urban) populations continuing Drews's dichotomous conception of folk religion as the religious elaborations of the faithful juxtaposed to the religion of self-designated official institutions and their functionaries. Other European regional ethnologists, such as southern Italian scholars influenced by Antonio Gramsci (e.g., Ernesto De Martino and Luigi Lombardi-Satriani) became especially interested in the autonomous devotions of the dominated classes, which they interpreted as a means of cultural and political resistance. Gradually throughout the century, archives and museums were established in Europe for the preservation, study, and display of the oral, literary, and material evidence of the people's traditional religious beliefs.

The American folklife scholar Don Yoder adapted the European approach to the study of the religion of folk cultures in the context of North America. His

A Haitian woman is possessed by spirits while dancing during a Vodou ceremony in Soukri, Haiti. (AP/Wide World Photos)

influential 1974 definition conceptualized folk religion as unorganized religion that is both related to and in tension with the organized religious systems in a complex society. It was, for him, the totality of people's religious views and practices existing apart from and alongside normative religious theological and liturgical forms. Yoder, therefore, conceived of folk religion primarily as unofficial religion. In this regard, his definition remains closely aligned to the official church-centered orientation of European scholarship. Yoder's two-tiered dichotomization of unofficial folk religion and official institutional religion pervades the scholarly description, conceptualization, and analysis of religion by American folklorists who emphasize folk religion's dependent, residual qualities in relation to formal cultural institutions.

When folklorists such as Yoder discuss folk religion or religious folklore appearing in the context of a religious folk group, the implication is that religion somewhere exists as a pure element that is in some way transformed, even contaminated, by its exposure to human communities. This tendency is emblematic of how folklorists consistently have devalued folk religion by assigning it unofficial religious status. Religious belief should be viewed as the integrated ideas and

Manism

Belief in the deification of deceased ancestors or the hypothesis that ancestor worship is a primary source of religion. The term *manism* is derived from the Latin *manes*, meaning 'departed spirits, ghosts, souls of the deceased.' The concept implies both the practice of worshipping deceased ancestors and the theoretical orientation that suggested this worship was the origin of religion. According to this hypothesis, ghosts developed into gods, with remote and important deceased ancestors becoming divinities and their offering places developing into the shrines for ritual propitiation.

As a belief in a continual relationship between the spirits of the deceased and the community of the living, manism was thought, during the nineteenth century, to have characterized the primal forms of religion, the religion still to be found among 'the primitives.' According to the British philosopher Herbert Spencer (1820–1903), manism offered a sort of rational explanation for otherwise mysterious or inexplicable events and phenomena. The unilineal scheme of evolution had become a dominant theory by Spencer's time, a time of increasing interest in the comparative study of mankind and its religions. His theory of religion was both psychological and evolutionary in its style. Spencer, who was the first to advocate the theory of manism, claimed that ancestor worship was the root of every religion, and he hoped that knowing the origin of religion would reveal the later developments in its unilineal evolution. He further believed that the idea that worship of ancestors or ghosts gradually developed into the belief in gods clarified the general direction of cultural evolution. However, as an explanation for the origins of religion, manism never enjoyed great popularity, not even during Spencer's lifetime.

Juha Pentikäinen

---

practices of individuals living in human society. It is this elemental aspect of the interface of individual religiosity and folklore that can never be categorized into a genre or identified primarily because of group affiliation or regional association. Indeed, though this would seem to be a major concern of the scholar of religion and folklore, it, in fact, has been the least examined element.

Yoder's approach to studying folk religion as religion instead of as oral genres or lore of religious people represented an attempt to break the practice of nineteenth- and early twentieth-century folklorists who were more interested in collecting and cataloging religious, magical, occult, fantastic, medical, or fatalistic beliefs as examples of "superstitions." Such beliefs were not studied and analyzed with an eye to their cultural context or their place within the fabric of community or individual lives but were bracketed as cultural aberrations. Folk religion is an item-centered, as opposed to context-centered, orientation more interested in the transmission and variation of oral forms than in the constitution or influence of systems of belief. Folklorist Wayland D. Hand was the chief

American exponent of this approach throughout much of the twentieth century. His insight was to collect, preserve, geographically classify, and annotate such material, but these "popular beliefs" were given little ethnographic contextualization. Some contemporary folklorists studying religion still depend on a religious folklore approach to center their study of religion, and even ethnographically based studies of religious communities emphasize the oral components of religious culture (testimony, preaching style, song, life story) as a foundation for analysis.

It was Yoder's student David J. Hufford, who, in reaction to such sources as the work on memorates by the Finnish folklorist Lauri Honko, expanded the folkloristic approach to narratives concerning supernatural experience by studying the relationship of such experiences to belief. Employing what he has termed the *experience-centered approach*, Hufford worked to establish the integrity of the connection between beliefs and lived experiences. At first emphasizing health belief contexts and then expanding into work on the epistemology of the supernatural, Hufford noted the importance of systems of belief as the foundation both for the variety of expressions of belief and the subsequent variety of healing contexts that individuals consider valid. In the context of folk medicine, Hufford focused on the systematic, dynamic, logical, and coherent qualities of folk medical traditions and individual health beliefs. Such systems are in a constant state of tension and negotiation with other culturally related health systems, such as allopathic Western medicine. He suggested an approach for understanding such beliefs that centers on the believers themselves, the variety of their life experiences, and the general capacity for variation as individual systems of belief incorporate and integrate other systems. In the case of religion or, more specifically, religious healing, Hufford recognized the same dynamism and the same tensions as he saw in other health systems. His conceptions of folk religion and folk medicine share such similar qualities as a reliance on oral tradition, regional variation, group identification, and the unofficial status of particular systems or beliefs in relationship to an official, normative tradition.

Influenced by the work of Hufford, the more specific study of folk religion within contemporary folkloristics should now be classified under the rubric of *belief studies*, which also includes such categories as medical and political belief. Belief itself can be defined as the confidence of individuals and communities of individuals in the truth or existence of something not immediately susceptible to rigorous empirical proof. A belief system is the combination of thoughts, opinions, or convictions held by an individual or group of individuals about a particular topic or topics. Individuals hold belief systems and express them in personal and communal manifestations. Furthermore, several systems of medical, political, religious, and other types of belief can coexist within the same individual, with individuals often mixing such systems. It is within this context of studying systems of religious belief that folklore and folklife today encounter the innumerable and wondrous variations of human religiosity.

Folklorists have left a considerable amount of potential religiosity out of consideration if all religion need be traditional, inherited, group-oriented, deliberate, and involved in performative verbal art to be considered folk religion. Surely, in an effort to study such religion in the context of holistic systems, folkloristic attention needs to be focused not only on the products of religious lives but also on their processes. It is, of course, well within the domain of folklore and folklife scholars to be concerned with the creative products of religious lives, and, indeed, this is a major contribution of the discipline to the study of religious culture. Manifestations of religious ideas and practices should not only be studied as products (e.g., narratives with a religious theme or about a religious context) and performance genres (e.g., the study of the verbal art of conversion testimonies).

The notion of folklore as expressive culture is a concept often espoused by folklorists but not explicitly defined within the discipline's literature. Folklorists usually study belief as expressive culture, through its contextual manifestations (oral, material, aural, ritual, kinesic, or proxemic). The entirety of expressive culture, however, is not to be found merely in its manifestations or outward phenomena but also in the holistic study of these products of communication as dynamic processes within their attendant conscious, unconscious, aesthetic, and affective contexts. The actual human activity of believing something is itself a form of expression and self-communication before it is manifested into particular products. Thus, belief and the action of personally believing also should be considered as expressive culture, not immediately to be gentrified and studied as products. Through exhibiting a sensitivity to the integrity of the very act of believing by the individual, the term *expressive culture* can identify for scholars the internal processes as well as products of human religiosity, a notion that folklorists have pursued in the later half of the twentieth century under the rubric of performance theory.

A potentially useful new term that focuses upon the process of belief and the believing individual is *vernacular religion*, which may serve as a methodological tool for studying the conjunction of religious, folklore, and folklife studies. Vernacular religion is, by definition, religion as it is lived: as human beings encounter, understand, interpret, and practice it. Since religion inherently involves interpretation, it is impossible for the religion of an individual not to be vernacular. Vernacular religious theory involves an interdisciplinary approach to the study of the religious lives of individuals, with special attention to the complex process of acquisition and formation of beliefs that is always accomplished by the conscious and unconscious negotiations of and between believers; to the verbal, behavioral, and material expressions of religious belief; and to the ultimate object of religious belief.

It is relatively easy for the folklorist to understand the vernacular nature of the religion of the common people. It is less easy for folklorists, as well as other scholars of religion, to grasp the vernacular nature of the institutionalized elements of organized religion: their clerical functionaries, their oral and written statements, and their ritualized or sacramental occasions and observances. A vernacular religious viewpoint shows that designations of institutionalized religion as official are inaccurate. What scholars have referred to as official religion does not, in fact, exist. The use of the term *official religion* as a pedagogical tool has helped explain scholarly perspectives to the uninitiated, but it remains an inadequate explanation for the nature of religion. Although it may be possible to refer to various components within a religious body as emically official, meaning authoritative when used by empowered members within that religious tradition, such a designation when used by scholars is limited by the assumption that religion is synonymous with institutional or hierarchical authority.

"Official religion" as a Western scholarly concept has been sustained partly out of deference to the historical and cultural hegemony of Christianity, which has set the dominant tone for Western culture. Through a process of reification, "institution" has become equated for both believers and scholars, whether lay or clerical, with Church/church, with valid, and with official. Religion as institution has been mistakenly identified as the religious reality itself and not as an ideal type. We must be aware that this process of reification has taken place when we consider the concretization of the human religious impulse. There are bodies and agencies of normative, prescriptive religion, but there is no objective existence of practice that expresses official religion. No one—no special religious elite or member of an institutional hierarchy, not even the pope in Rome—lives an "officially" religious life in a pure, unadulterated form. The members of such hierarchies themselves are believing and practicing vernacularly, even while representing the most institutionally normative aspects of their religious traditions. There is always some passive accommodation, some intriguing survival, some active creation, some dissenting impulse, or some reflection on lived experience that influences how these individuals direct their religious lives.

Scholars have studied and continue to study institutional religion as official religion, maintaining it as the standard against which the varieties of people's religious impulses are measured. To continue to compare the vernacular religious ideas of people of any culture to the construct "official religion" is to perpetuate the value judgment that people's ideas and practices, because they do not represent the refined statements of a religious institution, are indeed unofficial and fringe. This attitude is particularly faulty because it is believers' ideas that inspire the formation of institutional religion in the first place. Vernacular religion takes into consideration the individual convictions of official religious membership among common believers, as well as the vernacular religious ideas at the root of the institution itself. In such a situation, the concept of vernacular religion can highlight the creative interpretations present in even the most ardent, devout, and accepting religious life, while also being sensitive to the context of power that makes the validity of "official" religion so convincing. The possible evolution of the folkloristic study of religion would be the adoption of this new terminology in lieu of the term *folk religion* and the dichotomous conceptualizations that it has carried with it.

Leonard Norman Primiano

See Also Belief, Folk; Belief Tale; Divination; Magic; Medicine, Folk; Religion, Comparative; Supernatural/Supranormal.

References

Badone, Ellen, ed. 1990. *Religious Orthodoxy and Popular Faith in European Society*. Princeton, NJ: Princeton University Press.

Bruckner, Wolfgang. 1968. Popular Piety in Central Europe. *Journal of the Folklore Institute* 5: 158–174.

Byrne, Donald E., Jr. 1988. Folklore and the Study of American Religion. In *Encyclopedia of the American Religious Experience*, eds. Charles H. Lippy and Peter W. Williams, vol. 1. New York: Charles Scribner's Sons.

Christian, William A., Jr. 1981. *Local Religion in Sixteenth-Century Spain*. Princeton, NJ: Princeton University Press.

Clements, William M. 1983. The Folk Church: Institution, Event, Performance. In *Handbook of American Folklore*, ed. Richard M. Dorson. Bloomington: Indiana University Press.

Danielson, Larry. 1986. Religious Folklore. In *Folk Groups and Folklore Genres: An Introduction*, ed. Elliott Oring. Logan: Utah State University Press.

De Martino, Ernesto. 1968. *La Terra del rimorso* (The land of remorse), 2nd ed. Milan: Alberto Mondadori.

Drews, Paul. 1901. Religiöse Volkskunde, eine Aufgabe der praktischen Theologie (Religious folklore: A challenge to applied theology). *Monatsschrift fur die kirchliche Praxis* 1: 1–8.

Hand, Wayland D. 1961. Introduction to Popular Beliefs and Superstitions from North Carolina. In *The Frank C. Brown Collection of North Carolina Folklore*, ed. Newman Ivey White, vol. 6. Durham, NC: Duke University Press.

Honko, Lauri. 1964. Memorates and the Study of Folk Beliefs. *Journal of the Folklore Institute* 1: 5–19.

Hufford, David J. 1982. *The Terror That Comes in the Night: An Experience-Centered Study of Supernatural Assault Traditions*. Philadelphia: University of Pennsylvania Press.

Hufford, David J. 1985. Ste. Anne de Beaupré: Roman Catholic Pilgrimage and Healing. *Western Folklore* 44: 194–207.

Isambert, François-André. 1982. *Le Sens du sacré: Fête et religion populaire* (The sense of the sacred: Festivity and popular religion). Paris: Les Éditions de Minuit.

Lawless, Elaine J.1988. *God's Peculiar People: Women's Voices and Folk Tradition in a Pentecostal Church.* Lexington: University Press of Kentucky.

Lawless, Elaine J. 1988. *Handmaidens of the Lord: Pentecostal Woman Preachers and Traditional Religion.* Philadelphia: University of Pennsylvania Press.

Lombardi-Satriani, Luigi. 1978. Attuale problematica della religione popolare (Current problems of popular religion). In *Questione meridionale religione e classi subalterne* (Matters of southern religion and the lower classes), ed. Francesco Saija. Naples: Guida.

Noy, Dov. 1980. Is There a Jewish Folk Religion? In *Studies in Jewish Folklore*, ed. Frank Talmage. Cambridge, MA: Association for Jewish Studies.

Pleigel, Hilding. 1959. *Kyrklig Folklivsforskning: Fragelista I* (Folklife studies in religion: Issues I). Meddelanden fran Kyrkohistoriska Arkivet i Lund (Bulletin from the archives of church history in Lund), Vol. 1. Lund, Sweden: Gleerup.

Primiano, Leonard Norman. 1993. Intrinsically Catholic: Vernacular Religion and Philadelphia's "Dignity." PhD dissertation, University of Pennsylvania, Philadelphia.

Primiano, Leonard Norman. 1995. Vernacular Religion and the Search for Method in Religious Folklife. *Western Folklore* 54: 37–56.

Titon, Jeff Todd. 1988. *Powerhouse for God: Speech, Chant, and Song in an Appalachian Baptist Church.* Austin: University of Texas Press.

Tyson, Ruel W., Jr., James L. Peacock, and Daniel W. Patterson, eds. 1988. *Diversities of Gifts, Field Studies in Southern Religion.* Urbana: University of Illinois Press.

Vrijhof, Pieter, and Jacques Waardenburg, eds. 1979. *Official and Popular Religion: Analysis of a Theme for Religious Studies.* The Hague: Mouton.

Williams, Peter W. 1989. *Popular Religion in America: Symbolic Change and the Modernization Process in Historical Perspective.* Urbana: University of Illinois Press.

Yoder, Don. 1974. Toward a Definition of Folk Religion. *Western Folklore* 33(1): 2–15. Reprinted in 1990 in *Discovering American Folklife: Studies in Ethnic, Religious, and Regional Culture*, ed. Don Yoder. Ann Arbor, MI: UMI Research.

Religious Folk Heroes

This large category includes heroes of all kinds: founders of faiths, martyrs, saints, the pious, the brave, the compassionate, and the wise. The religious traditions of most cultures and peoples, whether written or oral, are full of heroic stories, many of which appear as discrete narratives in other cultures, usually disassociated from their religious significance. The Christian Bible, notably the Old Testament, the Koran, the Torah, and many other such holy books are vast repositories of folk heroism. As is well known, many of these works share common characters and incidents, even though these may be interpreted in different ways according to the various belief systems in which they appear. In addition to such authorized works, there usually exist considerable bodies of apocryphal material that contain even more lore.

Religious belief is a fertile ground for the creation of folk heroes. Those who are celebrated may be founders of their religions (Nanak Chand, founder of

Sikhism; Jesus of Nazareth, founder of Christianity), helpers of the founder (Mary, the Apostles), or those who are martyred to its creed—a large group in all religious systems—or any combination of these. Frequently such individuals, real and mythic, receive the official approbation of their belief system, sainthood in one form or another. Around many such figures form folk traditions, beliefs, and customs that in the case of the major religions have become the foundations of complex social and cultural systems. In the generally more humble realms of the folkloric, religious heroes are celebrated in down-to-earth ways, with the stories of their deeds often being humorous, ridiculous, or even irreverent. Tales told of many Jewish holy men, for example, often emphasize their shortcomings as well as their virtues.

The spread of some religious belief systems, especially Christianity, around the world has led many religious figures to take on folkloric roles in different cultures. St. George is one such example, while Saint James, known as Santiago, is the patron saint of Spain and also identified by some South American Indian groups who experienced Spanish colonization as the thunder god. In the New World, the legendary doings of saints are told among immigrant groups and their descendants, in part as a means of continuing their links with the homeland where the stories are located. Other groups, such as Mexicans of Spanish descent, locate the traditions of their saints and holy people in the New World itself. Such legends tend to concentrate on the spiritual or supernatural powers of the saint or

Woodcut depicting the legend of Santiago (St. James), which tells of the saint appearing to Christian troops during their battle with Muslim forces, 1503. (Library of Congress)

holy man. One example given by Dorson is the south Texas folk healer Pedro Jaramillo of Los Olmos, celebrated as a miraculous healer among Mexican families from the 1880s. Stories of Jaramillo emphasize his magical ability to effect cures, often involving prescribed actions being performed nine times.

Christian religious figures often have a role in folk drama, especially in Latin cultures. Jesus, Mary, and Joseph, for example, are found in the Nativity and also in other forms of traditional theater. God is also featured in some traditions, often those of a humorous nature.

Religious heroes are frequently found in folklore as helpers, sometimes as healers, and generally combine their status as official figures of veneration with the unofficial tales and beliefs that are popularly held or told about them. Like most folk heroes, they straddle the boundaries between different, often oppositional, cultural spaces, in these cases between the spiritual and the mundane.

Graham Seal

See Also Culture Hero; Drama, Folk; Helpers, Folk; Religion, Comparative; Religion, Folk.

References

Ausubel, N., ed. [1948] 1972. *A Treasury of Jewish Folklore*. London: Vallentine, Mitchell, pp. 104–223.

Blum, R. and E. 1970. *The Dangerous Hour: The Lore of Crisis and Mystery in Rural Greece*. London: Chatto and Windus, pp. 88–94.

Dorson, R. 1964. *Buying the Wind: Regional Folklore in the United States*. Chicago: University of Chicago Press, pp. 500–508.

El-Shamy, H., coll., trans., ed. 1980. *Folktales of Egypt*. Chicago: University of Chicago Press, pp. 149–169.

Espinosa, A. 1985. *The Folklore of Spain in the American Southwest: Traditional Spanish Folk Literature in Northern New Mexico and Southern Colorado*, ed. M. Espinosa. Norman: University of Oklahoma Press, pp. 201–213.

Frazer, Sir J. 1918. *Folk-Lore in the Old Testament*, 3 vols. London: Macmillan.

Gaer, J. 1951. *The Lore of the Old Testament*, Boston: Little, Brown.

Gaer, J. 1952. *The Lore of the New Testament*, Boston: Little, Brown.

Heath-Stubbs, J. 1975. The Hero as a Saint: St. George. In *Legends of Icelandic Magicians* (with an introduction by B. Benedikz), trans. J. Simpson. London: Brewer/Rowman and Littlefield, The Folklore Society, pp. 1–15.

Hunt, M., trans. and ed. 1884. *Grimm's Household Tales* (with the author's notes and an introduction by Andrew Lang), 2 vols. London: George Bell and Sons, pp. 312–324, 440–452.

Ivanits, L. 1989. *Russian Folk Belief*, Armonk and London: M. E. Sharpe Inc., pp. 136–153.

Lüthi, M. 1976. *Once upon a Time: On the Nature of Fairy Tales*, trans. L. Chadeayne and P. Gottwald. Bloomington: Indiana University Press, pp. 35–46.

Paredes, A. 1970. *Folktales of Mexico*. Chicago: University of Chicago Press, pp. 176–177.

Porter, R. 1975. Heroes in the Old Testament: The Hero as Seen in the Book of Judges. In *Legends of Icelandic Magicians* (with an introduction by B. Benedikz), trans. J. Simpson. London: Brewer/Rowman and Littlefield, The Folklore Society, pp. 90–111.

Sabar, Y., trans. and ed. 1982. *The Folk Literature of the Kurdistani Jews: An Anthology*, New Haven/London: Yale University Press, pp. 104–134.

Revenant

A home-wanderer, a deceased person believed to appear to the people of his or her own community after death. People usually express their encounters with revenants in memorates and legends. The existence of the belief in revenants is closely linked to the understanding of the notions of life and death in a community. Different systems of beliefs and their messages concerning death clearly establish grounds for human ethical expectations and the appropriate behavior and social roles of community members. In this perspective, the existence of revenants is interpretable as the result of an unfulfilled duty on the part of either the deceased or the community of the living: Either the deceased behaved in an unacceptable way during his or her life or the community of the living neglected or improperly conducted the necessary rites for the dead person, either during life or after death.

Ideas about death and the afterlife vary greatly, according to culture and area, as do the ceremonies associated with the dead. There are communities, for instance, whose religious behavior is characterized by the belief in reincarnation, when one's birth means a rebirth in a new body. Some religio-philosophical doctrines, however, regard reincarnation as a punishment, and attempts are made to avoid any afterlife. In many cultures, the cult of the dead is a central religious institution. The bonds between the family and its dead are not broken by death and burial; their collective interaction is believed to continue.

On the basis of Finnish and Scandinavian materials, revenants can be divided into two main groups: the guilty and the innocent. The former includes those dead people whose lingering is understood to be the punishment imposed on them for an offense committed during their lifetimes. By tradition, the necessity for such a punishment is stressed at the time of death or when the body is carried to the grave. Among the innocent dead, by contrast, we may count all those whose lingering is not explained as being a punishment for offenses committed during their lives. Among them, the following three groups are distinguished: (1) the solicitous, such as a mother who died in childbirth; a jealous or protective husband; a betrothed man or woman; a person who comes to look after his or her relations, children, or property; a person who hid his or her money; or someone who left behind a task undone or a promise unfulfilled; (2) the avengers, for instance, people who were maltreated, bewitched, or murdered; slaughtered children; aborted fetuses; or unaccepted potential children; and (3) those dissatisfied with the manner of their burial, burial place, or the behavior of the mourners, for example, those negligently or wrongly shrouded, unburied, or buried in unconsecrated ground; those not buried as they wished; those mourned for excessively or not mourned at all; and those buried with incomplete body or belongings. Members of the third group also might be termed the "unprovided." Ancestor worship has always been a central cult in the societies that hold beliefs in figures such as home-wanderers and revenants. The dead are conceived as guardians of morals, arbiters of behavior, and supporters of an organized society. The dead who reveal themselves to the living people fulfill their obligations to proper norms.

Deceased children of Nordic tradition provide an illustrative example of revenants who interfere in the life of their community. This category of revenant—a wandering, placeless soul lacking a position or status in the twin community of the living and the dead—is in a permanent transition phase. The basic problem concerning the majority of the Nordic deceased children is that they have no status either among the living or the dead. These "supranormal dead children" may be divided into many categories, such as those murdered or abandoned, those who died before being baptized or given a name, those who were stillborn, those prematurely born, and so on. What is common to all of them is that they all died before the completion of the rites necessary for establishing their first status in the society. Their position is problematic, as they did not have time to join any living social group. A common means of signaling membership is naming. In fact, the name was the most important symbol of status long before the advent of Christianity, with its emphasis on the Christian baptismal rite as the entrance of a newborn child into legitimate status. So vital was the name that Icelandic sagas and Old Nordic provincial laws of the missionary period state that abandoning a child with a name was considered murder. If a child had not belonged to the community of the living, he or she could not be incorporated among the dead. Burial rites were either not performed at all or performed in a special way.

Juha Pentikäinen

See Also Belief, Folk; Religion, Folk; Vampire.

References

Pentikäinen, Juha Y. 1968. *The Nordic Dead-Child Tradition: Nordic Dead-Child Beigns—A Study in Comparative Religion.* Helsinki: Academia Scientiarum Fennica.

Pentikäinen, Juha Y. 1989. The Dead without Status. In *Nordic Folklore: Recent Studies*, eds. Reimund Kvideland and Henning K. Sehmsdorf, with Elizabeth Simpson. Bloomington: Indiana University Press.

Reversal

The common view that the spirit world is an opposite version of the phenomenal world, in both form and function. In the spirit world of the Hopi, "everything is the other way around, just the opposite." According to Mircea Eliade, "The peoples of North Asia conceive the otherworld as an inverted image of this world. Everything takes place as it does here, but in reverse. When it is day on earth, it is night in the beyond (this is why festivals of the dead are held after sunset; that is when they wake and begin their day); the summer of the living corresponds to winter in the land of the dead; a scarcity of game or fish on earth means that it is plentiful in the otherworld." The dead may be buried face down (a reversal of the sleeping position of the living), so as to ensure their passage to the other world, or their clothing may be put on (or, in ancient Egypt, be put into the tomb) inside out. Clothing also may be reversed to undo the effects of the evil eye. Since the spirit world is frequently consulted by means of reflecting surfaces—mirrors, water, oil, crystal balls—it is likely that the phenomenon of mirror image brings this conception into being.

The reversed quality of the spirit world reveals itself not only in actions but also in the distinction between left and right. Perhaps because most people are right-handed (but their reflection is left-handed), the left is taken to be the side of the spirits, and left-handed people are often viewed with suspicion. In Henri Boguet's sixteenth-century account, the werewolf was said to eat only from the left side of the children it killed. In Paleolithic impressions of the human hand, according to G. Rachel Levy, "the negative impressions, produced by painting or blowing colour on to the rock surface round the flattened member, are generally of the left hand; the positive records of the paint-covered palm and fingers are chiefly of the right." The plastic *mani cornute*, or horned hands, which are worn to ward off the evil eye, always represent the left hand. It is easy to see why the left is associated with awkwardness, as is suggested by such words as the French (and English) *gauche*, German *linkisch*, and Norwegian *keitet*: Most people are right-handed and less "adroit" with their left. But because of its association with the spirit world, the left also has a spooky quality, as is suggested by the Latin word for "left" that has given us *sinister* in English. Latin *scaevus* means "left, awkward, unlucky," as does Greek *skaiós*. In Hungarian, the word for "left" is *bal. Balfogás* is "blunder" or "mistake," but *baljóslatú*is "ill-omened" or "ominous."

The distinction between right and left shows up in a great deal of folklore. Traditionally in Europe, people were enjoined to get out of the right side of the bed in the morning, rather than the left. But the word *right*, since it is associated with the human world rather than the world of the spirits, has come to have the meaning of "correct," so that it is opposed not just to *left* but also to *wrong*, and nowadays one hears the remark, when someone shows ill temper, that he or she must have "gotten out of the wrong side of the bed."

Relics of this sort of reversal are still common, as when one wishes an actor well by telling him or her to break a leg. In *Popular Beliefs and Superstitions*, an informant from Ohio says, "You should always say, 'I hope you break a leg.' If you wish them good luck, it means bad luck for them." That is, the spirits may respond with a reversal of the outcome that is appealed for. Thus, there is a common belief that it is unwise to praise anything good or valuable, as such praise is apt to spoil it. Such a custom as *couvade* (in which a father-to-be may dress in women's clothing and feign birthing) is probably to be understood in terms of this reversal of the spirit world, and this may be true also of the transvestitism sometimes practiced by shamans.

Paul Barber

See Also Belief, Folk; Shamanism.

References

Boguet, Henri. 1590. *Discours des sorciers* (Passage on werewolves). Translated in 1986, *A Lycanthropy Reader: Werewolves in Western Culture*, ed. Charlotte F. Otten. Syracuse, NY: Syracuse University Press.

Courlander, Harold, ed. 1982. *Hopi Voices: Recollections, Traditions, and Narratives of the Hopi Indians*. Albuquerque: University of New Mexico Press.

Eliade, Mircea. 1972. *Shamanism: Archaic Techniques of Ecstasy*. Princeton, NJ: Princeton University Press.

Levy, G. Rachel. 1963. *Religious Conceptions of the Stone Age*. New York: Harper & Row.

Puckett, Newbell Niles. 1981. *Popular Beliefs and Superstitions: A Compendium of American Folklore*, eds. Wayland D. Hand, Anna Casetta, and Sondra B. Thiederman. Boston: G. K. Hall.

Revitalization

A deliberate attempt by some members of a society to construct a more satisfactory culture by the rapid acceptance of a pattern of multiple innovations. Sociologically, individuals and groups withdraw to escape when primary ties of culture, social relationships, and activities are broken and force is imposed. But when value systems get out of step with existing reality, a condition of cultural crisis is likely to build up, which may breed some form of reactive movement. A drastic solution is attempted when a group's anxiety and frustration have become so intense that the only way to reduce the stress is to overturn the entire social system and replace it with a new one. Not all suppressed, conquered, or colonized people eventually rebel against established authority, although when they do, resistance may take one of several forms, which are varieties of revitalization movements.

A culture may seek to speed up the acculturation process in order to share more fully in the supposed benefits of the dominant cultures. Melanesian cargo cults of the post-World War II era have generally been of this sort, although earlier ones stressed a revival of traditional ways. Movements that try to reconstitute a destroyed but not forgotten way of life are known as nativistic or revivalistic movements. In such cases, it is commonly expressive culture (i.e., folklore) that is revived most easily to represent traditional lifeways, and narratives such as myth and folk history are commonly used as the means of characterizing and advocating the "golden age" that is to be revived. The Native American Ghost Dance religion of the Paiute prophet Wovoka demonstrates these principles.

A movement that attempts to resurrect a suppressed pariah group, which has long suffered in an inferior social standing and which has its own special subcultural ideology, is referred to as "millenarian"; perhaps the most familiar examples are prophetic Judaism and early Christianity.

If the aim of the movement is directed primarily at the ideological system and the attendant social structure of a cultural system from within, it is called revolutionary. As an example, revitalization movements have been common in the history of the United States whenever significant segments of the population have found their conditions in life to be at odds with the values of the "American Dream."

The revitalization sequence follows a predictable pattern. First, there is the normal stage of society, in which stress is not too great and there are sufficient cultural means of satisfying needs. Second, under domination by a more powerful group or under severe economic depression, stress and frustration will be steadily amplified to create a period of increased individual stress. Third, if there are no significant adaptive changes, a period of cultural distortion follows, in which stress becomes so chronic that socially approved methods of releasing tension begin to break down. Fourth and finally, the steady deterioration is checked by a period of revitalization, during which a dynamic cult or religious movement grips a sizable proportion of the population. Characteristically, the movement will be so out of touch with reality that it is doomed to failure from the beginning. Rarely, a movement may tap long-dormant adaptive forces underlying a culture, and a long-lasting religion may result, for example, Mormonism, Christianity, Islam, or Judaism.

Margaret Bruchez

See Also Religion, Folk; Revivals.

References:

Aberle, David F. 1966. *The Peyote Religion among the Navaho*. Chicago: Aldine Press.

Burridge, Kenelm. 1969. *New Heaven, New Earth: A Study of Millenarian Activities*. New York: Schocken Books.

Durkheim, Émile. 1957. *Elementary Forms of Religious Life*. Glencoe, IL: Free Press.

Spier, Leslie. 1935. *The Prophet Dance of the Northwest and Its Derivatives: The Source of the Ghost Dance*. Menasha, WI: Banta Press.

Wallace, Anthony F. C. 1969. *The Death and Rebirth of the Seneca*. New York: Random House.

Wilson, Bryan R. 1973. *Magic and the Millennium*. New York: Harper and Row.

Revivals

The conscious use of folklore *as* folklore to express or represent ideas about identity and/or art. The term *revivals* has been used most frequently to describe practitioners of folk music, storytellers, and craftspersons. Although sometimes it is a straightforward descriptive term for certain kinds of social movement, it frequently implies a judgment about authenticity.

An early appearance of *revival* in connection with folklore came in the writings of Cecil Sharp, who, in 1907, called for a revival of English folk music. Following his lead, the English Folk Dance and Song Society became the center of the social movement called "the first British folksong revival"—although the eighteenth-century English interest in the ballad also has been characterized retrospectively as a revival—and led indirectly to later twentieth-century folksong revivals in Britain and elsewhere. Sharp used *revival* metaphorically (its oldest sense) to describe the refurbishment of a repertoire or genre, as when we speak of the revival of a Shakespeare play or some other historical work of art. *Revival* also has been used as a metaphor for the awakening of religious spirit since at least the time of Cotton Mather. Folklorists are interested in religious revivalism as a social phenomenon with folkloric aspects, but they have viewed this area of inquiry as essentially different from that of secular revivalism and have generally treated it as an aspect of the folk-organized religion continuum.

By the 1960s, when folklore emerged as a professionalized discipline, folklorists read *revival* literally rather than metaphorically, and, having shifted their focus outward from cultural products to include cultural producers and contexts, they saw the word as referring to the resuscitation of "living" traditions in these new terms. Consequently, they employed it to describe the uses of insiders' cultural products by outsiders—individuals from "other" cultural contexts. This perspective coincided with the apogee of the commercial folk music boom of the 1960s. *Revival* thus became a pejorative or judgmental term for folklorists, referring to the contextually inauthentic or spurious, and it was used, characteristically, to describe situations in which individuals or groups perform texts, enact customs, or create objects that are based on traditions from outside their own personal historical and/or cultural experience.

The concept of revival, whether literal or metaphorical, has been problematic to folklorists for another reason as well. Although folklorists typically have defined their materials as emerging from a matrix of "unselfconscious" cultural production or enactment, attempts to revive such materials imply some degree of "non-unselfconsciousness." Those most interested in the revival of folklore tend to have, like Sharp, conscious (and articulated) political, artistic, or cultural agendas that extend far beyond the original contexts of production. Ironically, then—given their pejorative use of the term—folklorists have been among the principal folklore revivalists.

Folklorists, analyzing situations where differing degrees of awareness about such matters occur, create categories of classification that differentiate on the basis of awareness and agendas. Ellen Stekert speaks of four groups in the urban folksong movement: imitators (or emulators), utilizers, new aesthetic singers, and traditional singers, or those who "have learned their songs and their style of presentation from oral tradition as they grew up." Joe Wilson and Lee Udall, addressing folk festival organizers and managers, present similar though more detailed categories. Separating performers into two categories, they distinguish those "reared in the culture from which the performed materials are drawn" from those "who adopt elements of style and materials from cultures into which they were not reared." This allows them to split Stekert's category of traditional singer three ways: traditional folk performer, aware traditional performer, and evolved traditional performer. These subdivisions allow for the idea that traditional performers might lose the unselfconscious quality in their performance. Wilson and Udall split their second category, nonreared, into subdivisions resembling Stekert's other three.

Such categorization admits the possibility of non-unselfconsciousness, but it overlooks the frequent collaboration among the reared and the nonreared for conscious revival. Examples abound within the domain of music: Since the 1960s, for example, the growth of old-time fiddle music associations has been characterized by the participation of individuals who grew up hearing and performing fiddle music together with those who did not. They share a perception of this music culture as being threatened by outside forces and collaborate to protect and promote the tradition. In a more general way, collaboration between insiders and outsiders occurs whenever folklorists conduct research into a tradition.

Today, folklorists recognize the necessity and ethical imperative for dialogue with their informants in the process of research and publication. As scholars become aware and evolved in their attitudes about the traditions they study, so too do the tradition bearers. Consequently, the possibility of revival always exists whenever anyone identifies something as folklore.

Neil V. Rosenberg

See Also Authenticity; Fakelore; Folklorismus/Folklorism; Revitalization.

References

Boyes, Georgina. 1993. *The Imagined Village: Culture, Ideology and the English Folk Revival.* Manchester, England: Manchester University Press.

Stekert, Ellen J. 1993. Cents and Nonsense in the Urban Folksong Movement: 1930–66. In *Transforming Tradition: Folk Music Revivals Examined,* ed. Neil V. Rosenberg. Urbana: University of Illinois Press.

Wilson, Joe, and Lee Udall. 1982. *Folk Festivals.* Knoxville: University of Tennessee Press.

Rhetorical Analysis

In its most general terms, the study of the relations between language and intention, especially the function of discourse in communicating ideas and shaping knowledge. Rhetoricians since Plato have placed emphasis on the speaker, the audience, the nature of the message, and the constitution of persuasive form. Each historical period has created its own configuration of primary rhetorical issues, such as the relation of rhetorical principles to pedagogy, treatment of the rhetorical processes of composition (that is, canons of invention, arrangement, style, memory, and delivery), and attention to either performance or text. Since the classical period, rhetoricians have remained committed to the following assumptions: (1) The rhetorician must have a command of conventional discourse forms and a complementary understanding of the contextual variables that define and constrain performance occasions; (2) although they recognize the conventional nature of language, rhetoricians have typically assumed that human nature could be defined in universal terms, thus allowing the rhetorician to predict how to create certain persuasive effects; (3) rhetoricians have promoted the study of rhetorical theory and practice as a pursuit that is fundamental to the development of intellectual skills and moral character; and (4) rhetoricians in every era have associated an education in rhetorical skills with the development of a literate citizenry.

Rhetorical analysis had its greatest impact on folklore scholarship of the second half of the twentieth century when Dell Hymes, Roger Abrahams, and others, adapting rhetorical principles of situations and strategies as outlined by Kenneth Burke, reconceptualized folklore as a study of performance. Abrahams saw Burke's concept of persuasion and performance as a means to integrate diverse approaches to the study of art. The introduction of the concept of performance provided an alternative to the text-centered perspective scholars had previously utilized; now, scholars considered questions of form and the relation between components as part of a larger performance context involving the relations between performer, text or object, and audience. With the influence of Burke's rhetorical approach to art as persuasive communication, folklore studies was able to integrate literary, text-centered, historic-geographic studies with ethnographic, culturally contexted studies.

Interestingly, two of the most provocative Burkean concepts, *consubstantiation* and *terministic screen*, have not been incorporated into folklore's rhetorical approach to performance. In *Grammar of Motives*, Burke described consubstantiality as a state in which persons feel themselves to be "substantially one." Burke argued that it is the aim of rhetoric to create this state through language acts in which the addressee identifies substantially with the speaker. In *Language as Symbolic Action*, Burke defined the very nature of language as a "screen" that defines reality as much through what is filtered out as what is filtered in. Language acts or rhetoric performs this function at the level of discourse. Folklorists have utilized similar concepts under the general heading of context without realizing the theoretical rapprochement between folklore performance theory and these other Burkean rhetorical principles.

Rhetoric and folklore are joined most meaningfully in performance studies in which communication is viewed in a cultural context. However, though rhetorical principles, especially principles of arrangement and style, are well suited to the close analysis of cultural performances, the field of rhetoric itself has more often made universal rather than culturally specific claims. Further, even though rhetoricians long have recognized communication to be a crafted, artistic construction rather than a decontextualized truth, the principles of construction have been assumed to be universal rather than locally situated and contested. Thus, one consequence of the appropriation of rhetorical principles in performance studies has been a challenge to the universalist claims made by rhetoricians.

Between the late 1960s and late 1980s, the performance model became established as a dominant paradigm of folklore research. During that period, the role of rhetorical studies lost some emphasis as folklore models turned increasingly to anthropological, structural, and sociolinguistic models of communicative performance. In the 1990s, as performance studies turned toward addressing the politics of culture and larger performance stages rather than face-to-face interaction in small groups, rhetoric and the politics of persuasion again became integral to folklore research. By this time, rhetorical studies too had also been influenced by poststructural and, to a lesser extent, ethnographic cultural approaches of the past decades. These influences have resulted in the articulation of the social constructionist approach to rhetoric, a position that argues that communities define the nature of rhetorical practices and also argues that interpretation replaces truth. However, the social constructionist approach to rhetoric maintains that the communal nature of rhetoric is knowable; therefore, codes of practice can still be defined and taught. One of the attractions of the social constructionist approach to rhetoric for folklore studies is that this position attempts to dismantle the rhetoric's historical allegiance to the promulgation of dominant discourses.

In addition to the value of traditional rhetorical principles such as speaker, message, and context to folklore performance analysis, the social constructionist approach to rhetoric holds particular promise for another point of intersection between rhetoric and folklore because this position recognizes the politics of culture. Whereas the historical bias toward high culture on the part of rhetoricians and the bias toward a limited concept of the folk as low culture on the part of folklorists separated the two fields for most of the twentieth century, both fields are currently investigating the substance of those biases and are similarly committed to an ongoing exploration of the dynamics of language in use.

Nan Johnson and Amy Shuman

See Also Linguistic Approach; Performance.

References

Abrahams, Roger D. 1968. A Rhetoric of Everyday Life: Traditional Conversational Genres. *Southern Folklore Quarterly* 32: 44–59.

Abrahams, Roger D. 1968. Introductory Remarks to a Rhetorical Theory of Folklore. *Journal of American Folklore* 81: 143–158.

Abrahams, Roger D. 1977. Toward an Enactment-Centered Theory of Folklore. In *Frontiers of Folklore*, ed. William R. Bascom. Boulder: Westview Press.

Burke, Kenneth. 1961. *The Philosophy of Literary Form*. New York: Vintage.

Burke, Kenneth. 1962. *A Grammar of Motives*. Berkeley: University of California Press.

Burke, Kenneth. 1966. *Language as Symbolic Action: Essays on Life, Literature and Method*. Berkeley: University of California Press.

Conquergood, Dwight. 1992. Ethnography, Rhetoric, and Performance. *Quarterly Journal of Speech* 78: 80–123.

Hymes, Dell. 1972. The Contribution of Folklore to Sociolinguistic Research. In *Toward New Perspectives in Folklore*, eds. Américo Paredes and Richard Bauman. Austin: University of Texas Press.

Schaffer, John D. 1989. The Use and Misuse of Giambattista Vico: Rhetoric, Orality, and Theories of Discourse. *The New Historicism*, ed. H. Aram Veeser. New York: Routledge.

Shotter, John. 1993. *Cultural Politics of Everyday Life: Social Constructionism, Rhetoric, and Knowing of the Third Kind*. Toronto: University of Toronto Press.

Riddle

The best-known and best-studied form of traditional enigma. The riddle is generally agreed to consist of a description and its referent—the first posed by the riddler, the second guessed by the respondent. The enigma comes from the incorporation of a "block element" in the description: an ambiguity that prevents the description from being obvious. The ambiguity may occur at any level of the linguistic code from the phonological to the semantic, and it is often presented as an opposition or paradox within the description ("What has eyes but cannot see?—A potato").

The "true riddle," as it is often called, relies on concrete, familiar objects in the culture, and it equates two things through the use of a metaphor. The implications of favorite metaphors are elaborated through numerous riddles in a given tradition. In Finnish riddles, for example, women are commonly compared to trees:

> Rowan tree on a sacred hill, sacred leaves in the rowan tree. *(Bride)*
> A sacred rowan tree, on the edge of a sacred field, a sacred berry in the rowan tree.
> *(Pregnant woman)*
> A widow in the fall, a widow in the winter, a new bride in summer.
> *(Deciduous tree)*
> A thousand-year-old woman has a child every year. *(Pine tree with cones)*

The recurrence of metaphors makes it possible for riddles to be guessed by persons familiar with a given tradition, thus making the riddling session a true contest of wits. It also lets riddling make larger cultural assertions. The tree metaphor, for example, suggests that the focus of women's lives around marriage and childbearing is as natural and inevitable as the life cycle of a tree. Other Finnish riddling metaphors further reinforce traditional gender roles by matching women to kitchen tools and men to farming tools.

Many scholars have claimed that the use of metaphor to bring different cultural domains together functions to establish higher-order similarities and thus to imply an overarching coherence and rightness to the culture. When correspondences are established between nature, humanity, and human-made objects, riddling can serve, as James Fernandez says, as a kind of "edification by puzzlement"—a way of leading members of a culture from the diversity of their experience to a sense of a higher integration. In certain traditions, this power of riddles is appropriated for religious purposes, and riddling becomes a means of initiation into cosmology.

However, riddles often seem to disturb the coherence of culture by pointing out anomalies in its categories—there are some eyes that cannot see. Thus, some riddles relativize rather than reinforce culture: Their messages have to do with the limits of any system attempting to impose order on experience. Respondents are led to question the cultural taxonomies they have so painstakingly acquired and to investigate situations empirically.

John McDowell has suggested that these two functions of the riddle are not mutually exclusive but that they seem to prevail in different types of society. The "true" or metaphorical riddle flourishes in "traditional," relatively small-scale, and homogeneous societies, where the narrow range of material culture limits the universe of riddle referents and, more important, where a common system of beliefs and values can be taken for granted.

The riddles of paradox and anomaly belong to heterogeneous societies in which paradox and anomaly are likely to figure prominently in everyday experience. Riddle anomalies tend to occur at the level of language rather than in the world referred to: They are problems in the code ("What room can no one enter?—A mushroom"). Indeed, as W. J. Pepicello and Thomas A. Green suggest, the real referent of contemporary riddles is the linguistic code itself. And the question of code is perhaps the real challenge of contemporary culture; before any debate on the nature of reality can take place, a common language has to be established. The presence of conflicting cultural codes may enter riddling directly. In one session, a Chicano child asked the Anglo folklorist John McDowell, "Why do you need a moustache?—So you won't be a *bolillo* [white]."

Generalizing broadly, then, members of traditional societies use riddles to propound their culture's rules and to integrate these rules into a larger synthesis. In complex societies, in which riddling is generally limited to children, riddling teaches the importance of message form and the particular context. The analytical skills and cognitive flexibility learned in riddling prepare children for the pitfalls inherent in reading contemporary messages.

Dorothy Noyes

See Also Enigma, Folk.

References

Fernandez, James. 1986. Edification by Puzzlement. In *Persuasions and Performances*. Bloomington: Indiana University Press.

Köngäs-Maranda, Elli. 1971. The Logic of Riddles. In *The Structural Analysis of Oral Tradition*, eds. Elli Köngäs-Maranda and Pierre Maranda. Philadelphia: University of Pennsylvania Press.

McDowell, John. 1979. *Children's Riddling*. Bloomington: Indiana University Press. Pepicello, W. J., and Thomas A. Green. 1984. *The Language of Riddles*. Columbus: Ohio State University Press.

Taylor, Archer. 1951. *English Riddles from Oral Tradition*. Berkeley and Los Angeles: University of California Press.

Riddle Joke

A joke in the form of a traditional enigma. Although the riddle joke is couched as a question, the respondent is not expected to arrive at a solution; rather, the poser follows up with the answer after a short pause.

Riddle jokes often circulate in cycles relating to a current event, such as the 1986 explosion of the U.S. space shuttle *Challenger*, the 1986 meltdown at the Chernobyl nuclear plant in the Ukraine, a political campaign, or a celebrity scandal. Other foci of cycles include stigmatized social groups (such as Polish immigrants in the United States); powerful public figures (such as the hated Romanian dictator Nicolae Ceaușescu); an action frame (screwing in a light bulb); and such absurd or horrific dramatis personae as elephants and dead babies. The poser often tops one joke with another, and jokes build on the form of earlier jokes in a kind of dialogue. Such cycles circulate rapidly and enjoy wide popularity while the topic or the jokes themselves are current.

Riddle joke cycles address, whether openly or in symbolic disguise, matters that deeply trouble a society. Disasters and scandals undermine the claims of the established order to competence and integrity. Dominated populations, by their very existence and certainly by their movements to gain equal treatment, threaten the position of those already inside the structures of power. The anxieties of the privileged persist even when overt prejudice has been eschewed: Roger D. Abrahams and Alan Dundes, observing that the vogue of elephant jokes in the United States coincided with the rise of the civil rights movement, suggest that the images of elephant footprints in refrigerators or elephants in treetops expressed unconscious fear of African Americans "forgetting their place." Finally, unsettling social change emerges in such cycles as the dead-baby jokes of the 1970s, apparently linked to the new visibility of divorce, contraception, and abortion in North America.

Children's riddle joke cycles are particularly apt to test the margins of the speakable, as in the well-known "gross jokes." Their covert circulation in classrooms and schoolyards challenges the world of euphemism and normative conduct constructed in children's textbooks. In the same way, the much-condemned brutality of the *Challenger* jokes ("What was the last thing that went through Christa McAuliffe's head?—Her ass") is seen by Elliott Oring as a critique of the media's banalization of disaster. He notes the jarring effect of commercial interruptions upon images of catastrophe and how the jokes play upon this juxtaposition by frequent use of advertising slogans and brand names. "Sick" or obscene jokes, then, restore the horror of the world suppressed in official discourse. Unprintable, they resist co-optation into that discourse.

The performance of riddle jokes is often buffered by disclaimers on both ends. The joke is presented as something heard recently, thus not originating with the poser; the poser may add further distance by disparagement ("I heard an awful one yesterday"). The respondent mitigates his or her laughter by exclamations of disgust or by apology ("I shouldn't laugh, but it's such a bad pun").

The form of the riddle joke may ease the broaching of these delicate matters in conversation. Its brevity and tight construction (rendering it impersonal and almost aphoristic) and its topicality (giving it the status of news) remove the burden of responsibility for its content from the poser. Moreover, the collaborative form of the riddle, which demands at least a ritual grunt of interest after the question is posed, implicates the respondent in the joke. Both parties have collaborated in allowing the unspeakable to be spoken.

The riddle joke is one of the most common joking forms today, and individual jokes are probably the most widely transmitted items of folklore in the contemporary United States. The same formal qualities that allow them to speak of controversial matters make them memorable and conducive to rapid transmission. Moreover, the focus on topics made general throughout a national population by the mass media allows jokes to be passed between comparative strangers. Although community-specific riddle joke cycles do exist, local background knowledge is unnecessary for the appreciation of most riddle jokes. Thus, riddle jokes are widely used as social icebreakers. Dealing with general issues, they can serve as a basis for broad consensus and become a means of testing the waters in the establishment of provisional solidarities between new acquaintances. The respondent's appreciation or disapproval of a joke is a measure of social and political affiliations—it indicates the respondent's willingness to form an alliance with the poser in the face of a putative Other.

Dorothy Noyes

See Also Enigma, Folk; Ethnic Folklore; Joke; Popular Culture.

References

Dundes, Alan. 1987. *Cracking Jokes: Studies of Sick Humor Cycles and Stereotypes.* Berkeley, CA: Ten Speed Press.

Oring, Elliott. 1987. Jokes and the Discourse on Disaster. *Journal of American Folklore* 100: 276–286.

Wolfenstein, Martha. 1954. *Children's Humor: A Psychological Analysis.* Glencoe, IL: Free Press.

Ritual

A repeated socioreligious behavior; a chain of actions, rites, or ritual movements following a standard protocol. The important symbols and values of the people are used, provoked, communicated, or expressed in ritual. A ritual is easily observed in a community and is a major expressive form of any religion. Anthropologists and other students of culture have focused their attention on the description and interpretation of rituals to such a degree that it can be argued that many modern theories of religion are primarily theories of ritual. The meaning of a ritual entails more than merely the code of behavior it manifests. The predetermined set of events is well known to the participants of the ritual, and there are certain conventionalized expectations concerning their behavior. Although very important symbols and central values of a group are evoked, it would be false to assume any direct link between the outward expressions and inner states of the participants in a ritual. In order to find a satisfactory definition of the term *ritual*, the participants' attitudes concerning the ceremony, social custom, and religious doctrine should be taken into consideration.

Ritual as a category of action is characterized by predictable structure over time, a structuring that is commonly labeled repetitive. In distinguishing ritual from other behavior, it is imperative to establish the difference between compulsive actions, private repetitive idiosyncrasies, and ritual per se. Ritual is separable from individual compulsive behavior by reference to the social dimension of the former.

Initiation

Rites formalizing the passage of an individual or group into a new social or religious status. Puberty rites, ceremonies that symbolize the transformation of youths into adults, are the most common form of initiation worldwide. However, formal ceremonies of initiation precede admission into communal organizations of all kinds, including priesthoods, military orders, schools, sodalities, secret societies, and clubs.

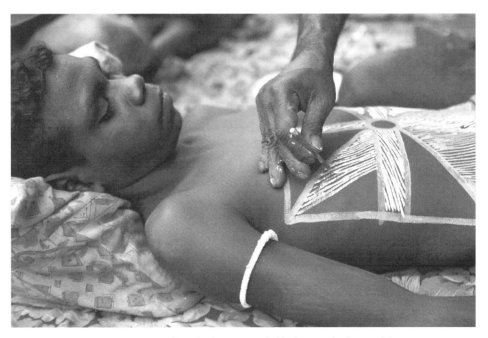

Aboriginal boy being painted for his important initiation and circumcision ceremony at Yathalamarra, Arnhem Land, Australia. (Penny Tweedie/Corbis)

The nature of initiation rites varies widely. Some are intensely public occasions distinguished by ritual scarification or circumcision. Others, especially if initiation entails the acquisition of secret or special knowledge, take place away from the public eye under remote or private circumstances. Extraordinary ordeals and rigorous group tests are commonly part of the initiation procedure if solidarity among initiates and the organization they are entering is a primary goal. Still other initiations merely signal the altered status of the initiates with unexceptional rituals little removed from ordinary social behavior. Among occupational groups, initiation may take the form of pranks in which the new person on a crew is made the butt of a work-related practical joke.

The French folklorist Arnold van Gennep (1873–1957) was the first to recognize that, despite specific differences in content, initiation rituals throughout the world tend to have similar, tripartite structures. According to him, such rites invariably consist of an initial phase that symbolically separates the initiates from their former status, a marginal or liminal period of transition, and a final phase of reincorporation with the group at the new status. Van Gennep also noted that initiation rituals share this tripartite form with weddings and funerals, two other key *rites de passage* that ritually symbolize and sanctify progressive transit through life and society.

D. Bruce Dickson

A ritual may be defined as a combination of the actions called rites (socioreligious ceremonies following specific traditional patterns), which, in their turn, may be divided into smaller ritual units in the structure of a ritual. In this definition, the conative (i.e., purposeful) level of religiosity comes to the fore. Rites commonly include both verbal and nonverbal communication. Religious concepts are displayed in the ceremony, and they are manifested not only in speech but also through kinesic channels.

The analysis of rites demands the analysis of both verbalized meanings and nonverbal elements in ritual behavior. Nonverbal does not mean, of course, noncognitive, although it may seem to be more difficult to get at the cognitive dimensions of the nonverbal acts of communication.

Rites commonly are divided into three categories: *crisis rites*, *calendrical rites*, and *rites of passage*. *Crisis rites* are understood to be occasional ritual acts, performed in order to remove some crisis phenomena, for example, a disease that torments the individual or community. These rites occur under unique circumstances and are attempts to organize the behavior of the community in such a manner that the crisis situation can be safely passed over and the normal order of life restored. Crisis rites include healing dramas. *Calendrical rites* are periodic, recurring, and form a clearly distinguishable group of their own. They include various ceremonies performed according to the time of the year or in conjunction with the shifts in seasonal employment, such as rites for sowing and harvesting grain and ceremonies for opening a new year. The third group consists of *rites of passage*, rituals that are associated with different phases of human life such as birth, childhood, puberty, initiation or entry into adult status, engagement, marriage, maternal confinement, fatherhood, transfer into another social status, and death. Lauri Honko defines rites of passage as traditional ceremonies organized by the community through which the individual is transferred from one social status to another.

The focus of each of the types differs not only in terms of occasion but also in terms of the subjects of the rites. Rites of passage focus tightly on changes in the social position of the individual, whereas calendrical rites or ceremonies concerning changes in seasonal employment generally affect the entire community

Rites of Passage

A category of rituals or rites that accompany change of place, state, social status, and age. A human life cycle is marked by these passages from one social and physical position to another, in a pattern determined by the physiological and psychological maturation of an individual as well as the cultural socialization pattern and worldview of the community. Some of these transitions take place only once in an individual's life (e.g., birth, initiation, death), and some may occur repeatedly (transition from a profane role to the holy one as a specialist of the sacred).

This theory was set forth by anthropologist Arnold van Gennep in his influential book *The Rites of Passage*, published in 1909. Van Gennep was particularly interested in crossing territorial borders. According to him, all the rites of passage fall naturally into three phases: *rites of separation*, when the individual is removed from a previous status; *rites of transition*, when one is prepared to transfer to a new position; and *rites of incorporation*, when the individual takes on a new status role. In rites of passage, both the individual, as a ritual subject, and those present at the rites undergo a clear-cut change in their social relationships and, in this way, are afforded formal acceptance and recognition. The transfer does not take place suddenly but is a gradual process when the individual who is going through this stage takes on a temporary and intermediary role during the process of transition (e.g., the role of an initiate).

Van Gennep's basic model is structural. According to his definition, rites of passage accompany every change of place, state, social position, and age. In many traditional communities, these changes generally are made public, with their importance reinforced by specifically structured rites. First comes the stage of *separation* in which the individual is removed from a previous social position. This is followed by an interim period, *marge*, during which the individual is poised on the borderline between two positions (a previous status and a new one). The third and last phase is the full entry into the new status (*aggregation*). The impact that van Gennep's theory has had on the study of ritual and religions is wide ranging, having influenced scholars in a variety of disciplines.

Juha Pentikäinen

or occupational group. Another significant distinction involves the cycles of recurrence of the ritual types. Calendrical rites recur regularly in the life of the community, but most rites of passage take place only once in the life of an individual.

There are at least two important points of view on the nature of a ritual. The first perceives ritual as an important constituent of religion; the second views ritual as psychologically interpretable irrational behavior distinct from pragmatically oriented behavior. The former perspective is popular with anthropologists and historians of religion. From the latter, primarily psychoanalytic viewpoint, ritual is contrasted to science as a non-pragmatic and irrational action.

Nonetheless, it is always possible to consider a ritual in terms of "latent" social goals or the explicit religious meaning of ritual symbolism, bearing in mind that ritual acts do endow culturally important cosmological conceptions. The balanced view of ritual must encompass two polarities—the explicit and the implicit meanings of ritual.

Like any human activity, ritual is experienced through the human body as well as through the intellect. Ritual symbolism often is closely linked to intense sensory experiences and primary forms of bodily awareness, such as sexual or metabolic processes.

Newlyweds tour on boats during a traditional Chinese group wedding in the Shajiabang Scenic Spot in Changshu, east China's Jiangsu Province, 2008. The couples wear the traditional red. (AP/Wide World Photos)

Ritual is a repetitive action and can be participated in by generation after generation because it follows a restricted model. Yet it seems quite obvious that ritual responds to the overall situation in which it is performed and is not confined by a static, exclusive procedure without any adaptive potential. An interesting issue regarding traditional communication in rituals focuses on this adaptive potential. The fact that the overall quality of a ritual remains the same but simultaneously undergoes changes leads to the very center of different views on ritual and requires special attention.

When considering the adaptive qualities of ritual, it is possible to classify them in functional descriptive terms or analyze them in structural terms. The functional approach emphasizes the empirical and precise observation of ritual action; the structural approach centers on the underlying nature of rituals. The functional-enumerative approach, for example, is more a detailed description than a serious attempt at classification. By comparison, a structuralist analysis may attempt a classification of confirmatory and transformatory rituals in order to understand the changes that any particular ritual imposes on the structure maintenance or transformation of a given community. In this approach, ritual is understood as a goal-oriented and reactive

---

Transition Ritual

A category of ritual by which a symbolic threshold is crossed; a status-free period in which participants enter a betwixt and between state that is trespassed upon and left behind, and the status structure is set anew. Transition rituals are transformatory by nature. In the course of a transition ritual, the status of the participant is transformed to a new and ordered one. In that respect, a transition ritual might be viewed as a means of safeguarding culturally patterned structures and overcoming the difficulties of status changes and other periods of potential confusions. In the terminology suggested by Arnold van Gennep, transition rites are a subcategory of rites of passage. Crossing a threshold is a necessary minimal criterion for the definition of transition rites.

According to social anthropologist Victor W. Turner (1920–1983), a shift from a temporary liminal phase is accomplished by means of transition rituals. Using a symbolic approach, Turner attempts to identify the essential and primary attributes of a ritual as perceived by participants in that ritual. A transition rite can be conceived of as a process of transformation that, in Turner's opinion, could be compared to heating water to the boiling point or the change a pupa goes through to become a moth. Transitional rituals can take a variety of forms, including calendrical rites, consecration rituals and conversions, initiations (or confirmations), and funeral rites.

Juha Pentikäinen

activity that, under specific circumstances, either confirms or transforms the relationships and boundaries that prevail between the individual, community, and cosmos.

Various other areas of ritual research remain viable. The historical approach is mainly centered on the role that ritual plays in the process of transmitting the cultural and religious knowledge and symbols and in the formation of the identity and invention of the past of the society, community, or group. Related to the historical approach is the problem of the relation of myth to ritual; there is no universal pattern or consistent theory on the priority of either myth or ritual. A final group of approaches compares ritual actions and means of performance to the means and modes of dramatic actions.

Juha Pentikäinen

See Also Anthropology, Symbolic; Divination; Liminality; Magic; Medicine, Folk; Myth-Ritual Theory; Religion, Folk.

References

Grimes, Ronald. 1985. *Research in Ritual Studies: A Programmatic Essay and Bibliography*. Metuchen, NJ: Scarecrow.

Kusch, Rodolfo. 2010. *Indigenous and Popular Thinking in America*. Durham, NC: Duke University Press.

Lewis, Gilbert. 1980. *Day of Shining Red: An Essay on Understanding Ritual*. Cambridge, UK: Cambridge University Press.

Pentikäinen, Juha. 1978. *Oral Repertoire and World View: An Anthropological Study of Marina Takalo's Life History*. Helsinki: Academia Scientiarum Fennica.

Pentikäinen, Juha Y. 1986. Transition Rites. In *Transition Rites*, ed. Ugo Bianchi. Rome: L'Erma di Bretschneider.

Pilgrim, Richard B. 1978. Ritual. In *Introduction to the Study of Religion*, ed. William T. Hall. San Francisco: Harper and Row.

Skorupski, John. 1976. *Symbol and Theory: A Philosophical Study of Theories of Religion in Social Anthropology*. Cambridge: Cambridge University Press.

Stavans, Ilan, ed. 2010. *Quinceañera*. Santa Barbara, CA: Greenwood.

Turner, Victor W. 1969. *The Ritual Process: Structure and Anti-Structure*. Chicago: Aldine.

Turner, Victor W. 1974. *Dramas, Fields and Metaphors: Symbolic Action in Human Society*. Ithaca, NY: Cornell University Press.

van Gennep, Arnold. 1960. *Rites of Passage*, trans. Monika B. Vizedom and Gabrielle L. Caffee. Chicago: University of Chicago Press.

Zuesse, Evan M. 1987. Ritual. In *Encyclopedia of Religion*, vol. 12, ed. Mircea Eliade. New York: Macmillan.

Zumwalt, Rosemary Levy. 1988. *The Enigma of Arnold van Gennep (1873–1957): Master of French Folklore and Hermit of Bourg-la-Reine*. Helsinki: Academia Scientiarum Fennica.

British Railways poster showing Robin Hood in Sherwood Forest. Artwork by Frank Newbould, ca. 1950. (Getty Images)

NOTTINGHAMSHIRE

BRITISH RAILWAYS   SEE ENGLAND BY RAIL

Robin Hood

English outlaw hero and archer who first appears in Langland's *Piers Plowman* (ca. 1377). This source is not explicit on Robin's status as a robber of the rich, but by the first half of the following century, his persona as a noble robber and friend of the poor and oppressed is commonplace. The means of Robin Hood's early celebration are a number of early ballads and the major work known as *A Mery Geste of Robyn Hoode*. Although Robin is a commoner in these works (he is not elevated to the aristocracy until the seventeenth century), the world of the *Geste* is that of the rich and powerful. The Sheriff of Nottingham appears in his role of arch villain. There are knights, abbots, nobles, and notables, as well as the king himself. In the end, Robin helps the king and is received into his service. But after a while, Robin's nostalgia for the greenwood compel him to ask the king for permission to visit his old haunts again. The king grants him a week. Robin returns to the forest, rejoins his band, and his week's holiday extends to twenty-two years, during which time he refuses to accept the monarch's authority. Finally, he is betrayed to death by the prioress and Sir Roger. As given by F.

J. Child, the various versions of the *Geste* present Robin as a heroic figure and usually conclude unequivocally with the verse:

Cryst haue mercy on his soule,
That dyed on the rode!
For he was a good outlaw,
And dyde pore men moch god.

The *Geste* is a literary work of some sophistication, either compiled from existing ballads or using the same materials on which these ballads may have been based. The early ballads of the fifteenth century are certainly less literary (many perhaps being in oral circulation before their capture in print) and also tend to be more proletarian in orientation. While Robin has the scoundrelly but still relatively high-born Sheriff of Nottingham to outwit and corrupt members of the clergy to deal with, he also has encounters with commoners, as in "Robin Hood and the Potter." Here the potter bests Robin, after which Robin symbolically exchanges clothes with him and, in this trickster disguise, goes off to Nottingham for further adventures with the sheriff and, as it turns out, his wife. This story is similar in some ways to the later "Robin Hood and the Pedlar," in which a peddler defeats Robin and Little John in a fight and is incorporated into the "band of merry men." In this ballad, Robin is still a leader of ordinary men, his heroic status dependent on his bravery, courteousness, fairness, and skill. The greenwood hero of the ballads and the *Geste*, then, despite his increasing aristocratic connections, is still quite a way removed from the eighteenth-century identification of Robin Hood as the "Earl of Huntingdon," Robert Fitzooth, supposedly and conveniently descended from both Norman and Saxon forbears. This latter-day fabrication, derived from sixteenth- and seventeenth-century suggestions that the outlaw was a noble down on his luck, influenced much subsequent thinking about Robin as a wronged aristocrat.

Regardless of the historicity of Robin Hood, his folkloric image is that of the outlaw hero, and he is clearly viewed in such terms from an early period. The courteous archer in Lincoln green, the fabric he allegedly wore, is therefore the archetype against which all subsequent Anglophone outlaw heroes are measured. That this is so is made elegantly clear in Child's account and editing of the Robin Hood ballads, where he presents evidence that these songs celebrating the real or mythical outlaw's exploits were widely sung in England, and beyond, around 1400 and, given the *Piers Plowman* reference, almost certainly earlier. While, according to Child's view, the later balladic treatments of this figure "debase" it in various ways, this "debasement" is in fact a sharpening and refining of the image of Robin Hood. Whereas he is certainly a friend of the poor in the *Geste* and, presumably, in the earlier traditions, by the time of a seventeenth-century treatment titled "The True Tale of Robin Hood" (1632), he is a full-fledged outlaw hero and definitely a morally upright friend of the poor—"all poore men pray for him, / And wish he well might spede." He helps distressed travelers on the road, assists widows and orphans, protects women, generally operates against the established power and corruption of the church, and robs the rich, particularly those who "did the poore oppresse." He does not harm the humble workers nor any man "that him invaded not." He is finally betrayed to death by "a faithlesse fryer."

Much time and learned effort has been devoted to the study of this character—sometimes with the aim of discovering his true identity, sometimes with an interest in the more general mythic significance of the green archer. The conclusions of some research are that Robin remains a figure of uncertain historicity but is a cultural symbol of considerable potency in the English-speaking world. Dobson and Taylor's revised and reissued *Rymes of Robin Hood* discusses Robin Hood place-names, linguistic terms, films, and other evidence of the enduring popularity of the outlaw, as well as a representative selection of mostly literary Robin Hood ballads. Stephen Knight has provided a comprehensive overview of this hero's numerous roles in a variety of cultural forms, old and new. In a comprehensive and careful study, *Robin Hood: A Complete Study of the English Outlaw*, Knight traced the outlaw's career in literature, film, and popular culture up to the present. He showed how the Robin Hood mythology has undergone changes related to social, economic, and ideological pressures. Robin's original folkloric presence is in legends, place-names, proverbs, drama, and, presumably, ballads as a symbolic figure of resistance to authority and of communal solidarity. While these notions have persisted, they have been overlaid and extended by narrative treatments that variously gentrify, politicize, nationalize, and romanticize the hero. At first Robin Hood is a forest fugitive, a common figure in the twelfth and thirteenth centuries. In this guise, Robin is a shadowy opponent of authority and law. These resistant elements, consistent with the image of the outlaw hero, are developed and refined in the ballads of the fourteenth century and after, and also in the widespread Robin Hood plays and games first recorded in the early fifteenth century (at Exeter, 1426–1427). These performances were closely associated with the folk calendar and with traditional activities, including raising funds, sports, competitions, and other festive activities. Records of Robin Hood plays, and of official concern about them, increase throughout the 1500s. By around 1600, most of these plays had quietly faded away or been actively suppressed through a combination of growing Puritanism and civic alarm.

As well as proving his virility in past as well as present popular and high culture, Robin Hood has persisted to some extent in folksong. A few oral versions of Robin Hood ballads were retrieved by English folksong collector Alfred Williams early in the twentieth century and provide evidence, if in somewhat fragmentary form, of the persistence of Robin Hood's image in British tradition. It seems from these partial texts, from Williams's observations on them, and from the age of their singers that Robin Hood may have been in decline as a central figure of rural English folksong by the early part of the twentieth century. As A. L. Lloyd pointed out in *Folksong in England*, only seven or so of the nearly forty Robin Hood ballads noted by Child in the 1880s had been collected in British oral tradition, and a further three in America. These ballads turn up in various states of completeness in the collections of the late and early nineteenth centuries, usually derived from nineteenth-century broadside versions, especially those printed by Such and Catnach. It seems fair to say from the available evidence that while Robin Hood retained a definite niche in oral tradition, he can hardly be said to be a major figure of British, American, or any other English-language folksong.

However, the catalogues of broadside printers of the 1830s show that Robin Hood lived on in printed ballads, and it is in media, literary, and artistic representations that Robin Hood is most alive today. Numerous film versions of Robin Hood continue a Hollywood tradition of regularly celebrating the English outlaw, a tradition dating from 1909 with the film *Robin Hood and His Merry Men* and involving well over thirty productions to date. The outlaw has also had an enduring career in the theater, in dramatic, comic, and musical forms, and in a still-remembered television series of the 1950s and 1960s. There are three tourist theme parks and recreations of the Robin Hood myth in and around Nottingham. Robin Hood remains the English-language archetype of the outlaw hero.

A substantial number of other folk heroes—though few heroines—are skilled with bow and arrow. William Tell is perhaps the best known of a number of heroes who shoot apples or other objects from the head of someone close to them, either a family member, close companion, or a lover. Other heroes carry out legendary feats involving bow and arrow, including the Russian Dunai Ivanovich and the Japanese Yuriwaka. Archers generally use their skills to avert catastrophe of some kind, as in the case of the Chinese Hou Yi and his Mongolian counterpart, Erkhii Mergen. Closely related to archers are spear-throwers, such as the Torres Strait Island hero, Kwoiam. The ability to use such missiles with skill and accuracy is not in itself heroic but, as with Robin Hood, forms a defining element of the archer hero's legendry.

Graham Seal

See Also Ballad; Folksong, Narrative; Hero/Heroine, Folk; Legend.

References

Chappell, W. [1859] 1965. *Popular Music of the Olden Time*, 2 vols. New York: Dover Publications.

Child, F. J. [1882–1898] 1965. *The English and Scottish Popular Ballads*, 5 vols. New York: Dover.

Dobson, R. B., and J. Taylor. [1976] 1989. *Rymes of Robin Hood: An Introduction to the English Outlaw*, 2nd. rev. ed. Gloucester, UK: Allan Sutton.

Keen, M. 1961. *The Outlaws of Medieval Legend*. London: Routledge and Kegan Paul.

Knight, S. 1994. *Robin Hood: A Complete Study of the English Outlaw*. Oxford, UK: Blackwell.

Lloyd, A. [1967] 1970. *Folksong in England*. New York: International Publishers, 1970.

Maddicott, J. R. 1978. The Birth and Setting of the Ballads of Robin Hood. *English Historical Review* 93.

Page, D. 1973. *Folktales in Homer's* Odyssey. Cambridge, MA: Harvard University Press.

Purslow, F., ed. 1965. *Marrow Bones: English Folk Songs from the Hammond and Gardiner Mss*. London: EFDS Publications.

Vaughan Williams, R., and A. Lloyd, A., eds. 1959. *The Penguin Book of English Folk Songs*. Harmondsworth, Middlesex: Penguin, esp. pp. 88–89 for "Robin Hood and the Pedlar."

Williams, A. 1923. *Folk Songs of the Upper Thames*. London: Duckworth & Co.

Romantic Nationalism

A cultural movement combining the romantic focus on the primitive or the common man or woman and older literary forms with the advocacy of national and ethnic pride through the development of the literature, language, and traditions of the group. Romantic nationalism led to the collection and literary imitation of traditional art forms, and as a consequence, it gave impetus to the discipline of folklore during its formative stage.

Ideas of romanticism and romantic nationalism developed toward the end of the eighteenth century. By the beginning of the nineteenth century, this phenomenon already had become a large-scale movement that had deeply influenced ideas and ideals of individuality, creativity, and personal experience. Romantic trends also played a significant role in the development of nationalism and the concept of nation-state. The ideals of romantic nationalism inspired an interest in antiquity, ancient traditions, and folklore. The works of philosophers such as Johann Wolfgang von Goethe, A. W. and Friedrich von Schelling, Friedrich von Schlegel, and Jean-Jacques Rousseau formed part of the necessary ideological background of romanticism. Among a number of emerging nations arose a need for re-creating or reconstructing indigenous mythical pasts, poetic landscapes, and golden ages, often for the purpose of supporting a case for nation-state status. Idealistic initiatives inspired an interest in folklore, and thus awoke wide-scale activity for collecting folklore materials in nineteenth-century Europe.

By 1765, Thomas Percy already had published a collection entitled *Reliques of Ancient English Poetry*. This work provided great impetus for the publishing of subsequent collections in the eighteenth century. Another example of such publications is the pioneering collection of the folk poetry and literature of quite a range of peoples compiled by Johann Gottfried von Herder under the title *Stimmen der Völker in Lieder* (1778). Also, *The Poems of Ossian* (1765) by James Macpherson, purported to be translations of poems by the Gaelic poet Ossian, had an immense impact on the romantically inspired interests in folklore, despite the fact that the poems later appeared, for the most part, to have been composed by the author himself. Perhaps most significant to the discipline of folklore was Jacob and Wilhelm Grimm's work of collecting and publishing folktales (*Kinder- und Hausmärchen* [Children's and household tales], 1812–1822), which served as an epoch-making impetus for the recording and publishing of folklore materials all over Europe. Their collection was a kind of blueprint, serving as one further model for other collections in the period of romantic nationalism and as a guide for selecting and editing such collections of literary-influenced fairy tales.

Interest in folklore has passed through similar stages among different nations regardless of the social system. The basic scheme of these stages could be simplified as follows: (1) idealistic initiative directed at interest in folklore, (2) wide-scale activation of collection, (3) development of forms of high culture based on traditional culture, and (4) establishment of applied traditional culture as part of cultural life.

There are abundant examples of Stage 2 in the large collections of folklore from the nineteenth century; the work of Krišjānis Barons, the compiler and publisher of close to 218,000 Latvian folksong texts in six volumes, *Latvju dainās* (1894–1915), is particularly worthy of note, as are Norwegian folktales by Peter Asbjørnsen and Jørgen Moe (1841) and collections of Russian *bylina* epics by P. N. Rybnikov (four volumes in 1861–1867) and A. F. Gil'ferding (1871). There are some 2 million lines of poetry in *Kalevala* (the Finnish national epic) meter in the archives of the Finnish Literature Society, collected mainly in the nineteenth century. About two-thirds have been published in the thirty-three-volume *Suomen Kansan Vanhat Runot* (Ancient poems of the Finnish people) (1908–1948). In the years 1841, 1845, 1846, and 1862, a selection of Vuk Karadzic's collections, *Srpske narodne pjesme* (Serbian folksongs), were published as four volumes, comprising a total of 1,045 songs.

As a rule, only small selections of these and other important bodies of oral literature have been translated into other languages. These collections continue to have immense importance for folklore research—an importance that extends beyond the national level.

Romantic nationalism also provided inspiration for the creation of national epics. Romantic idealists held the epic as the very beginning of literature. Virgil's *Aeneid* had been the dominant epic model in the Middle Ages and during

The Anger of Kallervo, from *The Kalevala* edited and compiled by Elias Lönnrot (1802–1884) and published in Finland, 1908. Illustration by Akseli Valdemar Gallen-Kallela (1865–1931). (Archives Charmet/The Bridgeman Art Library International)

the Renaissance (serving as a model for *Paradise Lost* by John Milton). This was the case especially in western and southern Europe. German romanticism, however, took Homer's works as the primary pattern for the epos at the end of the eighteenth century. Examples following this model are the national epics of some Finnic and Baltic peoples. Elias Lönnrot compiled the Finnish national epic, *The Kalevala*, on the basis of folk poetry. The first edition appeared in 1835, the second and greatly enlarged edition in 1849. The Estonian counterpart of the Finnish *Kalevala* was the epic called *Kalevipoeg* (1857–1861), compiled by F. R. Kreutzwald. He used as building material local legends and tales of origin. Andrejs Pumpurs, the author of the Latvian national epos *Lāčplēsis* (Bear slayer; 1888), created his epic poem on the basis of Latvian etiological tales, folktales, local legends, wedding songs, and other items excerpted from folklore. *The Song of Hiawatha* (1855), by Henry Wadsworth Longfellow, also follows a similar pattern of development.

In Germany, Wilhelm Jordan created the epic *Die Nibelunge* (The Nibelungs [a family name]), consisting of two parts: *Die Sigridsage* (The story of Sigrid; 1868) and *Hildebrands Heimkehr* (1874). In his *Epische Briefe* (Epic epistle), Jordan declared that he was in fact "the German Homer," a kind of embodiment or incarnation of an epic poet, matured in the right stage of development of the people.

A similar phenomenon, though one based within a different ideological framework, was characteristic of numerous ethnic minorities in the former Soviet Union. Romantic nationalism in its Soviet incarnation sprang originally from a statement emphasizing the creation of a high culture national in form, socialist in content, and international in spirit. Cultural life in many of the Soviet Union's socialist republics was, for the most part, based on traditional forms. Many of the peoples in these areas did not previously have arts based on so-called modern civilization. The culture witnessed a merging of old forms and new contents. Cultural clubs and circles began to form, especially during the mid 1930s. At its inception, the program consisted of pure folk performances. Gradually, texts propagating the new system began to be devised according to the traditional schemes, and new melodies greatly reminiscent of folksongs were composed.

During the Soviet period, a great number of epics were published. Those compositions created on the basis of diverse versions of the *Köroglu* (*Korogly, Gurguli*) epics known, among others, to the Azers, Uzbeks, Turkmens, and Tajiks serve as examples. There are also epics based on a version by a particular singer. The Uzbek epics *Alpamы̌s* and *Rustamhan,* published on the basis of versions performed by Fazil Çoldas-ogli (F. Juldǎševič), serve as examples. During the Soviet period, these and many other epics were subjected at times to censure and became the focus of ideological debate, but this is something that seems to be the fate of epics in general.

During the twentieth century, various manifestations of romantic and political nationalism have flourished in Asia, Africa, and South America. The role folklore has played in the cultural and social processes of these continents varies from preliminary efforts in collecting folklore items to diverse uses of folklore in cultural and national movements. Nationalism is unique to the specific contexts in which it develops, and the historical and political conditions under which it may arise are diverse. However, it may not be appropriate to use the term *nationalism* in an excessively wide range of contexts.

For numerous nations, folklore collections have been crucial for the creation of indigenous identity, cultural life, and fine arts; in some cases, collections have provided an impetus for the development of the written language. An interest in traditional culture characteristically has been stimulated by a romantic idealistic current represented by a nucleus group of cultural activists or some idealistic organization. The wide-scale collection and publication of folklore arising out of such stimuli has often been the last opportunity to record a nation's vanishing cultural heritage. Generally speaking, the wide-scale activation of interest in folklore has emerged from a desire to reinforce the nation's self-esteem and to arouse respect for the nation's own language and culture. Wide-scale collection has been the starting point for the creation of archives and collections and for publications of folk material. It also has acted as a source for a mainstream in which literary epics and other literary products based on folklore are born and for pictorial, musical, and dramatic art drawing on traditional themes and elements. Arguments that the collection does not displace attention to the past but rather that the past is in service of the collection are contradicted by a broad knowledge of cultural history across national and historical contexts. In fact, folklore should be studied not only in "pristine" but also in applied forms.

According to some authors, the discipline of folklore arose partly from backward-looking or anti-modern perspectives. It is possible that the feeling of "over-civilization" in the West during the modernization period was in the air in the western regions of nineteenth-century Europe or the United States, but that was not the case in central, eastern, and northern regions of Europe.

The discipline of folklore arose in the period of romantic nationalism from an essentially modern perspective. It was the aspiration toward modernity in eastern and northern Europe that led intellectuals to promote broad interest in folklore, language, and heritage. Thus, toward the end of the nineteenth century, national awakening and social mobility—and, as a consequence, education in the native tongue—represented the road leading to modernity. Peoples without their history, language, and identity created national literature and literary language, discovered or re-created their roots in the past, and formed a compendium of (modern) national myths and symbols, including flags, anthems, and national festivities. Romantic nationalism has not only been able to resist the rational and secular force of modernity, it has also been part of the modernization process and complemented political, technical, and scientific development of the period. It was an inspiring force in the creation process of nations, especially among peoples struggling for independence in nineteenth-century Europe and also in countries striving for national unity.

It is true that, in many cases, nation-states are composed of more or less heterogeneous cultural, economic, linguistic, ethnic, or religious elements. Furthermore, it is necessary to keep in mind that the romantic movement developed and was manifested in many different ways, and nationalism has taken distinct phenotypes at different times and in diverse types of states. It is possible to make the distinction between *cultural nationalism*, aiming mainly at the creation of cultural identity through the use of folklore, art, music, literature, and *political nationalism*, striving for national identity through political movements and in times with uncompromising imperatives. In the nineteenth century, the most powerful ideological bases were the Herderian humanist cultural and national idealism and (especially toward the end of the century) the Hegelian doctrines of national spirit and its evolutionary power. The expansionist forms of political nationalism periodically rushed forward during the twentieth century with different applications, the results of which are well known. Such forms of political nationalism seem to show up regularly, despite the fact that some scholars have thought that the impulse was already past its peak.

In our times, the resurrection or actualization of romantic nationalism, often based on ancient mythic and heroic figures and symbols, is, in many cases, a response to the decline of the modernist identity. In its entirety, the situation is very complex, with traditionalist, religious, and ethnic variations. But as we have witnessed, during this new era as well, national identity takes on many forms according to the political situation—from forms of peaceful rediscovery or creation of cultural identity to expansionist tendencies leading, in the worst cases, to situations wherein we can no longer speak about romantic but only about tragic nationalism. Romantic nationalism is not a homogeneous or unitary phenomenon, and all nationalistic uses of folklore materials are not necessarily romantic. The rhetoric of nationalism is based on diverse cultural, social, and political processes, and the role that folklore (and folklorists) plays in them is dependent on varying political aims and sociohistorical and sociocultural contexts.

Lauri Harvilahti

See Also Ethnic Folklore; Folklorismus/Folklorism; Literary Approach.

References

Abrahams, Roger. 1993. Phantoms of Romantic Nationalism in Folkloristics. *Journal of American Folklore* 106: 33–37.

Anderson, Benedict. 1983. *Imagined Communities: Reflections on the Origin and Spread of Nationalism.* London: Verso.

Friedman, Jonathan. 1992. Narcissism, Roots and Postmodernity: The Constitution of Selfhood in the Global Crisis. In *Modernity and Identity,* eds. S. Lash and J. Friedman. Oxford: Blackwell.

Hobsbawm, E. J. 1990. *Nations and Nationalism since 1780: Programme, Myth, Reality.* Cambridge, UK: Cambridge University Press.

Hobsbawm, Eric J., and Terence Ranger. 1983. *The Invention of Tradition.* Cambridge, UK: Cambridge University Press.

Hroch, Miroslav. 1985. Der Wachen kleiner Nationalen als Problem der komparativen sozialgeschichtlichen Forschung. In *Nationalismus,* ed. H. A. Winkler. Königstein, Germany: Athenäum.

Oinas, Felix J. 1978. *Folklore, Nationalism and Politics.* Columbus, OH: Slavica Publishers.

Smith, Anthony D. 1984. Ethnic Myths and Ethnic Revivals. *European Journal of Sociology* 25: 283–305.

Trapāns, J. A. 1989. Krišjānis Barons: His Life and Times. In *Linguistics and Poetics of Latvian Folk Songs,* ed. Vaira Vikis-Freibergs. Kingston, Ontario: McGill-Queen's University Press.

Wilson, William A. 1976. *Folklore and Nationalism in Modern Finland.* Bloomington: Indiana University Press.

Rumor

Unsecured information. People have a strong desire to make sense of the ambiguities of their world; certainty is a human goal. In this way, rumor serves as the cornerstone of epistemology. People make an "effort after meaning" and strive to explain uncertain or unknown events. Rumors frequently emerge in the aftermath of the breakdown of normal communication channels and become, in the words of sociologist Tamotsu Shibutani, "the cooperative improvisation of interpretations."

Because of its centrality as a sense-making device, rumor has been examined from a wide spectrum of disciplines, including psychology, sociology, anthropology, political science, journalism, business, social work, law, and, of course, folklore. The classic definition of *rumor* proposed by Gordon Allport and Leo Postman is "a specific (or topical) proposition for belief, passed along from person to person, usually by word of mouth, without secure standards of evidence being present." The key to the definition is the fact that the transmitter of rumors is not relying on secure standards of evidence, although what constitutes secure standards may be contested.

In the discipline of folklore, the study of rumor has been closely linked to that of contemporary legend, so much so that the lines between them are often blurred. In general, contemporary legends are traditional and have more complex narrative structures than rumor. A rumor is often a briefer and more evanescent communication than a contemporary legend. Yet there is considerable overlap between these two discursive genres.

The intensity of rumor has traditionally been expressed in the basic law of rumor, as proposed by Allport and Postman, which can be represented as follows: $R = i \times a$. That is, the amount of rumor in circulation varies with the importance of the subject matter multiplied by the ambiguity of the evidence. Despite the appeal of this equation, the data on the effects of ambiguity are generally stronger than the effects of importance per se. Some have argued that the critical ability of the listeners needs to be considered; those with lower critical ability are more likely to believe and spread rumor. As a result, rumor transmission may be linked to personality or emotional state.

Most rumors are brief, often no more than three related propositions. This is consistent with the processes of rumor memory and transmission: leveling, sharpening, and assimilation. In rumor transmission, most details of an original event are quickly forgotten (leveled). After most of the potential information has been lost, a rumor kernel remains, which is fairly stable. The second feature of rumor recall (sharpening) consists of the selective perception, retention, and reporting of a few details. Sharpening is the inverse of leveling: Sharpened details remain when others have been leveled. The extent of leveling and sharpening is a result of narrative content, the circumstances of transmission, and the abilities of the narrator. The final component of recall, assimilation, refers to how details become altered as a consequence of personal interest, emotion, or prejudice. Rumors assimilated to prejudice include those spread in times of ethnic or racial tension in which one group alleges that another has committed a heinous atrocity—a ritual castration or some claim of blood libel. A cynical viciousness may not motivate these reconstructions; rather, the story is "better" (makes more psychological sense), from the prejudiced person's viewpoint, with the hated group seen as the attacker. Assimilation assumes that memory operates through a process of "social constructiveness," in which uncertain details are transformed into a compelling story.

One of the challenges for narrators who spread unverified information is to provide a textual frame by which the information can be interpreted without negative attributions made to the narrator. The fact that rumor often carries with it a moral attribution means that care needs to be taken so as not to be attacked for spreading false information. These opening frames can bolster the credibility of the remark ("I have it on good authority that . . . "), or, more often, can be used to distance oneself from the information ("I heard an interesting rumor that . . . "). Similarly, these framing markers can be placed in the middle of the report ("they say") or at its conclusion ("What do you think about that?"). These markers cue the audience as to how they should treat the information to follow.

The discussion of rumor to this point assumes that there is common agreement on what constitutes unverified information. Actually, credibility is a social construction created by the parties to the rumor. How are narratives taken as true or false when they are presented as "truth claims"? The question that emerges centers around who has the authority to describe a claim as unsecured, unverified, and suspect. Although one might assert that there is "good" information and that there are "authoritative" voices, this only restates the problem. The choice of what constitutes an authoritative voice and good information is problematic and should not be taken for granted.

Obviously, characteristics of a source are important in our judgments of how to treat information. We judge narrators on remove, realm, and motive. Remove refers to how close the narrator is to the events being described or to trustworthy sources. In short, is the narrator in a "position to know," or is he or she far removed from the events being described? Realm refers to the class of information being transmitted. Some realms of knowledge are considered legitimate, whereas other realms (extrasensory perception, unidentified flying objects [UFOs], and "miracles") are considered by many to be suspect. Information in these zones of knowledge is barely considered, no matter the extent of the evidence. When considering motive, we ask if the narrator has some reason to shade information. The assumed motivation of a speaker influences how audiences will interpret the claims. The attribution of motivation will be a function of the narrator's reputation as a credible source and of whether she or he has a clear interest in the topic and in our belief in the claims being put forward.

Truth is not handed to us; truth claims are. Our goal as an audience is to make reasonable judgments, while at the same time making the conversation flow as smoothly as possible. Rumor, being entertaining discourse, plays an important role in the free flow of communication.

Gary Alan Fine

See Also Gossip; Legend; Legend, Contemporary; Legend, Urban.

References

Allport, Gordon, and Leo Postman. 1947. *The Psychology of Rumor*. New York: Holt.

Fine, Gary Alan. 1992. *Manufacturing Tales: Sex and Money in Contemporary Legends*. Knoxville: University of Tennessee Press.

Kapferer, Jean-Noel. 1990. *Rumors: Uses, Interpretations, and Images*. New Brunswick, NJ: Transaction Press.

Koenig, Fredrick. 1985. *Rumor in the Marketplace: The Social Psychology of Commercial Hearsay*. Dover, MA: Auburn House.

Morin, Edgar. 1971. *Rumor in Orleans*. New York: Pantheon.

Rosnow, Ralph, and Gary Alan Fine. 1976. *Rumor and Gossip: The Social Psychology of Hearsay*. New York: Elsevier.

Shibutani, Tamotsu. 1966. *Improvised News: A Sociological Study of Rumor*. Indianapolis, IN: Bobbs-Merrill.

S

Sacred

An ineffable, universal sense of ultimacy, holiness, and truth apprehended through experience. The phenomenologist of religion Mircea Eliade has written that the sacred is an element in the structure of human consciousness and not a stage in the history and development of that consciousness. This statement identifies differences in scholarly evaluations of the sacred in the discussion of its validity as an essential category within human culture. Folklorists who approach subjects related to the sacred—such as saints' legends; narratives on healing miracles; beliefs about the protective power of verbal prayer or material objects such as Roman Catholic sacramentals, Jewish talismans, or the Bible; or the numinous quality of a natural environment or hallowed human habitation—do not wish to argue in support of the reality of the sacred as much as to present its existence as a widely considered possibility that invites rational discussion.

The sense of the sacred has, in the West, been strongly identified and associated with religion, either in religious institutions, in communities, or in the lives of believing individuals. The sacred has been used prominently in English as an adjective describing the unique status and distinctive power of an action, place, time, language, or aspect of material culture. The verbal, behavioral, and material systems of the sacred within religious belief encompass a variety of instruments and occasions of expressive culture that can be categorized under the rubric of visual or performed arts, public and private cultural performances, and individual acts.

As a theoretical subject area, the concept of the sacred has not been widely treated within folklore and folklife scholarship. However, ethnographic contexts and specific expressions of reverence for the sacred in traditional communities as well as in the individual lives of the common people have been of great interest to folklorists. Public display events and festivals, domestic and public architecture, foodways, costume, objects of devotion carried on the person or found in the home or place of work, and a multitude of individual and systematic beliefs and actions all manifest a relationship with the sacred that folklorists have studied at its cultural source.

The pioneering phenomenologist of religion Rudolf Otto, author of *Das Heilige* (1917; [The Idea of the Holy]), possessed a keen folkloristic sense of the expression of the sacred/holy in daily life. Otto focused on the instinctive feelings and responses in humans toward the mysterious and uncanny—terror and fear, fascination and attraction. These feelings are engendered, he contended, by the presence of the holy or sacred, the *numen*, or numinous objects and signs that participate with or represent the holy. He claimed that the experience of the holy or sacred by people is itself the source that generates folktale, myth, saga, legend, supernatural belief, and memorate, sometimes by direct experience and sometimes because of the stimulation of the numen as the mysterious, which he called the *mysterium tremendum*. Otto felt that language actually fails to provide an adequate medium through which to describe the numinous experience. Working from the heritage established by Otto, folklorist David J. Hufford has made similar claims in his experience-centered approach to supernatural assault traditions. Hufford has carefully examined the language of belief, whether it be testimony, memorate, or other narrative structure, noting the individual's tendency to rely on simile and metaphor in an effort to provide an adequate description of a particular phenomenon.

Lauri Honko, Leea Virtanen, Hufford, Christine A. Cartwright, Gillian Bennett, and Diane E. Goldstein have contributed to the debate about academic traditions of belief and disbelief. This debate assumes that belief traditions involving feelings of the mysterious or supernatural grounded in awareness of the sacred are either true or arise from certain kinds of error. These folklorists have been especially interested in the analysis of the reasoned use of evidence within believers' narratives, and their testing of alternatives falls within the context of narration regarding supernatural experience. Another area of special interest in contemporary folkloristics is fieldwork within communities of believers who actively engage with the sacred as a serious and important part of their lives. This situation is especially challenging for folklorists who are themselves believers or who, though not believers, are nonetheless impacted by the strength of such beliefs due to their empathy with their informants.

Leonard Norman Primiano

See Also Belief, Folk; Religion, Folk; Supernatural/Supranormal.

References

Bennett, Gillian. 1987. The Rhetoric of Tradition. *Talking Folklore* 1(3): 32–46.

Bennett, Gillian. 1987. *Traditions of Belief: Women, Folklore and the Supernatural Today*. London: Penguin Books.

Cartwright, Christine. 1982. "To the Saints Which Are at Ephesus . . .": A Case Study in the Analysis of Religious Memorates. *New York Folklore* 8: 47–55.

Eliade, Mircea. 1969. Preface. In *The Quest: History and Meaning in Religion*, Mircea Eliade. Chicago: University of Chicago Press.

Goldstein, Diane E. 1991. Perspectives on Newfoundland Belief Traditions: Narrative Clues to Concepts of Evidence. In *Studies in Newfoundland Folklore: Community and Process*, eds. Gerald Thomas and J. D. A. Widdowson. St. John's, Newfoundland: Breakwater.

Goldstein, Diane E. 1983. The Language of Religious Experience and Its Implications for Fieldwork. *Western Folklore* 42: 105–113.

Honko, Lauri. 1964. Memorates and the Study of Folk Beliefs. *Journal of the Folklore Institute* 1: 5–19.

Hufford, David J. 1982. *The Terror That Comes in the Night: An Experience-Centered Study of Supernatural Assault Traditions*. Philadelphia: University of Pennsylvania Press.

Hufford, David J. 1985. Commentary. In *The World Was Flooded with Light*, ed. Genevieve W. Foster. Pittsburgh, PA: University of Pittsburgh Press.

Hufford, David J. 1982. Traditions of Disbelief. *New York Folklore* 8: 47–55.

Otto, Rudolf. 1958. *The Idea of the Holy: An Inquiry into the Non-Rational Factor in the Idea of the Divine and Its Relation to the Rational*. Trans. John W. Harvey. New York: Oxford University Press. Originally published as *Das Heilige*, 1917.

Schoemaker, George H. 1990. Folklore and Religion: Approaches to Folklore Research. In *The Emergence of Folklore in Everyday Life*, ed. George H. Schoemaker. Bloomington, IN: Trickster.

Virtanen, Leea. [1977] 1990. *"That Must Have Been ESP!" An Examination of Psychic Experiences*. Trans. John Atkinson and Thomas DuBois. Bloomington: Indiana University Press.

Sacrifice

Killing with a spiritual or religious motivation, usually, but not exclusively, accompanied by ritual and performed in a sacred place. Indeed, the term *sacrifice* is derived from a word meaning "to make sacred." The practice of sacrifice follows no historical pattern in cultures—levels of incidence can remain fairly constant for long periods, or the use of sacrifice may wax and wane over time. Accounts of sacrifices include seventeenth-, eighteenth-, and nineteenth-century eyewitness reports by English officers in India, visitors to Africa, and Spanish chroniclers in Central America, as well as cryptic texts from the Mediterranean world and China.

The purposes of sacrifice include purification, renewal, atonement, and unification. According to Edward Westermarck, sacrifice may include burying the living with the dead to memorialize; burning or burying family members and slaves to accompany an individual in the afterlife; making offerings to ensure success in wars or to stave off epidemics of disease thought to be punishment from the gods, including the making of medicine from the bodies of sacrifice victims; and interring adults or children in the foundations of new buildings or under city gates and bridges as peace offerings and as a means of protection, springing from a fear of anything new or doing an act for the first time.

Sacrifice can involve one or many bodies or the body parts of both humans and animals. Human sacrifice, in its highest expression, is a voluntary act, undertaken as a pledge for the common good, and suffering is often a preparation for the death.

Animals substitute for humans and for other animals as sacrificial victims regardless of the complexity of the civilization. Claude Lévi-Strauss insists that the choice of victim varies widely in accordance with what is available at the time. According to E. E. Evans-Pritchard's study of the Nuer religion, differences in substitutes are minimized. Romans, Greeks, Vikings, and Druids frequently offered humans and animals together on the same altar, to the same god, to obtain the same favors. And W. Robertson Smith has pointed out that human life is not viewed as more sacred than animal life in all contexts: For example, the eighteenth-century English would hang a man for stealing a sheep. Humans and beasts are leveled at the sacrificial altar when there is an unshakable belief in the blessings in store in the hereafter.

Sacrifice for purification purposes can be motivated by a fear of supernatural powers or by the desire to win favor or achieve a state of closer union with the god whose protection is sought. Or victim and sacrificer can join in seeking to bring about a better world as an act of hope. The rite can affect the sacrificer as much as the victim in the sense that the sacrificer is transformed as well and moved to a new sacred place.

Sacrifice for the purpose of renewal is inextricably linked to a belief that provisions will cease unless gods are propitiated. Fertility rites include sprinkling blood or burying pieces of human flesh in the fields before sowing to obtain a good harvest or ward off famine; making sacrifices to river gods for the necessary water; or sacrificing the firstborn, in the belief that if one child were given back to the gods, more would be provided.

The act in which one dies for the many is an act of atonement. In the hopes of saving their own lives, individuals may offer a human sacrifice as a method of life insurance—giving the one for the many, sacrificing an inferior individual to prevent the death of one more privileged, or offering one held personally responsible for a calamity.

H. Hubert and M. Mauss, French sociologists, contend that sacrifice is aimed at cementing the bonds between humans and gods in an act of communion through which the victim becomes an intermediary between the human and the divine. By means of the rite, the victim becomes part of the divine, and the sacrificer is brought into a state of union with the god.

Modern scholars accept varieties of these premises of purpose with a difference in emphasis or with a combined emphasis. According to René Girard, for instance, the main aim of sacrifice is to bring back social union and to restore the cosmic order. In the absence of a true judicial system to deal with violence, counterviolence is part of the divine order, in which case a scapegoat is found. Tension reduced, the crisis is resolved. Mircea Eliade proposes that blood sacrifices replay the original act of creation and restore equilibrium by reenacting the original deed of violence, catering to the specific needs created by the deed.

Margaret Bruchez

See Also Myth-Ritual Theory; Ritual.

References

Eliade, Mircea. 1954. *The Myth of the Eternal Return*. Princeton, NJ: Princeton University Press.

Evans-Pritchard, E. E. 1956. *Nuer Religion*. Oxford: Clarendon.

Girard, René. 1977. *Violence and the Sacred*. Trans. Patrick Gregory. Baltimore, MD: Johns Hopkins University Press.

Hubert, H., and M. Mauss. 1964. *Sacrifice: Its Nature and Function*. Trans. W. E. Halls. Chicago: University of Chicago Press.

Lévi-Strauss, Claude. 1966. *The Savage Mind*. Chicago: University of Chicago Press.

Smith, W. Robertson. 1889. *Lectures on the Religion of the Semites*. Edinburgh: Black.

Westermarck, Edward. 1932. *Ethical Reality*. New York: Harcourt, Brace.

Saga

A medieval narrative genre of northwest Europe. Although Mody Boatright extends the term to American frontier chronicles, most folklorists use *saga* to refer solely to texts from Scandinavia (principally Iceland) and Ireland. The medieval saga is a literary genre, but it drew on oral tradition and was performed aloud. Saga material sheds light on medieval life in Scandinavia and Ireland, helps clarify the development of other narrative genres in Europe (e.g., the romance, the *Märchen*, the ballad), and provides a fascinating case for researchers in orality and literacy.

Irish Sagas

The Irish saga tradition predated the Scandinavian. Latin biographies (*vitae*) concerning Irish saints appeared during the seventh century, and court poetry and prose writing began in the following century. As manuscripts deteriorated, scribes recopied them, often altering the narratives markedly. Since the earliest extant manuscripts date from the twelfth century, their textual history is a complex web of superimposed oral and literary influences.

The oldest prose material in the tradition, the mythological cycle, depicted Celtic mythology from an antiquarian perspective. Tales of the Tuatha Dé

Danann, an otherworld people associated with ancient burial mounds, predominated.

The term *saga* generally refers to the subsequent Ulster cycle, narratives produced in the eighth and ninth centuries. These focused on heroes of the province of Ulster (the *Ulaidh*) and their battles with the people of Connacht. The Ulaidh were led by King Conchobhar mac Neasa and his champion Cú Chulainn. The textual cornerstone of the cycle was the *Táin Bó Cuailnge* (The cattle raid of Cooley), a prose epic made up of a variety of tales. Important features of the cycle included its strong female characters, embedded poetry, and striking motifs.

The king cycle focused on the quasi-historical kings of Ireland, the last of whom was Cathal mac Finghuine (died 742). Narratives of this group differed in terms of hero, event, and villain, and journeys to the otherworld and encounters with the supernatural figured prominently. The Fionn (Fenian) cycle became popular in the twelfth century. Earlier texts depicted the hero as a powerful seer, but the twelfth-century *Agallamh na Seanórach* (Colloquy of the old men) showed Fionn mac Cumhaill in his familiar form as a brave outlaw, leading a band of trusted followers, the Fianna. The heroes made frequent visits to the otherworld, and Fionn's son Oisín played a central role.

Cú Chulainn carries Ferdiad across the river in *Irish Iliad*. (Squire, Charles. *Celtic Myth & Legend, Poetry & Romance*, 1905)

Many of the Fenian tales were recognizable *Märchen* types, and Fenian ballads began appearing in the twelfth century as well. The popularity of the cycle is demonstrated by its persistence in twentieth-century oral tradition.

The sagas were performed in the evening, with a single saga sometimes lasting many nights. The basic narrative frame was often overshadowed by long descriptive asides, fanciful etymologies regarding place-names, and meticulous descriptions of warriors or retinues. Such "digressions" are often dismissed as professional pedantry, but they may equally have reflected different aesthetics with regard to narrative form and content.

Icelandic Sagas

The term *saga* derives from the Old Norse verb meaning "to say," connoting a lengthy reported narrative. A number of subgenres were recognized, varying in focus, historicity, tone, and style. Some of this variation stemmed from historical changes in both the saga and Scandinavian culture from the twelfth through the fourteenth centuries. Regional differences existed as well.

As in Ireland, the earliest Scandinavian sagas were written in Latin and focused on saints. Icelandic clerics soon opted for the vernacular, however. Closely related to the saints' lives were the sagas of kings (*konungasögur*), royal biographies set in various parts of Scandinavia. Composed primarily in the twelfth and early thirteen centuries, these sagas often had lay authors. *Heimskringla*, for instance, a compendious saga of the kings of Norway, was authored by Snorri Sturluson.

This biographic tendency carried over into the *Íslendingasögur* of the thirteenth century—sagas concerning famous Icelanders. The text often focused on heroes (*Njáls saga*), outlaws (*Grettis saga*), explorers (*Eiríks saga rauða*—the saga of Eirík the Red), districts (*Laxdoela saga*), or poets (*Egils saga*). Often termed *family sagas*, the narratives sometimes followed several generations within a family or district. In addition, they often included poetry, legendary material, and other items of folklore. In contrast to the kings' sagas, they were usually anonymous works.

As western Scandinavia came into greater contact with Europe, the sagas changed. On the one hand, authors turned to the legendary and mythological past of their people, writing sagas about ancient times (*fornaldursögur*). On the other hand, the European romance became a prime court entertainment, and derivative or translated sagas known as *riddarasögur*, or "knights' sagas," were produced both in Norway and in Iceland. *Märchen* elements figured prominently in these late works.

On saga performance and use, we know relatively little. Evidence from the thirteenth-century *Sturlunga saga* indicates that traditional storytellers recounted sagas orally; performers in the cosmopolitan court of Norway may have read aloud from manuscripts. Performance occurred in the evening, and a single narrative could stretch over days or weeks. Further, sagas could be commissioned or presented as gifts.

Thomas A. DuBois

See Also Epic; Hero/Heroine, Folk.

References

Boatright, Mody. 1958. *The Family Saga and Other Phases of American Folklore.* Urbana: University of Illinois Press.

Boberg, Inger. 1966. *Motif-Index of Early Icelandic Literature.* Copenhagen: Munksgaard.

Carney, James. 1955. *Studies in Irish Literature and History.* Dublin: Dublin Institute of Advanced Studies.

Clover, Carol, and John Lindow, eds. 1985. *Old Norse—Icelandic Literature: A Critical Guide.* Ithaca, NY: Cornell University Press.

Mitchell, Stephen. 1991. *Heroic Sagas and Ballads.* Ithaca, NY: Cornell University Press.

Nagy, Joseph. 1985. *The Wisdom of the Outlaw: The Boyhood Deeds of Finn in Gaelic Narrative Tradition.* Berkeley: University of California Press.

Ó Corráin, Donnchadh, Liam Breatnach, and Kim McCone, eds. 1989. *Sages, Saints and Storytellers.* Maynooth, Republic of Ireland: An Sagart.

Ó hÓgáin, Dáithí. 1991. *Myth, Legend & Romance: An Encyclopaedia of the Irish Folk Tradition.* New York: Prentice-Hall.

Wolf, Lois. 1991. Medieval Heroic Traditions and Their Transitions from Orality to Literacy. In *Vox Intexta: Orality and Textuality in the Middle Ages,* eds. A. Doane and C. Pasternack. Madison: University of Wisconsin Press.

Scatology

Folklore concerning excrement, flatulence, urine, and bodily organs involved in the process of defecation. Although many would assume scatological folklore is uniformly obscene or jocular, the range of meanings associated with defecation spans a broad spectrum and varies cross-culturally. Within many traditional cultures, for example, excrement is carefully studied to determine aspects of an individual's health and well-being, and in parts of agrarian Germany, the size of one's cow manure pile served as an index of social standing and wealth. Medieval European texts and church iconography indicate an association of defecation with brazen sinfulness or the devil. Navajo coyote tales often contain scatological humor, as do trickster tales from other Native American and African cultures.

Scatological terms function in many cultures as mild or extreme verbal obscenities. The study of scatological lore from culture to culture furnishes insights into the variety of human responses to even the most basic of physical experiences. Serious inquiry has been hampered at times, however, by folklorists' or editors' disinclination to publish scatological materials or broach the topic in detail.

Scatological folklore, even if left unpublished, has been collected in Europe and the United States for a long period. Folktale collectors such as the Russian A. N. Afanas'ev or the Norwegians Peter Christen Asbjørnsen and Jørgen Moe recorded numerous *Märchen* and anecdotes relating scatological themes. Afanas'ev eventually published his materials, although most nineteenth- and early twentieth-century collectors refrained from doing so. Occasionally, erotic and scatological humor was published privately in small, limited editions intended for a small circle of scholars. Classic folklore indexes such as the *Motif-Index of Folk-Literature* acknowledge the existence of such material in their numbering systems (e.g., X700–799, "Humor Concerning Sex") but avoid citing examples.

Within agrarian society, traditional folktales often possess both polite and bawdy versions, to be used in different contexts. The romantic tale type entitled "The Birthmarks of the Princess" (AT 850), for instance, frequently contains ribald scatological humor. In a Norwegian version of the tale, a peasant pig herder wins the right to see the princess naked and uses his knowledge of the color of her pubic hair to certain advantage. In a suitor contest later in the same narrative, the lad tricks his opponent into consuming human excrement, thereby rendering his breath so distasteful that the princess cannot countenance him during the night but must turn to face the lad instead.

Many folksongs contain scatological versions as well, as do riddles and jokes. Folktale and folksong collections that avoid such material run the risk of presenting an inaccurate picture of folk humor and entertainment.

Throughout agrarian Europe and North America, riddles often contain both an "innocent" answer and one based on erotic or scatological details. The scatological reference may be the first to spring to mind, creating humor when the riddle poser cites the innocent answer instead. A familiar example is provided by the following riddle: "What does a man do on two feet, a dog on three, and a woman sitting down?—Shake hands."

Native American myths and tales contain scatological motifs as well. The motif of magic birth from bodily secretions (T541.8), for instance, occurs among Northwest Coast tribes. In addition, trickster figures (e.g., Coyote, Raven) often display their social ineptitude through improper defecation. Thus, in a Navajo myth, Coyote's improper urination pollutes his wife's home and drives away all her family, and Coyote's brothers-in-law climb higher and higher into the neighboring trees in order to find firewood unsoiled by the trickster. Mention of scatological errors was perceived as hilariously funny by native audiences, who were extremely decorous about the act of defecation.

Medieval texts from Europe allow us to examine changes in scatological concepts in one cultural area over a long period. In theological writing and art during both the medieval and the Reformation periods, fecal imagery served as an important metaphor for sin and sinfulness. Church paintings and manuscript marginalia often depicted sinners kissing the buttocks of the devil, and anticlerical folklore of the period often used this same "brownnosing" image. Illustrations of this sort sometimes represented sexual acts, but many references and illustrations depicted persons consuming or collecting feces. Martin Luther's sermons, too, made numerous references to the devil as an entity who feasts upon human excrement and hell as a place pervaded by the foul odor of defecation. These references may strike the modern reader as coarse or inappropriate, but they appear to have been normal, albeit vivid, metaphors in earlier eras.

Scatological humor from the medieval period apparently drew upon serious, theological uses of fecal imagery. Chaucer's "Summoner's Tale," for instance, concerned an effort to divide a fart into twelve equal portions—a parodic reference to the Last Supper. Similarly, the medieval poem *Audigier* parodied high court romance texts through the substitution of a turd hero for the typical knight in armor. Scatology undoubtedly furnished more vivid metaphors in earlier times, when commodes, outhouses, and primitive sewer systems imprinted the smells and memories of defecation more clearly on people's minds. Latrine humor is still common in armies, where the construction and maintenance of toilet facilities during field maneuvers approaches the experiences of traditional societies.

Folk speech reflects popular attitudes toward scatological matters. In many cultures, terms for both excrement and the body parts responsible for defecation constitute rich sources of obscene expressions as well as euphemisms. In North American English, for instance, polite or clinical terms (e.g., *penis, vulva, anus, feces, urine*) covary with a host of obscene or off-color terms (e.g., *dick, cunt, ass, shit, piss*), which in turn vary with respect to gravity and usage. Terms differ both in the degree to which they are permitted in normal conversation and in the extent to which they evoke their original referents. The terms *shit, crap*, and *turd* ostensibly denote the same referent (i.e., feces) but have different connotations and customary uses. Scatological terms may be used to comment metaphorically on a given situation (e.g., "What's all this shit around here?" in reference to a messy room) or may occur as simple expletives (e.g., "Shit!" in reference to a surprising turn of events). In either case, the decision to use such language helps speakers portray themselves in public, maintain community solidarity, or differentiate themselves or the moment from others.

In addition to such obscene terms, Americans—like others the world over— employ a host of euphemisms when referring to scatological phenomena.

Expressions such as "visit the restroom," "powder one's nose," or "pass wind" constantly come in and out of fashion, as speakers grapple with whether to sound coarse or prudish. Additional terms are used when discussing scatology with children (e.g., *kaka, poop, doo-doo, pee-pee*). Using euphemisms or child speech in unusual contexts leads to humor, as in the case of a police officer saying, "You're in deep doo-doo" for the expected "You're in deep shit" (i.e., "You're in trouble"). Despite this pattern of historical shifts, however, certain terms (e.g., *fart, shit*) have existed in the language for millennia and will certainly remain part of North American culture in the future.

Children's folklore offers some of the richest stores of scatological material. Feces and urine figure prominently in the narratives of young children, and scatological terms become important in insults and jokes throughout childhood and adolescence. The "hand-fart," made with the hand under the armpit, or the "raspberry," made with the lips, constitute potent comments and put-downs. Jokes and folk sayings about flatulence (e.g., "He who smelled it, dealt it") offer young performers the opportunity to match situation with witticism. Telling scatological "dirty jokes" can build solidarity among children vis-à-vis their teachers or other adults, who usually disapprove of the subject or performance. Taunts averring misuse of excrement or problems in defecation abound as well. Folklore of this sort, once common to adult and preadult communities alike, has apparently grown more taboo among adults during the last several centuries throughout Europe and North America.

Scatological imagery pervades folk perceptions of other communities or cultures. Interethnic stereotypes often focus on the means of defecation as well as the sexual habits and diets of strangers. Unwelcome outsiders are said to use restrooms incorrectly or to dispose of excrement in foolish or dangerous ways. They are accused of attracting rodents and insects through their lack of hygiene and their ignorance of toilets. Interethnic scatological humor reflects deep misgivings about the nature of people of differing cultures and is widespread throughout the world.

Often, such stereotyped scatological lore becomes compared in jokes shared by two communities. In an English-French interethnic joke, for instance, an Englishman criticizes a Frenchman for France's deplorable restrooms. The Frenchman's reply uses scatology as a prime metaphor for cultural imperatives: "We eat well, you shit well. It's all a question of priorities." The joke encapsulates both English and French stereotypes about each others' cuisines, toilets, and obsessions. Occasionally, groups will depict themselves as coarser than their counterparts in other cultures, as in Australian interethnic jokes in which the hypermasculine Australian hero displays sneering disregard for societal rules of hygiene and decorum, such as where to urinate and how to refer to excretions. Seemingly self-denigrating humor of this type often occurs in postcolonial situations, in which one culture (i.e., that of the colonized) has long been viewed as inferior to another (i.e., that of the colonizer). The Australian joke allows tellers to embrace their country's negative stereotype and transform it into a virtue, with a frankness superior to the supposedly overly refined and delicate manners of the English.

Scatological folklore is closely linked to sexual folklore and obscenity. All of these topics have posed difficulties to folklorists since they are traditionally taboo subjects in academic discourse. Many of the contributors to the journal *Maledicta*, for instance, use pseudonyms when publishing their studies. Folklorists run the risk of upsetting their informants as well when they transform remarks made in an intimate context into a scholarly text available for all to read. And newspaper journalists surveying the proceedings of academic conferences may ridicule the profession by citing scatological references as illustrations of the triviality or perversity of folklore studies. Despite these drawbacks, however, scatological folklore offers intriguing insights into the transformation of human physical experiences into cultural symbols and perceptions.

Thomas A. DuBois

See Also Belief, Folk; Joke; Obscenity.

References

Afanas'ev, A. N. 1966. *Russian Secret Tales: Bawdy Folktales of Old Russia.* New York: Brussel and Brussel.

Alford, Richard D., and William J. O'Donnell. 1983. Linguistic Scale: Cursing and Euphemisms. *Maledicta* 7: 155–163.

Allen, Irving Lewis. 1983. *The Language of Ethnic Conflict: Social Organization and Lexical Culture.* New York: Columbia University Press.

Brians, Paul, ed. 1972. *Bawdy Tales from the Courts of Medieval France.* New York: Harper & Row.

Davies, Christie. 1990. *Ethnic Humor around the World.* Bloomington: Indiana University Press.

Fine, Gary Alan. 1981. Rude Words: Insults and Narration in Preadolescent Obscene Talk. *Maledicta* 5(1-2): 51–68.

Haile, Berard. 1984. *Navajo Coyote Tales: The Curly Tó Aheedlíinii Version.* Lincoln: University of Nebraska Press.

Lancashire, I. 1981. Moses, Elijah, and the Back Parts of God: Satiric Scatology in Chaucer's *Summoner's Tale. Mosaic* 14(3): 17–30.

Legman, Gershon. 1982. *No Laughing Matter: An Analysis of Sexual Humor.* Bloomington: Indiana University Press.

Lindahl, Carl. 1987. *Earnest Games: Folkloric Patterns in* The Canterbury Tales. Bloomington: Indiana University Press.

Oberman, Heiko. 1988. Teufelsdreck: Eschatology and Scatology in the "Old" Luther. *Sixteenth Century Journal* 19(3): 435–450.

Sutton-Smith, Brian. 1981. *The Folkstories of Children.* Philadelphia: University of Pennsylvania Press.

Wentersdorf, Karl P. 1984. The Symbolic Significance of *Figurae Scatologicae* in Gothic Manuscripts. In *Word, Picture, and Spectacle,* eds. K. Wentersdorf, R. Ellis, C. Davidson, and R. Hanning. Kalamazoo, MI: Medieval Institute Publications.

Semiotics

The study of signs used to communicate. Folklore studies and semiotics, both of which offer interdisciplinary or transdisciplinary perspectives on human communication, have mutually influenced each other as they have developed over the last century or so. Each, of course, has various schools and traditions, but there are important convergences between them, both in the history of the disciplines and in current practice. Within semiotics, we can usefully distinguish an Americanist tradition drawing its insights and methods from the polymath Charles Sanders Peirce, a French (and, more broadly, European) tradition inspired by the Geneva linguist Ferdinand de Saussure (often denominated by Saussure's preferred term, *semiology*), and a Slavic tradition—elaborated especially in Prague, Moscow, and Tartu—whose prominent practitioners include several with strong interests in folklore traditions. Common to all three schools of thought is a concern with the functioning of signs as the means for interpersonal communication, especially the highly elaborated sign systems that characterize artistic communication. Although each school conceives the sign in slightly different ways, all might agree to define the sign as something that stands for something else, to some person and in some respect. Signs may be typologized differently by each tradition (sign versus symbol, symbol versus icon versus index, arbitrary versus motivated sign, and so on), but semioticians share an interest in understanding how people and societies utilize signs to embody meanings and values and to communicate them to one another. Each intellectual tradition offers certain insights or approaches of potential use to folklorists, and each has been influenced to greater or lesser degree by their application to folklore materials.

Of the three trends, the Slavic tradition is most heavily indebted to the work of folklorists, who had a formative role in its evolution. Developing first in the Moscow Linguistic Circle and then in the Prague Linguistic Circle, Slavic semiotics numbered among its founders several individuals with strong interests in folklore texts and traditions. The most prominent figure, Roman Jakobson, later made contributions to linguistics, ethnology, cognitive science, philology, and literary studies, but he began his lifelong inquiries into the sign by studying Russian folklore texts, to which he returned periodically throughout his life. One of Jakobson's close colleagues was the folklorist Petr Bogatyrev, who remained focused on folk traditions throughout his career, from his early days studying folk theater and puppetry in cooperation with Jakobson to his later concern with folk costume, folk poetry, magic, and ritual laughter. The two men were founding members of both the Moscow and the Prague circles. Jakobson's folkloric concerns centered on the poetics of traditional Slavic verse, wherein he noticed a pervasive use of poetic parallelism—the repetition from line to line of a stable phrase with variable contents. In the folk poetry traditions he studied, Jakobson saw parallelism as a canonical feature defining the construction of verse; this became the key to his broader explorations of parallelism in the artistic verse of various authors.

Bogatyrev's most important contributions to folklore theory grew out of his attention to the function of folklore materials and texts in social interactions. Reacting to the excessive ahistoricism and decontextualization of the emerging trend of formalist literary criticism, Bogatyrev insisted on the variable meanings that any sign may have when situated in concrete sociohistorical and social-interactional contexts or when moved from one to another. Drawing examples from folksong, folk costume, and especially folk theater and puppetry, Bogatyrev explored, with rich ethnographic detail, the interactions of structure and function in folklore. Studying the folk costumes of Moravian Slovakia, he showed how costumes indexed certain social statuses (e.g., single versus married, male versus female) and how the costume system generated a larger sense of ethnic identity, of "our-ness." His works on folk theater genres contributed both to the emerging Prague Circle theories of theatrical semiotics and to the avant-garde experimentations of interwar Prague.

Two other important Russian thinkers of the same generation significantly contributed to the development of semiotics and folklore, although both took care to distance themselves in certain ways from formalism and semiotics. Vladimir Propp devised a method of morphological analysis and applied it to Russian magic tales; he found that, despite their quite different surface features of character and plot, the tales shared a single compositional framework or morphology. His book, once translated into English in 1958, had very wide influence on both literary theorists and folklorists as they sought to articulate structural analyses of both artistic and folkloric narratives. Mikhail Bakhtin never counted himself a folklorist but took advantage of the contemporary fascination with folk culture among Soviet cultural commissars to argue his theories of dialogism in language and life. He traced styles and elements of folk humor as they were incorporated historically into the emergent literary genres and offered a brilliant analysis of Rabelais that indeed constituted a richly detailed ethnography of the folklife of Europe in the Middle Ages and Renaissance.

Jakobson left the Soviet Union for exile in Prague and the United States; Bakhtin suffered many years of internal exile during which he had few opportunities to publish or teach. Bogatyrev returned from Prague to the Soviet Union, where he, like Propp, taught for decades but in relative obscurity; neither again achieved the kind of insights or influence they had had in their earlier days. The conjunction of folklore and semiotics was picked up again only in the 1960s, when a circle of scholars in Tartu and Moscow once more turned to folkloric texts, especially myths, as elements in constructing a semiotics of culture.

The Slavic semioticians were inspired by Saussure's crucial programmatic work suggesting a transdisciplinary semiology to be developed from the science of linguistics, although they soon found fault with Saussure and explored other conceptions of the sign. But Saussure had continued to have both direct and indirect influence, especially among francophone scholars. One of the foundational figures of modern structuralism, Claude Lévi-Strauss, employed folkloric texts (especially myths) in his elaboration of a method of structural anthropology (drawing inspiration as well from Propp's morphological method but criticizing it as inadequate). His contemporary, Roland Barthes, employed folklore and, more often, popular culture in propagating a Saussurean semiology that profoundly influenced literary and cultural theory in the 1960s and later. Extending Lévi-Strauss's and Barthes's structural method—some would say to the point of reductio ad absurdum—A. J. Greimas continued to employ folkloric texts as the testing ground of a theory and a method that were briefly in vogue but now seem to be of little interest (especially to American scholars).

The giant of American semiotics, Charles S. Peirce, had virtually nothing to say about folklore in his massive oeuvre, which, in any case, remained little known until recent decades. But his systematic investigation of the sign in all its aspects and functions provided an analytical tool and perspective that crystallized the thinking of contemporary American semioticians in crucial ways. Two figures were pivotal here: again Jakobson, who discovered Peirce upon arriving in the United States during World War II, and Thomas A. Sebeok, who has been both an intellectual and an institutional father of modern semiotics. Jakobson did not incorporate Peirce's ideas into his own analyses of folkloric or literary texts to any great extent but instead celebrated Peirce and promoted interest in his writings.

Within a vast and complex schema of sign modes and functions, Peirce distinguished three ways in which a sign can relate to its object: An *icon* is related by similarity, an *index* is related by real connection, and a *symbol* is related by convention. Jakobson took up this triple distinction to refocus his long-standing concerns with the nature of signs in social and especially artistic communication. Revising Peirce's tripartite scheme, Jakobson took the two oppositions of actual versus imputed and similarity versus contiguity and elaborated a four-way distinction between *icon* (actual similarity), *index* (actual contiguity), *symbol* (imputed contiguity), and *artifice* (imputed similarity, which for Peirce would be subsumed under "symbol"). Whether we retain Peirce's triad or adopt Jakobson's revisions, the division of sign relations and Peirce's corollary divisions of sign functions, modes, and effects have been employed as powerful tools to organize analyses and discussions of complex folklore texts and events.

A scholar whose breadth of expertise parallels that of Peirce himself, Sebeok followed Jakobson's example of employing folkloric texts (especially oral poetry and other verbal art forms) as the material on which to hone semiotic methods of analysis. Equally influential as his own writings has been Sebeok's entrepreneurial work as the organizer of seminars and institutes (including the Folklore Institute at Indiana University) and as the publisher and editor of folkloric and semiotic works of all kinds. Sebeok edited, for instance, such key articles as Lévi-Strauss's "The Structural Study of Myth" (1955) and Jakobson's "Linguistics and Poetics" (1960) and served as editor of the *Journal of American Folklore*.

Although few contemporary folklorists self-identify as semioticians and few contemporary semioticians give as much attention to folklore as those just discussed, the influence—both direct and indirect—of semiotics on folklore theory in recent decades has been profound. The traces are varied: Though few folklorists today engage in structural analyses of folktales or myths, all are expected to know of the approaches of Propp and Lévi-Strauss. The concern with ethnopoetics and the methods used to carry out detailed analyses of the compositional strategies of oral poets and poetic traditions derive, in very large part, from Jakobson's example. Students of folk theater and puppetry must begin with the work of Bogatyrev and his Prague Circle colleagues. And Bakhtin's celebration of the culture of resistance of medieval and Renaissance peasants, the carnivalesque and transgressive, and his contribution to writing a "history of laughter" offer a reinvigorating inspiration to today's folklorists. Finally, the complex semiotic schema elaborated by Peirce can provide a very powerful apparatus around which to organize analyses of those complex, multivocal, multichannel, and multisensory experiences that constitute the folkloric arts.

Frank Proschan

See Also Linguistic Approach; Structuralism.

References

Bakhtin, Mikhail. 1968. *Rabelais and His World*. Cambridge, MA: MIT Press.

Bakhtin, Mikhail. 1981. *The Dialogic Imagination*. Austin: University of Texas Press.

Bauman, Richard. 1982. Conceptions of Folklore in the Development of Literary Semiotics. *Semiotica* 39: 1–20.

Bogatyrev, Petr. 1971. *The Functions of Folk Costume in Moravian Slovakia*. The Hague: Mouton.

Jakobson, Roman. 1987. *Language in Literature*. Cambridge, MA: Harvard University Press.

Lévi-Strauss, Claude. *Structural Anthropology*. New York: Basic Books.

Lucid, Daniel P. 1988. *Soviet Semiotics: An Anthology*. Baltimore, MD: Johns Hopkins University Press.

Matejka, Ladislav, and Irwin R. Titunik, eds. 1976. *Semiotics of Art: Prague School Contributions*. Cambridge, MA: MIT Press.

Propp, Vladimir. 1968. *The Morphology of the Folktale*, 2nd ed. Austin: University of Texas Press.

Propp, Vladimir. 1984. *Theory and History of Folklore*. Minneapolis: University of Minnesota Press.

Proschan, Frank, ed. 1983. *Puppets, Masks, and Performing Objects from Semiotic Perspectives*. Special issue of *Semiotica*, Vol. 47.

Steiner, Peter, ed. 1982. *The Prague School: Selected Writings, 1929–1946*. Austin: University of Texas Press.

Shamanism

The worldview system in northern cultures, particularly those in which a religious leader, a shaman, plays a central role as the mediator between this world and the upper and nether realms of the universe, the leader's main role being that of a healer, an officiant at sacrifices, or a divine prophet. The phenomenon of shamanism is extremely complex and multifaceted. The word *saman* is derived from a Tungus word meaning "a person with special supranormal skills" (the Tungus are an indigenous people of Siberia). When the concept of shamanism was introduced into international literature, its meaning was significantly broadened.

In the cultures where it is practiced, shamanism is not a religion in the narrow sense of compartmentalized Western thinking, which rigidly separates realms of experience; rather, it is a worldview system or a "grammar of mind" that is closely interrelated with ecology, economy, and social structure. Mythic knowledge in shamanic societies is partly collective knowledge shared by the clan and partly esoteric property owned solely by the shamans. This specific knowledge is particularly important to the status of the shaman and is transmitted from one shaman to another in an initiatory education process.

A special grammar of mind is typical of shamanism and designates a way of life and a culture in which the chosen leader, the shaman, occupies a central role. This grammar implies competence in a certain shamanic folklore repertoire, specific skills in performing ritual acts, and knowledge of the shamanic language and the rules of the generic and ritual grammar observed not only in the shamanic sessions but also in the behavior and everyday life of this kind of society. In order to understand shamanism as a religious, social, and cultural phenomenon, it should be analyzed as a whole, taking into consideration both the visible, manifest elements of

Ecuadorean shaman directs solstice festivities in Cochasqui, north of Quito, Ecuador, June 26, 2005. (AP/Wide World Photos)

shamanism and the invisible, latent meanings and messages in the depth structure motivating the behavior of the people who share a shamanic culture as a basis for their societies.

Recently, the concept of shamanism has been extended to an unwarranted degree in the popular press. The term *shamanism* has not only been used to characterize certain ecstatic and other traditional rituals of so-called primitive peoples but also to describe phenomena of Christianity and even the personae cultivated by popular rock musicians. Experts in shamanistic research regard this trend as a devaluation of the concept. Many criticize the overemphasis on ecstasy as a religious experience par excellence, as described, for example, by Mircea Eliade.

Since the middle of the nineteenth century, attempts have been made to account for shamanism as a mental disorder (e.g., schizophrenia or epilepsy). In such hypotheses, however, the problem has been oversimplified. Although the aptitude for exceptional experiences is one of the criteria of "shamanhood," and though periods of madness seem inherent in shamanic initiation, shamans usually are ordinary men and women who, often involuntarily, have to accept the painful vocation of shamanizing.

Phenomenologically, shamanism could be defined on the basis of a number of criteria. Ecstatic techniques are used to find a way into other worlds or dimensions of reality. There is a belief in more than one soul; therefore, a free soul is believed to leave the body in trance to make trips to the other world, where it assumes various shapes (e.g., animal shapes). There is a three-level model of the universe, and the role of the shaman is to mediate between these levels. There is also a belief in helping spirits who assist the shaman. In addition, the shaman achieves his or her ends by using ritual paraphernalia, which vary culturally: drum, dress, bag, mask, and so forth.

When using shamanic categories, it is important to make a distinction between such cultures as that of a number of Mandshu-Tungusian peoples who have the concept of *saman* as a linguistic entry in their native lexicon and those who know parallel phenomena but do not have a lexical entry for the concept (e.g., most Arctic peoples or the Ob-Ugric people of the Khanty). Furthermore, many cultures have neither the word nor the phenomenon. According to the proposed definition, African American spirit possession cults, for example, are not shamanistic.

Generally speaking, the ideological aspect of shamanism has been underestimated in research into the phenomenon. The transmission of the traditional knowledge from one shaman to another is a major element of shamanistic initiation. One of the most important criteria in the choice of a new shaman is certainly the candidate's expertise in the ideological traditions of the culture.

Efforts toward a more holistic interpretation of shamanic folklore texts should determine their cosmological and astral mythical background and the way this relationship is revealed in rituals, expressed in mythic narratives, and interpreted and understood by the members of the culture.

Juha Pentikäinen

See Also Divination; Medicine, Folk; Religion, Folk.

References

Aboensis XII. 1989. *Kalevala Mythology*, trans. Ritva Poom. Bloomington: Indiana University Press.

Aldhouse-Green, Miranda. 2005. *The Quest for the Shaman: Shapeshifters, Sorcerers and Spirit-Healers of Ancient Europe*. London: Thames & Hudson.

Blackburn, Stuart. 2010. *The Sun Rises: A Shaman's Chant, Ritual Exchange and Fertility in the Apatani Valley*. Boston: Brill.

Edson, Gary. 2009. *Shamanism: A Cross-Cultural Study of Beliefs and Practices*. Jefferson, NC: McFarland.

Eliade, Mircea. 1971. *Shamanism: Archaic Techniques of Ecstasy*. Princeton, NJ: Princeton University Press.

Harner, Michael. 2009. *The Way of the Shaman: The Definitive Handbook*. New York: Harper.

Hoppal, Mihaly, ed. 1984. *Shamanism in Eurasia*. Göttingen, Germany: Herodot.

Hoppal, Mihaly, and Juha Y. Pentikäinen. 1992. *Northern Religion and Shamanism.* Budapest: Akedémiai Kiadó.

Lewis, I. M. 1989. *Ecstatic Religion: A Study of Shamanism and Spirit Possession.* London: Routledge.

Pentikäinen, Juha Y. 1987. Saami Shamanic Drum in Rome. In *Saami Religion*, ed. Tor Ahlback. Scripta Instituti Donneriani. Abo, Finland: Almqvist & Wiksell International.

Siikala, Anna-Leena. 1978. *The Rite Technique of the Siberian Shaman.* Helsinki: Academia Scientiarum Fennica.

Siikala, Anna-Leena, and Mihaly Hoppal, eds. 1992. *Studies on Shamanism.* Budapest: Akedémiai Kiadó.

Tolley, Clive. 2009. *Shamanism in Norse Myth and Magic.* Helsinki: Academia Scientiarum Fennica.

Shape-Shifters

Also known as transmogrification or transforming, shape-shifting involves characters with the ability to change themselves into animal, vegetable, mineral, and supernatural forms. Such characters are commonly encountered in hero traditions. Shape-shifting may occur in many ways and for a variety of purposes. A common situation involves a man's attempts to win a woman. Tales and songs of this type often involve a contest, as in the ballad usually known as "Twa Magicians," in which the "lusty smith" eventually wins the woman's maidenhead when she turns herself into a bed and he shape-shifts into a green coverlet or eiderdown. The ability of a hero or heroine to maintain a hold on the beloved while he or she is being changed into all manner of usually loathly or uncomfortable things is also met with quite often, as in the ballad of "Tam Lin."

Another frequent use of shape-shifting occurs in the form of contests between sorcerers or between the hero and the villain, as in the Scandinavian tale of Farmer Weathersky, in which Weathersky—in reality the Devil—is out-shifted by a young hero named, in English translation, Jack. In ballads such as "The False Knight" and its variants, the Devil, in the form of a knight, appears to a small boy on the road and asks questions that the young boy artfully parries, thus, it is implied, escaping damnation.

Shape-shifting may also be used for disguise in order to escape from bondage, elude pursuers, or enter otherwise impenetrable castles. The wicked queen in "Snow White" uses a number of disguises in her attempts to kill the heroine. Often a human will take animal form as a disguise, a theme that is well attested in classical and other mythologies, as well as in folklore.

Shape-shifting is a standard element in trickster traditions around the world. In Native American traditions, the ability of heroes to shape-shift, or transform, is extremely widespread and usually associated with trickster figures such as Coyote, Hare, and Rabbit. The African Anansi, or Spider, is a great shape-shifter. In Chinese and Japanese tradition, shape-shifting is common, especially in relation to the fox.

Graham Seal

See Also Magic; Magicians; Magic Tale; Trickster.

References

Aldhouse-Green, Miranda. 2005. *The Quest for the Shaman: Shapeshifters, Sorcerers and Spirit-Healers of Ancient Europe*. London: Thames & Hudson.

Del Negro, Janice M. 2007. *Passion and Poison: Tales of Shape-shifters, Ghosts, and Spirited Women*. New York: Marshall Cavendish.

Porter, J., and W. Russell, eds. 1978. *Animals in Folklore*, London: Brewer/Rowman and Littlefield, The Folklore Society, pp. 113–182.

Radin, P. 1956. *The Trickster: A Study in American Indian Mythology*, New York: Philosophical Library.

Seki, K., ed. 1963. *Folktales of Japan*. Trans. R. Adams. London: Routledge and Kegan Paul.

Sleeping Beauty

Usually titled in books of fairy tales "The Sleeping Beauty," this widespread, ancient, and well-known folktale is almost always told in English simply as "Sleeping Beauty." Known in one version or another since at least the fourteenth century, "Sleeping Beauty" has had a long literary as well as folkloric life. Successive tellers of the tale, such as Perrault ("*La Belle au Bois Dormant*") and the Grimms (in English, "Little Briar Rose"), have added to it or subtracted from it in various ways, leaving us with the modern version as more-or-less solidified in the Disney animated feature film.

Most readers will be familiar with the Grimm plot, in which a queen, after many years of unsuccessful attempts, finally gives birth. Overjoyed, the king and queen invite everyone in the kingdom to come to the palace to celebrate the birth of their daughter. There are thirteen wise women in the kingdom, and all must be invited. Unfortunately, the king has only twelve gold plates and so, to avoid embarrassment, invites only twelve. While these women bestow gifts of beauty and happiness on the royal baby, the offended thirteenth wise woman angrily curses the child, saying that she will die at fifteen years of age through a prick in her finger. One of the invited wise women is able to lighten the curse from death to one hundred years of sleep.

Spinning machines and their sharp spindles are immediately banned in the kingdom, but in her fifteenth year, the princess comes across an old woman

The Prince awakens the Sleeping Beauty in this illustration by Gordon Frederick Browne for *Children's Stories from Tennyson* by Nora Chesson, 1914. (The Bridgeman Art Library International)

spinning in a castle tower. The princess picks up the spindle and pricks herself, bringing the prophetic curse into effect. She falls asleep, and so does everyone else in the palace, from the king and queen down to the lowliest servant and even the flies on the wall. A great thorn hedge grows around the palace, cutting it off from the world. The legend of the sleeping beauty attracts many young men to the palace, but despite their skill, strength, and determination they all fail to break through and waken the sleeping beauty with a kiss. Eventually, one hundred years pass, and a prince does succeed in breaking through. He kisses the sleeping princess, and she wakes, along with everyone and everything else in the palace. Life returns to normal, and the young prince and Sleeping Beauty marry.

Some elements of the story can be traced to Greek myth, though the motifs of a sleeping princess and magic sleep in general are widely distributed in the world's folktale traditions. The popularity and wide spread of this story and its variants have attracted extensive comment and analysis. Psychological and psychoanalytic approaches generally interpret the story as a metaphor of the sexual awakening of young women that, whatever the parents may think or do about it, is bound to occur sooner or later. In Bettelheim's *The Uses of Enchantment*, for example, there is an extended discussion of the Sleeping Beauty stories along these lines, stressing that the theme of the futility of trying to prevent the child's sexual maturity is common to all versions of the story.

Folklorists would perhaps be more inclined to argue that it is unlikely that every version of "The Sleeping Beauty," past and present, revolves around this theme or that the story was or is told with such intentions. While Bettelheim and other psychoanalysts may be right about some, even many, tellings of this tale, it is not likely to have the same significance in all the societies and in all the periods in which it has been told, a notion akin to the Jungian "one-symbol-does-for-all" archetype. Only on-the-ground fieldwork can determine the significance of any particular telling of "The Sleeping Beauty," or any other folktale. The fact that there have been and continue to be so many differing interpretations of the story is a testament to its popularity, longevity, and wide distribution. That so many meanings can be found within it is due to that peculiar magic we continue to find in those reworked folktales known as "fairy tales."

Graham Seal

See Also Cinderella; Fairy Tale Heroes; Shape-Shifters; Snow White.

References

Bettelheim, B. 1976. The *Uses of Enchantment: The Meaning and Importance of Fairy Tales*, New York: Knopf.

Bottigheimer, R., ed. 1986. *Fairy Tales and Society: Illusion, Allusion, and Paradigm*. Philadelphia: University of Pennsylvania Press.

Calvino, I. [1956] 1980. *Italian Folk Tales: Selected and Retold by Italo Calvino*. Trans. G. Martin. New York: Harcourt Brace Jovanovich, Penguin.

Einfeld, Jann, ed. 2001. *Fairy Tales*. San Diego, CA: Greenhaven Press.

Lüthi, M. 1976. *Once upon a Time: On the Nature of Fairy Tales*. Trans. L. Chadeayne and P. Gottwald. Bloomington: Indiana University Press.

Massignon, G., ed. 1968. *Folktales of France*. J. Hyland. Chicago: University of Chicago Press, pp. 133–135.

Tatar, M. 1987. *The Hard Facts of the Grimms' Fairy Tales*. Princeton, NJ: Princeton University Press.

Snow White

In their version of this favorite and widely known fairy tale, "Little Snow White" (no. 53), the Grimms begin like this: "Once upon a time, in the middle of winter when the snow flakes fell like feathers from the sky, a queen sat at a window which had a frame of black ebony. And as she was sewing while looking at the snow, she pricked her finger with the needle and three drops of blood fell on the snow. The red looked so beautiful on the white snow that she thought to herself, 'I wish I had a child as white as snow, as red as the blood, and with hair as black as the wood of the window frame.'"

Thus the scene is set for the birth of Snow White, the death of her mother, and the taking of a new wife by the king, Snow White's father, one year later. All goes well until Snow White turns seven. Then the trouble begins. The stepmother turns out to be of the wicked variety and is insanely envious of Snow White's beauty, imploring the magic "mirror, mirror on the wall" to tell her "who is the fairest of them all" and receiving the answer she does not wish to hear.

As most children know from either the Disney animated feature (the first version of which was released in 1937) or from any number of children's books, Snow White is expelled from the castle. The wicked queen orders a woodsman to murder the young girl in the forest, but the man cannot bring himself to commit this cold-blooded deed and instead leaves Snow White alone in the wilderness. Here she is found and looked after by seven dwarfs. But the wicked queen discovers that Snow White is not dead and disguises herself in various forms in attempts to kill her. At her third attempt, the queen tricks Snow White into eating a poisoned apple, and the girl dies. She is laid out in a crystal coffin and mourned over by the dwarfs and birds until a handsome prince arrives. He kisses her and, bumping the coffin in the process, wakens her from what was only a deeply drugged sleep after all. She marries the prince, and the wicked stepmother is punished by being made to wear red-hot shoes in which she must dance until her death. The young couple lives happily ever after and, in the manner of most fairy tales and folktales, the cultural equilibrium is reestablished with the defeat of evil and the succession of the generations.

This version of Snow White is satisfyingly complete, with its elaborated narrative structure, its deployment of many ancient and widespread motifs of myth and legend (including the helpers, the wicked stepmother, the narcissistic streak of the queen, the sleep of the heroine, and her awakening with a kiss), and its just rewards and deserts for heroine, hero, and villainess. Most of the many other versions of the tale are less refined and extended, though they tend to retain the symbolic elements of blood, whiteness, and black hair and the motivations of the wicked stepmother as essentially sexual jealousy.

Differences between various versions of Snow White–type tales are highlighted in a number of analyses undertaken from various perspectives. Steven Swann Jones, for instance, shows how the pattern of action varies in three different versions of "Snow White." Nevertheless, comparison of the versions reveals an underlying structure. The heroine may be killed by a poisoned apple in one version, by a raisin in another, or by a poisoned needle in yet another; nonetheless, she is killed, and the narrative proceeds to the next significant action. In comparing the Grimms' version of Snow White with French and Italian versions, Jones points to the quite different ways in which each of the significant actions within the story is accomplished.

In the Grimms' opening situation a queen learns from a magical mirror that the heroine is more beautiful than she. In the Italian version, it is a stepmother

Postcard from 1812 showing the seven dwarves finding Snow White asleep in their bedroom. (Hulton Archive/Getty Images)

who resents her new stepdaughter. In the French version, the stepmother is jealous of her husband's apparent preference for the stepdaughter. In the second significant action, the Grimms' version has the queen ordering a servant to kill the heroine, but instead the servant leaves her in the forest. In the Italian version, the stepmother commands the stepdaughter to tend a dangerously located basil plant. In the French version the stepmother asks her husband to abandon the heroine on a distant mountain.

The third significant action in the Grimms' version involves the dwarfs taking in the heroine. In the Italian version an eagle carries her to a fairy palace. In the French version, the heroine surreptitiously performs domestic chores in the palace of forty giants until they find her out and adopt her. In the fourth significant action the Grimms have the wicked queen discover her location by the magic mirror. In the Italian version, the eagle tells the stepmother the heroine's whereabouts. The French story has the stepmother consulting the sun about any woman more beautiful than herself and discovering the heroine's whereabouts accordingly. In the fifth significant action the Grimms' persecuting queen attempts to murder the heroine, first with a poisoned staylace and comb; eventually she succeeds with the poisoned apple. In the Italian tale, the stepmother enlists the aid of a witch, who fails to kill the heroine with poisoned sweetmeats but succeeds with a poisoned dress. Finally, in the Grimms' version a prince obtains the heroine's body. He bumps her coffin, and Snow White revives and marries him. In the Italian version, the prince obtains the heroine's body, and his mother then removes the poisoned dress in order to wash it, thus causing the heroine to return to life. Heroine and hero are married. In the French conclusion, the father of the prince who discovers the body presses the heroine's chest, causing her to regurgitate the raisin and to breathe again. Prince and heroine then marry.

Jones's purpose in carrying out this enlightening analysis is to pursue a larger argument about narrative structure in folktales, but his analysis also usefully reveals the extent to which all versions of a particular tale are essentially different ways of telling the same story. The means by which the significant actions that make up the core story are brought about is not as important as the carrying out of the actions themselves. The actions, usually strung together in the same sequence, lead inexorably to the climax of the story and to its resolution in the traditional happy ending in which hero and heroine are united in marriage. This narrative structure and its culmination are a symbolic parallelism of the male and female principles that motivate many folktales, especially those of the fairy tale variety. Similar comparisons are possible between different versions of most folktales.

Like most fairy tales, Snow White has numerous international parallels, including the Jewish story of Romana. In her tale, of Middle Eastern origin and perhaps the archetype of "Snow White and the Seven Dwarves," Romana falls in with forty thieves rather than the seven dwarves. The rest of the story is remarkably similar to that of Snow White, with much the same happy ending. Likewise, the theme of the mother, or stepmother, attempting to harm her children or stepchildren is found in many traditions. The brothers S'ad and Sa'id, the sons of a poor woodworker, feature in Persian and Middle Eastern tradition. Their mother falls in love with a wealthy man and, in order to please him, plots to kill her two sons. They escape and after many adventures become rich and honored rulers.

Graham Seal

See Also Cinderella; Fairy Tale Heroes; Shape-Shifters; Sleeping Beauty.

References

Bettelheim, B. 1976. *The Uses of Enchantment: The Meaning and Importance of Fairy Tales.* New York: Knopf.

Briggs, K., ed. 1970–1971. *A Dictionary of British Folk-Tales in the English Language,* 2 vols. London: Routledge and Kegan Paul.

Dawkins, R., comp. and trans. 1974. *Modern Greek Folktales.* Oxford: Clarendon Press, 1953; reprint Westport, CT: Greenwood Press.

Einfeld, Jann, ed. 2001. *Fairy Tales.* San Diego: Greenhaven Press.

Hallett, M., and B. Karasek, eds. 1996. *Folk and Fairy Tales,* Ontario: Broadview Press, pp. 65–73.

Jones, S. 1986. The Structure of "Snow White." In *Fairy Tales and Society: Illusion, Allusion, and Paradigm*, ed. R. Bottigheimer. Philadelphia: University of Pennsylvania Press, pp. 165–186.

Klipple, M. 1992. *African Folktales with Foreign Analogues*. New York: Garland, pp. 244–248.

Kurti, A., trans. [1958] 1971. *Persian Folktales*. London: Bell and Sons, pp. 96–108.

Zipes, J. 1997. *Happily Ever After: Fairy Tales, Children, and the Culture Industry*. New York and London: Routledge.

Speech, Folk

The expressive language use of any group of people sharing a greater or lesser number of local cultural traits. In any living language, there is constant tension between forces promoting stability and uniformity and forces promoting fragmentation and diversity. This essentially dynamic situation is especially evident in languages that have many speakers occupying a large territory and engaged in a wide variety of occupations and activities. In such a context, public education systems and the media consciously or otherwise promote a standard form of speech or forms of speech thought to approach what is considered to be standard and desirable. One of the principal agents of linguistic diversity is the expressive speech of homogeneous groups of people whose geographic location, ethnic background, religion, and occupations, to name the most important features, allow them to be distinguished from other speakers of the same language.

It should be stressed that regional or local speech characteristics, however distinctive, rarely modify the underlying structure of the dominant language; even peculiarities of sound usage (phonology), word shape (morphology), and word order and sentence structure (syntax) do not disguise the fact that a regional or local variety of language belongs to the acknowledged standard tongue. When such changes do operate over a long period of time, new languages come into existence. This is how Latin, once the common language of most of Western Europe, evolved into such modern languages as French, Spanish, Portuguese, Italian, and Romanian, with their numerous regional varieties.

Although these questions of language evolution, regional varieties of language, and the mechanics of language are chiefly the domain of linguists and dialectologists, the folklorist has a nonetheless valid interest in them, too. Dialectologists map the distribution of words, both from the perspective of the varying meaning of a given word and from that of the different words used to identify a specific object or concept; folklorists may do much the same thing or make use of such linguistic mapping in order to cast light, for example, on the movements of peoples and the cultures they carry with them. Careful comparisons, taking

Argot

A special linguistic code whose purpose is to conceal and to exclude. Also called *cant*, this genre of folk speech differs from standard language principally in vocabulary. However, argots based upon a language (the use of *Romanes* by Gypsies in English-speaking societies, for instance) or dialect differing from that in mainstream social use may diverge from standard speech in more complex ways. Argot's nonstandard diction allows its users to communicate with one another secretively. Hence, it most usually occurs among speakers with reasons to hide what they are saying from uninitiated listeners. Argots may merge with other folk speech genres such as jargons and slang.

Groups that have developed argots include persons whose activities are regarded as either illegal or immoral in some social contexts—for example, professional criminals, drug users, and homosexuals. Other groups may develop argots because their activities, though not illegal, require secrecy. Occupations that depend, in part, on tricking clients—gambling and carnival operations, for instance—may generate argots, as may competitive activities in which one team of players wishes to conceal its intentions from another team. Some ethnic groups use their native language as an argot in occupational contexts. Others may employ their language in the same way in social situations to guarantee the privacy of their communication. Argots also may have generational significance; adolescents, for example, often adopt vocabulary usages that exclude their parents from their communications. Argots may also develop in ritual situations, thus allowing religious specialists to deal with topics of esoteric spirituality without revealing sacred secrets to the profane masses. Another possible context for argot development involves communication among members of one sex that is designed to exclude persons of the other sex.

Argots received scholarly attention as early as the fifteenth century, though the first formal dictionary of a cant was probably issued in the 1700s. Francis Grose's *Classical Dictionary of the Vulgar Tongue,* first published in 1785, remains an important source of vocabulary usage by British criminals. Folklorists had included argot in their new discipline by the late 1800s. In 1890, the *Journal of American Folklore* published materials on *Shelta*, an argot used by British tinkers. Most studies of argot by folklorists and others (many of which have appeared in the periodical *American Speech*) have focused only on the compilation of word lists and their definitions. These glossaries may provide general comments about the group that uses the argot but often do not deal with specific usages in particular contexts.

More contextually oriented research could identify (1) particular situations in which groups employ specific words and phrases from the argot vocabulary, (2) whom such groups intend to exclude through their use of argot, and (3) the sociopsychological functions, such as group integration, that argots may perform in addition to their practical role in promoting secrecy and privacy of communication. Moreover, the playful dimension of argot, though noted by several commentators, has not received the attention that it deserves. Often, what appear to be attempts at communicative concealment may be artful linguistic flourishes that demonstrate the verbal agility of the speakers more than their desire for secrecy.

William M. Clements

into account other cultural and historical phenomena, enable the folklorist to understand the social pressures involved in producing cultural change or cultural conservatism.

Furthermore, some knowledge of regional forms of speech and the history of a given language is useful, not to say essential, for the complete understanding of the texts of narratives and songs, rhymes, proverbs, riddles, and other forms of verbal expressive folklore in which nonstandard vocabulary and nonstandard usages are embedded. It is axiomatic that the field-worker embarking on the study of the folklore of a particular group must make every effort necessary to master the local idiom. Without a thorough familiarity with the subtleties of local usage, the researcher will be deprived of the insights to be gained from such knowledge, and he or she may miss the significance of words and nuances of meanings in the very texts that are the subject of study. Without such knowledge, the student of a regional or local folklore will focus on what seem to be curious words or phrases (which may be a good deal less curious than the field-worker thinks) and give them more emphasis than they merit.

An important corollary to the issue of nonstandard speech is the question of transcription. On the one hand, some scholars believe regional forms should be standardized when setting the spoken word into a written form, retaining peculiar local words and phrases for "local color." Such scholars maintain that the use of "eye dialect"—approximate renderings of nonstandard pronunciations based on the transcriber's own speech habits (e.g., writing "wuz" for "was")—unnecessarily portrays the original speaker in a demeaning fashion and, in any case, is rarely an accurate rendering of a phonological reality. On the other hand, some scholars, for theoretical reasons, prefer to attempt as accurate an approximation of the spoken word as is possible. The best of these approximations are usually based on a solid grounding in phonetics and the history of the language. It is certain that a standardized version of a text and a so-called folkloric transcription of the same text give two very different visions of the material. It is clearly important both to justify the approach one adopts on theoretical grounds and to provide a clear guide to the system of written conventions used to render the nonstandard forms. Of immediate interest to the field-worker exploring the traditions of a social group is the specialized vocabulary related to the group's primary and other occupations. One cannot appreciate the creative artistry involved in the making of a loggers' song or a song about (and by) members of any other occupation without some familiarity with the technical terms and phrases that are part and parcel of that occupation. The folklorist will need to know the names of tools used by potential informants. For example, to the average person, a plane is a plane, but to a carpenter, it may be no more than a generic term for which the profession has five or six specialized names, each referring to a particular type; to most people, snow is snow, but to the Inuit of the high Arctic, there may be no single word for snow at all but thirty or forty different words describing particular kinds of snow.

Similarly, it is important to list the folk names for animals, fish, insects, or plants (in addition to learning about the traditional uses to which these may be put); in other words, establishing the local names for things is a first step in defining local taxonomies and a preliminary to understanding the relationship of the social group to the world around it. And lest the impression be given that there is too great a preoccupation with the rural or marginal in society, it should be stressed that scholars have long been preoccupied with creating vocabularies peculiar to urban groups—there are gay lexicons and lexicons of the underworld, of the church, of the military, of airline pilots, and the like. If in the beginning was the word, then the word—the vocabulary of a social group—is one of the first things to be studied.

Also of interest in this area is the field of naming. Nicknames, pet names, names given to domestic animals, the calls used to summon animals, and the vocabulary of animal husbandry all reflect sets of preoccupations. Local history is echoed in the place-names of an area, and not infrequently, local sayings allude to local references, be they to places or people. Thus, the form of the widespread proverbial comparison "as big a liar as . . ." may simply be concluded with the name of a local teller of tall tales. Or the comparison "as deep as Dead Man's Pond" will allude to a local body of water believed to be bottomless, for example. There are many such reports of traditional genres, including proverbs and riddles, whose effectiveness depends on knowledge of local events or characters. Not infrequently, demands for explanations of the meanings of such local sayings will lead to a variety of anecdotes—some humorous, others serious—knowledge of which further adds to the investigator's appreciation of the cultural texture of the community under examination.

Many characteristic forms of folk speech are embedded in rhymes. Children's lore is replete with rhymes, beginning with the nursery rhymes and jingles used by adults or older children with small infants. Then, as children enter school, they learn the teases, the jeers, the taunts and reproofs, the retorts and parodies, the rhymes meant to shock and upset, the epithets and euphemisms, the insults, the tongue twisters, the catches, the wisecracks, and, sometimes, the secret languages shared by their peers, all of which may involve rhyme in part or in whole, not infrequently rhymes that are rhymes only because of the peculiarities of local pronunciation.

Rhyme often goes hand in hand with naming customs. This has long been attested in the area of *blasons populaires*, the nicknames attributed by the members of one community to the inhabitants of neighboring communities. *Blasons populaires* are not, of course, necessarily in rhyme, and folk speech will incorporate pejorative forms of epithet in all manner of colorful sayings. Indeed, an interesting though relatively little studied area of folk speech is that of oaths and

Tongue Twister

A linguistic sequence with difficult phonological combinations. Also called *tongue tanglers*, *tongue teasers*, and *jaw busters*, tongue twisters require agility in articulating sequences of similar sounds at a rapid rate. Sound similarities usually involve long strings of alliteration (the repetition of initial consonant sounds, as in "Peter Piper picked a peck of pickled peppers"), assonance (the repetition of vowel sounds, as in "How now brown cow?"), consonance (the repetition of final consonant sounds, as in "He thrusts his fists against the posts / And still insists he sees the ghosts"), or a combination of these and other sound patterns. Sometimes, tongue twisters utilize elaborate sound inversions in complex juxtapositions—for example, "How much wood would a woodchuck chuck if a woodchuck could chuck wood?" Homophones (words and syllables that sound the same) also often occur in tongue twisters ("I saw Esau sitting on a seesaw"). Frequently, tongue twisters rhyme, and most evince regular rhythmic qualities. Some are extremely short, amounting to only a phrase ("rubber baby buggy bumpers"), and others extend for several sentences.

Tongue twisters seem to flourish most among children, who delight in challenging one another to demonstrate their speaking ability. If the tongue twister is brief, the challenge may be to say it several times as quickly as possible. For longer tongue twisters, the challenge is simply to get through it rapidly without making a mistake. A competitive element figures in the performance of tongue twisters when one child recites a difficult text and then calls upon another to do likewise. Some tongue twisters assume the form of a question and answer, one child articulating a traditional alliterative question and expecting another to respond in kind. Often, children delight most when a pronunciation error occurs, especially if that error involves the utterance of a taboo word. For example, a slight juxtaposition of vowel sounds in "I'm not a fig plucker nor a fig plucker's son, but I'll pluck figs till the fig plucker comes" can allow a child to say with impunity a word that might otherwise be forbidden.

Though competitive in their own right, tongue twisters may figure into other games, particularly those requiring the payment of a "forfeit." Drinking games, popular with high school and college students, often focus on the proper enunciation of a tongue twister to an increasingly accelerated rhythm. When someone makes an error, he or she must quickly consume a quantity of beer or other alcoholic drink, thus further impairing the ability to articulate. Some traditional songs incorporate tongue twisters. These verbal challenges may serve as informal, semiserious measures of one's ability to speak a foreign language. Tongue twisters also have served as formal exercises in elocution, speech therapy, and foreign language instruction.

Though many studies of tongue twisters by folklorists simply provide lists, others have investigated the linguistic patterns and the geographical and generational distribution of the tongue twister. Among topics that merit further attention are studies of similarities and differences in tongue twisters from different languages, the relationship between the popularity of particular texts and the demographics of the children who perform them, and the use of tongue twisters in informal educational contexts.

William M. Clements

swearing. More tastefully, folk speech also includes a variety of blessings and graces, prayers, and toasts, which may be both serious and humorous.

Two types of folk speech that have received attention from scholars are proverbs and proverbial speech and the riddle and riddling question. In the past, scholars tended simply to make lists of examples of proverbs, rarely providing the contextual data essential to understanding how the proverbs were used; yet such data are clearly essential since proverbs may make use both of local words and of allusions to local events or characters. One of the most distinctive features of folk speech, indeed, is the colorful imagery embedded in proverbial similes, exaggerations, metaphors, retorts, and Wellerisms, in which the "color" is an expression of the group's relationship to its own world and its own worldview.

The same comment can be made about the language of riddles and related forms. The so-called true riddle—a riddle that asks a question in metaphorical terms but that the listener may take literally and that has an answer involving the same opposition between the literal and the metaphorical—frequently refers to local realities. A person unfamiliar with kerosene lamps, for instance, will be stumped when asked what it is that drinks its blood and eats its own guts. The outsider learns not only what is a familiar feature of a local environment but also the characteristic ways in which such features are expressed locally, that is, the nature of local imagery.

A final aspect of folk speech worthy of examination is the relationship between speech and communication. All speech attempts to communicate, but not all communication is necessarily in the form of speech. Much communication is made through gesture, and all cultures have an unwritten code of gestural communication. It is important to take note of the vocabulary of gesture in any community, not because the body of gestures that are locally meaningful may differ greatly or be in some way alien to the dominant culture (though they may be) but because without such a vocabulary, the researcher is denied complete access to local speech. Thus, although gestures signaling greeting or farewell, anger or insult, or directions may be common beyond the local context, some may have evolved specific to a given occupation or activity. Gestures made during card games may not, for example, be noticed by an outsider observing the play, or they may be misinterpreted; similarly, there may be formalized gestures with local significance embedded in traditional performance contexts such as storytelling or singing.

The idiom of any social group emerges in the many kinds of discourse characteristic of the communicative contexts proper to that group. Some of these contexts, in which well-established folkloric genres are embedded, have been well documented and carefully studied from a variety of perspectives. Others have been, until recently, somewhat neglected because of the apparent absence of easily recognizable genres in such discourse contexts. Yet most speech is conversational rather than performative, and it is in conversational speech that local idiom is given its most natural expression. In performative genres, it is not uncommon to find archaic words and expressions, as if frozen in time; folksong collectors frequently encounter words whose meanings are unclear not only to the collector but to the singer as well. A methodological lesson for the folklore field-worker using a tape recorder is to let the tape recorder run, even when the informant or informants are not actually "performing," and to have constantly at hand a notebook in which to jot down words and phrases that seem significant.

Gerald Thomas

See Also Language, Play; Language, Secret.

References

Botkin, B. A. 1944. *A Treasury of American Folklore*. New York: Crown.

Brunvand, Jan Harold. 1978. *The Study of American Folklore. An Introduction*. 2nd ed. New York: W. W. Norton.

Butler, Gary. 1991. *'Saying Isn't Believing': Conversation, Narrative and the Discourse of Tradition in a French Newfoundland Community*. St. John's, Newfoundland: Institute of Social and Economic Research, Memorial University of Newfoundland.

Dundes, Alan. 2008. *"The Kushmaker" and Other Essays on Folk Speech and Folk Humor*. Burlington: University of Vermont.

Maurer, David W. 1981. *Language of the Underworld*, eds. Allan W. Futrell and Charles B. Wordell. Lexington: University Press of Kentucky.

Murray, Thomas E. 1993. The Folk Argot of Midwestern Gangs. *Midwestern Folklore* 19: 113–148.

Preston, Dennis R. 2003. *Needed Research in American Dialects*. Durham: Duke University Press.

Thomas, Gerald, and J. D. A. Widdowson, eds. 1991. *Studies in Newfoundland Folklore: Community and Process*. St. John's, Newfoundland: Breakwater Books.

Thompson, Harold W. [1939] 1962. *Body, Boots & Britches: Folktales, Ballads and Speech from Country New York*. New York: Dover Publications.

Spirit

An insubstantial replica, usually invisible, of an object or person. The spirit is often thought to function as a kind of servo-mechanism of the body that it mimics and as a source of its will or other animating or vital principle, so that unconsciousness and sleep may be interpreted as the temporary loss of the spirit and death as its permanent absence. Often, as expressed in Plato, it is believed that there is a pool of spirits somewhere that, from time to time, become incorporated in new bodies. At birth (or during the rituals associated with the newborn), it is important that an appropriate spirit enters the new body and that inappropriate ones be warded off; at death, it is vital that the old spirit successfully makes its way out of the body.

Anything that creates images may be taken for a conduit into the separate, normally invisible world where spirits live. In other words, spirits may manifest themselves in dreams (as Patroclus's spirit appears to Achilles in the *Iliad*); in mirrors (such as the magic mirror in *Snow White*); in water (which has a reflecting surface and is commonly used in divination); or in the figures seen in tea leaves or coffee grounds, which can be interpreted by someone familiar with the ways of spirits. Mental imagery, induced through a variety of methods—sensory deprivation, hallucinogenic drugs, fasting, meditation, repetitive sounds—is often taken for a manifestation of the spirit world.

In industrial societies, some of these methods have lived on in the belief system known as "spiritualism." Spiritualism stresses one aspect of the traditional beliefs, namely, the idea that one can consult the spirits of specific dead people, which is done at séances. Such consultation is an ancient tradition and has often been done at burial places, as in the early Russian steppes, where figures known as "stone women" were erected on grave mounds; relatives would sleep at the graves and communicate with the dead through their dreams.

Such figures illustrate a common quality of spirits: They have an affinity for anything that has their shape. To capture a spirit, one may create an image in the shape of its corresponding body. Since spirits also have an affinity for reflecting surfaces, mirrors and vessels of water are often used to hold them in place. These may be placed in or above graves to prevent the spirit of the deceased from wandering about.

Perhaps because they may be manifested in reflections, spirits are taken to be exact opposites (that is, mirror images) of the phenomenal world. Therefore, the spirit world is typically appealed to and approached by means of reversals: The shaman may enter his or her hut backwards in preparing to make contact with the spirits. Traditional dream interpretation, as far back as Artemidorus's *Interpretation of Dreams*, has assumed that the meaning of a dream is based on such reversal—to dream of sorrow means happiness and vice versa.

What is commonly called the "soul" differs from the traditional spirit. Whereas the spirit has a loose connection to the body and, when on temporary furlough from it, is capable of acting on its own, the soul is generally assumed to maintain its connection to the body until death. But like spirits, souls also may stay around after death, sometimes haunting the location where death occurred, and then, once disembodied, they are referred to as "ghosts." Both the term *ghost* and the term *spirit* also are used to refer to the third member of the Trinity in Christianity: the Holy Ghost (or Holy Spirit).

Paul Barber

See Also Assault, Supernatural; Divination; Medicine, Folk; Religion, Folk.

References

Brain, James L. 1979. Ancestors as Elders in Africa—Further Thoughts. In *Reader in Comparative Religion: An Anthropological Approach*, eds. William A. Lessa and Evon Z. Vogt. New York: Harper & Row.

Downs, James F. 1985. Spirits, Power, and Man. In *Magic, Witchcraft, and Religion: An Anthropological Study of the Supernatural*, eds. Arthur C. Lehmann and James E. Myers. Palo Alto, CA: Mayfield.

Furst, Peter T. 1976. *Hallucinogens and Culture*. Novato, CA: Chandler & Sharp.

Goodman, Felicitas D. 1990. *Where the Spirits Ride the Wind: Trance Journeys and Other Ecstatic Experiences*. Bloomington: Indiana University Press.

Storytelling

The definition crafted in 2000 after much debate by the board of directors of the National Storytelling Network, the principal professional storytelling organization in the United States, reads: "Storytelling is the interactive art of using words, vocalizations, and/or physical movement and gesture to reveal the elements and images of a story to a specific live audience." The definition is suggestive in what it excludes as well as what it includes. It does include interactivity, the reciprocal flow of energy between teller, audience, and narrative in the moment of live performance. It thus excludes writing, filmmaking, television, video gaming, and other mediating frameworks that interpose between teller and listeners. These later arts, however, grounded as they are upon the genres and principals of storytelling, are ever willing to appropriate the hallowed name of their ancestor for its intimacy and mythic resonance. In its essence, storytelling as we will use the term here is a live and living art, a process of communication and communion between teller and listeners, shaped by various traditions but mediated as little as possible by distancing technologies.

The difficulty in maintaining a definition of storytelling *as* storytelling and not as a metonymy for something quite different is to be found less in the word or the process it denotes than in the cultural mindset within which the act of definition must be attempted. Walter Ong has pointed out that the assumptions of literacy-based civilization have so permeated our thought processes as to breed unchallenged oxymorons such as "oral literature" (or "literary storytelling"). In *Image, Music, Text*, Roland Barthes has beautifully enumerated how narrative (as opposed to storytelling) can exist in "a prodigious variety of genres, themselves distributed among different substances—as if any material were fit to receive man's stories." Marshall MacLuhan postulated that "environments are invisible"; and the environment of literature- and media-saturated culture has certainly hidden in plain sight our dependence on the technological artifacts of

Storyteller Rosie Chapman, second from right, tells the story of "Molly the Mouse" as Tatyanna Todd, Khadidja Ngom, and Aryanna Young act out characters during the 2002 Storytelling Festival at the Detroit Public Library. (AP/Wide World Photos)

the story-making process. Storytelling, both as concept and as artistic/political movement, would refocus our attention on the process in its unencumbered form.

Historically, storytelling in primarily oral cultures has functioned as an expression of any and all social castes but takes on distinctive characteristics depending on the nature and functions of a particular group. Thus, storytelling of and for elites or ruling castes tends toward what we know as bardic storytelling, its principal genres being epic, praise song, and genealogy. Whether Homeric epics, the Irish legends of Cuchulain and the *Tain bo Cuiligne*, or the African Mwindo epic, these stories are generally highly formalized and formulaic, passed on by hereditary professional lineages, and often chanted to the accompaniment of stringed instruments such as the harp, lyre, gusle, rebec, or kora.

Storytelling in occupational groups (warriors, hunters, fishermen, pastoralists, and agriculturists, among others) or religious groups revolves around the hero types and activities of that group, whether the genre be epic, tall tale, wonder tale, or sacred teaching tale. These show wide variation in form, ranging from ceremonial or ritual tellings resembling those of traditional epic performances to less formal exchanges in coffeehouses, homes, barracks, or courtyards of monasteries or prayer houses.

Storytelling in peasant or servant groups tends toward the wonder tale, as Max Lüthi, Jack Zipes, and others have shown, to provide imaginative release from the harsh conditions of workaday life. They are often performed as an accompaniment to repetitive menial tasks, such as food storage (picking, canning, drying, and threshing), cloth-weaving, or net-mending, as Appalachian, Hebridean, and Hungarian storytellers have testified. Or they can be just vessels to carry community spirits across the long winter nights. The hero or heroine's journey from outcast wayfarer through magical trials to blessed estate seems designed to lift the laboring heart and mind and to anaesthetize sore fingers. Animal tales are widespread in African, African American, Native American, European, and Asian traditions. Stories in which human and divine traits and conflicts are embodied in animal forms, these tales range in function from simple children's fables and jests to sacred creation myths. *Märchen* and animal tales may thrive in less-formal contexts than bardic or ritual tellings; yet there remains something ceremonious about the repetition of traditional stories, whether in ceili houses (the houses where neighbors gather in rural Irish and Scottish communities for music, dancing, and storytelling) or fishing shacks, around a shaman's fire or a child's bed, or, more recently, at library story hours or revival storytelling festivals.

The storytelling process is often imprecisely understood from opposite sides of the orality/literacy divide. Milman Parry and Albert B. Lord reported that the illiterate bards from whom they collected South Slavic epics naturally assumed that their literate interlocutors could perform such feats of memory as the singers themselves had just demonstrated, and much more as well, since the educated folk had the additional power of literacy. And literate persons often still make the error of assuming that oral traditional storytellers are reciting their stories and verses word for word, as literates would memorize a play or a poem.

Only since we have transited into the epoch of electronic recording and transmitting media has it become possible to examine such notions with any precision, as Parry and Lord were able to in the Balkans in the 1930s and again in the 1950s with their early recording devices. They recognized that oral memory is a process of stitching together performances out of formulaic elements—traditional images, metaphors, stylized action passages, and a range of other syntactic and discursive chunks, arranged with some improvisatory freedom to fit the audience and the occasion. A traditional storyteller learns from hearing these elements repeated in sufficient variety yet stylistic consistency that he or she can make use of their patterns to freely reproduce the community's repertoire of tales, adding their own variations, reflections, and responses to the pressures of the environment. Thus, oral storytelling performances can emerge rather fluidly from the language web of community talk, as Henry H. Glassie beautifully elucidates in the Irish ceili storytelling in *Passing the Time in Ballymemnone* (1982). A particular tale may appear in multiple variants, from different narrators in different settings, yet each variation can be experienced by the group authentically as "the story."

While tellers in bardic or religious orders are often trained to what amounts to professional standards and lineages, and perform a distinct high-status social function, tellers in rural or peasant communities can be equivalently recognized and valued by their own peers. In cultures around the world where orality remains a dominant force of cultural transmission, tellers such as the *seanachies* of rural Ireland recorded by the Irish Folklore Commission, or Jack tale tellers of the Hicks-Harmon-Ward extended family of Beech Mountain, North Carolina, are well known as cultural resources and authorities both within and beyond their immediate communities. Yet, as these redoubts of oral culture are increasingly encroached upon first by literacy and then still more disruptively by electronic culture, the practices and repertoires of traditional storytelling are subject to the twin perils of attrition or revival.

The vanishing subject has been both the lamentation and driving force of folklore scholarship since its inception with Johann Gottfried Herder and Jacob and Wilhelm Grimm. When Hector Urquhart, friend and informant of the great Scottish folktale collector John Francis Campbell, was a young man in the early nineteenth century, he wrote of the common custom in the Gaelic Highlands of his childhood of gathering to listen to folktales and fairy tales (or *sgeulachd*) as told by itinerant tailors, shoemakers, or other traveling folk. "It was also the custom," he wrote, "when an *aoidh*, or stranger, celebrated for his store of tales, came on a visit to the village, for us, young and old, to make a rush to the house where he passed the night . . . just as I myself have seen since when a far-famed actor came to the Glasgow theater" (Campbell, 5). Yet Urquhart goes on to report that, after the minister and the schoolmaster came to the village in the 1830s, their disapproval of the practice and their teaching of the written word caused oral storytelling to die away almost completely.

More than a century later, African storyteller Raouf Mama described a similar turn in his native Benin: In the space of twelve years—from 1960, when Benin was granted independence, to 1972, the year of the Beninese revolution—storytelling evenings in Beninese homes declined considerably. Today, that time-honored tradition has gone out of existence. Much of the blame for this must be laid on the colonial educational system, which sought to make the Beninese look down on his native tongue, customs and tradition, culture, and folklore (MacDonald, 9–10).

Similarly, the Appalachian storyteller Ray Hicks, an iconic fixture at the National Storytelling Festival from 1973 to 2000, often said that the doctrinaire ministers of the hardshell Baptist churches drove the traditional wonder tales out of his region of the mountains. "They teached 'em out," he would say. "Said they's wrong." The coming of television to rural areas has had a particularly corrosive impact on the customs of social gathering and listening that are the necessary habitat of extended-form storytelling sessions in the home. These factors and others have driven the transposition of storytelling to more formally constructed contexts, such as libraries, schools, and storytelling revival festivals.

Anthony Wallace placed revivals as one class of revitalization movement, which he defined in general as "the deliberate, organized, conscious effort on the part of members of a society to construct a more satisfying culture" (Wallace, 265). Revival movements celebrate values, customs, and rituals that are thought to have been part of the everyday lives of earlier generations, and whose eclipse is held to symbolize a larger decline in the cultural health of the present. Such movements have long been part of the self-regenerating fabric of cultural life. They tend to emerge in periods when social, political, economic, or technological changes put great stress on cultures and individuals. Though their explicit agenda is to bring back practices belonging to an idealized past, their actual mechanisms are usually homeostatic, and serve to integrate contemporary innovations in context and process by buffering them with traditional imagery and reassuring ritual.

Folk arts in general and storytelling in particular have regularly served as grist for the cultural revival mill. The revival of storytelling in the latter three decades of the twentieth century was part of a pattern that reaches back to include the fairy tale enthusiasm at the court of Versailles that produced the works of Charles Perrault, Marie-Catherine d'Aulnoy, and their peers; the Hasidic movement in eighteenth and nineteenth-century Judaism, which gave a central sacred role to storytelling and generated both the legends of the Baal Shem Tov and the mystical fairy tales of his great-grandson Nachman of Bratslav; the German Romantic movement, fired by the folkloristic proclamations of Herder and the Brothers Grimm; and the Romantic-nationalist movements that followed the German lead in nearly every country in Europe and the Americas, producing great collections of national and regional folklore and often serving as cultural cover for significant political and social consolidation and change.

In the United States, there was an important if now nearly forgotten revival of storytelling in the 1890s and the first decades of the 1900s that neatly mirrored the storytelling movement at the century's close. It began in the emerging library and public school systems. Library story hours were established in the Carnegie and New York Public Library systems in the 1890s, and the training of children's librarians came to include storytelling as an essential vocational skill (Alvey). The National Story Tellers' League was founded in 1903 by Richard Wyche at a summer school for public school teachers in Knoxville, Tennessee, to promote storytelling in schools. Manuals and inspirational tracts on storytelling as an art form were published by Sarah Cone Bryant, Marie Shedlock, Wyche, and others, all recommending folktales, fairy tales, and literary fairy tales by the likes of Hans Christian Andersen, Oscar Wilde, or Howard Pyle, and biblical stories,

Arthurian legends, and Greco-Roman myths. Storytelling was regarded as an important resource for settlement schools, which were being established in urban areas to serve the children of burgeoning immigrant populations, as well as in isolated rural areas such as the southern Appalachians.

Both these institutions, libraries and schools, provided secular vocational paths for passionate, idealistic young adults, primarily female. They served an urgent social purpose, namely the socialization of poor children to the cultural norms of the literate middle class. It is suggestive of the implicit agendas of this storytelling movement (and their eventual fulfillment, diversion, or cancellation) that its fervor began to wane in the 1920s in synchrony with laws granting women the vote (1919) and restricting immigration (1924). Yet its accomplishments were to create institutional bases for organized storytelling in the United States and northern Europe—albeit in primarily book-centered, oral interpretive contexts— which were in place and ready to support resurgences of fervor around the art at the end of the century.

In 1973, in a small town on the edge of the Blue Ridge Mountains, a festival was organized that became a focus for such a resurgence. The National Storytelling Festival in Jonesborough, Tennessee, offered safe haven to young women and men fresh from the countercultural movements of the 1960s, hungry for a cultural vehicle that promised reconciliation, social connectedness, and artistic healing. Over the succeeding decades, performers and listeners have been drawn to the festival and others like it around the United States, Canada, and Western Europe. Many of the tellers have discovered storytelling independently, sometimes in the earlier contexts of community oral traditions, library work, or teaching, but more often as voyagers from related art forms, such as theatrical impersonation, oral interpretation, performance poetry, mime or New Vaudeville, stand-up comedy, singer/songwriting, or folk music. They came together in Jonesborough and similar sites under a banner of a revival of oral tradition; yet, like many a crusade or parade banner, it served to camouflage even as it exalted the diversity of backgrounds and motives beneath it.

At the outset at least, revival storytelling repertoires have been dominated by folktales and fairy tales, often buttressed by Freudian, Jungian, or Campbellian cross-cultural interpretive frameworks (see Psychological Approach). Traditional tellers with distinctive community repertoires of wonder tales, such as Ray Hicks in the United States, Joe McNeil in Canada, and Duncan Williamson in Scotland, have had formative influences on storytelling revival performers and repertoires; and many important younger tellers, such as Diana Wolkstein, the late Jackie Torrence, Laura Simms, and the English teller Ben Hagerty have based their careers at least initially on the telling of folktales (though recent festival repertoires in the United States have been increasingly dominated by personal memoir). In part this renaissance of folktale telling was due to these stories' easy identification with tradition and their naturalness in solo and small group performance; but it may also owe to the fact that the form of the wonder tale as described by Joseph Campbell or Vladimir Propp uncannily mirrors the process of a revitalization movement itself.

Wallace described periods of increasing individual or communal stress (separation), followed by a revealed vision of a new way of life (initiation), often based on earlier, forgotten forms and rituals. These revitalizing breakthroughs lead to the creation of organizations, such as the National Story Tellers' League or the National Storytelling Network, to communicate the new path and assimilate it into existing social forms (return). Revival storytellers tend to see themselves as heroes or heroines of their own wonder tale quests, with storytelling as the magical gift enabling them to vanquish the glass mountain of alienated labor, and to make a meaningful living from their art in order to live "happily ever after." Regardless of the status of the ever after, storytelling as a potential of human expression promises to remain with us for as long as we remain human.

Joseph Daniel Sobol

See Also Animal Tale; Epic; Folktale; Legend; Myth; Oral-Formulaic Theory; Oral Tradition.

References

Alvey, Richard G. 1974. The Historical Development of Organized Storytelling for Children in the United States. Dissertation, University of Pennsylvania.

Barthes, Roland. 1977. *Image, Music, Text*. New York: Noonday.

Campbell, J. F., trans. 1994. *Popular Tales of the West Highlands: Orally Collected.* New edition. 2 vols. Edinburgh: Birlinn.

Glassie, Henry. 1982. *Passing the Time in Ballymenone*. Bloomington: Indiana University Press.

Lord, Albert M. 1960. *The Singer of Tales*. Cambridge, MA: Harvard University Press.

MacDonald, Margaret Read, ed. 1999. *Traditional Storytelling Today: An International Sourcebook*. Chicago: Fitzroy Dearborn.

McLuhan, Marshall. 1965. *Understanding Media: The Extensions of Man*. New York: McGraw.

Ong, Walter. 1982. *Orality and Literacy: The Technologizing of the Word*. London: Routledge.

Pellowski, Anne. 1990. *The World of Storytelling*. Expanded and revised edition. Bronx, NY: Wilson.

Schneider, William. 2008. *Living with Stories: Telling, Re-telling, and Remembering.* Logan: Utah State University Press.

Sobol, Joseph Daniel. 1999. *The Storytellers' Journey: An American Revival.* Urbana: University of Illinois Press.

Wallace, Anthony F. C. 1956. Revitalization Movements. *American Anthropologist* 58: 264–281.

Structuralism

Various methods of analysis based on the reduction of phenomena into cognitive models referred to as *structures*. It is probably best to approach the term *structuralism* through an attempt to understand the concept of *structure* within this theoretical point of view. Traditionally, the major problem with the term *structure* has been its concreteness. The word typically refers to phenomena or entities (e.g., buildings) that are quite physical in their essence. Needless to say, structures in structuralism are neither concrete nor physical. Rather, such structures are mental models built after concrete realty. Furthermore, these models are not obvious but demand an understanding of hidden or deep aspects of the matter at hand. Following this approach, structuralism is an attempt to build models that can help understand or, as structuralists would put it, explicate the materials at hand.

The most difficult aspect of structuralism is that these structures are not based on concrete or physical phenomena as they are in biological or other sciences but on cultural realities, such as kinship organization or mythologies. These structures and their structuralist models exist only in human minds and not in nature as, for example, a Marxist would claim.

The ranks of the structuralists include Ferdinand de Saussure, Roland Barthes, Michel Foucault, Jacques Lacan, and Claude Lévi-Strauss. It is even possible to claim that some important social and/or psychological theoreticians and certain sciences are structuralist in character because they build models of psychological or social reality. This seems to be particularly true of Sigmund Freud and Karl Marx. But a distinction is made between what may be called "surface structure" (consciousness, superstructure) and "deep structure" (unconscious, infrastructure). It is also worth noting that structuralists claim that to understand the surface structure, one has to understand the deep structure and the ways in which it influences the surface structure. Of all the structuralists, undoubtedly the best known and most influential is Lévi-Strauss.

Structuralism, however, is not a unified school or methodology; Lévi-Strauss does not have a monopoly on structural studies in anthropology or other disciplines. Furthermore, the work done by structuralists is extensive, diverse, and difficult. However, because of Lévi-Strauss's influence, his work may serve as an example of structuralist approaches in general. In anthropology, the use of the concept of structure is far older than Lévi-Strauss; A. R. Radcliffe-Brown, George Peter Murdock, and many others have used the term in different ways. But it is important to note that Lévi-Strauss's work is multifaceted and that he was influenced not only by other anthropologists but also by linguists, geologists, and others. Lévi-Strauss brings into anthropology these and other influences that have shaped his thinking and anthropological thought through his work. The main aspects of Lévi-Strauss's work can be summarized under three headings: (1) alliance theory, (2) human mental processes, and (3) structural analysis of myth.

Alliance Theory

Alliance theory stresses the importance of marriage in society as opposed to the importance of descent. Its basic supposition is that the exchange of women between groups of related men results in greater social solidarity and that the product of this cohesion is a greater chance of survival for all members of the resultant kin group. Lévi-Strauss claims that the regulating of marriages through prescription and preference and the proscription of other types of marriage create an "exchange" of women in simple societies. This, accompanied by exchanges of gifts, ensures the cooperation of the members of these groups.

His analysis of the incest taboo is seminal. For Lévi-Strauss, the link between nature and culture in humankind comes from this universal proscription. In the incest taboo, nature transcends itself and creates culture as the controlling element of human behavior. Sex and other drives are regulated by culture; humankind has become a cultural entity.

Human Mental Processes

There is unity in the way the human mind functions. Lévi-Strauss claims that, although the manifestations may be very different, the human mental processes are the same in all cultures. The unity of the mental processes results from the biology and operations of the human brain. As a result of this unity, for example, the classification of the universe by "primitive man" has the same basis as classifications by any other groups—through models. The fact that resultant models of this classification may be different is irrelevant for him. The analysis of myth in Lévi-Strauss's work also is based on the premise of the unity of the human mind.

Structural Analysis of Myth

Lévi-Strauss's work on myth parallels his interest in mental processes; he attempts to discover the unconscious regularities of the human mind. The use of the structuralist models of myth allows for the reduction of material studied to manageable levels. The dominant manner to accomplish this goal is based on the use of the following concepts: (1) surface and deep structure, (2) binary oppositions (culture/nature), and (3) mediation.

To discover the model/structure of a myth, one must explore the myth's deep structure. The surface structure provides us with the narrative, but the deep structure gives us an explication of the myth. This is accomplished by discovering the major binary opposition(s) in the deep structure.

Binary oppositions occur in nature and, naturally, in the human mind. They are such things as night and day, left and right, or nature and culture. Nature and culture often function as a binary opposition in tales. However, depending on the tale or myth, the binary opposition changes. For example, the binary opposition life and death is useful in explicating *Sleeping Beauty*. Here, the deep structure of the story suggests that when the thirteenth fairy declares that Sleeping Beauty is to die at her fifteenth birthday, a life-versus-death binary opposition is posited. A mediation to solve the problem is now necessary.

A binary opposition can be mediated by finding a solution to the opposition created by the binary. The mediation to the culture/nature binary opposition is that culture transcends nature. In the case of *Sleeping Beauty*, the nature of the mediation is quite different but equally embedded within the subject matter. Here, the life-versus-death binary opposition is mediated by the twelve fairies' actions: Death is transformed into a hundred-year sleep.

In *Sleeping Beauty* or in any myth, the deep structure of the narrative is analyzed through the discovery of a binary opposition and the resultant mediation. This process may, in itself, create new binary oppositions in the story that need to be followed until one arrives at a final mediation for the narrative.

Structuralism is an intellectual movement that bases its analyses on the reduction of materials into models referred to as structures. These structures are not concrete manifestations of reality but cognitive models of reality. Lévi-Strauss stresses that all cultures (not just scholars) understand the universe around them through such models and that humankind comprehends the world on the basis of these mental structures.

Mark Glazer

See Also Linguistic Approach; Semiotics.

References

Barthes, Roland. 1967. *Elements of Semiology*. London: Cape.

Barthes, Roland. 1973. *Mythologies*. London: Paladin.

Barthes, Roland. 1975. *S/Z*. London: Cape.

de Saussure, Ferdinand. 1966. *Course in General Linguistics*. New York: McGraw-Hill.

de Saussure, Ferdinand. 1972. *The Archaeology of Knowledge*. London: Tavistock.

Foucault, Michel. 1970. *The Order of Things: An Archeology of the Human Sciences*. London: Tavistock.

Hawkes, Terence. 1977. *Structuralism and Semiotics*. Berkeley: University of California Press.

Lacan, Jacques. 1968. *The Language of the Self: The Function of Language in Psychoanalysis*. Baltimore, MD: Johns Hopkins University Press.

Lévi-Strauss, Claude. 1967. *Structural Anthropology*. Garden City, NY: Anchor Books.

Lévi-Strauss, Claude. 1967. The Story of Asdiwal. In *The Structural Study of Myth and Totemism*, ed. Edmund Leach. London: Tavistock.

Lévi-Strauss, Claude. 1969. *The Elementary Structures of Kinship*. Boston: Beacon.

Turner, Bryan. 2009. *The New Blackwell Companion to Social Theory*. Chichester, UK: John Wiley & Sons.

Style

Textual pattern or the exploitation of available patterns within given contexts. The concept of *style* and the scholarly pursuit devoted to its study, *stylistics*, are slippery intellectual commodities. A positive assessment of their characteristics might describe such patterns as multifaceted; in less optimistic terms, they might be called indefinable. With regard to the description and analysis of this complex phenomenon, folklorists might be wise to be guided by important developments in linguistic stylistics, although not all the concerns of value to the student of language in this respect are also of interest to the investigators of folk culture. For example, of the three types of style that Donald C. Freeman highlights—style as deviation from the norm, style as recurrence or convergence of textural pattern, and style as a particular exploitation of the grammar of possibilities—the first is clearly inapplicable in the absence of any normative element in folk culture, the second has limited applicability but cannot be discarded altogether, and the third would appear to be of special significance in the study of the variety and range of actualizations of the "grammar" of tradition. Or, as John Spencer puts it, "a writer's style may be regarded as an individual and creative utilization of the resources of language which his period, his chosen dialect, his genre and his purpose within it offer him." Substitute storyteller, singer, fiddle player, potter, house builder, or weaver for writer and tradition/folk culture for language, and this statement could easily have been made by a folklorist. Add the notion of *usage*, as the sum of individual or particular "utilizations," and we find ourselves beneficially borrowing ideas from yet another area of language study—sociolinguistics—which has, as one of its focal interests, the study of variation or variants, which also goes to the heart of practically every manifestation of folklore ever investigated.

As has often been pointed out with justification, folklorists have, in the past, paid comparatively little attention to matters of style, except for students of folk narrative who have, in some measure, investigated the performance style of storytellers or the style of given texts. A notable exception is Max Lüthi who, in his overview of the form and nature of the European folktale, devotes a whole chapter to what he terms the "abstract style of the folktale," which, for him, is a concept that goes far beyond mere linguistic considerations. It was not until 1980, however, that the question of "appropriateness" was added to the study of "usage" by W. F. H. Nicolaisen, opening the door for yet another sociolinguistic concept—that of *register*, which refers to the use of language appropriate to any given situation, especially with regard to the kind of people present on the occasion. This seems to be a useful concept to replace the older notion of "levels of culture"—elitist, normative, folk, primitive—with its hierarchical implications and lack of accommodation for dynamic cultural features. Going beyond the basic consideration of stylistic elements, the "folk cultural register" (in contrast to other cultural registers) thus becomes the appropriate behavioral response, the right kind of action, under those circumstances in which a traditional tale might be told, a folksong sung, a fiddle tune played, or a rug woven, and it emerges as the register in which artists, creators, and virtuosi are allowed full realization of their creative powers within the bounds of tradition and within the shelter of the group. The concept of register acknowledges that most of us—one might be tempted to say all of us—operate in several different registers from time to time and from place to place, and there is not and never has been any place or niche in society that has been "folk" through and through.

W. F H. Nicolaisen

See Also Performance; Text.

References

Ball, John. 1954. Style in the Folktale. *Folklore* 65: 170–172.

Dorson, Richard M. 1960. Oral Styles of American Folk Narrators. In *Style in Language*, ed. Thomas A. Sebeok. Cambridge, MA: MIT Press.

Freeman, Donald C. 1970. Linguistic Approaches to Literature. In *Linguistics and Literary Style,* ed. Donald C. Freeman. New York: Holt, Rinehart and Winston, pp. 3–17.

Jansen, Wm. Hugh. 1952. From Field to Library. *Folklore* 63: 152–157.

Lüthi, Max. [1947] 1982. *The European Folktale: Form and Nature (Das europäsche Volksmärchen: Form und Wesen)*. Reprint translated by John D. Niles. Philadelphia: Institute for the Study of Human Issues.

Nicolaisen, W. F. H. 1980. Variant, Dialect and Region: An Exploration in the Geography of Tradition. *New York Folklore* 6: 137–149.

Spencer, John. 1964. Introduction. In *Linguistics and Style,* eds. Nils Erick Enkvist, John Spencer, and Michael J. Gregory. London: Oxford University Press.

Thompson, Stith. 1946. *The Folktale*. New York: Holt, Rinehart and Winston.

Supernatural/Supranormal

The entities, beings, or other phenomena that form, control, and manifest humanity's ultimate concerns, those that are believed to be beyond human control but that can be experienced in ritual encounters and within other supranatural spheres of activity or circumstances.

Many theories of religion point out that the belief in a supernatural order is a sign *of* religion rather than a criterion *for* it. Religions usually use a power or powers beyond this world as a reference point—that is, the fundamental questions regarding humanity and its place in the universe are answered by projecting them against a supernatural background. This supernatural realm is populated by a variety of beings whose existence is manifested by various means cross-culturally.

The affective level of religiosity is particularly manifested in man's experiences with the supernatural. The difference between the definitions given by an official religion and those derived from individual perceptions is crucial. Such a distinction is necessary because experiences and the reporting thereof are products not only of religious myths, dogmas, and values but also of the individual idiosyncrasies that influence perception and interpretation, as well as the social situations that condition perception, interpretation, and other relevant dimensions of behavior.

Supernatural experiences may be classified as casual or ritual encounters with supernatural beings. A casual encounter generally is unexpected and, thus, surprising in nature. The experiencer feels he or she is both at the mercy of a supernatural being and the focus of its actions. Often, fright ensues, along with the realization that the experience is somehow "abnormal." Usually, the person flees and, in distress, resorts to some incantation, prayer, or other protective rite.

The elements of surprise and fright are lacking from ritual encounters. Here, a *Homo religiosus*, a religious person, seeks contact with the supernatural by means of traditional ritual formulas. For example, the fisher may offer a part of the first spring catch to the water spirit, the herder may sacrifice a cow's first calf to the spirit of the cow shed, or the residents of a household in mourning may take offerings of food to the graveside of the deceased. In these cases, believers are the subject of the activity, not the object. They command the ritual techniques needed and know beforehand how to act and why. The appearance of the supernatural being or some other influence exerted by it is believed to be favorable and thus serves a positive social function.

Traditions concerning casual encounters are transmitted primarily through memorates, whereas more formal ritual descriptions and incantations provide sources of information about ritual encounters with supernatural beings.

Juha Pentikäinen

See Also Assault, Supernatural; Belief, Folk; Religion, Folk.

References

Davidson, Hilda Ellis, and Anna Chaudhri. 2001. *Supernatural Enemies.* Durham, NC: Carolina Academic Press.

Pentikäinen, Juha Y. 1978. *Oral Repertoire and World View: An Anthropological Study of Marina Takalo's Life History.* Helsinki: Academia Scientiarum Fennica.

Pentikäinen, Juha Y. 1968. *The Nordic Dead-Child Tradition: Nordic Dead-Child Beings—A Study in Comparative Religion.* Helsinki: Academia Scientiarum Fennica.

Sharpe, Eric J. 1983. *Understanding Religion.* London: Duckworth.

Watson, Lyall. 1974. *Supernature: The Natural History of Supernatural.* London: Hodder and Stoughton.

Superorganic Theories

Postulates that hold culture at a unique level above the individualistic and the social. The perceiving of culture as a superorganic entity presupposes that although culture is created by human beings, it functions at a level above and beyond the individualistic organic and social levels of human existence. However, arguments on behalf of continuity between the organic (psychological), the social, and the cultural have led to reinforcement of racist ideologies. Within European anthropological schools, especially British social anthropology, that continuity was taken to mean that clearly superior cultures or nations (with technologically advanced bases, as those of civilized colonial Western powers) would necessarily be products of superior societies and, consequently, superior psyches (minds or individuals); coupled with the evolutionary doctrine of the survival of the fittest, this was also taken as justification for imperial European policies toward colonized peoples at the stages of so-called savagery and barbarism. This ideology coincided with the independent introduction of the psychoanalytic approach to the study of culture and society, which, along with similar psychological notions, comprised an influential trend in the study of humankind at the beginning of the twentieth century. Among anthropologists in the United States, a reinterpretation of the superorganic concept took place, and the postulated continuities among the organic, the social, and the superorganic (i.e., cultural) were to be negated. American cultural anthropology developed in contradistinction to British social anthropology.

The psychoanalytic approach to the study of culture has been attacked on theoretical grounds. The problem is a philosophical one, considering the ontological aspects of culture regarding allied levels of human activities, such as the psychological, social, and cultural. In 1911, Franz Boas observed that the social or cultural phenomenon is "in its very essence" nonindividualistic. He argued further that the explanation of cultural phenomena in terms of innate biological differences leads to the assumption that the whole problem of the development of culture is reduced to the study of psychological and social conditions, among other factors such as the effects of the natural environment.

Boas's criticism of the psychological treatment of culture as reductionism was persuasively expressed by Alfred Kroeber, one of his disciples. Kroeber's theory

Mentifact

A constituent of culture that exists primarily in the minds of the adherents of that culture. As a classificatory concept, the term *mentifact* overlaps with covert culture, or aspects of culture that are not directly observable, and nonmaterial culture, or aspects of culture that are not expressed via solid matter (e.g., stone, wood, ink). The term mentifact has been loosely applied to designate mentalistic, intellectual facts (e.g., sheer knowledge), as well as affective experiences involving feeling (e.g., biologically determined emotions, as well as learned sentiments).

The term emerged at the beginning of the twentieth century as part of the debate over the nature of culture in relation to humanity, and the introduction of the idea of culture as superorganic. Culture was perceived as referring to both the process of learning, or human self-cultivation (enculturation), and the resultant product of that process. Human beings, it was argued, cultivate not only their own natural potentialities but also the physical objects of the natural environment in which they live. Consequently, individuals invent instruments for the better satisfaction of their needs; these constitute a second class of cultural products, namely, artifacts. Since these objects or artifacts exist independently of their human inventors, all such culture products were designated, in Herbert Spencer's term, superorganic.

Two additional categories of superorganic products of the cultural process were identified: mentifacts and socifacts. The first word was introduced to label conceptual symbols comprising such products of culture as language, morals, aesthetics, religious ideals, intellectual aspects of scientific research, and similar mental phenomena. The second word labels aspects of social interaction within a community, such as social norms and organizations that serve to regulate the conduct of individuals within society, as well as the conduct of society as a whole in relation to other societies.

The sum total of the artifacts, socifacts, and mentifacts that comprise superorganic culture, it has been argued, constitutes the surplus resulting from cultural life. This total is commonly referred to as a given society's "social heritage" or "cultural capital."

Hasan El-Shamy

of the superorganic explained cultural phenomena without reducing culture to the plane of purely psychic activities and products. In 1917, Kroeber argued that mentality relates to the individual and that the social or cultural is, in its very essence, nonindividualistic; consequently, heredity has nothing to do with civilization (or culture). Contrary to Herbert Spencer's views, Kroeber denied that the three levels of human existence—the individual, the social, and the cultural—were linked together and maintained the complete disparity of biological and cultural evolution. For Kroeber, "the dawn of the social is not a link in any chain, not a step in a path, but a leap to another plane."

Thus, Kroeber contended, psychology could not be used to investigate the phenomena or measure the dimensions of culture, which he regarded as "the superpsychic product of special mental process." In other words, explaining such cultural phenomena as the mythology of a nation or the songs of an ethnic group in psychoanalytic terms of the ego and the subconscious would be as meaningless as measuring weights in feet and inches and distance in pounds and ounces. Culture is to be understood exclusively in terms of culture.

In folklore scholarship, efforts to account for the origin and stability of folklore—apart from the individual—seem to have grown without any contact with the concepts of European or American superorganicism. Among folklorists, awareness of the theoretical arguments concerning the superorganic is due to the influence of David Bidney, a passionate disciple of Kroeber, on his own students of folklore at Indiana University (e.g., Alan Dundes, Hasan El-Shamy, and Dan Ben-Amos, among others). Many arguments seemed to speak, wittingly or unwittingly, of folkloric processes in what may be characterized as superorganic terms.

One theory with a pronounced superorganic rationale is that of the "Epic Laws of Folk-Poetry," proposed by the Danish folklorist Axel Olrik and presented in 1908. Olrik postulated stylistic and structural laws to determine the conditions and aspects of the *Sagenwelt* (a label he applied to a category of folklore, that is, the verbal and narrative). The basic unit in this "epic world" is the *Sage* (or folk story, which may belong to one of a variety of literary genres, ranging from the epic to the *Märchen* or fairy tale). Among Olrik's "laws" are the following:

1. The "Law of Opening" and the "Law of Closing," which result in moving from calm to excitement and from excitement to calm; consequently, the *Sage* does not begin with sudden action and does not end abruptly.

2. The "Law of Repetition," which allows folk literature to compensate for the lack of techniques producing full-bodied detail through various sorts of repetition. By contrast, academic literature employs many means of producing "emphasis, means other than repetition." Thus, in European folk literature, we encounter the "Law of Three," whereas in Indic stories, it is "Law of Four."

3. The "Law of Two to a Scene."

4. The "Law of Contrast," according to which the *Sage* is always polarized and opposites or different but complementary qualities exist side by side.

5. The "Law of the Importance of Initial and Final Positions," which contributes to the "Unity of Plot."

6. The "Law of Concentration on Leading Character," which is, for Olrik, "the greatest law of folk traditions."

According to these laws, the *Sagenwelt* is completely autonomous of psychological and social forces. Thus, the human bearer (or composer) is simply an instrument through which these narratives express themselves.

In recent anthropological theory, a similar view was expressed by Claude Lévi-Strauss along morphological lines of thought concerning myth. He asserted that "man does not think himself through myths, but myths think themselves through man."

Another folkloristic postulate based on "superorganic" views is André Jolles's *einfache Formen* (simple forms), presented in 1930. Jolles claimed autonomy of origin, function, form (structure), and existence for certain folklore genres through language. As Jolles saw it, "The entire work, which fulfills itself [via] peasants, hand-workers, and priests, fulfills itself once more in language." Once this product of "peasants," "hand-workers," and "priests" enters a language, it is re-created by that language, language re-creating what life has produced.

For Jolles, the "simple forms" (religious legend, legend, myth, riddle, saying, *case/Kasus*, memorate, fairy tale, and joke) were formed not by human agents but by language, which extracts events from life and re-creates them as independent entities. Thus, folklore—through language—becomes an autonomous, abstract, cultural process sui generis, requiring no reference to social or psychological conditions for an explanation of its origin, development, or existence.

Clearly, superorganicism, on the one hand, and psychological, sociological, contextual, performance interpretation and analysis of materials, on the other, are mutually exclusive.

Whether the superorganicism in these and similar folklore theories is systemic or merely coincidental is not always overtly expressed. Human perception tends to be animistic; personification, or the speaking of inanimate objects and abstract concepts or forces as if human, is an outcome of such a perception. Academic arguments typically speak of how culture diffuses or migrates, how ideas meet, and so on. Actually, cultures do not diffuse or migrate, but human beings spread culture and carry cultural components from one place to another; also, cultures do not meet, but individuals who bear certain ideas get together and interact accordingly.

It is in this semantic vein of the predominantly animistic personification of culture and its products that certain folkloristic arguments may be judged as superorganic. Yet one significant folklore theory that is decidedly founded on nonsuperorganic factors has unjustifiably been judged superorganic because of its animistic title: "The Law of Self-Correction," formulated by Walter Anderson.

Hasan El-Shamy

See Also Audience; Epic Laws; Evolutionary Theory; Psychoanalytic Interpretations of Folklore; Worldview.

References

Boas, Franz. 1921. *The Mind of Primitive Man*. New York: Macmillan.

Bidney, David. 1953. *Theoretical Anthropology*. New York: Columbia University Press.

Dundes, Alan. 1965. *The Study of Folklore*. Englewood Cliffs, NJ: Prentice-Hall.

El-Shamy, Hasan. 1967. Folkloric Behavior. PhD thesis, Indiana University, Bloomington.

Jolles, André. 1958. *Einfache Formen: Legende, Sage, Mythe, Rätsel, Spruch, Kasus, Memorabile, Märchen, Witz* (Primary forms: Religious legend, legend, myth, riddle, proverb, Kasus, memorate, folktale, joke).Tübingen, Germany: Halle Saale.

Kroeber, Alfred. 1917. The Superorganic. *American Anthropologist*. 19: 183–213.

Lévi-Strauss, Claude. 1964. *Le Cru et le cuit* (The raw and the cooked). Paris: Plon.

Palombo, Joseph, Harold K. Bendicsen, and Barry J. Koch. 2009. *Guide to Psychoanalytic Developmental Theories*. New York: Springer.

T

Tale Type

A narrative plot identified by a name and a concise description of its contents. When defining a tale type, a folklorist presents an outline of the main events of a number of narrative texts resembling each other. For example, the stories depicting the imprisonment of two children in a witch's or devil's house and their clever escape represent the tale type "The Children and the Ogre"; its main sequences of action are "arrival at ogre's house," "the ogre deceived," and "escape."

Generally, the tale type is provided with a signifying label. The code number of "The Children and the Ogre" is AT 327 in Antti Aarne and Stith Thompson's international folktale index.

The tale type is always an abstract construction. The scholar's generalization is based on several concrete text variants or versions of the plot. Variants that closely resemble each other can be categorized as subtypes. The practitioners of the historic-geographic method have called the subtypes *redactions*. If only known in a particular region or an ethnic group, a tale type or its subtype can be called an *oikotype*.

The notion of the tale type (compare ballad type, rune, or byliny type) appeared in folkloristic discourse as early as the nineteenth century. Faced with the tasks of organizing collections of manuscripts and publishing anthologies, scholars had to identify and list recurring narrative plots and their variants. Several plots proved to be international. For example, "The Children and the Ogre" was recorded not only in German (as "Hansel and Gretel") but also in Scandinavia and Finland.

The Finnish folklorist Antti Aarne analyzed a vast number of Finnish, Danish, and German folktale texts in the early twentieth century. On the basis of this corpus, he defined 540 European tale types and published them in 1910 in his *Verzeichnis der Märchentypen* (Types of the folktale). The American scholar Stith Thompson enlarged Aarne's international index twice, in 1928 and 1961. In the latter revision, the number of folktale types exceeds 1,000. Aarne and Thompson's tale-type index provides information about "the folk-tales of Europe, West Asia, and the lands settled by these peoples." The work covers the following narrative genres with their subgenres: animal tales, magic (fairy) tales, novellas (romantic tales), and jokes.

Tale-type indexes are highly valuable. Using the indexes, a scholar can examine a certain narrative from a cross-cultural perspective. Regional indexes also offer an ample overview of a given culture's narrative tradition and its key themes in a concise form. Examples of regional type indexes are *The Types of the Norwegian Folktale* (edited by Ornulf Hodne) and *A Type and Motif Index of Japanese Folk-Literature* by Hiroko Ikeda. The concept of the tale type involves both empirical and theoretical problems. Foremost among the empirical problems is the issue of the universality of Aarne and Thompson's "international" tale types. Because these types were defined on the basis of tales collected in Europe and neighboring regions, their applicability when describing non-European tales is often limited. Examples of type indexes in which Aarne and Thompson's categorizations and plot definitions have been discarded are Lee Haring's *Malagasy Tale Index* and Patricia P. Waterman's *A Tale-Type Index of Australian Aboriginal Oral Narratives*.

As a theoretical reservation, it is useful to remember that the definition of tale types depends on the scholar's understanding of the semantics of the narratives and his or her interpretation of what kind of similarities (*homologies*) and differences appear in the texts. Thus, "scientific" or purely objective definitions and classifications of folktales are hard to attain.

The most articulate and insightful critics of the concept of the tale type were the Russian formalists Vladimir Propp and A. I. Nikiforov in the 1920s. According to Propp and Nikiforov, narrators do not rely on single, fixed plots to produce their tales. Instead, storytellers have a collection of episodes, sequences of events, and minor elements (motifs) at their disposal, and they use these components to fabricate their tales during narrative performances.

In later studies on storytellers and extensive text materials, scholars have reached a diplomatic solution concerning the problem of the stability of tale types by recognizing at least two ways of producing tales. The storyteller may use a well-known plot as the basic structure of his or her tale, or the narrator may create a new plot by combining traditional and individual elements.

Satu Apo

See Also Folktale; Magic Tale; Motif; Oikotype/Oicotype.

References

Aarne, Antti. 1910. *Verzeichnis der Märchentypen* (Types of the folktale). Folklore Fellows Communications, no. 3. Helsinki: Academia Scientiarum Fennica.

Aarne, Antti, and Stith Thompson. 1961. *The Types of the Folktale: A Classification and Bibliography*. Second revision. Folklore Fellows Communications, no. 184. Helsinki: Academia Scientiarum Fennica.

Azzolina, D. S. 1987. *Tale-Type and Motif-Indexes: An Annotated Bibliography*. Garland Folklore Bibliographies, no. 12. New York: Garland.

Haring, Lee. 1982. *Malagasy Tale Index*. Folklore Fellows Communications, no. 231. Helsinki: Academia Scientiarum Fennica.

Hodne, Ornulf. 1984. *The Types of the Norwegian Folktale*. Oslo: Universitetsforlaget.

Ikeda, Hiroko. 1971. *A Type and Motif Index of Japanese Folk-Literature*. Folklore Fellows Communications, no. 209. Helsinki: Academia Scientiarum Fennica.

Jason, Heda. 1970. The Russian Criticism of the "Finnish School" in Folktale Scholarship. *Norweg* 14: 285–294.

Krohn, Kaarle. 1971. *Folklore Methodology*. Trans. Roger L. Welsh. Austin: University of Texas Press. Originally published as *Die folkloristische Arbeitsmethode*, Oslo, 1926.

Nikiforov, A. I. 1975. Towards a Morphological Study of the Folktale. In *The Study of Russian Folklore*, eds. Felix J. Oinas and Stephen Soudakoff. The Hague: Mouton. Originally published as *K voprosu o morfologiceskom izucenii narodnoj skazki*, Leningrad, 1928.

Propp, V. 1970. *Morphology of the Folktale*, 2nd ed. Trans. Laurence Scott. Austin: University of Texas Press. Originally published as *Morfologija skazki*, Leningrad, 1928.

Waterman, Patricia P. 1987. *A Tale-Type Index of Australian Aboriginal Oral Narratives*. Folklore Fellows Communications, no. 238. Helsinki: Academia Scientiarum Fennica.

Text

The basic "object" of folklore research. Folklore texts can be recorded (and preserved) by using a variety of writing implements, electromagnetic or visual facilities, and other media. It is hardly possible to offer a definition for the term *text* in the study of folklore that is not ambiguous. If, for instance, the target of the research is diachronic, the texts that seem to unveil something of the earlier history of the phenomenon under research would be regarded as relevant. From the synchronic perspective, the requirements would concern the usefulness of the texts for the analyses of folklore as incorporated into living human interaction. There is no doubt that a text written in shorthand from a singer in the nineteenth century and a text recorded in a performance situation by means of modern technology are both folklore texts. The problem is whether there is a point of departure, according to which we may judge some texts as objects of research that ought to be regarded as more (or less) valuable than others.

The variety of criteria established for folklore texts arises from diverse methodological frameworks, and very often, research practice is a result of following axioms based on the scientific practices or dominant paradigms currently in fashion. A range of problems surround the concept of text in folkloristics.

To fulfill the demands of proper research as construed during the dominant period of the historic-geographic school, scholars were required to develop the complete body of text variants in their studies, taking into account the time and place of collection for each text and all available information on the tradition carrier's background. This was justified on the assumption that the geographic or typological distribution of the preserved texts would reveal the prehistory of the texts and that some texts might work as a "codex unicus," a unique and most original version, having a key importance. In the beginning of the twentieth century, the adherents of the historic-geographic school strove to reconstruct *metatexts*, *archetypes*, or *invariants*. Thus, for example, the typology of folktales proposed by Antti Aarne and Stith Thompson was originally based on the assumption that each type had a prehistory and an archetype. It is necessary, however, to note that variants assigned to the same typological category are not necessarily genetically dependent on one another. Furthermore, such a taxonomy cannot fully accommodate the constant variation of a living tradition. In practice, numerous codes are needed simultaneously for classifying the majority of folktale texts, and new types to which no existing codes apply are always being discovered.

In the structural analysis of folktales, or *morphology*, developed by the Russian formalist Vladimir Propp, the structure of the text consists of a syntagmatic order of narrative units called *functions*. For Propp, unlike many later structuralists or structurally oriented folklorists (e.g., Alan Dundes), the bias was diachronic, as the final purpose of the analysis was to reveal the archetype of folktales and the myth forming the original basis of this archetype. Propp's analysis of narrative was synchronic since he used a corpus consisting of 100 folktales and aimed at establishing the syntagmatic system of invariant functions of folktales on the basis of this corpus.

The French structuralists, by contrast, concentrated on deep structures of the narrative. In his analysis of myths, Claude Lévi-Strauss segmented the corpus into basic units called *mythemes* and attached these units into a paradigmatic matrix in order to extract the fundamental meanings of the myth. Algirdas Julien Greimas also strove to determine an abstract deep structure, which, according to him, might be exposed from beneath every narrative text.

Later, scholars who advocated the functionalistic paradigm rejected the value of texts dating from the nineteenth century or earlier, regarding them as dead artifacts; it was argued by folklorists such as Kenneth Goldstein and Linda Dégh that those texts were not collected in a natural social context (the proper context of functioning of the folklore in society) but in artificial situations. Folklore texts, according to Roger Abrahams, were regarded as folklore only if actually performed, and the folklore discipline was redefined (most notably by Dan Ben-Amos) as artistic communication in small groups. Suddenly, there was living folklore all around us: workplace lore, various contemporary tales, legends and anecdotes, rumors, gossip, graffiti, parodies on proverbs and riddles, the abundant children's tradition, jokes, tall tales and jests, and marketplace lore, for example. The springs of folklore texts certainly do not show any signs of running dry, despite the fact that scholars at the end of the nineteenth century felt everything of any importance already had been collected. The questions of where, when, and from whom the text originated were no longer regarded as sufficient. It was possible to discern active and passive tradition bearers, the event of performance, and the communication process; the whole context became important. The problem of how to define the context and how to cope with the text/context dichotomy arose—a concern that continues even now.

Consequently, many of the synchronically oriented approaches to textual analysis in folkloristics have been influenced since the 1970s by text linguistics, by sociolinguistics, and subsequently, by discourse analysis. During the development of text linguistics, the notions of context and the communicative function were emphasized as a counterbalance to the abstract models created by structuralists (such as Propp, Lévi-Strauss, and Greimas) or in opposition to the generative transformational theory developed by Noam Chomsky, based on the analysis of separate texts without context. The main bias of sociolinguistics is the use of language in social contexts as an empirical object of research. Text linguistics and sociolinguistics gave new impetus to folkloristics, and the birth of the performance (and contextual) school is, in many ways, connected with the development of modern linguistics and the sociologically oriented analysis of discourse. Through the approaches mentioned earlier, the social variation of texts becomes an important object of study. One of the key notions is communicative competence, the ability of the performer to produce texts (e.g., of a given genre) coherently and to relate them to the situation of performance, audience, and other elements of context.

Many other approaches have stressed the importance of the performance situation. Milman Parry and Albert Lord suggested that the performers of epic texts did not reproduce their poems as complete entities drawn from memory but used instead an internalized system of poetic devices of *oral-formulaic technique*, providing the basic tools (formulas, themes, and story patterns) for the production of folk poetry that varied from one performing situation to another (composition in performance). According to John Miles Foley, formulas and story patterns function not so much as compositional conventions but as cognitive immanent categories. One important branch influenced by oral tradition studies is the orality-literacy discussion and the theories of development (and coexistence) of orality, writing, and print.

The *ethnopoetic* approach has focused on revealing narrative patterns reaching from the level of stylistic features and other formal elements of surface structure up to the overall meaning structures or focused on transcription systems of recorded performances in order to visualize such "paralinguistic" meaningful features as pitch, quality of voice, loudness, or pause, for example.

One of the key issues in the debate concerning folklore texts is the notion of *genre*. The concept of genre and the practice of dividing folklore texts into a system of genres (e.g., for purposes of classification) have been among the fundamental functional tools used in the analysis of folklore. The majority of the genre terms used by folklorists are devised by researchers and refer to concepts aiming at universal use (e.g., in archives). From the point of view of the producer (performer) and the receiver (audience) of folklore, genres, however, are not, in themselves, important, and they are not recognized as systems. In analyzing folklore texts as genres, we are, in fact, analyzing the means of expression of different channels available to folk culture for describing, interpreting, or explaining life and the environment. Genre should not be an analytical fossil constructed by researchers and existing outside the realm of living folklore. If, for example, a commonly used archive classification does not seem to apply to the folklore of some ethnic minority or other special group, researchers should take heed of classifications to be found in the culture in question.

The processes of creating, collecting, and recording folklore texts are taking place in constantly changing sociohistorical, cultural, and political settings. For this reason, the texts are not products of arranging symbolic objects in any stable content, order, or structure having fixed meanings; rather, they constitute a multidimensional and multilevel network of forms of manifestation and interdependences. The different types of discourse and genres and the pertinent elements of texture serve the purpose of making distinctions, enabling the suitable choice in the jumble of possible realizations in a given situation.

During the history of folkloristics, folklore texts have been exposed to a methodological cross fire. A productive synthesis is needed. Since the 1960s, the integration of various approaches has yielded promising results in the study of folklore texts: structuralism, oral-formulaic theory, ethnopoetics, cognitive sciences, computer analysis, sociolinguistics and discourse analysis, the notions of folkloristic variation and intertextuality, and studies on gender and power.

The field is open to fruitful discussion, but the era of rigid axioms has not yet, it seems, come to an end. The biggest problem concerning future prospects for research on folklore texts appears to be how to prevent fruitless, authoritative discourse according to which only the approach presented by a given scholar or a dominant school or paradigm is the one leading to the "truth."

Lauri Harvilahti

See Also Literary Approach.

References

Bauman, Richard, and Américo Paredes. 1972. *Toward New Perspectives in Folklore.* Austin: University of Texas Press.

Ben-Amos, Dan. 1971. Toward a Definition of Folklore in Context. *Journal of American Folklore* 84: 3–15.

Briggs, Charles. 1993. Metadiscursive Practices and Scholarly Authority in Folkloristics. *Journal of American Folklore* 106: 387–437.

de Beaugrand, Robert, and Wolfgang Dressler. 1981. *Introduction to Text Linguistics*. New York: Longman.

Foley, John Miles. 1991. *Immanent Art: From Structure to Meaning in Traditional Oral Epic*. Bloomington: Indiana University Press.

Hymes, Dell. 1981. *"In Vain I Tried To Tell You": Studies in Native American Ethnopoetics*. Philadelphia: University of Pennsylvania Press.

Ong, W. J. 1982. *Orality and Literacy: The Technologizing of the Word*. New York: Methuen.

Siikala, Anna-Leena, and Sinikka Vakimo, eds. 1994. *Songs beyond the* Kalevala*: Transformations of Oral Poetry*. Studia Fennica Folkloristica 2. Helsinki: Finnish Literature Society.

Textiles

Cultural products of cloth. Often regarded as creative objects subject to the imagination and ingenuity of a community of creators, textiles reveal much about stylistic choice and the aesthetics of experience based on local ways of being creative. They are also practical objects. In the domestic realm, textiles cover floors, walls, furniture and people. They not only offer warmth and material comfort but also symbolize personal, ethnic, regional and national identities through artistic methods (weaving, sewing, plaiting, etc.) and the use of decorative motifs. The iconography of each textile is frequently based on symbolic patterning and is imbued with cultural meaning extending through space and time. Textiles have the capacity of "diffusing mythology into daily life" (St. George 2006).

In terms of creativity and construction, folklorists examine the range of inventive processes associated with textile making to determine the degree that genres such as weaving, bark cloth, felt, pieced quilts, painted fabric, embroidery, and so forth are cultural and social productions as well as technical ones. The notion of the textile as an interactive, performance-conditioned object—that is, a catalyst and agent—is also compelling. As such, it suggests an array of interpretive possibility from the pictorial narrative traditions of Southeast Asian story cloths with their visual portrayal of sequenced life experiences to South Pacific plant fiber cloaks bearing the physical imprint or traces of generations of owners and wearers, which evoke complex stories of lineage, legacy, and dispute. Folklore methodology with its emphasis on tradition, innovation, process, and performance is particularly effective when applied to textile interpretation and to the substantive yet fluid meanings of design patterns shifting within cultural contexts.

The term *textile* derives from *texere*, a Latin verb denoting "to construct," "to weave," or "to plait" (to braid). Both *textile* and *text* share this root verb and are linked to the notion of weaving (or composing) a tangible, visual or literary object virtually out of nothing in order to create an aesthetically or culturally intelligible entity. Folklorists discern cultural meaning from textiles by not only analyzing the way these objects are made but also by assessing how a society continues to regard and represent singular textiles in their narrative repertoire long after the objects have lost their usefulness or immediate relevancy. This is significant for understanding the symbolic power and value of textiles within a group context. For example, today Maori woven cloaks belonging to nineteenth-century chiefs are stored in museum collections out of social circulation. Nevertheless, in Maori oral tradition these cloaks have names. Stories are still recounted with allusions to events belonging to different cloak biographies. Hidden from public view but narratively "alive," these cloaks can be considered "objects in action." Stories are told about these objects as well as told in conjunction with these objects. Thus, relative to textiles and material culture, folklorists examine the resonance of objects activated through exchanges among makers, curators, chroniclers, collectors, viewers, and so forth with certain objects. The folklore theory of practice as applied to textiles addresses a range of human-object relations and performances inclusive of conception and production, cultural behavior around objects, social context, cultural discourse, and self-reflexivity.

Folktale Themes

Textile lore appears in many folktales as stories of magical performance and prowess (e.g., magic carpets, cloth of gold, etc.). One dominant theme in European folklore is a belief in clandestine nocturnal spirit helpers who perform tasks of spinning, weaving, and sewing during the night. Other tales narrate stories about naïve and inexperienced characters caught in untenable situations where they must spin, weave, and sew staggering amounts of raw material in record time (e.g., flax into gold). In these tales, dwarfs, supernaturals, and evil outcasts rescue the distressed spinner (weaver, stitcher, etc.) and drive dangerous bargains in exchange for their help. Regarding folklore analysis, textile themes also highlight contemporary cultural attitudes toward textile creation and bestow a kind of agency on textiles relative to human behavior vis-à-vis creativity, social relations, and historical circumstances (Schneider 2006).

Materials and Processes

Textile arts today employ the same materials, methods, and forms as they did in ancient eras. In addition to continuity, another unique characteristic is that textile creation involves creating the essential materials out of which cloth is made unlike carving wood or stone. Thus, fibers for weaving or plaiting are first painstakingly created through other processes such as spinning, scraping, peeling, pounding, and so forth, which involve converting rough, coarse materials into pliant fibrous strands suitable for cloth construction (Schoeser 2003).

A woman spins wool during the International Poncho Day in Nobsa, Colombia, June 21, 2009. Local craftsmen make sheep's wool ponchos using ancestral techniques. (AP/Wide World Photos)

Labor-intensive technologies utilized in fiber preparation and cloth construction are culturally dynamic processes. These encompass familiar techniques of spinning, dyeing, and weaving cotton, wool, and silk, as well as rare artisanal textiles created from layers of inner bark (e.g., flax, hemp, and ramie) and leaf fibers (sisal and raffia). Textile arts of all types are subject to ongoing concerns with artistic and cultural adaptations, innovation, synthesis, hybridity, authenticity, tradition, and change. Wool, cotton, and silk are the most versatile and widespread fibers. Throughout Central Asian areas like Uzbekistan and Turkestan, ancient felting techniques and textile designs in wool and silk exemplify enduring processes of bonding fibers and the artistic viability of patterns inspired by abstracting ancient animistic spirit-based motifs. In terms of current marketplace demands, these textiles have been modified from their original totemic functions to more universal and aesthetic adaptations relative to tourism and international trade.

At one time textiles made from plants comprised a sustainable resource for communities around the world. Nevertheless, many were eventually replaced by the internationalization of commercial trade fabrics and some became obsolete. Due to recent more favorable economic climates for plant fiber textiles, weavers have revived many of the old practices along with a resurgence of cultural pride and artistic identity. Whether vegetal fiber products such as rare Micronesian banana leaf loincloths and Buddhist ceremonial robes made from the leaf stems of the aquatic lotus plant are historically or iconographically rooted, they are not limited to solely reproducing or replicating cultural identity but also "mediate between self and society in ways that make visible how people reposition themselves in times of dramatic change" (Hamilton and Milgram 2007). By analyzing textile creation in terms of its social, political and religious significance, it is apparent that eclectic identities bound up with cloth production and display are diverse, often fragmented, in flux, and rarely stable. Within the interplay among textile creation, a community's value system and its history, the evolution and mutability of artistic, cultural and social domains define and determine the main constituents of continuity, change, and creative innovation.

Aesthetics

Folk aesthetics or ethnoaesthetics pertain to a micro-level of artistry in local or regional cultural zones and are grounded in "aesthetics of experience" where art and life are not necessarily separate realities. An internal (insider) understanding of ethnoaesthetics is shared by a community of textile makers and users and is based on personal and group identity, knowledge, and appreciation of technical skill and virtuosity, complexity, customary design concepts, and judgments about symbolically important themes. In Joyce Ice's study of aesthetics and quilting groups, she emphasizes the social considerations of reaching group consensus about pattern, choice of color, stitching, and so forth as part of the process of collective artistic decision making. The quilt becomes both the social and aesthetic product of this collaborative creative process (Ice 1993).

Sacred and Ceremonial Textiles

For time immemorial textiles have continued to play important ceremonial and symbolic roles. The sacred properties of textiles range all the way from decorative surface embellishments, which attest to the spiritual or social status of the wearer, to the concept of cloth as a container of spirits and ancestral power. Universally, cloth demarcates sacred and secular spaces (e.g., embroidered and appliquéd Ottoman tents and Cook Islands, *tivaevae*, multicolored appliqués used as backdrops for rituals such as weddings and hair-cutting ceremonies). Textiles and cloth are offered as gifts of grace and empowerment, while they also embrace and wrap (marriage veils and shrouds), deflect evil, and absorb an excess of spiritual power (talismanic robes, fabrics of a certain color, and Fijian chief's mats).

Gender

Worldwide there are variations on gender-based division of artistic labor in the traditional production of textiles. In various geographical locations, women weave and men decorate and embellish or vice versa. Today, however, the classic dichotomies counterbalancing women's work of weaving and dyeing with men's farming and fighting activities are now scrambled, where women are cultivators, processors, textile artists, innovators, and entrepreneurs. The old prevailing attitude in Indonesia where weaving symbolized the "women's warpath" as paired with men's headhunting battles (loom and spear) is now superseded by the reality and extent of women's multiple roles in commerce, finance, and creative areas of responsibility. Locally produced textiles' popularity in the global marketplace also offers more opportunities to women artists and marketers in distant places. At the same time, the dynamics and asymmetries of globalization shift and realign relationships between marginal or peripheral societies and world trade centers. Global developments figure in folklore theory where questions are asked from the vantage point of a scholarly tradition operating at microlevels of society. These queries are about power of place, centrality, regional, ethnic and national identities, subaltern groups, and social change.

Textile scholarship focuses on the object as agent ("objects in action"), where the engagement with the textile and the action of artistic creativity and its consequences are paramount (Gell 1998). Folklore has long been interested in communication and is ideally suited to explore the communicative power of textiles as well as their function, aesthetics, and performative associations.

Suzanne P. MacAulay

See Also Art, Folk; Material Culture.

References

Gell, Alfred. 1998. *Art and Agency: An Anthropological Theory*. Oxford: Clarendon.

Gillow, John, and Bryan Sentance. 1999. *World Textiles*. London: Thames & Hudson.

Hamilton, Roy W., and B. Lynne Milgram, eds. 2007. *Material Choices*. Los Angeles: Fowler Museum Textile Series, No. 8.

Ice, Joyce. 1993. Women's Aesthetics and the Quilting Process. In *Feminist Theory and the Study of Folklore*, eds. Susan Tower Hollis, Linda Pershing, and M. Jane Young. Urbana: University of Illinois Press.

St. George, Robert. 2006. Home Furnishings and Domestic Interiors. In *Handbook of Material Culture*, eds. Christopher Tilley et al. London: Sage Publications.

Schneider, Jane. 2006. Cloth and Clothing. In *Handbook of Material Culture*, eds. Christopher Tilley et al. London: Sage Publications.

Schoeser, Mary. 2003. *World Textiles: A Concise History*. London: Thames & Hudson.

Weiner, Annette B., and Jane Schneider. 1989. *Cloth and Human Experience*. Washington: Smithsonian Institution Press.

Thompson, Stith

Arguably "the father of American folklore," Stith Thompson (1885–1976) was for the five decades before his death the best known of American folklorists and the most influential force in the field. One cannot study American folklore without coming across his name innumerable times and always in important contexts.

He was born in Kentucky; attended Butler University, the University of Wisconsin (MA), and the University of California; and earned his PhD from Harvard in 1914. His dissertation, "European Borrowings and Parallels in North American Indian Tales," was directed by the illustrious George Lyman Kittredge, and the experience was to influence the rest of Thompson's professional life. Harvard was, at the time, a leading center for the study of folklore in America, and at the time, folklore study was based in the English Department. Kittredge, himself a student and colleague of the ballad scholar Francis James Child, was a distinguished scholar of medieval and Renaissance literature and knowledgeable about folklore. Thompson learned a great deal about those literary areas from his mentor, and his book *The Folktale* (1946) is laced with examples from medieval literature.

Thompson went to Indiana University in 1921 to teach courses in literature and folklore and there began efforts to establish folklore as a university subject. His efforts culminated in the formation of the country's first folklore PhD program in 1953, and since that time, many distinguished folklore scholars have graduated from Indiana University. Simultaneously, Thompson worked to establish folklore courses and programs at other universities around the country, and from them, as well, other prominent folkloric scholars have been produced. In these ways, he helped established folklore study as a serious American discipline.

During his decades at Indiana University, Thompson edited and saw through publication *The Types of the Folktale* (1964) and the monumental *Motif Index of Folk Literature* (1955–1958). These works alone would have established him as his nation's leading folklore scholar, but he also published *European Tales among the North American Indians* (1919), *Tales of the North American Indians* (1929), *The Folktale* (1946), and *One Hundred Favorite Folktales* (1968). The influence of his dissertation in several of these volumes is obvious.

Thompson introduced many American folklorists to the theories and methods of analysis being done on the folktale by the Finns, thus introducing the American scholarly community to European folktale scholarship. His lengthy and detailed essay on the Indian "Star Husband Tale" demonstrated the historic-geographic method to an English-speaking North American audience, and his editions of the folktale types and the motif index provided the tools that enable this research to be performed.

When the focus of folklore scholarship shifted in the 1950s away from a study of the folkloric item as text-based entity to the folkloric transmission act as a communicative event, Thompson's research, his scholarly editions, and his influence began to decline. Nevertheless, his contributions have been enormous; no other American scholar has been as important or as influential.

Warren Roberts

See Also Historic-Geographic Method.

References

Thompson, Stith. 1955–1958. *Motif Index of Folk Literature*. 6 vols. Rev. ed. Bloomington: Indiana University Press.

Thompson, Stith. 1929. *Tales of the North Americans Indians*. Cambridge: Harvard University Press.

Thompson, Stith. 1946. *The Folktale*. New York: Dryden Press.

Thompson, Stith, and Antti Aarne. 1964. *The Types of the Folktale: A Classification and Bibliography*. Folklore Fellows Communication no. 184. Helsinki: Academia Scientiarum Fennica.

Tourism

Tourism is an industry or set of linked businesses and infrastructure elements involving distance, geographical destinations, time, resorts, culture change, and human interaction. The essence of tourism, as John Urry (2002) notes, is difficult to grasp because of its multifaceted nature and its connection with a range of contemporary social and cultural processes. It is linked to consumer culture, to transnational movements of people from one part of the world to another for purposes of pleasure and travel, and to global capitalism.

One product of modernization and globalization has been the rise of a new leisure class and its quest for authenticity. Dean MacCannell (1989) conceives of tourism as the modern equivalent of the religious pilgrimage in that both involve looking for authentic experiences. He argues that in its quest for ultimate reality, the modern quest for authenticity resembles the concern for the sacred in traditional societies. Though acknowledging that such a quest is important, Urry rejects the idea of the search for authenticity as the primary motivation for tourism. He suggests instead that the contrast between one's workplace and residence and the tourist experience motivates tourism. Cohen (1984) and Smith (1989) have identified several types of tourists (elite tourists, off-beat tourists, unusual tourists, incipient mass tourists, mass tourists) for whom the question of authenticity does play an important role. Feifer (1985), though, has suggested that the tourist is not "a time traveler when he goes somewhere historic; not an instant noble savage when he stays on a tropical beach; not an invisible observer when he visits a native compound. Resolutely 'realistic,' he cannot evade his condition as outsider."

Several hypotheses have been developed to explain tourism. Many authors have linked tourism with consumption, while MacCannell sees the tourist as a sort of symbolic cannibal who "consumes not only resources and material goods but the very cultures in which they are located." Moreover, one of the dangers that tourism may create, according to Coleman and Crang (2002), is the conversion of places, people, and generally the world into something that can be "esthetically" used and consumed. They fear that tourism may transform places into exhibitions. Crick (1989) labels tourists "the sun-tanned destroyers of culture" and questions the positive impact of tourism on customs and the arts in general (including festivals and handcrafted products). Some commentators have seen tourism as a rupture and contaminating plague, which could destroy local customs and pristine places by converting them into commodities.

However, commodification in itself does not necessarily change customs or arts. In fact, in some instances, it may preserve them in the interest of tourism. The image of tourism as a destroyer of customs and arts, which leads to the emergence of what Cohen calls "phony-folk-culture" or to the mass production of cheap souvenirs adapted to tourist's expectations, is questionable. Tourism has been perceived as producing chains of identical resorts and reducing locals to servants. This negative concept of tourism may be defined as the "McDonaldization" of travel, which tends to homogenize and standardize tourist experiences. Meanwhile, though, more positive results are often neglected. In particular, tourism may generate the development of new local arts or styles. It may rediscover, preserve, and eventually enhance those local arts that modernization has tended to leave behind or forget. Also, workers in the travel business attempting to emphasize local differences in order to create distinctive products and market specificity have tried to correct the tendency to homogenize tourists' experiences. Rather than looking at transformations engendered by tourism in lifestyle, arts, and customs as merely negative, it is more useful to approach them as another stage in the continuous process of cultural change.

What makes and motivates a tourist? What are the relationships between local "hosts" and tourist "guests"? Is tourism an agent of social change? Early scholars of the anthropology of tourism, such as Louis Turner and John Ash (1975), help to understand tourists' behavior, though they tend to judge the tourist harshly. Initially, anthropologists studied only the effects of tourism on the host culture. Today, a growing body of research also investigates the interaction between hosts and guests in terms of social and environmental impact. Urry, for instance, contributes to an understanding of how the "tourist gaze" orders and regulates the relationship with the tourist environment. He claims that there are systematic ways of "seeing" what tourists look at. He writes, "When we 'go away' we look at the environment with interest and curiosity. It speaks to us in ways we appreciate, or at least we anticipate that it will do so. In other words, we gaze at what we encounter." Before they actually travel, tourists tend to have expectations about what should be present at their destinations. They want to see these things when they arrive.

Some case studies use tourist behavior on beaches and at seaside resorts to highlight what Nelson Graburn (1989) calls tourism's inversions, or the "non-ordinary experience." Inversions, according to Graburn, are shifts in behavior patterns away from usual norms, which are expressed as temporarily opposite behavior. Tourism, in this sense, serves as a form of escapism (Mazanec 1985) or pleasure seeking, as tourists take advantage of "the opportunity to temporarily become a nonentity, removed from a ringing telephone." The beach is a site of transgression—a place of license, bodily disclosures, and excess, according to Rojek (1993). At the seaside resort, normality seems to be suspended, the individual liberated from his or her ordinary preoccupations. Life at the beach is experienced as "out of time and place," as a relaxing existence, separate from the everyday life of the tourist and even of the local population. However, actual tourists differ notably from one another in their motivations, traveling styles, and activities.

The impacts of tourism are enormous not only for whole countries but also for small communities, rural districts, and wilderness areas. Even though it may not be the main source of change in a community, tourism has a role in precipitating or accelerating rapid changes. Tourism may help to revitalize towns and cities with successful strategic marketing plans. Place marketing succeeds when community members derive satisfaction from their community and when visitors and new businesses visit and invest in that area. Community involvement, for instance, has become accepted practice in planning and developing cultural-tourism projects. Most professionals in this field affirm that heritage development depends on high levels of community awareness and understanding. The need to consider the potential impacts of heritage tourism on local cultures and communities before beginning projects has received increasing attention. In fact, one of the major concerns and biggest challenges facing heritage-tourism programs, as reported by the National Trust for Historic Preservation (http://www.national trust.org/heritage_tourism/Services.html), is ensuring that tourism does not destroy the very heritage that attracts visitors. Understanding the need to protect certain local cultural areas from tourist visitation to preserve traditions and quality of life for the inhabitants is demonstrated in the attempt to develop noninvasive tourism. Burn (1999), for instance, cites Stanley Plog, who has elaborated a plan for a better tourism future called "Preserving," which aims to improve new global-local partnerships.

Tourism remains a complex phenomenon with social, cultural, political, and economic dimensions, and has elicited multidisciplinary interest from researchers, scholars, and practitioners. Tourism also provides an important tool for examining and interpreting globalization, the most transformative process in the world today. As a mode of travel, communication, visualization, and experience, tourism not only reaches isolated parts of the world but also transforms social life and identity at home. Tourism has become an integral part of all societies, and—perhaps, more importantly—the tourism industry is one of the largest and most dynamic economic forces in the world.

Francesca M. Muccini

See Also Beliefs, Folk; Folk Culture; Folklife.

References

AlSayyad, Nezar. 2001. *Consuming Tradition, Manufacturing Heritage: Global Norms and Urban Forms in the Age of Tourism.* New York: Routledge.

Bull, Adrian. 1991. *The Economics of Travel and Tourism.* New York: Longman Cheshire.

Burn, Peter. 1999. *An Introduction to Tourism and Anthropology.* New York: Routledge.

Clifford, James. 1997. *Routes: Travel and Translation in the Late Twentieth Century.* Cambridge: Harvard University Press.

Cohen, Erik. 1984. The Sociology of Tourism: Approaches, Issues, and Findings. *Annual Review of Sociology* 10: 373–392.

Coleman, Simon, and Mike Crang. 2002. *Tourism: Between Places and Performance.* Oxford: Berghahn Books.

Crick, M. 1989. Representations of International Tourism in the Social Sciences: Sun, Sex, Sights, Savings and Servility. *Annual Review of Anthropology* 18: 307–344.

Feifer, M. 1985. *Going Places.* London: Macmillan.

Feifer, M. 1986. *Tourism in History.* New York: Stein and Day.

Graburn, Nelson. 1989. Tourism: The Sacred Journey. In *Hosts and Guests: The Anthropology of Tourism*, ed. Valene Smith. Philadelphia: University of Pennsylvania Press, pp. 21–36.

Hanna, Stephen P., and Vincent J. Del Casino Jr. 2003. *Mapping Tourism.* Minneapolis: University of Minnesota Press.

Leed, Eric J. 1991. *The Mind of the Traveler: From Gilgamesh to Global Tourism.* New York: Basic Books.

MacCannell, Dean. 1989. *The Tourist.* New York: Schocken.

Mazanec, Josef A. 1985. Constructing Traveller Types. In *Change in Tourism: People, Places, Processes*, eds. Richard Butler and Douglas Pearce. New York: Routledge, pp. 137–158.

Ringer, Greg. 1998. *Destinations: Cultural Landscapes of Tourism.* New York: Routledge.

Rojek, Chris. 1993. *Ways of Escape: Modern Transformations in Leisure and Travel.* London: Macmillan.

Rojek, Chris, and John Urry. 1997. *Touring Cultures: Transformations of Travel and Theory*. New York: Routledge.

Rowan, Yorke, and Uzi Baram. 2004. *Marketing Heritage: Archaeology and the Consumption of the Past*. Oxford: Altamira Press.

Smith, S. L. J. 1989. *Tourism Analysis: A Handbook*. New York: Wiley.

Turner, Louis, and John Ash. 1975. *The Golden Hordes: International Tourism and the Pleasure Periphery*. London: Constable.

Urry, John. 1995. *Consuming Places*. New York: Routledge.

Urry, John. 2002. *The Tourist Gaze: Theory, Culture and Society Series*, 2nd ed. London: Sage Publications.

Toy, Folk

Play objects, often although not always, rendered in miniature. Toys belong to the realm of fantasy, even though they are material objects. The object may have been created for one purpose, but we only know it is actually a "toy" if we see someone playing with it. Stones can be toys, but clearly not all stones are toys, and dolls certainly can be toys, yet we cannot assume that every small, doll-like human figure is actually a toy. The oldest of what we now recognize as toys— balls, tops, and human doll figures—may have been utilized for magical-religious or healing purposes in one context and then used either for reenactment or for parody when placed in the hands of a child. The separation of the category "folk toy" from "toy" is itself controversial, reflecting basic disagreements over definitions, players, and usage.

Toys as Culture, an elaborate, book-length essay by Brian Sutton-Smith, makes the point that although toys are often thought of as realistic miniatures, they vary from "those which perfectly resemble that which they signify . . . to those which are quite schematic and convey only those salient traits of those objects they signify . . . to those which distort or have little realistic signification whatsoever." In the popular sense, the toy is considered, according to the *Oxford English Dictionary*, "a thing of little or no value or importance; a foolish or senseless affair, a piece of nonsense, a material object for children or others to play with (often in imitation of some familiar object); a plaything; also something contrived for amusement rather than for practical use." However, despite all their divergent views, scholars interested in folk toys would likely contend that the toy is anything but "senseless" or of "no value or importance." Rather, they would suggest, it is precisely in the small things—such as songs, poems, gestures, and toys—that one sees the larger cultural patterns.

The small but varied literature on folk toys can be divided into three main groups, each giving a different meaning to the term *folk toy*: the historical study of folk toys as artifacts; the exhibition of specific toy collections primarily consisting of photographic displays, often of specific ethnic groups or regions; and the hidden literature on folk toys, embedded in larger ethnographies. In the first genre of folk toy literature, the historical study of toys as artifacts, the emphasis is on the description of the object and its basic historical context. We can only speculate whether children played with toys or whether the toys they utilized merely did not survive the years like their sturdier adult counterparts did. In the second genre, toys as ethnicity on display, folk toys are seen alongside ritual objects as items made in a specific locale, and the makers of the toys are emphasized. In this view, toys are considered reflective of a specific cultural style or people, and they may be objects for either children or adults. In the third genre of folk toy literature, toys as a part of ethnographic description, folk toys are typically seen as those objects made exclusively by children for children of a specific culture.

In the literature that treats folk toys as artifacts, folk toys are generally handmade objects and are said to represent the daily life of specific peoples in history. The primary research tools in this literature are archaeological, and the texts are typically comparative. Some conjecture has been made evaluating which miniatures or instruments or dolls were used for recreational purposes and which were employed for religious or magical purposes.

Two classic texts examining toys through time, beginning with antiquity, are Antonia Fraser's *History of Toys* and Max von Boehn's *Dolls and Puppets*. Both Boehn and Fraser warn of confusing ancient dolls and ritual figures, and their pages are filled with photographs of ancient toys from a variety of world museums. Both texts mention the ancient throwballs, dolls, and animal figures found in Egyptian tombs, possibly for the entertainment of the dead, although these were not found in the tombs of children, only adults. Chapters on Greek and Roman toys consistently mention Roman dice, knucklebones, and other games of chance in archaeological finds, although these items also could have been used for divination. It seems that the first record of kite flying was made in China, in 206 BCE when General Han-Sin used kites to measure the distance from his camp to the royal palace. We are left questioning whether these objects were tools or toys or both.

Boehn, because of his focus on a particular type of toy, is able to include prehistoric idols, ancestor images, fetishes, amulets, talismans, funeral images, and mannequins. He then examines the early European doll and dolls in literature and proceeds to the most mobile of dolls: the automata, movable images, and the early puppet shows. Unfortunately, although it is rich with detail, much of the book has an evolutionary tone as the author makes logical leaps about the supposed developmental connections between ancient dolls, "exotic dolls," and the dolls of Western Europe. Fraser, too, links "ancient and primitive playthings" in a manner unacceptable in modern anthropology and folklore; however, there is much attention to detail in her chapters entitled "Toys of the Greeks and Romans," "Mediaeval Childhood," "Toys in the Age of the Renaissance," and "The Expanding Eighteenth Century World." "Movable toys" and "optical toys and the juvenile theatre" are also examined, followed by a peek at the beginning of the toy-making industry in the West, with its modern machines.

Throughout the scholarly literature that perceives the toy as artifact, the term *folk toy* is synonymous with *old toy*. Yet ironically, as Antonia Fraser suggests, folk toys in general are transient objects, often constructed from leftover material and not necessarily made to last. Furthermore, the best-loved toys may be too well used to survive as artifacts, whether the toy is the African American corn-husk doll, the Indian ceramic animal, the Japanese rice-paper kite, or the English adventure playground tree house. One could remark that the toys that survive may, in fact, be the ones played with the least, which suggests that we know even less about the history of actual toys than this small literature would indicate.

Folk toy books that represent the toys of one particular culture in pictorial form can be categorized as ethnicity on display. Often, these are books with beautiful pictures and little information; many simply display one particular museum or individual collection. Datta Birendranath's *Folk Toys of Assam* presents the Indian folk toy in relation to its place of production by organizing the photos and drawings by material, that is, "clay toys," "pith toys," and "toys made of bamboo, wood and other materials." This volume emphasizes the production of the toy and the adult use of the toy for religious or healing rituals. Another fine example of this approach is Emanuel Hercik's *Folk Toys: Les Jouets Populaires*, which, although it includes many drawings of folk toys throughout Europe in general, emphasizes Czechoslovakian folk toys spanning several centuries. It, like the *Folk Toys of Assam*, is dedicated to the makers of the toys, the artisans as culture bearers, and it leaves readers wondering about the objects' actual uses or connections to recreation as we know it.

Florence Pettit and Robert Pettit's *Mexican Folk Toys, Festival Decorations, and Ritual Objects* provides a sharp contrast to the Birendranath and Hercik volumes. *Mexican Folk Toys* places the toy in the larger world of celebratory material culture. The emphasis here is on the production and seasonal display of specific objects. The object as cultural reflection and production here includes Mexican wheeled pottery dating to the first or second century CE and "old traditional flutes" as toys, moving animal toys, jumping jacks made of wood and woven palm leaf rattles, animals, and figurines.

The Treasures of Childhood: Books, Toys, and Games from the Opie Collection represents another attempt to provide a context for toys—the world of English childhood. Unlike the other collections, its emphasis is on toys specifically used by children, and it goes beyond a focus on the toys' production. The volume presents childhood as its own subculture, and it leads to a consideration of questions of culturally based definition (i.e., what a toy is) and function (i.e., what a toy's role is in a specific culture).

There is a tension in many of these historical and regional compilations between the universality of the toys as archetypes—balls, tops, dolls, pull toys—and the uniqueness of toys in specific regions. Examples abound of regionalization by image (e.g., toy tigers in India, toy horses in New Mexico), regionalization by material used (e.g., carved ivory animals among the peoples of the far north, cotton and corn dolls among non-nomadic North American native tribes), or regionalization by storyline associated with the local hero toy (e.g., the soldier in England, the miner in Czechoslovakia). There is the implication that the "folkness" of a toy is to be found in its unique regionalization, and there is the further insinuation that it is possible to discern such a distinction between a toy and a folk toy, although these theses are not clearly stated.

The United Nations Educational, Scientific, and Cultural Organization (UNESCO), in a text based upon an exhibition of world folk toys, attempted to fine-tune a definition of the toy and discover which aspects of toys were universal across cultures. In this picture-focused book, *Toys and Games of Children of the World*, the toys and games are divided into four groupings: "representational" toys and games, toys and games with "skills and rules," those with a "connection with tradition," and "present day" toys and games. Although one could make a case for the division of fantasy play-oriented objects from rule-oriented game objects, all have their own "connection with tradition" and the "present day." Ultimately, the games and toys can be said to be inseparable from their traditions and cultural contexts.

Russian nesting doll, or "Matryoshka" doll. (Vladikpod/Dreamstime.com)

Ethnographies that have specifically examined the toy as part of a larger system are associated with ethnographies of child life or child cultures. These studies promulgate the view of the folk toy as a recreational object made by the children themselves—for developmental, functional purposes. Most significant among the authors writing in this vein is the neo-Freudian Erik Erikson, who, in his collection of essays entitled *Toys and Reasons*, argues that the body is the first toy and that toying and toys are involved with the child's attempt to master the environment in miniature.

Helen Schwartzman's *Transformations: The Anthropology of Children's Play* is an excellent source guide and leads the reader through the culture and personality studies and through comparative classics such as the *Children of Six Cultures: A Psycho-Cultural Analysis*, compiled in 1975 by Beatrice and John Whiting; Cora Dubois' 1944 Indonesian study called *The People of Alor*; T. Centner's 1962 *L'Enfant Africain et ses jeux*; Wayne Dennis's 1940 journal study *The Hopi Child*; and the early works of Margaret Mead and Gregory Bateson. In all of these studies, the emphasis is on the understanding of the entire culture of the child in order to examine cross-culturally the relationship of culture to personality in the development of humans. The details about toys may be sparse in any individual work, but each offers insights about the use of such objects in children's cultures—information not found in the first two categories of toy literature. Centner's study of the Bantu-speaking groups includes much on dolls, dollhouses, cars, weaponry, and a seasonal creation of a children's village. Schwartzman refers to Dubois' description of "ingenious" child-made squirt guns made of bamboo, tops, cats' cradles, marbles, and jacks. Dennis, too, has described "ingenious" child-made playhouses constructed of mud and sand, dolls made from found bones, and peach-seed sheep. In all of these examples, the "folk toys" have been made by the players themselves, with little or no guidance from the adults.

One modern American example of a work on folk toys as those made by the children themselves is Simon Bronner's *American Children's Folklore*. In an otherwise generalized text broadly collected across the United States with little ethnic or regional information, there is a wealth of information in a chapter entitled "We Made It Ourselves." Chewing gum wrapper chains, string friendship bracelets, paper fortune-telling squares, and slingshots and tree forts are given as examples of children's own folk toys and constructions, along with diagrams and photographs of the child as toy maker.

As with many other genres of traditional expression, perhaps we should focus not on origin but on issues of use in context to arrive at conclusions regarding the nature of the folk toy. If the child-made ingenious invention travels and is made by adults elsewhere, is it no longer a folk toy? If a hero toy is made by machine from another country but labeled as a local hero, is it not also a folk toy? Fraser and Boehn suggest that machine production and large-scale distribution of toys led to the disappearance of the folk toy, reinforcing the notion that the term refers to the handmade process distributed locally. But if the German top with Hebrew letters known as a dreidel is made in plastic and by machine in the United States, is it no longer a folk toy? Although some toys are indeed traditional in a certain locale and among a certain group of players, it is only the unused toy—unchallenged by any player and, therefore, divorced from both a performance context and ludic tradition—that may not become an actual folk toy.

Ann Richman Beresin

See Also Childbirth and Childbearing; Children's Folklore; Games, Folk.

References

Bronner, Simon J. 1988. *American Children's Folklore*. Little Rock, AR: August House.

Chanan, Gabriel, and Hazel Francis. 1984. *Toys and Games of Children of the World*. Paris and Barcelona: UNESCO and Serbal.

Erikson, Erik. 1977. *Toys and Reasons*. New York: W. W. Norton.

Datta, Birendranath. 1986. *Folk Toys of Assam*. Assam, India: Directorate of Cultural Affairs, Government of Assam.

Fraser, Antonia. 1966. *A History of Toys*. London: Wiedenfield and Nicolson.

Hercik, Emanuel. 1952. *Folk Toys: Les Jouets Populaires*. Prague: Orbis.

May, Roland. 1992. Les Jeux de table dans l'antiquité (Table games in antiquity). Special issue entitled *Jeux et jouets dans l'antiquité et au Moyen Age* (Games and toys in antiquity and the Middle Ages). *Les Dossiers d'archaelogie* No. 168, February.

Opie, Iona, Robert Opie, and Brian Alderson. 1989. *The Treasures of Childhood: Books, Toys, and Games from the Opie Collection*. London: Pavilion.

Pettit, Florence H., and Robert M. 1978. *Mexican Folk Toys, Festival Decorations, and Ritual Objects*. New York: Hastings House.

Schwartzman, Helen. 1978. *Transformations: The Anthropology of Children's Play*. New York: Plenum.

Sutton-Smith, Brian. 1986. *Toys as Culture*. New York: Gardner.

von Boehn, Max. 1966. *Dolls and Puppets*. New York: Cooper Square.

Tradition

Repeated pattern of behaviors, beliefs, or enactment passed down from one generation to the next. Traditions are culturally recognized and sustained; in general, folklorists have maintained a particular interest in those that are orally transmitted. Within the discipline of folklore, the historicity of tradition has been subjected to a variety of interpretations—for example, a set of cultural ideals regarded as a coherent unit in which past ideals influence the present patterns of behavior in the group, a recognized set of present practices with origins in the past, or a set of practices created in the past that is purposefully maintained by the group in the present.

Thus, the definition of the term *tradition* elicits a variety of responses. One definition would deem tradition as something passed down from one generation to the next, generally by informal means, with little or no change in the transmission of that item or in the item that is transmitted. However, particularly in the latter decades of the twentieth century, many folklorists have asserted that tradition entails a complex set of relationships between the past and the present, in which the past sets precedent for the present and the present reflects the past in its adherence to a particular tradition. *Tradition* is often defined as an adjective in relation to specific genres, such as a "traditional ballad," "traditional narrative," or traditional belief," or in terms of technical use, such as "traditional modes of transmission." In these and like constructions, tradition is understood as a set of preexisting values and materials particular to a genre, which have been passed from one generation to the next. In the performance of a traditional genre, these preexisting values are of greater importance than the performers' individual

Dia de Los Muertos celebrations have their roots in pre-Columbian Aztec and other native festivals memorializing departed loved ones. The celebration occurs annually on November 1 and November 2, coinciding with the similar Roman Catholic celebrations of All Saints Day and All Souls Day. During the holiday, departed friends and family return from the land of the dead to visit with the living. The living prepare special offerings of food and gifts, which are placed on the family altar, or *ofrendas*, either in the home, in the local parish chapel, or outside the family cemetery. (Zepherwind/Dreamstime.com)

tastes, and judgment of the relative success or failure of the performance is based on these constructs. As folklorist Jan Brunvand asserts, there is a relative fixity of form that causes these art forms to be regarded as traditional.

For the bearers of a particular tradition or set of traditions, the performance establishes a connection between the present group and their predecessors. There is an understanding that a tradition is important with linking the past to the present as a form of identity making. This continuity over time venerates the tradition as something of central importance to the group. Distinct from a custom, for example, a tradition bears the patina of time and takes on something of a near-sacred role within the group's worldview. A seemingly nonsensical activity can be elevated within a group if that activity is classified as a tradition. Markers such as "tradition dictates" or "it's part of our tradition" set the activity described apart from the day-to-day realities of the group and ascribe a special status to it.

Traditions remain recognizable through successive performances, but certain variations within group standards may be allowed. Traditions represent both continuity through time and innovation within particular performances. The continuity (or sedimentation, as it is defined by Paul Ricoeur) manifests itself through the consistently identifiable features within the tradition and its repeated performances. Innovation is manifest in each particular performance, wherein certain deviations from the tradition are allowed and even expected within group normative standards. How long it takes for an item to become a tradition—for sedimentation to produce a consistently identifiable core to the tradition—is subject to the dynamics of the group and the role that particular tradition fills. For a transient group such as college students, a particular cheer, hand gesture, or greeting may become a tradition relatively quickly. In these cases, the rapid turnover rate of group members dictates that the process of tradition creation be accelerated. For other groups, though, the development from simple repetition and handing down of a certain practice or belief into an accepted tradition may take several years, decades, or generations before it is understood and accepted to be a tradition.

Within the scholarly use, traditions represent a core set of traits handed down through succeeding generations, and they often identify and are identified with specific groups. The word *tradition* is used to define and to identify both methods of transmission and specific practices. As such, a definition of the term is based on two key elements. First, it is understood as something passed through succeeding generations in a relatively fixed form. There is an identifiable core within a specific tradition or mode of transmission that is identifiable through time and among various performances. Second, individual performances reflect a continuity in performance and an adherence to the central core of the tradition to a degree at which any given performance is recognized as fulfilling the dictums of that particular tradition. However, there may be certain variations on the core elements in the individual performances that are idiosyncratic to those performances. These variations, which are

Procession

The act of moving along in an orderly fashion or in a ceremonious or formal manner. The procession dates back to ancient times and serves as an official part of a ceremony during ritualistic activities or festivities. As a form of ritual, the procession can represent a public display of an established social institution. As a structural component of festival, the procession often provides the opportunity for positive group interaction in the community.

The procession is characterized by a display of individuals and institutions who, in the act of moving along in succession, reaffirm their place within the given social structure of a community. In this manner, dominant community values are expressed as a formal event in which the order of the procession is prescribed. Common examples include the processional in a wedding and the *procession générale* in eighteenth-century Montpelier, France, which, as Robert Darnton observed, symbolized the corporate order of urban society. That procession, composed of municipal officials, members of the clergy, and leading officials of the town, was a public statement taken to the streets, whereby the city represented itself to itself, to inspire both power and awe in its observers.

Processions differ from parades in their form and content. The Day of the Dead procession held throughout Mexico every October–November is a religious expression of the temporary merging of the living and spirit worlds to pay tribute to deceased family and friends.

In contrast, the parade is a more flexible and loose form of public display that often conveys sentiments opposed to those in power. Robert DaMatta demonstrated this difference by distinguishing between the ritualistic expressions of Brazil's Independence Day and the world of carnival. Independence Day is associated with the armed forces and national authorities, but carnival is associated with the common people. The procession of authoritarian figures on Independence Day represents the social mechanism of reinforcement that acts to strengthen social roles through the separation of elements, categories, or rules. In contrast, carnival employs the mechanism of inversion that works to unite normally separate social roles and relationships that are rigidly segregated in daily life.

Georgia Fox

framed by group standards, may be expected or accepted in performances of a tradition, but the core elements of the tradition remain identifiable.

There is a more recent trend to define *tradition* in a performance sense—as an interpretive, symbolic connection between the past and the present. In this sense, traditions may give meaning to current institutions and practices, through invented traditions and customs based on past practices. In this instance, tradition becomes a more symbolic and purposefully constructed idea to link with the past, which contrasts with the more traditional, naturalistic definitions that treat tradition as a continuum of practices and beliefs from the past to the present. Common to all of these definitions, though, is the idea that traditions represent a core set of practices or beliefs based on a connection with past practices and beliefs and that these are accepted by the group and fulfill a specific role in group identity.

Randal S. Allison

See Also Aesthetics; Family Folklore; Festival; Invented Tradition; Ritual; Transmission.

References

Bauman, Richard. 1992. Folklore. In *Folklore, Cultural Performances, and Popular Entertainments: A Communications Centered Handbook*, ed. Richard Bauman. New York and Oxford: Oxford University Press.

Beardslee, Karen E. 2004. *Translating Tradition: A Longman Reader*. New York: Pearson Longman.

Brunvand, Jan. 1986. The Field of Folklore. In *The Study of American Folklore*, 3rd ed. New York: W. W. Norton.

DaMatta, Roberto. 1991. *Carnivals, Rogues and Heroes: An Interpretation of the Brazilian Dilemma*. Notre Dame, IN: University of Notre Dame Press.

DeCaro, Frank. 2004. *Re-situating Folklore: Folk Contexts and Twentieth-Century Literature and Art*. Knoxville: University of Tennessee Press.

Graber, Christoph Beat, and Mira Burri-Nenova. 2008. *Intellectual Property and Traditional Cultural Expressions in a Digital Environment*. Northampton, MA: Edward Elgar.

Hobsbawm, Eric, and Terence Ranger, eds. 1985. *The Invention of Tradition*. Cambridge, UK: Cambridge University Press.

Jones, Michael Owen. 1989. *Craftsman of the Cumberlands: Tradition and Creativity*. Lexington: University Press of Kentucky.

De L'Estoile, Benoit, Federico Neiburg, and Lygia Sigaud, eds. 2005. *Empires, Nations, and Natives: Anthropology and State-Making*. Durham: Duke University Press.

Moore, Henrietta. 1990. Paul Ricoeur: Action, Meaning, and Text. In *Reading Material Culture: Structuralism, Hermeneutics and Post-Structuralism*, ed. Christopher Tilley. Oxford: Basil Blackwell.

Ruggles, D. Fairchild, and Helaine Silverman, eds. 2009. *Intangible Heritage Embodied*. New York: Springer.

Schneider, William. 2008. *Living with Stories: Telling, Re-telling, and Remembering*. Logan: Utah State University Press.

Stoeltje, Beverly J. 1992. Festival. In *Folklore, Cultural Performances and Popular-Entertainments*, ed. Richard Bauman. New York: Oxford University Press.

Toelken, Barre 1979. Describing Folklore. In *The Dynamics of Folklore*, by Barre Toelken. Boston: Houghton Mifflin.

Traditionalization

The active process by which people situate their creative acts within a history of similar acts either as part of a recognizable tradition or as imbued with the special status granted to acts deemed traditional. While processes of traditionalization are clearly evident in material and customary culture, the concept has been explored and applied most often in the study of oral narrative.

The idea of traditionalization emerged as folklorists were shifting their thinking from products to processes, from stable texts to creative acts. Where *context* could be identified by a checklist of situational and cultural factors, *contextualization* examined how people actively identified the contexts they deemed both relevant for interpretation and valuable for achieving their particular goals, all *within* their performances. The same was true of tradition. Rather than focus on tradition as an inherent but intangible collective of historical texts and acts, folklorists began to consider the ways in which tradition was accessed and recreated in the act of performance. When Dell Hymes introduced the concept of traditionalization to folklore studies in his 1974 presidential address to the American Folklore Society, he highlighted this paradigm shift: "Let us consider the notion, not simply as naming objects, traditions, but also, and more fundamentally, as naming a process. It seems in fact the case that every person, and group, makes some effort to 'traditionalize' aspects of its experience" (1975, 353).

At its most inclusive, traditionalization is an act of contextualization, grounding performance in specific situational, historical, social, and cultural contexts. When those contexts include past performances recognized as part of a coherent tradition, a person can be understood not only to be contextualizing their performance, but traditionalizing it. As often, however, traditionalization is defined more specifically, referencing not only a tradition, but the traditional. Meanings of "traditional" continue to be debated. Following scholars such as Hobsbawm and Ranger (1983) and Handler and Linnekin (1984), the concept can be understood as a symbolic quality granted to elements of culture in an ongoing interpretive process that establishes continuity with the past. The traditional becomes more than a dynamic constellation of objects, concepts, and practices, but a resource actively manipulated for specific ends. Further, the traditional indicates a conscious bestowal of status, elevating some aspects of culture above others. It is this elevation of status that makes traditionalization such a useful tool in performance.

In the act of traditionalization, people can draw upon the authority of past performers and performances to validate their own performance. Richard Bauman outlines some of the most common strategies for how traditionalization is accomplished in narrative performance, all of which depend on reproducing or referencing past performances, whether in terms of reported speech, participants, location, presentation style, diction, audience involvement, or formal structure (2004, 149). One of the most common means of traditionalization is attribution, linking current performances to past ones by referencing previous storytellers, storytelling events, and interpretations. By referencing the traditional and not just tradition, acts of traditionalization have even greater ability to claim authority, even authenticity (see Bauman 2004, 31; Mould 2005).

The dual move into the past and to the value-laden category of the traditional can be viewed as a reaction to modernity, responding, in Hymes's words, to "a world of technology and mongrelization of culture" (1975, 353). Traditionalization is a conservative move, reifying the past as a means of borrowing its authority for one's own performance. However, the process of traditionalizing one's performance by evoking the words, images, and ideas of the past can have the paradoxical effect of challenging the past rather than reifying it. By referencing the traditional, speakers introduce it into performance and therefore into negotiation. While the traditional can be supported and subtly reconstructed, it can also be challenged, both by upending the traditional in favor of modernity or by supplanting one conception of the traditional with another. Such a rhetorical or interpretive move should be viewed as a *result* of traditionalization, rather than part of the process itself.

While folklorists have typically addressed acts of traditionalization made by the individual performer in the act of performance, the process can also be co-opted and applied more broadly both by institutional powers and to entire genres of performance. Concepts of the traditional, particularly when implicated by what is deemed authentic, is often constructed by an elite hegemony (see Bauman 2004, 31 and Gilman 2004). People in positions of power—whether in the public sphere such as in governments or local arts councils, or the academic sphere such as among folklorists or art historians—may strive to traditionalize particular artistic forms, acts, and customs to serve their own interests whether altruistic or self-serving. In this way, the term can refer to any attempt to situate a particular act within a recognized tradition or to elevate a particular cultural practice to the status of the traditional.

Tom Mould

See Also Performance; Tradition.

References

Bauman, Richard. 2004. *A World of Others' Words: Cross-Cultural Perspectives on Intertextuality*. Malden, MA: Blackwell Publishers.

Gilman, Lisa. 2004. The Traditionalization of Women's Dancing, Hegemony, and Politics in Malawi. *Journal of Folklore Research* 41(1): 33–60.

Handler, Richard, and Jocelyn Linnekin. 1984. Tradition, Genuine or Spurious. *Journal of American Folklore* 97(385): 273–290.

Hobswam, Eric, and Terrence Ranger. 1983. *The Invention of Tradition*. Cambridge: Cambridge University Press.

Hymes, Dell. 1975. Folklore's Nature and the Sun's Myth. *Journal of American Folklore* 88(350): 345–369.

Mould, Tom. 2005. The Paradox of Traditionalization: Negotiating the Past in Choctaw Prophetic Discourse. *Journal of Folklore Research* 42(3): 255–294.

Ruggles, D. Fairchild, and Helaine Silverman, eds. 2009. *Intangible Heritage Embodied*. New York: Springer.

Tradition Bearer

A person who preserves traditional materials in memory and transmits them to other people. Traditional transmission occurs through only certain individual members of a given community. These persons can be classified either as *active* or *passive* bearers of tradition.

Carl W. von Sydow, in contrast to the romantic nationalists, claims that tradition does not lie in the depths of the soul of all the people of a given community but rather that it has its custodians, who generally form a minority of the total population. Among the bearers of tradition, von Sydow distinguished two polar types: the active and the passive. The former keep the tradition alive and pass it on via performance. The latter are generally aware of the content of a given tradition and, when asked, can partly recall it, but they do nothing either to spread the tradition or to keep it alive. In folkloristics, this dichotomy is considered to be of classical significance despite the fact that it is one-sided, attending only to a single criterion for classification of tradition bearers.

Another significant discovery made by von Sydow is that the boundary between an active (i.e., living) and passive (i.e., dormant) tradition is variable. An active tradition may, for various reasons, become passive. And every bearer can be active regarding several traditions but clearly passive in respect to others. Von Sydow notes the collective social nature of tradition when he stresses the importance of passive tradition bearers as "the sounding board of tradition" and as the controllers of the stereotyped nature of tradition who establish the acceptable limits of variation in folk performance. Von Sydow's basic thesis is that tradition does not spread by itself but is moved and transferred by human bearers. Thus, his work calls for a shift in focus from the superorganic transmission of folk traditions to the transmitters of these items.

Many studies of tradition bearers seem to have been troubled by an error in perspective, inasmuch as bearers of tradition often have been narrowly examined as gifted, creative personalities with no connection to any community. Psychological research has clearly centered on the individual. Yet even the consideration of recall and recognition has been disregarded. When the communication of oral tradition is analyzed as a pattern of social behavior, one should examine tradition bearers not only as individual transmitters of tradition but also as members of social groups, who are expected by the community to regularly play specific social roles. In creating a typology for tradition bearers in a community, their social roles and the role behavior actualized in the transmission of particular genres of folklore should especially be emphasized.

During the last decades of the twentieth century, the research on tradition bearers has widened its scope to include the roles they play in the transmission and perpetuation of age-group traditions, pop culture, and mass lore.

Juha Pentikäinen

See Also Tradition; Transmission.

References

Ben-Amos, Dan, and Liliane Weissberg, eds. 1999. *Cultural Memory and the Construction of Identity*. Detroit: Wayne State University Press.

Geertz, Clifford. 1973. *The Interpretation of Cultures*. New York: Basic Books.

Niles, John D. 1999. *Homo Narrans: The Poetics and Anthropology of Oral Literature*. Philadelphia: University of Pennsylvania Press.

Pentikäinen, Juha Y. 1978. *Oral Repertoire and World View: An Anthropological Study of Marina Takalo's Life History*. Helsinki: Academia Scientiarum Fennica.

von Sydow, Carl Wilhelm. 1948. *Selected Papers on Folklore: Published on the Occasion of His 70th Birthday*. Copenhagen: Rosenkilde and Bagger.

Transformation

The changing between human and animal. It is widely believed that some human beings are able to transform themselves into animals at will. In European lore, the lycanthrope, or werewolf, is a common form of this transformation, but such figures are common around the world, and they are thought to occur for a variety of purposes. Often (as with the wolf in Europe, the jaguar in South America, and the lion and leopard in Africa), it is a large and dangerous predator whose shape is taken on by a human being. In China and Japan, the fox often functions as a were-animal. Such animals, unlike the were-animals of the movies, look just like other animals of their type; they are not half-man, half-animal creatures. As Johannes Wilbert points out, "Jaguars being alter egos of shamans, one can never be sure whether a jaguar is really an animal, or, rather, a man." Because the transformation involves a substitution of spirits and because the spirit world is a reversed form of the human world, it is not uncommon for the animal transformation to involve an efficacious reversal of some sort: The shaman may somersault one way to turn into a jaguar, then the other way to regain his human form.

A common form of the belief involves a sorcerer who changes periodically into another creature and does terrible damage in animal form. He or she is usually

Thjassi, the giant in his eagle plumage, flies down and catches Iduna. Illustration from *The Book of Sagas* by Alice S. Hoffman, published in 1926. (The Bridgeman Art Library International)

gaining revenge on someone who has given offense. This version of the belief shows up in the following (typical) account: A woman is out in the woods with her husband, but he leaves her alone for a short time, whereupon a wolf attacks her. She defends herself, perhaps aided by another person, and injures the wolf, then sets out to find her husband. But when she finds him, she sees that he has a wound that corresponds to the one the wolf had suffered or has some of her clothing in his teeth. In Europe, the werewolf was believed to undergo transformation by means of a salve and a wolf skin or sometimes a girdle, and he or she might be condemned to live as a wolf for a specified period of time.

The crucial event in such transformations is a movement of the spirit from one body into another; the spirit is commonly viewed as a kind of interchangeable part. Therefore, a human spirit can enter a wolf, for instance, and operate its body, or the wolf's spirit can operate a human body (but in general, it is much more common for a human to turn into an animal). Because such exchanges of spirit occur also with other supernatural figures, it is not surprising that the were-animal belief is not strongly differentiated from some other beliefs that seem, at first glance, to be quite different. In some Slavic areas, werewolves may turn into vampires when they die. And though there are specific apotropaics for warding off werewolves (such as *A. lycoctonum*, or wolfsbane), many of the apotropaics for werewolves are the same as those for other manifestations of the spirit world. Garlic and sharp objects, such as thorns and knives, ward off not just werewolves but also witches, vampires, and the evil eye.

Another common type of animal transformation is that of the shaman who deliberately lets himself or herself be possessed by the spirit of an animal (or causes his or her own spirit to take over the body of the animal) in order to use its superior speed, strength, or sensory capabilities to gain knowledge or effect the cure of a patient. Often, the shaman takes the form of a bird since birds may be seen as manifestations of spirits. (The Slavic *vila* or *rusalka*, a type of fertility spirit believed to be the soul of a girl who died childless, is represented as a bird with a woman's head.)

Some cultures use the concept of transformation to account for the presence of animals. An animal may be explained as a person who committed a particular sin and was transformed into an animal as punishment. Here, there is often a relationship between the form or habits of the animal and the quality of the sin; in Morocco, for instance, the stork is seen in popular belief as a judge who married and then committed a sin and whose bearing and color are reminiscent of his former condition. Such a transformation may be a routine event. As Morris Opler notes, "The Jicarilla associate neighboring tribes with various birds and animals and believe that the ghosts of those belonging to a particular group turn, at death, to the condign form. The Navaho are the Mountain Lion People, the Ute the Owl People, the Pueblo the Prairie Dog People, the Mescalero the Wolf People, the Mexicans the Burro People, and the Americans the Mule People." The Jicarilla themselves turn into coyotes, but not all coyotes are former Jicarilla Apaches; some are just coyotes, and again, one cannot tell the difference between the real animal and the were-animal simply by appearance.

This process of transformation is just one form of the larger category of metempsychosis, or the passage of the spirit from one body to another. Some cultures take the view that a person's animating spirit—once it is ejected, at death, from its body—removes itself to a kind of spiritual holding tank, where it awaits incorporation into another body. If all goes well, it is incorporated into a child of its own clan, a process that is sometimes seen as an explanation for family resemblance. Through divination, the ancestor of the child may be determined, and the child may be named after this individual. Other cultures (and this is well known from Hindu tradition) take the view that the spirit, depending on its habits and character in this life, will be incorporated into a higher or lower form of life in the next. Animals, then, are seen as temporary repositories of the human spirit on its path toward perfection, and a human being who lives badly may be fated in the next life to take the form of an animal that shows the particular negative qualities (such as greed) that he or she showed during this existence.

Just as the spirits of human beings return to animate the bodies of later generations, the same is assumed to be true of the spirits of animals. It is important, therefore, to ensure that this process is not disturbed, so that culturally important animals are not depleted. Among the northern Eurasian peoples, the bones of animals that are used for food may be carefully kept together to allow another animal to come into existence. And since spirits have an affinity for anything that has their form, they may be encouraged to remain in the area by the use of images or drawings of the animal they represent, which hold them in place until they are reincorporated. Although we will surely never know much about the rationale behind the Paleolithic cave drawings, parallels from ancient and modern cultures suggest that they may have been intended as a kind of spiritual template for the physical body, designed to ensure its maintenance or return.

Paul Barber

See Also Assault, Supernatural; Magic; Shape-Shifters; Werewolf.

References

Opler, Morris E. 1960. Myth and Practice in Jicarilla Apache Eschatology. *Journal of American Folklore* 73: 133–153.

Otten, Charlotte F., ed. 1986. *A Lycanthropy Reader: Werewolves in Western Culture*. Syracuse, NY: Syracuse University Press.

Westermarck, Edward. 1926. *Ritual and Belief in Morocco*. London: Macmillan.

White, David Gordon. 1991. *Myths of the Dog-Man*. Chicago: University of Chicago Press.

Wilbert, Johannes. 1987. *Tobacco and Shamanism in South America*. New Haven, CT: Yale University Press.

Transmission

The process of passing on themes and symbols in language, music, design, movement, and action by which a society forms its tradition. The selection of subjects and forms for transmission is a conscious and unconscious social and individual creative act that ideology, cultural values, and personal emotions influence. The process empowers these subjects with the authority of the past. *Oral transmission*, in particular, is a key term in the conception and definition of folklore. Orality has become a central issue in most inquiries into the possibility of transmission as a natural process governed by natural laws.

Theoretically, in the formulation of Cecil J. Sharp, transmission is subject to three abstract principles: *continuity*, *variation*, and *selection*. Continuity operates through the cultural maintenance of narrative and poetic types and in the retentive memory of performing artists. Variation is a consequence of performance and its situational circumstances, inventive creativity, unconscious selection, taste, and memory and forgetfulness. Selection, following Charles Darwin's ideas of adaptation, is a function of conformity to community aesthetic and ethical values. Continuity and variations are dynamic forces within the society that culturally and historically operate at cross-purposes; selection becomes their synthesis.

Empirically, there have been two major concerns with oral transmission: its exclusiveness and its accuracy. In nonliterate societies, the exclusiveness of oral transmission is self-evident. However, when the subjects of transmission are sculptures and designs, their accompanied interpretation is verbal; there is an interdependence between oral and visual transmission even in the absence of literacy. In literate societies, such an interdependence intensifies.

It is possible to distinguish three forms of interdependence between oral and written transmission: diachronic, literary, and mnemonic. In diachronic interdependence, oral and written transmissions occur in successive periods. Oral transmission precedes literacy. With the advent of writing, scribes, printers, and learned members of the group select from their oral tradition themes and forms that serve their own purposes and commit them to writing. These texts, in turn, serve as a source upon which oral transmission could draw and to which it refers. The commitment of oral tradition to writing does not necessarily terminate its transmission in its own cultural channels; it continues to exist independently of or in mutual interaction with the written forms.

The motivations for writing down orally transmitted tales, songs, and other folklore forms can be religious, political, commercial, personal, commemorative, or scholarly. Religious functionaries select from oral tradition those themes that they deem most appropriate for their purposes to supplement their own texts. When their faith gains social and cultural acceptance, these texts, once transmitted orally, enjoy the status of a religious canon. Similarly, selectively written-down oral traditions affirm political orders. With the advent of print, local entrepreneurs circulated stories in chapbooks and ballads on broadsides. These have become a major link in the transmission of texts. The oral reproduction of typographical errors attests to singers' and narrators' reliance on printed versions. In other cases, oral artists have written down narrative and poetic texts for their own use, and subsequently, these writings have become publicly available in manuscripts or in other forms of print. In modern times, the folkloristic intervention itself has become a factor in transmission. Tales that scholars recorded have gained popular distribution in society; parents, teachers, and revival storytellers have then disseminated their knowledge either by reading aloud or by oral performances in a literate society.

Literary interdependence involves writers who draw upon oral tradition for their own creative purposes. For example, Sophocles in classical Greece and Boccaccio, Chaucer, and Shakespeare in the Renaissance drew upon oral tradition, either directly or through mediating sources. Leading writers in many languages have resorted to similar practices, transferring themes from oral tradition and recasting them in literary genres and styles appropriate for literate, urbane audiences. Only when they have maintained or tried to imitate folklore forms have their works had some influence on oral transmission itself. Otherwise, the literary dependence on oral transmission remains one-sided, documenting the knowledge of a particular theme in a specific historical period.

Mnemonic interdependence between oral and written transmission occurs among storytellers, preachers, and singers who jot down phrases, plot outlines, and sometimes complete texts to aid them in their oral performance. Though literate to a degree, these folk artists have learned and then transmitted their narratives and songs orally.

Although the interdependence between oral and written transmission has contributed to the stability of texts, narrators and singers do pass on the forms of their folklore orally from generation to generation and from group to group. The significant factor in oral transmission is memory. Psychological experiments on memory suggest the significance of a knowledge of cultural symbols and genres, formulaic expressions, and idiomatic language in the retention and transmission of folklore. Divorced from these elements and the general cultural context, memory fails and transmission flounders.

As an explanation for the worldwide dissemination of themes in recognized tale types, Walter Anderson has proposed the "Law of Self Correction" ("*das Gesetz der Selbsberichtigung der Volkserzählung*"). At the basis of this law is the assumption that the averaging of narrative versions tends to draw them toward their standard forms. Each narrator learns stories from many sources, reconciling the differences between them in individual renditions. In turn, in many tellings, the audience's response and the performer's own sense of narrative logic help construct a tale that approximates its standard version.

In the absence of community support—when, for example, people migrate and folklore forms are uprooted—there is a qualitative decline in the transmitted texts. There are two kinds of folkloric devolution in transmission, generic and literary. Hypothetical in nature as it is, such an observation suggests that, historically, themes shift from longer to shorter folklore forms, from epics to ballads, from tales to proverbs and jests, and from rituals to children's verses and games. English ballads that survived the Atlantic crossing, Tristram P. Coffin proposes, shed many of their narrative details, and their American singers retained only the "emotional core" of these ballads. However, once immigrants established their new communities, they developed their own folklore forms, and some of these suggest continuity with those that were transmitted from their countries of origin.

Transmission depends on agency. In every society, there are different cultural agents who transmit the society's respective forms of folklore. There is a broad range of folklore proficiency among these agents of folklore transmission, or "bearers of tradition," as Carl W. von Sydow calls them. They fulfill a variety of social roles. They are the mothers who sing lullabies and tell stories in the nursery, the social jokesters, the ballad singers, the village raconteurs, the market story-tellers, and the trained epic singers. The higher their proficiency, the more likely they are to retain their repertoire throughout their lives. Otherwise, they may shift, expand, or narrow the traditional forms they perform depending on their stage in life and social circumstances. As Linda Dégh and Andrew Vázsonyi point out, adequate transmission occurs when there is a fit between agent and genre. A narrator of legends does not necessarily sing ballads well or tell jokes successfully.

The transmission of folklore forms across social and linguistic boundaries may appear to occur as "ripples in the pond" or concentric circles without human migration, but actually, the transmission requires contact between agents from the respective groups. They meet each other in border areas where bilingualism is common or in ports, markets, and other trading posts where travelers from different geographic parts congregate. Within a stratified society, the lower classes aspire to attain the living standards and values of the upper classes, and through imitation, they cause cultural goods to be transmitted downward. Hans Naumann called these goods the *gesunkenes Kulturgut* (filtered down cultural goods). Such a characterization is appropriate for some specific historical forms, but it would not be an acceptable description of the whole peasant culture and nonliterate society.

Agents of transmission often achieve thematic and, in the case of religious texts, even verbatim accuracy. However, factual accuracy in the oral transmission of historical information over long periods of time is a rare phenomenon. First, oral tradition is inadequate for preserving chronology. Second, it tends to collapse events, figures, and actions into established cultural patterns and structures of thought, eliminating the historical texture of events and personalities. Third, since historical information often provides legitimacy for present political leaders, such individuals tend to manipulate it. Therefore, the more naive a speaker is (in terms of being removed from political arenas), the greater the historical reliability is, and the shorter the genres are, the less room they provide for textual manipulation.

Finally, transmission can reach the end of the line. This can occur with the death of a language or the disintegration of a community; it can result from a lack of agents, such as narrators and singers; and it can occur when an audience loses interest and ultimately disappears, having become bored by or oversaturated with isolated traditions that, given the lack of contact with other communities, are never replenished or renewed.

Dan Ben-Amos

See Also Performance; Tradition Bearer.

References

Anderson, Walter. 1923. *Kaiser und Abt: Die Geschichte eines Schwanks* (Emperor and abbot: The history of a joke). Folklore Fellows Communications, no. 42. Helsinki: Academia Scientiarum Fennica.

Ben-Amos, Dan, and Liliane Weissberg, eds. 1999. *Cultural Memory and the Construction of Identity*. Detroit: Wayne State University Press.

Bertrand H. 1954. The Morphology of the Ballad-Tunes: (Variation, Selection, and Continuity). *Journal of American Folklore* 67: 1–13.

Coffin, Tristram P. 1957. Mary Hamilton and the Anglo-American Ballad as an Art Form. *Journal of American Folklore* 70: 208–2 14. Reprinted in *The Critics and the Ballad*, eds. MacEdward Leach and Tristram P. Coffin. Carbondale: Southern Illinois University Press, 1961.

Dégh, Linda. 1995. *Narratives in Society: A Performance-Centered Study of Narration*. Folklore Fellows Communications, no. 255. Helsinki: Academia Scientiarum Fennica.

Dégh, Linda, and Andrew Vázsonyi. 1975. The Hypothesis of Multi-Conduit Transmission. In *Folklore: Performance and Communication*, eds. Dan Ben-Amos and Kenneth S. Goldstein. The Hague: Mouton.

Dorson, Richard M. 1972. The Debate over the Trustworthiness of Oral Traditional History. In *Folklore: Selected Essays,* by Richard M. Dorson. Bloomington: Indiana University Press.

Dundes, Alan. 1969. The Devolutionary Premise in Folklore Theory. *Journal of the Folklore Institute* 6: 5–19.

Finkelstein, Louis. 1941. The Transmission of the Early Rabbinic Tradition. *Hebrew Union College Annual* 16: 135–155.

Gerhardsson, Birger. 1961. *Memory and Manuscript: Oral Tradition and Written Transmission in Rabbinic Judaism and Early Christianity*. Trans. Eric J. Sharpe. Acta Seminarii Neotestamentici Upsaliensis XXII. Uppsala and Lund, Sweden: Gleerup and Copenhagen: Munksgaard.

Goldstein, Kenneth S. 1971. On the Application of the Concepts of Active and Inactive Traditions to the Study of Repertory. *Journal of American Folklore* 84: 62–67. Reprinted in *Toward New Perspectives in Folklore*, eds. Américo Paredes and Richard Bauman. Publications of the American Folklore Society Bibliographical and Special Series, Vol. 23. Austin: University of Texas Press.

Goldstein, Kenneth S. 1963. Riddling Traditions in Northeastern Scotland. *Journal of American Folklore* 76: 330–336.

Goody, Jack. 1985. Oral Composition and Oral Transmission: The Case of the Vedas. *Oralitè: Cultura, Letteratura, Discorso. Atti del Convegno Internazionale (Urbino 21–25 luglio 1980)*, eds. Bruno Gentili and Giuseppe Paioni. Rome: Ateneo.

Henige, David P. 1974. *The Chronology of Oral Tradition: Quest for a Chimera*. Oxford Studies in African Affairs. Oxford: Clarendon.

Labrie-Bouthillier, Vivian. 1977. Les Expériences sur la transmission orale: D'un Modèle individuel à un modèle collectif (Experiments in oral transmission: From an individual model to a collective model). *Fabula* 18: 1–17.

Naumann, Hans. 1922. *Grundzüge der deutschen Volkskunde*. Leipzig, Germany: Quelle & Meyer.

Ortutay, Gyula. 1959. Principles of Oral Transmission in Folk Culture. *Acta Ethnographica* 8: 175–22 1. Reprinted in *Hungarian Folklore: Essays*, by Gyula Ortuta. Budapest: Akadémiai Kiadó, 1972.

Richmond, W. Edson. 1951. Some Effects of Scribal and Typographical Errors on Oral Tradition. *Southern Folklore Quarterly* 15: 159–170.

Sharp, Cecil J. [1907, 1936] 1954. *English Folk Song: Some Conclusions*. 3rd ed. Revised by Maud Karpeles with an appreciation by Ralph Vaughan Williams. London: Methuen.

Stone, Kay F. 1986. Oral Narration in Contemporary North America. In *Fairy Tales and Society: Illusion, Allusion, and Paradigm*, ed. Ruth B. Bottingheimer. Philadelphia: University of Pennsylvania Press.

Vansina, Jan. 1965. *Oral Tradition: A Study in Historical Methodology*. Trans. H. M. Wright. Chicago: Aldine.

von Sydow, Carl W. 1948. On the Spread of Tradition. *Selected Papers on Folklore*. Copenhagen: Rosenkilde and Bagger.

Trickster

The central figure in one of the most characteristic worldwide myth cycles—a god, animal, and human all in one who is always duping others and is always duped in return and whose stories tell of experiences involving a lengthy series of dangerous, outrageous, and often obscene adventures and behaviors marked by trickery. The trickster as a character of myth—and the problems of interpreting the ambiguous nature of the figure presented—were noted and described at some length using comparative materials by Franz Boas in an introduction he wrote for a collection of Thompson River Indian stories, published in 1898. The best-known and most influential discussion of the trickster figure, however, is the 1956 book *The Trickster* written by Paul Radin, a later ethnographer much influenced by Boas. The book—actually a collaborative effort of Paul Radin, Karl Kerényi, and Carl Jung—contained the major Winnebago Native American trickster cycle, the secondary Winnebago Hare trickster cycle, and summaries of Assiniboine and Tlingit Native American trickster myth cycles extensively annotated by Radin. In addition, the book contained an article on the trickster in relation to Greek mythology by Kerényi, a well-known historian of religion of the time, and a psychological interpretation of worldwide trickster myths by Jung.

A special 1990 feature in the culture and folk wisdom section of *The World and I* contained seven articles on the trickster by scholars, offering a more recent discussion of the subject. Researchers from a number of disciplines also published studies and interpretations of trickster figures in many cultures in the years between Radin and the special magazine section. Despite using different approaches, all the researchers agreed on the fact that the trickster figure is found in clearly recognizable form among all known tribal cultures and in the folklore of most nontribal cultures as well. The researchers noted a host of central figures in trickster cycles: the Native American figure known as Coyote in some groups and Hare, Mink, Blue Jay, or Raven in others; African figures including Spider, Tortoise, Hare, and Jackal; the Japanese Fox; the African American Brer Rabbit and High John the Conqueror; and the Middle Eastern figures of Juha, Mullah Nasruddin, and Nasruddin Hoja.

The character and stories about the trickster show a good deal of variation from culture to culture in terms of the values they reflect, but they share a fine disregard for boundaries. In an Omaha tale noted by Roger Welsh, Rabbit saves members of the tribe from a hill that is destroying them and then sends his penis underwater to impregnate the women and humiliate the tribe.

Radin also noted that the trickster survived in the figure of the medieval jester and continues in Euro-American culture in such forms as Punch and Judy and clowns, and more recent scholarship has shown the trickster's continuing presence in American popular culture. Film tricksters include the central characters in the Keystone Cops series and the many *Police Academy* films, as well as Charlie Chaplin's "little tramp" character and Steve Martin's various comic creations. David Letterman and Johnny Carson, American television's most famous late-night hosts, are tricksters. American popular music stars Bob Dylan and Prince also fit the generally accepted definition of the trickster.

Research and interpretation concerning tricksters explain the appeal, persistence, and function of the figure either in terms of the culture from which a particular cycle of stories had been collected or in terms of all of humanity. The earliest explanations for the strange mix of the trickster figures who make the world safe for humans and ludicrously attempt the inappropriate were framed in terms of a universal history of religion or a universal human psychology, and many recent studies have followed the same path. David Brinton argued that the trickster figure came about as a degeneration of an older culture hero, whereas Boas claimed that the trickster was older than the serious culture heroes. Paul Radin agreed with Boas and initially attempted to find the meaning of the Winnebago trickster within Winnebago culture. Although he provided a careful set of notes that explained the stories in terms of ethnological detail, his final conclusions were psychological. Karl Kerényi noted the similarities between the Winnebago trickster and figures in Greek myth and explained the figure in Freudian terms. Jung himself explained the trickster figures in Native American narrative traditions in terms of his posited universal human psychology and especially in terms of his own theory of the etiology of the human mind and consciousness. Similarly, more recent interpretations of the trickster have explained

Illustration by Fred Kabotie from a San Ildefonso Pueblo tale, "The Coyote and the Blackbirds." (DeHuff, Elizabeth Willis. *Taytay's Tales Collected and Retold*, 1922)

the figure psychologically as a negative model of conduct, showing how not to behave while simultaneously affording a release through fantasy and humor from the strain of acting properly or as an example of how folklore serves human needs by creating a dream life.

Barbara Babcock examined the trickster as a worldwide, cross-cultural figure. Her article blended an interpretation of the trickster in terms of marginality with a close-reading, structural analysis of the Winnebago forty-nine–tale trickster cycle collected by Radin. Her general conclusion was that the trickster is tolerated and welcomed because the narratives of the trickster figure have the power to transform perceptions of reality.

The other major approach to understanding the trickster figure in world folklore, following the example given by Radin's meticulous notes, has been to explore the figure and stories as they have meaning for the people who are the usual and natural audience and performers of the individual traditions. Ellen B. Basso, John Roberts, and Barre Toelken applied this approach to the trickster cycles of the Kalapalo of the Amazon, African Americans, and Navajo coyote stories, respectively, and reached much the same conclusions. All three found the meaning of the trickster stories that they studied within the cultures in which the narratives existed, and Basso and Toelken were particularly alike in their insistence upon approaching tricksters as enablers whose actions—good or bad, sublime or obscene—in narratives turn abstractions into realities that can then be contemplated and evaluated and in their efforts to firmly ground their discussions in the actual languages in which the stories are told.

Both research traditions present ample, solid, and convincing evidence in support of their respective points of view. The only general conclusion possible is that the trickster—at once subhuman and superhuman, bestial and divine, creator and destroyer, giver and negator, wise and foolish—is of the past and the present, of folk and popular culture, culturally bound and a part of the psychology of all peoples. And it is this destruction of boundaries, the greatest trick of all, that is the essential nature of the trickster and that should serve as the principle for further studies of the figure.

Keith Cunningham

See Also Culture Hero; Shape-Shifters.

References

Babcock, Barbara. 1975. "A Tolerated Margin of Mess": The Trickster and His Tales Reconsidered. *Journal of the Folklore Institute* 11(3): 147–186.

Evans-Pritchard, E. E., ed. 1967. *The Zande Trickster*. Oxford: Clarendon.

M'Baye, Babacar. 2009. *The Trickster Comes West: Pan-African Influence in Early Black Disporan Narratives*. Jackson: University Press of Mississippi.

Radin, Paul. 1956. *The Trickster: A Study in American Indian Mythology with Commentaries by Karl Kerényi and C. J. Jung*. London: Routledge and Kegan Paul.

El-Shamy, Hasan M. 1980. *Folktales of Egypt*. Chicago: University of Chicago Press.

Welsch, Roger L., ed. 1990. All Fools' Month. *The World and I* 5(April): 612–669.

U

UFOs and Folklore

What place do real UFOs (unidentified flying objects)—if any exist—hold within the perennial fabric of folk belief? Folklorists cannot say whether UFOs are genuine spaceships or only Venus and airplanes mistaken for something more, but they have gained respect for human experience as a necessary source and sustainer of tradition. The former understanding of folklorists sided with tradition as the basis for apparent experiences. By hearing ghost stories an individual learned to expect ghosts at midnight in a graveyard. That same individual passing a cemetery at night and seeing moonlight on a patch of fog might reshape the vague form to fit his expectations and fears, with the outcome a ghost complete with shroud and chains. The "witness" would then reinforce the belief of others by adding his testimony to tradition, though in fact the ghost amounted to mist and misperception force-fitted into an imaginative preconception, nothing more.

In recent years, some investigators have turned this explanation upside down and argued that some traditions endure, even against the rationalistic opposition of official culture, because they have independent experience to back them up. Folklorist David Hufford investigated the "Old Hag" tradition of Newfoundland, a belief that a witch was responsible for experiences of people who wakened in the night unable to move while some evil presence entered the bedroom and choked the victim. The tradition with all its interpretations was well known and long established in Newfoundland, but Hufford found that some of his students in Pennsylvania had suffered similar experiences, even though they knew nothing of the tradition. If the experience was widespread but the tradition was not, the standard explanation that expectations create the experience quite simply fell apart. He established that "supernatural assault traditions" had worldwide distribution. The basic experiential features remained the same whatever the folk explanation might be, and included in part a physiological condition known as sleep paralysis. In this case, the tradition seemed to begin with experience and not the other way around.

A great deal of UFO lore depends on observation. Tens of thousands of people have seen something in the sky that they could not explain, and whether they reported the sighting or not, to them it became a UFO. In most of those cases the expectation led the way as it lent an aura of mystery and significance to an ordinary planet or meteor, a sight the witness would not imagine to be a spaceship without the preparation of tradition. In March 1967, a Soviet moon probe fell

A car topped with a model spacecraft, encouraging people to welcome extraterrestrial beings, is parked near Jamul, California, October 15, 2000. The surrounding land was purchased by the Unarius Academy of Science to serve as a future landing site for "space brothers" from other planets. (Getty Images)

back into the atmosphere and burned up over several Midwestern states. The U.S. Air Force received about 70 reports of this reentry, and most observers gave an accurate description of half a dozen flaming, meteor-like bodies high in the atmosphere. Some even recognized the nature of the objects. But there were a few individuals who saw something entirely different. One reported a UFO flying at treetop level with six lighted windows, fiery exhaust, and riveted steel plates along the hull. Either this witness misinterpreted the reentry in terms of UFO expectations, or two of the most spectacular aerial sights of a lifetime occurred at once, and this witness missed one of them. A great many UFO reports have an experiential basis, but not necessarily an extraterrestrial one. They originate in the eyes of believers and take the shape of a spaceship, where another observer not under the influence of the UFO tradition looks at the same sight and sees nothing more than the evening star.

At the same time, a remainder of reports continues to puzzle the investigator, and the most determined effort to find a conventional solution leaves behind evidence that refuses to fit. Even as fantastic a story as alien abduction defies the typical dynamics of folklore by varying very little from one narrator to another.

Folk narratives typically exist as clusters of variants swarming around a core of ideas. Even tightly constructed forms such as jokes and urban legends multiply as different content fits into the same plot form, or similar content aligns itself with a different plot. Abduction reports are long, loosely constructed, and fantastic—ideal candidates for rampant variation, ready to satisfy the personal needs of anyone looking to escape the dullness of everyday life in fantasies of romance and adventure. In fact, the accounts reflect few of these expectations. The episodes could exchange places and the story would make equally good sense, yet the episodes usually keep the same relative positions in one report after another. The same content recurs in story after story, down to some minor detail seldom if ever emphasized in any published or broadcast accounts, in some cases present in the reports for years before any investigators recognize or call attention to it. Despite all the aliens depicted in mass and popular culture, abductees limit their accounts to very few types and usually describe the rather bland and unimpressive small gray humanoids. All those opportunities for colorful fantasies languish unrealized as abductees usually depict themselves not as the heroes of their own adventure but as victims, taken and used and turned out with no sense of satisfaction, only feelings of resentment and confusion. Such an outcome is surprising for a fantasy, if these reports are truly fantasies. Proposals that abductees as a group are fantasy-prone or subject to suggestion while under hypnosis have proven doubtful when tested. Whatever they prove to be, abductions, like UFOs in general, appear more complicated than simple errors or creative imaginings.

Any final reckoning must balance the two sides that comprise the whole of the UFO mystery. On the one hand, Jung was right to call UFOs a modern myth. They answer big questions about life and the cosmos and tie them all together in a comprehensible whole with visitors from the sky at the center. They restore wonder and mystery, hope and dread to a world where modernization has stifled these emotions. UFOs challenge official knowledge with the grassroots experience of people who see things that the experts refuse to allow. In this rebellious resistance the folk assert the worth of their own knowledge and a democratic faith that officialdom holds less than full understanding of the world. Whatever else UFOs may be, they serve human uses. The vast lore accumulated around the UFO idea speaks less for the needs of reason than for the human needs of people who tell these stories.

On the other hand, there are the UFOs themselves, whatever they may be, much entangled in the myth surrounding them. Folk, popular, mass, and elite cultures take their own approaches to the phenomenon, and the cumulative effect obscures the reality behind a multitude of expectations, wishes, and preconceptions. The UFOs of reality become lost behind the UFOs of belief, to be glimpsed only in distorted versions. Folklorists cannot settle the issue, but whether UFOs crumble into a collection of conventional occurrences or exist as an independent phenomenon, no one can hope to study UFOs without recognizing the role of human beliefs and concerns in UFO lore.

James R. Lewis

See Also Belief, Folk; Folklore; Myth; Night Hag.

References

Lovern, Kyle. 2009. *Appalachian Case Study: UFO Sightings, Alien Encounters, and Unexplained Phenomena.* Chapmanville, WV: Woodland Press.

Saler, Benson, Charles A. Ziegler, and Charles B. Moore. 1997. *UFO Crash at Roswell: The Genesis of a Modern Myth.* Washington, DC: Smithsonian Institution Press.

Tumm, Diana G., ed. 2009. *Alien Worlds: Social and Religious Dimensions of Extraterrestrial Contact.* Syracuse: Syracuse University Press.

Yomtov, Nelson. 2010. *Secret American Places: From UFO Crash Sites to Government Hideouts.* Mankato, MN: Edge Books.

Urban Folklore

Folklore about cities and in cities; in recent scholarship, folklore generated by and about the modern urban experience. Even the most industrialized, urbanized, polluted, crime-infested city hosts countless examples of traditional folk creativity. Folklore, enhanced and expanded by the mass media and political or commercial interests, thrives in the urban context. The study of urban folklore alternates between the city as a location in which various forms of folklore may be discovered and the city itself as an object of study, illuminated by folklore: Attention shifts, according to Barbara Kirshenblatt-Gimblett, from "city as locus to city as focus."

The collecting of urban folklore began with the first oral and written descriptions of city life. For many centuries, travelers and chroniclers recounted legends about cities and their histories. Folklore enthusiasts of the past also documented the unique urban traditions they encountered in daily life: ballads sung and sold on cheaply printed broadsides, the street cries of vendors, folk speech of the lower classes, and street performances. Excellent collections of city children's folklore appeared in the middle of the nineteenth century. Scholars of typically rural forms of folklore often recorded materials from country craftspeople, traders, and peasants visiting urban markets. All of these traditions belong to the constantly changing repertoire of folklore that is remembered, maintained, and created in the city.

Folklore scholars in the nineteenth century typically fled from the city and modernity. The European romantics were interested in the traditions of rural peasants, ancient history, and poetry that could be transformed into national culture. The British anthropologists collected reports of archaic customs and superstitions surviving among the "uncivilized" people of the world. City traditions and urban culture as a whole were usually not addressed by these folklorists.

At the turn of the twentieth century, the folklore of the urban working classes attracted the attention of socialist agitators, who saw in the narratives and songs of factory workers powerful symbols that could be used to mobilize mass labor movements. The resulting popular publications contain a rich variety of urban labor lore, but they should be consulted with care. Just as peasants and rural folklore were idealized in the service of nationalist ideologies, so also was labor lore often romanticized, manipulated, or even invented by political activists. The same was true of the more recent publications in the Soviet Union, which selectively described the forms of workers' culture and urban traditions that corresponded to government ideology and the official cultural and economic programs.

During the 1920s and 1930s in Germany, pioneering research was published about workers and their traditions. At the same time in the United States, sociologists were turning to the study of city populations and producing the first studies of ethnic groups, criminals, and various members of the urban lower classes. Their research is still a useful source of information about everyday traditions and folklore in the city.

In the late 1960s and 1970s, American folklorists moved away from a past-oriented study of culture in the rural periphery, grappling instead with the topic of American folk culture in the modern world. Richard Dorson and Linda Dégh rejected the ideological manipulation of folklore characteristic of works by Benjamin Botkin and other American romantics and attempted instead to develop the methods needed for accurate ethnographic description of folklore in the city. The 1968 symposium entitled "The Urban Experience and Folk Tradition" posed the question, "Is there a folk in the city?" and answered it with the observation that there was indeed a "folk" but that the materials of folklore had changed. When rural people moved to the city, older genres of folklore lost the traditional performance occasions of the village community and had to either adapt to the urban context or be functionally replaced by other forms. Intensive fieldwork in the steel-mill region around Gary, Indiana, inspired the revision of earlier folklore theories and the recognition of new categories of folklore, such as "personal revelation" and "folklore of crime."

Urban folklore research led to a change in the approaches to fieldwork and the people to be studied. Urban folk are knowledgeable about recording technology and the uses or misuses of the folklore they perform; they are literate and read the results of research about themselves; they are articulate and forceful in their criticism of people writing about them. No longer could field-workers collect and publish whatever they pleased. After the urbanization of folklore research, discussions emerged about accurate description, rapport, respect, and responsibility toward the people studied.

Interest in urban culture also grew outside the academic discipline of folklore. Urban anthropology, urban geography, sociology, and social history produced many ethnographies of city life. Municipal governments became aware of the commercial potential (tourism) and political uses (multiculturalism) of urban folklore and hired folklorists to study, stimulate, and celebrate the aesthetically pleasing urban traditions.

In Germany during the 1950s, folklorists rebelled against the rural, preindustrial orientation of earlier scholars. Taking leads from sociology, they refashioned folkloristics as an "empirical science" and set as their goal the study of people in the contemporary world. In 1961, Hermann Bausinger demonstrated that modernity had not destroyed folklore, as generally believed, but that folklore had changed to encompass modern technology and the mass media of communication. Traditional magic, for example, was replaced in its functions by machines and science. Not limited to the study of urban folklore, the German theories nevertheless opened the city as the main setting in which folklore research continued.

The German shift to urban folklore settings culminated in a 1983 conference entitled "The Large City: Aspects of Empirical Cultural Research." Participants surveyed the history and goals of urban folklore research in nine European countries. The historical development of the modern city and its effect on everyday life, work, and leisure were recurrent themes. Like the earlier American discussions of urban folklore, conference papers described the survival, continuation, and transformation of pre-urban traditions. Others emphasized the city itself as a topic of study. Helge Gerndt, for example, called for the study of three aspects of the city: the city as a structure encompassing and bounding a specific world of everyday culture, the city as a mediator of culture or setting in which unique forms of everyday life are communicated, and the city as a cultural phenomenon with a specific meaning of its own.

The American and German conferences on urban folklore represent a turning point in Western folklore research, a point that has not been reached in many other parts of the world. East European critics observe that reality preceded theory in both cases. The traditional rural village communities and the gifted performers of archaic folklore could be found only with difficulty in modern Germany and the United States, and folklorists in these countries were forced to change their methods, theories, and object of research in order to survive in their professional careers. Whatever the case might be, the shift in approaches uncovered the rich world of urban folk culture and the unique traditions of gifted, creative individuals in urban communities. The urban setting remains a frontier in folklore research. The existing case studies of separate traditions and groups or even of entire cities have yet to be placed in a broad, internationally valid comparative theoretical framework.

Folklore emerges in the city in diverse contexts. Urban folklorists have favored the study of relatively small groups: families, ethnic or religious communities, associations based on occupation or leisure-time activities, and groups defined by geography—for example, the inhabitants of a building, a city block, a neighborhood, or a district. These enclaves provide a personal, mutually supportive environment based on face-to-face communication, in contrast to what is thought to be the anonymous, impersonal urban environment. Community events encourage the cohesion of these groups.

Communities in urban enclaves announce their presence in traditional actions charged with symbolism (processions, demonstrations, eating, dancing, music performance) and in tangible objects (clothes, flags, food, icons) representing the culture that both holds the group together and distinguishes it from the larger society. The urban context fosters conscious maintenance, revival, and traditionalization of folklore. Extra money and leisure time allow members of the middle classes to create new associations based on shared interests and to establish traditions that hold these groups together. Folklore, understood to be a symbol of a simpler, better way of life in the preindustrial past, is revived as an escape from the perceived evils of modern urban society. Thus, traditions that are being replaced by mass culture in their original rural settings—crafts, costume, custom, music, dance, song—are given a second life in the city.

Ethnic identity acquires special significance when people of many backgrounds must live and work in close proximity. The folklore of ethnicity is displayed in public settings where cultures meet, clash, or confront mainstream traditions. Dense urban housing is another factor leading to the creation of communities. Informal social programs and anticrime ("neighborhood watch") organizations, for example, set an area apart from the dangers of urban decay, welding coalitions of trust and familiarity among closely spaced but otherwise isolated households. In the city, events such as block parties, neighborhood picnics, or concerts and local outdoor markets (or sidewalk sales) are a few of the traditionalized occasions in which a sense of local community is constructed.

Material traditions mark off enclaves within the city. Municipal ordinances stipulate some degree of uniformity in house facades, but many more unofficial, traditional aesthetic norms produce, for example, similarities in house colors, exterior decorations, and front gardens. Residents learn which "weeds" should be removed and which vegetable- or fruit-bearing plants are appropriate for public view by observing other gardens in the community. Less-visible communities such as American street gangs leave visible signs marking their territory ("turf") in elaborate graffiti spray-painted on fences or walls.

National Puerto Rican Day Parade in New York City, 2010. (Shiningcolors/Dreamstime.com)

The urban setting gives a double stimulus to folklore: On the one hand, folklore is used to strengthen small communities, and on the other hand, it provides traditional ways for individuals to personalize and humanize the mass-produced, industrial setting of the city. Communal traditions provide their performers with a means of artistic creativity and the possibility to express individual identity. Within certain limits, individual artistic expression is prized in the city, and street performers—musicians, actors, jugglers, speakers, artists—are given money by admiring passersby. It is not, however, the most original art that extracts the greatest resonance (and financial gain) from the fleeting audience; folklore and folklorized elite or popular culture flourish here.

The personal revelation, an expression of individual experience, philosophy, and worldview, gains importance in the egalitarian urban context. In everyday conversations, persons set themselves apart from the faceless, anonymous millions by telling autobiographical stories (personal narratives). Folklore characteristics of these seemingly nontraditional narratives appear in the commonly held themes, beliefs, and fears that they contain. Narratives about rapes, muggings, robbery, and theft, told by the victims or their acquaintances, express both the widespread fears of encountering urban crime and the relief of sharing such fears with reliable, trusted persons.

Many other forms of urban folklore have been described in detail. Problems of terminology emerge whenever a specific genre is placed under scrutiny. For example, two of the most popular forms of folklore that have become known as "urban" are not exclusively urban. *Urban legend*, a term popularized during recent decades, denotes legends containing references to modern technology and circulating among urban populations. The term is misleading, for it refers to narratives that have been collected in urban, suburban, and rural areas alike and that contain both modern and archaic motifs. Moreover, other forms of folklore communicated by means of modern technology (via fax or "Xerox") are not found only in cities, as implied by the frequently used term *urban folklore*. These are primarily examples of folklore transmitted through the modern mass-media network, which is both urban and rural.

There are few qualitative differences between urban folklore and any other folklore touched by the modern world. All folklore found in cities is a part of modern urban culture, but it is usually not exclusively urban. Some forms of folklore, however, arise directly out of the urban experience.

Everyday life in cities follows many rhythms of work and leisure, acted out differently in various districts. Daytime and nighttime activities will follow identifiable schedules (clocked by factory whistles and the bells of churches and schools), and a calendrical cycle appears in the sequence of workdays and holidays. Business, shopping, and leisure habits are traditional, known by all but rarely prescribed by law. They give observable and recordable evidence about the urban dweller's perceptions of time.

There are also traditional divisions of space as known by people in a city. The geographical landscape of a city is sometimes printed on maps for use by visitors or municipal governments, but many other maps exist in the minds of people going about their daily existence. Different landmarks reveal different ways of looking at the city: For children, a street is punctuated by stones, gutters, and tree stumps used as markers in games of stickball; for a homeless beggar, the daily circuits revolve around places where money, food, and drink may be obtained, followed by a place to sleep. Other lives are passed on a circle joining home, work, a food store, and a community gathering place. A tourist imagines the city as a cluster of skyscrapers, museums, and parks. Persons in the city have a mental image of the city and the various districts that lie beyond the familiar neighborhood, but this traditional sense of place rarely resembles commercially produced maps. Informal place-names and stories about the city reveal a traditionally formulated landscape of wealth and poverty, work and leisure, history, beauty, and progress and decay.

Images of the city and its everyday life as perceived by the urban dwellers reveal contrasts between, for instance, the cultures of the city and the countryside. Whereas the stereotypical city rigidly follows the clock and calendar, the life of a rural farmer is governed by the weather and the seasons, regardless of dates. Other everyday traditions indicate that a historical break has occurred between urban and rural folklore. In the twentieth century, cities have fostered the growth and expansion of the middle social classes; it is no surprise, then, that the typically middle-class values concerning time, cleanliness, work, and leisure often predominate in urban culture as a whole.

Everyday culture reveals subtle changes in the characteristics of cities over time. Festivals place these differences in open view, to be identified by urban folklorists. Historical studies show, for example, that public celebrations moved from outlying districts into central areas of the city with the rise of liberal democracy and populist movements; family customs such as weddings, by contrast, have been transformed from public events in rural villages to private affairs among the urban middle classes. Changes in perceptions of openness and privacy signal that larger changes are taking place in cultures.

Images of the city appear in crystallized form in public festivals held by municipal organizations: Parades and pageants address the many cultures of the city, giving every inhabitant occasion to identify with the local government and to recognize its place in the local hierarchy of power. Public political demonstrations are recognized both from above and from below as traditional instruments of social change; memorials construct the city's history, re-creating the past to validate or challenge the present. The mass media and the tourism industry diffuse concentrated images of the city (silhouettes of the skyline, pictures of value-charged sites such as the Brooklyn Bridge in New York), identifying these symbols with the given city and its inhabitants. When the mass-produced images find resonance and are accepted by portions of the urban population, they folklorize, becoming part of the city's informally transmitted culture. Distinctive urban identities form through images constructed in political and commercial processes. Sports, weather, and news broadcasts on television and the other mass media have made people very aware of the existence of their city among many other cities in their country and abroad, intensifying their sense of belonging to a specific place in the transurban context. Audiences struggle and suffer with the eleven football players representing their hometown; sports rivalries between cities run deep in the identities of fans, sometimes even leading them to violence.

The study of urban folklore provides the views of the average city dweller on the great social and cultural changes currently taking place in the world. As people of many backgrounds continue to migrate to ever-expanding cities, rural identities are transformed by the traditions of the city, which are in turn tightly intertwined with national and international culture. If solutions to the world's intercultural conflicts exist at all, then they are to be found in the city.

Guntis Šmidchens

See Also Legend, Urban; Xeroxlore.

References

Bausinger, Hermann. 1961. *Volkskultur in der technischen Welt*. Stuttgart: Kohlhammer GMbH. Trans. Elke Dettmer, as *Folk Culture in a World of Technology*. Bloomington: Indiana University Press, 1990.

Botkin, Benjamin. 1954. *Sidewalks of America: Folklore, Legends, Sagas, Traditions, Customs, Songs, Stories, and Sayings of City Folk*. Indianapolis, IN: Bobbs-Merrill.

Dorson, Richard Mercer. 1981. *Land of the Millrats*. Cambridge, MA: Harvard University Press.

Dundes, Alan, and Carl R. Pagter. 1991. *Never Try to Teach a Pig to Sing: Still More Urban Folklore from the Paperwork Empire*. Detroit, MI: Wayne State University Press.

Düding, Dieter, Peter Friedmann, and Paul Münch, eds. 1988. *Öffentliche Festkultur: Politische Feste im Deutschland von der Aufklärung bis zum Ersten Weltkrieg*. Hamburg: Kohlhammer GMbH.

Frykman, Jonas, and Orvar Löfgren. [1979] 1987. *Culture Builders: A Historical Anthropology of Middle-Class Life*. Trans. Alan Crozier. New Brunswick, NJ: Rutgers University Press.

Kirshenblatt-Gimblett, Barbara. 1983. The Future of Folklore Studies in America: The Urban Frontier. *Folklore Forum* 16(2): 175–234.

Kohlmann, Theodor, and Hermann Bausinger, eds. 1985. *Großstadt: Aspekte empirischer Kulturforschung*. Berlin: Staatliche Museen Preußischer Kulturbesitz.

Mohrmann, Ruth-E. 1990. Die Stadt als volkskundliches Forschungsfeld. *Österreichis-che Zeitschrift für Volkskunde* 44: 129–149.

Paredes, Américo, and Ellen J. Stekert, eds. 1971. *The Urban Experience and Folk Tradition*. Austin: University of Texas Press.

Wachs, Eleanor F. 1988. *Crime-Victim Stories: New York City's Urban Folklore*. Bloomington: Indiana University Press.

V

Vampire

In European folklore, the spirit of a dead person that returns after death to haunt the living. This spirit (the body remains in the grave) attacks the relatives and friends of the deceased and is viewed as the party responsible for any number of disastrous and actual events, including bad weather, bad crops, sickness, and death. During epidemics, it was assumed that the first person who had died was a vampire, but otherwise, the suspects were commonly murder victims, suicides, alcoholics, and anyone who, during life, had fallen under suspicion of evildoing. In order to end the vampire's depredations, the living would exhume a suspect corpse and examine it for evidence that it was the guilty party. Because literate outsiders have occasionally attended such exhumations, we know what the vampire looked like as it reposed in its grave: The body had decomposed less than expected and was bloated; it was a darker color than it had been during life; the mouth was open and had blood in it; the skin and nails had peeled away, revealing fresh skin and nails; the hair and beard appeared to have grown after death; the blood had not coagulated; there was no evidence of rigor mortis; and the body had a strong smell. These accounts of the vampire in his or her grave, however startling they appear at first glance, have proven to be accurate descriptions of decomposing corpses in the grave, and they clear up some details of the folklore. For example, the belief that the vampire sucked blood appears to be an interpretation of the bloating and the blood at the lips of the corpse. As the corpse bloats from the gases given off by the microorganisms of decay, the pressure in the abdomen forces blood from the decomposing lungs out of the mouth and nose. This blood is taken to be the blood of the vampire's victims and the cause of the corpse's increased size. "Not without astonishment," says an eighteenth-century observer of the exhumation of a vampire, "I saw some fresh blood in his mouth, which, according to the common observation, he had sucked from the people killed by him."

If the corpse was found to be a vampire, it was "killed." Because its blood was thought to be dangerous, people commonly killed the vampire in ways that allowed them to keep their distance. If killed with a stake, the corpse might be covered with a hide or blanket to prevent its blood from spurting onto the people killing it. But staking was just one method of killing the vampire and perhaps not even the most common. In northern Europe, the corpse might be decapitated with a shovel—a tool that was already at hand and that kept some distance between the vampire and the person killing it. The vampire might also be cut into pieces, excoriated, cremated, or left out for scavengers. Often, several methods were used, the last of which was usually cremation, and the remains were then thrown into running water (water is believed to capture spirits, and running water carries them away). From one geographic area to the next, there are differences in the habits of the vampire, the interpretations of the body in the grave, and the methods of killing it. The Greek version of the vampire, for example, the *vrykolakas*, is not believed to suck blood.

The relationship of the vampire's spirit and corpse is also subject to great geographic variation. Often, the spirit is seen as an insubstantial version of the body, identical in appearance. It is commonly thought to function as a kind of servomechanism for the body, so that sleep, unconsciousness, and death are all taken for evidence of a separation of spirit from body. When someone dies properly and is given appropriate funeral and burial rites, his or her spirit makes its way to the afterworld. If death is violent or if the corpse does not undergo the usual rites, the spirit remains behind and returns to the body. Then, the body remains alive in some sense and functions as a dwelling place for the spirit during the day. At night, the spirit wanders about on its own and causes trouble. If the body is destroyed, the spirit has no dwelling place and departs for the afterworld. Alternately, one could destroy the vampire by capturing his or her spirit. In some areas, sorcerers made a living by claiming to be able to see and capture these spirits, even during daylight, although most people saw the vampire's spirit only at night, during sleep. In the Balkans, there was a common belief that vampires could be seen by their sons or by people born on a Saturday, a day when vampires were obliged to remain in their graves.

Among the many apotropaics reported for warding off the vampire are sharp objects (thorns, sickles, hair needles, awls, knives) and anything with a strong smell (incense, cow dung, garlic). A knife might be placed under the pillow to keep vampires away during sleep, and sharp objects might be buried with the corpse to prevent it from being reanimated. (The common practice of burying sickles with corpses has a reflex in our traditional personification of death: a skeleton in a shroud bearing a sickle or scythe.) Another traditional apotropaic is the rose, presumably because of its thorns (at the end of *Faust*, the angels strew roses to disperse the devils). In Slavic areas, roses were commonly embroidered onto the cuffs and neck openings of shirts and blouses, not just as decoration but also to protect against the spirits of the dead.

The vampire of European folklore bears little resemblance to the vampire in popular films and literature, although it provided the inspiration for them. Suave counts in evening dress, castles, and even bats were donated to the traditional lore by nineteenth-century writers of fiction. (The bat made its way into the

On board the *Demeter,* the vampire Count Orlok emerges from one of his coffins before they can be destroyed by the ship's first mate in a scene from F. W. Murnau's expressionist horror film *Nosferatu* (1922), based on Bram Stoker's novel *Dracula* (1897). (Hulton Archive/Getty Images)

fiction after a Central American bat, which lives on blood, got its name from the vampire of folklore.) Vlad Dracul himself, a Romanian hero of the fifteenth century, had no connection at all with the history of the vampire except that he contributed his epithet (*dracul* is the Romanian word for devil plus the definite article) to Bram Stoker's fictional character Dracula.

Paul Barber

See Also Assault, Supernatural; Revenant; Shape-Shifters; Werewolf.

References

Barber, Paul. 1988. *Vampires, Burial and Death: Folklore and Reality.* New Haven, CT: Yale University Press.

Blum, Richard, and Eva Blum. 1970. *The Dangerous Hour: The Lore of Crisis and Mystery in Rural Greece.* New York: Scribner.

Butler, Erik. 2010. *Metamorphoses of the Vampire in Literature and Film.* Rochester, NY: Camden House.

Lecouteux, Claude. 2010. *The Secret History of Vampires: Their Multiple Forms and Hidden Purposes.* Rochester, VT: Inner Traditions.

Noll, Richard. 1992. *Vampires, Werewolves and Demons: Twentieth Century Reports in the Psychiatric Literature.* New York: Brunner/Mazel.

Otten, Charlotte F., ed. 1986. *A Lycanthropy Reader: Werewolves in Western Culture.* Syracuse, NY: Syracuse University Press.

Perkowski, Jan L. 1989. *The Darkling: A Treatise on Slavic Vampirism.* Columbus, OH: Slavica.

Senn, Harry A. 1982. *Were-Wolf and Vampire in Romania.* New York: Columbia University Press.

Trigg, Elwood B. 1973. *Gypsy Demons and Divinities: The Magic and Religion of the Gypsies.* Secaucus, NJ: Citadel.

Vukanovic, Tatomir P. 1957–1960. The Vampire. *Journal of the Gypsy Lore Society* 36: 125–133, 37: 21–31, 38: 111–118, 39: 44–55.

Verbal Art

A branch of folklore encompassing all orally performed genres and ways of speaking. Verbal art has usually been defined according to its constituent varieties (e.g., myths, legends, *Märchen*, proverbs, riddles, song texts) and has been viewed in contrast with nonverbal folklore, on the one hand, and literary narrative genres, on the other. The inclusive sense of the term *verbal art* makes it of value to folklorists, especially those interested in broad, overarching aesthetic and performative features of oral culture. The study of verbal art draws on analytical methods such as ethnopoetics, discourse analysis, and linguistic approaches.

The term *verbal art* was proposed by William Bascom in 1955. Bascom's concern (still a problem in folklore research today) was that the term *folklore* does double duty, leading to confusion. On the one hand, *folklore* is used holistically to denote the entirety of the field, including verbal art, customs, material culture, and so on. On the other hand, many folklorists and anthropologists reserve the term *folklore* exclusively for the purely verbal genres. By using *verbal art*, Bascom argued, folklorists can avoid such confusion and further promote the use of the term *folklore* in its broadest sense.

In practice, the term *verbal art* has not spread as widely as Bascom might have hoped. It is used most extensively by folklorists with anthropological training, and it tends to be found in studies of African or Native American peoples. The fact that many of the most promising methods for verbal art analysis have come from studies of non-European communities may bode well for the term *verbal art* in the future.

Contemporary verbal art studies often focus on strategic and stylistic choices made during oral performance. For instance, a performer may express identity or attitude through code switching in a bilingual or diglossic community. Shifts in register and dialect may accomplish the same ends in monolingual communities. Many cultures also possess elaborate, specialized vocabulary or stylistic features for storytelling, poetry, speeches, or other forms of oral performance. These special ways of speaking constitute an important part of a culture's verbal art.

As a blanket term, *verbal art* allows folklorists to talk about all spoken or recited genres within a given culture. Recent folklore research demonstrates clearly that verbal art differs in substantive ways from written communication. At the same time, oral and written genres appear to borrow much more readily from each other in daily life than earlier folklorists assumed. Verbal art and written art fall along a continuum of expressive options and norms open to competent performers of a given culture.

Thomas A. DuBois

See Also Aesthetics; Ethnoaesthetics; Ethnopoetics; Folklore; Genre; Performance.

References

Bascom, William. 1955. Verbal Art. *Journal of American Folklore* 68(269): 245–252.

Bauman, Richard. 1977. *Verbal Art as Performance*. Rowley, MA: Newbury House.

Briggs, Charles L. 1988. *Competence in Performance: The Creativity of Tradition in Mexicano Verbal Art*. Philadelphia: University of Pennsylvania Press.

Finnegan, Ruth. 1970. *Oral Literature in Africa*. London: Clarendon Press.

Kofi, Anyidoho. 1983. Oral Poetics and Traditions of Verbal Art in Africa. PhD dissertation, University of Texas, Austin.

Verbal Duel

A bounded series of linked insults usually involving two combatants and performed before a wider audience of peers. The verbal duel genre is found most often among males and occurs in cultures throughout the world. It has been observed in various forms among indigenous peoples of the Americas, north Eurasia, and Africa, in agrarian European and Middle Eastern cultures, and in urban African American and Puerto Rican social life, as well as in certain historical sources (e.g., the Viking age *flyting* [exchange of personal abuse in verse form] of Scandinavia). The contexts for dueling vary cross-culturally, ranging from impromptu sessions during conversation to elaborate formal competitions performed at assemblies or weddings. In any case, the performance is set apart from normal discourse by formal bounds, including the use of poetic vocabulary, stock images or topics, exaggeration, overt innuendo and double entendre, rhythm, rhyme, or melody. Key to the competition is the ability of combatants to match the insults of their opponents with equal or preferably more effective retorts until one player loses temper, concedes defeat, or is unable to come up with a reply. Invariably, the audience plays a central role in judging the success of the insults and retorts, approving of the combatants' wit and monitoring the players' reactions. Often, reports of particularly artful or fierce verbal duels pass into narrative tradition and are recounted by former witnesses as evidence of an individual's wit or prowess. Such reports of verbal duels constitute a secondary narrative genre of great importance in determining the form and frequency of future duels and in creating folk heroes or cycles.

In the folklore research of the performance school, boundedness refers to the existence of verbal, paralinguistic, or behavioral markers that signal to the co-performer or audience a shift from ordinary discourse to active performance. In the most widely studied forms of verbal dueling—African American *dozens* and Turkish boys' rhymed insults—such signals include the use of metrically regular lines and rhyme as well as shifts in stance and voice quality. Similar features characterize the Chamula and Lebanese varieties of verbal dueling. In the north Eurasian cultural region, performance boundaries are created through adherence to musical conventions (e.g., melody, alliteration, rhyme, rhythm) and through the existence of clearly demarcated ritual contexts. The Faroese *drunnur* tradition, performed during weddings, as well as the wedding insult sessions of Karelian and Ingrian tradition, rely on a broader ritual context for justification and performative bounds. The Inuit song dance, performed at a communal assembly after a long period of preparation and composition, constitutes one of the most clearly demarcated and formal varieties of the genre. Similarly, the Ewe people of Ghana perform insult songs as part of an annual festival and rely on the genre as an important means of social control and community maintenance.

Performative boundaries permit combatants to invoke and maintain what the theorist Gregory Bateson terms a *play frame*, a marked departure from the rules of ordinary behavior during which all actions are interpreted as non-serious. Maintenance of the play frame allows opponents to broach topics otherwise taboo in ordinary conversation and to make accusations that would normally lead to serious conflict. Such topics include claims of sexual promiscuity on the part of the opponent or the opponent's family, accusations of homosexuality or incest, and assertions of culturally stigmatized characteristics (e.g., selfishness, conceitedness, physical deformity, impotence). As long as the accusations are made within the overt guise of play, the opponent must accept them as humorous or lose the game. Inevitably, the limits of decorum within such play are subject to negotiation and testing, and verbal duels may result in physical conflict in many cultures. Alternatively, remarks made in a verbal duel may permanently damage interpersonal relations, leading to long-standing grudges or even hatred. Success or failure in verbal duels may influence one's overall status in the community and determine one's success in future endeavors.

The topics covered in verbal duels vary cross-culturally but always indicate important concerns or taboos. Generally, the topics characteristic of the genre in any one culture are fairly restricted in number, consisting of three or four primary categories of frailty or transgression and usually closely tied to notions of face and status within the community. In African American dozens, for instance, insults often focus on the sexual promiscuity of the opponent's female relatives, particularly the mother. In Turkish duels, the insults may focus on homosexual tendencies. In Inuit song duels, insults may aver the opponent's lasciviousness, incest, or greed. Faroese duels center on such topics as marital conduct, sexual appetite, and impotence.

The successful retort usually continues the initiated theme, elevating the stakes of the competition by making more extreme accusations in the same vein against the opponent. Switching topics—that is, failing to produce a linked insult—can be interpreted as a loss of the competition and is thus avoided. Linkage is further achieved through metrical reproduction of the prior utterance, use of rhyme to bind utterances together, metaphoric plays or double entendres based on key words from the prior utterance, and other verbal patternings. Because many verbal dueling traditions demand speedy replies, retorts may be memorized and drawn upon by performers at appropriate moments. Memory becomes as important an attribute of the expert player as wit in such traditions, although the truly remarkable retort is always one that combines elaborate formal linkage with novelty and aptness.

As with other forms of joke, the verbal duel has been interpreted generally along functionalist and psychoanalytical lines. When the genre occurs among male adolescents—as in the case of African Americans, Turks, or Chamula—folklorists have viewed it as a testing ground for the development of adult oratory skills. When the genre exists among adult males bound together in ambiguous but important alliances—for example, in-law status in some African cultures or trading partnerships in Inuit communities—folklorists have viewed the genre as a safety valve for alleviating attendant strains and hostilities. Verbal dueling within the wedding context or shamanic system has been seen as expressive of conflicts of values or interests inherent in certain social institutions.

When examining folklore genres from a cross-cultural perspective, it is important to distinguish between genres that display clear evidence of diffusion across linguistic and cultural lines (e.g., *Märchen*, legends) and genres that appear to occur more or less independently in various cultures. Verbal dueling belongs to the latter category, although the overall origins of the genre may indeed lie in a single ancient tradition. Apparent similarities between verbal duels from culture to culture may mask marked differences in the symbolic or functional implications of the genre. Thus, in African American, Puerto Rican, Chamula, Lebanese, or Turkish cultures, community members may regard the genre as informal and inappropriate to more decorous occasions, whereas members of other cultures in northern Europe, Siberia, Africa, and North America may regard it as a central

Boast

Formulaic praise of self or one's property and associates. The boast as a distinct verbal art genre almost always occurs in association with other forms, and boasting may occur in folklore when the boast as genre is not present. In most cases, formulaic boasts are specific to particular contexts, especially those defined by age and gender. They are often a component of competitive displays that may be ends in themselves or that may lead to further competition, even physical violence.

Verbal dueling, usually an activity of adolescent males, provides an important context in which boasts occur cross-culturally. For example, the ritual exchange of insults that characterizes what is called "dozens," "joning," or "snaps" among young African American males focuses principally on derogating the opponent and his family. But frequently, boasts of one's prowess, especially sexual, contribute to the duel's outcome, which depends upon verbal agility and one's ability to undercut the opponent's masculinity. Reducing the opponent to an image of passivity can be achieved at least partially through boasting of one's active masculinity, a technique that also has been reported in verbal dueling among Turkish youths.

Boasts also occur in longer forms of folk literature. One characteristic of the epic hero, be he Achilles or Odysseus from Homeric Greece, Beowulf from Old English tradition, or the protagonists of the Balkan epics reported by Milman Parry and Albert Lord, is his boasting, an act that may figure into council scenes, serve as preparation for battle, or comprise a warrior's account of an action in which he has participated. The humor of the American frontier produced similar boasts, which probably served to burlesque the characters' uncivilized manners. Davy Crockett or Mike Fink would claim to be "half horse, half alligator" and able to "lick [his] weight in wildcats" before scuffling with an opponent. The toast, a long narrative poem recited by African American males, often features a boastful protagonist who extols his own violent disregard of convention. Among Native Americans of the plains, boasts became part of the formula for coup tales, stories in which warriors recounted their military exploits, especially those that evinced particular daring. The tall tale provides another folk literary context for the boast. The focus of tall tales, though, may not be praise of self as much as of the country where one lives. For example, tall tales often include boasts about a land's fertility and richness, the size and accessibility of its game, and the beauty of its women.

Boasts also may assume a negative cast, though their ultimate purport redounds to the boaster's credit. For example, American humor includes boasts about the excessively inclement weather and general insalubrity of rural areas and the toughness of city neighborhoods. On one hand, these boasts derogate, but on the other, they stress the speaker's prowess in being able to survive unpleasant, dangerous conditions.

Formulaic boasting seems to flourish in societies that stress the so-called "masculine" virtues of aggressiveness toward other males, women, and the environment. Folklore research has tended to examine such boasting in terms of its linguistic patterning and psychological importance, the latter usually informed by Freudian assumptions.

William M. Clements

means of social control. Folklorists must balance outward performative similarities with careful observation of use and significance.

The seeming paucity of female participants or forms of verbal duel raises methodological questions. It may be that female varieties of verbal aggression have been excluded from the usual definition of the verbal duel due to a reliance on male data or phenomena. African American women, for instance, often report knowledge of and even proficiency in verbal dueling, although their participation has not been ethnographically examined. Further, women may possess distinct forms of verbal aggression that display structural or functional similarities with male genres. The role of gender in verbal aggression in general and in folkloristic examinations of the topic deserves much more attention.

Thomas A. DuBois

See Also Joke; Obscenity; Scatology.

References

Abrahams, Roger. 1962. Playing the Dozens. *Journal of American Folklore* 75(297): 209–220.

Abrahams, Roger D. 1970. *Deep Down in the Jungle: Negro Narrative Folklore from the Streets of Philadelphia*. 1st rev. ed. Chicago: Aldine.

Awoonor, Kofi. 1975. *The Breast of the Earth*. New York: Doubleday.

Balikci, Asen. 1970. *The Netsilik Eskimo*. Garden City, NY: Natural History Press.

Bateson, Gregory. 1972. *Steps to an Ecology of Mind*. New York: Ballantine.

Boatright, Mody C. 1949. *Folk Laughter on the American Frontier*. New York: Macmillan.

Coffey, Jerome E. 1989. The Drunnur—A Faroese Wedding Custom. *ARV* 45: 7–16.

Dundes, Alan, Jerry W. Leach, and Bora Ozkok. 1970. The Strategy of Turkish Boys' Verbal Dueling Rhymes. *Journal of American Folklore* 83: 325–349.

Gossen, Gary. 1974. *Chamulas in the World of the Sun*. Cambridge, MA: Harvard University Press.

Haydar, Adnan. 1989. The Development of the Lebanese *zajal:* Genre, Meter, and Verbal Duel. *Oral Tradition* 4(1–2): 189–212.

Labov, William. 1972. *Language in the Inner City*. Philadelphia: University of Pennsylvania Press.

Lauria, A. 1964. *Respeto, Relajo* and Interpersonal Relations in Puerto Rico. *Anthropological Quarterly* 37: 53–67.

Murray, Stephen O. 1983. Ritual and Personal Insults in Stigmatized Subcultures: Gay-Black-Jew. *Maledicta* 7: 189–211.

Radcliffe-Brown, A. 1940. On Joking Relationships. *Africa* 13: 195–210.

Swenson, Karen. 1988. Verbal Duels and the Heroic Self: Genre Definition in Old Norse Literature. PhD dissertation, Cornell University, Ithaca, NY.

Vernacular

An analytic term applied to cultural forms or behaviors that are alternate to or held separate from those practices exhibited, regulated, or controlled by institutions. Sometimes used as a synonym for *folk*, the term more properly refers to cultural expression that is rooted in a specific community without necessarily suggesting any traditional features in the expression.

Derived from the Latin word for "home born," one of the earliest known uses of *vernacular* to describe expressive human behavior was around 49 BCE when the ancient Roman politician and philosopher Marcus Tullius Cicero suggested that the "vernacular" was a source of persuasive rhetorical power (Cicero 1971, 147). Linked to participation in a particular community, Cicero referred to the vernacular as an "indescribable flavor" in the political speeches of a successful politician of his day. Unlike the arts of oratory, however, Cicero's vernacular existed and was learned outside of formal education in Roman schools. Over 1500 years later, the term entered the English language as an outgrowth of this meaning to refer to the local languages of Europe in the seventeenth century. As a lingering result of Roman influence at that time, European institutional discourse including that of government, education, science, and the Catholic Church was conducted almost exclusively in Latin. Languages like English, French, Italian, Portuguese, and Spanish were termed "vernacular" to distinguish them from institutional Latin.

Then, in the nineteenth century, there was a surge of interest in the literature, practices, and beliefs expressed in the European vernaculars. Many individuals began to imagine nations as defined by local languages and regional practices. While occasionally referred to as vernacular during the nineteenth century, the English-speaking scholars and writers interested in these kinds of expression primarily used the term *folklore*. For them, this latter term captured the nationalist and Romantic implications of their time by linking local culture to an imagined ground of knowledge that was generally termed *tradition*. *Vernacular* began to come back into fashion in the 1950s when some architects began to use it to refer to local building styles. In 1960, the term was popularized for use in cultural theory more generally when anthropologist Margaret Lantis used it to refer to "the commonplace" (202). For her, "high" culture was only accessible by the elites of a society, but "vernacular culture" remained accessible to all. From this usage, two trajectories of meaning came to be associated with the term in cultural theory. On the one hand, vernacular forms are those available to individuals or groups who are subordinated to institutions, and, on the other, they are a common resource made available to everyone through informal social interaction. Based on this dual meaning, the vernacular came to refer to discourse that coexists with dominant culture but is held separate from it.

The term's most significant uses in folklore studies today are in three areas. First, *vernacular architecture* refers to those building designs that are known and practiced in specific communities instead of by professional architects such as nomadic peoples' tent-making practices (Rapoport 1969, 4). Second, *vernacular religion* refers to the everyday lived religion of specific individuals such as the communities of alternate Catholicism created by homosexuals (Primiano 1995, 51). Third, *vernacular discourse* refers to communication practices that are not necessarily traditional, but emerge dialectically distinguished from institutionally sanctioned communication (Howard 2008b, 490). With the emergence of network communication technologies, the term has gained new life as a way to designate the expression of communal authority that is often found embedded in or intertwined with institutional media communication (Howard 2008a, 192).

Origins of the Term

After the term came into regular use among folklore researchers in the twentieth century, it gave rise to some concern because of its origins as a term that referred to a specific kind of human slave. The Latin word *vernacular* is derived from the Classical Greek word *oikogenes* that literally means "home-genetic." In extant Greek writings, an *oikotrips* is a "home-born" slave. A distinguishing quality of the *oikotrips* was her or his ability to speak Greek. This meaning is made clear in Plato's "Meno" when Socrates asks Meno to provide a "retainer" for an experiment in learning. Meno brings a boy forward, and Socrates asks, "He is a Greek and speaks our language?" Meno responds, "Indeed yes—born and bred in the house [literally "yes, he is 'home-genetic'"]" (Plato 1989, 365). By the Roman period, Latin had come to dominate the colonial holdings of the Roman Republic and later the Empire. Latin speakers translated *oikogenes* as "vernacular." At this time, *Vulgar Latin* was a blanket term covering the many spoken dialectics of Latinate languages that were spread across Western Europe. These came to be called the "vernacular languages" of Europe in the seventeenth century.

Even in the sense of a "vernacular" language, however, the term relies on a distinction between an institutionally empowered language and a local or everyday language. In Roman society, most slaves were seized during wars, in the suppression of colonial insurrections, or even outright piracy. The vast majority of these slaves spoke one of the many forms of Vulgar Latin. Since any person born to a slave woman (regardless of the social position of the father) was automatically a slave, female slaves were encouraged to have children to increase the master's slave stock (Bradley 1987, 42). These *verna* became more valuable than their mothers because they were native speakers of Classical Latin and could be trained in more valuable skills. In this sense, the verna was vernacular not because she or he knew their own language natively but because she or he knew the institutional language natively. While some see this history of slavery as a reason to avoid using the term, others find that it renders the term more flexible. This flexibility emerges because the dialectical nature of the term suggests interdependence or even hybridity between everyday or folkloric cultural elements and institutional structures.

Accepting its hybridity, Henry Glassie has argued that the vernacular should be conceptualized as embodying "values alien to the academy" (Glassie 2000, 20). In this sense, vernacularity emerges into meaning only in relation to the institutional that must be logically prior to it. That is to say, its meaning relies on its apparent distinction from institutionally empowered cultural forms—what Glassie terms "the academy." The "alien" is alien precisely because it is found alongside the locally born. Accepting this interdependence, the vernacular cannot be fully disentangled from its opposite. As a result, the term can refer to one layer of meaning that resides among others—even in a single object or behavior. Because it can emerge as one layer among others, the vernacular can be a component part of the behaviors or products of institutions, their documents, or their officials just as easily as it can designate a more obviously folkloric expression. This sense of the vernacular was most vividly captured by Leonard Primiano's argument that when the pope or Dalai Lama performs a private personal prayer, even that expression is vernacular (1995, 46).

Three Theoretical Conceptions of the Vernacular

As the term is used in cultural theory today, it is conceived in three theoretically distinct ways. First, the vernacular is often imagined as local expression that is distinct from larger institutional discourses. In this "subaltern" view, the vernacular voice is that of the subordinate counter-agent seeking to be heard over hegemony. In a second theoretical conception, the vernacular is imagined as a shared resource, a *sensus communis*, or community *doxa*. In this "common resource" view, the vernacular is a communal chorus that emerges from the multiplicity of voices speaking in the noninstitutional discursive spaces of quotidian life. Both of these conceptions, however, rely on a strict division that fails to fully account for the interdependent nature of the vernacular and the institutional.

The third conception, the "dialectical" vernacular, addresses this concern by returning to the ancient origins of the word to emphasize that what is vernacular is only so when it is held distinct from what must come structurally prior to it—the institutional. As a result, the vernacular is always entangled with the institutional. This conception frees the vernacular from having to demonstrate authentic connections to a particular tradition or community. At the same time, it accounts for the appearance of vernacular meaning embedded in objects or expressive behaviors that are largely institutional. In this way, the dialectical conception of the vernacular resists essentializing any expression as entirely vernacular or folkloric.

The concept of the "subaltern" vernacular locates what is authentically vernacular in historically subordinated groups. Derived from a term for low-ranking officers in the British army, the concept of the "subaltern" refers to groups whose power is severely limited or denied by social structures. Researchers have sought to understand what discursive means are available for the subaltern to effect changes in their subordinated status. In 1988, Henry Louis Gates Jr.'s *The Signifying Monkey* described the vernacular as a source of discursive power for African Americans. In 1995, Kent Ono and John Sloop called for critics to explore such vernacular discourse because it "resonates within and from historically oppressed communities" (20). Ono and Sloop specifically define vernacular discourses as those that "emerge from discussions between members of self-identified smaller communities within the larger civic community" (2002, 13). From this perspective, the vernacular emerges in the expressive behaviors of individuals who are seen as being held outside of the larger "civic" community because they are identified with a historically subordinated or "subaltern" group. With this subaltern view of the vernacular, researchers have generated excellent scholarship focusing on the possibilities and limits of counter-agency.

While the subaltern view of the vernacular emphasizes a community of individuals who are alternate to institutions, the common resource view of the vernacular locates it in the contexts where the human expression occurs. The vernacular is that which is enacted or performed in places, times, or documents other than those that are institutionally empowered. Here, the vernacular is a common recourse that is available to everyone, but one held separate from institutional contexts. Associated with the informal expression of the community in this second conception, the vernacular is the communal and informal action of many individuals over time. The general association between communal or "public" action and the vernacular is fully articulated in Gerard Hauser's 1999 *Vernacular Voices*. Hauser argues that "Publics are emergences manifested through vernacular rhetoric" (1999, 14). Hauser's "vernacular rhetoric" is the dialogic force of the community. This force emerges in what Hauser calls the "mundane transactions of words and gestures that allow us to negotiate our way through our quotidian encounters" (11). From this perspective, the vernacular is equated with the *doxa*, s*ensus communis*, or "common sense" that is maintained and taught within a local community but held separate from institutional power structures.

The third or "dialectical" conception of the vernacular retrieves its meaning from the ancient texts where the term first appears. Because the verna was defined as a person who was held apart from but could still gain power from Roman institutions, the vernacular is here imagined as in a strictly dialectical fashion as anything that is marked as separate from the institutions that exercise control over it. Separated from a necessary association with any particular origin, the vernacular can emerge even in the behaviors of an institutional actor. For example, when a world leader such as a U.S. president uses a regional pronunciation or speaks in colloquial language, she or he is a fully institutional actor who is accessing a vernacular mode of expression. Here, the vernacular can support or contest the institutional because its definition is not based on any authentic counter-hegemonic or subaltern identity for the individual engaging it. Instead, the vernacular emerges even when a president or the pope seeks to express her or himself in terms that suggest they are alternate to the institutional structures of power.

Much as the verna was in the unique position of being able to introduce extra-institutional influence into the very institutions that rendered her or his enslavement, a dialectical conception of the vernacular imagines vernacularity as a quality of any expressive discourse that attempts to convey meaning by distinguishing itself from institutions to which it is subordinated. This paradoxical relationship is embedded in the historical meanings of the term *vernacular*, and it points away from the strict separation from the institutional in the both the subaltern and common resource conceptions of the vernacular.

Because access to vernacular authority is not granted based on participation in any specific local community, it is accessible to everyone. At the same time, however, this universal access does not diminish the authenticity of any specific vernaculars because vernacularity is granted whenever an individual performs her or his own position as subordinate to the institutional. Because this subordination is emergent in discourse, access to such authority is possible only in degrees as alterity from institutional power is asserted. Thus all that is vernacular relies on the institutional to make its meaning. As a result, vernacularity is always empowered by the very institutions from which it seeks alterity.

A subaltern vernacular sees noninstitutional expression as a means to empower marginalized groups. So doing, it locates an essential identity in the individuals enacting the vernacular as necessarily disempowered. The common resource conception locates its essential identification of the term in the situations that allow for informal social forces to shape the discourse of agents over time. Both conceptions of the vernacular seek to account for noninstitutional power by imagining a strict division between the vernacular and institutional that has probably never really existed. Distinct from these two theoretical conceptions, the dialectical vernacular accounts for hybrid expressions that are both institutional and vernacular even while it avoids the necessity of establishing an essential authentic identity or folkloric origin for the vernacular elements.

The Analytic Flexibility of the Vernacular

The dialectical conception of the vernacular is particularly useful when examining contemporary expressions that mix institutional and noninstitutional materials such as DJ performances. When commercially produced institutional recordings are remixed in a local live performance, the result is a hybrid of institutional and vernacular expression. Entanglements of mass media, commercial, and folkloric expression such as this are particularly common in Internet-based folk expression. There, individuals make hybrid "vids," "mashups," or "imagemacros" by combining commercially produced media objects to express their own everyday creativity. While short-term "traditions" have emerged in the communities where these artistic forms are created, they take as their main components mass media instead of traditional materials. In this sense, many of these new forms of expression do not seem folkloric. At the same time, they are the product of today's "folk"—everyday people using what is near at hand in their cultural repertoire to create meaning for themselves. In this situation, the dialectical conception of the vernacular has proved very useful.

The dialectical conception of the vernacular is more flexible than the term *folkloric* because it resists a romanticizing or essentializing of what it is identifying. It imagines individuals or groups of individuals who in any given case may be acting through some institutional and/or some vernacular means. Further, it imagines the locations of discourse made possible by institutional forces as potential locations for vernacular expression. At its base, this conception of the vernacular imagines a web of intentions moving along vectors of structural power that emerge as vernacular whenever they assert their alterity from the institutional. Because a dialectical conception of the vernacular asserts neither a purely noninstitutional object nor a verifiable traditional trajectory, vernacularity is far more flexible as an analytic term than is *folkloric* or *folklore*. This flexibility renders the vernacular better suited for situations where the traditional or institutional elements of specific expressions are difficult to disentangle. In the twenty-first century, the expansion of digital communication and reproduction technologies represent at least one realm of cultural analysis where the term will continue to serve as a significant analytic concept.

Robert Glenn Howard

See Also Folklore; Language, Play; Oikotype/Oicotype; Religion, Folk; Speech, Folk.

References

Blank, Trevor J., ed. 2009. *Folklore and the Internet: Vernacular Expression in a Digital World*. Logan: Utah State University Press.

Bradley, Keith R. 1987. On the Roman Slave Supply and Slave Breeding. In *Classical Slavery*, ed. M. Finley. London: Cass Publishers, pp. 42–64.

Cicero, Marcus Tullius. 1971. *Brutus and Orator*. Cambridge, MA: Harvard University Press.

Gates, Henry Louis. 1988. *The Signifying Monkey: A Theory of African-American Literary Criticism*. Oxford, UK: Oxford University Press.

Glassie, Henry. 2000. *Vernacular Architecture*. Bloomington: Indiana University Press.

Hauser, Gerard. 1999. *Vernacular Voices: The Rhetoric of Publics and Public Spheres*. Columbia: University of South Carolina Press.

Howard, Robert Glenn. 2008a. Electronic Hybridity: The Persistent Processes of the Vernacular Web. *Journal of American Folklore* 121(Spring): 192–218.

Howard, Robert Glenn. 2008b. The Vernacular Web of Participatory Media. *Critical Studies in Media Communication* 25(December): 490–512.

Lantis, Margaret. 1960. Vernacular Culture. *American Anthropologist* 62(2): 202–116.

Ono, Kent A., and John M. Sloop. 1995. The Critique of Vernacular Discourse. *Communication Monographs* 62(1): 19–46.

Plato. 1989. Meno. In *Collected Dialogues of Plato*, ed. Edith Hamilton and trans. W. K. C. Guthrie, pp. 353–384. Princeton, NJ: Princeton University Press.

Primiano, Leonard Norman. 1995. Vernacular Religion and the Search for Method in Religious Folklife. *Western Folklore* 54: 37–56.

Rapoport, Amos. 1969. *House Form and Culture*. Englewood Cliffs, NJ: Prentice-Hall, Inc.

Volkskunde

The description of the entire lifestyle of the folk or the interpretation of folk groups as revealed through the study of their traditions, customs, stories, beliefs, dances, songs, and other forms of folk art. Literally meaning "folklore," the word is derived from the German *Volk* (people or nation) and *Kunde* (information). Coined by Clemens Brentano and Achim von Arnim, *Volkskunde* as a concept achieved currency after Jacob and Wilhelm Grimm began using the term to discuss oral folk narratives and Germanic mythology in works such as their two-volume collection of German folk narrative, *Kinder- und Hausmärchen* (1812–1815).

Specifically, the early nineteenth-century German scholars such as the Grimms applied the term to describe the study of the entirety of the life of rural peoples, who were removed from modern culture by virtue of their habitat. These antiquarians viewed the peasant class as a something of a pure, original group and looked upon their traditions as remainders of an earlier time. By collecting these remnants and studying them, the antiquarians hoped to piece together a picture of the origin of the groups' traditions and lifeways. The emergence of romantic nationalism led its adherents to begin to focus on these remnants as a means of encapsulating national or ethnic identity. The term *folk* began to replace *peasant* as a preferred term, and the former term came to denote common unity rather than class distinctions.

Spurred on by the rise of romantic nationalism and an interest in antiquarian studies, the term *Volkskunde* was adopted by scholars outside of Germany as a cover term for folklore and folklore studies. In the early nineteenth century, the term *popular antiquities* was widely used among English-speaking scholars to denote the areas of study that the Grimms and others were undertaking. In a nod to the German term *Volkskunde* and the changing attitudes of the scholars, English antiquarian William John Thoms suggested in 1846 that the term *folklore* be adopted as the preferred term for antiquarian studies among English-speaking scholars.

Volkskunde, like *folklore*, is still an appropriate cover term for the field of folklore studies. However, both terms have fallen under attack as being too broad in meaning. As a result, in Germanic usage at least, terms denoting the specific areas of study are becoming more common and are often used in place of the overall term *Volkskunde*. Among these terms and areas are: *Volkerkunde* (ethnology), *Volkscharakter* (folk or national identity), *Volksleben* (folklife), *Volkslied* (folksong), *Volksmedizin* (folk medicine), *Volkssitte* (folk or national custom), *Volkssprache* (folk or vernacular speech), and *Volkstracht* (folk or national costume).

Randal S. Allison

See Also Folklife; Folklore; *Gesunkenes Kulturgut*.

References

Brunvand, Jan Harold. 1986. *The Study of American Folklore: An Introduction*. 3rd ed. New York and London: W. W. Norton.

Dorson, Richard M., ed. 1972. *Folklore and Folklife: An Introduction*. Chicago and London: University of Chicago Press.

Dow, James R., and Hannjost Lixfeld, eds. and trans. 1986. *German* Volkskunde*: A Decade of Theoretical Confrontation, Debate, and Reorientation (1967–1977)*. Bloomington: Indiana University Press.

Toelken, Barre. 1979. Introduction. *The Dynamics of Folklore*. Boston: Houghton Mifflin.

Werewolf

Literally, a "man-wolf" (from the Old English *wer,* or man, and *wulf,* or wolf); a human being transformed into a wolf by witchcraft or by the person's own power. The belief in werewolves is international. The first information comes from Herodotus (fifth century BCE) attributing lycanthropy (werewolfism) to the *Neuroi* (Proto-Slavs or Proto–Eastern Balts): "Scyths and Greeks who live in Scythia tell that every *Neuroi* is transformed once a year for some days to wolf, after which he resumes his former shape." In the Ukraine and Belorussia, the belief in werewolves is especially strong. It is believed there that werewolves can change themselves further to dogs, cats, bushes, or tree stumps.

The bloodthirsty werewolves primarily hunt animals, infrequently human beings. They move at night and must assume the human form before daybreak. If they are wounded, the wound appears on the human body of the person who was transformed into the wolf. This belief is widespread. James Frazer gives examples from Livonia, the mountains of Auvergne, Padua, and the French district of Beauce. The same belief also is encountered in Estonia, Finland, and Russia.

To change into a werewolf, a human throws on a wolf skin or puts on a magic belt. In Estonia, one can crawl through openings, such as the bow formed by the trunk of a tree and its top when it grows back to the earth, and say a magic formula. In Lithuania, a human changes into a werewolf by somersaulting over a tree stump, crawling backward under the space between a pine tree root and the ground, turning two somersaults in the area between two stakes driven into the ground, passing under the bow formed by four poles driven into the ground, and so forth. The Belorussians and Ukrainians turn into werewolves by going into the woods to somersault over a tree stump into which a knife has been driven. Among the Balts and Slavs, transformation can also be accomplished by putting on a magical belt or a wolf skin.

The ritual donning of the wolf skin can be understood as causing a radical change in the person's behavior, as the transformation from human to carnivore occurs. Crawling through a narrow opening can be explained as the imitation of rebirth, that is, the "sham birth," of the person into a new being because of the similarity of the opening to the birth canal.

To regain human form, the tricks for becoming a werewolf are usually performed in reverse. The lasting effect is achieved by burning the wolf skin used by

Engraving showing a werewolf devouring a young woman, ca. 1901. (Time Life Pictures/Getty Images)

the person for transformation or giving food to the werewolf. In the Baltic countries, a legend is told that a man offered a wolf a piece of bread on the tip of a knife. The wolf grabbed the bread together with the knife and ran away. When the man recognized his knife at a merchant's in Riga, he was amply rewarded by the merchant for the kindness he had shown to the werewolf. This legend reflects the popular belief that a supernatural being becomes human by eating human food.

Stories are told of wedding parties transformed into werewolves, who, as a group, roamed and plundered in neighboring countries. According to Felix Oinas, werewolves were called *viron sudet*, "Estonian wolves" in southeast Finland since they were believed to have come from Estonia, where they had been changed by a witch, a Russian, or a Latvian. The transformed wedding parties also came to Finland from Russia and Lapland. Such transformations also were known in Belorussia. In general, the people are inclined to consider werewolves as belonging to another nation or as having been transformed by foreign sorcerers. This conclusion is in line with the so-called out-group attitude that attributes everything negative to foreigners, especially to neighboring nationalities.

The werewolf eats the meat of the animal raw. In the Baltic area (Estonia, Livonia, Latvia), if someone asks the werewolf about this or curses the creature, the werewolf hits the person's face with the animal's leg or with another piece of meat. The meat gets instantly roasted and burns the face of the person who was hit. This incident signifies the werewolf's transition from the world of raw to the world of cooked, that is, from the supernatural world to the human world.

Among the south Slavs, werewolves have merged with vampires; the term for werewolf, *vukodlak*, *volkodlak* (literally, wolf's hair), has become the name for the combined werewolf-vampire. In Yugoslavia, there are only a few traces of the *vukodlak's* lycanthropy. Most often, however, the *vukodlak* appears as a vampire, which comes out of the grave at night to attack people at home.

In countries where there are no wolves, the place of the werewolf is taken by the fiercest wild animal in that region. Thus, there is the weretiger in India, Borneo, and western Asia; the tiger in China and Japan; the boar in Turkey and Greece; the hyena, leopard, and crocodile in Africa; and the jaguar in South America.

Lycanthropy, according to psychiatrists, is a kind of mental illness that causes the victim to feel like a carnivore, a predatory beast, and to act accordingly. Religio-phenomenologically, it is interpreted as being connected with the idea of the free or detachable soul that can leave the body, assume the shape of an animal, wander around, and return again to the body. This belief is attested in Serbia, Sweden, Livonia, and Estonia. It was reported from Livonia in the nineteenth century that when the soul of a werewolf was abroad on its particular business, its body was lying dead as a stick or stone. However, if during this time the body were moved to another place or even if the position were accidentally shifted, the soul could not find its way back and had to remain in the body of a wolf until death. Oskar Loorits reports that "the soul of an evil man or sorcerer wandered around as a wolf causing damage to other people, while the man himself slept."

Occasionally, Latvian werewolves function as protectors of communities. At a witch trial in 1691, as Leopold Kretzenbacher reports, an old Latvian, Thies (Matiss), claimed to be a werewolf, a "dog of God" (*Dievs*), and to work with his companions against the sorcerers, who were allied with the devil (*velns*). The devil, through sorcerers, took fertility (blessing) away into hell, but the werewolves stole it back. The preceding year, the Russian werewolves had arrived earlier at hell and had taken away the blessing of Latvian land. Therefore, there was a good crop in Russia, but the Latvians had a crop failure. This year, the Latvian werewolves had come sooner, and they expected Latvia to have a fertile flax year.

The tendency of people to believe in good werewolves who counteract the reign of evil through the powers of good can be compared with similar beliefs about vampires. Thus, according to Balkan belief, the classic vampire has an antagonist, a "good" vampire ("vampire's son"), who is destined to detect and kill the bad vampires. Kretzenbacher reports that the Russian villages are said to have two kinds of vampires—one bad and the other good: "More frequently encountered was the belief that while a dead vampire destroyed people, a live one, on the contrary, defended them. Each village had its own vampire, as if it were a guard, protecting the inhabitants from his dead companions."

Felix J. Oinas

See Also Assault, Supernatural; Magic; Shape-Shifters; Transformation; Vampire.

References

Frazer, James George. 1935. *The Golden Bough*, vol. 10. New York: Macmillan.

Kretzenbacher, Leopold. 1968. *Kynokephale Dämonen südosteuropäischer Volksdichtung*. Munich: R. Trofenik.

Loorits, Oskar. 1949. Grundzüge des estnischen Volksglaubens, I. Skrifter utgivna av kungl. *Gustav Adolfs Akademien*, 18: 1. Lund, Sweden.

Moszynski, Kazimierz. 1934. *Kultura ludowa slowian*. I. Krakow: Polska Akademja Umiejetnosci.

Odstedt, Ella. 1943. *Varulven i svensk folktradition* (Werewolves in Swedish folk tradition). Uppsala, Sweden: Lundequistska Bokhandeln.

Oinas, Felix J. 1979. Introduction to *The Werewolf*. In *The Golden Steed: Seven Baltic Plays*, ed. Alfreds Straumanis. Prospect Heights, IL: Waveland.

Oinas, Felix J. 1979. Viru susi. In *Kalevipoeg kütkeis*. Alexandria, VA: Mana. (This volume contains English summaries of each article.)

Pipe, Jim. 2007. *Werewolves*. New York: Bearport.

Senn, Harry A. 1982. *Were-Wolf and Vampire in Romania*. New York: Columbia University Press.

Women's Folklore

Folklore and "women" are terms that have been linked in scholarship only recently. Expressive, artistic behavior, whether verbal or plastic, used to be considered an activity exclusive to men. Women's expressive behavior was assigned categories such as "decorative" or "utilitarian," thus denying the conscious manipulation of form and content for effect or aesthetics.

The American Folklore Society was founded in 1888; from the beginning, women scholars were represented in its publications as well as in other popular and scholarly publications of the time. However, the perceptions of women's contributions, whether as scholars or consultant/informers, were limited by prevailing ideas about women and their abilities.

Today, women are actively challenging the preconceptions about themselves and their scholarship, sometimes with a strident rhetoric, sometimes with a comical or ironic attitude, but always with a plethora of knowledge and references. Indeed, the adage about women having to be "better than" to be considered "equal to" is demonstrated repeatedly in women's reports of their difficulties in being taken seriously and being published in premier outlets. While we like to think that our times are considerably different from those of a hundred years ago, in practice we now find many similarities to the situation that existed when folklore first became a scholarly presence on the American scene.

Early collectors, whether men or women, preferred to gather stories from men, unless, of course, the stories concerned hearth and home, charms or lullabies, children's games or cooking, which, it was believed, were the province of women. Despite the fact that the Grimm brothers reported collecting their fairy tales primarily from serving-women, men were believed to be the bearers of the important and lengthy traditions, while women were believed to be more capable of, and interested in, things that surrounded what was considered to be their primary role—household duties and child care. Even when women's knowledge was demonstrated to be superior to that of men in a particular genre, the words of men were preferred.

Gradually, during the 1950s and 1960s, information about women in journals or books was expanded to include their roles in cultures other than those founded on Western European models. At times some of this information related to folklore.

African American woman doing laundry with a scrub board and tub, girl stirring pot with three other children on the ground watching, and a woman in the background spreading laundry, ca. 1900. (Library of Congress)

But usually it was folklore *about* women rather then the kinds of expressive behavior in which women engaged, whether in groups of women, women with children, or mixed gender groups. Occasionally, there was a single publication focusing on the repertoire of this female storyteller or that woman singer; such publications were exceptions to an otherwise firm rule that significant folklore study was predicated on working with men's knowledge.

By the late 1960s and the early 1970s, the situation was changing rapidly. It is not a coincidence that this change occurred coterminously with the so-called women's movement and court cases affirming the rights of minorities and women. Many graduate school programs, previously de facto closed to women, began to reserve slots for women in order to ensure the continuance of federal funding for other sectors of the university.

Older women, those with children, and those who lived on the margins longing for the opportunities of their brothers and husbands were represented in disproportionate numbers in these early graduate classes. These women, predominantly in our country at the University of Texas in Austin, at Stanford University, at the University of Pennsylvania, and at Indiana University–Bloomington, had life experiences and artistic/folkloristic repertoires that were neither described in literature nor accorded legitimacy. These women began to be heard in the mid-1970s, when there was a sudden explosion of literature about women, their folklore, their roles, their self-perceptions, and even their bawdy jokes, stories, and tales—more often than not with men as the butt of the joke. With the increasing availability of funding for women and their concerns, stories began to circulate of the women's folklore from this country or that and its similarities and differences compared with American folklore. Much of this cross-cultural work, however, was not published until the late 1970s and early 1980s.

Also during the late 1960s and early 1970s, women's groups were formed; originally these were consciousness-raising or rap groups, but now they are termed support groups and have generalized to society as a whole. Women delighted in finding their commonalities, especially in sharing their ways of relating experiences about such commonalities in these groups. Some of the earlier published and scholarly work in women's folklore grew from such associations of women.

The numbers of books, articles, and chapters on women and their folklore being produced in the mid- and later 1980s reached such proportions as to make it impossible for any one person to keep adequate track of the literature without devoting full time to it. Primarily the work has focused on women's roles and women's expressions of and about them in cultures throughout the world as well as in our own country. There has also been a coming together of feminism and scholarship. Women have been freed, one hopes permanently, from the bonds of being passive to the recognition that women are active agents, often agencies as well, for the enactment of their lives. Even in repressed situations, such as can be seen in some back-to-the-past Middle Eastern cultures, women scholars are demonstrating the expressive ways in which women manipulate and comment upon their condition through folkloristic resources.

Theoretical work in women's folklore currently follows the same trends and paradigms as does any other subject in an academic discipline. There are those studies that focus on ethnography, on a Marxist perspective, on a structural presentation, on a semiotic interpretation, or on a performance enactment, as well as those that take a tone of literary criticism; additionally, many works reinterpret past canon on the basis of contemporary insight. Previously taboo topics, such as lesbianism, receive their fair share of scholarly attention and are now publishable, whereas a few years ago they were not—save in the so-called underground press. What were once accepted social "facts," as, for instance, the concept of universal male dominance, have recently been shown to be as much a product of our own mythology concerning proper roles of men and women as they were social reality. The genres and paradigms that have been utilized to discuss women and their folklore or to trivialize them both are more reflective of the scholars and the zeitgeist than they are of the actual situation obtaining in any one time or place.

In the late 1980s, attention is being given to the effects of colonialism, of cultural recidivism, of feminism, of text versus performance, of performance of text, and of alphabetic literacy on the production, recording, and interpretation of folklore and women. The topic of folklore and women now encompasses folklore of women, folklore about women, women's folklore, and metafolklore—the folklore about the folklore.

In 1888, understanding of folklore and women was a foregone conclusion: everyone knew the kinds of folklore women had and the areas in which they could be expected to demonstrate competency, and everyone knew that real folklore was a possession of men. It took almost one hundred years, until 1972, before the first scholarly session on women's folklore was presented at the American Folklore Society meetings; two years later, in 1974, the interest was so intense that there was a double session (four hours of papers). In 1986, the society's annual meeting featured an entire day of scholarly papers on women's folklore, with multiple sessions running concurrently. Unfortunately, few men attended the sessions. This précis of the American Folklore Society's record concerning folklore and women replicates the situation in other disciplines and scholarship in general.

Five women have had a significant impact upon the thinking of those who write about folklore and women: Barbara Babcock and Claire R. Farrer, whose books and articles are repeatedly cited; Marta Weigle, who presents images of women from many cultures throughout history; and, Michelle Zimbalist Rosaldo and Louise Lamphere, whose anthropological collection provided the stimulus for much of the research now seeing the light of publication.

Claire R. Farrer

See Also Family Folklore; Gender.

References

Babcock, Barbara, ed. 1978. *The Reversible World*. Ithaca, NY: Cornell University Press.

Farrer, Claire R., ed. 1986. *Women and Folklore: Images and Genres*. Prospect Heights, IL: Waveland Press.

Kailo, Kaarina, ed. 2008. *Wo(men) and Bears: The Gifts of Nature, Culture, and Gender*. Toronto, CA: Inanna Publications and Education.

Locke, Liz, Theresa A. Vaughan, and Pauline Greenhill. 2009. *Encyclopedia of Women's Folklore and Folklife*. Westport, CT: Greenwood Press.

Weigle, Marta. 1982. *Spiders and Spinsters*. Albuquerque: University of New Mexico Press.

Zimbalist Rosaldo, Michelle, and Louise Lamphere, eds. 1974. *Women, Culture and Society*. Stanford, CA: Stanford University Press.

Worldview

The way in which a person or group views the world; the complex interaction of culture, language, and mental constructs utilized to make sense of the world around us; alternately, *Weltanschauung*, or the view of life, philosophy of life, or ideology. Studies of worldview focus on how culture and language are utilized to interpret and mediate the experiences and sensory data from the world at large.

The concept of worldview is understood to be a complex idea that can vary greatly from group to group. Most research views worldview as a function of patterns of native language and group culture. The patterns are internalized within the members of a group by way of group interaction. These patterns are passed through each succeeding generation and become an integral part of the life of the group. Indeed, it is improbable that the people of any given culture can understand the world without these native patterns. The development of an individual's worldview begins in infancy and continues throughout life. Along with the complexities of linguistic development, the individual is subjected to a myriad of behavioral and perceptual norms. One group may develop fine distinctions between colors, another might focus on linear forms, and another might focus on temporal and spatial relations to each other and to other groups. Thus, each culture utilizes a different methodology for processing perceived reality; reality is processed through filters of language and culturally provided ideas. These learned patterns allow members of a group to orient themselves to the world around them in terms they understand. Euro-Americans, for example, tend to orient themselves in terms of linear relations to people and places, a concept they begin to internalize early on and that is reinforced through regular interaction with others from their group.

Linguist and anthropologist Edward Sapir developed a concept of culture as something internalized by the individuals who make up a given group to create a "world of meanings." This world of meanings was something that the individual abstracted through language and interaction with other members of the group, and it conditioned the way in which these individuals as a group were able to build a worldview. From this and the later Sapir-Whorf hypothesis, which holds that language affects the way in which worldviews are perceived, grew the more recent ideas on worldview.

One key to understanding the worldview of a group is through its folklore. If worldview can be understood to be the mediating filter through which an individual or group perceives the world, then traditional renderings of the group's orderly principles (e.g., myth, belief systems) can be utilized as the key to apprehending its worldview. More recent research attends to the fact that observers, too, have their own worldviews and that these act on what the observers perceive. This informed perspective, sometimes called "new reflexivity," builds the observer's bias into any discussion of worldview. By recognizing this double mediation, a more accurate picture of worldview is believed to emerge.

Randal S. Allison

See Also Acculturation; Linguistic Approach; Myth.

References

Dundes, Alan. 1971. Folk Ideas as Units of Worldview. *Journal of American Folklore* 84: 93–103.

Hodder, Ian. 1992. The Problem. In *Reading the Past: Current Approaches to Interpretation in Archeology*. New York: Cambridge University Press.

Langness, L. L. 1990. American Developments. In *The Study of Culture*. San Francisco: Chandler and Sharp.

Rabinow, Paul. 1977. Ali: An Insider's Outsider and Self-Consciousness. In *Reflections on Fieldwork in Morocco*. Los Angeles: University of California Press.

Toelken, Barre. 1979. Folklore and Cultural Worldview. In *The Dynamics of Folklore*. Boston: Houghton Mifflin.

Xeroxlore

Also known as *photocopylore*, signifies traditional items reproduced by xerographic or analogous means that subvert the primary intentions of those in ostensible control of such higher-level technologies. Examples of devices so employed include printing presses, photographic printing, mimeograph machines, photocopy machines, computer printers, computer networks, fax machines, and coin-minting presses. Any device that reproduces an item or transmits alphanumeric data may be employed in this folk practice, and most are known to have been so used.

Xeroxlore, because it is the product of the unofficial use of technology, reflects the customary practices of those who use it rather than the intentions of the institutions that own or control it. Xeroxlore is also affected by its host technology and often reflects folk attitudes to its institutional context. Thus, xeroxlore usually contains a visual component and often parodies the values of the host institution through fake memos or the values of dominant culture more generally through obscene Christmas cards and the like. An example of xeroxlore, reproduced by photocopy machines on paper, by coin-elongating machines on U.S. cents, and by private mints on one-ounce silver ingots, reads:

> Big cats are dangerous,
> [representation of a tiger]
> but a little pussy never hurt anyone.

Although the technology often serves more seemingly innocuous ends, such as the circulation of favorite recipes, chain letters, and favorite published cartoons, even these are reproduced despite official restrictions on what may be copied and in violation of copyright laws; their circulation may also violate postal regulations. It is a small step from such unofficial uses of the technology to the photocopying of body parts.

Just as the technology is an extension of human faculties, so also is xeroxlore an extension of traditional oral joking practices and of the making of material culture, novelty items in particular. The folk make their own uses of technological innovations as they become available, just as they always have. The fragmentary record of the past includes typeset folk verse and World War II–era blueprints of female nudes with their body parts labeled as if they were airplanes. Present practice includes use of facsimile machines to transmit photocopied materials, with an increasing proportion of pictorial material that the technology permits and wholesale circulation of xeroxlore by means of the Internet.

Although xeroxlore is an international phenomenon, the product of whatever technology is available for its duplication and dissemination, all items of xeroxlore are not equally widespread. Xeroxlore is frequently adapted to different cultural contexts, but many items are of interest to specific groups of people only, be they employees of a particular corporation, the citizens of a particular country, or the speakers of a particular language. Xeroxlore represents age-old human practices carried out by means of and influenced by modern inventions, but despite the international availability of identical technologies, xeroxlore exhibits the same types and perhaps as much variation, as any other traditional practice, based on race, color, creed, gender, sexual orientation, political ideology, and so forth.

Michael J. Preston

See Also Cyberculture; Legend, Urban.

References

Barrick, Mac E. 1972. The Typescript Broadside. *Keystone Folklore Quarterly* 17: 27–38.

Bell, Louis Michael, Cathy Makin Orr [Preston], and Michael James Preston, eds. 1976. *Urban Folklore from Colorado: Photocopy Cartoons*. Research Monographs, LD00079. Ann Arbor, MI: Xerox University Microfilms.

Dundes, Alan, and Carl R. Pagter, eds. 1975. *Urban Folklore from the Paperwork Empire*. Memoir Series, Vol. 62. Austin, TX: American Folklore Society.

Kofod, Else Marie, ed. 1988. *Chefens Sekretaer Og andre beske kommentarer til hverdagens fortraedeligheder*. Aalborg, Denmark: Det Schonbergske Forlag.

Kutter, Uli, ed. 1982. *Ich Kundige!!! Zeurnisse von Wunschen und Angsten am Arbeitsplatz—Eine Bestandsaufnahme*. Marburg, Germany: Jonas Verlag.

Orr [Preston], Cathy Makin, and Michael James Preston, eds. 1976. *Urban Folklore from Colorado: Typescript Broadsides*. Research Monographs, LD00069. Ann Arbor, MI: Xerox University Microfilms.

Preston, Michael J. 1974. Xerox-Lore. *Keystone Quarterly* 19 : 11–26.

Smith, Paul, ed. 1984. *The Complete Book of Office Mis-Practice*. London: Routledge & Kegan Paul.

Index